Religion's Influence in Contemporary Society

Readings in the Sociology of Religion

Edited by

Joseph E. Faulkner

The Pennsylvania State University

Charles E. Merrill Publishing Co.

A Bell & Howell Company

Columbus, Ohio

Merrill Sociology Series

Under the editorship of
Richard L. Simpson
University of North Carolina, Chapel Hill
and
Paul E. Mott
University of Pennsylvania

Published by
Charles E. Merrill Publishing Co.
A Bell & Howell Company
Columbus, Ohio 43216

ISBN: 0-675-09105-5

Library of Congress Catalog Card Number: 72-76586

1 2 3 4 5 6—77 76 75 74 73 72

Printed in the United States of America

For Babs

If we find a little difficulty today in imagining what these feasts and ceremonies of the future could consist in, it is because we are going through a stage of transition and moral mediocrity. The great things of the past which filled our fathers with enthusiasm do not excite the same ardour in us, either because they have come into common usage to such an extent that we are unconscious of them or else because they no longer answer to our actual aspirations; but as yet there is nothing to replace them. We can no longer impassionate ourselves for the principles in the name of which Christianity recommended to masters that they treat their slaves humanely, and on the other hand, the idea which it has formed of human equality and fraternity seems to us too Platonic; we desire another which would be more practicable; but as yet we cannot clearly see what it should be nor how it could be realized in facts. In a word, the old gods are growing old or already dead, and others are not yet born. . . . it is life itself, and not a dead past which can produce a living cult.

Emile Durkheim, *The Elementary Forms of the Religious Life*

Contents

Preface

A sociological study of religion may seem to reflect a peculiar attention to a moribund subject. After all, those most professionally responsible for propagandizing the latest news about God have themselves entered into serious debate over the state of His health. Some have announced His death. Others disagree, but feel, nevertheless, that the announcement is simply premature and that the future of religion is highly uncertain. The "death of God" debate and the genuine anxiety over the place of religion in contemporary society are manifestations of the secular nature of Western society. For some (more often the word is "many") religion has been relegated to an obscure corner of their lives. For others, adherence to the traditional aspects of religion, e.g., church attendance and participation,[1] remain necessary and important. For yet a third group (for whom an exact numerical determination is impossible) the traditional church and *its* practices have been abandoned, but a vigorous search for a new expression of the faith reflects their religious loyalties. Nonetheless, the institutional church *is* still there on the corner of 5th and Elm Streets[2] attempting to exercise some degree of influence in a secular society. On cursory examination religion may seem to be of minor importance in influencing behavior. The Roman Catholic who does, or does not, practice birth control is reacting not only to the influence of the Church's teaching in this matter but to several other sources of influence in his life as well. Or, as the many studies of the association between religious affiliation and voting have shown, not only religion but class, family traditions, regional location, and other variables must be considered before one can ascribe particular weight to the religious variable in voting behavior. Whether religion is more or less significant in influencing behavior than one's position in the economic order or one's political affiliation is better stated as an hypothesis rather than a foregone conclusion. The findings of the various studies in this book clearly show that in scientific interpretation of behavior religion does account for some of the variance.

The student should be aware at the beginning of this study of the sociology of religion that the data describing religion's influence upon behavior point to *both* desirable and undesirable consequences—depending upon one's own value system. Particular religious ideologies may lead to vigorous opposition to programs of sex education in the schools. Religious motivations of nuns and clergy resulting in their involvement in the civil rights struggle of this society may be considered desirable by some and undesirable by others. The current debate over tax-exempt status for church property often finds individuals and groups of very similar religious backgrounds arguing for opposing points of view. Some sociological studies of the association between religion and prejudice suggest that church members may be more highly prejudiced than nonmembers.[3] However, continuing research into the relationship of religion to prejudice (as well as other areas of behavior) has pointed to the need for enlarging the number of variables used in measuring religion and its influence. For example, church membership, considered as one measure of religion, may be related to prejudice. But church members who are deeply committed to their religious faith have been found to be less prejudiced than those members weakly committed to their faith.[4] Thus, the influence of religion is a function of several variables—each of which must be carefully specified in research studies. In sociological research, nevertheless, the purpose is to explore and define the nature of the relationship between religion and behavior rather than to proscribe or approve religion's influence in contemporary society. In this view, as in many others, the sociology of religion is the mainstream of that sociological tradition seeking to shed light upon the institutional influences which account for a large part of human behavior.

This book is an outgrowth of my own professional interest in both research and teaching in the sociology of religion. Unlike certain areas in sociology, especially the introductory, there is no need to apologize for "another book" in the sociology of religion. Research and teaching in the area have developed so rapidly in the last decade that there exists a need for a text which will draw together examples of the better work being done by those scholars studying changes and new developments in religion. A book attempting to present selections from the works of all those who have studied religion would fill several volumes, however, each of which would most appropriately be edited by those specializing in their respective fields. The purpose of the present work is more modest: to introduce the reader to the major thrust in the scientific study of religion in recent years, concentrating primarily on the work of sociologists.

Like any reader the present book has had to omit what some will think should have been included. None of the "classics" are presented here due to the book's avowed purpose. The major thrust of the book concentrates upon the religious scene in the United States (with which the reader is most likely to have familiarity), but a cross-cultural perspective is provided in several of the selections included (see, especially, the articles by Bellah in chapter 7, Wilson in chapter 9, and Luckmann in chapter 10). Since the orientation is sociological, no effort was made to include examples of the very fine research in religion being done by psychologists, for example. But while the majority of the selections were authored by professional sociologists, the choice was dictated by the method of treatment and content of the subject matter rather than the author's professional identification. Certainly one would expect to find a "sociological perspective" among some theologians writing today, and such is the case in certain of the studies presented in this book. On the other hand any explicit theological statement, irrespective of its merit, was not considered unless it contributed to the purpose of the book. Whatever limitations may be present due to the selective nature of a reader are, I trust, more than compensated for by the very high quality of work revealed in those writings finally chosen for inclusion.

Most of the studies chosen utilize sociological methods of analysis which will be readily grasped by any student who has had an introductory course in sociology. A few of the selections utilize such advanced techniques as factor analysis. To have omitted these studies because of the type of analysis involved would have resulted in by-passing some of the more creative efforts by contemporary sociologists to explain man's religious behavior. In a time when introductory courses and texts are introducing the student to both the substance and the methods of the discipline most students will be able to follow the logic of the argument in the articles utilizing a factor analytic or a multivariate analytic approach. However, in order to provide a more complete understanding of the scientific methodology employed in measuring religion, chapter 11 has been prepared especially for this volume by Professor Rex Warland of The Pennsylvania State University. It describes in relatively simple language the meaning and purpose of some of the more advanced methods being used in contemporary sociological analysis. With Professor Warland's article as a guide, along with the help of the instructor, the student will be adequately prepared to read and understand the respective articles involved.

The plan of the book is as follows: there are four sections, each with a brief introduction of its own. *Section One* contains both theoretical and empirical studies which seek to define the field of study. There is a continuing concern today with efforts to define and measure the religious variable in its many dimensions. The selections in chapter 1 represent recent efforts to conceptualize and measure the religious variable.

Section Two is based on the premise that a major manifestation of the religiosity of people is still centered in the institutional church. While there is growing discussion, and some evidence, of the "privatization" of religion in today's society, such a characterization is not the normative pattern. The studies in chapter two indicate that the best statistical information we have suggests that church membership and participation is still characteristic of a significant proportion of the population. So much for statistical data. If people do belong and participate, the question is, Why? The second and third articles of chapter two seek to provide some answers to this question. But, as any knowledgeable person will point out, statistics notwithstanding, they know *many* people who do not consider themselves religious at all. The next two studies of chapter two give attention to this admittedly neglected area of investigation in the sociology of religion: the "religious 'nones'" (as Glenn Vernon has aptly described them).

Chapter three examines the characteristics of those who provide the formal leadership in the church: the clergy. The four empirical studies in chapter three focus on the professional and personal identity crisis facing the modern clergyman as he endeavors to fulfill the various, and often conflicting, roles expected of him by those he is appointed to serve.

The fourth chapter presents a selection of studies which reveal a continuing interest among sociologists of religion in the organizational features of the church. The now vulnerable, and highly criticized, "sect-church" typology is examined to see what, if any, basis it may still provide for understanding the organizational structure of the religious institution.

The third section of the book examines the interrelationships of religion and society. *Section Three* is entitled "The Church in Society" rather than "Religion in Society" since it is religion as primarily manifest in its institutionalized aspects which is the object of concern here. The studies in chapters 5, 6, and 7 investigate, respectively, the church and the stratification system, the church and the political system, and the church and the economic order.

In *Section Four* attention is directed to the forces of social change which are altering the traditional forms of religion and, consequently, the structural forms of the church. The concentration of most church activity in an urban environment (chapter 8) and the increasing secularization of society (chapter 9) are examined as on-going processes which strongly suggest that religion in its traditional form is undergoing rapid change. Chapter 10 presents a collection of studies which some sociologists (and not a few theologians) feel represents the most "vital" or "significant" religious activity presently occurring in society. Phrases such as "the Second Reformation" and "religionless Christianity" (which means basically *non-church* religion) are common in the thinking of those who see the day of the institutional church as past. Whatever the final outcome of the changes which religion is undergoing, it is clear that the nature and influence of religion in mid-twentieth century, as presented in the three previous sections of this book, are not necessarily that which future generations may expect. An understanding by students of the material presented in all four sections of this book will itself, no doubt, contribute in some degree to the shape of religion in the future.

---

1. Simple attendance at the formal Sunday worship service constitutes the primary religious activity of many church members. Demerath reports that church attendance is the only measure of religiosity found to be "meaningfully associated" with the "highly discrepant" member. ("Highly discrepant" is a characteristic of individuals who find themselves uncomfortable under the prevailing status systems in a society. An example would be the Negro medical doctor or the female lawyer. Does one react to the former in terms of his status as a Negro or as a doctor?) See: N. J. Demerath, III, *Social Class In American Protestantism* (Chicago: Rand McNally & Company, 1965), especially chapters 6 and 7.

2. How *long* the church will remain as a viable religious institution on the corner is a question of serious import. According to the *New York Times,* August 23, 1970, an estimated 700 churches in England may be declared "redundant" and offered for sale in the next ten years. Interested individuals and/or groups may purchase any of these churches or they may be adapted as youth centers, libraries, or historic monuments to the past.

3. Such a conclusion is reached by Charles Glock and Rodney Stark in *Christian Beliefs and Anti-Semitism* (New York: Harper and Row, 1966).

4. See, for example, the excellent study by Russell Allen and Bernard Spilka, "Committed and Consensual Religion: A Specification of Religion-Prejudice Relationships," *Journal of the Scientific Study of Religion* 6 (Fall 1967): 191-206. See, also, Morton King, "Measuring the Religious Variable: Nine Proposed Dimensions," *Journal for the Scientific Study of Religion* 6 (Fall 1967): 173-90. A fine bibliography of the efforts to explore the multidimensional nature of religion is an appendix to this study.

Acknowledgments

No book is the product of one man's thinking. Like all authors I am indebted to many colleagues for their contribution to my work. I would like to acknowledge, with gratitude, the cooperation of the authors whose works are reprinted in this book. David Schulz provided valuable help in reading an early version of the complete manuscript. Paul Mott and Richard Simpson demonstrated an unusual degree of editorial sophistication in smoothing out the rough spots in the manuscript; and Roger Ratliff, sociology editor for Charles Merrill, sustained a high degree of interest in the project from the beginning and guided it through to a successful completion. The several revisions of the manuscript were carefully typed, without complaint, by Bonnie Johnstonbaugh and Jan Morring.

It is common in acknowledgments to comment on the "many hours" of play and conversation which one's wife and children were denied during the preparation of a book. I have both a wife and children. The children seem to enjoy playing as much (if not more) with the dog, rabbits, and frogs who live with us, as they do me, and my wife is so busy with her own teaching and fulfilling the multiple roles required of the modern woman that the best she could muster when it was all over was, "So, you finally finished it, huh?"

Efforts to Delimit the Field of Study

Following his study of the impact of religion on politics, economics, and family life in a modern metropolitan community, Lenski concludes that

> contrary to the expectations of the nineteenth century positivists, religious organizations remain vigorous and influential in contemporary American society.[1]

What was it that the nineteenth-century positivists expected would happen with regard to religion? Simply stated, man, in his evolutionary development, would by-pass the need for reliance on any transcendental power or powers. For the evolutionary scholars such as Tylor and Spencer the religious beliefs and practices of prescientific "primitive" man could readily be understood. As man and his society evolved, however, he would discard his religious superstitions and rely upon his rational faculties to understand his world and his behavior in it.

Lenski notwithstanding, it cannot be said that the evolutionists were "wrong." They were clearly overambitious in their predictions. More importantly, however, they failed to grasp an essential feature of primitive thoughtways which enabled primitive man to differentiate between two systems of action. Primitives often *did* behave as they thought the gods would have them do. Some, perhaps much, of that behavior we would today label "superstitious." But as the Parsonian analysis of the work of Pareto, Malinowski, Durkheim, and Weber in the first article in chapter 1 indicates, the primitive behaved quite rationally in those situations calling for scientific or technical knowledge. If canoes were to be built the primitive employed the best technical skills and knowledge available. Malinowski's field observations offer ample data to support this. On the other hand, many situations to which man must respond are not subject to the canons of science. Pareto suggested that deviations from the "logico-experimental" standards of science in such situations did not reflect ignorance on the part of the primitive but rather recognition that nonempirical elements, such as those found in religion, were not subject to positivistic interpretations. He also stressed the great importance of these nonempirical elements in understanding human behavior. This was especially true, Malinowski observed, when the primitive confronted death. While rational explanations for death were available, there were, nevertheless, ritual requirements to be met, also, in such a highly emotional matter as the loss of a tribal member.

Durkheim carried this analysis further by noting that primitive peoples often divided the world into "sacred" and "profane" things. The most "sacred" object for the primitive was society. After all, society commands and individuals obey as if the will of society were a moral imperative. Society enjoys our utmost respect; it is "eternal" (i.e., it continues beyond the life of the individual and precedes his life, also). The religious sentiments of the individual are developed as a result of the experiences which he has with others: the collectivity—the society. Thus, religion is the worship of society itself. (As Parsons observes, however, the proposition, simply stated, is not acceptable and has, unfortunately, tended to detract from Durkheim's larger theoretical perspective.)

The careful student should note, of course, that both Malinowski and Durkheim based their study of religion upon field observations of primitive peoples. It might be argued that what was true for the Melanesians or the Arunta is not necessarily applicable to modern, complex societies. This, of course, was the argument of the evolutionary scholars. But as Max Weber's contributions to the sociology of religion were to show, men in any society try to explain not only *how* things work but *why* things happen as they do. A child dies from leukemia; a young man is paralyzed as a result of wounds in combat. As pointed out by Weber these are highly emotional human involvements and rational explanations are not totally satisfactory. Thus, two levels of explanations are involved. Again, one is the causal or scientific explanation of disease or misfortune, but the second is what Weber has labeled the "problem of meaning." The individual wants to know "why" it happened, and in trying to answer the question of "why?" the influence of the individual's religious beliefs combines with his rational understanding to allow a coherent response to a given situation.

The work of Pareto, Malinowski, Durkheim, and Weber provides, then, a point of departure for a scientific investigation of the role of religion in society. It presents a clear recognition of the need for the study of both empirical and nonempirical elements in human behavior.

It is a tribute to the work of these "founding fathers" (and they may justly be called that) that their theories have been the subject of much empirical testing. An even greater tribute, however, can be seen in the fact that sociologists and theologians are today grappling with the central issues which Durkheim or Weber saw as imperative to understanding the religious interests of men. Section IV, for example, contains studies treating the meaning of the "sacred" and the "secular" which now suggest that the "sacred" is best expressed in the "secular" world and that men no longer draw much of a distinction between the two as Durkheim suggested. Peter Berger's understanding of what is happening with the secularization of theology (article 2, chapter 9) strongly suggests that, for many, an explanation of behavior on *two* levels is not binding on the masses nor today's "secular" theologians. Theology may yet be reduced to anthropology, and if so, Tylor and Spencer, and not Weber, Malinowski, or Durkheim will have been the more prophetic in their insights. Obviously the data needed for any final conclusion in this matter are not yet available, but as the works in this volume suggest there is a continuing need for careful investigation of Lenski's assertion about the "vigorous and influential nature of religious organizations" in American society. To ascertain the degree and nature of this influence it is first necessary to discuss the problem of the definition of religion.

Some would assert that all attempts to define religion are certain to be unsatisfactory at best. Others eagerly quote Weber[2] to the effect that definitions must come at the end of one's work and not at the beginning. In his article on the "Nature of Religion" Williams suggests that rather than evading the issue we at least cope with one of the basic problems confronting research into man's religious life: do we define religion in terms of its "essence" or its "functions"? (Religion, defined in terms of its "essence," emphasizes what religion *is,* e.g., religion is belief in supernatural powers. The "functional" definition of religion looks at the consequences of religion—what it *does,* e.g., religion enables man to face the uncertainties of life with courage.) Agreeing that measures of belief, emotion, willed behavior, and attitudes all constitute part of an acceptable definition of religion Williams argues that much of what is defined as religious behavior is secular instead—e.g., going to church, or holding church membership. Such measures are not measures of *real* religion. Real religion (a nebulous phrase at best) is subjective and concerns the inner man. We study religion only when we study the "true inner state" of man. This viewpoint may be contrasted with that expressed in other research. Joseph Fichter, for example, in his efforts to construct a typology of parishioners, argues that:

> The intangible and immeasurable inner perfection of the Christian can be judged only by God. The best that the scientific observer can do is to provide a rough description of a class of persons who tend to approach the ideal type of nuclear parishioner as defined by certain arbitrary criteria.[3]

Certainly neither of these viewpoints is sufficient. The "inner state" of man manifests itself in overt behavior, and the criteria by which overt behavior is measured are not wholly arbitrary, though much of the earlier empirical work in measuring religion did rely upon single indices such as church membership or some other arbitrarily selected criterion. Recognizing this fact, the contribution by Glock begins with the basic assumption that religion *is* diverse in its manifestations, and thus measures of religiosity must give recognition to the varied nature of religion. Glock proposes five dimensions which must be taken into account if one hopes to arrive at some operationally comprehensive definition of religion: ideological, ritualistic, intellectual, experiential, and consequential. In addition to operationalizing these "core dimensions" he states the necessity, also, of exploring the nature of their interrelationships. With few exceptions each of the remaining articles in this book incorporates one or more of these dimensions into their efforts to describe the influence of religion upon human behavior.

It is necessary at this point to digress for a moment and give brief attention to an important problem recognized by those attempting to conceptually define religion. How does one decide just what data he will use? Does he investigate the nature of the religious organization, i.e., an institutional approach, or is it the characteristics of the *individuals* both within and outside the religious organizations that are most important to delineate? The answer would seem to be, obviously, both—since religion occurs within an institutional setting as well as in the lives of individual adherents. But the record reveals that often sociologists have settled for an institutional approach, leading, sometimes, to the virtual identification of church and religion.[4] While such an identification is, of course, unacceptable, it is very important to keep in mind the ancient adage about throwing the baby out with the bath. An individual's religion is, more often than not, institutionalized, as Demerath and Hammond note:

> Clearly individual religion does not occur in a social vacuum; measurements of individual religion should reflect the institutional setting in which that religion is most generally conceived and acted out. In fact, this is precisely the difference between the relatively nonsociological treatments of religion . . . and the manifestly sociological treatments. . . . Whereas the former definitions tend to neglect or deemphasize the institutional setting, the latter, more empirical, treatments seek to take it into account. It is true that the accounting is often superficial and even opportunistic (because, after all, it is easier to ascertain an institutional identification than to probe the depths of the individual psyche). It is even true that many of these efforts go too far in the institutional direction, thus overemphasizing the impress of the "church" and giving short shrift to other factors. Still, the institutionalization of individual religious sentiment is undeniably crucial.[5]

It is not within the professional competence of sociologists to say whether noninstitutional religious sentiments are more or less important than "church" religion.[6] It is a fairly safe prediction, however, that the divergent religious sentiments of important groups of individuals will, without too much prodding, take on varying degrees of institutionalization themselves. The selections in section II, chapter 4, will treat this subject in more detail.

The final selection in chapter one by Faulkner and De Jong is an effort to construct scales designed to measure each of the five dimensions of religiosity outlined by Glock and to examine the nature of the interrelationships among them. Using a Guttman scale technique (see chapter 11), scales were constructed for the ideological, ritual, intellectual, experiential, and consequential dimensions. An analysis of the interrelationships among the dimensions revealed the critical importance of the ideological dimension (belief). The correlations of the consequential dimension with the other four dimensions were the lowest of all correlations and would tend to give support to those who see little association between religiosity and secular activities.

---

1. Gerhard Lenski, *The Religious Factor* (Garden City, New York: Doubleday, 1963), p. 319.

2. Max Weber, *The Sociology of Religion,* trans. E. Fischoff (Boston: Beacon Press, 1963), p. 1.

3. Joseph Fichter, *Social Relations in the Urban Parish* (Chicago: University of Chicago Press, 1954), p. 23.

4. As studies in political science sometimes overstress the identification of politics with governments; and economists, in studying the economic system, sometimes give primacy to business corporations and their importance in the total system.

5. N. J. Demerath, III and Phillip E. Hammond, *Religion in Social Context* (New York: Random House, 1969), p. 137.

6. Luckmann argues that the approximate identity of religion and church began to dissolve following the period of the Renaissance. He contends that religion in the modern period is best understood as nonchurch religion occupying the sphere of the "private":

> Religious themes originate in the "private sphere." They rest primarily on emotions and sentiments and are sufficiently unstable to make articulation difficult. They are highly "subjective"; that is, they are not defined in an obligatory fashion by primary institutions. They can be—and are—taken up, however, by what may be called secondary institutions. . . . Syndicated advice columns, "inspirational" literature ranging from tracts on positive thinking to *Playboy* magazine . . . articulate what are, in effect, elements of models of "ultimate" significance.

He is careful to point out, nevertheless, that "subjectively constructed and eclectic systems of 'ultimate' significance will have a somewhat precarious reality for the individual." See: Thomas Luckmann, *The Invisible Religion* (New York: Macmillan, 1967). This theme is developed more fully in chapter 10 of the present volume.

Chapter 1
The Dimensions of Religion

TALCOTT PARSONS

The Theoretical Development of the Sociology of Religion

The present paper will attempt to present in broad outline what seems to the writer one of the most significant chapters in the recent history of sociological theory, that dealing with the broader structure of the conceptual scheme for the analysis of religious phenomena as part of a social system. Its principal significance would seem to lie on two levels. In the first place, the development to be outlined represents a notable advance in the adequacy of our theoretical equipment to deal with a critically important range of scientific problems. Secondly, however, it is at the same time a particularly good illustration of the kind of process by which major theoretical developments in the field of social theory can be expected to take place.

Every important tradition of scientific thought involves a broad framework of theoretical propositions at any given stage of its development. Generally speaking, differences will be found only in the degree to which this framework is logically integrated and to which it is explicitly and self-consciously acknowledged and analyzed. About the middle of the last century or shortly thereafter, it is perhaps fair to say, generalized thinking about the significance of religion to human life tended to fall into one of two main categories. The first is the body of thought anchored in the doctrinal positions of one or another specific religious group, predominantly of course the various Christian denominations. For understandable reasons, the main tenor of such thought tended to be normative rather than empirical and analytical, to assure its own religious position and to expose the errors of opponents. It is difficult to see that in any direct sense important contributions to the sociology of religion as an empirical science could come from this source.[1] The other main category may be broadly referred to as that of positivistic thinking. The great stream of thought which culminated in the various branches of utilitarianism, had, of course, long been much concerned with some of the problems of religion. In its concern with contemporary society, however, the strong tendency had been to minimize the importance of religion, to treat it as a matter of "superstition" which had no place in the enlightened thinking of modern civilized man. The result of this tendency was, in the search for the important forces activating human behavior, to direct attention to other fields, such as the economic and the political. In certain phases the same tendency may be observed in the trend of positivistic thought toward emphasis on biology and psychology, which gathered force in the latter part of the nineteenth century and has continued well into our own.

Perhaps the first important change in this definition of problems, which was highly unfavorable to a serious scientific interest in the phenomena of religion, came with the application of the idea of evolution to human society. Once evidence from non-literate societies, not to speak of many others, was at all carefully studied, the observation was inescapable that the life of these so-called "primitive" men was to an enormous degree dominated by beliefs and practices which would ordinarily be classified according to the common-sense thinking of our time as magical and religious. Contemporary non-literate peoples, however, were in that generation predominantly interpreted as the living prototypes of our own prehistorical ancestors, and hence it was only natural that these striking phenomena should have been treated as "primitive" in a strictly evolutionary sense, as belonging to the early stages of the process of social development. This is the broad situation of the first really serious treatment of comparative religion in a sociological context, especially in the work of the founder of modern social-anthropology, Tylor,[2] and of Spencer,[3] perhaps the most penetrating theorist of this movement of thought. Though there was here a basis for serious scientific interest, the positivistic scheme of thought imposed severe limitations on the kind of significance which could be attributed to the observed phenomena. Within the positivistic schema, the most obvious directions of theoretical interpretation were two. On the one hand, religious phenomena could be treated as the manifestations of underlying biological or psychological factors beyond the reach of rational control, or interpretations in terms of subjective categories. Most generally this pattern led to some version of the instinct theory, which has suffered, however, some very serious scientific handicaps in that it has never proved possible to relate the detailed variations in the behavioral phenomena to any corresponding variations in the structure of instinctual drives. The whole scheme has on the level of social theory never successfully avoided the pitfalls of reasoning in a circle.

The other principal alternative was what may be called the "rationalistic" variation of positivism,[4] the tendency to treat the actor as if he were a rational, scientific investigator, acting "reasonably" in the light of the knowledge available to him. This was the path taken by Tylor and Spencer with the general thesis that primitive magical and religious ideas were ideas which in the situation of primitive men, considering the lack of accumulated knowledge and the limitations of the technique and opportunities of observation, it would reasonably be expected they would arrive at. With beliefs like that in a soul separable from the body, ritual practices in turn are held to be readily understandable. It is, however, a basic assumption of this pattern of thinking that the only critical standards to which religious ideas can be referred are those of empirical validity. It almost goes without saying that no enlightened modern could entertain such beliefs, that hence what we think of as distinctively religious and magical beliefs, and hence also the accompanying practices, will naturally disappear as an automatic consequence of the advance in scientific knowledge.

Inadequate as it is in the light of modern knowledge, this schema has proved to be the fruitful starting-point for the development of the field, for it makes possible the analysis of action in terms of the subjective point of view of the actor in his orientation to specific features of the situation in which he acts. Broadly speaking, to attempt to deal with the empirical inadequacies of this view by jumping directly, through the medium of anti-intellectualistic psychology, to the more fundamental forces activating human behavior, has not proved fruitful. The fruitful path has rather been the introduction of specific refinements and distinctions within the basic structural scheme with which "rationalistic positivism" started. The body of this paper will be concerned with a review of several of the most important of these steps in analytical refinement, showing how, taken together, they have led up to a far more comprehensive analytical scheme. This can perhaps most conveniently be done in terms of the contributions of four important theorists, Pareto, Malinowski, Durkheim, and Max Weber, none of whom had any important direct influence on any of the others.

It is of primary significance that Pareto's[5] analytical scheme for the treatment of a social system started precisely with this fundamental frame of reference. Like the earlier positivists, he took as his starting-point the cognitive patterns in terms which the actor is oriented to his situation of action. Again like them, he based his classification on the relation of these patterns to the standards of empirical scientific validity —in his terms, to "logico-experimental" standards. At this point, however, he broke decisively with the main positivistic tradition. He found it necessary, on grounds which in view of Pareto's general intellectual character most certainly were primarily empirical rather than philosophical, to distinguish two modes of deviance from conformity with logico-experimental standards. There were, on the one hand, the modes of deviance familiar to the older positivists, namely the failure to attain a logico-experimental solution of problems intrinsically capable of such solution. This may be attributable either to ignorance, the sheer absence of logically necessary knowledge of fact, or possibly of inference, or to error, to allegations of fact which observation can disprove or to logical fallacy in inference. In so far as cognitive patterns were deviant in this respect, Pareto summed them up as "pseudo-scientific" theories. Failure to conform with logico-experimental standards was not, however, confined to this mode of deviance, but included another, "the theories which surpass experience." These involved propositions, especially major premises, which are intrinsically incapable of being tested by scientific procedures. The attributes of God, for instance, are not entities capable of empirical observation; hence propositions involving them can by logico-experimental methods neither be proved nor disproved. In this connection, Pareto's primary service lay in the clarity with which the distinction was worked out and applied, and his demonstration of the essentially prominent role in systems of human action of the latter class of cognitive elements. It is precisely in the field of religious ideas and of theological and metaphysical doctrines that its prominence has been greatest.

Pareto, however, did not stop here. From the very first, he treated the cognitive aspects of action in terms of their functional interdependence with the other elements of the social system, notably with what he called the "sentiments." He thereby broke through the "rationalistic bias" of earlier positivism and demonstrated by an immense weight of evidence that it was not possible to deal adequately with the significance of religious and magical ideas solely on the hypothesis that men entertaining them as beliefs drew the logical conclusions and acted accordingly. In this connection, Pareto's position has been widely interpreted as essentially a psychological one, as a reduction of non-logical ideas to the status of mere manifestations of instinct. Critical analysis of his work[6] shows, however, that this interpretation is not justified, but that he left the question of the more ultimate nature of non-cognitive factors open. It can be shown that the way in which he treated the sentiments is incompatible in certain critical respects with the hypothesis that they are biologically inherited instinctual drives alone. This would involve a determinacy irrespective of cultural variation, which he explicitly repudiated.

It is perhaps best to state that, as Pareto left the subject, there were factors particularly prominent in the field of religious behavior which involved the expression of sentiments or attitudes other than those important to action in a rationally utilitarian context. He did not, however, go far in analyzing the nature of these factors. It should, however, be clear that with the introduction, as a functionally necessary category, of the non-empirical effective elements which cannot be fitted into the pattern of rational techniques, Pareto brought about a fundamental break in the neatly closed system of positivistic interpretation of the phenomena of religion. He enormously broadened the analytical perspective which needed to be taken into account before a new theoretical integration could be achieved.

The earlier positivistic theory started with the attempt to analyze the relation of the actor to particular types of situations common to all human social life, such as death and the experience of dreams. This starting-point was undoubtedly sound. The difficulty lay in interpreting such situations and the actor's relations to them too narrowly, essentially as a matter of the solution of empirical problems, of the actor's resorting to a "reasonable" course of action in the light of beliefs which he took for granted. Pareto provided much evidence that this exclusively cognitive approach was not adequate, but it remained for Malinowski[7] to return to detailed analysis of action in relation to particular situations in a broader perspective. Malinowski maintained continuity with the "classical" approach in that he took men's adaptation to practical situations by rational knowledge and technique as his initial point of reference. Instead of attempting to fit all the obvious facts positively into this framework, however, he showed a variety of reasons why in many circumstances rational knowledge and technique could not provide adequate mechanisms of adjustment to the total situation.

This approach threw into high relief a fundamental empirical observation, namely that instead of there being one single set of ideas and practices involved, for instance in gardening, canoe-building, or deep-sea fishing in the Trobriand Islands, there were in fact two distinct systems. On the one hand, the native was clearly possessed of an impressive amount of sound empirical knowledge of the proper uses of the soil and the processes of plant growth. He acted quite rationally in terms of his knowledge and above all was quite clear about the connection between intelligent and energetic work and a favorable outcome. There is no tendency to excuse failure on supernatural grounds when it could be clearly attributed to failure to attain adequate current standards of technical procedure. Side by side with this system of rational knowledge and technique, however, and specifically not confused with it, was a system of magical beliefs and practices. These beliefs concerned the possible intervention in the situation of forces and entities which are "supernatural" in the sense that they are not from our point of view objects of empirical observation and experience, but rather what Pareto would call "imaginary" entities, and on the other hand, entities with a specifically sacred character. Correspondingly, the practices were not rational techniques but rituals involving specific orientation to this world of supernatural forces and entities. It is true that the Trobriander believes that a proper performance of magic is indispensable to a successful outcome of the enterprise; but it is one of Malinowski's most important insights that this attribution applies only to the range of uncertainty in the outcome of rational technique, to those factors in the situation which are beyond rational understanding and control on the part of the actor.

This approach to the analysis of primitive magic enabled Malinowski clearly to refute both the view of Lévy-Bruhl,[8] that primitive man confuses the realm of the supernatural and the sacred with the utilitarian and the rational, and also the view which had been classically put forward by Frazer[9] that magic was essentially primitive science, serving the same fundamental functions.

Malinowski, however, went beyond this in attempting to understand the functional necessity for such mechanisms as magic. In this connection, he laid stress on the importance of the emotional interests involved in the successful outcome of such enterprises. The combination of a strong emotional interest with important factors of uncertainty, which on the given technical level are inherent in the situation, produces a state of tension and exposes the actor to frustration. This, it should be noted, exists not only in cases where uncontrollable factors, such as bad weather or insect pests in gardening, result in "undeserved" failure, but also in cases where success is out of proportion to reasonable expectations of the results of intelligence and effort. Unless there were mechanisms which had the psychological function of mitigating the sense of frustration, the consequences would be unfavorable to maintaining a high level of confidence or effort, and it is in this connection that magic may be seen to perform important positive functions. It should be clear that this is a very different level of interpretation from that which attributes it only to the primitive level of knowledge. It would follow that wherever such uncertainty elements enter into the pursuit of emotionally important goals, if not magic, at least functionally equivalent phenomena could be expected to appear.[10]

In the case of magic, orientation to supernatural entities enters into action which is directed to the achievement of practical, empirical goals, such as a good crop or a large catch of fish. Malinowski, however, calls attention to the fact that there are situations which are analogous in other respects but in which no practical goal can be pursued. The type case of this is death. From the practical point of view, the Trobrianders, like anyone else, are surely aware that "nothing can be done about it." No ritual observances will bring the deceased back to life. But precisely for this reason, the problem of emotional adjustment is all the greater in importance. The significance both practically and emotionally of a human individual is of such a magnitude that his death involves a major process of readjustment for the survivors. Malinowski shows that the death of another involves exposure to sharply conflicting emotional reactions, some of which, if given free range, would lead to action and attitudes detrimental to the social group. There is great need for patterns of action which provide occasion for the regulated expression of strong emotions, and which in such a situation of emotional conflict reinforce those reactions which are most favorable to the continued solidarity and functioning of the social group. One may suggest that in no society is action on the occasion of death confined to the utilitarian aspects of the disposal of the corpse and other practical adjustments. There is always specifically ritual observance of some kind which, as Malinowski shows, cannot adequately be interpreted as merely acting out the bizarre ideas which primitive man in his ignorance develops about the nature of death.

Malinowski shows quite clearly that neither ritual practices, magical or religious, nor the beliefs about supernatural forces and entities integrated with them can be treated simply as a primitive and inadequate form of rational techniques or scientific knowledge; they are qualitatively distinct and have quite different functional significance in the system of action. Durkheim,[11] however, went farther than Malinowski in working out the specific character of this difference, as well as in bringing out certain further aspects of the functional problem. Whereas

Malinowski tended to focus attention on functions in relation to action in a situation, Durkheim became particularly interested in the problem of the specific attitudes exhibited toward supernatural entities and ritual objects and actions. The results of this study he summed up in the fundamental distinction between the sacred and the profane. Directly contrasting the attitudes appropriate in a ritual context with those towards objects of utilitarian significance and their use in fields of rational technique, he found one fundamental feature of the sacred to be its radical dissociation from any utilitarian context. The sacred is to be treated with a certain specific attitude of respect, which Durkheim identified with the appropriate attitude toward moral obligations and authority. If the effect of the prominence which Durkheim gives to the conception of the sacred is strongly to reinforce the significance of Malinowski's observation that the two systems are not confused but are in fact treated as essentially separate, it also brings out even more sharply than did Malinowski the inadequacy of the older approach to this range of problems which treated them entirely as the outcome of intellectual processes in ways indistinguishable from the solution of empirical problems. Such treatment could not but obscure the fundamental distinction upon which Durkheim insisted.

The central significance of the sacred in religion, however, served to raise in a peculiarly acute form the question of the source of the attitude of respect. Spencer, for instance, had derived it from the belief that the souls of the dead reappear to the living, and from ideas about the probable dangers of association with them. Max Müller and the naturalist school, on the other hand, had attempted to derive all sacred things in the last analysis from personification of certain phenomena of nature which were respected and feared because of their intrinsically imposing or terrifying character. Durkheim opened up an entirely new line of thought by suggesting that it was hopeless to look for a solution of the problem on this level at all. There was in fact no common intrinsic quality of things treated as sacred which could account for the attitude of respect. In fact, almost everything from the sublime to the ridiculous has in some society been treated as sacred. Hence the source of sacredness is not intrinsic; the problem is of a different character. Sacred objects and entities are symbols. The problem then becomes one of identifying the referents of such symbols. It is that which is symbolized and not the intrinsic quality of the symbol which becomes crucial.

At this point Durkheim became aware of the fundamental significance of his previous insight that the attitude of respect for sacred things was essentially identical with the attitude of respect for moral authority. If sacred things are symbols, the essential quality of that which they symbolize is that it is an entity which would command moral respect.

It was by this path that Durkheim arrived at the famous proposition that society is always the real object of religious veneration. In this form the proposition is certainly unacceptable, but there is no doubt of the fundamental importance of Durkheim's insight into the exceedingly close integration of the system of religious symbols of a society and the patterns sanctioned by the common moral sentiments of the members of the community. In his earlier work,[12] Durkheim had progressed far in understanding the functional significance of an integrated system of morally sanctioned norms. Against this background the integration he demonstrated suggested a most important aspect of the functional significance of religion. For the problem arises, if moral norms and the sentiments supporting them are of such primary importance, what are the mechanisms by which they are maintained other than external processes of enforcement? It was Durkheim's view that religious ritual was of primary significance as a mechanism for expressing and reinforcing the sentiments most essential to the institutional integration of the society. It can readily be seen that this is closely linked to Malinowski's view of the significance of funeral ceremonies as a mechanism for reasserting the solidarity of the group on the occasion of severe emotional strain. Thus Durkheim worked out certain aspects of the specific relations between religion and social structure more sharply than did Malinowski, and in addition put the problem in a different functional perspective in that he applied it to the society as a whole in abstraction from particular situations of tension and strain for the individual.

One of the most notable features of the development under consideration lay in the fact that the cognitive patterns associated with religion were no longer, as in the older positivism, treated as essentially given points of reference, but were rather brought into functional relationship with a variety of other elements of social system of action. Pareto in rather general terms showed their interdependence with the sentiments. Malinowski contributed the exceedingly important relation to particular types of human situation, such as those of uncertainty and death. He in no way contradicted the emphasis placed by Pareto on emotional factors or sentiments. These, however, acquire their significance for specifically structured patterns of action only through their relation to specific situations. Malinowski was well aware in turn of the relation of both these factors to the solidarity of the social group, but this aspect formed the center of Durkheim's analytical attention. Clearly, religious ideas could only be treated sociologically in terms of their interdependence with all four types of factors.

There were, however, still certain serious problems left unsolved. In particular, neither Malinowski nor Durkheim raised the problem of the relation of these factors to the variability of social structure from one society to another. Both were primarily concerned with analysis of the functioning of a given social system without either comparative or dynamic references. Furthermore, Durkheim's important insight into the role of symbolism in religious ideas might, without further analysis, suggest that the specific patterns, hence their variations, were of only secondary importance. Indeed, there is clearly discernible in Durkheim's thinking in this field a tendency to circular reasoning in that he tends to treat religious patterns as a symbolic manifestation of "society," but at the same time to define the most fundamental aspect of society as a set of patterns of moral and religious sentiment.

Max Weber approached the whole field in very different terms. In his study of the relation between Protestantism and capitalism,[13] his primary concern was with those features of the institutional system of modern Western society which were most distinctive in differentiating it from the other great civilizations. Having established what he felt to be an adequate relation of congruence between the cognitive patterns of Calvinism and some of the principal institutionalized attitudes towards secular roles of our own society, he set about systematically to place this material in the broadest possible comparative perspective through studying especially the religion and social structure of China, India, and ancient Judea.[14] As a generalized result of these studies, he found it was not possible to reduce the striking variations of pattern on the level of religious ideas in these cases to any features of an independently existent social structure or economic situation, though he continually insisted on the very great importance of situational factors in a number of different connections.[15] These factors, however, served only to pose the problems with which great movements of religious thought have been concerned. But the distinctive cognitive patterns were only understandable as a result of a cumulative tradition of intellectual effort in grappling with the problems thus presented and formulated.

For present purposes, even more important than Weber's views about the independent causal significance of religious ideas is his clarification of their functional relation to the system of action. Following up the same general line of analysis which provides one of the major themes of Pareto's and Malinowski's work, Weber made clear above all that there is a fundamental distinction between the significance for human action of problems of empirical causation and what, on the other hand, he called the "problem of meaning." In such cases as premature death through accident, the problem of *how* it happened in the sense of an adequate explanation of empirical causes can readily be solved to the satisfaction of most minds and yet leave a sense not merely of emotional but of cognitive frustration with respect to the problem of *why* such things must happen. Correlative with the functional need for emotional adjustment to such experiences as death is a cognitive need for understanding, for trying to have it "make sense." Weber attempted to show that problems of this nature, concerning the discrepancy between normal human interest and expectations in any situation or society and what actually happens are inherent in the nature of human existence. They always pose problems of the order which on the most generalized line have come to be known as the problem of evil, of the meaning of suffering, and the like. In terms of his comparative material, however, Weber shows there are different directions of definition of human situations in which rationally integrated solutions of these problems may be sought. It is differentiation with respect to the treatment of precisely such problems which constitute the primary modes of variation between the great systems of religious thought.

Such differences as, for instance, that between the Hindu philosophy of Karma and transmigration and the Christian doctrine of Grace with their philsophical backgrounds are not of merely speculative significance. Weber is able to show, in ways which correlate directly with the work of Malinowski and Durkheim, how intimately such differences in doctrine are bound up with practical attitudes towards the most various aspects of everyday life. For if we can speak of a need to understand ultimate frustrations in order for them to "make sense," it is equally urgent that the values and goals of everyday life should also "make sense." A tendency to integration of these two levels seems to be inherent in human action. Perhaps the most striking feature of Weber's analysis is the demonstration of the extent to which precisely the variations in socially sanctioned values and goals in secular life correspond to the variations in the dominant religious philosophy of the great civilizations.

It can be shown with little difficulty that those results of Weber's comparative and dynamic study integrate directly with the conceptual scheme developed as a result of the work of the other writers. Thus Weber's theory of the positive significance of religious ideas is in no way to be confused with the earlier naively rationalistic positivism. The influence of religious doctrine is not exerted through the actor's coming to a conviction and then acting upon it in a rational sense. It is rather, on the individual level, a matter of introducing a determinate structure at certain points in the system of action where, in relation to the situation men have to face, other elements, such as their emotional needs, do not suffice to determine specific orientations of behavior. In the theories of Malinowski and Durkheim, certain kinds of sentiments and emotional reactions were shown to be essential to a functioning social system. These cannot stand alone, however, but are necessarily integrated with cognitive patterns; for without them there could be no coordination of action in a coherently structured social system. This is because functional analysis of the structure of action shows that situations must be subjectively defined, and the goals and values to which action is oriented must be congruent with these definitions, must, that is, have "meaning."

It is of course never safe to say a scientific conceptual scheme has reached a definitive completion of its development. Continual change is in the nature of science. There are, however, relative degrees of conceptual integration, and it seems safe to say that the cumulative results of the work just reviewed constitute in broad outline a relatively well-integrated analytical scheme which covers most of the more important broader aspects of the role of religion in social systems. It is unlikely that in the near future this analytical scheme will give way to a radical structural change, though notable refinement and revision is to be expected. It is perhaps safe to say that it places the sociology of religion for the first time on a footing where it is possible to combine empirical study and theoretical analysis on a large scale on a level in conformity with the best current standards of social science and psychology.

When we look back, the schemes of Tylor and Spencer seem hopelessly naive and inadequate to the modern sociologist, anthropologist, or psychologist. It is, however, notable that the development sketched did not take take place by repudiating their work and attempting to appeal directly to the facts without benefit of theory. The process was quite different. It consisted in raising problems which were inherent in the earlier scheme and modifying the scheme as a result of the empirical observation suggested by these problems. Thus Malinowski did not abandon all attempt to relate magic to rational technique. Not being satisfied with its identification with primitive science and technology, he looked for specific modes of difference from and relation to them, retaining the established interpretation of the nature and functions of rational technique as his initial point of reference. It is notable again that in this process the newer developments of psychological theory in relation to the role of emotional factors have played an essential part. The most fruitful results have not, however, resulted from substituting a psychological "theory of religion" for another type, but rather from incorporating the results of psychological investigation into a wider scheme.

In order for this development to take place it was essential that certain elements of philosophical dogmatism in the older positivism should be overcome. One reason for the limitations of Spencer's insight lay in the presumption that if a cognitive pattern was significant to human action, it must be assimilable to the pattern of science. Pareto, however, showed clearly that the "pseudoscientific" did not exhaust significant patterns which deviated from scientific standards. Malinowski went further in showing the functional relation of certain non-scientific ideas to elements of uncertainty and frustration which were inherent in the situation of action. Durkheim called attention to the importance of the relation of symbolism as distinguished from that of intrinsic causality in cognitive patterns. Finally, Weber integrated the various aspects of the role of non-empirical cognitive patterns in social action in terms of his theory of the significance of the problems of meaning and the corresponding cognitive structures, in a way which precluded, for analytical purposes, their being assimilated to the patterns of science.[16] All of these distinctions by virtue of which the cognitive patterns of religion are treated separately from those of science have positive significance for empirical understanding of religious phenomena. Like any such scientific categories, they are to the scientist sanctioned by the fact that they can be shown to work. Failure to make these distinctions does not in the present state of knowledge and in terms of the relevant frame of reference[17] help us to understand certain critically important facts of human life. What the philosophical significance of this situation may be is not as such the task of the social scientist to determine. Only one safe prediction on this level can be made. Any new philosophical synthesis will need positively to take account of these distinctions rather than to attempt to reinstate for the scientific level the older positivistic conception of the homogeneity of all human thought and its problems. If these distinctions are to be transcended it cannot well be in the form of "reducing" religious ideas to those of science—in the sense of Western intellectual history—or vice versa. The proved scientific utility of the distinctions is sufficient basis on which to eliminate this as a serious possibility.

---

1. It was far less unfavorable to historical contributions than to those affecting the analytical framework of the subject.

2. *Primitive Culture.*

3. Esp. *Principles of Sociology,* Vol. I.

4. See the author's *The Structure of Social Action,* Chaps. II and III.

5. *The Mind and Society.* See also the author's *The Structure of Social Action,* Chap. V–VII; and "Pareto's Central Analytical Scheme," *Journal of Social Philosophy,* I, 1935, 244-262.

6. Cf. *The Structure of Social Action,* 200 ff., 241 ff.

7. See esp. *"Magic, Science, and Religion,"* by Bronislaw Malinowski, edited by Robert Redfield, the Free Press, Glencoe, Ill.

8. *Primitive Mentality.*

9. *The Golden Bough.*

10. For example, the field of health is, in spite of the achievements of modern medicine, even in our own society a classical example of this type of situation. Careful examination of our own treatment of health even through medical practice reveals that though magic

in a strict sense is not prominent, there is an unstable succession of beliefs which overemphasize the therapeutic possibilities of certain diagnostic ideas and therapeutic practices. The effect is to create an optimistic bias in favor of successful treatment of disease which apparently has considerable functional significance.

11. *The Elementary Forms of the Religious Life.* See also *The Structure of Social Action,* Chapter XI.

12. Especially *De la division du travail* and *Le suicide.* See also *The Structure of Social Action,* Chap. VIII, X.

13. *The Protestant Ethic and the Spirit of Capitalism.*

14. *Gesammelte Aufsätze zur Religionssoziologie.* See also *The Structure of Social Action,* Chaps. XIV, XV, and XVII.

15. See especially his treatment of the role of the balance of social power in the establishment of the ascendancy of the Brahmans in India, and of the international position of the people of Israel in the definition of religious problems for the prophetic movement.

16. See the writer's paper, "The Role of Ideas in Social Action," *American Sociological Review,* III, 1938, for a general analytical discussion of the problem included in the present volume.

17. Every treatment of questions of fact and every empirical investigation is "in terms of a conceptual scheme." Scientifically the sole sanction of such a conceptual scheme is its "utility," the degree to which it "works" in facilitating the attainment of the goals of scientific investigation. Hence the conceptual structure of any system of scientific theory is subject to the same kind of relativity with "arbitrariness." It is subject to the disciplining constraint both of verification in all questions of particular empirical fact, and of logical precision and consistency among the many different parts of a highly complex conceptual structure. The "theory of social action" is by now a theoretical structure so highly developed and with so many ramifications in both these respects that elements structurally essential to it cannot be lightly dismissed as expressing only "one point of view."

J. PAUL WILLIAMS

The Nature of Religion

The fashion today among serious students of religion is to dodge responsibility for developing a comprehensive descriptive definition of religion. Many researchers tend merely to indicate how they will use the word in their particular project. In some disciplines, a consensus develops; these intradisciplinary consensuses unfortunately are sometimes used not merely as a basis for work in a particular field but also as an excuse for avoiding the labor of coming to grips with the use made of the word *religion* by scholars working in other fields.

My impression is that a large percentage of the papers presented at the meetings of the SSSR assume without defense a definition of religion which is narrow. Even at the Research Planning Workshop conducted at Cornell University by the Religious Education Association in the summer of 1961, an extremely able set of consultants fell into this error, at least in their public presentations.

From the *Journal for the Scientific Study of Religion* 1 (Fall 1962):3-14. Reprinted by permission of the publisher and author.

Excellent research in religion can no doubt be conducted on the basis of a limited view; a researcher need not see the woods in order to make significant discoveries about his particular tree. Perhaps a whole school of researchers can make significant contributions on the basis of an arbitrarily limited definition. But certainly no interdisciplinary society such as ours can do its job without wrestling to the limit of its capacity with the problem of developing comprehensive definitions of its basic category, common understandings of the object of its investigation. The supposed hopelessness of reaching an interdisciplinary consensus is often alleged as an excuse for avoiding the effort. Intellectual advance seldom results from such defeatism. Reaching an interdisciplinary consensus may indeed prove to be beyond our present abilities. But that possibility does not relieve us as responsible scholars of the obligation to bring all our present resources to an effort to solve the problem. If we fail, we will at least be made more aware of the limitations inherent in our various approaches and have gained a broader perspective from which to judge our various contributions. This article is offered as a starter; hopefully it will stimulate in our varied and talented membership a vigorous discussion.

How Shall We Begin?

In trying to identify the distinctive characteristics of religion, the serious student can approach the problem in various ways:

1. He can be so much impressed with the value of his own experience that he defines religion solely in terms of that experience. In this *Journal* surely, there is no need to cite reasons for rejecting this approach.

2. He can generalize from the characteristic religious phenomena of the West. This practice would reflect a parochialism which, if it is considered to be justified, should be the product, not the premise of serious study.

3. He can begin by examining the data which are ordinarily considered to be religious. Jane E. Harrison, for example, wrote that "we shall at the outset attempt no definition of the term *religion,* but we shall collect facts that admittedly are religious."[1] This approach tries to identify the common elements in such familiar systems as Christianity, Judaism, Islam, Hinduism, Buddhism, Confucianism, Shinto, and the religions of primitive societies. The difficulty with this method is that the data which are studied are limited arbitrarily and, moreover, limited according to a criterion which is accepted uncritically. If a scholar used this method, he would be "merely taking refuge in an implicit rather

than an explicit judgment of what constitutes the 'admittedly religious.' "[2]

4. He can begin by an examination of all the data which are alleged by serious students to be religious; he would then include in his consideration data which usually are thought to be secular but which some students consider to be religious—for example, such social systems as nationalism and Communism and under some circumstances such private concerns as miserliness and status-seeking.

5. He can begin by an examination of the many definitions of religion which have been proposed.

6. He can adopt a combination of 4 and 5; that is, he can attempt to consider together the many proposed definitions of religion and the mass of data which are alleged by serious students to be religious. During his study a recurring interplay between data and definition, between observation and generalization, would be established. Hypotheses concerning the essential and distinctive aspects of religion would then be proposed and appraised.

Difficult as it is, this last approach is the one proposed here; it does not fall into the error of assuming a definition at the beginning of the inquiry, nor into the error of limiting the data which are to be examined. I contend that this is the approach which all serious efforts should take when the purpose is to define religion in all its complexity, an apparently world-wide and history-wide set of phenomena.

The burden such an effort places on the individual scholar is of course overwhelming; no individual has the capacity to meet more than a portion of the requirements of such a study. But perhaps a society of scholars has this capacity. A society-wide approach, cooperative effort, probably can bring to bear on this difficult problem all relevant facts and all relevant insights, at least those which have been set down in print.

"Religion" or "Religious"?

After examining the data which are alleged to be religious, scholars generally have concluded that religion as such is not to be identified with any specific type of overt conduct or any specific set of objects. Two quotations may give the ring of authenticity to this proposition. Ruth Benedict wrote, "There is probably nothing that at some time and place has not been of fundamental religious importance."[3] George A. Coe wrote, "There is not a type of human conduct that has not been attributed by some religion to its god."[4] Even allowing for a bit of rhetoric in these statements, the proposition is surely true that the essence of religion is not to be found in any specific kind of institution, symbol, behavior, or physical object.

This conclusion leads directly into the thesis proposed by John Dewey and others that religion should not be viewed as an independent entity by itself but as an aspect of entities. Dewey wrote:

> There is a difference between religion, *a* religion, and the religious; between anything that may be denoted by a noun substantive and the quality of experience that is designated by an adjective. . . .
>
> There is no such thing as religion in the singular. There is only a multitude of religions. . . .
>
> In contrast, the adjective "religious" denotes nothing in the way of a specifiable entity. . . . For it does not denote anything that can exist by itself or that can be organized into a particular and distinctive form of existence. It denotes attitudes that may be taken toward every object and every proposed end or ideal.[5]

Unless some investigator can identify as religion some entity "that can exist by itself," the conclusion is justified that religion is an aspect of entities rather than entity in its own right. Thus in strict usage the adjective *religious* would be more accurate than the nouns *religion* or *religiousness.* However, abandoning the nouns in favor of the exclusive use of the adjective would hardly seem necessary. Nouns are frequently used to refer to aspects of existence which have no independent reality. We speak of temperature, color, location; they never exist by themselves; they exist only as qualities of things. In the same way we can speak of religion ("the religion of Christianity") recognizing that it has no independent manifestation, but is rather an aspect of the life of human beings, and preferring the adjective religious ("religious persons of the Christian type") where we wish to make sure we will not be misunderstood.

The adjective is often used to modify other things than human beings (religious books, religious institutions). Religiousness is of course *primarily* a human quality. The religiousness of other entities is *secondary,* it is derived from the religiousness of human beings. For example, one book is said to be religious and another is said to be secular. The difference is not in the type of paper used, nor in the printing, nor even in the ideas stated, but in the way the books are regarded by human beings. The place for us to look when we are trying to isolate *primary* religiousness is at human beings.

The only escape from this conclusion is through the adoption of some type of Platonism; that is, the adoption of the belief that true religion is one of the eternal *ideas,* or perhaps that it was created by Almighty

God and that everything else claiming to be religion is false. According to this view, religion cannot be merely an aspect of man's life. Persons who hold this view will not find the propositions contained in this article congenial.

What type of human quality is religiousness? No one has suggested that it is a quality of the human body, like tallness or swiftness. Everyone who regards religiousness as a human quality would agree that it is a quality of man's mental life. Walter H. Clark, for example, wrote of religion as an "inner experience."[6] Joachim Wach called it a "mental act."[7] Religion is often called a *consciousness,* as for example, by the recent program makers of this Society.

Thinking, Feeling, or Willing

The overwhelming majority of definitions of religion begin "Religion is. . . ." The next word or phrase tends to identify the genus of the definition; that word points to the sort of mental quality which is thought to be religious. The many theories which have been proposed at this point have sometimes been classified into those which emphasize either the intellectual, the emotional, or the volitional aspects of man's mental life.

In the nineteenth century, a popular view was the intellectualistic. Tylor used the word *belief;* Spencer, *hypothesis;* Hegel, *knowledge.* The cogency of this view is seen in the fact that such knowledgeable contemporaries as C. J. Ducasse and Peter A. Bertocci return to this usage. Ducasse wrote: "Religion is any set of beliefs that. . . ."[8] and Bertocci, "The essence or core of religion is the personal belief that. . . ."[9] Religiousness certainly has belief in it; that is, wherever religiousness is found, belief (explicit or implicit) of some sort is present. Therefore, "belief" should be a part of an adequate definition. But the word is not comprehensive enough to place as the third word of the definition.

An influential group of thinkers maintain that religion is some type of emotion. Friedrich Schleiermacher used the word *feeling;* H. N. Wieman, *devotion;*[10] Rudolf Otto wrote of religion as an experience of awfulness, overpoweringness, urgency, fascination.[11] Here again, religiousness certainly has emotion contained in it; wherever religiousness is found, emotion (in some degree) is also found. But the concept *emotion* by itself is also not comprehensive enough to indicate the genus of religion.

Another group of thinkers hold that religiousness is some kind of willing. In all the theories I am familiar with, this willing is assumed to be manifest in some kind of behavior. The author of the Letter of James said, "Religion . . . is this: to visit orphans and widows in their affliction, and to keep oneself unstained from the world." Matthew Arnold emphasized *morality.* J. G. Frazer used the word *propitiation;* James H. Leuba, *appeal;*[12] W. K. Wright, *endeavor;*[13] J. Milton Yinger, *effort.*[14] These men indicate in various ways that religion is more than willing; yet the emphasis is there. That some element of willing is present in religiousness seems clear; that is, wherever man is religious, he has the will in some degree to behave according to his religiousness. But is the implication justified that this willing always results in behavior of some kind? Is there not religiousness which does not come to fruition in behavior? The man, for example, who resists the impulse to pray; or even the man who has a mystical experience who yet does not permit it to affect his life—a not impossible eventuality if the mystical experience is a mild one. Behavior instead of being an adequate identification of the genus of religiousness is one of the entities through which religiousness can become manifest.

"Religion is . . . ," then, more than believing or feeling or willing, but contains all of them. This observation has been made by a number of students. Wach, for example, wrote that the religious experience involves "the total being . . . not just the mind, the emotion, or the will."[15] Gordon W. Allport wrote that "subjective religion . . . must be viewed as an indistinguishable blend of emotion and reason, of feeling and meaning."[16] Presumably most of the writers classified above as emphasizing thinking, feeling or willing would agree. If possible, a word or phrase should be used which tries to get across this idea at the beginning of the definition.

Still another class of definitions identifies religiousness as an *attitude.* Dewey,[17] James B. Pratt,[18] Kingsley Davis,[19] and Elizabeth K. Nottingham,[20] for example, use this word. Nottingham writes that "Sociologists . . . use the term attitude to designate habitual tendencies to act in particular ways toward particular objects."[21] This definition of *attitude* does not seem adequate to identify the type of mental quality which religiousness is. Belief, the center of so many definitions of religion, seems insufficiently accounted for. Moreover, in Nottingham's definition, religiousness is directed "toward particular objects." The word *objects* in this phrase becomes adequate when it is understood to include the nonmaterial aspects of reality as well as the material, since religiousness is often directed toward such nonmaterial "objects" as institutions, beliefs, acts, etc. If Nottingham's definition of attitude is amended to read as follows, then perhaps attitude is the best single word to use to identify religiousness: Attitude designates habitual tendencies to think, feel, and act in particular ways toward particular objects.

James B. Pratt's definition of *attitude* is more descriptive and, therefore, more adequate:

> The word "attitude" shall here be used to cover that *responsive* side of consciousness which is found in such things as attention, interest, expectancy, feeling, tendencies to reaction, etc. Thus it is contrasted with . . . "content," the relatively passive element in sensation, the accepted and recognized. It presupposes always an object of some sort, and involves some sort of content; but it is itself a relatively active state of consciousness which is not to be described in terms of the given but it is a subjective response to the given. Thus it is not to be confined to any one of the three traditional departments of the mind—"knowing, feeling, and willing"—but involves factors that belong to each of them.[22]

When careful thinking is called for, the chances of getting *attitude* used in this inclusive sense are not good enough, if there is an alternative. "It is regrettable," writes Allport, "that we have no term in the lexicon of psychology to designate this cognitive-affective fusion."[23] He uses *sentiment,* a word whose connotations are probably not as adequate as are those of *attitude.*

Another class of definitions expounds religion in terms of its *functions.* This type of study has produced valuable insights. But it does not tell us what religion is. Moreover, if the previous analysis is correct, religiousness could modify a large number of functions. Allan W. Eister has raised some serious question concerning the functional approach; he wrote:

> Any attempt to apply most of the available functional theories of religion to complex societies rather than to primitive ones is more likely to lead to frustration than to fruitful understanding or insight. . . .
>
> The situation is one which comes close to suggesting that the theoretically statable functions of religion are at least highly elusive if not paradoxical.[24]

See my comment near the end of this article on the effort to identify the functions of religion.

In this article religiousness will be called a mental quality which will be identified as a *belief-attitude;* the hope is that the connotations of *attitude* for the reader include something of both the emotional and the volitional. The expression *belief-attitude* is of course a monstrosity. In situations where all the exactness possible is not needed, the simple word *attitude* should be sufficient.

Here follows a proposed formal definition of primary religiousness; after presenting this definition, its terms will be expounded and some opposing theories will be appraised.

Religiousness is a mental quality which modifies certain aspects of the life of individuals (and through individuals of groups); this quality must have each of the following characteristics in some degree:

a belief-attitude that the Ultimate for man exists (however it may be conceived) and that certain aspects of life derive from the Ultimate;

a belief-attitude that the derivation (from the Ultimate) of these aspects of life is beyond empirical demonstration;

a belief-attitude that these aspects of life are of supreme importance (at least potentially) for the concern of the individual (and perhaps of groups and/or all men).

Derived from the Ultimate

The Ultimate for any religious person is the final reality which he believes affects man's life, the aspect of the universe which he believes needs no further referent. The Ultimate is believed to be the basic source of life, that which man cannot escape. Usually this reality is thought to be cosmic in scope, manifest throughout the universe. The Ultimate may, however, be thought to be the primary influencer (or determiner) of human life and destiny, dominant only in the microcosm which has reality for the believer. Polytheists, for example, sometimes believe that one god is ultimate for them even though they believe in the existence of other gods. Thus the term *Ultimate* does not necessarily mean cosmic; but it does mean final or basic for the believer.

Some persons conceive of the Ultimate as existing apart from man, as being distant, "out there." Many moderns, however, think of it as being manifest throughout the universe, manifest in the near and small as well as in the far and great, in the human as well as in the divine. On the other hand, the conception of the Ultimate has no room for the idea that it is created by man. Rather it is discovered; it is fact; it is there; it is given. It is not concocted or manufactured or devised by man. The religious person's *beliefs* about the Ultimate are of course in part devised by himself but the reality itself about which he has beliefs are thought by him to be existent prior to himself and to be discovered—by himself and/or others.

The Ultimate is conceived of in many ways. Obviously included among these conceptions are the various types of theism: monotheism, polytheism, deism. Included also are the various types of nontheism: naturalism, humanism, materialism, etc. The nontheist views the Ultimate in impersonal terms. It is an error to suppose that all nontheists —naturalistic humanists, for example—think that the Ultimate is man himself. This view is rare. Most nontheists affirm that in the universe is an impersonal reality—called perhaps natural law—which is in some sense beyond man and Ultimate for him.

Religiousness is not confined, moreover, to those who are willing to affirm some view of the *nature* of the Ultimate; most agnostics are also religious according to this definition. The word *agnostic* usually applies to a person who is unwilling to affirm whether the Ultimate is personal or impersonal. Such a person could be religious, according to the definition expounded here, if he believed that the Ultimate exists and that certain aspects of life derive from it. Also a person could be religious if he wished to avoid making any affirmation concerning the nature of the Ultimate other than that it exists. The person who could not be religious would be the person whose agnosticism extended to affirmations that human beings can properly express no convictions as to whether or not an Ultimate exists or as to whether or not certain aspects of life derive from the Ultimate. A person may be very unsure what the Ultimate is like and yet be willing to make affirmations that the Ultimate exists and that certain aspects of life have their source in it; such a person could be religious.

This view of religiousness takes sharp issue with the view which holds that religiousness *can* concern merely what is of supreme importance for the individual or group. Vergilius Ferm, for example, wrote that religiousness is adjustment "to w(W)hatever is reacted to or regarded implicitly or explicitly as worthy of serious and ulterior concern."[25] This view means that the source of religiousness *can* be (not "always is") believed to be man, and only man. Paul Tillich says religion is an "ultimate concern,"[26] and Charles Y. Glock uses "ultimate commitment" and "primary commitment."[27] These phrases, also, imply that religiousness *can* be believed to derive from man's choice alone. The phrases "ultimate concern" and "ultimate commitment" have in addition the implication that man is capable of an ultimate concern or commitment. In reality human beings are capable only of a human concern for or a human commitment to what they believe to be Ultimate. Tillich wrote, "The ultimate concern is unconditional. . . . The unconditional concern is total; no part of ourselves or of our world is excluded from it. . . . The total concern is infinite; no moment of relaxation and rest is possible in the face of a religious concern which is ultimate, unconditional, total, and infinite."[28] If these are the characteristics, what human being could ever have an ultimate concern?

The rejection of the view that religiousness *may* concern merely whatever is of supreme importance to an individual is wholly arbitrary; no logical analysis or no set of data requires the view that religiousness comes from a belief-attitude that certain aspects of life derive from that which is believed to be Ultimate for man. Rejection of the possible human-derivation view of religiousness is prompted by two pragmatic considerations. (1) Religion could be very transitory. On this view a religious value might be no more than what a person wants most at the moment—perhaps victory in a football game or election to the country club. (2) Belief-attitudes which are held to have only a human derivation have much less power to generate compelling motivations than have belief-attitudes which are held to derive from the Ultimate. I hold that adequate research would demonstrate that motivations of the latter type are probably the strongest which impel human beings. The conviction of being in line with the Ultimate, of fighting on the side of the angels, of conducting oneself in accordance with the true nature of man and his environment probably gives a person more staying power than anything else.

The potency of religious motivation is clearly seen when religious values conflict with physiological values. Experience has demonstrated again and again that the basic physiological drives can be (not "always are") subjected by values which are believed to be the way of the Ultimate: hunger bows to religious asceticism; sex to religious ideals of chastity; self-preservation to love of country. If a person has a conviction that his action fulfills a God-or-nature-intended purpose, he gains strength which can help him endure frustration, privation, pain, and death. Religious motivation, be it noted, also tends to make religious belief-attitudes hard to change; they tend to be "inexorably held under all circumstances and conditions."[29] If this thesis concerning religious motivation is true, then religiousness becomes an extremely important aspect of human behavior and the potential source of great discoveries in psychology and sociology. Evil as well as good can of course result from religious motivation.

This view of religion is contrary to that view which limits religion to supernaturalism. By supernaturalism is meant the view which divides the universe into two orders of reality: nature and supernature. Robert H. Lowie contrasted the "workaday world" with "something transcending the expected or natural, a sense of the Extraordinary, Mysterious, or Supernatural."[30] Edward Norbeck defined "religion as ideas, attitudes, creeds, and acts of supernaturalism. By 'supernaturalism' we mean to include all that is not natural."[31] The United States Supreme Court in Davis v. Beason spoke for the man on the street in the following proposition: "The term 'religion' has reference to one's views of his relations to his Creator, and to the obligations they impose of reverence for his being and character, and of obedience to his will."[32]

Including nonsupernaturalist views in religion is again arbitrary. Yet, an appeal can be made to data which usually are alleged by serious students to be religious; none of the following systems are supernaturalist: early Buddhism, early Confucianism, Jainism, Sankhya, left wing Unitarianism, Ethical Culture. Moreover, naturalistic views of the Ultimate function in life in much the same way as do supernaturalist views. They both furnish to individuals and to groups orientation, integration, motivation, dynamic. Surely a definition of religion is seriously defective if it rules out Confucius, The Buddha, Felix Adler, Henry Nelson Wieman, and Mordecai M. Kaplan. On the other hand, a definition which includes these men also includes a multitude of other phenomena not "usually" thought to be religious—nationalism and Communism, for example.

A prominent school of thought, among sociologists especially, anchors its definition of religion on the term *sacred.* This practice has no particular merit since the term *sacred* must then be defined. Economy of effort would seem to indicate the simple use of the terms *religious* or *religion.*

Tillich wrote in his *Systematic Theology* that he had "avoided terms like '*the* ultimate,' '*the* unconditioned,' '*the* universal,' '*the* infinite.' "[33] Here on the contrary the term *the Ultimate* is deliberately used with the implication that the one affirmation about the nature of the Ultimate which is essential to the religious person is that it exists.

Beyond Empirical Demonstration

The second characteristic which must be present before a mental quality can be called religious is a belief-attitude that the derivation of certain aspects of life from the Ultimate is beyond empirical demonstration and is, therefore, taken on faith.

The complex world of experience contains many aspects of life which are believed to derive from the Ultimate. Most people believe (explicitly or implicitly) that the ultimate derivation of some of these aspects can be demonstrated by empirical methods. The universe has us in its lap. The laws of gravity require us to base our lives on the surface of the earth. The laws of health require us to avoid the poisons which are everywhere about us. The laws of human nature require us to get along somehow with some other men and women. These aspects of life (and many others) are believed to be inescapable, to be given to man not concocted by him, to be God-or-nature-intended for man. They are part of the very structure of man's universe. They derive from the Ultimate. Beliefs of this sort are arrived at by empirical means of one sort or another.

On the other hand, empirical means are incapable of demonstrating beliefs about certain other aspects of life which also are affirmed to derive from the Ultimate. The dogmas stated in the Apostles' Creed, for example, or the belief in the "sanctity of all human life" are thought to have their source in the Ultimate but their inescapability for man, their reality, their ultimacy, is beyond empirical demonstration.

I dodge here a discussion of the nature of empirical demonstration. This topic, called perhaps the nature of scientific method, is of basic importance for our Society and should be a major object of our recurring discussion. Dealing with the topic here in a few sentences would be of doubtful value. However, I do want to assert that faith, called perhaps "assumption," is a part of empirical demonstration.

This emphasis on the "unprovable" nature of religiousness probably needs no defense. Do any theories deny it? Is not "faith" a part of all serious definitions of religion?

One adjective sometimes used to describe this characteristic of religiousness is *irrational.* This word is quite inadequate. It implies knowledge not faith, knowledge of the erroneous nature of religious belief. Particularly bad are the words *imaginary* and *fictitious,* words reiterated by Kingsley Davis.[34] Here the error of religious beliefs is flatly asserted. Davis' use of the word *superempirical* is quite different. The connotation of this word is "beyond empirical demonstration." On the other hand, the connotation of the words *imaginary* and *fictitious* is "contrary to empirical demonstration."

Of Supreme Importance

The third essential characteristic of religiousness is the belief-attitude that some aspects of life which derive from the Ultimate are of supreme importance. Religiousness does not concern the trivial, incidental, peripheral aspects of life, but the major, fundamental, central aspects of life.

A distinction must be made, however, between those aspects of life which are *actively* considered to be matters of supreme importance and other aspects which are only *latently* or potentially considered to be of supreme importance. For example, some of life's "supreme values" are only latent because they are not threatened. Maintaining the food supply, for example, is not an object of religious concern for most Americans and Europeans. Under changed circumstances, however, say after a nuclear war, methods of maintaining the food supply would become very uncertain and would become the object of active religious concern since these methods would then have "the power of threatening and saving our being."[35] Thus a distinction is necessary between *active* and *latent* religiousness.

Religious persons vary in the amount of effort they give to pursuing their active religious values. Some persons expend much time and energy; they are very religious. Others expend little time and energy; they tend toward the secular.

All Three Characteristics Essential

Each of the characteristics outlined above must be present before a mental quality is religious. For purposes of identification only, these characteristics are listed below in phrases too short to be quoted as an adequate summary:

I Derive from the Ultimate
II Beyond empirical demonstration
III Of supreme importance

If only I and II are present and III is absent, even in latent form, then the mental quality would not be religious. If, for example, a person believes that certain aesthetic values are I and II but if also he "couldn't care less," then his belief-attitude toward these values would not be religious.

If only I and III are present and II is absent, again the mental quality would not be religious. If, for example, a person believes that the laws of gravity are I and III but considers their derivation from the Ultimate to be demonstrable empirically, these laws would not be viewed religiously.

Lastly, if only II and III are present and I is absent, the mental quality would not be religious. If, for example, a person believes that for him the values to be had from "adventure" are II and III but do not derive from the Ultimate, these values would not be viewed religiously.

The definition of *secular* is the absence of one or more of the three characteristics affirmed to be essential to the presence of religiousness.

Some Consequences of Accepting this View of Religiousness

1. Religiousness is subjective; it concerns the inner man. The only way to discover which specific aspects of life (beliefs, activities, symbols, institutions, etc.) are the objects of a given person's religiousness is to study his true inner state.

The extent to which such a study can be successful is a problem for the psychologists. I express the conviction that methods for investigating primary religiousness can be devised, and that they would include the asking of masked questions. A test devised to measure the extent to which persons worship may be suggestive for researchers in this area.[36] Is not a major challenge to psychologists of religion the creation of tests which both measure the intensity of a person's religiousness and also indicate the objects toward which his religiousness is directed?

2. Many of the aspects of life which are usually thought to be inherently religious are in fact often secular—going to church for example. People can go to church in the interest of very human ends: to make friends, to impress business associates, to show off new clothing. On the other hand, behavior which is usually considered to be strictly secular is often religious—status-seeking, for example. However, not all efforts to achieve a higher position in society would be religious. The test would be whether the individual's belief-attitude toward this aspect of his life had the three characteristics specified as essential to religiousness.

3. A distinction should be made between *avowed* religiousness and *real* religiousness. The religious system a person avows (Roman Catholicism, Methodism, Islam) may be at sharp variance with his real religion.

4. The religiousness of almost every religious person is inadequately summarized by pointing to some one religious system. His real religiousness is a combination of belief-attitudes which he selects from stimuli which come from many sources.

5. Religious systems are simply religious belief-attitudes (and their products) which are *shared* in large measure by a significant number of individuals.

6. Some social systems which are often considered to be irreligious or antireligious are in fact religious in the view of many of their adherents—nationalism for example. Many patriots look upon their particular brand of nationalism as deriving from the Ultimate, as beyond empirical demonstration, and as of supreme importance; similarly with democracy, capitalism, Communism, and militarism. A major threat to man's survival is the adherence of most contemporary national leaders and of large sections of the peoples of many contemporary nations to militaristic and nationalistic religious systems. The strong motivations inherent in religiousness and the tenacity which characterizes them increase this threat.

7. Religiousness is not inherently good. On any scale of values which is held consistently, some religiousness would be evil.

Types of Religiousness

Among the many possible analyses of religiousness, a useful one would be into the following four *categories:* secret, private, denominational, and societal. *Secret* religiousness would be those belief-attitudes a person refuses to divulge to other people; *private,* those he divulges but actively shares only with his intimates; *denominational,* those he shares with members of a group within society; *societal,* those he shares with the members of his society. These categories are not mutually exclusive. Moreover, the lines separating the categories are often blurred; the same religious values can often be found in more than one category of a given person's religiousness.

The nature of secret, private, and denominational religiousness is probably clear. Societal religiousness is perhaps a new conception to some readers. It is one of the major social dynamics of our day. At the heart of every enduring society is a set of values. In a competitive world such as ours, some of these values must be religious else the society could not survive in the struggle against other societies which possess the vitality which springs from religious motivation. Societal religiousness is a shared system of mental qualities. It exists as a part of the psyche of individual men and women. It has reality only because it is embodied by individuals. But it is shared by at least the dominant members of a society. It furnishes an essential part of the cement which binds the discrete units of humanity into vital, cooperative groups. And yet societal religiousness comprises the whole religiousness of very few (if any) persons. Included also in the religiousness of almost every religious person would be secret, and/or private, and/or denominational religious values.

Individuals often do not manifest religiousness in all four of these categories. Many persons in our society, for example, give evidence of secret, private, and societal religiousness but give no indication of denominational religiousness. Such persons are often called "secular." This designation would be improper according to the definition of secular here proposed.

Our society is often called secular. This designation also is surely improper according to the usage proposed here. A society whose major values do not correspond to the avowed values of its religious denominations may possess a very strong societal religiousness.

Scholars who approach the study of religion from the angle of functional analysis should find the difficulties of their study to be somewhat eased by a differentiation between denominational and societal religiousness. The thesis is often stated, for example, that a major function of religion is "the integration of society."[37] This thesis is attacked by pointing to the obvious fact that what often passes for the whole of religion in Western society (denominationalism) is often divisive. If, however, a distinction is made between denominational and societal religion, the integrative function of religion (societal religion) in society becomes clear. A viable society must have some degree of integration around values; and in our day some of these values must have the support of religious belief-attitudes. Within all the categories, religiousness can probably be shown to serve the function of integration to some degree; that is, denominational religiousness does tend to integrate the denominational group, societal religiousness to integrate the society, private religiousness to integrate smaller groups, say families. Other functions of religion can probably be specified in the same manner.

A fifth category of religiousness needs to be added to the four categories stated above: to secret, private, denominational, and societal religiousness add *international* religiousness. If a viable society in our day demands integration in some degree around religious values, then a major task of our aborning international society is to develop among its dominant individuals and groups such shared religious belief-attitudes as will tend toward the preservation rather than toward the destruction of this society.

An adequate study of religiousness can neglect none of these five categories. In our day, however, a prime object of investigation must be societal and international religiousness. Here lie the major forces which work for and against man's survival.

---

1. Jane E. Harrison, *Themis* (Cambridge, 1912), p. 29.
2. Jack Goody, "Religion and Ritual: The Definitional Problem," *The British Journal of Sociology,* Vol. XII, No. 2, June, 1961, p. 142.
3. Ruth Benedict, "Religion," *General Anthropology,* Franz Boas, ed. (Heath, 1938), p. 634.
4. George A. Coe, "The Word 'Religion,'" *School and Society,* July 9, 1949, Vol. 70, pp. 17-19.
5. John Dewey, *A Common Faith* (Yale, 1934), pp. 3, 7, 9.
6. Walter H. Clark, *The Psychology of Religion* (Macmillan, 1958), p. 22.
7. Joachim Wach, *The Comparative Study of Religions* (Columbia, 1961), p. 29.
8. C. J. Ducasse, *A Philosophical Scrutiny of Religion* (Ronald, 1953), p. 130.
9. Peter A. Bertocci, *Introduction to the Philosophy of Religion* (Prentice-Hall, 1951), p. 9.
10. H. N. Wieman, *Normative Psychology of Religion* (Crowell, 1935), p. 29.
11. Rudolf Otto, *The Idea of the Holy* (Oxford, 1928).
12. James H. Leuba, *A Psychological Study of Religion* (Macmillan, 1912), p. 7.
13. W. K. Wright, *A Student's Philosophy of Religion* (Macmillan, 1948), p. 47.
14. J. Milton Yinger, *Religion, Society and the Individual* (Macmillan, 1957), p. 8.
15. *Op. cit.,* p. 32.
16. Gordon W. Allport, *The Individual and His Religion* (Macmillan, 1950), p. 16f.
17. *Loc. cit.*
18. James B. Pratt, *The Religious Consciousness* (Macmillan, 1921), p. 2.
19. Kingsley Davis, *Human Society* (Macmillan, 1949), p. 521.
20. Elizabeth K. Nottingham, *Religion and Society* (Doubleday, 1954), p. 4.

21. *Ibid.*, p. 14n.

22. *Op. cit.*, p. 2f.

23. *Op. cit.*, p. 17.

24. Allan W. Eister, "Religious Institutions in Complex Societies: Difficulties in the Theoretic Specification of Functions," *American Sociological Review*, August, 1957, Vol. 22, pp. 387-391.

25. Vergilius Ferm, *First Chapters in Religious Philosophy* (Round Table, 1937), p. 61.

26. Paul Tillich, *Systematic Theology* (University of Chicago, 1956), Vol. I, p. 12.

27. Charles Y. Glock, "Religion and the Integration of Society," *Review of Religious Research*, Fall, 1960, Vol. 2, pp. 53ff.

28. *Op. cit.*, p. 12.

29. Charles Y. Glock, *op. cit.*, p. 54.

30. Robert H. Lowie, *Primitive Religion* (Boni and Liveright, 1924), p. xvi.

31. Edward Norbeck, *Religion in Primitive Society* (Harper, 1961), p. 11.

32. 1890, 122 U.S. 333.

33. *Op. cit.*, p. 12.

34. Kingsley Davis, *op. cit.*, pp. 521ff.

35. Paul Tillich, *op. cit.*, p. 14.

36. See my "An Objective Approach to the Study of Worship," *Religious Education*, July-August 1945, pp. 218ff.

37. Charles Y. Glock, *op. cit.*, p. 49ff.

CHARLES Y. GLOCK

On the Study of Religious Commitment

Religion is not the same to all men—neither in modern complex societies nor in even the most homogeneous of primitive ones. Even within a single religious tradition, many variations can be found. This simple fact scarcely needs documentation. The evidence that people think, feel, and act differently when it comes to religion is all around us.

In the face of this great diversity, the student of the individual and his religion is faced, therefore, with the formidable task of deciding how to conceptualize the phenomenon of religion and how to distinguish people in terms of their religious orientations. These are not, certainly, questions that have been ignored by students of religion. There have been attempts to distinguish people religiously and to discover what leads people to be religious or not. But the efforts have been surprisingly few and, on careful examination, incomplete. All things considered, the

Reprinted from the July-August 1962 Research Supplement of *Religious Education*, pp. 98-110, by permission of the publisher, The Religious Education Association, New York City.

task of constructing a conceptual framework for the systematic study of differential commitment to religion still lies ahead of us.

The present paper[1] is an effort to move us closer to that goal. Taking past work into account, it considers the question of what is required for a comprehensive and operationally useful definition of religion and suggests a research strategy for meeting these requirements. The intrinsic importance of religion in the life of man would be enough to justify the study of individual religiosity. But having a way to measure differential commitment to religion would do more than simply satisfy our curiosity. It is a prerequisite to moving on to the more compelling questions of what are the sources and the consequences of individual religiosity both for individuals and for societies.

The Dimensions of Religiosity

A first and obvious requirement if religious commitment is to be comprehensively assessed is to establish the different ways in which individuals can be religious. With some few exceptions, past research has curiously avoided this fundamental question. Investigators have tended to focus upon one or another of the diverse manifestations of religiosity and to ignore all others. Thus, in one study attention will be confined to studying religious belief and in another to studying differences in religious practices. The particular aspect of religion being studied is rarely, if ever, placed within the broader context of its relations to other expressions of religiosity. Nor is the question raised of whether religiosity manifested in one way has anything to do with its being expressed in other ways.

If we examine the religions of the world, it is evident that the details of religious expression are extremely varied; different religions expect quite different things of their adherent. Catholics and Protestants, for example, are expected to participate regularly in the Christian sacrament of Holy Communion. To the Moslem such a practice is alien. Similarly, the Moslem imperative to undertake a pilgrimage to Mecca during one's lifetime is alien to the Christian.

In the midst of the great variation in detail, there nevertheless exists among the world's religions considerable consensus as to the more general areas in which religiosity ought to be manifested. These general areas may be thought of as the core dimensions of religiosity. Five such dimensions can be distinguished; within one or another of these dimensions all of the many and diverse manifestations of religiosity prescribed by the different religions of the world can be ordered. We shall call these dimensions the experiential, the ritualistic, the ideological, the intellectual, and the consequential.[2]

The experiential dimension gives recognition to the fact that all religions have certain expectations, however imprecisely they may be stated, that the religious person will at one time or another achieve direct knowledge of ultimate reality or will experience religious emotion. The emotions deemed proper by different religions or actually experienced by different individuals may vary widely—from terror to exaltation, from humility to joyfulness, from peace of soul to a sense of passionate union with the universe or the divine. The emphasis placed on religious feeling as an essential element of religiosity may also vary widely; even within Christianity, groups differ widely in their evaluation of mysticism or in the importance they attach to the experience of conversion. Nevertheless every religion places some value on subjective religious experience as a sign of individual religiosity.

The ideological dimension is constituted, on the other hand, by expectations that the religious person will hold to certain beliefs. Again, the content and scope of them will vary not only between religions but often within the same religious tradition. Every religion, however, sets forth some set of beliefs to which its followers are expected to adhere.

The ritualistic dimension encompasses the specifically religious practices expected of religious adherents. It comprises such activities as worship, prayer, participation in special sacraments, fasting, and the like.

The intellectual dimension has to do with the expectation that the religious person will be informed and knowledgeable about the basic tenets of his faith and its sacred scriptures. The intellectual and the ideological dimensions are clearly related since knowledge of a belief is a necessary condition for its acceptance. However, belief need not follow from knowledge nor, for that matter, does all religious knowledge bear on belief.

The consequential dimension, the last of the five, is different in kind from the first four. It includes all the secular effects of religious belief, practice, experience, and knowledge on the individual. Included under the consequential dimension are all those religious prescriptions which specify what people ought to do and the attitudes they ought to hold as a consequence of their religion. The notion of "works," in the theological meaning of the term, is connoted here. In the language of Christian belief, the consequential dimension deals with man's relation to man rather than with man's relation to God.

These dimensions, it is proposed, provide a frame of reference for studying religion and assessing religiosity. There is no single piece of research in the literature which has looked at all five dimensions simultaneously; with a few exceptions,[3] most research on the individual and his religion has taken a unilateral rather than a multi-dimensional approach. Aside from the early works of Hall, Leuba, Starbuck, and James, almost no attention has been given to the experiential dimension of religion.[4] There have been some denominationally sponsored studies of religious knowledge among Christians, but no major piece of research has focused primarily or even incidentally on this dimension. The indicators of religiosity most often used fall under the ritualistic and ideological dimensions.[5]

It is the nature of the consequential dimension of religiosity that it cannot be studied apart from the other dimensions. Attitudes and behavior in secular areas of life can be used as measures of religious commitment only where they are grounded in religious conviction—where they follow from religious belief, practice, experience, and knowledge. Studies of the consequences of differential commitment to religion have necessarily, therefore, followed the pattern of comparing the secular attitudes and behavior of churchgoers and non-churchgoers, believers and non-believers, in an effort to discover whether religion does, in fact, have its effects.

Until there is research which measures religiosity in all of its manifestations, the question of the interrelatedness of the five dimensions cannot be wholly explored. It is scarcely plausible that the various manifestations of religiosity are entirely independent of each other. However, several recent studies strongly suggest that being religious on one dimension does not necessarily imply religiosity on other dimensions.[7] Fukuyama found, using a sample of Congregationalists, that those who scored high on ritual observance and biblical literacy tended to score low on religious belief and religious feeling and vice versa.[8] Lenski, in his recent study, *The Religious Factor,* found a relatively low order of association between the four indicators of religiosity he used: ritual participation, doctrinal orthodoxy (religious belief), devotionalism (religious experience), and associationism (religious self-segregation).[9]

In this general connection, it has recently been suggested that some of the contradictory findings of past research on religion and social class may be the result of different investigators conceptualizing religiosity in different ways. Demerath, in a monograph on this topic, cites studies which show no relation between social class and religiosity, some which report a positive relation between class and religion, others which show a negative relationship, and still others which show a non-linear relationship between the two.[10] In his discussion, Demerath points out that the way religiosity is manifested varies by social class. Thus, findings can be expected to vary from study to study if the indicators of religiosity used also vary, sometimes measuring one dimension, sometimes another.

The confusions that result from conceptualizing religion in unilateral terms and failing to recognize its other dimensions also characterized recent discussions on the state of religion in America. Several years ago, some observers claimed that a major postwar revival was occurring in American religion.[11] Others, while agreeing that interest in religion had heightened in recent years, argued that the increase did not represent a revival so much as a continuation of the long term upward trend in the religiosity of Americans.[12] Still others contended, to the contrary, that the long term trend in America is toward increasing secularization.[13] And, finally, the idea was expressed that over the past century and more the remarkable quality of American religion has been its stability, there having been a propensity neither toward greater religiousness nor toward greater secularization.[14]

These disagreements over whether or not a revival had in fact occurred and over the nature of the long term trend in American religiosity were, at least in part, attributable to a failure to specify the dimensions of religiosity that had allegedly decreased, increased, or remained the same. Different observers were defining religion in different ways. Some were equating it with belief, others with church attendance, and still others with the consequences of religiosity.

The mere identification of the different ways in which religiosity may be expressed thus turns out to be useful in a number of respects. It provides a perspective for locating the gaps in past and present research. It clarifies some of the discrepancies in what has been observed and reported about religiosity. And it establishes, at least roughly, the requirements to be met if we are to study the phenomenon of religion comprehensively.

It does not, however, afford a prescription as to how to go about studying religiosity. This is the task to which we now wish to turn. The premise which will inform our efforts is that insofar as the comprehension of religiosity in its whole is possible, this can only follow from an understanding of its parts. Consequently, principal attention will be given to considering how religiosity may be studied within each of its core dimensions. How it might be studied across dimensions will be briefly considered in a conclusion. The orientation in the following pages is toward the study of religion in societies which are in the Judaic-Christian tradition. However, on occasion, some of the special problems that arise in the cross-cultural study of religion will be mentioned.

It would ease the burden of analysis and research if each of the core dimensions delineated above could be assumed to be itself unilateral.

Such an assumption would allow us to ignore the question of subdimensions and to move directly to discussing ways of distinguishing more religious people from less religious ones. Unfortunately, the matter is not so simple. Within every dimension it is necessary to make distinctions in kind as well as in degree.

Religious Belief (The Ideological Dimension)

Religious belief may be studied in a number of ways. It may be approached from the perspective of the doctrines of institutionalized religion or from the point of view of a definition of religion which transcends traditional doctrine. In studying religious belief, one may inquire simply into what people believe. Or, one may go on to inquire into the saliency of belief, or going even farther, into the functions of belief for the individual. To understand belief, it will probably be necessary in the end to adopt all of these perspectives.

For the most part, past research has studied religious belief from the standpoint of traditional church doctrine and has asked, simply, "How do people differ with respect to their acceptance of church doctrine."[15] A number of scales and indexes have been developed, some simple and some complex, whose purpose usually is to order people along a continuum ranging from traditional belief to liberal or modern belief to unbelief.[16] Almost always, these measures are conceived in unilateral terms and assume, implicitly at least, that the greater the number of beliefs that a subject holds, the stronger is his belief.

Such an approach, while useful for certain purposes, obviously avoids the problems of assessing the saliency and the function of religious beliefs for the individual. Before discussing the questions of saliency and function we should first like to consider the appropriateness of conceiving of religious belief, even traditional belief, in a unilateral way. The failure to make distinctions in kind within the general category of religious belief may obscure some fundamental differences in *types* of belief and in *types* of unbelief.

The belief structure of any particular religion may be divided into three parts. First of all, every religion has beliefs whose primary role is to warrant the existence of the divine and to define its character. Within Christianity, such warranting beliefs would be represented by belief in God, in Christ and his miracles, in the virgin birth, and so on. Those who accept these beliefs are, in effect, accepting the existence not only of God but of a personal God. To be distinguished from warranting beliefs are those which explain divine purpose and define man's role with regard to that purpose. Within Christianity, purposive beliefs would include belief in original sin, in the possibility of man's redemption, in a day of final judgment, in eternal salvation or damnation. Purposive beliefs give rise, in turn, to a third category of beliefs, namely, those which bear on the means by which the divine purpose is to be implemented. Implementing beliefs establish what is the proper conduct of man toward God and toward his fellow man for the realization of the divine purpose. Implementing beliefs thus provide the ground for the ethical strictures of religion.

Different religions give different emphases to these three components of belief. Jainism, for example, stresses the implementing component as does Confucianism. Hinduism, on the other hand, places high value on the purposive element. These components are also given different emphases in Christianity. Lutheranism stresses the warranting and purposive components, the Society of Friends the implementing one.

The conclusion that emerges from these considerations is that in all probability degree of religiosity cannot be measured simply by the sheer number of beliefs that are assented to. Just as different religions stress different beliefs, so we can expect to find some individuals whose religious creeds encompass primarily implementing beliefs and others who place major emphasis on warranting and/or purposive beliefs. Future research will probably reveal the need to develop typologies of religious belief within which degree of religiosity can be measured rather than a single scale of religious commitment on which all individuals can be measured.

It seems equally inappropriate to conceive of non-believers as a single type, as most past studies have done. Perhaps in these studies there were too few atheists and agnostics to justify distinguishing between them. Yet, on the face of it, it would appear that a person who openly rejects religious belief is radically different from one who contends that the question of belief is beyond his ability to decide.

The question of saliency—how important the beliefs he holds are to the individual—is, of course, inexorably bound up with the problem of measuring the range and degree of religious conviction. There are many people who acknowledge holding a belief without its being important to them. Between 95 and 97 per cent of Americans acknowledge a belief in God, for example. It is possible, of course, to ask people directly to assess how important their beliefs are to them. But the saliency of belief is more appropriately studied in terms of the kind of religiosity individuals express on other dimensions. How active one is ritualistically, the kinds of religious experiences he has, how well informed he is religiously, and the extent to which he acts out his beliefs in practice are all measures of the saliency of belief.

These suggestions, while moving us toward a more sophisticated operational definition of religious belief, do not touch on the problem of discovering the functions of beliefs for individuals. Here, the objective is not to know what people believe or how salient their beliefs are to them, but to understand the role of religion in their psychological and social adjustment. To probe into the functions of religion is to attempt to answer the question: "Why are people religious?" in terms of the psychological and social benefits of religious commitment. It is a question which cannot be answered by asking people directly. They are likely either to find the question incomprehensible or to give an answer which is irrelevant to the concept of function, for example, "I believe in Christ because he died for my sins." The direct approach is faced with the fact that individuals are seldom consciously aware of the latent functions of their belief, though depth probing of a qualitative kind by a skilled interviewer could conceivably provide clues to them.

A functional approach to religious belief transcends particular religious traditions and focuses on the more generic functions of belief. Many hypotheses have been and will be proposed as to what the functions of religion are. In all likelihood, religious belief performs a variety of functions, depending on the belief itself and on the individuals who hold it.

One hypothesis offered is that all religions provide the individual with an interpretation of his existence. In a world whose purpose cannot be ascertained by reason, religion stands ready with an explanation, however partial it may be, to fill the vacuum. One significant aspect of belief in religious doctrine, therefore, may be that it resolves the problem of ultimate meaning for those to whom it is a concern.

Supporting such an hypothesis would be evidence to the effect that believers are actually more deeply concerned than non-believers with the problem of meaning and that religious doctrine actually allays the "metaphysical anxiety" of its adherents. Should it be found, as it may very well be, that religious belief is only one way of resolving the concern about meaning, the question would still remain as to whether religion is a more or less satisfactory way to do so than its functional alternatives.

It has also been suggested that religious beliefs help individuals to transcend many of the deprivations they experience, to meet their needs for being the object of someone else's concern, to overcome loneliness, and so on. Such meanings will clearly be latent to the believer. That they exist can be established only by methods that must rely for their cogency on the existence of an association between need and deprivation, and manifest expressions of belief.

Until now, we have analyzed belief largely within a framework which defines religion in traditional ways. However, religious belief may also be conceptualized in other ways. One alternative, implicit in what has just been said, is to conceptualize religion in terms of the individual's concern with discovering the purpose and meaning of life and of the beliefs he adopts to resolve that concern. Believers would then be represented by all those who have experienced this concern and have resolved it. Those who have the concern but who have not resolved it may be thought of as seekers. Non-believers would be those for whom the concern does not even exist.

Another alternative, suggested by the work of Durkheim and Tillich, might equate being religious with having a deep and ultimate commitment to a set of values.[17] From this view, any deep and ultimate commitment is regarded as defining what is "sacred" to the individual whether or not he also regards it as grounded in divine or supernatural authority. Whether a person subscribes to traditional religious doctrine becomes, then, essentially irrelevant to an assessment of his religiosity.

That alternative definitions of religious belief are possible raises the question of how religion is to be defined and by whom. From the point of view of research, there are no true and false definitions of religion, but only more and less fruitful ones. The justification for any conceptualization does not depend on how widely it is accepted. Religionists, by and large, reject Durkheim's conceptualization of religion. In the last analysis, however, what counts is how well the conceptualization works in adding to our understanding of men and society.

Religious Practice (The Ritualistic Dimension)

In the case of religious belief, the main research interest has been in what people believe rather than in the meaning of belief for those who have it. A parallel situation obtains with regard to research on religious practice. Again, the primary focus has been on what people do rather than on the meaning of their activity to them. However, even within this framework, the effort has been neither systematic nor comprehensive.

Reliance is usually placed on church membership and frequency of church attendance as indicators of religiosity within the ritualistic dimension, and there exists a plethora of studies describing the social correlates of these indicators.[18] Participation in sacraments has been studied occasionally as has the recitation of prayers. Probably the closest approximation to an effort to be comprehensive is Joseph Fichter's study of the degree to which Roman Catholic parishioners in a New

Orleans parish participate in the prescribed rituals of the church.[19] Fichter, however, did not study the interrelatedness of different forms of participation nor did he look at private religious practice in contradistinction to public practice.

Taking a fresh view of the problem, three possible approaches to studying the religious practices of individuals suggest themselves. First, one may give attention to distinguishing individuals simply with respect to the frequency with which they engage in ritualistic activity and to investigating the interrelatedness of various practices. A second approach is to study variations in the nature of a particular practice—prayer, for example. Thirdly, there exists the possibility of studying the meaning of ritual acts for the individuals who engage in them.

The study of the frequency and the patterns of religious practice is perhaps the simplest of the three. It would require, to begin with, a specification of the variety of religious practices which exist. Since different religions have different practices, one would have to decide whether to focus on practices common to different traditions or to take account of differences as well. A study in the United States limited to Christians and Jews would encompass a considerable variety of practices—worship, prayer, scripture reading, penance, obeying dietary laws, confession, tithing, and many more.

No study has yet been made of patterns of religious practice either within a particular religious group or within a total population. Aside from its descriptive interest, a study of this kind would provide an empirical basis for deciding whether religious practice can be conceived of in unilateral terms or, whether like religiosity itself, it must be conceived of in multidimensional terms. It would also provide a basis for deciding whether a distinction has to be made between being religiously active and being religiously involved.

The possibility for confusion between activity and involvement is perhaps best conveyed by an example. Two persons may be equally diligent about attending worship services every Sunday. They are equally active ritualistically on this measure. However, for one, this may be the only form of religious practice engaged in during a week. For the other, attendance at worship may be one of a wide variety of religious acts performed during the week. It is evident that to equate the two on the grounds of their equal participation in worship services is to obscure a major difference in their involvement in ritualistic activity. This illustrates the inherent weakness of relying on a single indicator to distinguish individuals on this, as well as other dimensions of religiosity. What combination of indicators might best be used to provide a reliable measure would be one of the questions which could be resolved by the research suggested above.

Studies of the frequency and the interrelatedness of religious practices need to be paralleled by studies which look at the phenomenon of religious practice more deeply. It is one thing to investigate variations in the frequency of prayer among different religions and among different people in the same religious group. It is quite another thing to investigate variations in the nature of the prayers themselves. We have remarkably little empirical knowledge of the occasions on which people pray or of the content of their prayers. Qualitative differences in the practice of praying may conceivably be of such a magnitude as to invalidate the use of the simple act of prayer as an indicator of religiosity.[20]

Knowledge of the variations which exist in particular forms of religious practice is perhaps a first step to understanding their meaning for the individual. Prayers of praise, for example, suggest a meaning different from prayers of petition. Knowledge of the varying meanings with which individuals invest religious acts is, in turn, a first step toward explaining differential religious participation and experience.

Religious Feeling (The Experiential Dimension)

There has been a tendency to associate religious feeling with the more extreme forms of religious expression—the conversion experience, talking in tongues, being visited by the Holy Spirit, and the like. In the little research done in the past on religious experience, it is precisely such expressions of religious feeling that have been focused on. That there are more subtle and less public feelings which accompany religious belief and practice has also to be recognized. Faith, trust, and communion connote these kinds of feelings.

The difficulties of studying the experiential dimension of religiosity, even in its extreme forms, are reflected in its research history. The flowering of interest in the subject occurred around the turn of the last century. As early as 1881, the psychologist Stanley Hall was engaged in empirically studying religious conversion and two of his students, Leuba and Starbuck, carried on the tradition he had established.[21] At the time, their work enjoyed wide acclaim. With the appearance in 1902 of James' classic *Varieties of Religious Experience,* it might have been supposed that the psychological study of religion had truly come of age.[22] Yet, despite the seeming promise of this early work, the leads suggested were not followed up and, since James, there has been no major and memorable work on religious experience.

Finding a way to begin anew the study of the experiential component of religion is complicated not only by the absence of a strong research tradition but by the relative lack of everyday experience with the phenomenon which could provide the empirical raw material for developing concepts. Except where they are expressed in overt and extreme forms, the individual's feelings toward or sensitivity to the divine are not likely to be openly expressed in everyday life. The research strategy proposed below must be viewed, therefore, as tentative and in need of the kind of refinement which only experience with its use can provide.

To begin with, it seems self-evident that religious feelings may be expressed in more than one way. We would suggest a fourfold ordering around the notions of concern, cognition, trust or faith, and fear. Individuals, we suspect, differ in their concern or need to have a transcendentally based ideology. Where there is a concern, it may find expression in a wish to believe, a seeking after a purpose in life, and a sense of deprivation with the world as it is. How concerned one is in this sense would be one component of his religiosity within the experiential dimension.

A second component would be the individual's capacity for cognition or awareness of the divine. Reverend J. Moran Weston has suggested the possibility of there being spiritual talent much as there is musical or artistic talent.[23] Insofar as he may be right, this is likely to be manifested in one's subjective experience of a divine presence, of a closeness to God, of being saved. The cognition may be intense, as in the case of conversion, or mild, as when an individual senses God in the beauties of nature. It may be manifested publicly—in a religious service—or privately—in isolation from others.

The third—trust or faith—bears on the individual's sense that his life is somehow in the hands of a divine power in which trust can be reposed. This component is not present in some religions though it has a primary place in Christianity. The problem of measuring faith is obviously a complex one. One can ask individuals directly concerning their sense of being watched over and cared for by the divine. Studying the matter indirectly may be more fruitful, however. Freedom from worry, having a feeling of well being, and the like are possible indicators of the fruits of faith.[24]

Though there is an admixture of fear and trust in most religions, one is likely to predominate over the other. The fear component, though present in Christianity, is not as strongly emphasized by it as by Islam, for example. As with faith, it can be studied directly by asking people whether they fear the divine and in what ways. Again, a more productive approach is to see whether and how fear is represented on other dimensions of religiosity—in beliefs about the nature of God, for example.

The experiential dimension of religion is inextricably bound up with the other dimensions. It can be studied effectively, therefore, only in the broader context of the individual's religiosity as it is manifested on other dimensions.

Religious Knowledge (The Intellectual Dimension)

The expectation that the religious person will be informed about his faith is common to all religions. There is considerable variation, however, in the kind of knowledge valued by different religions. Classical knowledge was esteemed by the Confucianists. Knowledge of Jewish history and of the law is highly regarded in Judaism. Within the most proselytizing of all religions—Christianity—communicating the Gospel is given great emphasis but being highly informed about the origin and history of the faith is not. Attitudes toward secular knowledge and higher criticism also vary in different religions. In some Christian sects, an effort is quite consciously made to limit exposure to secular knowledge and only literal interpretation of the "facts" of the faith is tolerated.

This great variation within and between faiths as to what the religious person ought to know and what should be the quality of his knowledge makes it difficult to judge what kinds of knowledge ought to be considered as indicators of religious commitment. It may be that attributions of religiosity based on knowledge cannot be made without reference to the individual's orientation on the other dimensions of religiosity, particularly religious belief. It is certainly not inconceivable, and perhaps even likely, that the atheist will tend to be highly informed religiously. Yet, by definition, he is a non-believer. It becomes a matter of considerable research interest to learn the relationship between how much and what kinds of religious knowledge the individual possesses and his patterns of belief, practice, and experience.

In evolving ways to measure this component of religiosity, we are obliged to start without the benefit of past research. There may be a dissertation literature on this subject, and perhaps it has been given attention in unpublished denominational studies. The published literature, however, is almost wholly devoid of research on religious literacy.

We may begin by asking just what it is that we wish to measure. First of all, it would be of interest to learn simply how much people know about what. Thus, religious literacy tests could be constructed to include a wide range of questions on the origin and history of the religion in which a subject was reared as well as questions about other religions. A variety of types would undoubtedly emerge from the administration of such tests. There would, of course, be those who are religiously illiterate. Many would be found who are knowledgeable about their own faith and not about others. Knowledge about origins, at least in Christianity and Judaism, would probably be much greater than knowledge about subsequent history. As already suggested, it is unlikely that greater and broader knowledge will be uniformly associated with stronger religious feelings, more regular religious practice, and greater adherence to religious beliefs. On the contrary, those with limited knowledge about their own faith will probably be found to be more religious in these other ways than either those with no knowledge or those with great knowledge. It is also likely that people hold to many misconceptions about the origin and history of their religion, and that these misconceptions are associated with certain patterns of religious belief, practice, and feeling.

Attitudes toward knowledge are also likely to be relevant. How much time is spent in reading religious literature—one indicator of an interest in acquiring knowledge—would ordinarily be studied within the area of religious practice. Beyond this, however, it would be useful to discover the importance given to knowledge and the kind of knowledge considered appropriate. We have in mind here distinguishing between those who would consider it inappropriate to become informed about the critical literature on religion as over against those who are willing to expose themselves to all that has been said and thought. Open- and closed-mindedness in this respect could conceivably help to account for types of religious belief and unbelief.

Finally the factor of religious knowledge could be further probed by inquiring into the degree of intellectual sophistication brought to the reading of scripture and other religious literature. This is measurable in terms of the degree to which there is, for example, an uncritical acceptance of scripture as literally true. Looking at religious knowledge from these different perspectives and relating what is learned to differential religious commitment on the other dimensions seems a necessary part of coming to understand the religious side of man. Its seemingly obvious importance makes the absence of research on what we have called the intellectual dimension of religiosity all the more surprising.

Religious Effects (The Consequential Dimension)

The implications of religion for practical conduct are stated very explicitly in some religions and very abstractly in others. The more integrated a religion is into the social structure, the more likely it is that the everyday actions of man are defined by religious imperatives. In Hinduism, for example, how a man deports himself from the time that he arises in the morning until he goes to bed at night is defined by customs which have the support of religious authority. In the more highly institutionalized religions, which have an existence in large measure independent of the social structure, religiously inspired imperatives are less likely to inform the conduct of daily life in explicit ways. General standards are set by the religion which the individual is left to interpret for himself as he confronts the decisions of daily existence. Thus, in Christianity, man is exhorted to be "a steward of God," "to exercise choice and initiative in his use of leisure time in keeping with the new life in Christ," "to manage economic wealth in terms of Christian responsibility and leadership," "to accept the political responsibilities of Christian citizenship on the basis of his citizenship in the Kingdom of God." But how these general injunctions are to be interpreted in concrete circumstances is left for the individual to decide.

Despite these differences, there is agreement among religions that consequences follow, or should follow, from religious commitment. These consequences have to do both with what the individual can expect to receive as a result of being religious and with what he is expected to give. The rewards may be immediate or promised for the future. Immediate rewards would include such things as peace of mind, freedom from worry, a sense of well being, or even, in some religions, material success. Among future rewards would be included salvation, promises of eternal life, reincarnation in a higher social category, and the like. Expectations about what a person will do as a result of being religious include both avoiding certain kinds of conduct and actively engaging in others. As in the Ten Commandments, there are always both "thou shalt" and "thou shalt not" injunctions.

As we have had occasion to point out before, research on religious effects cannot be done in isolation from research on other aspects of religiosity. How religious a person is on these other dimensions provides the warrant for asserting that a given act is, in fact, a religious effect. By definition, an act can be a religious effect only if it flows from religiosity.[25]

In this light, then, what research has been done on religious effects? On the reward side of our "reward-responsibility" dichotomy, research on the actuality of future rewards is, of course, automatically excluded. Research into the saliency of such promised rewards is important and feasible though it is most appropriately studied within the framework of religious beliefs. Research on the immediate rewards of religion has been relatively sparse.[26] For the most part, research on religious effects has focused on the "responsibility" side of the dichotomy, on what the individual does or does not do as a consequence of his religion.[27] A number of studies have examined the effect of religious adherence on individual attitudes and values. The work of Hartshorne and his associates, during the 1930's, on the effects of Christian education are relevant here.[28] They found no religious effect, though the indicators used to define religion were limited to attendance at worship services or at Sunday School. Joseph Fichter, in the final chapter of his book, *Southern Parish,* examines the degree to which parishioners judged to be highly religious in their ritualistic behavior subscribe to certain moral and ethical standards of the Roman Catholic Church.[29] His general conclusion is that adherence to the standards of the church is high only where they do not conflict with secular values. In his study, *Communism, Conformity, and Civil Liberties,*[30] Samuel Stouffer found, contrary to his expectations, that the religious are less civil libertarian in their attitudes than the nonreligious. In this instance, frequency of church attendance was the indicator used to judge religiosity.

The most ambitious attempt to study religious effects is Lenski's *The Religious Factor.*[31] Lenski adopts four indicators as measures of religiosity and relates each of them to a series of questions having to do with respondents' political, economic, and family values. His conclusions show generally that religiosity is related to the values studied, though the nature of the relationship varies according to the indicator of religious commitment used.

These studies, even Lenski's, are less than comprehensive in the indicators used to measure the religious commitment of their subjects. And, because they are all cross-sectional studies done at one point in time, they do not allow warranted conclusions as to the causal direction of the associations they find. Though Stouffer concluded that church attendance leads people to be less civil libertarian, the opposite conclusion is just as plausible, namely, that being non-civil libertarian leads people to more church attendance.

Despite their limitations, these studies are suggestive of the possibilities for more systematic research on the consequences of religion. However, precedence ought probably be given to studying the nature of religiosity in its "man to God" dimensions. For until we have established more adequate grounds for distinguishing people on these dimensions, the study of consequences will necessarily be tentative and incomplete.

Nevertheless, the potentialities seem very great indeed. Religion in our society would not be so viable had it no consequences for the individual. We suspect that these consequences are more of the "reward" than the "responsibility" variety. Yet both possibilities warrant further study. It would obviously be of major significance to know how and in what ways religion contributes to mental health. It would also be important to know more about what it implies for morality, for altruistic behavior, for the decisions people make as they move through the life cycle.

Conclusions

We are still far from an adequate understanding of the individual and his religion. The burden for this must rest primarily on our failures, thus far, to comprehend the nature of religion. In our zeal to explore the correlates of religion and to understand its effects, we have somehow ignored the phenomenon itself. It may turn out that there is no greater depth to religion than the simple indicators which have been used to measure it. However, until the effort is made to comprehend religion in all of its manifestations, we can neither rest easy in this thought nor have confidence in our research.

What is required first is a slow process of beginning to build more adequate measures of religion within and between dimensions. We cannot assume *a priori,* as previous research has tended to do, either that the dimensions are unilateral or that a single indicator will be sufficient to distinguish religious orientations within a dimension. Nor can we assume that religiosity expressed on one dimension automatically assures its being manifested on other dimensions as well. Recent research has already begun to suggest that different modes of religious expression may, in fact, be quite unrelated.[32] This lead needs to be followed up by examining, more systematically, the interplay between different aspects of religiousness.

It is quite conceivable that we shall end up with not one but a set of operational definitions of religion whose correlates and whose effects may vary very much from one another. On reflection, it seems very unlikely indeed that so complex a phenomenon as religion can be wholly understood either in unidimensional terms or within a framework borrowed exclusively from the expectations of traditional religion. The possibilities of doing research using concepts of religion which are informed by sociological and psychological theory have not been explored. Yet there is, perhaps, as much promise in following up such leads as continuing to rely too exclusively on more traditional conceptualizations of religion.

For the future, the real challenge probably lies in the cross-cultural study of religious commitment. However, until we have found a more adequate way to study commitment in our own culture, it would perhaps be unwise to plunge headlong into comparative research. The potentialities, though, seem exciting indeed.

1. This paper elaborates on certain ideas which were first presented in the author's paper, "The Religious Revival in America?", Jane Zahn, ed., *Religion and the Face of America.* Berkeley: University Extension, University of California, 1959. Reprinted in French under the titles "Y A-t-il Un Reveil Religieux Aux États-Unis?" in *Archives de Sociologie des Religions,* No. 12, 1961. The author is deeply grateful to his colleague, Gertrude Jaeger Selznick, for editorial assistance and advice.

2. The intellectual dimension represents an addition to those postulated in *op. cit.* The suggestion for the addition was made by Yoshio Fukuyama.

3. For example, Fichter, Joseph H., *Dynamics of a City Church: Southern Parish,* Chicago: University of Chicago Press, 1951; Lenski, Gerhard, *The Religious Factor,* New York: Doubleday and Co., 1961.

4. Hall, Stanley, "The Moral and Religious Training of Children and Adolescents," *Pedagogical Seminary,* June 1891.
Leuba, J. H., *A Psychological Study of Religion.* New York: The Macmillan Co., 1912.
Starbuck, E. D., *The Psychology of Religion.* New York: Charles Scribner's Sons, 1899.
James, William, *The Varieties of Religious Experience.* New York: Longmans, Green and Co., 1902.

5. For example, Bultena, Louis, "Church Membership and Church Attendance in Madison, Wisconsin," *American Sociological Review,* 47, March 1952, and Lenski, Gerhard, "Social Correlates of Religious Interest," *American Sociological Review,* 15, 1950.

6. Lenski, *op. cit.,* and Stouffer, Samuel, *Communism, Conformity and Civil Liberties.* New York: Doubleday and Co., 1955.

7. These studies rely only on single indicators to place people within particular dimensions and hence a question may be raised as to the adequacy of those indicators to represent a dimension.

8. Fukuyama, Yoshio, "The Major Dimensions of Church Membership," *Review of Religious Research,* Spring 1961.

9. Lenski, *op. cit.*

10. Demerath, Jay, *Religious Orientations and Social Class.* Berkeley: Survey Research Center, University of California, mimeo., 1961.

11. Herberg, Will, *Protestant-Catholic-Jew.* New York: Doubleday and Co., 1955.

12. Argyle, Michael, *Religious Behaviour.* London: Routledge, Kegan and Paul, 1958.

13. Whyte, William H., *The Organization Man.* New York: Simon and Shuster, 1956.

14. Lipset, Seymour M., "Religion in America: What Religious Revival?" *Columbia University Forum,* II, 2, Winter 1959.

15. For example, Allport, Gordon, Gillespie, J. M., and Young, J., "The Religion of the Post War College Student," *The Journal of Psychology,* XXV, 1948; Katz, Daniel and Allport, F. H., *Students' Attitudes,* and Barnett, Lincoln, "God and the American People," *Ladies Home Journal,* September 1948.

16. Allport, *op. cit.,* Lenski, *op. cit.,* Ross, Murray G., *Religious Beliefs of Youth.* New York: Association Press, 1950.

17. Durkheim, Emile, *The Elementary Forms of the Religious Life.* Glencoe, Ill.: The Free Press, 1947.
Tillich, Paul, *The Dynamics of Faith.* New York: Harper and Bros., 1958.

18. For example, Lenski, *op. cit.,* Bultena, *op. cit.,* Demerath, *op. cit.,* Goldschmidt, Walter, "Class Denominationalism in Southern California Churches," *American Journal of Sociology,* 1949.

19. Fichter, *op. cit.*

20. The same point can, of course, be made with reference to each kind of ritual activity. It cannot be assumed that even attendance at worship services connotes the same thing for different individuals.

21. Hall, *op. cit.,* Leuba, *op. cit.,* Starbuck, *op. cit.*

22. James, *op. cit.*

23. This suggestion was made personally to the author by Rev. Dr. Weston.

24. They are also, of course, indicators of the function of religion for the individual and of its consequences. Given the interrelatedness of the different dimensions, it is impossible to examine them each in a completely independent way and it is inevitable that some indicators will have significance for assessing religiosity in more than one of its dimensions.

25. It is possible, of course, to define religion only in terms of the degree to which its ethical principles are acted out in everyday life, leaving out all consideration of belief, ritual, feeling, and knowledge. While the utility of such a definition might be questioned, adopting it would provide, perhaps, the one condition under which consequences may be studied apart from the other dimensions of religiosity.

26. It is difficult to draw the line between the functions that religious belief serves for the individual, as discussed under the ideological dimension, and the idea that religion provides immediate rewards to the individual. For example, religion may function to give the individual peace of mind, or its psychological equivalent. At the same time, one of the promised rewards of religion may be peace of mind. Insofar as a distinction may be thought necessary, we may define as consequences of religion, those promised rewards of religion which are, in fact, produced. The functions of religious belief, on the other hand, would be the needs which religion serves which are not explicitly or implicitly stated in promised rewards.

27. It is sometimes difficult to distinguish between consequences which follow from explicit expectations formulated in the implementing beliefs of a religion, consequences which follow from an expectation expressed in abstract terms in an implementing belief, e.g. "The Christian should be a steward of God," and consequences which follow from the associations which the individual forms in his religious practice, or from the feelings he experiences in his response to the divine. A finding that Roman Catholics practice birth control would represent a clear consequence of the first kind. A finding that believers are more likely to engage actively in community affairs might represent a consequence of the second kind. A result showing that believers are more likely to vote Republican than non-believers might represent the third kind of consequence. In our discussion of past research, we shall not try to distinguish between the three types of consequences though the reader may wish to make his own interpretation as to the category in which specific findings fall.

28. Hartshorne, H., and Maller, J. B., *Studies in Service and Self Control.* New York: The Macmillan Co., 1929; Hartshorne, H., and May, M. A., *Studies in Deceit.* New York: The Macmillan Co., 1928; Hartshorne, H., and Shuttleworth, F. J., *Studies in the Organization of Character.* New York: The Macmillan Co., 1930.

29. Fichter, *op.cit.*

30. Stouffer, *op.cit.*

31. Lenski, *op. cit.*

32. Fukuyama, *op. cit.,* Lenski, *op. cit.*

JOSEPH E. FAULKNER
GORDON F. DE JONG

Religiosity in 5-D: An Empirical Analysis

The scientific study of religion has increasingly become a recognized object of theoretical and empirical interest for sociologists. A paramount problem of this undertaking has concerned methodological issues. What is the nature of religiosity, that is religious involvement? What are the characteristics of the religious devotee? The works of such early theorists as Tylor[1] and Frazer[2] revealed concern with man as a believer in spiritual beings who were believed to direct and control the course of nature and human life. R. R. Marett recognized the need for a multidimensional understanding of religion as an "organic complex of thought, emotion, and behavior."[3] William James stressed the need for an emphasis upon the "feelings, acts, and experiences" of religion,[4] and Durkheim's study of the religious life stressed the beliefs and practices of those who were collectively united into a church.[5]

However, as Charles Glock has pointed out, while researchers may be familiar with the necessity of conceptualizing religion in several dimen-

---

From *Social Forces* 45 (December 1966):246-54. Reprinted by permission of the University of North Carolina Press.

sions, most research tends to focus upon one or two dimensions to the exclusion of others.[6] That is, attendance at church may be utilized as the identifying factor of the religious devotee. Or, affirmations of belief in God plus a measure of attendance at church may be combined to provide an index of religiosity. With such variations in measures of religiosity it should not be surprising that there are divergent, and sometimes contradictory, findings with respect to such matters as the influence of religious involvement upon political preferences. Thus, Glock proposes that an investigation of religiosity should include five dimensions about which there is some consensus among world religions. Religious devotees, then, should be characterized by these dimensions which Glock identifies as experiential (feeling, emotion), ritualistic (religious behavior, i.e., church attendance), ideological (beliefs), intellectual (knowledge), and consequential (the effects in the secular world of the prior four dimensions).

The Problem

Based on the framework suggested by Glock the problem is to develop measures of religiosity for each of the five dimensions using the Guttman scale technique. Previous work in this area has undertaken similar goals, but has not given consideration to each of the dimensions suggested by Glock.[7] A major purpose for developing scales for different aspects of religiosity is to investigate the nature of the interrelationship among the five dimensions. There is no way to predict in advance the nature of the interrelationships among the various scales. Analytically they may be considered discrete, but as Glock states: "It is scarcely plausible that the various manifestations of religiosity are entirely independent of each other."[8] Fukuyama,[9] in a study of the dimensions of church membership among Congregationalists, found negative correlations between certain dimensions. Those who scored high on one dimension, ritual, tended to score low on belief and feeling. An investigation of the nature of interrelationships among the five dimensions will be a step in the direction of a comprehensive analysis of the religious phenomena.

Research Procedure

An immediate problem in developing a measure of religiosity is the delineation of what is considered more religious and what is less religious. In other words, an underlying continuum must be identified along which individual responses can be ranked. After careful analysis of responses to prior studies and extensive discussions with colleagues, it was decided to develop a scale based on traditional Judaeo-Christian beliefs.[10] An advantage of measuring religiosity along a traditional-nontraditional continuum is the discernible commonality among Catholic, Jewish, and major Protestant bodies on the more universalistic religious issues. This, of course, is not true at the more particularistic level. As a consequence, test items are designed to tap the more universalistic Judaeo-Christian beliefs.

The development of items to be included in each dimension followed the basic guidelines provided by Glock. To enhance the reliability and validity of the instrument several items were garnered from prior studies of religious attitudes. Notably, items in the ideological and experiential dimensions are modifications of those used by Allport *et al.*,[11] in their study of the religion of the postwar student. Certain items in the intellectual dimension parallel those of Lenski in *The Religious Factor.*[12] Additional items were constructed primarily to tap the intellectual, ritualistic, and consequential dimensions.

An initial pretest of the instrument was made by interviewing 89 randomly selected Pennsylvania State University students. On the basis of the interviews, some items were found to be ambiguous and were either revised or eliminated. Further analysis utilizing the Guttman scale procedure resulted in the elimination and revision of those items which did not meet the criteria of unidimensionality. As a special case of latent structure analysis, the unidimensional character of the Guttman scale method offers evidence to the validity of items.

Based on the pretest, the instrument was revised and administered to students in Introductory Sociology classes at The Pennsylvania State University during the fall of 1964. Out of a total of 375 students, 362 usable responses were obtained. Freshmen and Juniors were equally represented in the sample with about 25 percent each; Sophomores with 38 percent composed the largest grouping, while the proportion of Seniors was expectedly smaller, 12 percent.

Scale Items

From these data, dichotomized responses in each dimension were analyzed for scalability (Table 1).[13] This procedure yielded items which were most promising on empirical and logical grounds.[14] For the ideological dimension, a five-item scale yielded a coefficient of reproducibility of .94. Included were belief questions concerning the end of the world, the nature of the Deity, the necessity for repentance of sins, the

TABLE 1. *Items and Scale Criteria for Five Dimensional Scales of Religiosity*

Items	Percent Positive Responses	Percent Error	Scale Criteria
IDEOLOGICAL SCALE			
End of the world	36.5	2.7	
Idea about the Deity	56.9	5.5	
Necessity of repentence	62.2	8.5	
God in history	75.7	6.4	
View of the Bible	81.2	4.9	
Coefficient of Reproducibility			.94
Total responses			362
Expected no. of exact scale type responses			148
Observed no. of exact scale type responses			265
*Chi Square = 98.9, p. < .01			
†Coefficient of Scalability			.76
INTELLECTUAL SCALE			
Creation story	23.2	2.3	
Miracles	44.2	6.6	
Religious truth	50.0	7.5	
Books of the Bible	71.3	10.6	
Coefficient of Reproducibility			.93
Total responses			362
Expected no. of exact scale type responses			190
Observed no. of exact scale type responses			268
Chi Square = 37.0, p. < .01			
Coefficient of Scalability			.71
RITUALISTIC SCALE			
Religion apart from church	21.3	9.4	
Time reading Bible and other religious literature	29.8	7.6	
Attendance	45.9	6.0	
Prayer	63.8	8.9	
Marriage ceremony	73.8	8.6	
Coefficient of Reproducibility			.92
Total responses			362
Expected no. of exact scale type responses			157
Observed no. of exact scale type responses			234
Chi Square = 41.9, p. < .01			
Coefficient of Scalability			.74
EXPERIENTIAL SCALE			
Purpose to life	21.3	4.7	
"Union" with the Divine	50.0	8.9	
Security in face of death	67.1	10.6	
Interpretation of existence	70.7	8.2	
Faith is essential	78.2	8.7	
Coefficient of Reproducibility			.92
Total responses			362
Expected no. of exact scale type responses			160
Observed no. of exact scale type responses			229
Chi Square = 33.0, p. < .01			
Coefficient of Scalability			.74
CONSEQUENTIAL SCALE			
Business on the Sabbath	26.2	9.9	
Attitude about sex	32.6	10.3	
Political candidate	44.8	11.8	
Lying	65.5	7.8	
Coefficient of Reproducibility			.90
Total responses			362

TABLE 1, *continued*

Items	Percent Positive Responses	Percent Error	Scale Criteria
Expected no. of exact scale type responses			187
Observed no. of exact scale type responses			228
Chi Square = 10.5, p. < .01			
Coefficient of Scalability			.71

*This is a technique suggested by Festinger (See L. Festinger, "The Treatment of Quantitative Data by Scale Analysis," *Psychological Bulletin*, 44 (1947), pp. 149-161) which is designed to test the probability that the items would form a scale by chance. It involves computing the exact probability of each scale-type response, given the marginal of each item. The expected number of exact scale type responses is then compared with the observed number of exact scale type responses in a Chi-Square analysis.

†Herbert Mensel, "A New Coefficient for Scalogram Analysis", *Public Opinion Quarterly*, 17 (Summer 1963), pp. 268-280.

acting of God in history, and the view of the Bible. A four-item intellectual dimension scale was composed of items concerning the Biblical story of creation, miracles in the Bible, religious truth as compared to other forms of truth, and the identification of books of the Bible. These items yielded a coefficient of reproducibility of .93.

The scale designed to measure the ritualistic dimension of religiosity was composed of five items which had a coefficient of reproducibility of .92. Questions concerned time spent reading the Bible and other religious literature, church attendance, prayer, the possibility of developing a well-rounded religious life apart from the institutional church, and the choice between a religious or a civil marriage ceremony.

The experiential dimension was composed of five items pertaining to purpose in life, security in the face of death, interpretation of existence, the importance of faith, and a sense of "union" with the divine. These items composed a scale with a coefficient of reproducibility of .92. Finally, the consequential dimension included four attitudinal items about operation of nonessential businesses on the Sabbath, premarital sexual relations, lying on income tax, and religious orientation of political candidates. The coefficient of reproducibility for these items was .90.

All five scales met the .90 minimum standard for the coefficient of reproducibility and all items included in the scales met the .85 minimum single item standard established by Ford.[15] The observed number of exact scale-type responses exceeded the expected number by a statistically significant margin in all five scales. Results from the coefficient of scalability, a measure of the extremeness in the marginal distribution of items and individuals, ranged from .71 to .76, well above the minimal level suggested by Menzel (see footnote to Table 1).

Securing items which met the criteria for scalability was easiest for the ideological dimension and most difficult for the consequential dimension. We had anticipated using primarily behavioral items (such as incidence of cheating, premarital sexual relations, etc.) in the consequential dimension. Not too unexpectedly, however, these items failed to meet scale criteria, thus leaving attitudinal questions with respect to behavior.

The failure of the behavioral items to scale leaves us with a less than satisfactory composition of items in the consequential dimension. The use of behaviorally oriented items was considerably more successful in the ritualistic dimension where such items as church attendance, prayer, and reading the Bible and other religious literature met scale criteria.

TABLE 2. *Percentage Distribution of Student Scores for Guttman Scale Types on Five Dimensions of Religiosity*

Religiosity Dimension	No. of items in scale	Total (N = 362)	(low) 0	Scale Type 1	2	3	4	(high) 5
Ideological	5	100	12	6	19	13	16	33
Intellectual	4	100	16	32	16	16	20	--
Ritualistic	5	100	14	15	25	22	15	9
Experiential	5	100	11	9	16	23	26	15
Consequential	4	100	23	28	27	9	13	--

FINDINGS

Although these five scales of religiosity obviously have not been standardized, a few salient features of the distribution of student scores can be mentioned. Perhaps the most prominent feature is the rather significant grouping of high scores on the ideological dimension, indicating support of previous findings that there is not a marked departure from traditional beliefs by college students. To a lesser extent a similar skew is noted for the experiential dimension. This finding is of particular interest in that it suggests continuing support for the role of religion in providing answers to questions relating to emotional security, i.e., death, purpose in life, and religious faith.

On the other hand, the distribution of scale scores on the intellectual dimension shows a small but discernible grouping toward low scale types. With a student population this is not an unanticipated finding. Neither is the markedly low grouping of scores in the consequential distribution. It is clear that the majority of students are not greatly differentiated with respect to the consequential dimension as measured here. This perhaps suggests the presence of a strong humanistic element among college students. Scale scores on the ritualistic dimension more nearly follow a normal distribution.

The salient question, however, is the interrelationship among the five dimensions of religiosity. Hypothetically, a positive relationship would be expected among the five dimensions. However, if some aspects of religiosity are of more significance than others, complementary variations would be expected in the pattern of interrelationship.

The hypothesized interrelationships were tested by computing correlation coefficients among the five dimensions of religiosity. For all students, the correlation coefficients ranged from a high of .58 between the ideological and intellectual dimensions to a low of .36 between the experiential and consequential dimensions (Table 3). Although all the correlations were positive and statistically significant, some rather notable patterns of relationships did emerge.

TABLE 3. *Correlation Coefficients Between Five Dimensions of Religiosity by Characteristic of Students*

		Dimensions of Religiosity†									
Characteristic	Number	Ide-Int	Ide-Rit	Ide-Exp	Int-Rit	Int-Exp	Exp-Rit	Rit-Con	Int-Con	Ide-Con	Exp-Con
ALL STUDENTS	362	.58	.57	.49	.49	.48	.44	.43	.40	.39	.36
Sex											
Male	196	.58	.60	.39	.49	.37	.42	.44	.37	.38	.32
Female	166	.59	.54	.60	.49	.59	.46	.43	.45	.39	.42
Religious Affiliation											
Catholic	86	.48	.45	.42	.41	.46	.32	.47	.35	.43	.33
Jewish	37	.32	.57	.33	.28*	.45	.38	.07*	.24*	-.11*	.18*
All Protestants	160	.53	.43	.40	.45	.32	.31	.34	.28	.28	.20
Lutheran	40	.50	.25*	.09*	.32	.25*	.11*	.41	.49	.19*	.14*
Methodist and E.U.B.	30	.63	.46	.49	.46	.36	.24*	.25*	.03*	.31*	.38
Presbyterian	44	.52	.47	.45	.52	.46	.43	.34	.13*	.28*	.21*
Episcopal and Church of Christ	29	.50	.33*	.44	.57	.16*	.22*	.44	.54	.35*	.31*
Parents' Church Membership											
Neither parent	42	.57	.38	.51	.26*	.53	.07*	-.03*	.23*	.22*	.37
One parent	50	.57	.65	.29	.51	.32	.33	.50	.46	.57	.13*
Both parents	263	.56	.55	.49	.47	.46	.44	.42	.37	.33	.37

†Ide – Ideological
Int – Intellectual
Rit – Ritualistic
Exp – Experiential
Con – Consequential

*Not statistically significant at the .05 level.

If the size of the correlation coefficient is indicative of importance of a dimension, the ideological dimension was unmistakably of pervasive importance. Correlations between the ideological and the intellectual, ritualistic, and experiential scales, respectively, ranked one, two, three, out of a total of ten correlations. In many ways, the pervasive importance of the ideological dimension lends *post hoc* substantiation to some prior studies which relied primarily on this dimension as a measure of religiosity.

At the other extreme in terms of size of correlations was the consequential dimension. Correlations between the consequential dimension and the other four were all lower than correlations between any other dimensions. Along with the previously mentioned difficulties in scaling consequential items, the low correlations would seem to indicate that this dimension may reflect a qualitatively different measure of religious involvement. The remaining three dimensions (intellectual, ritual, and experiential) fall between the two extremes in importance. If the correlation analysis indicates any differences among these three, the intellectual dimension is slightly above average and the experiential dimension is slightly below average as indicators of religiosity.

In an attempt to further specify the interrelationships of the religiosity dimensions, student responses were divided on the basis of sex, religious affiliation, and parents' church membership. Correlation coefficients among the five dimensions were then computed for the various subsample groupings. In this way it was possible to see if certain dimensions of religiosity were of greater or lesser importance for certain groups of respondents. Lacking any other standardized basis for evaluation, subgroup correlations were compared with those for all students.

The most notable variation was the low correlations for Jewish respondents on nearly all interrelationships, particularly for the consequential dimension. Low consequential dimension correlations were also observed for all Protestant groups. For Lutheran affiliates, the experiential and ritualistic dimensions were unusually low. The ritualistic dimension was also below average for Methodists, while for Episcopalians and members of the Church of Christ, the experiential dimension showed weak correlations. For Catholic respondents all but two of the ten correlation interrelationships were below the average for all students.

Concerning religious background as indicated by whether or not the parents were church members, responses of students from homes where neither parent was a church member indicated particularly low ritualistic and consequential dimension correlations. On the other hand, responses of students from homes where one parent, usually the mother, was a church member showed particularly high consequential dimension correlations and rather low experiential dimension relationships. This was the only subgroup for which the consequential dimension correlations were consistently above average.

Supporting the popular image, the experiential dimension correlations were above average for females and below average for males.

SUMMARY AND CONCLUSIONS

The purpose of this research was to develop and empirically test the interrelationships among scales for five dimensions of religiosity as identified by Glock. These dimensions were the ideological, the intellectual, the ritualistic, the experiential, and the consequential. All the scales met the Guttman scaling criteria, and were well above the minimal level of the coefficient of scalability.

The findings from the correlations among the five dimensions of religiosity indicate the interdependent nature of these measures of religious involvement. That these dimensions are positively related is indeed what one would theoretically anticipate. However, the degree of relationships differ for the various dimensions. This diversity in the degree of relationships lends empirical support to the view that religious involvement is characterized by several dimensions—some of which are more closely related than others.

The highest correlations were, in every case, associated with the ideological dimension while the lowest correlations were associated with the consequential dimension. The importance of the ideological dimension as seen in its high positive correlations with other dimensions suggests that perhaps even more attention may be given to studying the importance of belief in the life of the religious devotee. Indeed this finding empirically substantiates Nottingham's[16] observation that Western religion has stressed belief in its intellectual aspects more so than other dimensions of religiosity.

The low correlations characteristic of the consequential dimension supports Glock's suggestion that this dimension is different in kind from the other four. The findings concerning the experiential dimension were the least anticipated in the study. The importance of this dimension seems to be in contradiction to some contemporary theological thinking, especially on university campuses, which would tend to emphasize the intellectual and minimize the experiential. However, it was a very volatile dimension for various subgroupings of students as was the ritualistic dimension.

These measures of religiosity were, of course, developed using a college student population. A further task is to test their applicability with nonstudent populations. Nevertheless, this research is a step toward alleviating a major problem in the scientific study of religion—the development of measures of religious involvement.

---

1. E. B. Tylor, *Religion in Primitive Culture* (New York: Harper & Bros, 1958).
2. J. G. Frazer, *The Golden Bough* (New York: The Macmillan Co., 1941).

3. R. R. Marett, *The Threshold of Religion* (London: Methuen, 1909), p. xii.

4. William James, *The Varieties of Religious Experience* (New York: Random House, 1936), p. 53.

5. E. Durkheim, *The Elementary Forms of the Religious Life* Swain, trans. (Glencoe, Illinois: The Free Press, 1947).

6. Charles Y. Glock, "On the Study of Religious Commitment," *Religious Education,* Research Supplement, 42 (July-August 1962), pp. 98-110.

7. Notable exceptions are the multidimensional approaches used by Ruth Goldsen *et al., What College Students Think* (Princeton: D. Van Nostrand, 1960); and G. Lenski, *The Religious Factor* (New York: Doubleday & Co., 1961).

8. Glock, *op. cit.,* pp. 99-100.

9. Yoshio Fukuyama, "The Major Dimensions of Church Membership," *Review of Religious Research* (Spring 1961).

10. The scale items are designed to measure deviation from the traditional Judaeo-Christian responses to such matters as belief in God, attendance at church services, and personal communion with the Divine. With this emphasis on traditional beliefs, item response categories permitted the student to answer in a fashion which in certain instances would be considered liberal, or in others, irreligious. For example, in the question concerning the idea of the Deity, the response "I am an atheist" is more of an irreligious than liberal position. Both positions, nevertheless, represent a departure from the accepted traditional response.

11. Gordon Allport *et al.,* "The Religion of the Post-War College Student," *The Journal of Psychology,* 25 (1948).

12. Lenski, *op. cit.*

13. The assistance of The Pennsylvania State University Computation Center is gratefully acknowledged. A program for Guttman scale analysis was written by C. B. Broderick, based primarily on the technique devised by Ford. (See Robert N. Ford, "A Rapid Scoring Procedure for Scaling Attitude Questions," *Public Opinion Quarterly,* 14 (1950), pp. 507-532.) For those not familiar with Guttman scaling, it is an attempt to reproduce a respondent's full set of answers from his rank on the scale. Cf., Louis Guttman, "The Cornell Technique for Scale and Intensity Analysis," *Educational and Psychological Measurement,* 7 (Summer 1947), pp. 247-280; Edward A. Suchman, "The Logic of Scale Construction," *Educational and Psychological Measurement,* 10 (Spring 1950), pp. 79-93; Samuel A. Stouffer *et al., Studies in Social Psychology in World War 2* (Princeton: Princeton University Press, 1950), Vol. 4, chapts. 1-9.

14. For the complete scales, see the appendix.

15. Ford, *op. cit.*

16. Elizabeth Nottingham, *Religion and Society* (New York: Random House, 1954), pp. 5-6.

Appendix

The exact wording of items included in the religiosity scales is shown below with an asterisk (*) marking the response defined as indicating a traditional religious response.

Ideological Scale

1. Do you believe that the world will come to an end according to the will of God?

*1. Yes, I believe this.
2. I am uncertain about this.
3. No, I do not believe this.

2. Which of the following statements most clearly describes your idea about the Deity?
*1. I believe in a Divine God, creator of the Universe, who knows my innermost thoughts and feelings, and to whom one day I shall be accountable.
2. I believe in a power greater than myself, which some people call God and some people call Nature.
3. I believe in the worth of humanity but not in a God or a Supreme Being.
4. The so-called universal mysteries are ultimately knowable according to the scientific method based on natural laws.
5. I am not quite sure what I believe.
6. I am an atheist.

3. Do you believe that it is necessary for a person to repent before God will forgive his sins?
*1. Yes, God's forgiveness comes only after repentance.
2. No, God does not demand repentance.
3. I am not in need of repentance.

4. Which one of the following best expresses your opinion of God acting in history?
*1. God has and continues to act in the history of mankind.
2. God acted in previous periods but is not active at the present time.
3. God does not act in human history.

5. Which of the following best expresses your view of the Bible?
*1. The Bible is God's Word and all it says is true.
*2. The Bible was written by men inspired by God, and its basic moral and religious teachings are true, but because writers were men, it contains some human errors.
3. The Bible is a valuable book because it was written by wise and good men, but God had nothing to do with it.
4. The Bible was written by men who lived so long ago that it is of little value today.

Intellectual Scale

1. How do you personally view the story of creation as recorded in Genesis?
*1. Literally true history.
2. A symbolic account which is no better or worse than any other account of the beginning.
3. Not a valid account of creation.

2. Which of the following best expresses your opinion concerning miracles?
   *1. I believe the report of the miracles in the Bible; that is, they occurred through a setting aside of natural laws by a higher power.
   2. I do not believe in the so-called miracles of the Bible. Either such events did not occur at all, or, if they did, the report is inaccurate, and they could be explained upon scientific grounds if we had the actual facts.
   3. I neither believe nor disbelieve the so-called miracles of the Bible. No evidence which I have considered seems to prove conclusively that they did or did not happen as recorded.
3. What is your view of the following statement: Religious truth is higher than any other form of truth.
   *1. Strongly agree
   *2. Agree
   3. Disagree
   4. Strongly disagree
4. Would you write the names of the four Gospels?
   What are the first five books of the Old Testament?
   (The second question was used for Jewish respondents.)
   *Three or more books correctly identified.

Ritualistic Scale

1. Do you feel it is possible for an individual to develop a well-rounded religious life apart from the institutional church?
   *1. No
   2. Uncertain
   3. Yes
2. How much time during a week would you say you spend reading the Bible and other religious literature?
   *1. One hour or more
   *2. One-half hour
   3. None
3. How many of the past four Sabbath worship services have you attended?
   *1. Three or more
   *2. Two
   3. One
   4. None
4. Which of the following best describes your participation in the act of prayer?

*1. Prayer is a regular part of my behavior.
*2. I pray primarily in times of stress and/or need, but not much otherwise.
3. Prayer is restricted pretty much to formal worship services.
4. Prayer is only incidental to my life.
5. I never pray.

5. Do you believe that for your marriage the ceremony should be performed by:
   *1. A religious official.
   2. Either a religious official or a civil authority.
   3. A civil authority.

Experiential Scale

1. Would you say that one's religious commitment gives life a certain purpose which it could not otherwise have?
   *1. Strongly agree
   2. Agree
   3. Disagree
2. All religions stress that belief normally includes some experience of "union" with the Divine. Are there particular moments when you feel "close" to the Divine?
   *1. Frequently
   *2. Occasionally
   3. Rarely
   4. Never
3. Would you say that religion offers a sense of security in the face of death which is not otherwise possible?
   *1. Agree
   2. Uncertain
   3. Disagree
4. How would you respond to the statement: "Religion provides the individual with an interpretation of his existence which could not be discovered by reason alone."
   *1. Strongly agree
   *2. Agree
   3. Disagree
5. Faith, meaning putting full confidence in the things we hope for and being certain of things we cannot see, is essential to one's religious life.
   *1. Agree
   2. Uncertain
   3. Disagree

Consequential Scale

1. What is your feeling about the operation of nonessential businesses on the Sabbath?
   *1. They should not be open.
   2. I am uncertain about this.
   3. They have a legitimate right to be open.
2. A boy and a girl, both of whom attend church frequently, regularly date one another and have entered into sexual relations with each other. Do you feel that people who give at least partial support to the church by attending its worship services should behave in this manner? Which of the following statements expresses your opinion concerning this matter?
   *1. People who identify themselves with the church to the extent that they participate in its worship services should uphold its moral teachings as well.
   2. Sexual intercourse prior to marriage is a matter of individual responsibility.
3. Two candidates are seeking the same political office. One is a member and a strong participant in a church. The other candidate is indifferent, but not hostile, to religious organizations. Other factors being equal, do you think the candidate identified with the church would be a better public servant than the one who has no interest in religion?
   *1. He definitely would.
   *2. He probably would.
   3. Uncertain.
   4. He probably would not.
   5. He definitely would not.
4. Suppose you are living next door to a person who confides in you that each year he puts down on his income tax a $50.00 contribution to the church in "loose change," even though he knows that while he does contribute *some* money to the church in "loose change" each year, the total sum is far below that amount. Do you feel that a person's religious orientation should be reflected in all phases of his life so that such behavior is morally wrong—that it is a form of lying?
   *1. Yes
   2. Uncertain
   3. No

SECTION II

Religion in the Church: Members, Leadership, and Organizational Structure

If there are difficulties in agreeing upon what elements best describe the religious person and the measurement of these constituent elements it might seem a relatively easy thing to describe certain characteristics of those who claim membership in some religious body. Such is not the case. Religious statistics of such a simple order as who does and who does not belong to a church are notoriously unreliable and are not readily comparable from one denomination to another. Some churches list as members any person who has been baptized into that particular faith—from infants to old people. Other churches list as members only adults who have been confirmed into membership. Some churches retain on their membership rolls individuals whose residences have been unknown for years and who, in fact, may no longer be alive. Since some churches do not remove from their membership rolls any persons except those known to be dead, individuals who have transferred from one denomination to another may well be enumerated more than once in a count of church membership. And then there is the problem of Jewish identification. A precise definition of who is a "Jew" presents difficulties which need not be discussed here. Morris Kertzer, for example, shows that there are several possible definitions of a Jew:

> A Jew is one who accepts the faith of Judaism. That is the *religious* definition. A Jew is one who, without formal religious affiliation, regards the teachings of Judaism—its ethics, its folkways, its literature—as his own. That is the *cultural* definition of a Jew. A Jew is one who considers himself a Jew or is so regarded by his community. That is the *"practical"* definition of a Jew.[1]

Notwithstanding these difficulties many social scientists still feel that efforts to carefully delineate a population into church members and those not formally belonging to any church constitute an important point of departure for ascertaining the degree of influence of religion in a society. Others, of course, disagree and argue that formal church membership and participation is of no more significance than membership and participation in other voluntary organizations, or is more a function of other variables (e.g., class) than it is of religious concern. That people *do* belong to and participate in church activities is, however, a social fact in the Durkheimian sense and cannot be simply dismissed as irrelevant to the understanding of the religious phenomenon.

The first article in chapter 2 by Sidney Goldstein is an analysis of the socioeconomic differentials among the various religious groups in the United States. It is important not to interpret the data reported by Goldstein as representing church *membership* in the United States. These data were gathered by the 1957 Current Population Survey of the United States Census Bureau in response to the question, "What is your religion?" As Goldstein notes, the data do not represent actual church membership and do not indicate any degree of church activity. They do, however, "provide one of the best bases for determining the religious composition of the American population. . . ." In addition, as the analysis indicates, the data provide valuable information necessary to construct a picture of the social and economic characteristics of those individuals who identify themselves as Protestants, Catholics, or Jews.

The next two selections in chapter 2 examine the motives for those individuals who join and participate in the activities of the church. Nash and Berger in their study of a Protestant suburban church interviewed adults who had joined the church during a three-year period prior to the study. In a majority of the cases the reason given for joining the church centered around parental concern for the children of the family and their moral instruction in matters of right and wrong. Acknowledging that this finding does not come as any great surprise the authors then raise the question as to why the *parent* would join also. The answer here was quite specific: if the children go the parents should too: ". . . commitment to one's children is more important than a personal commitment to religion at the time of joining."

In the study by Gorlow and Schroeder an attempt is made to identify "religious types" among those reporting some participation in religious activity. Utilizing an initial sample of 175 active church members "87 relatively nonoverlapping and unambiguous reasons for religious participation" were derived. These were then rated by 100 students who had described themselves as involved to some degree in religion. A factor analytic technique (see chapter 11) produced eight clusters of persons and their motivations for participation. The analysis reveals that Protestants, Roman Catholics, and Jews do not share equally the various motivations to participate. Roman Catholics, for example, but not Jews, are motivated "to be redeemed," or "to receive assurance of everlasting life" (Factor V). On the other hand, Jewish devotees, but not Roman Catholics, may be termed *religious eggheads* (Factor VIII). Such individuals are motivated to participate for intellectual reasons (studying religious and biblical writings) rather than in anticipation of some confrontation with God. Protestants are similar to Catholics but also are described as the *socially oriented servants of God.* They participate to "serve others" and to have an opportunity for "sharing one's faith with others" or for "sharing one's 'goods' with others." While there are differences for participation among Catholic, Protestant, and Jewish groups the authors are careful to point out that this "finding . . . must be interpreted cautiously since this investigation was not a study of various religious populations, and the sampling procedures prohibit generalizations to such populations."

Unlike the Faulkner and De Jong study (article 4, chapter 1), Gorlow and Schroeder did not specifically seek to test the theoretical dimensions of religion proposed by Glock (article 3, chapter 1), but they do call attention to the resemblance between the clusters which resulted from their analysis and the "core dimensions" of religion as proposed by Glock. The student should carefully examine the relationship of all three studies to the various dimensions of religion.

While there is an abundance of sociological studies describing characteristics of those participating in religious organizations, other voices persist in pointing to the decline of religion and lack of participation by a minority of the population (usually described as an "influential" or "significant" minority). Certainly there has been, as pointed to by Vernon in his study of the religious "nones," an insufficient amount of attention given to those who are often categorized as having "no religion"—a designation which ordinarily means the respondent does not hold membership in a church. But as Vernon remarks, it also adds the "gratuitous implication of a nonreligious person." Certainly not all religious activity nor all those who would identify themselves as religious are found in the churches. Nevertheless, much social science research describing the religious phenomenon has omitted from its analysis the "nones." Vernon's study is a valuable contribution designed specifically to see what degree of religiosity is found among the religious "nones."[2]

If sociological studies have tended to overemphasize the institutionalized facets of religion, one strong supportive reason lies in the observation by Demerath and Thiessen that "irreligion has failed to replace the churches." Nevertheless, there is a need for a sociology of irreligion and their study of a small-town Wisconsin free-thought movement is a beginning step in this direction. A careful examination of the "Church News" section of any Saturday edition of a metropolitan newspaper will reveal the existence of a considerable number of humanitarian, rational, ethical, or free-thought societies which conduct meetings on a regular basis like the more traditional churches. As Demerath and Thiessen point out, however, such organizations exist in what may fairly be described as a "hostile environment," and this results in an "organizational precariousness" of those which do manage to carry on their activities. Even students who firmly decline to participate in church activities are unlikely to be aware of the problems which this study points out, e.g., how does an irreligious organization go about the task of recruiting new members? What type of activities can it publicize and pursue? Can it openly proselytize among the traditional churches' membership—as the latter commonly do? If irreligious groups are unable to engage in these routine organizational activities they face, of course, eventual extinction or a thoroughgoing change in their nature to be more akin to the prevailing religious ethos. The authors conclude with regard to their study that it "is no surprise that the Freie Gemeinde is on the verge of disbanding."

Having examined selected characteristics of church members and nonmembers in some of the religious activity of this society, chapter 3 presents a series of studies of those professionals—the clergy—whose work it is to direct much of society's religious activity. The image, activities, and self-identity of the clergy today represent one of the dramatic examples of occupational change which has occurred over the past one hundred years. While historians of religion have put to rest both the popular image of the piety of our forefathers and the clergy's influence in colonial and later periods of American history, nevertheless, the former position of an educated clergy serving a largely uneducated populace resulted, no doubt, in the exercise of a greater degree of authority and influence in community life than is the case today.[3] Indeed the basis of the clergyman's authority and the exact nature of his role constitute the "crisis of identity" pointed to in the study of Jeffrey Hadden. Hadden suggests that the layman finds it hard to understand the clergyman for a variety of reasons. Clergymen are a highly heterogeneous group with regard to what they believe and what they do in their professional functions. Many clergy no longer view themselves as "set apart" from the laity—some of whom tend to persist in maintaining social distance from them. And both laymen and clergy have definite expectations of the role which the church is to perform in contemporary society. Unfortunately, these two views do not always coincide. While some clergy (especially the younger ones) view the church as an instrument of reform in society many laymen tend to think of it primarily as a source of comfort. Compounding all of these difficulties is the fact that the clergyman finds many of his traditional roles taken over in contemporary society by other professionals. This latter point is the subject of research in the selection by Cumming and Harrington.

The study by Cumming and Harrington investigates one of the vulnerable roles of the clergy, i.e., the counselor. Implicit in most studies which have discussed the clergyman as counselor is the assumption that this role has greatly increased in modern times. While longitudinal data are not available to see just what the degree of increase may be, contemporary studies do seem to agree that the clergyman is one of the professionals most often sought by those in need of resolution of their individual problems. Of course, in contemporary society the minister is only one of many sources of help for the distressed, and he often finds it necessary to refer to other professionals those who may have first come to him. Referrals among professionals in many fields is a common practice, but Cumming and Harrington found that the clergy in their study were particularly frustrated by the fact that they are quite willing to refer clients to other professionals but rarely experience the reverse of this situation. This "asymmetry of referrals" was found to be offset, however, by the satisfactions experienced by the minister in the fulfillment of this traditional role.

The role problems experienced by the clergy in counseling and other traditional areas might well receive a sympathetic hearing from the layman. After all, as the study by Cumming and Harrington indicates, the laity still do seek out the clergy in times of emotional stress. But the study by Campbell and Pettigrew is of a different order. In the racial upheaval experienced in this society for more than a decade now, neither clergy nor laity are certain of the proper role for the leadership of the church. This is not true for *some* of the clergy and laity, however. In both groups there are those who are adamant in their position that "religion and politics" should not "mix." An equally strong opinion is held by some clergy and laity that religion and politics cannot be divorced. The study by Campbell and Pettigrew of the role of Little Rock ministers in the 1957 effort to integrate Central High School highlights some of the problems faced by the clergy in trying to determine the nature of their involvement in the reformation of the society.

How is the clergyman to behave when confronted with specific moral and political decisions involving himself and the members of his local parish? Should he preach sermons devoted to the problem? Should he meet with his fellow clergymen and offer public statements as to what should or should not be done? Should he settle for prayers that "all will be well" in working out the crisis? Should he *personally* involve himself in the resolution of the problem? Campbell and Pettigrew found that each of these options was undertaken by some of the ministers in Little Rock. Others, of course, remained inactive throughout the entire crisis period.

In an effort to answer the question as to why the individual minister acted as he did in the Little Rock crisis, Campbell and Pettigrew point to the need to consider three systems "as relevant to his behavior: the self-referent system (SRS), the professional reference system (PRS), and the membership reference system (MRS)." While they suggest that the net effect of all three systems predisposed the minister to favor integration, conflicting strains in the systems resulted in only 8 of the sample of 29 ministers being classified as *active integrationists;* 16 were *inactive integrationists,* and 5 were classified as *segregationists*—though "none was avidly so." All of the 29 ministers had one thing in common, however: a segregationist congregation, which tended to produce inaction as the typical response of the minister.

The final selection in chapter 3 is an empirical examination of a new and evolving role for some clergy in this society: the campus minister. As stressed by Hammond the *campus* minister's role expectations and behavior clearly differentiate him from the local parish minister. The campus minister is politically more liberal, less ethnocentric and more ecumenically minded than his parish counterpart. He is, furthermore, better educated, more critical of the organized church, and more predisposed to the church's involvement in social action. Thus, there exists a "campus ministerial mind" which is representative of the campus clergy, but not the local parish minister. But, even in this specialized ministry there is not total uniformity among the clergy.[4] Hammond creates an index to measure *undifferentiated* conceptions from *differentiated* conceptions of those serving in the campus ministry. The undifferentiated ministers' conceptions of their role are more akin to that of a traditional "pastor" than are the differentiated. The latter tend to view themselves as on the "frontiers" of service to the church. They are willing, therefore, to risk "losing" the student if it means that he is questioning and striving to grow in understanding of his faith. The denominational support of both the differentiated and the undifferentiated in the campus ministry suggests, however, an evolution of new church structures to meet the needs of its adherents—at least on the university campuses. The understanding of the existing structure of the church as an organization is the subject of chapter 4.

Among the church's friends and foes alike there are those who argue that the strong organizational characteristics of the church represent, not its strength, but its weakness. The phrase, "religionless Christianity" (which means "Christianity without an institutional church") is popular in the writings of many contemporary theologians. But from the sociological perspective the church is not so much the "body of Christ" as it is the "General Motors" of religion. This is not, of course, a critique of the church—it is simply a social fact and as such necessitates an analysis of the church's organizational structure. The three selections in chapter 4 examine the "sect" and "church" characteristics of institutional religion.

The selection by Benton Johnson examines the extensively criticized church-sect typology developed by Ernst Troeltsch to see what, if any, utilization of it may be helpful in classifying the major religious groups in America today. It is by now a well established proposition in sociology of religion that no religious groups are "pure" church types or sect types. Whatever variables are utilized in constructing a modification of the Troeltsch typology will result still in overlappings. Johnson suggests, nevertheless, that if an effort is made to distinguish between church and sect on a "very high level of generality" it will have some heuristic value in attempting to classify the different religious groups in this society as well as providing a basis for cross-cultural comparisons. Basing his distinction of church and sect upon the "acceptance" or "rejection" of the social environment in which it exists (the church accepts the environment; the sect rejects it), Johnson then proceeds to point to the more "subtle distinctions" which must be analyzed in the acceptance or rejection of the social environment. While with "varying degrees of enthusiasm the great majority of American religious bodies support the dominant values" of the society, there are cleavages within both church and sect-type groups which are closely related to the liberal-conservative political divisions in the country. One must consider "the liberal-conservative split within Protestantism" if he "wishes to investigate the actual manner in which religious bodies are related to the value climate of the contemporary United States. For many research purposes it will yield far more positive and meaningful results than will breakdowns based on denomination or any distinctions in the extent to which groups enthusiastically endorse the dominant values." Recent overt political protests in the United States by Presbyterian James McIntyre and his followers and Fathers Daniel Berrigan and James Groppi of the Roman Catholic Church support the fruitfulness of this approach to understanding church-sect typologies.

The student should note, of course, that the theoretical features of church and sect types are closely related to the previous discussion of leadership characteristics. Certainly the campus ministerial mind outlined by Hammond would find it impossible to provide leadership in extreme right-wing sect-type groups. On the other hand, Hadden's assertion that a "significant proportion of young men who are choosing the ministry today are doing so out of a commitment to the solution of critical social problems in society" has strong implications for the future leadership of those conservative church-type groups which tend to accept the social environment in which they exist.[5]

Steinberg's discussion of Reform Judaism as a "church movement" is a further elaboration of the effort by Johnson to refine the church-sect typology. Reform Judaism has always presented particular problems for the original Troeltsch typology. It has some sectarian tendencies but is absolutely divorced from other major characteristics often associated with sects: literal adherence to the biblical teachings, for example. And perhaps most important, Reform Judaism is not dedicated to the radical alteration of societal norms and/or values, but rather is concerned with bringing its own norms and values into harmony with those of the larger society. Is it, then, a church or sect?

Steinberg stresses, consistent with the Johnson thesis, that the degree of tension between a religious body and the surrounding society provides the basis for differentiation between church and sect-type groups. A Church is a religious group which has low tension with the surrounding society while the Sect is characterized by high tension with the surrounding environment. He feels that this conceptualization is preferable to the Johnson statement since either society or the religious group may be the party which rejects the other. Reform Judaism is best understood as a church movement since it has been characterized by its efforts to modify its own institutional norms and values to bring them into harmony with those of the larger society. In contrast, Orthodox Judaism, at first in relative harmony with its surroundings, later experienced difficulties and thus moved toward a higher state of tension. It would, accordingly, be classified as a sect-type movement.

Bryan Wilson's study of the strains and role conflicts of Pentecostal ministers might very well have been included with the discussion of leadership characteristics in chapter 3. It is, however, a study of leadership problems with an evolving sect-type religious group and stresses, accordingly, the *dynamic* nature of the church-sect typology. As noted by Johnson, one of the criticisms of the Troeltsch typology is that it is a static concept. Wilson's study clearly reveals the growth pattern and consequent problems of a religious group with strong sectarian tendencies moving toward a degree of institutionalization as a church type. In the Pentecostal group studied by Wilson (and in similar other groups), there is a long-standing tradition of leadership by the Spirit, the priesthood of all believers, and speaking-in-tongues. The appointed minister shares this ideology but, at the same time, must meet the most institutionalized demands of his superiors. If the religious group has a strong hierarchy but a weak local organization—as was the case in the Elim Foursquare Gospel Alliance—the minister faces special difficulties in mediating the demands of the hierarchy to the local congregation. His is a contradictory status since there is little consensus among those he is to serve as to his proper role. It is no surprise, as Wilson states, that the "tradition of the leadership of the Spirit is ill-matched with a paid ministerial order. . . ."

---

1. Morris N. Kertzer, "What is a Jew?" in Leo Rosten (ed.), *A Guide to the Religions of America.* New York: Simon and Schuster, 1955, p. 65.

2. The religious "nones" may be irreligious, i.e., hostile to religion in the sense discussed by Demerath and Thiessen in article five, chapter 2. They may, of course, be simply un-religious, i.e., having no concern either way with religion.

3. See, for example, F. L. Littell, *From State Church to Pluralism* (Garden City, New York: Doubleday and Company, 1962); and, Clifton E. Olmstead, *Religion in America Past and Present* (Englewood Cliffs, New Jersey: Prentice-Hall, 1961).

4. An important point to bear in mind in studying the reports of attitudes and behavior of ministers in the Hadden, Campbell and Pettigrew, and Hammond studies is that there are differences *within* as well as *between* groups. Hammond's stress on the differences *between* campus ministers and those serving in the local parish should not obscure the differences which Hadden (as well as Campbell and Pettigrew) found *within* his study of the local parish minister. Indeed, Hadden stresses the fact that the perplexity of the layman stems, in part, from his inability to understand how "the carriers of God's 'eternal truth' can come wrapped in so many different packages."

5. Although Hadden reports elsewhere in *The Gathering Storm in the Churches: The Widening Gap Between Clergy and Laymen* that the high status congregations with members whose class position predispose them to conservatism tend to hire the more theologically and politically liberal clergy.

Chapter 2
Characteristics and Motivation for Church Participants and Nonparticipants

SIDNEY GOLDSTEIN

Socioeconomic Differentials among Religious Groups in the United States

On November 16, 1966, the director of the U.S. Bureau of the Census announced that the 1970 census will not include a question on religion. In his words, "The Bureau has been considering a number of requests from individuals and organizations which proposed that a question on religion be added to the nationwide census which is to be taken beginning in April, 1970. The decision not to add this question is based on the fact that a substantial number of persons again expressed an extremely strong belief that asking such a question in the decennial population census, in which replies are mandatory, would infringe upon the traditional separation of church and state."[1]

Reprinted from the *American Journal of Sociology* 74 (May 1969):612-31, by permission of the author and The University of Chicago Press.

Thus, in 1970, as in previous decennial censuses, information on religion will not be included among the data collected on the social, economic, and demographic characteristics of the American population. For at least another ten years, therefore, religion will retain its distinctiveness as being "the most significant social characteristic that is not now included in the decennial census."[2] Despite the fact that, "like the factors of educational attainment, occupation, and income, it [religion] is the axis around which much of a person's life is oriented,"[3] social scientists will be unable to obtain information on religious identification from the 1970 decennial census that would enhance their analyses of the demographic and social characteristics and behavior of the American population. This will be in sharp contrast to the situation in many other countries. In the 1964 United Nations *Demographic Yearbook,* out of a total of 214 independent nations and dependencies listed, as many as eighty-five present statistics on religious affiliation as part of their regular official census tabulations.[4] The United States does not.

Serious consideration was also given to this issue in the 1960 census.[5] In fact, in March, 1957, the Bureau of the Census included the question, "What is your religion?" in its monthly Current Population Survey. Unlike the decennial census, this survey, which encompassed approximately 35,000 households in 1957, is voluntary. The purpose of including a question on religion was twofold: (1) to ascertain the public reaction to such a question, and (2) to evaluate the quality of the answers obtained to the specific wording of the question. But even before the first results of the survey were made available to the public in February, 1958, the director of the census announced, in December, 1957, that the 1960 census of population would not include any inquiry on religion. The reason given was the same one cited in 1966, namely, that "a considerable number of persons would be reluctant to answer such a question in the census where a reply is mandatory."[6] This decision was reached despite the fact that the 1957 voluntary Current Population Survey indicated that only 1 per cent of all persons 14 years old and over had made no report on religion, thereby suggesting that the American people were quite willing to reply to such a question, at least on a voluntary basis.

In the absence of any question on religion in 1960 and in the forthcoming 1970 census, the data from the 1957 Current Population Survey still provide one of the best bases for determining the religious composition of the American population and the social and economic characteristics of individuals in the various religious groups. Until recently then, the only source of statistics from the 1957 survey was the Current Population Report of February 2, 1958, "Religion Reported by the Civilian Population of the United States: March 1957."[7] Other nationwide statistics on religious composition are, of course, available from various surveys undertaken by public opinion polls and other organizations. Extensive use of such data was made by Donald Bogue in *The Population of the United States.*[8] In addition, insights into the characteristics of particular religious groups and the differences between the members of these groups and those of the total population are available from a number of community population surveys, many of which are sponsored by specific religious bodies. These do not, however, give a national picture. Finally, data have in the past also been available from the Census of Religious Bodies, which was taken periodically as a separate census between 1906 and 1936 by means of a questionnaire mailed to the pastors and clerks of the parishes or congregations. It was limited to an enumeration of the membership of the various religious groups and did not, therefore, provide any information on their social and economic characteristics.

The data published in the February, 1958, Current Population Report were restricted to an enumeration of persons 14 years old and over by religion, cross-tabulated by color and sex, by region of residence, by urban-rural residence, and by age and sex. Information was also presented on (1) related children under 14 years old, cross-tabulated by religion reported for the family head and his wife, thereby providing insights into the religious composition of the total population; and (2) married couples by religion reported, thereby permitting determination of the number of persons married to individuals belonging to the same or different religious groups at the time of the census, a crude measure of intermarriage since it overlooks marriages in which one spouse converted to the religion of the other.

When the February, 1958, Report was released, it was generally assumed that other reports would follow. Because of various pressures on the Bureau of the Census, this did not happen. As a result, a wealth of data on the social and economic characteristics of Protestants, Catholics, and Jews, and of various denominations within each of these three major religious groups have not been available from this national survey. In 1967, the Freedom of Information Act was passed by Congress.[9] In accordance with the provisions of the Act, the Bureau of the Census made these unpublished tabulations available upon request. Unfortunately, the original survey records and tabulation materials have been destroyed, but the unpublished tabulations are now available for analysis. Although they do not provide all of the possible cross-tabulations which might be desired, they do provide a new source of data on the social and economic characteristics of religious groups in the United States. Referring to 1957, they are obviously already outdated. Yet, in the absence of more recent data from the 1960 or the forthcoming 1970 census, they represent a major source of information on the demographic characteristics of religious groups in the United States and provide important base data against which future changes in composition can be measured. Since the published statistics are readily available and have already been analyzed,[10] they will be used here only incidentally. This analysis will focus on differentials by religion with respect to education, labor force participation, occupation, and income.

THE DATA

The data are based on information collected in the monthly population sample survey conducted by the Bureau of the Census in March, 1957.[11] At that time, the sample was spread over 330 sample areas, comprising 638 counties and independent cities. A total of about 40,000 dwelling units and other living quarters are designated for the sample at any time, and completed interviews are obtained each month from about 35,000 households. Of the remainder, about 1,500 are households from which information should be obtained but is not, and the rest are vacant dwellings or other dwellings, such as households with usual residence elsewhere, that are not available for enumeration by the survey. The final estimates, based on the survey, involve the adjustment of weighted sample results to independent estimates of the civilian non-institutional population of the United States. These estimates were made separately for the various age, color, and sex classes.

Since the estimates are based on sample data, they are subject to sampling variability.[12] The sampling variability may be relatively large in the case of the smaller figures and in the case of small differences between figures. In addition to sampling variation, the estimates are subject to bias due to error in response and to non-reporting. Thus, where the household members differ in their religion but only one member gives the information, there may have been a tendency to report the same religion for all of the household members. Also, a few persons may have misreported their religion.

The figures relate primarily to the civilian population. Approximately 809,000 members of the armed forces living off-post or with their families on-post are included, but all other members of the armed forces are excluded. For convenience, the population covered is referred to by the Bureau of the Census as the civilian population.

The data on religion are based on voluntary answers to the question, "What is his religion—Baptist, Lutheran, etc.?" The answer given for each person indicated what he regards as his religion and not whether the person is an active member of a church or synagogue. The question was asked only of persons 14 years old and over. These persons were classified as "Protestant," "Roman Catholic," "Jewish," "Other Religion," "No Religion," and "Religion Not Reported." Persons reported as Protestant are further classified into one of the four largest Protestant denominational groups—Baptist, Lutheran, Methodist, or Presbyterian —or as "Other Protestants," but data on these denominational groups are not included in the recently released tabulations. The group "Other Religion," consists largely of persons reporting such organizations as the Eastern Orthodox Church, the Polish Catholics, and the Old Catholics. It also includes the relatively few persons who are Buddhists, Moslems, and other non-Christians. The group "No Religion" includes persons who reported that they are atheists, agnostics, or said that they had no religion.

Both the published data and the newly released statistics based on the 1957 survey dichotomize the Protestant group into white and non-white. Non-whites constituted 10 per cent of the total sample and 13.3 per cent of the Protestant group. Only 2.5 of the Roman Catholics and 0.2 per cent of the Jews were non-whites. Their numbers in the residue categories, Other Religion, No Religion, and Religion Not Reported ranged between 10.6 and 13 per cent, closely reflecting their proportions in the total population. But the major point is that nearly all non-whites (88 per cent) were Protestant, so that any statistic on the non-white Protestant group essentially refers to non-whites as a whole. Comparison of non-white Protestants, on the one hand, with the white Protestants, the Roman Catholics, and the Jews, on the other, therefore points out racial differentials rather than religious ones. Since this analysis is directed toward differentials among religious groups, it was decided to restrict the comparisons to white Protestants, Roman Catholics, and Jews. To permit the reader to compare the characteristics of these three major groups with those of the non-white Protestants, the data for the latter are included in the tables. The statistics for the total population include both the non-white Protestants and the other three small residue categories.

FINDINGS

Before turning to the major focus of this analysis, the evaluation of socioeconomic differentials by religion, a brief overview of the distribution of the American population by religious group and of the ecological and demographic features of the major religious groups is in order (Table 1). Of the total population 14 years old and over in 1957, two-thirds were identified as Protestant and one-fourth as Roman Catholic.

TABLE 1. *Selected Social Characteristics of Persons 14 Years Old and Over by Religion, United States**

Religion	Number (in 1,000's)	Percentage Distribution by Religion	Percentage in Urban Areas	Percentage in Urbanized Areas of 250,000 or More	Percentage in Northeast	Percentage in South	Percentage Non-white	Males per 100 Females
Total	119,333	100.0	63.9	36.6	26.2	30.6	10.0	92.9
Protestant	78,952	66.2	56.6	27.2	16.8	38.3	13.3	89.0
White	68,475	57.4	55.2	24.5	17.1	35.1	--	89.4
Non-white	10,477	8.8	66.1	44.6	14.8	59.3	--	86.2
Roman Catholic	30,669	25.7	78.8	53.9	46.0	13.9	2.5	92.7
Jewish	3,868	3.2	96.1	87.4	69.1	7.7	0.2	92.7
Other Religion	1,545	1.3	77.4	52.9	41.9	17.4	11.7	100.9
No Religion	3,195	2.7	54.2	29.5	11.2	34.7	13.0	281.3
Religion Not Reported	1,104	0.9	68.2	49.5	23.3	33.7	10.6	98.6

*Based on data in U.S. Bureau of the Census, "Religion Reported by the Civilian Population of the United States: March 1957," *Current Population Reports,* Series P-20, No. 79 (February 2, 1958).

Just over 3 per cent of the total gave Jewish as their religion; and 2.7 per cent (an overwhelming majority of whom were men) reported no religion. Under 1 per cent of the total did not report religion in answer to the question. This group was about equally divided between men and women, but it was more heavily concentrated in urbanized areas.

The different religious groups vary considerably in the distribution of their respective populations between urban[13] and rural places. In 1957, 64 per cent of the total U.S. population 14 years old and over lived in urban areas. But among the three major religious groups, the concentration in urban areas varied from 55 per cent of the white Protestants to 79 per cent of the Catholics and to virtually all (96.1 per cent) of the Jews. The differentials were, in fact, even sharper, since 87.4 per cent of all Jews lived in urbanized areas of 250,000 or more persons, in contrast to 53.9 per cent of the Catholics and only 24.5 per cent of the white Protestants.

These urban-rural differentials parallel the variations among the four major regions of the United States—Northeast, North Central, South, and West. The white Protestants are most concentrated in the South, which accounted for just over one-third of all white Protestants in the United States. Two-thirds of all those living in the South were white Protestants, in contrast to only 37 per cent of those in the Northeast. In fact, the Northeast accounted for only 17 per cent of all white Protestants in the United States compared with 46 per cent of all Roman Catholics and 69 per cent of the Jews. Like the South, the West and the North Central regions were heavily white Protestant (65 and 63 per cent, respectively). Thus Protestants constituted a minority in the population only in the Northeast, being exceeded by the larger group of Catholics with 45 per cent of the total. The heavy concentration of Jews in the Northeast, reflecting its highly urban character, also accounts for their being 8.5 per cent of the population living there in 1957, compared to less than 3 per cent of the population in each of the other three regions. In fact, Jews constituted less than 1 per cent of the population living in the South. These differentials in urban-rural residence and in regional concentration help to explain the variations to be noted later in socioeconomic composition.

Variation in age composition is also a key factor in influencing social and economic differentials among population groups (Table 2). In 1957, the median age of those 14 years old and over in the United States was 40.4 years. The median age of white Protestants (41.3) was close to that of the total population.[14] In contrast, Roman Catholics had a median age of 38.7; their younger population reflects the effects of their higher-than-average fertility levels over the preceding decades. The higher median age of the Jewish group, 44.5 years, no doubt results from their low fertility, reinforced by the residue effects of high levels of immigration in earlier decades, resulting in a disproportionate number of older persons in 1957.[15] Thirteen per cent of the Jews were 65 and over compared with 10 per cent of the Catholics; but the Protestants had the highest concentration of older persons: 13.6 per cent of those 14 years old and over.

TABLE 2. *Percentage Distribution by Age of Persons 14 Years Old and Over by Religion, Total United States**

Religion	Total 14 Years and Over	14-19 Years	20-24 Years	25-44 Years	45-64 Years	65 Years and Over	Median Age (Years)
Total	100.0	11.7	8.2	39.0	28.8	12.3	40.4
Protestant	100.0	11.8	8.0	38.1	29.0	13.0	40.8
White	100.0	11.5	7.7	37.7	29.5	13.6	41.3
Non-white	100.0	14.2	10.0	41.0	26.0	8.9	37.2
Roman Catholic	100.0	12.1	8.7	42.3	27.0	10.0	38.7
Jewish	100.0	9.0	6.0	35.9	36.0	13.0	44.5
Other Religion and Not Reported	100.0	10.6	7.9	34.2	32.0	15.4	43.5
No Religion	100.0	9.0	9.2	37.1	30.9	13.8	42.0

*Based on data in U.S. Bureau of the Census, "Religion Reported by the Civilian Population of the United States: March 1957," *Current Population Reports,* Series P-20, No. 79 (February 2, 1958), Table 4.

EDUCATION

A major mechanism for social and occupational mobility in the United States is education. Various immigrant groups have placed differential emphasis on use of this mechanism for moving ahead.[16] Jews, in particular, have traditionally placed a very high value on education, including, in modern times, secular learning. In part, this stems from the intellectual content of Judaism; in part, it results from their perception of education as a means of social mobility. This high level of motivation for a good education is clearly reflected in the statistics (Table 3) that show the number of years of school completed by persons in the various religious groups. The median school years completed by Jews was 12.3 years compared with 11.3 for white Protestants and 10.4 for Roman Catholics. Thus, almost two full years of schooling separate the medians of Jews and Roman Catholics. But even these differentials mask sharp variations with respect to the proportion who have achieved certain levels of education. For example, 59 per cent of all Jews had at least a

TABLE 3. *Percentage Distribution of Years of School Completed by Persons 25 Years Old and Over by Religion and Sex, Total United States**

Years of School Completed and Sex	Total	White Protestant	Non-White Protestant	Roman Catholic	Jewish
Males:					
Elementary: 0–7	23.2	18.7	55.4	22.9	14.7
8	18.5	19.3	10.9	18.9	13.1
High school: 1–3	17.3	18.1	15.4	18.2	9.7
4	22.1	24.0	10.0	24.0	21.5
College: 1–3	7.3	8.2	2.8	6.6	12.6
4 or more	9.4	10.4	2.3	8.1	25.6
Not Reported	2.2	1.3	3.2	1.3	2.8
Total percentage	100.0	100.0	100.0	100.0	100.0
Median school years completed	10.3	10.9	Under 8	10.3	12.5
Females:					
Elementary: 0–7	20.3	15.7	48.7	21.1	16.6
8	17.4	17.6	13.5	18.9	13.1
High school: 1–3	18.1	18.9	17.6	18.4	10.2
4	29.5	31.5	12.7	31.4	35.8
College: 1–3	7.4	8.9	3.3	5.0	12.8
4 or more	5.7	6.5	3.0	4.1	9.7
Not Reported	1.6	0.9	1.2	1.1	1.8
Total percentage	100.0	100.0	100.0	100.0	100.0
Median school years completed	10.9	11.6	8.1	10.5	12.3
Total:					
Elementary: 0–7	21.7	17.1	51.8	22.0	15.6
8	17.9	18.4	12.3	18.9	13.1
High school: 1–3	17.7	18.5	16.6	18.3	10.0
4	26.0	27.9	11.4	27.8	29.0
College: 1–3	7.3	8.6	3.1	5.8	12.7
4 or more	7.5	8.4	2.7	6.0	17.3
Not Reported	1.9	1.1	2.1	1.2	2.3
Total percentage	100.0	100.0	100.0	100.0	100.0
Median school years completed	10.6	11.3	Under 8	10.4	12.3

*Data in this and the remaining tables in this paper are based on information in U.S. Bureau of the Census, "Tabulations of Data on the Social and Economic Characteristics of Major Religious Groups, March 1957" (unpublished).

high school education, and 17 per cent had four years of college. In contrast, 44.9 per cent of the white Protestants and 39.6 per cent of the Roman Catholics had educational levels equal to at least a high school diploma, and only 7.7 and 6 per cent of the persons in these two major religious groups had graduated from college.

These differentials characterize both men and women. For example, among Jewish males, 38.2 per cent had some college education in contrast to 14.7 per cent of the Catholic men and 18.6 per cent of the white Protestant men. Among Jewish women, 22.5 per cent had some college education compared with 9.1 per cent of the Catholic women and 15.4 per cent of the white Protestant women. In all religious groups, it was more common for men to complete their college education than for women. In fact, considerably higher proportions of men, especially in the Jewish group, completed college education than received only some college training, whereas among women, proportionately more had only one to three years of college education than received a college degree.

Unfortunately, the data on education by religion are not cross-tabulated by age; it is, therefore, not possible to ascertain the extent to which these religious differentials are narrowing among the younger age groups. In the United States as a whole, the over-all increase in the level of education among the younger segments of the population is evidenced by the data from the March, 1967, Current Population Survey, which show a continuous rise in the median school years completed, from 8.5 among males aged 65 and over to 12.6 among men aged 25–29, and from 8.7 to 12.5 for females.[17] In addition, community survey data have indicated that the median education level among the younger members of a religious group is considerably above that of the older segments. In the Providence, Rhode Island, metropolitan area, for example, the median education for Jewish males aged 25–44 was 15.9 years compared with 8.3 for those aged 65 and over.[18] In the general population the corresponding medians for these two age groups were 12.1 and 7.9, respectively. Although confirming a considerable improvement in educational level among younger segments of the population, these data do not, in comparison with the Jewish medians, suggest a narrowing of differentials. They may, however, be too restricted to provide a fair basis for testing this hypothesis.

Labor Force Participation

For the United States as a whole in 1957, 81.1 per cent of all males 14 and over and 35.1 per cent of all females were in the labor force (Table 4). The proportion for males varied only minimally among the three major religious groups, between the narrow range of 81.1 and 81.6 per cent. For the females, there was slightly greater variation. The lowest

TABLE 4. *Labor Force Participation Rates of Persons 14 Years Old and Over by Religion, Age, and Sex, Total United States*

Age and Sex	Total*	White Protestant	Non-white Protestant	Roman Catholic	Jewish
Both sexes	57.0	55.8	60.3	57.6	55.1
Male	81.1	81.1	80.3	81.6	81.5
14–17 years	30.5	32.7	32.7	26.7	†
18–24 years	79.1	78.5	82.1	80.0	53.9
25–34 years	97.0	96.9	96.4	97.2	97.0
35–44 years	97.8	97.9	96.9	98.1	99.1
45–64 years	92.7	93.4	89.3	92.5	96.1
65 years and over	37.4	38.7	37.0	34.1	46.9
Female	35.1	33.7	43.3	35.8	30.7
14–17 years	17.7	18.5	11.5	19.1	†
18–24 years	45.5	42.3	40.2	54.4	57.2
25–34 years	34.8	33.6	48.5	32.8	25.5
35–44 years	42.6	41.2	58.1	40.5	33.5
45–64 years	41.1	40.3	51.3	39.9	38.2
65 years and over	11.5	11.6	13.2	11.0	8.5

*Includes, in addition to the groups shown separately, persons with Other Religion or Religion Not Reported.
†Base is less than 150,000.

level characterized Jewish women, of whom 30.7 per cent were in the labor force. Intermediate were the white Protestant women, with 33.7 per cent in the labor force, followed by the Roman Catholics with 35.8 per cent.

The over-all similarity in the labor force participation rate of males masks some significant differences by religion within specific age groups. Reflecting the higher educational achievement of Jews which results in many remaining in school instead of entering the labor force, the levels of labor force participation by Jews aged 18–24 is considerably below that of Roman Catholics and Protestants—only 53.9 per cent in contrast to approximately 80 per cent of the Protestants and Roman Catholics. By ages 25–34, however, and continuing through the 35–44-year group, all groups had very high labor force participation rates. Differences become apparent again in the 45–64-year group and are accentuated in the 65 and over age group. In particular, these latter differences largely involve the higher participation rates of older Jewish males in contrast to older Protestants and Roman Catholics. Whereas only 34.1 per cent of the Catholic men and 38.5 per cent of the Protestant men 65 years old and over remained in the labor force, this was true of 46.9 per cent of the older Jewish males. This differential reflects the higher proportion of professional and self-employed persons among Jews. To the extent that retirement from the labor force is more voluntary for professionals and the self-employed generally, the disproportionate number of Jews in these categories contributes to their higher-than-average labor force participation rates in the older age groups.[19]

For females, too, the age-specific labor force participation patterns of Jews differ from those characterizing the total adult groups. In the 18–24-year age group, Jewish women have the highest labor force participation rate, with 57 per cent in the labor force compared to 54 per cent of the Roman Catholics and 42 per cent of the Protestants. In all succeeding age groups, however, the labor force participation rates of Jewish women are below those of the other two religious groups. Also noteworthy, the labor force participation rate of Catholic women 18–24 is higher than that of Protestants and not far below that of Jewish women. The differences between Roman Catholics and white Protestants are not great, however, for age groups above 25. The reasons for the fairly close similarity in the relatively high labor force participation rates of Jewish and Roman Catholic women aged 18–24 are not clear. The high rates for the Jewish group may reflect their relatively high educational achievement accompanied by a somewhat later age at marriage with the consequent greater opportunity to use the skills obtained by education. Greater and more successful use of family limitation may also contribute to this pattern.[20] However, these factors are not operating to the same degree in the Roman Catholic female population, and other explanations for the similarity must be sought. Since this difference persists even when the comparison is restricted to the urban population,[21] it does not seem to stem from the higher concentration of Catholics or Jews in urban places, although greater refinement by size of urban place might reduce some of the differentials.

Further insight into the extent of religious differentials in labor force participation can be gained from examination of participation rates of (1) married women with varying numbers of children present in the household (Table 5). The over-all levels of participation vary only minimally by religious group for all married women whose husbands were present in the household (between 27.3 and 29.6 per cent). But for each of the age groups under 45 years, whether or not the women participated in the labor force, varied considerably by religion and consistently for all age groups under 65 years. Especially for those between 25 and 45, the participation rates of Jewish women were lowest, followed by those of Roman Catholic women, then white Protestant women. Over-all, these data suggest, therefore, that the underlying factors accounting for the low participation rates of Jewish women and somewhat low rates for Roman Catholic women permeate all age groups under 45. For those groups 45 and over, for whom there are sufficient numbers of cases to calculate rates, the differences among the three major groups are minimal.

TABLE 5. *Labor Force Participation Rates for Married Women Living in Same Household as Husband, by Religion, Age, and Presence of Children, Total United States*

Age and Presence of Children	Total	White Protestant	Non-white Protestant	Roman Catholic	Jewish
Total married women, husband present	29.6	29.6	40.4	27.3	27.8
Age:					
Under 25 years	29.1	29.2	26.0	30.6	*
25–34 years	27.2	28.1	38.2	22.6	18.7
35–44 years	35.7	36.1	51.1	31.5	24.5
45–64 years	32.3	31.6	45.0	30.9	30.6
65 years and over	6.4	6.2	*	6.7	*
Presence of children:					
No own children under 18 years	35.6	34.1	47.7	36.6	30.0
With children 6–17 years, none under 6 years	36.7	36.2	52.6	35.3	28.6
With children under 6 years	17.0	18.2	23.6	13.2	11.8

*Base is less than 150,000.

Religious differentials also persist when the participation rates are examined for the presence or absence of children of different ages. In all three religious groups, the presence of children under 6 years of age reduces the participation levels considerably. For example, in all religious groups the participation rates of women with children under 6 years is 50 per cent or less than the rates of those with children 6–17 years but with none under 6 years of age.

Yet, the participation levels of Jewish women for each category of number of children present at home is below that of Roman Catholic and Protestant women, even in the group with no children under 18 years of age. For example, among those with children under 6 years old, only 11.8 per cent of Jewish women, compared with 18.2 per cent of white Protestant women, were labor force participants. For this category, the level of participation of Roman Catholic women is more similar to that of Jewish women than to white Protestant women. In contrast, in those categories with children 6–17 years of age only and with no children under 18 years of age, the levels for Roman Catholic women were much more similar to those of white Protestant women than to the Jewish women.

The lower participation levels of Jewish women at all ages except 18–24 (Table 4), and for all categories of family status (Table 5), as measured by presence of children, suggests that their higher socioeconomic status plays a key role in influencing participation levels; but the impact of SES is augmented by the presence of small children. The cross-sectional data suggest that for Jews, as for members of other religious groups, marriage and especially the presence of children under age 6 leads to a considerable exodus from the labor force. Participation levels generally rise again with increasing age of women (through the 45–64 group). However, they do not reach the high levels characterizing the 18–24 age group, although they closely approach it for white Protestants. Among Catholics the low level of participation by women with children under age 6 may stem from the larger number of young children in these families and the need to remain home to care for them. But as these children grow up and go to school, the sharp rise in participation rate of Catholic women suggests that the pressure to go to work to help support the family may be greater than in other groups of higher status. Moreover, even when some increase in labor force participation occurs, as among Jews, it may be for somewhat different reasons as, for example, the desire to utilize occupationally the special skills obtained in higher education. In short, variations in SES, coupled with differences in the presence of young children and the size of family, may be key factors in influencing the pattern of religious differentials in levels of labor force participation of women at various points in the life cycle.

Occupational Composition

Paralleling the earlier noted differentials in educational achievement, the major religious groups are also characterized by sharp differentials in occupational composition, particularly those between the Jewish group, on the one hand, and the Protestant and Roman Catholic groups, on the other (Table 6). Three-fourths of all Jewish employed males work in white-collar positions compared with just over one-third of the Roman Catholic and white Protestant males. This large differential extends to three of the four subcategories of white-collar employment. The proportion of Jewish males in the professions was approximately twice as large as those of Roman Catholics and white Protestants. The proportion who were managers, officials, and proprietors (35 per cent) was almost three times as great as the corresponding proportion of Roman Catholics and two and one-half times as great as the proportion of white Protestants. Among both the professional and the managerial groups, the proportion of males who were self-employed varied significantly by religious group. Among white Protestants and Catholics, about one out of eight professionals was self-employed; among Jews this was true of one out of three. Within the managerial group, self-employment was more characteristic of all three groups, but differentials persisted, although at a lower level. About five out of every ten Protestant and Catholic males were self-employed compared with seven of every ten

TABLE 6. *Percentage Distribution of Employed Persons 18 Years Old and Over by Major Occupation Group, by Religion and Sex, Total United States*

Major Occupation and Sex	Total	White Protestant	Non-white Protestant	Roman Catholic	Jewish
Males:					
Professional	9.9	10.9	2.6	8.9	20.3
Wage and salary workers	8.4	9.5	2.3	7.5	12.8
Self-employed	1.5	1.4	0.3	1.3	7.5
Farmers and farm managers	7.3	9.5	5.8	3.8	0.1
Managers and proprietors	13.3	14.1	2.2	12.5	35.1
Wage and salary workers	6.3	7.3	0.5	5.7	10.8
Self-employed	7.0	6.7	1.7	6.8	24.3
Clerical workers	6.9	6.8	4.1	8.4	8.0
Sales workers	5.4	6.0	0.5	4.8	14.1
Skilled laborers	20.0	21.2	9.7	22.5	8.9
Semi-skilled laborers	20.9	19.7	27.0	22.4	10.1
Service workers	6.1	4.3	14.1	7.7	2.3
Farm laborers	2.5	2.2	7.6	1.7	0.1
Unskilled laborers	7.7	5.4	26.4	7.4	0.8
Total percentage	100.0	100.0	100.0	100.0	100.0
Total white collar*	35.5	37.8	9.4	34.6	77.5
Total blue collar†	57.2	52.8	84.8	61.7	22.2
Females:					
Professionals	12.2	13.7	6.2	11.4	15.5
Wage and salary workers	11.6	12.8	6.1	11.0	15.1
Self-employed	0.7	0.9	0.1	0.4	0.4
Farmers and farm managers	0.7	0.8	1.4	0.3	0.2
Managers and proprietors	5.5	6.5	1.4	4.3	8.9
Wage and salary workers	2.3	3.0	0.4	1.3	3.2
Self-employed	3.2	3.5	1.1	3.0	5.7
Clerical workers	30.3	32.1	7.2	35.6	43.9
Sales workers	6.9	8.0	0.9	6.4	14.4
Skilled laborers	1.0	1.1	0.3	1.3	0.7
Semi-skilled laborers	17.1	15.8	14.1	21.8	11.2
Private household workers	9.6	5.6	43.8	4.9	0.5
Service workers	13.1	12.7	19.4	11.6	4.6
Farm laborers	3.0	3.3	4.1	1.9	--
Unskilled laborers	0.6	0.5	1.3	0.5	--
Total percentage	100.0	100.0	100.0	100.0	100.0
Total white collar	54.9	60.3	15.7	57.7	82.7
Total blue collar	44.4	39.0	83.0	42.0	17.0

*Includes professionals, managers except farm, clerical, and sales workers.
†Includes skilled, semi-skilled, household, service, farm, and unskilled laborers.

Jews. In clerical work Roman Catholics had a slightly higher proportion of males than did the Jewish group, and both were higher than the white Protestant group; but Jews had from two to three times as many males employed as sales workers than was true of the white Protestant and Catholic groups. In part, the latter may reflect the high proportion of Jews who owned their own businesses and who employed family members as workers.

Conversely, the proportion of males employed as blue-collar workers (craftsmen, operatives, service workers, and laborers) was highest for Roman Catholics (61.7 per cent), followed by white Protestant males (52.8 per cent). Only one out of every five Jewish males held a blue-collar job. The one remaining category, not included in the white-collar group, is that of farmers and farm managers. This occupation was most prevalent among white Protestants of whom 9.5 per cent were farmers or farm managers, compared to only 3.8 per cent of Roman Catholics and just a sprinkling of Jews. Over-all, therefore, these differences show rather small variations between Roman Catholics and white Protestants in occupational distribution of males but considerable differentials between the Jews and the two Christian groups.

Compared with males, women in the labor force are much more concentrated in white-collar positions. This is true of all three religious groups. Although concentration in white-collar jobs is more prevalent for Jews than for either Roman Catholic or white Protestant women, the differentials among the women are less marked than was true among the men. Just over four out of every five Jewish women are in white-collar jobs compared with about three out of every five Catholic and white Protestant women. Examination of the specific occupational categories also points to a narrowing of differentials among women. For example, the number employed as professionals varies only between 11.4 and 15.5 per cent among the three groups. About twice as many Jewish women as Roman Catholic women are employed as managers, but the difference between Jewish and white Protestant women is considerably smaller. Among professionals, self-employment is far less common among women than among men. It ranges between 3 and 7 per cent of professional women in the three religious groups and is about equally high for white Protestant and Jewish women. Within the managerial group, self-employment characterizes a majority of the women in each group: among Catholics, seven out of ten are self-employed; among Jews, six out of ten, and among white Protestants, five out of ten. In contrast to men, therefore, Jewish women are not as disproportionally represented among the self-employed, especially in view of the fact that, if they were working without pay in businesses operated by their husbands, they would be counted as self-employed. This may be related to the tendency for Jewish women to withdraw from the labor force to a greater degree following marriage and family formation and not to return as often once children grow up; self-employment is more likely to be associated with continued participation in the labor force. But the relatively small percentage of women employed as managers and proprietors and the even smaller proportion which the self-employed constitute of the total female labor force precludes attaching too much significance to the religious differences noted.

One-third or more of the women in each of the three major groups hold jobs as clerical workers, but the proportion so employed is higher for Jewish women (43.9 per cent), compared with non-Jewish women (32.1 and 35.6 per cent). One of the sharpest differences characterized the proportion of women in the three religious categories who are employed as sales workers. Among Jewish women, 14.4 per cent hold such jobs, compared with 8 and 6.4 per cent of the white Protestant and Roman Catholic women. As with males, the proportion of Jewish women in blue-collar jobs is very small, only 17 per cent of the total, whereas for the white Protestant and Catholic women, approximately two out of every five hold blue-collar jobs.

Special tabulations of survey data from the National Opinion Research Center show quite similar patterns of occupational distribution among the three religious groups.[22] These statistics also show, for heads of households, the occupational distribution of the major denominations within the Protestant group. They demonstrate clearly that the Protestant group is by no means homogeneous; in many respects the distribution of Episcopalians and Presbyterians resembled that of the Jewish group. Unfortunately, the census data do not subdivide the Protestant group beyond the distinction between white and non-white, and it is not possible therefore to pursue this kind of comparison. An advantage of the census tabulations, however, lies in that the occupational data have been refined by showing the composition for the urban population, standardized by years of school completed. By restricting the data to a more homogeneous social and economic environment and by holding constant the wide differences in educational achievement, it becomes possible to ascertain more clearly the extent to which occupational differences are directly related to religious affiliation and to what extent they may simply be a reflection of differential opportunities, available to persons of various religious affiliation because of the place in which they live and the level of education they have achieved.

Restricting the data to the urban population and standardizing this population by years of completed schooling results in a considerable narrowing of differentials and to actual reversal in the case of some occupational categories (Table 7). With residence and education controlled, 69.7 per cent of the Jewish males are shown to be white-collar workers compared with 42.7 per cent of the white Protestant males and 39.1 per cent of the Roman Catholics. Thus, the concentration of Jews in white-collar positions remains far above that of white Protestant or Catholic males, but the difference is no longer in the ratio of two to one as was the case with the unstandardized data. Moreover, for selected occupation categories there is also a dramatic change. For example, with residence and education controlled, only 9.9 per cent of the Jewish males

TABLE 7. *Percentage Distribution of Employed Persons 18 Years Old and Over by Major Occupation Group, by Religion and Sex, Urban United States (Standardized by Years of School Completed)*

Major Occupation and Sex	Total	White Protestant	Non-white Protestant	Roman Catholic	Jewish
Males:					
Professionals	11.5	12.1	10.2	11.2	9.9
Wage and salary workers	9.7	10.5	8.9	9.5	6.3
Self-employed	1.8	1.6	1.3	1.7	3.6
Farmers and farm managers	0.4	0.6	0.2	0.1	--
Managers and proprietors	14.6	15.3	2.8	12.8	36.8
Wage and salary workers	7.3	8.4	0.6	6.3	9.3
Self-employed	7.3	6.9	2.2	6.5	27.5
Clerical workers	8.6	8.3	9.0	9.8	8.0
Sales workers	6.3	7.0	0.8	5.3	15.0
Skilled laborers	21.3	23.9	11.0	22.2	11.7
Semi-skilled laborers	21.7	21.3	28.1	22.2	14.0
Service workers	7.7	5.9	16.2	8.5	3.4
Farm laborers	0.3	0.3	0.2	0.3	0.1
Unskilled laborers	7.7	5.2	21.6	7.5	1.1
Total percentage	100.0	100.0	100.0	100.0	100.0
Total white collar*	41.0	42.7	22.8	39.1	69.7
Total blue collar†	58.7	56.6	77.1	60.7	30.3
Females:					
Professionals	12.5	12.6	9.5	13.9	8.9
Wage and salary workers	11.7	11.6	9.3	13.4	8.5
Self-employed	0.8	1.0	0.2	0.5	0.4
Farmers and farm managers	--	0.1	--	--	--
Managers and proprietors	5.3	6.3	1.9	3.9	8.9
Wage and salary workers	2.4	3.1	0.5	1.3	3.0
Self-employed	2.9	3.2	1.4	2.6	5.9
Clerical workers	33.5	33.6	15.7	37.1	41.3
Sales workers	7.1	8.4	1.6	6.1	19.0
Skilled laborers	1.1	1.3	0.3	1.2	1.0
Semi-skilled laborers	17.7	16.8	16.5	21.6	15.1
Private household workers	8.8	6.3	29.9	4.4	0.4
Service workers	13.3	14.0	23.2	11.2	5.5
Farm laborers	0.1	0.1	0.1	--	--
Unskilled laborers	0.5	0.5	1.1	0.5	--
Total percentage	100.0	100.0	100.0	100.0	100.0
Total white collar*	58.4	60.9	28.7	61.0	78.1
Total blue collar†	41.5	39.0	71.1	38.9	22.0

*Includes professionals, managers except farm, clerical, and sales workers.
†Includes skilled, semi-skilled, household, service, farm, and unskilled laborers.

are professionals in contrast to 11.2 per cent of the Roman Catholics, and 12.1 per cent of the Protestants. On the other hand, the earlier sharp differentials with respect to the managerial and the sales-worker categories remain about the same. Also, the standardized data do not lead to any change in the earlier noted distribution of professional and managerial persons between self-employed and wage and salary workers. Similar conclusions hold for occupational differentials for females after the data are restricted to urban residence and standardized by education. Over-all, therefore, controlling for both education and residence suggests that both these factors explain some of the variation in religious differentials in occupation composition. Yet, despite narrowing, differentials persist, suggesting that other factors contribute to the variation in occupational composition among religious groups, and particularly between the Jewish group, on the one hand, and the white Protestant and Roman Catholic groups, on the other.

In a further attempt to assess the role of education in occupation for the major religious groups, the census made a special tabulation of the occupational distribution of employed college graduates in urban areas (Table 8). The data are not presented separately by sex. It will be recalled that 8.4 per cent of the white Protestants, 6 per cent of the Roman Catholics, and 17.3 per cent of the Jews were college graduates. Of these three groups of college graduates, the Roman Catholics have the highest proportion, 66.1 per cent, employed as professionals, compared with 62 per cent of the white Protestants and 58.2 per cent of the Jews. In contrast a significantly higher proportion of Jewish college graduates earn their living as managers, proprietors, and officials—22 per cent, compared with only 12.4 per cent of the Roman Catholics and 16.3 per cent of the white Protestants. The absolute differentials for most of the remaining categories are relatively small, with only slightly higher proportions of Jews being employed in clerical and sales work. These data for college graduates alone, therefore, suggest more homogeneous patterns of occupational composition within the college graduates of the three major religious groups. But the fact that differentials persist, as they did for the total male population with education standardized, indicates that religion itself, or at least other factors associated with religion, do have an impact on occupational composition.

TABLE 8. *Percentage Distribution of Employed College Graduates in Urban Areas by Major Occupation Group, by Religion*

Major Occupation Group	Total	White Protestant*	Roman Catholic	Jewish
Professional	63.2	62.0	66.1	58.2
Managers and proprietors	15.7	17.1	12.4	22.1
Clerical workers	8.2	8.3	7.4	8.9
Sales workers	5.8	5.8	6.1	7.8
Skilled laborers	3.2	3.6	3.8	0.9
Semi-skilled laborers	1.5	1.3	1.5	1.3
Other occupations	2.4	1.8	2.9	0.9
Total percentage	100.0	100.0	100.0	100.0

*Non-white Protestant group is not shown because base is less than 150,000.

Income

For each person in the sample, information was solicited on the amount of money income received in 1956. This included income from wages and salaries, from self-employment, and from such other sources as pension payments, interests, dividends, net rental income, unemployment benefits, and public assistance (Table 9). Income differentials among the religious groups are to be expected on the basis of variations in occupational composition and educational achievement. Since both high educational achievement and concentration in high white-collar positions are highly correlated with income, the fact that the $4,900 median income of Jewish males is well above that of the white Protestant and the Roman Catholic males ($3,728 and $3,954, respectively) is largely explainable in these terms. This sharp differential is also reflected in the more detailed statistics on distribution by income class. Incomes of $10,000 and over in 1956 were reported by 17 per cent of the Jewish males, compared with only 3.9 per cent of the white Protestants and 2.7 per cent of the Roman Catholics. On the other hand, just

TABLE 9. *Percentage Distribution of Persons 14 Years Old and Over by Income in 1956, by Religion and Sex, Total United States*

Income and Sex	Total*	White Protestant	Non-white Protestant	Roman Catholic	Jewish
Males:					
Under $1,000	17.2	16.5	31.6	14.0	10.0
$1,000–$1,999	11.7	11.2	18.3	10.5	9.0
$2,000–$2,999	12.1	11.6	20.0	11.0	7.4
$3,000–$3,999	14.8	14.7	16.1	15.2	11.0
$4,000–$4,999	15.9	16.2	9.4	18.3	14.0
$5,000–$5,999	11.9	12.2	3.1	14.6	13.4
$6,000–$9,999	12.7	13.7	1.5	13.7	18.0
$10,000 and over	3.6	3.9	0.1	2.7	17.2
Total percentage	100.0	100.0	100.0	100.0	100.0
Median income	$3,608	$3,728	$2,005	$3,954	$4,900
Females:					
Under $1,000	46.9	46.1	64.4	41.3	39.0
$1,000–$1,999	19.3	19.7	20.2	18.5	16.6
$2,000–$2,999	15.7	15.6	9.8	18.6	15.2
$3,000–$3,999	11.0	10.6	4.4	14.3	15.1
$4,000–$4,999	4.3	4.7	0.9	4.8	6.5
$5,000–$5,999	1.5	1.7	0.2	1.6	3.6
$6,000–$9,999	0.9	1.2	0.1	0.7	2.3
$10,000 and over	0.2	0.3	––	0.2	1.5
Total percentage	100.0	100.0	100.0	100.0	100.0
Median income	$1,146	$1,198	$ 776	$1,470	$1,663

*Includes, in addition to the groups shown separately, persons with Other Religion and those with No Religion or Religion Not Reported.

over one-fourth of the Jews, but one-third of the Catholics, and almost 40 per cent of the white Protestants, had incomes under $3,000.

These differences extended to females as well. The median income of $1,663 of Jewish women was about one-fifth higher than that of Roman Catholic women ($1,470) and almost 50 per cent more than that of white Protestant women ($1,198). Again, this probably reflects differentials in occupational composition. The differences in medians reflect variations in the over-all income distribution. Considerably fewer women had incomes above $5,000—only 2.6 per cent of the total population. Yet, this was true of 7.4 per cent of the Jewish group, compared with only 3.2 per cent of the white Protestants and 2.5 per cent of the Roman Catholics. A majority of the women in every religious group had incomes under $2,000, but this range encompassed 55.6 per cent of the Jewish women, 59.8 per cent of the Roman Catholics, and 65.8 per cent of the white Protestants.

In an attempt to make income data more comparable, the Bureau of the Census presents income data for the urban employed population standardized for major occupational group (Table 10). Doing so eliminates considerably the sharp differentials noted for the unstandardized data for the total United States. For males, the standardized data show a median income for Jews of $4,773, just slightly above the $4,553 for white Protestants and the $4,509 for Roman Catholics. For women, standardization also eliminates the major part of the differential; the median income of Jewish women becomes $2,352, compared with $2,-282 for Roman Catholics and $2,263 for white Protestants.

The narrowing of differentials suggested by the similar median income figures extends to the over-all distribution by income level. For the standardized data, 18 per cent of the Jewish males, compared with 21 per cent of both the Roman Catholics and the white Protestants had incomes below $3,000. At the other extreme, the proportion of Jewish males with incomes of $10,000 and over is reduced to 8.7 per cent from the unstandardized 17.2 per cent, that of white Protestant males is raised to 5 per cent, and that of Roman Catholics to 3.9 per cent. The same narrowing in the distributions appears for women. In the standardized data, 41 per cent of the Jewish women, compared with 43 per cent of the Roman Catholics and 44 per cent of the white Protestants, had incomes under $2,000. At the other extreme, 5.2 per cent of the Jewish women, 3.8 per cent of the Roman Catholics, and 5.0 per cent of the white Protestants had incomes of $5,000 and over.

Clearly, then, with only slight differences apparent both in the median income and in the distribution among income groups, the considerably higher income level characterizing Jewish males and females, compared with white Protestant and Roman Catholic men and women,

TABLE 10. *Percentage Distribution of Employed Persons 14 Years Old and Over by Income in 1956, by Religion and Sex, Urban United States (Standardized for Major Occupation Group)* *

Income and Sex	Total†	White Protestant	Non-white Protestant	Roman Catholic	Jewish
Males:					
Under $1,000	5.6	5.8	12.4	5.2	4.1
$1,000–$1,999	6.1	5.5	12.7	6.2	6.4
$2,000–$2,999	10.8	9.7	24.1	10.0	7.6
$3,000–$3,999	17.4	17.1	21.2	17.1	13.9
$4,000–$4,999	21.4	21.5	19.2	22.6	23.3
$5,000–$5,999	16.0	16.4	6.4	17.3	17.0
$6,000–$9,999	17.6	19.0	3.5	17.7	18.9
$10,000 and over	5.0	5.0	0.5	3.9	8.7
Total percentage	100.0	100.0	100.0	100.0	100.0
Median income	$4,472	$4,553	$3,038	$4,509	$4,773
Females:					
Under $1,000	23.2	23.5	25.0	23.8	22.5
$1,000–$1,999	20.6	20.1	30.1	19.4	18.8
$2,000–$2,999	24.3	24.3	20.7	24.1	24.7
$3,000–$3,999	19.6	18.7	18.2	21.8	19.1
$4,000–$4,999	7.8	8.5	4.3	7.2	9.7
$5,000–$5,999	2.7	3.0	0.9	2.4	2.8
$6,000–$9,999	1.4	1.7	0.7	1.0	1.7
$10,000 and over	0.3	0.3	––	0.4	0.7
Total percentage	100.0	100.0	100.0	100.0	100.0
Median income	$2,255	$2,263	$1,831	$2,282	$2,352

*Standard used was distribution by major occupation group within each sex group of total urban employed in the three major religious groups combined.

†Summation of groups shown separately only; information not available for urban residents of other religions.

is a function of both their concentration in urban areas and in high white-collar positions. Taking these two variables into account greatly reduces and virtually eliminates whatever income differences otherwise exist. This suggests that, as educational differentials among Protestants, Roman Catholics, and Jews narrow, and that, as increasing proportions of both white Protestants and Catholics enter white-collar positions, the existing income differentials between Jews and the two Christian groups will also diminish.

This conclusion is justified by the data showing median income according to years of schooling completed (Table 11). For all three groups, the median income level rises consistently with increasing education. For those with less than an eighth-grade education, the median income varies between $2,609 for Jews to just over $2,800 for white Protestants and Roman Catholics. Except for the group with one to three years of high school, the difference in median income for Jews, white Protestants, and Catholics is less than 10 per cent for all educational categories

TABLE 11. *Median Income in 1956 of Urban Men 14 Years Old and by Religion and Years of School Completed*

Years of School Completed	Total	White Protestant	Non-white Protestant	Roman Catholic	Jewish
Elementary:					
0–7	$2,654	$2,812	$2,249	$2,819	$2,609
8	3,631	3,712	2,864	3,729	3,844
High school:					
1–3	3,858	3,850	2,849	4,170	4,672
4	4,563	4,684	3,092	4,567	4,913
College:					
1–3	4,526	4,712	*	4,361	5,026
4 or more	6,176	6,375	*	5,727	8,041

*Base is less than 150,000.

below the college level. For the college groups, however, the range increases, with Jews having the highest median incomes and Catholics the lowest. The differential is particularly sharp at the four-year or more educational level, at which the median income of Jews is $8,041 compared with $6,375 for white Protestants and $5,727 for Roman Catholics. But this sharp differential may be somewhat misleading since that particular educational category includes those who have gone on to postgraduate work, which survey data has shown to be true of a considerably higher proportion of Jews than of Catholics or Protestants.[23] This differential in education and the corresponding differential in median income are both related to the likelihood that a higher proportion of Jews who have postgraduate education and who are in professional categories hold high-income positions, such as doctors or lawyers. The higher educational achievement of the Jewish group may also permit them to hold more responsible managerial positions in commerce, manufacturing, or as self-employed proprietors in wholesale and retail establishments.[24] For analytic purposes, it would be desirable to have a more detailed breakdown of the college-educated group, particularly in the future, when proportionately more persons in the population will have a postgraduate education.

The question of whether religion, occupation, and/or education is a more important factor in determining the income level of individuals cannot be clearly determined without further controls. Control for major occupation groups and for place of residence reduces considerably the income differentials in the three major religious groups, but it does not eliminate them completely, particularly with respect to the distribution among income categories. Similarly, comparisons of income level (judged by the median) among various educational categories suggest minimal differences among most categories. Even where large differences exist, they may be largely attributable to the heterogeneous educational and occupational composition of the particular education category, that is, those with four years or more of college. Obviously, a number of intervening variables operate, and full evaluation of their effect must await more comprehensive statistics. Yet, standing out above these differences is the fact that the range of differences by education within each of the three major religious groups is far greater than the differences in median income level among the three religious groups. For example, whereas the median income level for the total males varied between a low $3,728 for white Protestants and a high of $4,900 for Jews, the range in median incomes between the highest and lowest educational levels of each of the religious groups is considerably greater: from $2,812 to $6,375 for white Protestants, from $2,819 to $5,727 for Roman Catholics, and from $2,609 to $8,041 for Jews. On this basis, the conclusion suggested by Donald Bogue—that education is a much more potent factor than religious preference in determining the income level of households—seems fully justified.[25]

Summary

The availability of hitherto withheld tabulations from the 1957 Current Population Survey, in which a question on religion was asked, provides a unique opportunity to examine a nationwide sample of the U.S. population for the relation between religion and socioeconomic status, as measured by education, occupation, and income. Earlier published data had already demonstrated the significant differentials in the distribution of the population by religion among the various regions of the United States and between urban and rural places of residence. This differential residential pattern could in itself account for significant variations in socioeconomic status, since economic opportunities vary considerably by place of residence. Urban residence in itself may stimulate proportionately more persons to obtain a higher education; it may also serve as a major attraction to persons from other places who have achieved high education. Recognizing both the interrelation between place of residence and socioeconomic status, the Bureau of the Census attempted, in a limited fashion, to control for these factors in several of the tabulations. Unfortunately, in the absence of the detailed data themselves, further manipulation of the materials was not feasible in this analysis.

Over-all, without controls, the data show significant differences among the religious groups with respect to socioeconomic status. Judged by median income, median education, and the proportion of white-collar workers, Jews occupied considerably higher status positions than did either Protestants or Catholics. The relative position of Protestants varies, depending on the measure used but, generally, white Protestants occupied a second place among the three religious groups. The heterogeneity of the Protestant group makes any conclusion about it difficult. Previous research has demonstrated that within the Protestant group there is a significant range of variation and that in many respects the socioeconomic characteristics of Episcopalians and Presbyterians closely resemble those of Jews.

Controlling for place of residence by restricting the analysis to the urban population and controlling for education as well in examining the occupation data, and for occupation and education separately in controlling for the income data, suggest that, when these controls are introduced, there is a considerable narrowing of the differentials in socioeconomic status among the three religious groups. In fact, for several subcategories of each of the groups, the income differentials virtually disappear, as do some of the striking differentials in occupational composition. These controls suggest that many of the differences among the three religious groups to which the crude data point are in fact a function of the differential educational achievement and/or occupational composition of the members of these groups, as well as a result of their differential concentration in urban and rural places. With these factors controlled, although admittedly in a somewhat crude fashion, the conclusion seems warranted that both education and occupation play a much more crucial role than does religion itself in influencing the income levels of members of the three religious groups.

The differences in education were originally a function of both the value placed on education itself and on the recognition given to the important role that education plays as a mechanism for social and occupational mobility. The high educational achievement of Jews is understandable in these terms. But high educational achievement in itself is not fully adequate to account for the high concentration of Jews in white-collar positions. Especially among older generations of Jews, for example, a disproportionate number are in high white-collar positions even among those with low educational achievement.[26] These persons, most of whom were immigrants, continued the tradition, developed by their forebears in Europe under restrictions of occupational choice, of gaining a livelihood through engaging in trade. On the American scene, their drive to achieve middle-class status coupled with the reduced need for farmers and blue-collar workers, accentuated their entry into the occupational strata represented by the managers and proprietors of retail, wholesale, and manufacturing establishments.

It seems reasonable to assume that, as the over-all educational level of the general population rises, with a consequent decline in education differentials among members of the three religious groups and, as discriminatory restrictions on occupational choice weaken further, there will be a corresponding decline in occupational differentials. In turn, this should lead to greater homogeneity among the three religious groups with respect to income levels. The fact that the data for 1957 demonstrate relationships among religious groupings, education, occupation, income, and residential distribution suggests the importance of obtaining information on religion as a part of census and other social surveys.

---

1. U.S. Bureau of the Census, "1970 Census Will Not Contain Question on Religion" (news release CB66-134, November 16, 1966).

2. Recommendation of the Committee on Population Statistics of the Population Association of America, quoted by Conrad Taeuber, "The Census and a Question on Religion" (paper presented at a Conference on the Census, sponsored by the National Community Relations Advisory Council, the Synagogue Council of America, and the Council of Jewish Federations and Welfare Funds, New York, October 22–23, 1967), pp. 5-6.

3. Donald J. Bogue, *The Population of the United States* (New York: Free Press, 1959), p. 688.

4. United Nations, *Demographic Yearbook, 1963* (New York: United Nations, 1964), Table 11; *Demographic Yearbook, 1964,* Table 32.

5. Taeuber, *op. cit.,* pp. 4-5.

6. *Ibid.,* p. 5.

7. U.S. Bureau of the Census, "Religion Reported by the Civilian Population of the United States: March 1957," *Current Population Reports,* Series P-20, No. 79 (February 2, 1958).

8. *Op. cit.*

9. Public Law 89-489.

10. See, e.g., Bogue, *op. cit.,* pp. 688-709; Paul C. Glick, "Intermarriage and Fertility Patterns among Persons in Major Religious Groups," *Eugenics Quarterly,* VII (March, 1960), 31-38; Erich Rosenthal, "Jewish Fertility in the United States," *Eugenics Quarterly,* VIII (December, 1961), 198-217.

11. U.S. Bureau of the Census, "Tabulations of Data on the Social and Economic Characteristics of Major Religious Groups, March, 1957" (unpublished). For a fuller, published discussion of how the Current Population Survey of 1957 was conducted and the definitions used, see U.S. Bureau of the Census, "Religion Reported by the Civilian Population of the United States: March 1957," *op. cit.,* pp. 1-4.

12. U.S. Bureau of the Census, "Religion Reported by the Civilian Population of the United States: March 1957," *op, cit.,* p. 4.

13. The urban population comprised all persons living in (*a*) places of 2,500 inhabitants or more incorporated as cities, boroughs, and villages; (*b*) incorporated towns of 2,500 inhabitants or more except in New England, New York, and Wisconsin, where the term "town" is used to designate minor civil divisions of counties; (*c*) densely settled urban fringe areas, around cities of 20,000 or more, and (*d*) unincorporated places of 50,000 or more outside of any urban fringe. The remaining population is classified as rural. U.S. Bureau of the Census, *ibid.,* p. 3.

14. Wilson H. Grabill, Clyde B. Kiser, and Pascal K. Welpton, *The Fertility of American Women* (New York: John Wiley & Sons, 1958), pp. 51-79.

15. Glick, *op. cit.,* pp. 36-37.

16. Milton M. Gordon, *Assimilation in American Life* (New York: Oxford University Press, 1964), pp. 185-87.

17. U.S. Bureau of the Census, "Educational Attainment: March 1967," *Current Population Survey,* Series P-20, No. 169 (February 9, 1968).

18. Sidney Goldstein and Calvin Goldscheider, *Jewish Americans: Three Generations in a Jewish Community* (Englewood Cliffs, N.J.: Prentice-Hall, Inc., 1968), pp. 67-70.

19. *Ibid.,* pp. 71-91.

20. Pascal K. Whelpton, Arthur A. Campbell, and John E. Patterson, *Fertility and Family Planning in the United States* (Princeton, N.J.: Princeton University Press, 1966), pp. 69-124 and 221-99.

21. For the urban data, see Table 11 in "Characteristics of Major Religious Groups, March, 1957" (see n. 11 above).

22. Bogue, *op, cit.,* pp. 702-5.

23. E.g., in the Providence study of the Jewish community, 25.3 per cent of the adult Jewish population had four or more years of college compared with only 6.5 per cent of the total population (Jews and non-Jews). But of the 25.3 per cent, just over half (13.4 per cent) had some postgraduate education, a percentage which in itself was twice as high as the proportion of the total population which had four or more years of college education, and even slightly above the total proportion in the population who had had any college education (13.1 per cent) (Goldstein and Goldscheider, *op. cit.,* p. 65).

24. Bogue, *op. cit.,* p. 704.

25. *Ibid.,* p. 708.

26. Goldstein and Goldscheider, *op. cit.,* pp. 95-100.

DENNISON NASH
PETER BERGER

The Child, the Family, and the "Religious Revival" in Suburbia

Though recent critics have whittled down the latter-day figures, the recent historical trend—particularly since 1940—shows that an increasing number of Americans have been committing themselves to church rolls.[1] This dramatic surge of Americans into the churches has been cited frequently as one aspect of an American "Religious Revival." But while the *quantitative* nature of this movement seems to be generally accepted, its *quality* has been the subject of a series of lively polemics centered for the most part on the question of religious authenticity.[2] Considering the widespread interest, it is remarkable that there have been no first-hand empirical studies of the *qualitative* nature of the

From the *Journal for the Scientific Study of Religion* 1(Fall 1962):85-93. Reprinted by permission of the publisher and authors.

The study on which this article is based was made possible by grant M-4821A from the National Institute of Mental Health, administered by the Hartford Seminary Foundation. We are indebted to the pastors and staffs of the churches involved for their cooperation, to Mary Forman for help with the interviewing, and to Mona Bachlund and Lillian Jockheck for clerical assistance.

"Revival." The answer to the question of why more people are committing themselves to churches than ever before so far has escaped us.

This paper, based on a study which explored the reasons why some Americans have been joining a denomination in one community, opens up our approach to the question. The locale of the study is a suburb (town) of Hartford, Conn. The denomination is the Congregational-Christian, the three churches of which draw their clientele from what may be described loosely as the middle class. We drew our sample from people who had joined these churches recently. Our selection of the suburb was prompted by the knowledge that recent religious gains have been associated particularly with an expanding suburbia.[3] We chose a Protestant denomination because Protestantism tends to prevail in suburbia.[4] The Congregational-Christian is the leading Protestant denomination in New England.[5] Though we will confine our generalizations to new Congregational church members in one suburb, the selection of a typical, rather than an atypical, universe should make speculation about broader areas feasible and provide a better springboard to additional studies.

Though many hypotheses have been offered to account for the "Religious Revival," there appeared to be no grounds for accepting one at the expense of others in our study.[6] However, we did take them into account in constructing the research instrument, the guiding question of which was: "What factors are associated with the decision to join?" These factors fell into two conceptual categories: the occasion or cue and the needs which the person sought to satisfy by joining the church.[7] Largely because of the serendipitous nature of the findings, we decided to treat the occasion of joining separately in this paper. A later article will deal comprehensively with the whole decision-making process.

Method and Techniques

By confining ourselves to one community and one denomination we have controlled these variables. Our churches, however, vary in character. One, the largest and oldest, was the first church of the community. It is situated in the center of the town and draws most of its clientele from the upper reaches of the middle class. The second largest is the "community" church of the industrial section of the suburb. Its membership is predominantly lower-middle class. The third and smallest church is a recently-formed congregation in an affluent "New Suburban" section of town. Its church building has not yet been raised. Because of the differences between these churches the class background of our respondents appears to vary more than would be the case in the single-class suburbs which have become famous in the literature.[8]

The total membership of all three churches in 1960 was 5.2 percent of the town's population. The sample was drawn from the people who joined the churches during a three-year period ending in October, 1960 (when the study began). This time span was selected to get a period short enough not to impede recall and long enough to provide data for statistical manipulation. We reduced the size of the potential universe by ruling out Transfers and young people who joined from the Pastor's Class.[9] The remaining adults had joined by Confession of Faith or Reaffirmation of Faith. These people had not been on a church roll recently and were now adding their name to one, or they were affecting a radical crossing of denomination lines (e.g., Roman Catholic-Congregational). We felt that the process of decision would be sharpened among these people.

A twenty-three percent random sample of the adults who joined by Confession of Faith or Reaffirmation of Faith was drawn.[10] Each person selected constitutes an instance of joining. If the person selected and his spouse joined at the same time the two were taken to be a single instance of joining. Thus the sample consists of more than twenty-three percent of our universe, but only twenty-three percent were randomly selected.

The joiners, with one exception, were interviewed at home. Husbands and wives were interviewed separately where possible. The interview consisted, first, of a series of questions designed to get at simple facts about the respondent and his situation, and second, of a series of only-slightly-directed questions (followed by probing where necessary) related to the decision to join and attitudes toward the church and religion.[11] A schedule was used for the first part, and a tape recorder for the last part, of the interview. The respondents were almost invariably friendly and cooperative. Some (usually from the better-educated ranks) were interested in the study. For a few, the interview seemed to spark some self-searching, but we doubt that our interviewing activities have caused more than a ripple on the suburban waters.

The Locale

Our suburb doubled (mostly by migration) in population from 1940 to 1960.[12] This growth appears to be related to the expanding economy—based particularly on insurance and aircraft industries—of the Hartford area. The town is a suburb of mixed character—principally residential, but also employing. One finds (toward the Hartford line) "Old Suburban" homes on tree-lined streets and (toward the periphery) the sprawl of standardized "New Suburban" developments of various income levels. With the exception of the south-eastern industrial section the community wears the aura of the affluent middle class. It is a Republican stronghold. There are the station wagons and foreign cars, plenty of police, country clubs, trucks of landscape gardeners. An expensive and expanding school system turns out significant numbers of National Merit Scholars. These are some of the signs of its style of life.

There are twenty-three churches. Thirteen of these are Protestant, five Catholic, three Jewish, and two Undenominational. Protestant church members, who are numerically superior to the other faiths, comprised about 14 percent of the town's population in 1960. Since 1940 Protestant church membership increased from 3732 (about 11 percent of the town's population) to 8500. During the period 1940–1960 Congregational church membership doubled, and data from the largest church show that increased joining, not increasing longevity of membership, has been responsible for this increase.[13]

Though church life in the Congregational churches centers around the Sunday morning services, the churches are hives of (mostly womanly) club and committee activity throughout the week. Of major concern is the education and organization of children who are drawn from the expanding cohort of young people in the town's population.[14] Thus, women and children receive most of the churches' attention and carry on most of their activities. This family-centeredness of the church has been noted elsewhere.[15] It is to be expected in the milieu of suburbia where a child-centered familism appears to be developing.[16]

The Joiners

There were 35 instances of joining. (The number of people interviewed was almost double this figure.) 32 of these were married couples when they joined. The modal cases had lived in their present home 2–5 years and in their present community slightly longer. They were Old Americans (fourth or later generation) whose parents were Protestants (but, for the most part, not Congregationalists). The average age of the men in the sample was 40, of the women, 38.

Considering the occupation of the family head, 21 were in the upper white collar bracket (professionals, proprietors of substantial businesses, members of top management in some corporation, and lesser managers and officials). Only 6 were self-employed. Eighteen had been in their present position three years or less. Sixteen (the mode) had a gross family income in 1959 of $6000–12000 (range: $4000–$25000). Adding an average education of about two years of college, we gain the impression of a well-educated, upwardly-mobile group of white collar people.

The modal family of procreation had 4 members at the time of joining. Sixteen of the families had children younger than five years old and 23 had children aged 5–14. Forty three children of the families in the sample were affiliated as church or Sunday School members at the time of joining. In this group it is the usual thing for all of the family, who are old enough, to become affiliated with the same church. This impressive display of formal commitment to a church is not matched by affiliation with other voluntary associations, however. We gained the impression that the family is emphasized to the exclusion of most voluntary associations, and where many voluntary associations are joined it is because family life is not particularly satisfying. Since family life appears to center around the children we think that these people may increasingly commit themselves to association life as their children leave the nest. Meanwhile, informal visiting appears to satisfy some of the need for broader association.

William Whyte describes the modal man of his well-educated, highly mobile, associationally-active Park Foresters as "a twenty-five-to-thirty-five-year-old white-collar organization man with a wife, a salary between $6000 and $7000, one child, and another on the way."[17] Our joiners seem to be of the same stamp, though a bit older, wealthier, more stable and less committed to association life. We attribute their lesser commitment to associations to the greater stability of their lives. Finally, there appears to be more of a status spread among our joiners than among the Park Forest natives. This seems to be due to the difference in the nature of the class range in the two communities.

The Occasion of Joining

It is possible from our interview material to discern the needs related to the decision to join and thus the function of that decision. But though this will explain *why* joining occurred, it does not tell us *when.* In this article we seek to answer the "when" in terms of the occasion which prompted the decision.[18] There was very little difficulty in discerning the occasion which led to the act of joining. In 32 cases joining was prompted by a consideration for some other person(s).[19] In 31 cases it was a gesture of solidarity within a proposed or established family. In 25 cases it was the prospect or presence of children which wholly or partly occasioned the act of joining by their parents. We will concentrate on this modern version of the biblical notion that "a little child shall lead them."

Here are some typical responses:

"My daughter started in Sunday school. I decided that as long as we were bringing up the children in the church we ought to join."

"It was mainly after we had a child that I thought of the child being brought up in the church . . . At that time we looked into religion much more for that reason."

". . . my daughter. Well, I thought I might as well go to the same church she was. A few of her girl friends went down there, and of course she kept egging us on—that we should too. So, she was the instigator, probably."

When we asked these respondents why it was so important for children to be brought up in a church we found ourselves dealing with what we take to be a cultural article of faith, i.e., a largely unquestioned postulate. When we pressed them for an explanation we got responses such as the following:

"I think that a Christian education which one gets from Sunday School—there is a certain direction in it. . . . , a certain training of right and wrong which is not being done in other activities for young boys."

"It rounds out their education."

"By attending Sunday School he's taught how to go along the right paths." Such responses suggest that the church is conceived as a necessary adjunct to the family (in this case, an ethical agency) in the task of socializing the children.

But why must the parents join too? Again we are confronted by what appears to be a cultural article of faith. For these people it is a largely unquestioned postulate that if one's children go to church or Sunday School one does also. Pressed on this particular point, here is what some of our respondents had to say:

". . . and the first thing he (the child) would say is, 'Why do I have to go to Sunday School and you don't go to church?' You just can't say, 'Well, I'm grown up. I don't need it anymore'."

"She'd have a much stronger feeling for the church if she knew that I belonged."

"I felt that if I wanted the kids to go to Sunday School and to be active in church later . . . I should be a member to at least set an example for them." In other words, if the church is to perform its socializing function properly these people feel that they must commit themselves to it. By doing so they are fulfilling themselves as parents.

In Park Forest, according to Whyte, the "new suburbanites customarily approach the church through their children."[20] Our data support this hypothesis. We see that for the suburbanite commitment to one's children is more important than a personal commitment to religion at the time of joining. Most of the parents see nothing wrong with a superficial or even hypocritical involvement with organized religion, if it is conceived to benefit the children. It is not the usual thing for parents to show evidence of conflict in this area, but for one independent-minded young matron of humanist leanings the "triumph" of her devotion to her children over her personal beliefs has brought out some guilt feelings. After telling of the pressures from her daughter, her daughter's friends, and relatives and detailing her own lack of religious conviction she was asked by the interviewer to explain why she had joined. She replied:

"When I joined the church I said that it was hypocritical on my part . . . I don't feel quite as clean as I did before—to be honest with you—because I didn't do it for me—I mean trying to do something for someone else that I should have done for my own feelings, for my own reasons."

This excerpt demonstrates the strength of the ethic of child-centered familism which seems to be the key to the style of life in modern suburbia. It also brings out the element of "vicariousness," i.e., doing something for someone else, in a society in the grip of the Social Ethic.

In Crestwood Heights we learn that "the institutions . . . tend to converge on the family."[21] Of the principal institutions, however, the church is the only one to which people can commit themselves *en famille.* In turn, the church, by addressing itself to the family (especially the women and children) has benefited *quantitatively* from the solidarity of its members. Granted the need to have children and to bring them up properly, the prospect or presence of children becomes the cue which elicits the response of joining.[22] What other needs are involved in the decision and why the Congregational-Christian church satisfies them better than others are questions which we will answer in another paper. Finally, joining is one thing; staying on as a member is another. Will these parents remain as members after their children have grown? If so, what other needs will be activated to keep them there? These would seem to be fruitful questions for further research.

The Cause of the "Religious Revival": An Hypothesis

If what has happened in our churches is representative of America during the period of the "Religious Revival," we suggest that the upsurge in church membership is due at least partly to an increase in the number of children who enter the church *and* parents who follow. Three factors could, individually or collectively, produce this phenomenon: 1) An increase in the number of families with children. 2) An increase in parents' tendency to follow their children to church. 3) An increase in the percentage of families whose children go to church.[23] How many of these factors have been operative, and in what way they are interrelated, we do not now know.

Statistics from our churches are both tempting and exasperating. The more adequate data from the larger of the two which have been in existence through the period 1940–1960 show that the number of families belonging to the church almost doubled (850–1540), but data on the number of families with children in Sunday School are lacking for 1940.[24] Because of this we cannot say whether the increase in Sunday School pupils (539–956) is due to an increase in the number of families with children or to an increase in the number of children per family in Sunday School. As for an increase in parents' tendencies to follow their children to church, the data show a decline in the number of nonaffiliated families of Sunday School children, but (again) data are lacking for the number of families with children in Sunday School in 1940. Therefore, we cannot say that the proportion of church-affiliated families with children in Sunday School has increased. If it were so it would establish the increasing tendency of parents to follow their children into this church.[25] There are many "ifs" in the line of argument for our hypothesis, but we feel that the "ifs" are likely to be true. If the number of families with children in Sunday School has not changed or has increased, and if the number of children per family with Sunday School children has declined, remained unchanged, or increased only slightly, the hypothesis would be confirmed for this church. If the same holds true for other churches in the community, and if the percentage of families whose children are in the church has remained the same or increased, the hypothesis would be proved for our suburb. And if other suburban communities are like ours in this regard, the explanation of the American "Religious Revival"—at least in the major denominations—would be something more than a "Just So" story.[26] We need data badly to test this argument.

Summary and Conclusion

In order to explore the reasons why Americans have been committing themselves increasingly to organized religion we interviewed a sample of adults who recently joined the Congregational-Christian church in a fast-growing Connecticut suburb. The joiners presented a picture similar to that of suburbanites studied elsewhere. For most of these people the decision to join was promoted by the prospect or presence of children in the family. The parade of parents into the church because of the children confirms Whyte's Park Forest hypothesis and reflects the childcentered familistic ethic of suburbia. We speculated that this movement has been responsible for the increase in church membership which has been one aspect of the American "Religious Revival."

Though Whyte's hypothesis was supported, other hypotheses were not confirmed by our data. Herberg's suggestion that the turn to religion actually is a *re*-turn to religion by the third generation clearly does not apply to our sample in which the modal category is the fourth or later generation.[27] Since Lenski in the Detroit study found that (with the possible exception of Jews) there is a progressive increase in religious commitment as measured by church attendance through the generations, the third generation notion would seem to fail as an all-embracing explanation.[28] A second hypothesis sees the turn to religion as a product of life crisis.[29] We explored this area with our respondents, but only in the exceptional case were we able to connect a life crises with the decision to join. For most of our joiners their life was at least tolerable and their outlook favorable at the time of joining. Moreover, conversion experiences such as those reported in detail by William James are almost non-existent.[30] We do not mean to imply that these people were all models of psychological well-being when they joined nor that religion does not play a part in dealing with personal difficulties, but that a crisis does not usually stand at the beginning of their commitment to the church. Joining, for most of these people, appears to be an ordinary, to-be-counted-on occurrence—a rite of passage—in the unfolding of their family life.

In summary, the approach of these people to membership in a religious organization appears to have been a smooth one and rational. Nor should we expect it to be otherwise in a middle-class milieu informed by the "secularized Protestant Ethic" and the form of religious organization called the denomination. We can speculate on the function of the act of joining for these people on two levels. First, on the level of culture, the act of joining will further commit the individual to the values of the middle class. Second, on the level of society, to the degree that the individual commits himself to organizational activities in the church, he will be broadening his social participation and, presumably, satisfying the need for belonging which Whyte found to be so important among his Park Foresters and which may increase when the children leave home. We see, therefore, that the direction in which "the little child shall lead them" may be into further commitment to the "O.K. World" which is the psychological environment which suburbanites have created out of existence.[31]

---

1. See *Yearbook of American Churches,* 1956, 1960, B. Landis (ed.), New York: National Council of Churches, 1955, 1959. Data from the *Yearbook* are not adequate for a number of reasons, one of which is a lack of a standardized minimum age in reported church membership. Refinements of these data have cut down the long-term upward trend in church membership, but the upward surge in membership since 1940 still remains. See M. Argyle, *Religious Behavior,* Glencoe, Ill.: The Free Press, 1959, 28-29; S. Lipset, "Religion in America: What Religious Revival?", *Columbia University Forum* (Winter, 1959), 17-21.

2. See, e.g., A. Eckardt, *The Surge of Piety in America,* New York: The Association Press, 1958; P. Hutchinson, "Have We a 'New' Religion?", *Life* (April 11, 1955), 138-140; R. Niebuhr, "Is There a Revival of Religion?", *The New York Times Magazine* (November 19, 1950); S. Rowland, *Land in Search of God,* New York: Random House, 1958.

3. G. Winter, *The Suburban Captivity of the Churches,* New York: Doubleday, 1961, 39-58.

4. See W. Whyte, Jr., *The Organization Man,* New York: Doubleday Anchor Book, 1957, 407-408.

5. The Congregational-Christian is the oldest extant church in much of New England. It is the largest Protestant denomination in Connecticut, Massachusetts, and Vermont, second largest in Maine, and third largest in Rhode Island. See *Churches and Church Membership in the United States,* New York: National Council of Churches, 1956.

6. We tapped the following sources for hypotheses: H. Gans, "The Origin and Growth of a Jewish Community in the Suburbs: A Study of the Jews of Park Forest," in M. Sklare (ed.), *The Jews,* Glencoe, Ill.: The Free Press, 1958, 205-248; W. Herberg, *Protestant, Catholic, Jew,* New York: Doubleday Anchor Book, 1960; R. Goldsen, M. Rosenberg, R. Williams Jr., E. Suchman, *What College Students Think,* New York: Van Nostrand, 1960; H. R. Niebuhr, *The Social Sources of Denominationalism,* New York: Holt, 1929; R. Niebuhr, *op. cit.;* T. Parsons, *Structure and Process in Modern Societies,* Glencoe, Ill.: The Free Press, 1960, 317-319; J. Seeley, R. Sim, E. Loosley, *Crestwood Heights,* New York: Basic Books, 1956; M. Weber, "The Protestant Sects and the Spirit of Capitalism," in H. Gerth and C. W. Mills (eds.), *From Max Weber,* New York: Oxford University Press, 1946, 302-322.

7. A discussion of this scheme and the theories from which it is derived is included in footnote 18.

8. See D. Riesman, "The Suburban Dislocation," *The Annals,* CCCXIV (November, 1957), 123-146; Whyte, Jr., *op. cit.,* 330-344.

9. A Transfer is simply taken off one church roll and put on another. Thus he could not have contributed to the nationwide increase in church membership. The Pastor's class is made up almost entirely of young people moving up into the church from Sunday School. We felt that their Confession of Faith would not be so much a personal decision as a normal rite of passage out of Sunday School to which they probably had been committed by their parents.

10. A letter from the pastor was sent to each person. It explained the nature of our study and made clear that cooperation would be a voluntary matter. If one of these people could not be interviewed he was replaced by another chosen at random from a list of randomly-selected "reserves." We have interviews from eighty-four percent of the people selected in the original sample. As for the sample size, we think that, considering the homogeneity of the respondents, it probably is larger than necessary.

11. E.g., "Would you tell me the story of how you came to join the church?"

12. *Community Monographs,* Hartford, Conn.: The Connecticut Development Commission 1956; U.S. Bureau of the Census, *Census of the Population, 1940, 1950, 1960.*

13. Data were obtained from the membership records of individual churches and from a study of churches in the community by The Connecticut Council of Churches.

14. In 1940 19.1 percent of the population were younger than age 14, in 1960, 24.9 percent. U.S. Bureau of the Census, *op. cit.*

15. P. Berger, "The Second Children's Crusade," *The Christian Century* (December 2, 1959).

16. See W. Bell, "Familism and Suburbanization: One Test of the Social Choice Hypothesis," *Rural Sociology,* XXI (September, 1956), 276-283; E. Jace and I. Belknap, "Is a New Family Form Emerging on the Urban Fringe?", *American Sociological Review,* XVIII (October, 1953), 551-557; E. Mowrer, "The Family in Suburbia," in W. Dobriner (ed.), *The Suburban Community,* New York: Putnam's, 1958, 147-164; Seeley, Sim, Looseley, *op. cit.;* Whyte, Jr., *op. cit.,* 378-379, 423-434.

17. Whyte, Jr., *op. cit.,* 311.

18. The scheme for viewing the decision-making process can be derived from reference group theory. See M. Sherif and M. O. Wilson (eds.), *Group Relations at the Crossroads,* New York, Harper, 1953; R. K. Merton, *Social Theory, and Social Structure,* Glencoe, Ill., Free Press 1957; and especially, T. Shibutain, "*Reference Groups* as Perspectives," *American Journal of Sociology,* LX (1955), p. 562ff. The biography of the individual is a process of transition through a series of reference groups that not only determine his behavior but his perspectives on society and on his own existence. We assume that, in this case, the prospect or presence of children marks the parents' transition into a new reference group, i.e., the world of fulfilled suburban families. The act of religious affiliation is then part and parcel of the acquisition of this new group's norms. The role of the individual's needs in joining is discussed by Festinger. See L. Festinger, *"Group Attraction and Membership"* in D. Cartwright and A. Zander (eds.), *Group Dynamics,* Evanston, Ill.: Row Peterson, 1953, 92-101.

19. The general part which vicariousness plays in suburban religion will be treated in another paper.

20. Whyte, Jr., *op. cit.,* 421.

21. Seely, Sim, Loosley, *op. cit.,* 11.

22. That the need is not simply our fortuitous construction to fit the response of joining for the sake of the children is indicated by Bell's data which show that for 83 percent of his suburban respondents a familistic orientation entered into their decision to move to the suburbs. Bell, *op. cit.,* 282.

23. Census data show that the number of husband-wife families with children under 18 increased from 1940 to 1960, but the percentage of such families of all husband-wife families followed a "U"-shaped trend (59 percent in 1940, 54.7 percent in 1950, 59.3 percent in 1960). The decline from 1940 to 1950 probably is due to the increase in married people who had not yet had a child. The decline of the marriage rate in the 50's and the birth of children to those married in the late 40's (when the peak marriage rate occurred) would account for the subsequent increase. These data are not incompatible with our finding that the prospect or presence of children leads to joining by the parents. See U.S. Bureau of the Census, "Family Characteristics," *Special Reports* (1940, 1950) *Current Population Reports,* Series P-20, No. 106 (March, 1960).
We know of no data which may be cited in relation to factors 2 and 3.

24. Data provided by the church clerk. Children who are church members are omitted from the tabulation because they are not recorded separately in the church records. This does little harm as far as our hypothesis is concerned since most joining in our sample was tied up with a child going to Sunday School.

25. Data concerning the percentage of church-going families with children in the community are not available, but it would be relevant only if our study included all churches in the community.

26. There has also been a "Religious Revival" in sects which is decidedly not a suburban phenomenon. This suggests that it has different causes. By confining ourselves to the major denominations we are dealing with a growth which is associated primarily with the rapid expansion of suburbia and which is accompanied by central city losses. See Winter, *op. cit.*, 39-58.

27. Herberg, *op. cit.*, 56-57.

28. G. Lenski, *The Religious Factor*, New York; Doubleday, 1961, 40-43.

29. See E. Nottingham, *Religion and Society*. New York: Random House, 1954, 28-40. We are referring only to specific incidents, not more generalized stress such as fear of a nuclear war, anxiety, fear of communism, etc. Such factors may be associated with the "Religious Revival," but we reserve the discussion of them for a later paper.

30. W. James, *The Varieties of Religious Experience*, New York: Mentor Books, 1958, 157-206.

31. P. Berger, *The Noise of Solemn Assemblies*, New York: Doubleday, 1961, 93ff.

LEON GORLOW
HAROLD E. SCHROEDER

Motives for Participating in the Religious Experience

The present study aimed at (1) an empirical identification of self-reported motives for participation in religious activities and (2) an examination of the relationships between those motives, and personal, social, and demographic variables. We especially attempted to identify an *exhaustive* set of statements individuals report as reasons for participation in religious activity. The empirical literature provides no such complete set of statements. We anticipated that, given such an exhaustive range of reasons, individuals would cluster themselves into meaningful groups—"religious types"—sharing similar constructions about the religious experience. This would accord with everyday experience and with the work of Glock (1954), Fukuyama (1961), Lenski (1963), and King (1967), suggesting that religious motives and religious experiences are not unidimensional.

Finally and most importantly, it was anticipated that the extent to which one belonged to a "type" would be related to variables such as

From the *Journal for the Scientific Study of Religion* 7 (Fall 1968):241-51. Reprinted by permission of the publisher and authors.

religious denomination, socio-economic status, and political affiliation and that these relationships would lend construct validity to the typology.

Method

Generating Statements

One hundred seventy-five active church members in central Pennsylvania were used to generate an initial set of statements of "reasons for participating in religious activities." They consisted of clerical and lay members of liberal, orthodox, and pentecostal Protestant denominations (e.g., Unitarian, Mormon, Lutheran, Episcopalian, Methodist, Baptist, Church of God, Nazarene), and the Roman Catholic Church. Each person was asked to respond in writing to the following:

> As a participant in church activities, you are a person who attaches significance to the religious domain of your life. We are trying to identify dimensions of importance and need your assistance. What feeling, act or experience in this realm has been, is, or continues to be of greatest personal significance or meaning to you?

This procedure yielded several hundred responses which preliminary review reduced to 87 relatively non-overlapping and unambiguous reasons for religious participation. The reasons were cast into the infinitive form, producing such items as "to obtain forgiveness of sins," "to gain inner peace," "to be challenged," "to follow higher principles," "to experience the mystery of God."

A further review of these items by a group of 40 young college adults who were participating in a three-hour-long religious discussion group failed to produce additional reasons beyond the 87 already abstracted.[1]

Rating of Items

The final set of items was administered as a 13-pile Q-sort task to 129 subjects drawn from introductory psychology classes at The Pennsylvania State University. In the Q-sort, a given subject's task was to place in Pile 1 the reason "of least importance" to him and place in Pile 13 the statement "of greatest importance" to him. Distribution was forced so that the 13 piles would contain 1, 2, 4, 8, 10, 12, 13, 12, 10, 8, 4, 2, 1 statements, respectively.

On a questionnaire administered immediately prior to the Q-sort task, subjects were asked to indicate the strength of their religious involvement on a single-item scale. One hundred subjects indicated at least "some involvement," and they were selected as subjects since the purpose of the study was to explore orientations toward religious *participation.*

All of the subjects were undergraduates ranging in age from 17 to 22; there were about equal numbers of each sex; they came from a wide variety of curricula in the university and represented variations in religious denomination, political philosophy, and social class.

Factor Analysis

The item placements in the Q-sorts were used to generate a matrix of correlations among persons; each cell of the matrix (the correlation coefficient) represents the degree of correspondence between the Q-sorts of all possible pairs of individuals (Stephenson, 1953). This matrix was then subjected to a principal components inverse factor analysis, utilizing a Varimax rotation. In contrast to *R* technique which yields clusters of *measures* which go together, the inverse analysis (*Q* technique) yields clusters of *persons* defining a hypothetical type (Cattell, 1950).

In order to characterize these types, correlations are computed between loadings on the factors which emerge and the Q-sort placements of the items. (Since the *inverse* analysis provides all individuals with loadings for all the factors, it is possible to correlate individuals' loadings on a given factor with their Q-sort placements for a given motive. This procedure identifies those motives whose placements relate significantly to a given factor and aids in identifying the character of that factor.)

In a similar fashion, correlations were also calculated between factor loadings and the variables included in the questionnaire which asked subjects to provide social, personal and demographic information. (Table 2 reports all such correlations significant beyond the .05 level.)

Results

The factor analysis was programmed to yield eight factors because experience suggests that additional factors account for a negligible amount of variance. Seven of these factors proved to be readily interpretable by examining the item placements associated with each of them. Table 1 contains all of these statements which correlated positively and negatively beyond the .01 level of significance with the factor loadings.

TABLE 1. *Reported Motives Correlating with Loadings on Each Factor*

r	Motive
Factor I: Humble servants of God	
.64	To be redeemed.
.52	To obtain forgiveness of sins.
.52	To gain the promise of salvation.
.52	To receive assurance of everlasting life.
.49	To have personal communion with God.
.48	To be an obedient servant.
.46	To be instructed about God and His revelation to man.
.45	To experience God's love.
.42	To experience the presence of God.
.34	To praise God.
.33	To grow in reliance on God.
.32	To experience the power of God.
.32	To feel a renewal of one's life.
.31	To have a refuge for relaxation.
.30	To participate in the sacraments.
.29	To pray.
.28	To experience the mystery of God.
.26	To feel a part of God's plan and purpose.
–.50	To maintain traditions.
–.42	To gain personal security.
–.42	To gain freedom from anxiety.
–.42	To gain freedom from the triteness of life.
–.41	To heighten one's goals.
–.40	To find a way to deal with one's personal limitations.
–.39	To meet personally with others in small group activity.
–.39	To grow in the ability to value other people.
–.38	To feel close to other people.
–.34	To gain an attitude that puts life in an ultimate perspective.
–.34	To moderate society's demand for success.
–.30	To remain true to one's family teaching.
–.30	To examine one's self.
Factor II: Self-improvers	
.47	To increase self-understanding.
.44	To find a way to deal with one's personal limitations.
.42	To grow in the ability to value other people.
.39	To heighten one's goals.
.38	To gain an attitude that puts life in an ultimate perspective.
.35	To gain freedom from anxiety.
.34	To receive the strength to deal with adversity.
.33	To be challenged to follow higher principles.
.32	To gain personal security.
.32	To examine one's self.
.32	To receive assurance of everlasting life.
.29	To gain freedom from the triteness of life.
.28	To moderate society's demand for success.
.27	To develop a greater concern for others.
.27	To receive help for everyday problems.
.26	To strengthen a set of beliefs on which to act.
.26	To obtain a greater knowledge of moral obligations.
–.41	To be redeemed.
–.40	To experience the presence of God.
–.38	To praise God.
–.38	To experience the power of God.
–.36	To experience the mystery of God.
–.36	To have personal communion with God.
–.35	To stand in awe and wonder of God.
–.34	To experience God's love.

TABLE 1, *continued*

r	Motive
Factor II	
–.33	To sing hymns.
–.29	To be instructed about God and His revelation to man.
–.29	To be an obedient servant.
–.29	To grow in reliance on God.
–.28	To gain the promise of salvation.
–.28	To pray.
–.27	To obtain forgiveness of sins.
Factor III: Family guidance seekers	
.49	To gain personal security.
.42	To find courage to face the certainty of death.
.38	To receive guidance for the conduct of family relationships.
.34	To gain freedom from anxiety.
.32	To strengthen family life.
.32	To receive help for everyday problems.
.32	To set an example for others.
.31	To have a refuge for relaxation.
.29	To receive the strength to deal with adversity.
.28	To have an opportunity for healing.
.26	To remain true to one's family teaching.
–.39	To read and discuss the Bible.
–.39	To exchange ideas about beliefs.
–.35	To be instructed about God and His revelation to man.
–.35	To evaluate one's self in terms of scriptural teaching.
–.34	To reinforce one's religious convictions.
–.34	To experience the presence of God.
–.33	To study Biblical writings.
–.32	To experience the power of God.
–.31	To gain a stronger faith.
–.30	To stand in awe and wonder of God.
–.29	To discuss religious writings.
–.28	To study religious writings.
–.27	To experience the mystery of God.
–.27	To have personal communion with God.
Factor IV: Moralists	
.38	To set an example for others.
.35	To feel close to other people.
.34	To be an obedient servant.
.33	To maintain a moral standard for conduct.
.30	To have an opportunity for sharing one's "goods" with others.
.28	To receive guidance for instructing others.
.28	To instruct the young by setting an example.
.26	To grow in the ability to forgive others.
.26	To develop a greater concern for others.
–.46	To evaluate one's self in terms of scriptural teaching.
–.39	To gain inner peace.
–.38	To add a spiritual dimension to the rest of life.
–.31	To sing hymns.
–.30	To hear religious music.
–.28	To lift one's spirits.
–.26	To read and discuss the Bible.
Factor V: God-seekers	
.53	To gain the promise of salvation.
.51	To receive assurance of everlasting life.
.48	To feel a renewal of one's life.
.47	To be close to the source of truth.
.46	To be redeemed.
.40	To be instructed about God and His revelation to man.

TABLE 1, *continued*

r	Motive
Factor V	
.39	To find courage to face the certainty of death.
.38	To receive hope for mercy.
.37	To experience the mystery of God.
.35	To lift one's spirits.
.35	To have personal communion with God.
.31	To gain inner peace.
.30	To search for the meaning of life.
.28	To add a spiritual dimension to the rest of life.
–.47	To maintain traditions.
–.45	To instruct the young by setting an example.
–.44	To strengthen family life.
–.43	To feel close to other people.
–.42	To set an example for others.
–.40	To develop a greater concern for others.
–.39	To serve others.
–.37	To be challenged to grow in unselfish feelings.
–.36	To heighten one's goals.
–.36	To grow in the ability to forgive others.
–.35	To have an opportunity for sharing one's faith with others.
–.34	To be motivated to do good works.
–.32	To meet personally with others in small group activity.
–.30	To remain true to one's family teaching.
–.29	To participate in worship with others.
–.29	To hear a sermon.
Factor VI: Socially-oriented servants of God	
.45	To experience God's love.
.45	To be an obedient servant.
.36	To discuss religious experience.
.34	To have an opportunity for sharing one's faith with others.
.30	To serve others.
.30	To have an opportunity for sharing one's 'goods' with others.
.28	To set an example for others.
.27	To experience the power of God.
.27	To be redeemed.
.27	To grow in reliance on God.
–.53	To search for the meaning of life.
–.51	To examine one's self.
–.45	To hear a religious interpretation of current events.
–.37	To obtain a greater knowledge of moral obligations.
–.34	To become aware of current events through the sermon.
–.33	To find a way to deal with one's personal limitations.
–.33	To maintain traditions.
–.29	To strengthen a set of beliefs on which to act.
–.29	To gain freedom from the triteness of life.
–.28	To grow in the ability to value other people.
–.28	To grow in humanitarian ideals.
–.27	To be challenged to follow higher principles.
Factor VIII: Religious eggheads	
.58	To study religious writings.
.47	To study Biblical writings.
.45	To instruct the young by setting an example.
.44	To read and discuss the Bible.
.44	To receive guidance for instructing others.
.44	To exchange ideas about beliefs.
.43	To participate in lectures and seminars.
.43	To have an opportunity to teach religious classes.
.41	To have an opportunity for sharing one's faith with others.

TABLE 1, *continued*

r	Motive
Factor VIII	
.40	To have fellowship with others of similar belief.
.38	To strengthen family life.
.37	To maintain traditions.
.34	To discuss religious experience.
.33	To become aware of current events through the sermon.
.32	To serve others.
.31	To be challenged to grow in unselfish feelings.
.30	To hear a sermon.
.29	To obtain a greater knowledge of moral obligations.
.29	To hear a religious interpretation of current events.
.29	To receive guidance as a family unit.
.28	To meet personally with others in small group activity.
.28	To set an example for others.
.26	To grow in humanitarian ideals.
–.55	To gain inner peace.
–.49	To receive inner strength.
–.49	To receive hope for mercy.
–.47	To stand in awe and wonder of God.
–.47	To gain inner contentment, security and trust.
–.47	To obtain forgiveness of sins.
–.47	To gain the promise of salvation.
–.43	To receive assurance of everlasting life.
–.43	To experience God's love.
–.42	To be redeemed.
–.40	To feel a renewal of one's life.
–.39	To find courage to face the certainty of death.
–.36	To feel a part of God's plan and purpose.
–.35	To experience the mystery of God.
–.34	To experience the presence of God.
–.32	To have personal communion with God.
–.30	To gain freedom from anxiety.
–.30	To gain personal security.
–.29	To experience the power of God.
–.28	To grow in reliance on God.

Factor I, accounting for 16 per cent of the variance, is identified by the statements giving prominence to a passive, subordinate relationship to a nurturant superior being. Persons loading high on this factor may be identified as *humble servants of God.*

When the correlations between loadings on Factor I (reflecting degree of membership in this cluster) and the personal, social, and demographic variables are examined (Table 2), the following relationships are observed: these persons are likely to be Roman Catholic and not Jewish; they rate themselves as having strong religious feelings; they are not enrolled in the Liberal Arts college; they are not likely to have a high parental income, nor are they likely to have parents who have a good deal of formal education; they are likely to be Republican politically; and finally, they indicate that their participation at religious services is likely to be more frequent and regular than others.

Persons clustering together in Factor II tend to value the religious experience for the purpose of increasing self-understanding, finding a

TABLE 2. *Correlations Between Factor Loadings and Personal, Social Demographic Variables.* ***

Variable	I Humble Servants God	II Self-Improver	III Family Guid. Seeker	IV Moralist	V God-Seeker	VI Soc. Serv. God	VIII Rel. Egg-head
Protestant*				−.40		.22	
Catholic*	.35			.43	.34		−.30
Jewish*	−.50				−.57		.25
Strength. Rel. Invlnt.**	.37	−.35				.26	
Frequency Attend. Rel. Services**	.63	−.47			.37	.29	−.37
Participation in Other Rel. Acty.**					−.22	.30	.22
Liberal Arts Curriculum*	−.25	.33					
Business Administration Curr.*			.23				
Science Curriculum*		−.27					
Father's Occ. as Professional*					−.22		
Father's Occ. as Bus. Mang.*		.22				−.26	
Father's Occ. as Skill. Work.*		−.32					
Father's Income**	−.27				−.23		.24
Father's Education**	−.29				−.20		.24
Mother's Education**	−.24				−.34		.36
First Born*					−.24		−.30
Political Affiliation (Rep.)*	.22						
Political Affiliation (Dem.)*		.26					
Political Philosophy (Liberal)*		.23					

*Point biserial correlations were computed between loadings and membership-nonmembership in the relevant class, viz: protestant-nonprotestant; catholic-noncatholic, etc. For reasons of computer data format, the classes of "conservative-nonconservative" and "liberal-nonliberal" appear in lieu of their equivalence "conservative-liberal."

**Product-moment correlations were computed.

***Five variables (sex, membership in the home economics or engineering curriculum, father's occupation as a semi-skilled worker, and conservative political philosophy) failed to produce significant correlations and are not indicated in the table.

way to deal with one's limitations, heightening goals and gaining freedom from anxiety. They lend less value to redemption and experiencing the presence and power of God. This factor accounted for 16 per cent of the variance, and we have identified persons loading high on this factor as *self-improvers.*

These persons describe themselves (Table 2) as less involved in religion than others and likely to be enrolled in the Liberal Arts college rather than in a science curriculum; the occupation of the father is more likely to be in business and management, and the father is not likely to be a skilled worker. In addition, these individuals are more likely to be Democrats, liberal in political philosophy and not engaged in a great deal of attendance at religious services.

Factor III, accounting for 3.7 per cent of the variance, defines a group of persons who tend to assign high value to personal security as a consequence of participating in religious activities. A very important theme for them is achieving the proper conduct of family life. They want to receive guidance for the family; they are pragmatists who seek help for everyday problems. These individuals may be termed *family guidance seekers.*

Only one of the demographic items turned out to be related to degree of membership on this factor. Individuals are more likely to be enrolled in the business curriculum.

Factor IV defines another rationale for participating in the religious experience. The central theme appears to be service to others, and this group may be identified as *the moralists.* The factor accounted for 3.3 per cent of the variance. These individuals are likely to be Roman Catholic and not Protestant.

Factor V, accounting for 5.8 per cent of the variance, represents a cluster of individuals who appear to attribute high value to confronting the Ultimate. This factor in many ways is similar to Factor I and is somewhat difficult to discriminate from the first factor. Unlike Factor I, however, persons loading high on Factor V place higher value on an active, seeking relationship with God, although both factors include a relationship of submission and dependence. This group of persons may be termed *the God-seekers.*

These individuals are likely to be Roman Catholic and not Jewish; they are not likely to have parents with professional employment and they are likely to have low family income and mothers and fathers of little formal schooling. They report high frequency of attendance at religious services, but are not likely to participate in other religious activities such as religious study groups, religious social groups, etc. They are likely, in addition, to be later born, rather than first born.

Factor VI, with 3.6 per cent of the variance, defines a cluster of individuals in which there appears to be two dominant themes. There is, first of all, the theme of experiencing God, his power, his example, his redemptive love. This is similar to Factors I and V. On the other hand, there is the theme of participation with others in social life, i.e. sharing one's faith with others, serving others, setting an example for others and sharing one's goods with others. This is similar to Factor IV. This group of persons may be termed *the socially-oriented servants of God.*

The demographic material yields the following: persons loading highly here are likely to be Protestant, to represent themselves as having strong religious involvement and to be frequent attenders at religious services. In addition, they are likely to be attenders of other religious functions, and finally, they are not likely to be offspring of parents at the business-management level.

Factor VII was uninterpretable as a result of the fact that only a few of the Q-sort placements turned out to be significantly related to the factor loadings. The demographic data also did not correlate significantly with these factor loadings.

In Factor VIII, accounting for 11.4 per cent of the variance, a cluster of individuals was encountered quite different from all of the others. Interest here appears to be focused on studying religious and biblical writings, readings and discussion, exchanging ideas and participation in lectures and seminars. Gaining inner peace, receiving mercy and inner strength, standing in awe of God, salvation and redemption are all given less value. This group of individuals may be termed *the religious eggheads.* These are individuals for whom the religious experience is valued not for its focus on God but rather for its focus on intellectual research.

Individuals loading on this factor are not likely to be Roman Catholic, but are likely to be Jewish and to come from families with higher income and more formal education. While they are likely to have infrequent attendance at religious services, they are likely to have more frequent attendance at other religious activities. Finally, they are likely to be later born.

Discussion

Correspondence with Other Studies

It is important to acknowledge at the outset that the clusters and their relationships are of interest to the extent that one can presuppose some generalizability and reliability to the factors which have emerged. In the absence of a cross-validating replication providing *direct* evidence of factor stability, one may examine the correspondence between the results of the present study with those of other studies. Such correspondence would constitute evidence for reliability.

Some rather striking parallels are observed when the factors of this study are compared with those which emerged in Monaghan's (1967) analysis of religious motivations among members of a fundamentalist church. Upon subjecting his Q-sort to analysis, Monaghan found three types of persons in his sample—*autonomy-seekers, comfort-seekers* and *social participators.* The first group of individuals seeks to learn God's word and shares in "a strong and consistent desire for a submissive relationship to authority." The autonomy-seeker of Monaghan is the humble servant of God in the present study. Similarly, the comfort-seeker whose motives involve seeking peace of mind corresponds to the self-improver who seeks personal security, freedom from anxiety and strength to deal with adversity. Finally, the social participator who desires friendly social interaction and human companionship resembles the socially-oriented servant of God, one of whose major interests is in participation with others in social life.

Fukuyama's work (1961) in testing Glock's multidimensional hypotheses (1954) is also worth noting for its correspondence with the present study. His *creedal, cultic, intellectual* and *devotional* dimensions are our humble servants, socially-oriented, religious eggheads and God-seekers, respectively.

King's factor analysis (1967) of a broadly conceived questionnaire on religious beliefs, attitudes and behaviors, and involvement in a congregation yielded nine dimensions, a number of which (*creedal assent and personal commitment, personal ties in the congregation* and *talking and reading about religion*) appear congruent with ours (humble servants, socially-oriented servants of God and religious eggheads, respectively). It does indeed appear that the factors adduced in the present study appear elsewhere, and are, therefore, of general interest.

Relationship of Factors with Other Variables

It appears that socio-economic level is highly associated with the type of religious motivation. It has widely been recognized that an individual's social status is a good predictor of the denomination to which he will belong. But the relationship apparently goes deeper than the social status of the church. Individuals from the same social level want to gain similar benefits from their religious participation. In our study, the most God-oriented motivations (Factors I and V) occurred in the lower socio-economic groups, as indicated by lower family income, less formal education of the parents and non-professional parental employment. On the other hand, high socio-economic status (measured by income, education, and employment status) appears to be associated with self-improvement, either intellectual or personal (Factors II and VIII).

Attendance at religious services also appears to be associated with types of motivation. Individuals clustering in Factors I, V and VI—all factors placing much emphasis on the experience of God—are likely to participate frequently in religious services. On the other hand, individuals clustering in Factors II and VIII, i.e., those interested in personal or intellectual improvement, are likely not to participate frequently. Possibly those motivated by a desire to experience God in some transcendental way find no other avenue than the worship service whereas those motivated toward self-improvement find other avenues more conducive to their desires. Indeed, the latter do indicate a frequent attendance at other religious activities while the former indicate little participation in such activities.

In addition, it appears that certain motivations have a differential appeal for different religious groups. This finding, however, must be interpreted cautiously since this investigation was not a study of various religious populations, and the sampling procedures prohibit generalizations to such populations. Such studies are, however, now possible.

Development of Questionnaire

Inasmuch as it is desirable to have an instrument for studying individual differences in religious motives and since a Q-sort does not readily serve this purpose, the data of this study have been utilized to define items for a new instrument which permits scoring subjects on each of the seven dimensions which have been identified.[2] The reliability of the instrument is under study and scores are currently being correlated with personal, social, and demographic data. In addition, relationships are being sought between religious motives and personality variables as measured in such instruments as the Cattell *Sixteen Personality Factor Questionnaire* and the Gough *California Personality Inventory.*

1. The complete set of 87 motives is available from the authors on request.
2. The instrument and scoring key are available from the authors on request.

References

Cattell, Raymond B., *Personality,* New York: McGraw-Hill, 1950.

Fukuyama, Yoshio, The Major Dimensions of Church Membership. *Rev. Relig. Res.,* 1961, 2, 154-161.

Glock, Charles Y., *Toward a Typology of Religious Orientation.* New York: Bureau of Applied Social Research, Columbia University, 1954.

King, Morton, Measuring the Religious Variable. *J. Sci. Study Relig.,* 1967, 6, 173-190.

Lenski, Gerhard, *The Religious Factor* (Revised edition, Anchor Book No. A-337). Garden City: Doubleday, 1963.

Monaghan, Robert R., Three Faces of the True Believer. *J. Sci. Study Relig.* 1967, 6, 236-245.

Stephenson, William, *The Study of Behavior.* Chicago: The University of Chicago Press, 1953.

GLENN M. VERNON

The Religious "Nones": A Neglected Category

The language which any group uses inevitably betrays evaluation, even when only description is intended, and much more than referent identification may be implied by a particular label. This appears to be the case with the "none" label, as when it designates the last category, following "Catholic, Jew . . .," in a list headed by "Religion."[1] It provides a negative definition, specifying what a phenomenon is not, rather than what it is. Intentionally or not, such a use implies that only those affiliated with a formal group are religious. In fact, the label "No religion" is used in the 1957 U.S. Census and by some researchers[2] to identify those who do not belong to a formal church.

By way of contrast, the social scientist classifies as *"independent"* those who do not report affiliation with a particular political party. The use of the "independent" label suggests that the lack of political party affiliation does not mean that one is apolitical or has no political convictions. He is still viewed as a political person. Perhaps this is because the

From the *Journal for the Scientific Study of Religion* 7 (Fall 1968):219-29. Reprinted by permission of the publisher and author.

act of voting serves as the primary validation of political participation. There is no comparable religious phenomenon, no clearly recognized religious behavior other than membership, attendance, or other identification with a formal religious group. Thus, "none" is used in religious research, designating no religious affiliation, but also adding the gratuitous implication of a nonreligious person.[3]

Like the "nones," the political independents have no visible organization; however, political independents do not suffer as greatly from nonvisibility as do the religious independents. In fact, they are assiduously polled, heeded, and courted. But there is no recognized voice or spokesman or ready audience for the religious independent. The "nones" are less likely to be heard on social issues, and public awareness of the position of such individuals is low. As Nathanson[4] has indicated, whenever moral or religious questions are being considered, opinions of Catholics, Protestants, and Jews are sought, while the unchurched are almost never consulted. Lipman and Vorspan[5] suggest that the atheist, agnostic, and nonbeliever to some degree have become second-class citizens. The public media are less likely to take the "nonaffiliated" into account in stories designed for public consumption. Visibility of the group is reduced accordingly; the public image is blurred and indistinct.

Scientific Neglect

Much attention has been given to research which explores the differential characteristics of various religious groups and the correlates of religious affiliation. Considerable attention has also been given to differences which are related to various types or degrees of religiosity. Nonaffiliates may be included among those studied, but they are rarely singled out for specific analysis. A somewhat extensive, though certainly not exhaustive, search of the literature has identified approximately 80 cases where they are essentially ignored in the analysis of the data. In this respect, "nones" are a neglected category, included in research designs so that percentages might total 100, rather than because it is a category worthy of analysis.

For any particular research the "nones" may be a small group, and primarily for this reason considered a residual category. However, there are a large number of independents available for and worthy of research. The fruitfulness of testing hypotheses about the functions or consequences of religion by comparing religious and nonreligious is suggested by Magill and Campbell[6] in their study of religious and intellectual values. In their pretest they checked the validity of their questions by the "method of known groups." Religious individuals were represented by Sisters in a religious order and nonreligious individuals were represented by self-defined atheistic university students. The two groups had "completely different response patterns" on the questions, and their scores on the composite index were on different ends of the scoring continuum. However, very little research of this nature has been done. Even in the Magill-Campbell report, the differences were reported in a footnote, and apparently once the research instrument had been pretested the atheists were forgotten. The only research effort of which this author is aware in which the "nones" were the major focus of attention was the Green and Vetter study of atheists in 1932.[7]

O'Dea[8] and others who endorse the premise that religion is functional for society might also have considered the function of "nones" for society, a question which is usually ignored, implying a negative answer. There is little research upon which to base any conclusions or even to suggest that such a question be entertained. Herberg[9] and others who speak of the "American Religion" (or societal religion) might have considered whether the nonaffiliated are stronger or weaker than the affiliated religionist on such measures. The strong endorsement of the democratic way of life by a humanist such as Sidney Hook[10] suggests that at least some of the "nones" would score high on an "American Religion Orthodoxy Scale." Although Herberg essentially ignores the "nones," he does suggest that

> Through the nineteenth century and well into the twentieth, America knew the militant secularist, the atheist or "free-thinker" as a familiar figure in cultural life, along with considerably larger number of "agnostics" who would have nothing to do with churches and refused to identify themselves religiously. These still exist, of course, but their ranks are dwindling and they are becoming more and more inconspicuous, taking the American people as a whole.[11]

He also suggests that many second generation Americans tend to draw away from the religion of their fathers and become "religionless."[12] Here he seems to equate "religion" with organized religion, but nothing more is done with the category.

Relationship Between Non-Affiliation and Other Religious Factors

If, as we have suggested, the scientific study of religious "nones" has been neglected, it follows that definitive answers are not available for whether the "nones" are as characteristically "nonreligious" as the name implies. But we turn now to some limited research providing information about some of the characteristics of independents. The material presented is only suggestive—selected because the findings *suggest* relationships quite contrary to many assumptions, rather than because its findings are conclusive or even representative of all available research.

Religious behavior

Religious beliefs. Studies concerning "belief in God" usually include atheists and agnostics in the "none" category.[13] Evidence from a study by the author[14] (Table I) questions the premise that all "nones" do not believe in God, and conversely that all agnostics and atheists should be classified in the "none" category if this implies an absence of religious belief. The "none" category in Table I includes anyone who did not provide a label for himself, even the broad label of "Protestant." (Groups which had less than 35 members were not included in the tabulation.)

The percentage of "nones" in the two categories most strongly endorsing a belief in God was lower than that for any of the "religious" groups. Conversely, the per cent of "nones" in the two categories most strongly rejecting or questioning such belief was higher than for any other group. At the same time, there were 17.7 per cent of the "nones" in the two most positive categories, and there were some from every formal group endorsing the agnostic position, and even, in most cases, the "I don't believe in God" alternative.

Other research suggests a similar pattern with respect to other religious beliefs. Cuber,[15] for instance, in his 1940 study of four Metropoli-

Table I. *Per cent Selecting Specific Answer to Question: "Which of the Following Statements Comes Closest to What You Believe About God?"*

Religious Affiliation	N	No[1] doubt	Some[2] doubt	Some[3] times	No[4] personal God	Agnostic[5]	Atheistic[6]	No Answer
None	85	7.1%	10.6%	8.2%	18.8%	27.1%	23.5%	4.7%
Roman Catholic	466	53.2	30.7	5.4	5.8	3.6	.6	.6
Methodist	269	34.6	40.9	8.6	7.1	5.9	1.5	1.1
Presbyterian	35	28.6	40.0	2.9	11.4	14.3	2.9	–
Episcopal	73	26.0	42.5	15.1	6.8	6.8	–	–
Congregational	208	24.5	35.6	13.0	13.5	8.2	2.9	2.4
Lutheran	58	46.6	36.2	8.6	5.2	3.4	–	–
Baptist	181	50.8	35.9	5.5	2.8	2.8	.6	1.7
Mormon	275	81.5	13.1	1.5	.7	2.5	.4	.4
Protestant	43	44.2	27.9	2.3	7.0	4.7	9.3	4.7
Jews	84	53.6	21.4	8.3	7.1	3.6	5.0	4.8

1. I know God really exists and have no doubts about it.
2. While I have doubts, I feel that I do believe in God.
3. I find myself believing in God some of the time, but not at other times.
4. I don't believe in a personal God, but I do believe in a higher power of some kind.
5. I don't know whether there is a God and I don't believe there is any way to find out.
6. I don't believe in God.

tan churches in Detroit, emphasized that nonmembers who were nonattenders manifested many traditional moral and doctrinal views and favored churches as institutions. In another study, DeJong and Ford[16] found that religious fundamentalism was negatively correlated with class level among the 9.3 per cent of Southern Appalachian respondents classified as "no religion or religion not reported," like the pattern which obtained for affiliated religionists. Also, those in the "no religion or religion not reported" category were more liberal than the total sample. These findings seem to add support to the premise that there are similarities between the religious beliefs of "nones" and those of affiliated religionists which need to be explored.

PARTICIPATION IN FORMAL RELIGIOUS ACTIVITIES. Cuber[17] also found that from 18 to 37 per cent of those attending church were nonmembers. He also indicated that almost every clergyman interviewed stated that he received numerous requests from nonmembers for religious ceremonies at weddings and funerals. Likewise, a 1949 census of Madison, Wisconsin[18] found that about 10 per cent of the "no church" group were regular church attenders.

RELIGIOUS EXPERIENCES. The findings presented in Tables II and III suggest that some individuals classified as "nones" have had religious experiences. Compared with members of religious groups, these figures are low—as would be expected. Yet using this one question as our criterion of religiousness, certain of the "nones" are more religious than certain of the members of formal groups.

SUMMARY. The "nonreligion" implication of the "none" label does not seem to find complete validation from the material which we have analyzed. Some of those categorized as "none" may, in fact, at least on

TABLE II. *Answers to Question: "Have You Ever Had a Feeling That You Were Somehow in the Presence of God?"*

Religious Affiliation	N	"Yes, I'm sure I have" (percent)	"Yes, I think I have" (percent)	"No" (percent)	No Answer
None	85	5.9	20.0	70.6	3.5
Roman Catholic	466	40.8	39.7	17.4	1.9
Methodist	269	31.6	46.5	20.8	.7
Presbyterian	35	28.6	42.9	28.6	–
Episcopal	73	27.4	53.4	17.8	1.4
Congregational	208	27.4	44.2	26.9	1.4
Lutheran	58	41.4	39.7	19.0	–
Baptist	181	37.6	45.9	15.5	1.1
Mormon	275	47.3	28.4	22.9	1.5
Protestant	43	41.9	23.3	32.6	2.3
Jewish	84	36.9	42.9	15.5	3.6

TABLE III. *Have You Ever Had a Feeling That You Were Being Punished by God for Something You Had Done?*

Religious Affiliation	N	"Yes, I'm sure I have" (percent)	"Yes, I think I have" (percent)	"No" (percent)	No Answer
None	85	7.1	16.5	72.9	3.5
Roman Catholic	466	30.7	42.1	26.0	.9
Methodist	269	18.6	43.5	36.1	1.5
Presbyterian	35	22.9	40.0	37.1	—
Episcopal	73	11.0	42.5	45.2	1.4
Congregational	208	15.9	42.8	40.4	1.0
Lutheran	58	29.3	46.6	24.1	—
Baptist	181	33.7	39.8	26.0	.6
Mormon	275	31.3	30.5	37.8	.4
Protestant	43	30.2	20.9	46.5	2.3
Jewish	84	39.3	36.9	20.2	1.2

certain religious measures, be more "religious" than some of those categorized as affiliated. On certain types of analyses, those usually classified as "nones" clearly fall within a "religious" category. That there is a difference between the "nones" as a group and affiliated religionists is certainly documented here; however, it seems as inaccurate to consider all "nones" to be "of one piece" as it is to consider all Methodists to be alike in all religious matters.

Relation Between Non-Affiliation and Other Behavior

If religious beliefs and practices contribute to socially approved behavior, we would not expect, on the basis of the evidence presented here, to find such behavior the monopoly of either group. We turn, therefore, to consider whether related social behavior of "nones" is different from that of affiliated individuals.

SOCIAL BEHAVIOR. Functional analyses of religion frequently suggest that religion contributes to societal integration and sanctifies or validates society's value definitions. Are affiliates, then, more law-abiding than "nones"? Lunden[19] presents the following answer from a survey of available research.

> In spite of the general opinion that religion creates "good" conduct and irreligion causes delinquency the statistical data available tend to prove the contrary almost to the point of paradox. Accepting the Bonger hypothesis in a 1916 study, "as irreligion increases, crime tends to decrease" the advocates of this position can now declare after almost fifty years "hypothesis proven."

Independents, then, appear to contribute as much as affiliates to socially approved behavior.

PREJUDICE. Do affiliates evidence less socially disruptive racial and ethnic prejudice than independents? Many studies have indicated a higher frequency of expressed prejudice toward racial or ethnic outgroups among members of organized religious bodies than among nonmembers and similarly greater prevalence of such prejudice among persons who frequently attend religious services than among those who do not. On the other hand, there are studies that present data suggesting a curvilinear association—both the completely inactive and the highly active being less prejudiced.[20] Independents, then, apparently are as free from racial-ethnic prejudice as affiliated religionists.

SECURITY AND ANXIETY. If as Sapir[21] suggests, "religion is omnipresent fear . . . paradoxically turned into bedrock security," are independents less secure or more anxious than affiliates. Death is one area with high fear potential. The author's research posed the question, "Do you feel that you could currently adequately face the death of a loved-one?" While 46.4 per cent of the total group answered "yes," 50.6 of those in the "none" category did. The Mormons (62.2%) were the only group exceeding the "nones." Independents apparently evidence as much "bedrock security" as affiliates.

MARITAL ADJUSTMENT. If religion serves an integrating function, not only for society, but for subgroups within society as well, does the marital adjustment of affiliates exceed that of "nones"? Peterson,[22] in a study of 420 persons in the Los Angeles area, worked out an overall marital adjustment score which he found to be related to his religious classifications as seen in Table IV.

TABLE IV

Religious Classification	Adjustment Scores	
	Men	Women
Liberal	78	82
Jewish	77	85
No-Church-Agnostic	77	65
Sect-Conservative	72	77
Institutional-Authoritarian	55	68

According to these data, being a religious independent does not seem to depress the adjustment score of the males, who in fact evidence a higher adjustment level than either the sect-conservative or the institutional-authoritarian categories. Lack of church affiliation does depress the female adjustment score, but these scores are not very different from those in the institutional-authoritarian category. The female pattern may be related to the tendency for the female to exceed the male on most measures of religiosity.

Analysis of other research related to the family suggests that the following relationships may obtain. When compared with affiliated individuals, independents attach less importance to religious endogamy as a contributor to marital happiness, but are still more likely before marriage to express doubts about the future success of their subsequent marriage. When married, they are less likely to experience certain types of sexual problems. They are more likely to experience divorce, although there is a high likelihood of the marriage enduring. In contrast to an affiliated-affiliated marriage, an independent-independent marriage, is more likely to have children low on ritualistic and consequential dimensions of religion, and an independent (female)-affiliated marriage to have children high on the consequential dimension and low on the ritualistic dimension of religion.[23]

The question of positive correlation between social behavior and religious beliefs and practices as a characteristic distinguishing the affiliates from the independents appears to warrant further investigation. The consequences of a lack of affiliation may not be what some have assumed. Independents do not seem disproportionately to evidence socially disapproved behavior. Theory about the functions of religion, then, may involve unwarranted interpretations if "religion" is interpreted to mean "organized religion."

Some Methodological and Theoretical Considerations

Variation within the "None" Group

Affiliation: membership or preference? In order to increase our understanding of religious phenomena, there is a need to refine both the affiliated and the independent categories.

The categories most consistently used to classify religious affiliates have been Protestant, Catholic, and Jew. In recent years, extensive subdivisions of each of these categories have been made, particularly in the Protestant category. Accordingly, research has been directed to within-group variation as well as to between-group variation, finding that on many variables the within-group variation is the greater of the two. As a result, alternate methods of classification have been suggested.[24]

This within-group variation obtains for independents as well as for affiliates, and without doubt the "none" category needs considerable refinement also. One meaningful distinction is that between those who have "no affiliation" according to the official records of the churches and those who do not themselves report any identification with or a preference for any particular group. The per cent of those who will provide an affiliation identification when asked is much higher than the per cent who are carried on the official records. Comparison of official church membership statistics with population figures for the U.S. indicate that around one-third of the population is not considered to be an official member of an established religious group.[25] It is apparently to this group that the *Lutheran Witness Reporter* referred when it reported that the unchurched outnumbered the churched in 29 states, with the highest percentage of the unchurched to be found in Oregon, Washington, and West Virginia, and the lowest percentage of the unchurched in Rhode Island, Utah, and Massachusetts.[26] This contrasts sharply with the 95-97 per cent who provide an identification or a preference when asked by researchers. The difference between these two labels needs to be explored. Having a preference for a formal grouping is not the same as belonging to it.

Other distinctions calling for further research include atheist, agnostic, nonaffiliated participant, nonaffiliated believer, "no-preference," committed and noncommitted independents, converted and lifelong independents, as well as, independents with various social characteristics such as prejudiced or nonprejudiced, secure or insecure, deviant or conforming, etc.

Some of this has been done within studies, such as the analysis of poll data relating to religious affiliation and social class shown in Table V. Schneider[27] found a difference between those classified as "no preference" and those classified as "atheist, agnostic." Although the number in the second category is small, the data do suggest that meaningful differences would be found between various types of independents.

TABLE V. *Social Class Profile of American Religious Groups*

	Upper	Middle	Lower	N
No Preference	13.3%	26.0%	60.7%	466
Atheist, Agnostic	33.3%	46.7%	20.0%	15

AFFILIATED-INDEPENDENT INTERRELATIONSHIPS

Discussion of affiliation usually assumes that nonaffiliation is the reciprocal of affiliation. We have tended to dichotomize the two terms, or to conceive of an affiliation-nonaffiliation continuum. Are these two types of phenomena in fact the obverse of each other, or do measures of affiliation and of independence really get at two somewhat different phenomena?

Analogous research in Industrial Sociology may clarify this issue. Research by Herzberg *et al.*[28] indicates that factors that lead to job satisfaction are not the same as those that lead to job dissatisfaction. Studying employees of nine organizations in the Pittsburgh area, they concluded that the most satisfying aspects of the work experience were those associated directly with the actual doing of the job—achievement, recognition, responsibility, advancement, and the work itself. The absence of these factors, however, did not cause dissatisfaction. On the other hand, the factors which contributed to job dissatisfaction were peripheral—company policy and administration, supervision, interpersonal relations and working conditions. In this case the improvement of these conditions did not necessarily cause satisfaction. Friedlander and Walton[29] arrived at similar conclusions from their interviews with engineers and scientists.

A similar hypothesis might be entertained with reference to religious phenomena the reasons one remains with a formal religious organization are different from and not merely the opposite of the reasons one leaves or does not affiliate with such an organization.

If the "content" of religion is beliefs about God, for instance, then there are those who accept such beliefs while staying outside the formal structure. Perhaps the context in which the affiliated religionist is expected to display or make public such beliefs is not the context in which the nonaffiliate desires to do so. Likewise, individuals may stay within a religious organization for "context" reasons—"good business" or family pressures for example—even though the "content" (beliefs) may diminish in importance.

The research generated by the Herzberg-Friedlander hypothesis has not all been confirmatory.[30] Further, the pretest research involving atheists by Magill and Campbell seems to contradict this hypothesis. However, so little evidence is available that the relationship between affiliation and nonaffiliation warrants further consideration.

Functional Analysis

Discussions about the functions of religion in society imply that everything labeled "religious" has the same consequences in a given system at any given time, and conversely, that everything that is "nonreligious" lacks these consequences or functions. This paper challenges these assumptions. The "nones" may serve some societal functions similar to those served by the affiliated religionist.

Herberg,[31] Luckmann,[32] and others suggest a distinction between societal religion and formal religion. *Societal religion* incorporates the high-intensity value definitions which hold society together and thus fulfill a societal integrative function. *Formal religion* maintains a set of beliefs and rituals which may or may not serve to integrate the society, even though they may integrate the church group. The "nones," who may 'belong' to the societal religion, even though they do not 'belong' to a formal church group, may contribute to the integration of a society as well as the affiliates.

The more intriguing question for sociology, however, is whether those in the "none" category serve a unique and distinctive function for society. For instance, does the presence of nonaffiliated individuals in a society reduce the intergroup conflict between established religious groups? What are the consequences of having "nones" as an appropriate other toward whom missionary or proselytizing efforts of the church may be directed? Or, when nonaffiliated are considered to be intransigents who have repeatedly resisted evangelistic approaches or to be immoral, unreliable, irresponsible, and "without self respect," as Vidich and Bensman[33] suggest is the case in small communities, and are therefore neglected in church recruiting and evangelism, what are the results? Does religious group identification take on increased meaning to those who do belong as a result of the presence of a negative reference group with which to compare themselves? Or, does the presence, or opposition, of a negative reference group facilitate the achievement of certain goals? It may be suggestive that the "ideal society" envisioned by most religious groups is a stratified society in which distinct differences are recognized and taken into account.

When religious affiliation is a norm, the "nones" are deviant individuals. To what extent do the conclusions about the functions of deviant behavior apply to the religiously deviant "nones"? Durkheim, for instance, says of crime:

> To classify crime among the phenomena of normal sociology is not to say merely that it is an inevitable, although regrettable phenomenon, due to the incorrigible wickedness of men; it is to affirm that it is a factor in public health, an integral part of all healthy societies.[34]

And Mead suggests:

> The criminal does not seriously endanger the structure of society by his destructive activities, and on the other hand he is responsible for a sense of solidarity, aroused among those whose attention would be otherwise centered upon interest quite divergent from those of each other.[35]

Does the conclusion of Mead, Durkheim, and other sociologists that crime as a universal phenomenon never could and *never should* be eliminated apply also to the religious "nones"? Does the existense and presence of "nones" in a society contribute to the 'health' of existing religions? To what extent does the existence of "nones" facilitate the accommodation of religious groups to society and society to the religious groups? Does the existence of "nones" encourage religious groups to attempt to relate their 'eternal' truths to the existing conditions in which their members are living and dying?

CONCLUSIONS

The "none" label carries negative evaluative implications, unwarranted by the limited research, and unproductive of further research. The "independent" label carries neutral implications, with research suggesting that such individuals have the following characteristics:

1. Independents reject membership in formal religious groups, but a limited percentage do attend formal services. These are nonaffiliated participants.
2. Independents may have experiences defined as involving the supernatural, but they tend to de-emphasize the relationship to the supernatural, apparently with a concomitant humanistic emphasis.
3. Independents are ethical and moral, but they relate their morality less than affiliates to supernatural or church-related variables.
4. Independents should be classified as religious along with those affiliated with church groups. Differences between various types of religious people should, of course, be studied.
5. There are different types of independents. Subcategories need to be developed.
6. Independents are more oriented toward and influenced by societal religion than by formal religion.
7. The reasons for being an independent may not simply be the obverse of the reasons of the affiliate for belonging to a formal group. The influence of societal religion on the behavior of affiliates may, accordingly, be inaccurately and unknowingly attributed exclusively to church or affiliation variables.
8. Independents in a pluralistic society may have latent functions for church groups and society per se.

Functional interpretations of religious behavior are inadequate to the extent that 'religion' is equated with formal religion. Furthermore, functional theory would better facilitate the investigation and understanding of both independents and affiliates if the basic premise were presented as, "There are certain functional requisites *of society* which formal religion *may* fulfill," rather than, "There are certain functions *of religion* which contribute to societal integration."

1. Frequently included under this label are atheists, agnostics, those with "no preference," those with no affiliation, and also members of small groups and others who, for one reason or another, do not fall within the classification scheme being used and who more properly belong in a residual or "other" category. The discussion in this article concentrates on those who have no affiliation.

2. Such as Kaare Svalastoga, *Social Differentiation.* New York: David McKay Co., 1965.

3. At times other terms such as "free thinker" and "non-affiliated" have been used. Norman Thomas used the label "Independent Christian" in a classification of conscientious objectors in his book *The Conscientious Objector in America.* New York: B. W. Huebsh, Inc., 1923. p. 48.

4. Jerome Nathanson, "Sixty-Four Million Americans Do Not Go To Church: What Do They Believe?" in Leo Rosten, *A Guide to the Religion of America,* New York: Simon and Schuster, 1955, pp. 166-172.

5. Eugene J. Lipman and Albert Vorspan, eds., *A Tale of Ten Cities,* New York: Union American Hebrew Congregations, 1962, p. 315.

6. Dennis W. Magill and Douglas F. Campbell, "Commitment to Religious Values and Intellectual Values among University Students," paper presented at the annual meeting of the Canadian Sociology and Anthropology Association, June, 1967, mimeographed.

7. G. B. Vetter and M. Green, "Personality and Group Factors in the Making of Atheists," *Journal of Abnormal and Social Psychology,* Vol. 27, 1932, pp. 179-194.

8. Thomas F. O'Dea, *The Sociology of Religion,* Englewood Cliffs, N.J.: Prentice-Hall, Inc., 1966.

9. Will Herberg, *Protestant-Catholic-Jew,* Garden City, N.Y.: Doubleday & Co., Inc., 1956.

10. Sidney Hook, "Religious Liberty From the Viewpoint of a Secularist Humanist," in Earl Raab, ed., *Religious Conflict in America,* Garden City, N.Y.: Doubleday and Co., 1964, pp. 138-151.

11. Herberg, *op. cit.,* pp. 59-60.

12. Herberg, *Ibid.,* p. 32.

13. Vetter and Green (*op. cit.*) found it meaningful to subdivide atheists into "certain atheists" and "uncertain atheists" depending on how committed respondents were to an atheistic position. Moberg (David O. Moberg, *The Church as a Social Institution,* Englewood Cliffs, New Jersey: Prentice-Hall, Inc., 1962. p. 66) suggests using the concept "marginal non-membership." Putney and Middleton (Snell Putney and Russell Middleton, "Rebellion, Conformity, and Parental Religious Ideologies," *Sociometry,* June 1961, 125-136) combined atheists, agnostics, and deists under a label of "skeptic."

14. A study of attitudes toward death. Analysis of the data is currently underway. The respondents involved in the data presented here include mainly students from several colleges and universities in the U.S. The questions analyzed here are taken from Rodney Stark, "Social Context and Religious Experience," *Review of Religious Research,* Fall, 1965, Vol. 7, No. 1, pp. 17-28. See also, Charles Y. Glock and Rodney Stark, *Religion and Society in Tension,* Chicago: Rand McNally & Co., 1965.

15. John F. Cuber, "Marginal Church Participants," *Sociology and Social Research,* September–October, 1940, pp. 57-62.

16. Gordon DeJong and Thomas R. Ford, "Religious Fundamentalism and Denominational Preference in the Southern Appalachian Region," *Journal for the Scientific Study of Religion,* Vol. V, No. 1, Fall, 1965, pp. 24-33.

17. Cuber, *op. cit.*

18. Louis Bultena, "Church Membership and Church Attendance in Madison, Wisconsin," *American Sociological Review,* Vol. 14 (1949) pp. 384-389.

19. Lunden, Walter A., *Statistics on Delinquents and Delinquency,* Springfield, Ill: Charles C. Thomas Publisher, 1964, p. 154.

20. See for instance Robin M. Williams, Jr., *Strangers Next Door,* Englewood Cliffs, N.J.: Prentice-Hall, Inc., 1964, p. 21 and George E. Simpson and J. Milton Yinger, *Racial and Cultural Minorities,* 3rd ed., New York: Harper & Row, 1965, pp. 397-403. Allport has suggested that it is those with an "extrinsic" orientation toward religion as contrasted with those with an "intrinsic" orientation, who tend to be most prejudiced. It would be worth checking to see if the Independents tend to have an "intrinsic" orientation. See Gordon Allport, *Religion in The Developing Personality,* Academy of Religion and Mental Health, New York University Press, New York, 1960, p. 33.

21. David G. Mandelbaum, ed., Selected Writings of Edward Sapir, in *Language Culture and Personality,* University of California Press, Berkeley, California, 1951, pp. 346-356.

22. James A. Peterson, *Education for Marriage,* 2nd ed., New York: Charles Scribner's Sons, 1965, Chapter 18.

23. See Glenn M. Vernon, "Marital Characteristics of Religious Independents," *Review of Religious Research,* Vol. 9, no. 3, Spring 1968, pp. 162-170.

24. See for instance, Seymour Martin Lipset, "Religion and Politics in American History" in Earl Raab, *op. cit.,* pp. 60-89; Charles Y. Glock and Rodney Stark, *Religion and Society in Tension,* Chicago: Rand McNally & Co., 1965, "The New Denominationalism," Chapter 5; Glenn M. Vernon, *Sociology of Religion,* New York: McGraw-Hill Book Co., 1962, Chapter 13, and Peterson, *op. cit.*

25. See Vernon, *op. cit.,* Chapter 12.

26. *Lutheran Witness Reporter,* December 4, 1966.

27. Herbert Schneider, *Religion in Twentieth Century America,* Cambridge, Mass.: Harvard University Press, 1952, appendix p. 228.

28. Frederick Herzberg, Bernard Mausner and Barbara Snyderman, *The Motivation to Work,* New York: John Wiley and Sons, Inc., 1960.

29. Frank Friedlander and Eugene Walton, "Positive and Negative Motivations Toward Work," *Administrative Science Quarterly,* 9 (1964) pp. 143-207.

30. Research by students of B. S. Bolaria at the University of Maine has provided both support and nonsupport for aspects of the Herzberg-Friedlander hypotheses.

31. Herzberg, *op. cit.*

32. Thomas Luckmann, *The Invisible Religion,* New York: The MacMillan Co., 1967.

33. Arthur J. Vidich and Joseph Bensman, *Small Town in Mass Society,* Princeton, N.J.: Princeton University Press, 1958, pp. 251-52.

34. Emil Durkheim, *Rules of Sociological Method,* 8th ed., The Free Press of Glencoe, copyrighted 1938 by the University of Chicago, p. 67.

35. George Herbert Mead, "The Psychology of Punitive Justice," *American Journal of Sociology,* Vol. 3, No. 5, March, 1918, p. 591.

N. J. DEMERATH III
VICTOR THIESSEN

On Spitting against the Wind: Organizational Precariousness and American Irreligion

This paper[1] offers a belated diagnosis of an organization that is currently in its death trance. The analysis follows the development and demise of a small-town Wisconsin free-thought movement or Freie Gemeinde which began in 1852, reached its zenith in the 1880's, and then began to atrophy with the pursuit of legitimacy. The study is intended as both a perverse chapter in the sociology of religion and a paragraph in the theory of organizational change. It has two primary justifications.

First, in focusing on irreligion it directs attention to a neglected phenomenon on the American religious scene. Although the sociology of religion has been born again, the sociology of irreligion remains in the womb[2] despite the current talk of secularization and the steady flow of theological amendments to nineteenth-century orthodoxy and despite the predictions of Weber, Marx, and Durkheim that the twentieth century would witness the decline of the religious establishment.[3] Cer-

Reprinted from the *American Journal of Sociology* 71 (May 1966):674-87, by permission of the author and The University of Chicago Press.

tainly irreligion has failed to replace the churches. At the same time, studies of irreligion may provide insight into its difficulties and a new comparative basis for analysis of the churches themselves.

A second justification is more abstract. Irreligious groups are precarious by dint of their dissidence and their illegitimacy. Examination of this precariousness may inform the study of organizational dynamics generally. Most organizational analysis follows in the wake of Weber's concern with the bureaucratic monolith. While the topic of organizational growth is common, studies of organizational demise are rare. While the conservative organization has been compelling, the deviant organization is frequently ignored and often shunted to the less attended realm of collective behavior. There is, of course, a range of studies on religious sects[4] as well as the literature on political extremism[5] and social movements.[6] And yet the freethinkers have features that distinguish them from each of these.

Unlike religious sects, the free-thought movement lacks any crystallized doctrine and falls beyond the pale of American religious tolerance. Unlike political movements, the freethinkers have no sharply defined organizational goals, and pressures against them are more informal than the sanctions of the electorate or the courts. Finally, unlike the Townsend movement, the Women's Christian Temperance Union, or an educational reform group, irreligion has neither a natural population from which to recruit nor a set of values which are in any way consistent with the normative mainstream.

Because the Freie Gemeinde is peculiar in these and other respects it points to considerations that are largely mute in previous work. These include community structure and differentiation as they relate to expressed hostility; the effect of social class on the response to hostility; the difficulties of nurturing charisma as well as its importance in sustaining an illegitimate group; the problems of rallying commitment around a nihilistic doctrine and a goalless program; and the conflict between commitment and recruitment as organizational imperatives. Precisely because irreligion taxes previous frameworks without falling wholly outside of them, it should provide important additions to our current knowledge. Still, the study has no illusions of definitiveness. Since both irreligion and organizational precariousness have been little explored, our errors may be as instructive as our insights.

The paper comprises five sections. The first describes the study's methodology. The second offers a brief historical account of the group at issue. Third, we shall discuss some general characteristics of organizational precariousness and the range of adaptations to it. Fourth, we shall show how adaptation is influenced by external community factors. Fifth and finally, we shall discuss adaptation to dissidence and precariousness in the light of internal organizational characteristics.

METHODOLOGY

The study invokes three methodological strategies: observation, historical records, and lengthy personal interviews. Although we intend more rigorous research in the future, this first study is undeniably "soft." Accordingly, we shall heed Howard S. Becker's advice[7] and present a chronology of the investigation as one slim basis for evaluation.

As is frequently the case in exploratory research, the analytic problem which finally emerged was not the one that launched the study. Our first information on the Freie Gemeinde included only its location in the small, predominantly Catholic community of Sauk City and its shrinking size. This suggested conflict between the group and its context, a conflict which was to be the focus of the research.

It took only a few visits to teach us otherwise. We soon discovered that actual conflict had seldom occurred and that even past hostility had evanesced as the group began to camouflage its principles and seek survival instead of reform. Thus, the study quickly shifted from static to dynamic. Rather than focus on the contemporary scene, we were led to the historical problem of a changing organization and its changing community relations.

This was the result of the research's first stage, involving lengthy conversations with strategic members of the organization. A second stage quickly followed and persisted. This involved "quasi-participant observation"[8] in the society's affairs, ranging from Sunday afternoon meetings held twice monthly to more informal gatherings. Third, we took advantage of the group's unique but dusty library to read and translate historical documents on nineteenth-century free thought. Fourth, we interviewed members of the movement more systematically. By this time we were aware of most of the key issues in the group's development. We had formed a number of hypotheses around which to probe for information.

Because the current membership is less than fifty, we decided to interview the entire population. But many members are no longer in the community, and others are so old as to be non-communicating. We completed interviews with twenty. Although these span all significant viewpoints within the group, there is no way of accurately assessing their representativeness. This together with the small number precludes statistical analysis and confines the yield to qualitative insights and illustration. In addition, we also interviewed apostates and non-affiliates in the community to gain a wider perspective. There was no formal community survey for fear of artificially reviving rancor and friction.

Finally, after the study was completed, we submitted drafts to several respondents for their comments. This revealed a few minor errors of fact, but all agreed that the basic theoretical points were sound, even those based on our own deductions rather than any direct mention in the interviews. Of course, acceptance of this sort may raise as many issues as it settles. It may be that our critics are too kind, especially to two outsiders who were giving them rare attention. It also may be that we suffered the analytic seduction that lurks for any observer. Nevertheless, these evaluations do confer one small stamp of validity, and validity is a precious commodity in a study of this sort.

The Freie Gemeinde in Historical Review

As the analysis shifted from current conflict to organizational dynamics, history became a crucial ingredient. American irreligion has enjoyed more historical than sociological attention,[9] but even so, work on ethnic irreligion in the tradition of the Freie Gemeinde is sparse.[10] This brief chronology draws heavily upon personal recollections and untranslated documents. Some of the details await the theoretical discussion to follow.

The Freie Gemeinde emerged out of the religious and social unrest in Germany and Eastern Europe of the 1840's. Upon the excommunication of one Johannes Ronge for doubting the sacramental validity of a "holy robe" in Trier, a number of Catholics severed their ties with Rome and founded Free Christian or German-Catholic churches. The movement was neither united nor homogeneous. Ronge himself was anti-institutional rather than anti-doctrinal. Yet some were more radical than others, and upon persecution, many fled the country. The emigration was accelerated by the German Revolution of 1848; hence the term "forty-eighters" to refer to this first major wave of German settlers.

The first Freie Gemeinde in the United States began in St. Louis in 1850. Other communities formed in Pennsylvania; California; Washington, D.C.; New York; Illinois; and Wisconsin. In Wisconsin there were some thirty groups by 1852 ranging from Milwaukee and Madison to Polktown and Koshkonong. The Sauk City group in question organized on October 24, 1852. Its declared purpose occurs in its articles of incorporation:

> The United German Free Congregation is our name for our organization, for we wish to unite the enemies of clericalism, official hypocrisy and bigotry, the friends of truth, uprightness and honesty to be found scattered among all religions, creeds, churches and sects.
>
> By means of such united strength we intend to erect a strong fortification against the pernicious power of the churches, sects and clericalism.
>
> The foundation of this organization is *reason,* which is defamed by the priests of all "revealed" religions, and the book of nature and world

history, feared and repudiated by clericals, but loved and honored by the wise of all nations and all times.

Obviously we do not recognize as "godless" those so called on account of their views (theoretical atheists) but rather the godless in fact—practical atheists, who behave as though there were no universal law to which they are obliged to submit, and no moral cosmic law to which they must conform. We dictate neither belief nor disbelief in God or immortality.[11]

Despite its stridency, the early Freie Gemeinde was a strong and cautiously respected element in the local community throughout the nineteenth century. Not only did they help to guide secular affairs, but they were often called in to mediate disputes within the churches themselves. The freethinkers were also an important cultural force. Their activities emphasized music, drama, poetry, ethics, and philosophy. Their periodic festivals drew capacity crowds and guest lecturers from all over the country.

All of this reached its zenith under the guidance of one leader in particular, Eduard Schroeter. He had received theological training in Germany but was later forced out of the country to the United States. From 1853 to his death in 1888, he was the rallying point for Wisconsin free thought. Not only was he the leader of the Sauk City group, but he also started the Milwaukee Freie Gemeinde and made yearly visits to many of the other free congregations.

At the time of Schroeter's death, the Sauk City organization had an active membership of over one hundred. Its militancy was pronounced. For example, one prominent freethinker bequeathed land for use as a cemetery and stipulated only that priests and ministers were never to set foot on the plot. A current member describes his grandfather this way: "He wasn't too tactful a person. He was a Bible scholar; he knew as much about religion as any preacher, and he'd just walk up to the preacher and argue with him about it. . . . I've seen some of the letters to the editor my grandfather wrote. I don't know of anyone now who would write things like that."

Indeed, with Schroeter's death and the turnover from first to second generation members, the Freie Gemeinde began to lose its momentum. Gradually, its membership decreased, its activities grew less frequent, and its militancy subsided. The Freie Gemeinde began to co-operate more and condemn less. Its members began to attend the services of the orthodox churches whose own members were increasingly present at the Free Congregation's meetings. Some freethinkers began contributions to the Catholic church, and intermarriage increased. All of this is reflected in the group's changing constitution. Gradually it became less vindictive. The constitution drafted in 1917 lacks any polemic against the church, and a 1951 revision drops all reference to atheism. While nineteen of our twenty respondents are admitted atheists, organizational imperatives demand a less stigmatizing public stand.

Finally, consider the Sauk City group in contrast to its Milwaukee counterpart. Both were founded by the same man, at the same time, and with the same purpose. Yet the two are now estranged. The Milwaukee Freie Gemeinde has cleaved more closely to its original ideals and is more aggressive in pursuing them. To this end, it has joined the American Rationalist Federation (ARF): a lower-class, militant association that embraces Madalyn Murray and *The Realist,*[12] together with rationalist societies in St. Louis, Philadelphia, New York, Baltimore, Cleveland, Chicago, and elsewhere. The ARF has repeatedly invited the Sauk City group to join. The invitations have never been answered. Instead Sauk City has chosen a different alliance. In order to legitimate itself and boost its recruitment potential, it became a member of the Unitarian-Universalist Fellowship in 1955. The move has had none of the salutary consequences expected and has even led to an unintended disruption. Recruitment and activities have remained at the same low ebb. The affiliation provoked sharp opposition from some members who felt betrayed and bolted to form a smaller but less compromising circle of their own. Hence this predominantly Catholic community of some 4,000 now hosts *two* irreligious groups. Although one is moribund and the other militant, the latter may very well follow the path of its predecessor. Free thought is neither big business nor aggressive associationalism.

Organizational Precariousness and Adaptive Strategies

In a society in which a leading liberal politician can assert, "I don't care what a man's religion is as long as he believes in God," it is no surprise to consider the Freie Gemeinde a precarious organization. The term "precarious" is appropriate for any organization that confronts the prospect of its own demise. The confrontation need be neither intentional nor acknowledged. The important criterion is a threatened disruption of the organization such that achievement of its goals and the maintenance of its values are so obstructed as to bring on a loss of identity through deathly quiescence, merger, or actual disbandment.

There is no single source of precariousness. It may arise out of structural weaknesses concerning leadership, communication, compliance, or role differentiation. It may emerge from poor recruitment or from low commitment. It may stem from abrasive relations with a hostile environment, even relations that fall short of blatant conflict. The last is plainly the most conspicuous source for the precariousness of the dissident Freie Gemeinde. It is also a central factor in Burton Clark's insightful analysis of "precarious values."[13] Clark argues that a value may be precarious because it is undefined, because its functionaries are illegitimate, or because the value itself is "unacceptable to a 'host' population." All three of these conditions apply to the Freie Gemeinde at one time or another. And yet Clark's suggestion that groups with precarious value are led into strenuous social service in the search for acceptance is less apt. There are other forms of adaptations and other factors that govern the pressure to adapt in the first place.

In general the possible responses to a hostile environment may be ranged along a continuum. The alternatives move in two directions. On the one hand, the group may follow Clark's scheme and pursue legitimation by changing or camouflaging its values, switching its functionaries and public spokesmen, or performing redeeming services for the community. Many groups attain stability in precisely this fashion. But for others the path may lead to organizational death. This is especially likely in groups like the Freie Gemeinde for whom dissidence itself was an original *raison d'être.*

On the other hand, a second adaptation involves increased militancy. Selznick, Nahirny, and Bittner have all pointed to the organizational gains that may be had by widening the gulf between the group and its context.[14] If membership commitment is a concern, one way to bolster it is to make commitment irrevocable by burning the members' bridges behind them and precluding competing allegiances to more legitimate organizations. Thus, a radical group's effectiveness may be judged by its ability to turn external hostility to an internal advantage. As we shall see, however, this ability is difficult to come by.

But is it necessary to adapt drastically in either direction? Certainly some organizations are able to compensate for hostility without radical shifts in either tactics or character. Some have no design on their context, and its hostility is therefore less urgent. Organizational structure and commitment may provide an imperviousness to opposition. Finally, the hostility itself may be poorly communicated, non-consensual, or effectively blunted. In short, there are really two issues involved in the adaptation to a hostile environment: is a major adaptation necessary and, if so, in which direction? To explore these questions further, let us return to the Freie Gemeinde in theoretical rather than historical relief. The problem is to account for the Sauk City group's adaptation in the direction of legitimacy. Possible solutions lie in two artificially distinguished clusters, one having to do with the community itself, the other relating to the group in particular.[15]

Differentiation and the Community Context

There is perhaps no concept more central to community analysis than that of "differentiation." Yet there are at least two dimensions to this concept, both of which are important to the changing position of the Freie Gemeinde. First, one can speak of *vertical* differentiation, referring to social class and the ability to sustain class distinctions and elites. Second, there is *horizontal* or "structural" differentiation,[16] referring to the degree of autonomy between various institutional spheres, including economics, politics, education, religion, and, indeed, irreligion.[17]

The relevance of vertical differentiation is discernible in two propositions. One is that strong elites may thwart the sentiments of the wider community by resisting or rechanneling their expression. Another is that a small town like Sauk city is unlikely to retain effective elites under the encroachments of the current "mass society."[18] In all of this, the contrast between the Sauk City group of 1865 and 1965 provides an illustration. Recalling the diatribe against the church in the Freie Gemeinde's original statement of principles, one might have expected countermeasures from the local Catholics. And yet the reciprocity was frustrated by an aristocratic class allegiance between the freethinkers and the most influential Catholics. Sauk City Catholics were originally polarized into two groups occupying the same church. The "old" Bavarian Catholics—wealthy, prominent, and educated—knelt in sharp contrast to the "new" Prussian Catholics who were lower rather than upper class and had migrated for economic rather than political reasons. One member of the Catholic church had this to say about the situation:

> There was more in common between the "Old Catholics" and the Freie Gemeinde than between the "Old Catholics" and the lower-class Catholics. . . . The freethinkers were a powerful force in the community. For many years they provided a cultural leadership. . . . The "Old Catholics" are contemptuous of many of the young priests who come in here who are ignorant, who have no real grasp of theology for all the preaching they do. So although the Catholics grew till they represented 70 per cent of the population of this community, they were never in a position to challenge the Freie Gemeinde. The bond between the "Old Catholics" and the Freie Gemeinde was too great.

Although the lower-class Catholics commonly had the priest as ally in their intended war against the freethinkers, the upper-class Catholics had the church coffers as a weapon in their opposition. As long as the elite retained its distinctive power in the church and community, the Freie Gemeinde was protected. By the turn of the century, however, this protective kinship had decreased. With acculturation and both upward and downward mobility, the Catholic church grew more homogeneous. Later we will note the downward mobility of the Freie Gemeinde itself. As both Catholics and freethinkers lost their upper-class character, pressure intensified and made an adaptive strategy necessary for the Freie Gemeinde.

But why a strategy of legitimation rather than increased militancy? Here the horizontal dimension of differentiation offers insight and Milwaukee offers a comparison. As a structurally differentiated urban center,[19] it affords its dissident groups both autonomy and a structured irrelevance. We would expect the Milwaukee Freie Gemeinde to choose the adaptive tack of militancy for several reasons. It not only must if it is to be heard, but it is allowed to since few are listening. Despite its bluster and intent, its disruptiveness is more threatened than real. Its militance is generally ignored because its activities do not impinge upon other community sectors or even upon the Milwaukee churches. But the less differentiated small town of Sauk City poses a different situation for its freethinkers. Because Sauk City forces an interpenetration of the activities of the Freie Gemeinde and every other institution, hostility increases and legitimation becomes a more likely response. In a small town, an irreligious group that occupies a prominent building on a large lot in the center of the community is more visible, more stigmatizing, and more consequential. Where this group is a dwindling minority, legitimation is the only recourse in the struggle for survival.

In all of this, there is a paradox and two tainted alternatives. In a differentiated community, the dissident group may be militant precisely because its militance goes unnoticed or ignored. In an undifferentiated community, the dissident group is much more noticed and, therefore, must put a damper on its pronouncements. Thus, one may have militancy at the cost of neglect or one may have attention at the price of legitimation. Of course, after a point, militancy may stimulate attention and legitimacy may bring on neglect. The latter is a major tactic of the Sauk City group. We mentioned earlier that the Freie Gemeinde joined the Unitarian-Universalist Fellowship to facilitate its recruitment by increasing its legitimacy. Even so, the group has qualms about risking a cultivated anonymity by launching a membership campaign of any sort. One member puts it this way: "If we ever battled for a member with one of the churches, then we might antagonize them. Our methods of obtaining members are far from the hard-sell type so that we don't antagonize any other group by trying to take members away from them." Of course, the churches have confronted the same problem among themselves. In many cases, they have evolved a complex set of recruitment boundaries to insure that every church has access to potential members without encroaching upon each other. The Freie Gemeinde is hardly eligible for the arrangement.

Organizational Characteristics and the Pursuit of Legitimacy

Other things being equal, a dissident group in an undifferentiated context will move toward legitimacy. But, of course, other things are seldom equal. Another set of factors that may mediate the influence of the community concerns internal characteristics of the dissident organization itself. Although we can assume that most groups would like to remain true to their original goals and values, we cannot assume that every group is up to the task.

Consider first the *social status of the membership.* In general, the higher the status of the members, the more militant a dissident group can be. This is so for several reasons. For one, the aura of prestige confers a certain license in itself. For another, high status often implies a crucial role in the community that redeems one's illegitimacy. For a third, high status makes the person more eligible for the support and tolerance of the community's wider elite. The early members of the Free Church had unequivocably high status in the community. In addition, they had power as editors of the local press, members of the community council, leaders of the local clubs, representatives on the village planning commission, and officers of the school board. We have already seen how these early freethinkers won the succor of the aristocratic Catholics. They also had leverage on the community as a whole, despite its hostility. A quote from Martin Marty's analysis of nineteenth-century Deism makes the point well for another irreligionist in another community: "Judge Driscoll could be a free thinker and still hold his place in society because he was the person of most consequence in the community, and therefore could venture to go his own way and follow his own notions."[20]

But, paradoxically, although the upper classes *can* be more militant they frequently opt not to be. Lacking the mutual reinforcement of the ethnic freethinkers, they may be concerned about overreaching the tolerance threshold and they may be co-opted by conservative elements in the community. On the other hand, the lower classes are more militant in spite of the greater likelihood of arousing hostility. They have less to lose, and continued frustration may lead them to spurn rather than eat the pie in the sky. In all of this, it is the middle class that is most constrained. Here, occupations depend on the good will of the community. Insurance agents, small businessmen, barbers, and others in personal services cannot afford to antagonize their customers. One member of the Freie Gemeinde explained, "In a small town, a tradesman can't afford to be anti-anything." As this suggests, the Sauk City freethinkers are now more middle than upper class and this has been a factor in their increased pursuit of legitimacy. Of course, none of this is new or surprising. Homans comments on the license of high status;[21] middle-class constraint has become a sociological cliché; and Gusfield corroborates the relationship between dissidence and low status.[22]

Now, however, we turn to a more theoretically provocative area, that of *leadership.* Leadership is obviously crucial in a dissident group.[23] It is here that Weber makes some of his most important contributions to theories of social change. For Weber, charisma was a key factor in producing innovations and "breakthroughs" in the social order.[24] It was only by rallying around the magical that the membership could escape the mundane. And yet once the breakthrough had occurred, it was important to consolidate the gains. At this point, Weber discusses the shift from charismatic to noncharismatic authority as a way of stabilizing the movement and insuring its orderly march into future generations.

As apt as this theory may be for other groups, it must be amended for the Freie Gemeinde. Unlike the religious sect, irreligion provides poor soil for the nurturance of charisma. Weber puts strong emphasis on charisma's magical component, but freethinkers are vehemently oriented to science and rationality. Weber also stresses the importance of sacramental trappings for routinized charisma, yet freethinkers explicitly repudiate all ceremony let alone any doctrine resembling apostolic succession. This is a first instance of the way in which irreligious organizations are betrayed by irreligious tenets. Charisma is crucial to any dissident group's success, but free thought frustrates its development. Note, however, that the Freie Gemeinde did have an early approximation. Schroeter was charismatic in most respects save the magical. Indeed, his case points to several additional elaborations of Weberian theory.

It is important to recall that German immigrants had organized Wisconsin free thought *before* the emergence or arrival of a charismatic leader. This suggests that charisma is not always necessary for the inception of social movements. While charisma may be crucial in launching movements among an *indigenous* and rooted population, it may be less important for movements occurring among uprooted transplants or those who are sufficiently alien to band together without having to be rallied. Further, charisma may be more important in sustaining a militant movement than in starting it. Although a shift away from charisma may be salutary once a group has been *accepted* by its context, it may be fatal if the group remains stigmatized. Certainly Schroeter's primary contribution was to persistence rather than inception. With his death in 1888, the group began its slow demise. Although the current leader is responsible and efficient, he makes no pretense of serving charismatic functions. Unlike Schroeter, he lacks the glamor of previous persecution, and his work as an insurance salesman brands him as all too ordinary. He has no prophetic role and even avoids ethical or intellectual leadership. Here then is one more reason why the group has opted for legitimacy rather than militancy.

But note that once legitimation is pursued, the pursuit itself has further consequences for the leader. Under conditions of militancy and consequent duress, the leader's power is centralized and maximized. Under conditions of legitimation, he faces increasing difficulty in maintaining his authority since his decisions and programs are less urgent. Sensing the compromise of legitimation, the group is apt to hark back to the time when its original ideals were being forged and defended militantly. It may then idealize past rather than present leadership and confer a wishful "charisma in absentia" upon one long gone. This cultivation of the past has the best of both worlds. It reminds the group of its militant strain but locates this militancy safely in a bygone age where it can provoke no contemporary disruptions. In this regard it is important to note that although Schroeter was crucial to the Freie Gemeinde in both Milwaukee and Sauk City, he is given much less attention in the former. Milwaukee's militance has more nearly obviated such wistful glances into the heroic past.

A third organizational variable concerns values and goals or, more properly, their absence. As Clark has suggested, undefined values are one condition of precariousness. Unattainable or unrealistic goals may be another. Certainly conventional religious groups suffer on both counts since salvation is neither clear cut nor easily achieved. For this reason churches have long suffered from goal displacement or what could be termed the "means-ends inversion" in which means such as recruitment replace goals such as salvation. All of this underscores the importance of charisma; it may serve as an antidote by providing an alternative source of meaning and a more immediate rallying point. It is hardly surprising that religious groups have long outdistanced more pragmatic organizations in their production of charismatic types.[25]

But if undefined and unattainable goals are a vulnerability of the churches, they are doubly so for the freethinkers. Here the problems escalate since values tend to be wholly relativistic and goals are rarely stipulated at all. The freethinker's high regard for individual autonomy makes an organizational creed anathema. The following quotations illustrate the members' amorphous conception of the Freie Gemeinde's purpose:

> Well, I think we're looking for something we can believe in.
>
> We try to educate people in cultural things, in anything that's above and beyond the average humdrum existence. When I talk about "above

and beyond," I mean above and beyond our lives, the way we live now, where we came from and where we're going. . . . I think we all look for meanings; if there are any we hope to find them. We don't presuppose that there are meanings, however, that there are always answers. There may not be.

We are a group of seekers rather than a body of believers. We think that through advancements of science the truth will change. We are prepared to accept this, and we can change our beliefs very easily, because if it follows the truth, then we believe we are right in changing it in contrast to other religions.

With such vague goals, passion dissipates. There are no concrete actions, no gauges by which to measure progress. There is little worth suffering for, and legitimacy is seductive to those who are dissident for no compelling reasons, and with no measurable end in view.

Like the churches, then, the Freie Gemeinde has indeed witnessed an inversion of means and ends. Many respondents confessed that their participation was motivated more by social reasons than anything else. The combination of "mighty fine food" and German "egg coffee" has supplanted the reformist zeal of overturning the churches and emancipating their parishioners. Insofar as substantive issues occur, one member comments upon their deliberation as follows:

In our meetings we never talk about the Freie Gemeinde as such, or try in any way to belittle the beliefs of others. We don't do anything except maybe we have a meditation or reading with the idea that they're not too strongly worded so that they won't cause any friction or hard feelings. Some ideas appeal to us more than others, but we don't use them because we don't want people to feel that we are trying to ram our ideas down their throats.

Part of this is due to the natural legacy of free thought; part of it is a redounding effect of legitimation. For whatever reason, irreligion has been replaced by areligion, and an organization has become a collectivity.

All of this leads in turn to the further factor of *commitment.* Obviously, membership commitment is another pre-condition to organizational militancy.[26] The commitment of most Sauk City members has flagged to the point where increased militancy would tax it beyond its breaking point. Nor does the decreasing strength of the organization bother them. One member shrugged and commented as follows:

If the Free Church does disintegrate, fine, let it go; I've had it for fifty years, it's given me a lot of personal happiness. Let's make it pleasant for ourselves. I wouldn't want any people to join with very vehement feel-

> ings. . . . We had two or three who did that and everyone felt rather uncomfortable. It's a lot more pleasant just to let it go and not worry about it.

Certainly commitment is affected by the unattainability of goals above, but there are other factors as well. One is the generation of membership. Despite their differences, the Freie Gemeinde and the religious sect are similar in that second- and third-generation members are generally less sensitive to the original ideals and less militant in maintaining them.[27] One elderly freethinker recalled the change this way:

> The Freie Gemeinde was more antichurch at that time because the people had come from Europe and were more opposed to it and were more eager to further their education. . . . Our forebears, when they first came, were getting away from something . . . there was something to fight for, there was much more. These things were fresh in their minds, and now there is an entirely different attitude.

Yet the members of later generations must not be confused with the convert. There is a difference between those whose membership is a family legacy and those who join out of independent conviction. Those respondents whose parents had *not* been members of the group were much more disgruntled with the current complacency. Most of them favored a more militant and more active program. However, as outsiders to a familistic organization, they lacked the influence to effect a change.

Finally, it is important to consider commitment alongside recruitment. One can relate the two hypothetically. Thus a militant group maximizes the commitment of its existing members but jeopardizes the recruitment of new adherents; a legitimizing group maximizes recruitment opportunities but minimizes commitment. In short, a dissident group cannot maximize commitment and recruitment at the same time. In order to secure commitment the group must adhere strongly to its dissident values, thereby alienating a flock of potential recruits who are not prepared to go so far. In order to enhance recruitment, the group must widen its appeal by reducing its dissidence, thereby betraying the allegiances of many of its original members.

The Freie Gemeinde offers a partial illustration. It is true that the group failed to take advantage of the recruitment opportunities afforded by their affiliation with the Unitarian-Universalist Fellowship. And yet merely securing the advantage at all had the predicted consequence of decreased commitment. Two lifelong members expressed their reactions as follows:

> I didn't like it very well, and I know that our forefathers wouldn't have agreed to it at all. I would rather that the group were like the way our forefathers had it.
>
> The Free Church now is a negative force—even in my youth it was still a positive force culturally . . . they are not a free church anymore; they are now a segment of the Unitarian church.

The dissension's denouement was a splinter movement that followed the classic path of the religious sect except that it moved to the radical left instead of the fundamentalist right. While the new group has only a dozen members, it is both more active and more militant. It also elicits envious reactions from older members of the parent Freie Gemeinde who did not make the jump but could understand it.

> One of the reasons they don't come anymore is that the *Freie Gemeinde* isn't as outspoken as it used to be. The group wasn't active enough to suit them. They became discouraged and therefore started a more active discussion group. . . . When Madalyn Murray was here last year, she was not invited to speak to the Free Church. She spoke to the other discussion group though, and many of us would have liked to talk to her.

Summary

The preceding section isolated four distinct intra-organizational factors which inform adaptation to dissidence and precariousness: social status, leadership and charisma, organizational goals and values, and commitment and recruitment.[28] At this point it is worth considering their mutual relations. Although the four are intimately associated, this is not to say that they will always be consistent in leaning toward militancy or legitimation, growth or decline. Some organizations will maximize the conditions for growth in all four respects; some will maximize conditions in one factor but fall short on others; finally, there will be organizations like the Sauk City group that come a cropper on each. The Sauk City Freie Gemeinde's entire history reveals a succession of disasters as it systematically loses first one and then another factor in its favor. In its early phase it had an upper-class membership, a quasi-charismatic leader, a compelling goal in the revolt against the churches, and the high commitment of first-generation membership. Gradually each of these advantages fell away.

Nor has the community been of recent help, as was seen in the section on differentiation and the external context. The early alliance between the Freie Gemeinde and the aristocratic Catholics has dissipated and there is no longer a defending elite. Sauk City has never had the structural differentiation of Milwaukee, and therefore the freethinkers have always had to contend with a hostile community sensitive to their actions and declarations. In all of this, it is no surprise that the Freie Gemeinde is on the verge of disbanding. It may have a fling at immortality in the continued existence of its splinter movement. But even this may soon follow the path of its forerunner and convert current militancy into proximate legitimacy and ultimate demise.

---

1. This is an expanded version of a paper delivered at the American Sociological Association meetings in Chicago, September 1, 1965. We are indebted to the Danforth Study of Campus Ministries and to Dr. Kenneth Underwood for research support. We are grateful to the members of the Sauk City Freie Gemeinde for their patience, their candor, and their hospitality. Finally, we have profited from the suggestions of a number of colleagues, including Kenneth Lutterman, Roberta Goldstone, Gerald Marwell, Phillip Hammond, and Berenice Cooper.

2. Organizational studies of irreligion are nonexistent, although there have been several surveys that tap irreligion in wider populations. See, e.g., Russell Middleton and Snell Putney, "Religion, Normative Standards, and Behavior," *Sociometry,* XXV (June, 1962), 141-52, and Putney and Middleton, "Ethical Relativism and Anomia," *American Journal of Sociology,* LXVIII (January, 1962), 430-38.

3. Max Weber, *The Protestant Ethic and the Spirit of Capitalism* (New York: Charles Scribner's Sons, 1958), pp. 181-83; *General Economic History* (New York: Collier Books, 1961), p. 270. Emile Durkheim, *The Elementary Forms of the Religious Life* (New York: Collier Books, 1961), pp. 427-29; *Professional Ethics and Civic Morals* (Glencoe, Ill.: Free Press, 1958), esp. pp. 55-56. See, e.g., Karl Marx, "Anti-Church Movement—Demonstration in Hyde Park," in *Marx and Engels on Religion* (New York: Schocken Books, 1964), pp. 127-34. Although all of these predictions are refuted in that the church remains strong, they are partially confirmed in the preconditions of that strength. Thus, the church has staved off irreligion by becoming increasingly secular and allowing room for potential irreligionists within its own ranks. The establishment may not have passed, but it certainly has changed.

4. For the classic statement on the religious sect, see Ernst Troeltsch, *The Social Teachings of the Christian Churches* (New York: Harper & Bros., 1960), I, 328-54. Several recent treatments include Bryan R. Wilson, "An Analysis of Sect Development," *American Sociological Review,* Vol. XXIV (February, 1959); Benton Johnson, "On Church and Sect," *American Sociological Review,* XXVIII (August, 1963), 539-49; and Scott Grant McNall, "The Sect Movement," *Pacific Sociological Review,* VI (Fall, 1963), 60-64. See also Leon Festinger, Henry W. Riecken, and Stanley Schachter, *When Prophecy Fails* (Minneapolis: University of Minnesota Press, 1956), for a more psychological analysis of a precarious religious cult.

5. Much of the literature on political extremism is more polemical than academic. Some of the better works include: Daniel Bell (ed.), *The Radical Right* (Garden City, N.Y.: Doubleday & Co., 1963); Irving Howe and Lewis Coser, *The American Communist Party: A Critical History* (New York: Praeger Books, 1962); Philip Selznick, *The Organizational Weapon* (Glencoe, Ill.: Free Press, 1960); Vladimir C. Nahirney, "Some Observations on Ideological Groups," *American Journal of Sociology,* LXVII (January, 1962), 397-405; Egon Bittner, "Radicalism and Radical Movements," *American Sociological Review,* XXVIII (December, 1963), 928-40; and Neil J. Smelser, *Theory of Collective Behavior* (New York: Free Press, 1963), pp. 270-382.

6. The term "social movement" is, of course, a catchall. Several broad theoretical treatments include the divergent perspectives of Smelser, *ibid.*, and Hadley Cantril, *The Psychology of Social Movements* (London: Chapman & Hall, Ltd., 1941). Case studies include Burton R. Clark, "Organizational Adaptation and Precarious Values: A Case Study," *American Sociological Review,* XXI (June, 1956), 327-36: Joseph R. Gusfield, "Social Structure and Moral Reform: A Study of the Women's Christian Temperance Union," *American Journal of Sociology,* LXI (November, 1955), 221-32; Sheldon I. Messinger, "Organizational Transformation: A Case Study of a Declining Social Movement," *American Sociological Review,* XXIV (February, 1955), 3-10; and C. Eric Lincoln, *The Black Muslims in America* (Boston: Beacon Press, 1961). Finally, for related treatments of delinquency and lower-class culture, see J. Milton Yinger, "Contraculture and Subculture," *American Sociological Review,* XXV (October, 1960), 625-45, and Lewis Yablonsky, "The Delinquent Gang as a Near-Group," *Social Problems,* VII (Fall, 1959), 108-17.

7. Howard S. Becker, "Problems of Inference and Proof in Participant Observation," *American Sociological Review,* XXIII (December, 1958), 652-60.

8. Participant observation is not quite apt since we were conspicuous as outsiders and made no attempt to hide our research objectives. At the same time, we were graciously received, invited to every meeting, and witnessed no inhibitions. It is a commentary on the group itself, however, that it no longer discusses issues about which inhibitions might arise.

9. Most of this historical attention has been devoted to early American deists such as Jefferson, Franklin, and Paine, together with the East Coast offspring of Unitarianism, including the ethical-culture movement. See, e.g., Stow Persons, *Free Religion: An American Faith* (New Haven, Conn.: Yale University Press, 1947); Sidney Warren, *American Freethought: 1860-1914* (New York: Columbia University Press, 1943); and Martin Marty, *The Infidel* (New York: Living Age Books, 1961).

10. Most of the literature here was locally published in limited editions and in German. For the European background of the free-thought movement, see Friedrich Schuenemann-Pott, *Die Freie Gemeinde* (Philadelphia: B. Stephen Publishers, 1861), and Johannes Ronge, *Rede Gehalten beim Ersten Gottesdienste der Freien Christlichen Gemeinden zu Schweinfurt am Palm Sonntag* (Schweinfurt, 1849). For historical materials on the Wisconsin movement, see Karl Heinzen, *Deutscher Radikalismus in Amerika* (distributed by the "Verein zur Verbreitung radikaler Prinzipien," 1879); Max Hempel, *Was Sind die Freien Gemeinden von Nord-Amerika?* (Philadelphia, 1877); Freidrich Schuenemann-Pott (ed.), *Blaetter fuer Freies Religioeses Leben* (Wisconsin, 1855-71), Vols. I–XVI; J. J. Schlichter, "Eduard Schroeter the Humanist," *Wisconsin Magazine of History* (December, 1944, and March, 1945); Freidenker Convention zu Milwaukee, *Blitzstrahlen der Wahrheit* (Milwaukee Freidenker, 1872). A good recent summary is provided in Berenice Cooper, "Die Freien Gemeinden in Wisconsin," *Wisconsin Academy of Science, Arts and Letters,* LIII (Fall, 1964), 53-65.

11. Clara Rung, "The Free Congregation of Sauk City" (unpublished manuscript, 1940), p. 11. Note that the statement is bitingly opposed to the church but somewhat ambiguous concerning doctrine. This Kierkegaardian syndrome was characteristic of early free thought, but two things are worth noting about its subsequent development in the Sauk City group. First, there is an ever widening gap between the statements of the organization and the beliefs of the individual members—perhaps an operationalization of both precariousness and bureaucracy. Confining ourselves to the former, the organization was forced to become more publicly accepting of both church and doctrine while its members increased their opposition to doctrine in particular. This leads to a second point. Over time the Kierkegaardian position has been reversed: the members' original hostility toward the church has ebbed, but their atheism has become more *pro*nounced if less *an*nounced. This tendency to accept the church while rejecting its doctrine has, of course, cut a swath through the religious establishment as well, accounting for the concomitant rise of both secularization and church participation.

12. Madalyn Murray is an outspoken and formidably aggressive atheist who has used her legal background to push for wider separation of church and state through the courts. Her recent moves from Baltimore to Hawaii and to Texas have left behind a cloud of legal proceedings and embittered former colleagues. *The Realist* is a magazine of free-thought satire that covers issues from homosexuality to foreign policy in the unflinching manner of a literary Lenny Bruce.

13. Clark, *op. cit.*

14. See also the general literature on the sociology of conflict, including Lewis Coser, *The Functions of Social Conflict* (Glencoe, Ill.: Free Press, 1956), pp. 87-104, and Kenneth E. Boulding, *Conflict and Defense: A General Theory* (New York: Harper & Row, 1962), esp. pp. 162-64.

15. At this point it is instructive to compare the approach to follow with Smelser's landmark, *Theory of Collective Behavior, op. cit.* Although the Freie Gemeinde fits into Smelser's category of the "value oriented movement," it cannot be understood in Smelser's terms. Because of his emphasis on political revolutionism, Smelser puts a great deal of stress on repressive control by formally constituted authorities. He gives little attention to either informal control from the wider context or to "self-control" through internal organizational characteristics. Both of these are crucial to the free-thought movement, and this is one of a number of ways in which irreligion departs from previous cases and previous theories.

16. The theoretical literature on structural differentiation is burgeoning. For a critical exchange on its applicability to social change, see Talcott Parsons, "Evolutionary Universals in Society," *American Sociological Review,* XXIX (June, 1964), 339-57, and S. N. Eisenstadt, "Social Change, Differentiation and Evolution," *American Sociological Review,* XXIX (June, 1964), 375-85. For two discussions of its applicability to religion in particular, see Robert Bellah, "Religious Evolution," *American Sociological Review,* XXIX (June, 1964), 358-74, and Richard A. Peterson and N. J. Demerath III, "Introduction to Liston Pope," *Millhands and Preachers* (New Haven, Conn.: Yale University Press, 1942; 5th ed., 1965), pp. xxv-xxxii.

17. Note that differentiation can be seen *within* each of these spheres as well as *between* them. This is even the case for irreligion itself. Thus, St. Louis hosts both a strong Ethical Culture Society (middle class and churchlike) and the headquarters of the ARF (lower class and more sectlike). The groups seldom communicate, and there is virtually no overlap in membership.

18. For a discussion of the role of elites in the contemporary small town, see Arthur J. Vidich and Joseph Bensman, *Small Town in Mass Society* (Garden City, N.Y. Doubleday & Co., 1960), esp. pp. 114-39, 287-89.

19. For an account of the role of structural differentiation in urban centers, see Delbert C. Miller, "Decision-Making Cliques in Community Power Structures: A Comparative Study of an American and English City," *American Journal of Sociology,* LXIV (November, 1958), 299-310; Robert A. Dahl, *Who Governs* (New Haven, Conn.: Yale University Press, 1961); Robert O. Schulze, "The Role of Economic Dominants in Community Power Structure," *American Sociological Review,* XXIII (February, 1958), 3-9; and Linton Freeman *et al.,* "Locating Leaders in Local Communities," *American Sociological Review,* XXVIII (October, 1963), 796.

20. Marty, *op. cit.,* p. 76.

21. George C. Homans, *Social Behavior: Its Elementary Forms* (New York: Harcourt, Brace, & World, 1961), pp. 349-55.

22. Gusfield, *op. cit.*

23. Yet there is a tentative qualification here concerning the relation between leadership and ideology. This is based on comparative observations of other irreligious groups, including the ethical movement and the ARF, together with the senior author's current analysis of civil rights organizations and their student volunteers. Where leadership is

absent a strong ideology may fill the void by becoming doubly rigid and compelling. Where leadership and efficient organization occur, the ideology need be less compulsory and may be more flexible. The first case characterizes both the ARF and the Student Non-Violent Coordinating Committee. The second describes the ethical movement and the Southern Christian Leadership Conference.

24. Max Weber, *The Theory of Social and Economic Organization* (Glencoe, Ill.: Free Press, 1947), pp. 358-92. See also the critical piece based upon new evidence by Peter L. Berger, "Charisma and Religious Innovation: The Social Location of Israelite Prophecy," *American Sociological Review,* XXVIII (December, 1963), 940-50.

25. Note the reference here to the "production of charisma." This is intended to suggest that charisma is often more imputed than claimed and that it relates more to group needs than to the psychology of leadership. In this interpretation, Weber is hardly an advocate of the "great man theory of history." For an analysis in this vein, see Festinger *et al., op. cit.,* and their implicit treatment of charisma as a response to collective dissonance.

26. The emphasis here is on the consequences of undercommitment for the pursuit of legitimation. And yet *overcommitment* is a pathology that may disrupt the militant group. Its symptoms are a penchant for the spectacular rather than the efficient and a tendency to grapple with the first task at hand instead of considering other tasks with more delayed but more important effects. Overcommitment is visible not only in the ARF as the most militant irreligious group but in civil rights organizations as well.

27. Clearly ethnic acculturation has taken its toll in this connection. Originally the Freie Gemeinde served an ancillary function in providing an island of old-world identity in the new-world sea. As ethnic lines blurred, the movement lost this role. Since then it has had to "make it" on the basis of irreligion alone. But, while this is an undeniable factor in the organization's decline, it is hardly a sufficient cause. Other ethnic free-thought movements in Milwaukee, St. Louis, and Philadelphia have maintained their militancy and conserved their strength in spite of acculturation.

28. What is the basis of four factors, only four factors, and these four factors? They are not random choices, and they are recommended by two considerations. First, of course, they resonate in the interviews and documents that provide the data. Second, they articulate with broader theoretical schemes. E.g., there is a contrived but provocative parallel between status, leadership, commitment, and values, on the one hand, and A-G-I-L, on the other. Certainly Parsons' model can be employed in the analysis of precariousness and dissidence, as Smelser has indicated. Yet our present intention is more to elucidate a single case than to engage in higher-order systematics.

Chapter 3
Leadership Characteristics and Role Conflicts

JEFFREY HADDEN

The Clergyman's Crisis of Identity

INTRODUCTION

The central theme of this volume has been that the Protestant churches are in the midst of a web of crises. These crises are seen as emerging out of serious doubt about the most basic theological doctrines of Christianity and from a growing struggle over the meaning and purpose of the church. These two crises have in turn resulted in a third crisis, namely a crisis of authority. In this chapter I want to argue that these three crises have led to yet a fourth crisis: a *crisis of identity* for the Protestant clergyman. Having elaborated this final development, I will then attempt to look at these crises in perspective and speculate about their implications for institutionalized religion in contemporary society.

THE CLERGYMAN'S CRISIS OF IDENTITY

The crisis of identity emerges out of the clergyman's *internalization* of the other crises. The problem of identity, in essence, is the confrontation of the self with the question, "Who am I?" As the vast literature of social psychology and philosophy will attest, the processes by which the self internalizes a sense of identity is enormously complex. Yet we need not go into a full explication of the theoretical literature to understand the clergyman's crisis of identity.

Identity emerges as a product of social interaction whereby the individual internalizes the attitudes and values of others toward the world around him as well as toward himself. While identity is not solely the product of what one internalizes about himself from others, social interaction is an integral part of the process by which the individual gains a sense of who he is. *Socialization* is the process by which human communities transmit values and modes of conduct to the individual which are essential for the survival of society. From the perspective of the individual, socialization is the learning of what is valued by the human community, what is expected in the way of conduct, and a built-in (internalized) desire to conform to the community's values and patterns of conduct. To the extent that socialization succeeds in internalizing the values and patterns of behavior of a society, it succeeds in giving the individual a sense of identity, for he not only understands the nature of the social order, he is able to see where he "fits in."

But what happens when a human community's values are in a state of flux or transition? To be sure, if the changing values are central to every individual, the entire community experiences some strain. But the strain is most acute for those whose responsibility it is to define, sustain, and transmit the values in question. When the values in flux are as basic as the ultimate meaning of life itself, the amount of strain is understandably great.

The clergyman's crisis of identity emerges out of the fact that the value system he has the responsibility of defining, sustaining, and transmitting is in a most serious state of flux. The evidence presented in this volume leaves little room to doubt that this is so. The society is not sure what it believes and it is uncertain as to what the meaning and purpose of the church ought to be. Lacking a clear and coherent notion of the role of religious faith and religious institutions in a changing world, it also is confused about the role of the clergyman. The failure to ascribe clearly defined roles to the clergyman, in turn, leaves the clergyman with considerable ambiguity and lack of clarity as to his role in society.

Many of the factors which contribute to this identity crisis have been implicitly elaborated in our discussion of the crises of belief, meaning and purpose, and authority. These need to be underscored and others further elaborated.

Social roles and identity grow out of the process of interaction with other persons who are important in the development of a self or a sense of identity. George Herbert Mead, one of the early and great contributors to the field of social psychology, referred to such persons as *significant others.* In early childhood the significant others may be very limited, but as the individual approaches adulthood, the range and number of significant others increase sharply. The number and range of significant others will be influenced by social status, residence, occupational choice, etc. A miner in an isolated rural community, for example, will obviously encounter both a smaller number and narrower range of significant others who contribute to the development of his sense of self-identity than will a high-status urban resident who aspires to a career in public life. Those who choose the ministry as an occupation are exposed to a wide range of significant others, both in the process of training and in the fulfillment of their roles in this occupation. Their sense of identity, thus, comes not from a single source, but from many sources.

The clergyman's identity crisis does not grow out of the fact that he encounters so many significant others, but rather that (a) the significant others often lack a sense of what the clergyman's role is, and (b) to the extent that they do define the role, there is broad disagreement and conflict. In short, the clergyman encounters a world that tells him that his role, and hence identity, is ambiguous. This can perhaps best be understood by elaborating some of the conditions and factors which contribute to this ambiguity. We will begin with some of the factors that contribute to the layman's lack of understanding, which of course are fed back to the clergyman, and then move to some factors that are more easily attributed to the occupation itself.

To begin with, the layman finds it difficult to understand the role of the clergyman precisely because clergymen are such an extremely heterogeneous group with respect to what they believe, what they do, and their presentation of self in society. As we have seen in this volume, the beliefs of clergymen range all the way from the Bible-slapping fundamentalists who hold forth in revival tents to the *avant-garde* men of the collar who proclaim that "God is dead" and think of themselves as Christian atheists. While the numbers at either extreme are probably not very large, there is still a very large variation in beliefs existing within the middle range. There is, for example, the conservative position, which, while not accepting the Bible as literal truth, holds a great deal of it as divine revelation which fundamentally informs man of the meaning of truth. The language and style of this position may not be easily distinguishable from the neo-orthodox position, where interpretation of religious doctrine has undergone a considerable degree of transvaluation of meaning. Most laymen are aware that there is a difference, but being theologically unsophisticated, they are not very clear as to exactly what the differences are or what they imply.

Ministers engage in an extremely wide range of activities. In recent years they have been conspicuously present in the civil rights movement. Others have developed styles of ministry and approaches to life which make it difficult to distinguish their work from that of the clinical psychologist or psychiatrist. Others are slaves to a church calendar filled with ladies' aid societies, Sunday school picnics, midweek prayer meetings, and youth chalk talks. And still others seem to be indistinguishable from the executive secretary of the chamber of commerce. They are busy from sunup until late at night making speeches and serving on committees that "make their community a better place in which to live."

The ministers' presentation of self today also involves striking variation. Some have the clean-cut, smooth style of the Madison Avenue executive. At the other extreme is a pious presentation of self which could leave little doubt in anyone's mind that the parson has arrived on the scene.

In short, ministers are an extremely diverse group of people who defy the historical stereotype of the country parson, and cannot be pigeonholed into some simple typology. All of this is perplexing to the layman. Can the carriers of God's "eternal truth" come wrapped in so many different packages? Not fully understanding what this range of styles represents, the layman does not know how to respond to the clergyman and hence the clergyman does not get a very clear reflection from the layman as to what his role behavior ought to be.

Historically speaking, the clergyman has been viewed as a professional holy man. He was God's representative on earth charged with the responsibility of manifesting pious, godly virtues. He was not supposed to be like other men. To reveal his doubts and anxieties, to interact with other men as colleagues or intimate friends, or to manifest his "humanness" would represent a betrayal or evidence of weakness of his calling. His authority to speak in behalf of the Lord was intricately linked to his pious posture and was protected by maintaining a social distance from laymen.

Today, most clergymen no longer consciously maintain this "holy posture" and social distance from their congregations. Yet many, if not most, of them find that they are still unable to communicate with many laymen and relate to them openly. This is probably in large part due to the fact that laymen have internalized the stereotypical view of the clergyman and respond to him as if he were a holy man apart from others. When they interact with a clergyman they must "put on" their most polished pietistic style.

But possibly even more significant is the fact that the social distance is now being created by the layman. He is afraid to get too close to the minister because he fears that the minister will ask him for commitments of his time and money that he is unwilling to make. One avoids a minister as one avoids the leaders of any voluntary association who are constantly on the lookout for persons who can be coerced to serve on committees or make larger financial contributions to the organization.

The average church layman wishes to maintain an active but nominal commitment to the church in the same sense as he desires nominal membership in his lodge and professional organization. They are there for his convenience, benefit, and comfort, but it is necessary to preserve social distance to avoid being saddled with too many responsibilities for the system-maintenance tasks of the organization.

But perhaps an even more important reason the layman maintains social distance from the clergyman is his desire to escape what I have called the crisis of meaning. To him, the church *is* a source of comfort and meaning and he does not wish to engage in a dialogue on the meaning of meaning. He does not wish to be confronted with questions regarding the implications of his faith for his daily life and the troubled world he lives in.

Interaction, thus, seldom goes beyond the minimal formal role requirements. While the minister may desire to move beyond this level of interaction and find out who his layman is as a person, and reveal to the laymen that he is also a person, the layman is reluctant to do so because of the uncertainties of what this kind of relationship might lead to.

Another critical underlying factor in understanding the ambiguity of the clergyman's role is the very nature of the changing world. Science and technology have pushed men to become increasingly concerned with the secular. The varieties and opportunities for new human experience have never been greater. Where once the church had a monopoly, it is now in competition for man's mind and his time. Moreover, there is too much which man doesn't know, but which he views as within his grasp to learn, for him to be overly concerned about those things that appear beyond the domain of human knowledge. Science has challenged the clergyman's claim to relevance in all matters of life. Often when clergymen are viewed as relevant at all by much of contemporary society, their competence is thought to be restricted to moments of grief and great exultation, such as death and birth.

The changing world is also at the root of the clergyman's crisis of identity, because it has necessitated a re-examination of the doctrines of religious institutions. While theologians have been seriously involved in this re-examination for a long time, it is not easy to communicate to laymen. Clergymen are caught in a dilemma between proclaiming a doctrine of truth which presumably transcends the ages and being forced to adapt and reinterpret this doctrine in light of man's increasing understanding of the empirical world. For the clergyman as well as the layman, it is often difficult to differentiate between the reinterpretation of enduring truth and the more precarious and fatal procedure of peeling away layers of the onion until nothing is left. What fundamental truths are there which the church proclaims which will abide through the ages? The clergyman fears to let go of doctrine before having subjected it to the most careful scrutiny for fear that having done so will leave him in a logically indefensible position. At the same time he feels pressed to discard irrelevant baggage which may get in the way of others understanding the essential features of his faith. Compounding this dilemma is the lack of consensus as to what the bedrock fundamental truths are.

As the physician who has difficulty diagnosing a rare disease does not find it easy to speak frankly with his patient, so the clergyman who is caught up in the turmoil of re-examining the canons of his faith finds it difficult to communicate clearly and honestly with his client. If his utterings appear to be unclear it may be because, in fact, his own beliefs are in a state of animated suspension.

In their quest for continuity with the past and relevance for the present many clergymen have retained much of the traditional language of the faith while reinterpreting its meaning. They are anxious to communicate this new meaning to those who will listen. At the same time, they are fearful of upsetting the faith of many who find meaning only in inflexible, absolute world views. They know that questioning this faith may cause considerable psychological distress and may risk losing the layman's support, as well as creating strife and discord in the congregation.

The young minister's own imperfect socialization to the nuances of Tillich or the latest *avant-garde* theologian at the seminary, combined with the difficult task of communicating new meaning with old vessels, has often left laymen in bewilderment. To the theologically unsophisticated, it is frequently not clear just what the differences are between a Billy Graham, a Norman Vincent Peale, and a James Pike; between a conservative, a neo-orthodox, and a liberal.

In a world that presents increasing opportunities for the utilization of time, the laity often find other uses for time traditionally reserved for religious activities. If worship and participation in church functions are preserved at all, they are likely to be rigidly compartmentalized. The minister who demands more time from his laity and pleads that they join with him in examining the meaning of the faith in a changing world is likely to find himself left with only a handful of faithful followers.

We can further point to the increasing division of labor and specialization in contemporary society as a factor contributing to the ministers' crisis of identity. The roles that were once exclusively or nearly exclusively the tasks of clergymen have been taken over by a proliferation of other helping professions. Teaching, administering aid, counseling the troubled, and advising the young are examples of tasks for which clergymen once assumed major responsibility, but which are now the domain of others.

This does not mean, however, that the clergyman in his search for relevance and meaningful activity has abandoned these earlier roles. On the contrary, he has expanded them, and usually does so without the benefit of specialized knowledge developed by other professional groups. As counselor, for example, he may engage in helping persons with emotional disturbances, marital problems, occupational choice, alcoholism, financial distress, and aging. Each of these areas has developed a highly particularized knowledge and practitioners who devote full time to this kind of helping relationship. The typical parish minister may very well be called upon to help in all of these situations within a reasonably short period of time. Thus, he is simultaneously sharing old roles while broadening them into other areas. It is increasingly difficult for him as well as others to discern what is uniquely the role of a clergyman.

He probably has not taken on this multiplicity of activities solely out of his search for identity and relevance, for many of these roles have been thrust upon him. Contemporary men are probably less reluctant than were men of earlier generations to turn to others for solutions to their problems. Man's practical and pragmatic orientation toward life leads him to seek to resolve or eliminate tensions that result in unhappiness. Unaware of where to look for specialized help or unable to afford professional services, he frequently turns to the clergyman. A national survey taken a few years ago found that 42 per cent of the American population indicated they would turn first to their clergyman if they experienced emotional stress.[1] This exceeds by a considerable amount the proportion who would turn to any other source of help, including the family physician.

Another factor involved in the clergyman's crisis of identity is his isolation from colleagues. The country doctor can work in isolation from colleagues because he has an image of who he is and what he does and this identity is shared by the community. But where the image is cloudy, as in the case of clergymen, isolation may increase the crisis of identity, or, alternatively, contribute to the individual's avoidance of the problem.

For example, when there is no other professional around to question the justification of his activities, the minister may find it easier to take on a motif of busyness that is psychologically rewarding to him and acceptable to his congregation, but which neglects many of the long-range problems of the church. Filling his life with so much activity that he never has the time to be troubled with the question "why," is the path of least resistance. While this may be functional for the immediate needs of the individual, it is dysfunctional for the larger task of reinterpreting the essential meaning of the faith and the role of the minister in contemporary society.

The isolation of the minister may also discourage him from straying too far from the parish and the activities that have been thrust upon him. The clergyman who ventures too far out of the ghetto of his parish is not unlike the American Negro. He cannot always be certain that he is welcome, and it is sometimes difficult to distinguish between genuine acceptance and a polite but patronizing tolerance.

What I am suggesting here is that while there are structural factors that make it possible for individual clergy to avoid a crisis of identity, and many may very well take this route, this does not alter the fact that the profession itself is caught up in a gathering storm.

It would be an oversimplification to argue that the society is totally ambiguous in its understanding and expectations of the clergy. While a significant proportion of the public lacks a clear conception of the clergyman's role, there is also another significant proportion who have a very clearly defined set of role expectations. The problem emerges out of the fact that different subgroups have different expectations. As has been demonstrated throughout this book, one of the major schisms of expectations is between clergy and laity. I have also tried to demonstrate that the depth of the schism is increasing. A significant proportion of young men who are choosing the ministry today are doing so out of a commitment to the solution of critical social problems in society. The seminaries reinforce and help internalize this commitment, because a large proportion of the seminary professors share this set of values and role expectations for the clergy. The same is true of many church administrators who seek to create structures in which the new breed can work.

But the vast majority must carve out their ministry within the structure of the local parish. While the seminary socialization may provide some realistic orientation to the parish ministry, for many it comes as a cruel awakening to discover the realities of parish life and the disparity between their expectations of the ministry and those of their congregation. But even when the young seminarian knows what he is in for, it probably doesn't significantly cushion the trauma of his exposure to the parish. Somehow he had hoped that his style and sincerity would bring laymen to see the purpose and meaning of the church in his terms. Not only is he confronted with the rude awakening that it didn't turn out as he had hoped, he must also confront the reality that he is pretty powerless to do much about it.

For some, the disparity between their expectations and the expectations of their laity is so great that they leave the ministry. Others seek to relieve the conflict by locating a non-parish position, but within the institutional church. For the large majority, there is nowhere else to go, so they attempt to solve their identity crisis by bringing their own views more in line with the expectations of their congregation. Resocialization may take many forms, but it usually involves taking a more "mature" and "realistic" view as to how much or how fast the church can change. Filling one's life with work is another way in which the resocialization occurs. One simply doesn't have time to think about all the problems that once bothered him. But for others, the resocialization is never quite complete. There is the lingering awareness of dreams once held. The increasing number and high visibility of clergy in non-parish structures also serves to remind the parish pastor of visions and expectations he once held. Thus, he must live with another dimension of his crisis of identity: the disparity between his expectations and the expectations of his congregation.

In summary, the reasons why clergymen are not understood and, in fact, often misunderstood, are intricately related to and a part of their crisis of identity. In the past, the clergyman's role was relatively unambiguous. He was the spiritual leader of his congregation, charged with the responsibility of proclaiming religious truth, tending to the propagation and preservation of the institutional church, administering the holy sacraments, and tending to the individual spiritual needs of the congregation. These traditional responsibilities were exercised in the roles of preacher, teacher, priest, and pastor.

Modern man is less certain of what the role of religion is or ought to be in his own life, and concomitantly is uncertain as to who the clergyman is and what his business is about. He is not satisfied with the traditional role of the pastor, but he doesn't understand or approve of the role of the new breed.

The clergyman faces a crisis of belief, yet he is required to maintain some kind of coherent and consistent posture from the pulpit and in other aspects of his ministry. Laity make multiple and often conflicting demands of him, and he is required to spend a great deal of time engaged in activities for which he is ill prepared. He is not only isolated from parishioners by social distance, but he is also physically isolated from other clergy from whom he might gain support and some sense of identity. Finally, he is caught in a conflict between his own concept of a clergyman's role and the purpose of the church, and the expectations of his congregation.

All of these factors contribute to the demise of the clergyman's authority in terms of the traditional order of the social system. If he is to achieve more than token authority and loyalty, he must rely heavily upon his own charismatic qualities. But charisma breaks down quickly when his direction of leadership strays too far from the expectations of his congregation. Which way does he go? How does he develop a life style that gives him a sense of identity and fulfillment which is acceptable to those whom he serves and who control his life?

---

1. Richard McCann, *The Churches and Mental Health,* Joint Commission on Mental Illness and Health Monograph Series, No. 8 (New York: Basic Books, 1962).

ELAINE CUMMING
CHARLES HARRINGTON

Clergyman as Counselor

This is the second report from a group of studies designed to discover how the task of controlling deviance in society is divided among the various integrative agents and agencies.[1] In this paper we report a study of the clergyman's description of his counseling role and an analysis of this role with emphasis upon its articulation with the rest of the controlling system.

Helping is a traditional activity of the clergy[2] and, as such, has received considerable attention from social scientists. Recent studies have shown that a large number of people turn to clergymen when they are in trouble.[3] Studies of our own have shown that the clergyman ranks with the doctor as the first contact made outside the kinship and friendship circle during the onset of mental illness.[4] Most people appear to be satisfied with the help that they get from the clergyman.[5] As Eaton and his co-workers point out, "Clergy are close to many people during

---

Reprinted from the *American Journal of Sociology* 69 (November 1963):234-43, by permission of the authors and The University of Chicago Press.

crucial periods of the life cycle. . . . For those who know they need help the clergy is accessible without a waiting list or an intake worker to screen applicants. And going to a clergyman does not require a self-admission of helplessness on the part of the client."[6] In spite of his popularity, the clergyman's counseling role appears to some who have studied it to be "poorly defined," "diffuse," and "conflicted."[7] Other observers have suggested that the clergyman has a peculiarly difficult role because of his sensitivity to the values and norms of his congregation.[8] Indeed, the clergyman is probably alone among integrative agents in being a member of the group he controls.[9]

In some respects the clergyman resembles the other helping and controlling agents in the community. All have policies and norms governing who may call upon them for what kinds of help and who should be referred for more specialized attention. These policies and norms set the agent apart as a recognizable system of action and define the "boundary conditions" that both separate him from, and relate him to, other systems. Concretely, an agent's boundary conditions determine the accessibility of his services to clients and other agencies, and help to regulate the patterns of mutual dependency—that is, the division of labor—among agents.

The clergyman's relationships with the remainder of the controlling system, the permeability of the boundary around his role as counselor, and his own helping practices can all be expected to resemble those of other agencies in some ways, but the major hypothesis tested in this study is that, *because the clergyman differs from other agents of social control in being normatively involved with his congregation, his behavior, including his articulation with these other agents, should be influenced by the characteristics of that congregation.*

The Study

In Syracuse, New York, a sample of sixty-one churches was selected. They included ten Roman Catholic, six Episcopal, three Lutheran, three Eastern Orthodox, eight Methodist, seven Presbyterian, five Baptist, ten fundamentalist, three Jewish, and six churches of other Protestant denominations. The sample was selected from the total universe of churches in Syracuse after they had been stratified by size, neighborhood status, and denomination, the latter grouped into five categories —Roman Catholic, liturgical Protestant, other Protestant, fundamentalist Protestant, and Jewish. The stratification yielded eighty cells; the sixty-one that contained churches were randomly sampled.[10] One clergyman from each of fifty-nine churches was interviewed as a representative of that church.[11] In churches with more than one clergyman, a pastor was allocated for interview by the clergyman in authority, usually on the basis of his interest in counseling. The results, therefore, should be generalized to the counseling activities of churches in Syracuse, not to the city's clergymen.

Three types of variables were examined: the characteristics of the clergyman and his congregation, the nature of the problems counseled, and the articulation of the clergyman's counseling role with the remainder of the system. Each clergyman was asked to describe his congregation in terms of his age, income, residence, and occupation. With this information, the socioeconomic statuses that had been assigned to the churches on the basis of neighborhood reputation alone were modified. Finally, thirty-one of the fifty-nine churches were classified as upper or middle class and twenty-eight as working class.[12] The size of the congregation and the age and education of the clergyman himself were noted.

Each clergyman was asked to describe the problems brought to him for counseling and the extent of his counseling activities. Forty-one different types were distinguished from these descriptions. In Table 1 they have been divided into problems that more than half of the reporting clergymen counsel, and those that more than half of those reporting refer for service elsewhere. The problems are also grouped, in terms of their social characteristics, into three categories: (1) transition states, (2) deviant behavior, and (3) exigencies. The categories are rough, and decisions to include types in one category rather than another are sometimes based on the interviewer's interpretations, but they are an attempt to develop theoretical classifications of problems that can be expected to be differently handled by the clergy.

Transition states are the adjustment problems inherent in the life-cycle that everyone can expect to encounter. They include adolescent sex problems, need for vocational guidance, loneliness in old age or widowhood, bereavement, and transient maladjustments. Clergymen would be expected to deal with these problems frequently.

Deviant behavior includes infidelity, criminal or quasi-criminal behavior, unwed motherhood, severe marital conflict, mental, emotional, and sexual disturbances, psychoses and neuroses, and chronic inability to get along with others. It would be reasonable to expect clergymen to refer many of these "pathological" problems.

Exigencies are essentially environmental; they include lack of money, unemployment, cultural conflicts and discontinuities, and adjustments to physical illness. The clergyman would be expected to refer those problems that he lacks concrete resources for solving and to counsel those not needing concrete help.

TABLE 1. *Incidence and Disposition of Problem Types*

	CLERGY REPORTING No.	CLERGY REPORTING Per Cent (N = 59)	Per Cent Referring (of those Reporting)
Problems less than half reporting clergy refer:			
Transition states:			
Premarital counseling	49	83.1	42.9
Marriage and parent-child counseling	38	64.4	18.4
Counseling adolescents	29	49.1	17.2
Loneliness in old age or widowhood	29	49.1	13.8
Bereavement	14	23.7	00.0
Adjustment to puberty	14	23.7	00.0
Problems associated with the menopause	6	10.2	16.7
Adjustment to retirement	4	6.8	00.0
Deviant behavior			
Marital conflict	37	62.7	48.6
Parent-child conflict	32	54.2	18.8
Criminal and quasi-criminal behavior	28	47.5	28.6
Infidelity	25	42.5	20.0
Depression and pathological guilt	21	35.6	47.6
Hostility, aggression, acting out	11	18.6	45.4
Sexual deviations	9	15.3	44.4
In-law and intergenerational disputes	9	15.3	11.1
General interpersonal conflict	9	15.3	33.3
"Neuroses" and "phobias"	7	11.9	42.8
Irresponsibility and immaturity	7	11.9	14.3
Neglect of children	6	10.2	33.3
Exigencies:			
Adjustment to interfaith marriages	16	27.1	6.3
Adjustment to physical illness	14	23.7	14.3
Adjustment to interethnic marriages	9	15.3	00.0
Unemployment (temporary financial aid)	7	11.9	28.5
Counseling kin of ill clients	6	10.2	16.7
Adjustment to economic dependency	3	5.1	00.0
Problems more than half reporting clergy refer:			
Transition states:			
Problems of child-bearing and adoptions	7	11.9	85.7
Deviant behavior:			
Vague mental disorders	45	76.3	71.1
Unwed mothers	42	71.2	78.6
Alcoholism	36	61.0	69.4
Sexual problems in marriage	22	37.3	63.6
"Psychoses," "paranoia," "schizophrenia"	15	25.4	73.3
Divorce and separation	15	25.4	66.7
"Psychopaths" and "mental defectives"	4	6.8	100.0
Exigencies:			
Insufficient income	42	71.2	57.1
Physical illness	18	30.5	88.9

TABLE 1, *continued*

	CLERGY REPORTING		Per Cent Referring (of those Reporting)
	No.	Per Cent (N = 59)	
Child care and support	18	30.5	55.6
Legal problems (non-criminal)	11	18.6	63.6
Housing problems	9	15.3	77.7
Senility	8	13.6	62.5
Transients	6	10.2	83.3

Each clergyman in the sample reported collaborating with others in the deviance-controlling system. These collaborations include contacts with nonprofessionals acting as informal sources of social control as well as with those professionally concerned with the control of deviance. A clergyman who participates in a system of divided labor with others can be thought of as having a high level of activity across the boundary of his counseling role.

A boundary activity score was computed from the clergyman's responses. Each clergyman was given one point for each of three signs of articulation with the larger controlling system. Thus, a score of two or three reflects relatively high boundary activity, while a score of zero or one, low activity and a relatively impermeable role boundary. The three indexes themselves form a Guttman-type scale. The items are:

1. *Receipt of referrals or information about clients from sources outside the congregation.* This characteristic was considered to reflect the accessibility of the clergyman as a helper, and also others' recognition of this role in the helping system. Forty-two clergymen reported this item.

2. *At least one referral by the clergyman to an outside agency in the month prior to the interview.* This activity was taken to indicate that the clergyman perceives certain problems as outside his competence. Referrals indicate that he allows people to leave his sphere of influence and also that he perceives himself as acting with others in a system of divided labor. Twenty-eight clergymen reported this item.

3. *An active rather than a passive form of referral.* Some clergymen participate more actively in the referral process than others; these report that they telephone agencies to inquire if a service is available, make appointments for parishioners, or even accompany them to the agency. Other clergymen suggest to a client or parishioner where he may go for help but make no actual contact with the agency. These we call passive referrals. A passive style of referral suggests that the clergyman is less accessible for co-operative solutions of problems and is less influenced by the norms of the agency world. Twenty-six clergymen reported active participation in referrals.

The counseling of non-parishioners is another indication of the clergyman's accessibility, and forty-nine of the fifty-nine clergymen report this activity. While it does not discriminate well among them, and is therefore not included in the boundary score, this accessibility of the clergyman distinguishes him, together with some church-sponsored charitable agencies, from secular helping agencies, all of which have formal criteria of admission.

FINDINGS

As the articulation of the clergyman's counseling role was the focus of this study, the boundary activity score was examined for its relationship with the other variables. It is not, however, considered to be an independent variable. All the relationships reported appear to be causally reversible.

As Table 2 shows, boundary-activity score is independent of denomination, except for the eight fundamentalists, all of whom have scores of 0 or 1. It seems reasonable to attribute the low scores of these pastors to the fact that they are leaders of small exclusive sects, but we will return to this point later. For the remainder of the clergymen in our sample, the boundary characteristics of the counseling role must be dependent on factors other than denomination and its associated theological differences.

TABLE 2. *Number of Clergymen by Boundary-Activity Score and Denomination*

Denomination	Total No.	Boundary Score* 0–1	Boundary Score* 2–3
All clergymen	59	25	34
Roman Catholic	10	2	8
Liturgical Protestant	12	5	7
Other Protestant	26	10	16
Fundamentalist	8	8	0
Jewish	3	0	3

* Fundamentalists have a significantly higher proportion of 0 and 1 scores than all other clergymen. $P = .0005$ by Fisher's exact test.

Among the social-structural variables that have been linked to the clergyman's practices and attitudes are congregation size and socioeconomic class.[13] In Table 3 we see that boundary score is directly associated with the socioeconomic level of the congregation, and that within the working-class churches size is also associated. It may be, however, that size is itself related to status; the larger working-class churches tend to have stable congregations while the smaller ones are more likely to be "store-front" churches with impoverished or transient congregations.

TABLE 3. *Number of Clergymen by Boundary-Activity Score and Congregation Size and Class*

Congregation Type	No.	Boundary Score 0–1	Boundary Score 2–3
All congregations	59	25	34
Middle-class congregations	31	3	28*
More than 1000 members	16	1	15
Less than 1000 members	15	2	13
Working-class congregations	28	22	6*
More than 1000 members	8	3	5†
Less than 1000 members	20	19	1†

* Middle-class clergy have more high scores than working-class. $\chi^2 = 25.8$, degrees of freedom = 1, $P < 0.0001$.

† Clergymen of large working-class congregations have more high scores than those of small congregations. $P = 0.003$, Fisher's exact test.

Bearing in mind that clergymen of the largest middle-class churches have the most permeable role boundaries and those of the smallest working-class churches the least, we note that the twenty small working-class churches include seven of the eight fundamentalists, the remaining thirteen being distributed among all the remaining denominations except Roman Catholic. Controlling for church size and socioeconomic level, we find that although six of these seven fundamentalists have scores of zero, compared with six of the thirteen other remaining clergymen, this difference is not significant.[14] In short, for all churches, differences in the boundary activity appear to be associated with differences in characteristics of congregations other than denomination.

When the characteristics of the clergymen are examined, differences in boundary score are not found to be significantly associated with age. The proportion of young clergymen, 23-34 years of age, having high boundary scores is 60 per cent, which is approximately the same as the comparable proportion of 67 per cent of the clergy who are 60 years of age and older. The proportion having high boundary scores of those who are 35-44 is 52 per cent, and of those who are 45-59, 62 per cent. This is surprising because younger clergymen might be expected to have received training for their counseling roles that would bring them into contact with social workers, physicians, psychologists, and so on, and, because of this, might possibly have become integrated into the deviance-controlling system. Details of each clergyman's training as a counselor were not available, however, so a direct test of this hypothesis is not possible.

The clergymen were divided into two groups according to whether or not they had received higher education at other than a theological or

Bible school. While their level of education was found to be associated with boundary score, a much closer association was found between boundary score and the *concordance* between the clergyman's education and the socioeconomic status of his congregation.[15] Educated clergymen in middle-class churches and less-well-educated clergymen in working-class churches are considered concordant with their congregations. Educated clergymen in working-class congregations were considered discordant. There were no less-well-educated clergymen in middle-class congregations. An examination of the boundary scores of the clergymen classified according to their concordance with their congregation reveals that twenty-eight of the thirty-one clergy concordant with their middle-class congregations have high boundary scores, as compared with six of the fifteen clergy discordant with their working-class congregations and none of the thirteen clergy concordant with their working-class congregation. Comparing just the two working-class groups, the boundary score is significantly higher ($P=0.018$, Fisher's exact test) among the discordant group than among the concordant group. The clergymen of middle-class congregations have been shown in Table 3 to have higher boundary scores than those of working-class congregations. We see, then, that boundary score is strongly associated with concordance between the clergyman and his congregation, even when class is held constant.

Clergymen with high boundary scores report a higher rate of counseling activity[16] than those with low scores. Of the seventeen with a large case load, fifteen have high boundary scores. At the other extreme, only three of the fifteen with small case loads have high boundary scores. The group with medium case loads occupies an intermediate place with sixteen of the twenty-seven having high boundary scores. These differences are statistically significant ($z=3.91$; $P<.00005$, Wilcoxon signed ranks). In addition, the clergy with high boundary scores also report more types of problems in all three categories. This may mean that the impermeable boundary reduces the number of applicants, or it may mean that there are few applicants and thus the clergyman is not called upon to make the kind of contact that would give him a high boundary-activity score. Furthermore, those clergymen who have more contacts with the rest of the deviance-controlling system and who also see a larger number of clients may discriminate more finely between similar problems and thus tend to report a larger number of types. For example, a clergyman who counsels one marital problem a year calls it just that; a clergyman counseling fifty marital problems and referring ten of them to other agencies may differentiate those associated with cultural conflict from those arising from sexual maladjustment, and so on.

The clergymen from this sample of churches, regardless of their boundary conditions, report that they refer many more clients to other agents than are referred to them and they refer to many agencies that never reciprocate with referrals to them. In all, they report referring to more than 50 agencies—and the average clergyman refers to 5.4. The most popular referral targets are Planned Parenthood Association, County Welfare Department, Alcoholics Anonymous, and physicians—all agencies specializing in a specific concrete service. The clergy themselves receive referrals from an average of only 0.63 agencies, most commonly from physicians. Many Protestant clergymen expressed discontent with this asymmetry of referrals.[17]

In other studies in this series, it has been noted that social workers appear to consider clergymen "too judgmental" and have complained of their inability to "give up" the client. Clergymen, on the other hand, appear to suspect social workers of an "amorality" that will undermine their parishioners' spiritual values. Some clergymen say that social workers "hold onto" clients longer than is necessary; they complain that social agencies will not give them information that they need in order to help the parishioner.

In summary, we have found the following:

1. The hypothesis that the articulation of the clergyman's counseling role to the remaining deviance-controlling system is related to the characteristics of the congregation is lost regarding denomination, but upheld regarding size and socioeconomic status. This relationship is not, however, a simple one—concordance between education and socioeconomic status predicts boundary activity quite accurately, but discordance does not predict at all.
2. Clergymen with low boundary scores report less counseling and describe fewer types of problems brought for counseling. Nevertheless, clergymen from all types of congregations report counseling all of the three major types of problems. Deviant behavior is referred frequently; transitional problems and exigencies, less frequently.
3. The clergyman refers more clients than he receives and he uses more agents than use him. This asymmetry is related to both the readiness of the average person to approach a clergyman for help and the tensions between clergymen and some other supporting and controlling groups.

We can now discuss some possible interpretations of these findings and in particular suggest new variables that might throw more light on the clergyman's counseling role. Before doing so, however, it should be repeated that the analysis rests upon the clergyman's image of his counseling role, and although for some purposes this does not matter, systematic distortions might lead to an erroneous picture of the clergyman's position in the total integrative system.

Discussion

The findings of this study might be interpreted in a number of ways. It might be proposed that different norms develop in congregations of different social-structural types and that these norms might differ in regard to the amount of time properly spent by the clergyman on non-spiritual matters. Perhaps the most parsimonious interpretation, however, can be developed by considering the clergymen's role in the greater system and particularly the strain to which it is subject. These strains are of two kinds—those concerned with disparities between the clergyman's reference groups and his membership groups and those concerned with the position of the clergyman as counselor in the larger deviance-controlling system.

Strains between reference groups and membership groups. The clergyman's membership in his congregation can be expected to have three important outcomes. First, he will develop, in interaction, some sentiments that he shares with them. Second, he will develop, again through interaction, diffuse, solidary bonds with some members, and third, he will be identified with his congregation by those outside it.

If the clergyman has a college education he will be likely to share some attitudes with other college-trained professionals including social workers, psychologists, and physicians; such a clergyman might be expected to appear on committees with other professionals and also to know them socially.[18] Referrals from clergymen of middle-class churches should be facilitated by shared values and personal friendships, and the larger the church, the more such bridges it is likely to have. Finally, social workers and psychiatrists who know a clergyman personally are more likely to exempt him from the stigma of "judgmental clergyman," and to consider him "professionalized" or "sophisticated," and thus to co-operate with him in the management of some clients. Such a relatively conflict-free situation may well lie behind the high boundary scores of the educated clergymen of middle-class congregations.

In contrast to these educated clergymen, those in working-class congregations cannot expect so high a level of compatibility among their own attitudes, those of their congregations, and those of the agency system. Such clergymen will not have access to outside resources through overlapping memberships, although they may have personal friendships among other professionals, share many viewpoints with them, and use them as reference groups. Many studies have shown, however, that these same professionals prefer middle-class clients,[19] and the clergyman, if he has personal contacts among agency professionals, will know this and perhaps be reluctant to risk a rebuff by interceding for his parishioners. Such a situation has the conditions necessary for a classical role conflict and may be the reason for the lesser use of the agency system reported by this group of clergymen. If, on the other hand, the clergyman does not have personal contacts among professionals, he will not be subject to the same conflict, but the professionals will tend to identify him with this congregation and be doubly reluctant to accept referrals of working-class clients from an unknown, working-class, and "judgmental" clergyman. If this is so, these latter clergymen should resemble the final group, the less-well-educated clergymen in the working-class churches, and a critical test of the formulation would lie in seeing whether the discordant clergymen who referred clients had personal contacts in the target agencies while those who did not refer had none.

In working-class churches where the clergyman's lack of higher education renders him concordant with his congregation, we would expect the clergyman to have a solidary relationship with his congregation but little access to the agency system. This, together with the agencies' own preference for middle-class clients, may explain the scant use made of outside resources by these clergymen.

It is interesting that less-well-educated clergymen do not appear in our sample in middle-class churches, although it is a theoretical possibility for some Protestant denominations. Such a situation may be inherently unstable because the clergyman would be expected to have difficulty establishing bonds with either the congregation or the agency system while at the same time bonds that existed between the latter groups might be expected to exclude him.

Strains between the clergyman and the rest of the controlling system. We have hypothesized that role conflicts arise when certain kinds of clergymen minister to certain kinds of congregations. Some other types of strains can be thought of as affecting all clergymen because of the relationship of their role to the rest of the system.

The first type of strain seems to arise just because the clergyman is a familiar and accessible figure whom people feel they can approach. His accessibility forces him into a referral role. He sorts and sifts those who come to him, and allocates those that he cannot help to other services —often after a period of trial-and-error counseling. This allocation process involves defining the parishioner as sick or deviant, and he is almost always reluctant to do this when the problems are transitional or arise in exigencies. For example, clergymen often give financial help during temporary unemployment so that parishioners will be spared the humiliation of applying for public assistance. In other words, unless the clergyman is totally isolated from the control system, his position in it imposes on him the obligation of allocating clients to services, and this involves him in decisions that are difficult to make. It also involves him in an automatic asymmetry with respect to the rest of the agency system. He cannot at once be the allocator and the target agent,[20] and so he perceives himself as giving more than he gets.

Besides the strain arising from the clergyman's position, strains inhere in the counseling function. Although there is an increasing specialization among agencies offering the so-called face-to-face services, it is questionable that counseling can be distinguished clearly from intensive casework. Because of haziness about where one leaves off and the other begins, considerable attention is paid to the training required for each. Pastoral counseling is perceived as requiring less training than casework, and so the social worker tends to regard the clergyman as an amateur. His feeling of responsibility for the total client is interpreted as "incomplete professionalization" and his willingness to deal with the respondent's moral well-being is seen as judgmental—a term of anathema. All of this need not lead to conflict if the clients qualifying for casework services were clearly different from those qualifying for counseling. Our studies suggest, however, that the clergyman and the social agency compete for what is often called the "motivated client," and this competition exacerbates the tension between the two groups. The helping task might be divided between clergymen and social workers either on the basis of function or on the basis of the target population, but as neither is done, each tends to regard the other redundant. Such solidarity as exists between clergyman and social worker is based on a commonality of interest, as we have argued above, and not on interdependence. The clergymen of this study appear to have much less strain in their dealings with physicians, lawyers, housing authorities, and other agents whose specific functions do not overlap with their own.

Finally, the membership of the clergyman in the group he counsels puts him in a position similar to that of the physician who will not treat his family and dislikes treating his friends. For all clergymen, this strain may act as an encouragement to refer. Those whose structural situation cuts them off entirely from the world of social agencies may be reducing the strain by circumscribing their counseling activities.

Returning to our point of departure—the division of labor among the integrative agents—we can see that the clergyman's position in the system involves him in a dual role. He is a counselor, but because he is approached so early in the search for help, he is called upon to allocate many clients to other agencies. The frustration that the clergyman experiences because of the asymmetry of his relationship with other agents appears to be offset by the rewards attendant upon his historic role as counselor—a role that he views as an intrinsic part of his ministry.

1. A revision of a paper read to the annual meetings of the American Sociological Association, Washington, D.C., 1962. The research reported was supported in part by NIMH Grant 4735, principal investigator, Elaine Cumming. Acknowledgment is made of the assistance of the staff of the Mental Health Research Unit, Syracuse, N.Y., and its director, John Cumming, under whose auspices the studies are taking place.

2. See Benton Johnson, "The Development of Pastoral Counseling Programs in Protestantism: A Sociological Perspective," *Pacific Sociological Review,* I (Fall, 1958), 59-63, and Robert S. Michaelsen, "The Protestant Ministry in America: 1850 to the Present," in H. Richard Niebuhr and Daniel D. Williams (eds.), *The Ministry in Historical Perspective* (New York, 1956).

3. *Action for Mental Health: The Final Report of the Joint Commission on Mental Illness and Health* (New York, 1961).

4. See Elaine Cumming, "Phase Movement in the Support and Control of the Psychiatric Patient," *Journal of Health and Human Behavior,* III (Winter, 1962), 235-41 (also see Bruce D. Dohrenwend, "Some Aspects of the Appraisal of Abnormal Behavior by Leaders in an Urban Area," *American Psychologist,* XVII, No. 4 [1962], 190-98).

5. Gerald Gurin, Joseph Veroff, and Shiela Feld, *Americans View Their Mental Health,* Vol. IV of a series of monographs published by the Joint Commission on Mental Illness and Health (New York, 1960).

6. Joseph W. Eaton *et al., Pastoral Counseling in a Metropolitan Suburb* (Pittsburgh: Southeastern Community Guidance Association [4232 Brownsville Rd.], 1961).

7. See Samuel Blizzard, "Role Conflicts of the Urban Parish Minister," *City Church,* VII (September, 1956), 13-15, and Allan W. Eister, "Religious Institutions in Complex Societies: Difficulties in the Theoretic Specifications of Functions," *American Sociological Review,* XXII (August, 1957), 387-91; see also Warren O. Hagstrom, "The Protestant Clergy as a Profession: Status and Prospects," *Berkeley Pub. Soc. Instit.,* III, No. 1 (Spring, 1957), 1-12; Waldo Burchard, "Role Conflicts of Military Chaplains," *American Sociological Review,* XIX, No. 5 (1954), 528-35; and Blizzard, *op cit.*

8. See Joseph H. Fichter, S.J., *Social Relations in the Urban Parish* (Chicago: University of Chicago Press, 1954), chap. x; Burchard, *op. cit.;* Ernest Campbell and Thomas F. Pettigrew, "Racial and Moral Crisis: The Role of Little Rock Ministers," *American Journal of Sociology,* LXIV (March, 1959), 509-16; Michaelsen, *op. cit.,* Lee Braude, "Professional Autonomy and the Role of the Layman," *Social Forces,* May, 1961.

9. For a general discussion of this point see Talcott Parsons, *The Social System* (Glencoe, Ill.: Free Press, 1950), chap. x; Charles Kadushin, "Social Distance between Client and Professional," *American Journal of Sociology,* LXVII (March, 1962), 517; and Campbell and Pettigrew, *op. cit.*

10. Church names and addresses were taken from the City Directory; local church officials contributed further details. Size was classified as follows: small, up to 150 total members; medium, 150-500; large, 500-1,000; and very large, over 1,000. Neighborhood status was taken from Charles V. Willie, "Socioeconomic and Ethnic Areas" (unpublished Ph.D. dissertation, Syracuse University, 1957). The neighborhoods were classified as upper, middle, lower and mixed metropolitan. The empty cells in the stratification plan are accounted for chiefly by the absence of small Roman Catholic churches and large fundamentalist churches. The latter group included the so-called store-front churches, seven of which no longer existed at the time of the research. These were replaced by further random choices from the cells. The sample included 10 of the 22 Roman Catholic churches, 6 of the 12 Episcopal, 3 of the 7 Lutheran, 3 of the 11 Eastern, 8 of the 17 Methodist, 7 of the 8 Presbyterian, 5 of the 15 Baptist, 10 of the 21 fundamentalist, 3 of the 8 Jewish, and 6 of the remaining 15 churches of other Protestant denominations. This represents, in terms of the grouping used, 45 per cent of the Roman Catholic, 40 per cent of the liturgical, 47 per cent of the other Protestant, 48 per cent of the fundamentalist, and 37 per cent of the Jewish churches.

11. Two fundamentalist clergymen refused to be interviewed, although eight attempts were made in each case.

12. Downtown churches with congregations of mixed economic status were classed as middle class, while those with only a few elderly wealthy people and a majority of very poor parishioners were classed as working class. The latter churches were once fashionable, but have been left in areas of transition and decay.

13. See Fichter, *op. cit.*, and Russell R. Dynes, "Church-Sect Typology and Socioeconomic Status," *American Sociological Review*, Vol. XX (October, 1955); Thomas F. Hoult, *The Sociology of Religion* (New York, 1958); Max Weber, *Essays in Sociology* (New York, 1946); Louis Bultena, "Church Membership and Church Attendance in Madison, Wisconsin," *American Sociological Review*, XIV (1950), 364-388; and Walter Goldschmidt, "Clan Denominationalism in Rural California Churches," *American Journal of Sociology*, LXI (1944), 348-55.

14. We have suggested above that the fundamentalists are qualitatively different from other denominations, but it is possible that, as they are the smallest and poorest churches, they represent only the final type in a series with graded boundary permeability. The numbers are so small, however, that the issue remains open.

15. The middle-class concordant clergy includes: four Roman Catholic, five Episcopal, three other liturgical, sixteen Protestant, and three Jewish. The working-class discordant group includes: six Roman Catholic, one Episcopal, two other liturgical, five Protestant, one fundamentalist. The clergy concordant with working-class congregations includes: five Protestant, seven fundamentalist, and one liturgical.

16. The size of the clergyman's case load was ranked by two coders independently, using answers to all relevant interview questions. All differences were then resolved between the coders.

17. For a discussion of this strain see George Todd Kalif, "Pastoral Use of Community Resources," *Pastoral Psychology*, November, 1950.

18. Seven clergymen within our sample are board members of agencies affiliated with the Community Chest. Of these, six are from middle-class congregations, as we would expect. The lone clergyman from a working-class congregation seems a special case. He has retired from administrative positions in denominational agencies and has recently agreed to come out of retirement to minister to a small congregation that cannot afford to hire a full-time clergyman because it is in a depressed transitional area of town. His position in an agency board—a church affiliated one—seems to be a function of his past activity in agencies rather than his present ministry.

19. See Jerome K. Myers and Leslie Schaffer, "Social Stratification and Psychiatric Practice: A Study of an Out-Patient Clinic," *American Sociological Review*, XIX (June, 1954), 307-10.

20. In this he differs from the physician. In our own studies we have found (see, e.g., n. 4) that the general practitioner is also a gatekeeper in the sense that people turn to him when informal resources fail, but he receives as many patients by referral as he sends to other agencies, and thus does not perceive himself as supplying other people with patients and receiving none in return.

ERNEST Q. CAMPBELL
THOMAS F. PETTIGREW

Racial and Moral Crisis: The Role of Little Rock Ministers

This paper[1] analyzes the conduct of the ministers in established denominations in Little Rock, Arkansas, during the crisis over the admission of Negro students to the Central High School in the fall of 1957. How do ministers behave in racial crisis, caught between integrationist and segregationist forces?

One might expect that Little Rock's clergymen would favor school integration. All the major national Protestant bodies have adopted forceful declarations commending the Supreme Court's desegregation decision of 1954 and urging their members to comply with it. And southern pastors have voted in favor of these statements at their church conferences—and sometimes have even issued similar pronouncements to their own congregations.[2] But the southern man of God faces serious congregational opposition if he attempts to express his integrationist beliefs publicly in the local community. The vast majority of southern whites—even those living in the Middle South—are definitely against racial desegregation.[3]

The purpose of this study is to determine how the ministers of established denominations in Little Rock behaved in the conflict. In analyzing their behavior, we treat self-expectations as an independent variable. This is contrary to the usual course, in which the actor is important analytically only because he is caught between contradictory *external* expectations. The standard model of role conflict treats ego as forced to decide between the incompatible norms of groups that can impose sanctions for nonconformity. This model—which is essentially what Lazarsfeld means by cross-pressures—skirts the issue of whether ego imposes expectations on itself and punishes deviations. Pressure and sanction are external to the actor. Hence the typical model tends to be ahistorical in the sense that a finite number of cross-pressuring groups are used to predict the actor's behavior. It is assumed that the actor cannot have developed from periods of prior socialization any normative expectations for his behavior which would have an independent existence.[4] This additional variable—the actor's expectations of himself —is especially meaningful in the analysis.

Though it is a city of approximately 125,000, Little Rock has much of the atmosphere and easy communication of a small town. It is located in almost the geometric center of the state, and physically and culturally it borders on both the Deep South–like delta country to the east and south and the Mountain South–like hill country to the west and north. Thus Little Rock is not a city of the Deep South. Its public transportation had been successfully integrated in 1956, and its voters, as late as March, 1957, had elected two men to the school board who supported the board's plan for token integration of Central High School. And yet Little Rock is a southern city, with southern traditions of race relations. These patterns became of world-wide interest after Governor Faubus called out the National Guard to prevent desegregation and thereby set off the most publicized and the most critical chain of events in the integration process to date.

Only two ministers devoted their sermons to the impending change on the Sunday before the fateful opening of school in September, 1957. Both warmly approved of the step and hoped for its success. Other ministers alluded to it in prayer or comment. It was commonly believed that a majority of the leading denominations' clergy favored the school board's "gradual" plan. This impression seemed confirmed when immediately after Governor Faubus had surrounded Central High with troops fifteen of the city's most prominent ministers issued a protest in, according to the local *Arkansas Gazette,* "the strongest language permissible to men of God."

When Negro students appeared at the high school for the first time, they were escorted by four white Protestant ministers and a number of prominent Negro leaders. Two of the four whites are local clergymen, one being the president of the biracial ministerial association, the other, president of the local Human Relations Council. Many of the more influential ministers of the city had been asked the night before to join this escort. Some demurred; others said they would try to come. Only two appeared.

On September 23, the day of the rioting near Central High School, several leaders of the ministerial association personally urged immediate counteraction on the mayor and the chief of police. Later, support was solicited from selected ministers in the state to issue a declaration of Christian principle, but dissension over the statement prevented its publication. Indeed, *no* systematic attempts were made by the clergy to appeal to the conscience of the community. Such statements as individual ministers did express were usually—though not always—appeals for "law and order" rather than a Christian defense of the principle of desegregation.

Several weeks after the rioting, plans for a community-wide prayer service began to develop. Care was taken to present this service in as neutral terms as possible. Compromise and reconciliation were stressed: never was it described as organized prayers for integration. And indorsements came from both sides of the controversy—from President Eisenhower and from Governor Faubus. As one of the sponsors put it: "Good Christians can honestly disagree on the question of segregation or integration. But we can all join together in prayers for guidance, that peace may return to our city." The services in the co-operating churches were held on Columbus Day, October 12. All the leading churches participated, with only the working-class sects conspicuously missing. The services varied widely from informal prayers to elaborate programs, and attendances varied widely, too, and totaled perhaps six thousand.

These "prayers for peace" may best be viewed as a ritualistic termination of any attempts by the clergy to direct the course of events in the racial crisis. The prayers had met the national demand for ministerial action and the ministers' own need to act; and they had completed the whole unpleasant business. Despite sporadic efforts by a small number to undertake more effective steps, the ministers lapsed into a general silence that continued throughout the school year.

We began our work in Little Rock in the week after the peace prayers. Following a series of background interviews and a careful analysis of ministerial action as recorded in the press, twenty-nine detailed interviews with ministers were held.[5] Twenty-seven of them are Protestants and two are Jewish; the Roman Catholics did not co-operate.

This sample was not selected randomly; the so-called "snowball technique" was used in order to include the most influential church leaders. This involves asking each interviewee to name the members of the Little Rock clergy that he considers to be "the most influential." The first interview was made with an announced leader of the peace prayers, and interviewing was continued with all the men mentioned as influential until no new names were suggested. We added a number of ministers who were not named but who had taken strongly liberal positions during the crisis. Thus our sample is most heavily weighted with the pastors of the larger churches with the greatest prestige and the pastors of smaller churches who had assumed active roles in the conflict. These two groups, we anticipated, would have to contend with the greatest amount of incompatibility in role.

Most of the interviews were held in the church offices. Rapport, which was generally excellent, was partly secured by the authors' identification with southern educational institutions. A detailed summary, as nearly as possible a verbatim account, was placed on Audograph recording equipment shortly after the completion of each interview. Information in three broad areas was sought, and to this end a series of open-ended questions was developed. A series of questions was aimed at determining whether the respondent was a segregationist or an integrationist. A segregationist here is defined as one who prefers racial barriers as presently constituted; an integrationist is one to whom the removal of legal and artificial barriers to racial contact is morally preferable to the present system.[6]

Each interviewee was asked to give a complete account of what he had done and said in both his parish and in the community at large regarding the racial crisis. If he had not been active or vocal, we probed him for the reason and to learn if he had felt guilty over his failure to state the moral imperatives.

A final set of questions dealt with the pastor's perception of his congregation's reaction to whatever stand he had taken. If pressure had been applied on him by his parishioners, we probed him to learn exactly what pressure had been used and how.

The Segregationist

Only five of the twenty-nine clergymen we interviewed were segregationists by our definition. None was avidly so, and, unlike segregationist ministers of the sects, none depended on "chapter-and-verse Scripture" to defend his stand. All men in their late fifties or sixties, they did not think that the crisis was a religious matter. One of them was a supervising administrator in a denominational hierarchy. Although all five were affiliated with prominent denominations, they were not among the leaders of the local ministerial body.

These five men have not been publicly active in defending segregation.[7] Each was opposed to violence, and none showed evidence of internal discomfort or conflict. All five co-operated with the neutrally toned prayers for peace. As one of them commented, "You certainly can't go wrong by praying. Praying can't hurt you on anything."

The Inactive Integrationist

Inactive integrationists had done enough—or believed they had done enough—to acquaint their congregations with their sympathy with racial tolerance and integration, but during the crucial weeks of the crisis they were generally silent. These, representing as they do all major denominations, varied considerably as to age and size of church served. Included among them were virtually all the ministers of high prestige, many of whom had signed the protest against Governor Faubus at the start of the crisis and later were advocates of the peace prayer services. Some had spoken out in favor of "law and order" and in criticism of violence. They had not, however, defended the continued attendance of the Negro students in the high school, and they had not challenged their members to defend educational desegregation as a Christian obligation. They were publicly viewed as integrationists only because they had supported "law and order" and had not defended segregation.

Altogether, the inactive integrationists comprise sixteen out of the twenty-nine of our sample. Because it was not a random sample, we cannot draw inferences regarding the division of the total ministerial community or of ministers of established denominations into integrationist and segregationist camps. However, since the sample under-represents the uninfluential minister who had not been in the public eye during the crisis, we may conclude that a large majority of Little Rock's men of God did not encourage their members to define the issue as religious, nor did they initiate actions or participate in programs aimed at integration.

The Active Integrationist

Eight of our respondents can be designated as active integrationists because they continued to defend integration in principle and to insist that support of racial integration is nothing less than a Christian imperative. They were, on the whole, young men who have headed their small churches for only a few years. Most were disturbed that the churches of the city were segregated; some have urged their churches to admit Negroes.

Most of the active integrationists had serious difficulty with their members because of their activities, evidence of which was lowered Sunday-morning attendance, requests for transfer, diminished giving, personal snubs and insults, and rumors of sentiment for their dismissal. One had concluded that his usefulness to his congregation had ended and accordingly had requested to be transferred. By the end of 1958, several others had been removed from their pulpits.

One thing all twenty-nine of the sample had in common was a segregationist congregation.[8] Without exception, they believed that the majority of their members were strong opponents of racial integration. The highest estimate given by any integrationist of the proportion of his congregation which supported his views was 40 per cent; the median estimate for segregation was 75 per cent. Only three interviewees thought that a majority of their members would "accept" a strong public defense of integration by their minister.

Personal integrity, alone, would lead the liberal Little Rock minister to defend integration and condemn those who support segregation. However, the minister is obligated to consider the expectations of his church membership, especially inasmuch as the members' reactions bear upon his own effectiveness.

When an individual is responsible to a public, we distinguish three systems as relevant to his behavior: the self-reference system (SRS), the professional reference system (PRS), and the membership reference system (MRS). The SRS consists of the actor's demands, expectations, and images regarding himself. It may be thought of as what the actor would do in the absence of sanctions from external sources. We have already seen that typically the SRS would support racial integration.[9] The PRS consists of several sources mutually related to his occupational role yet independent of his congregation: national and regional church bodies, the local ecclesiastical hierarchy, if any, the local ministerial association, personal contacts and friendships with fellow ministers, and, probably, an image of "my church." Finally, the MRS consists simply of the minister's congregation. We have already seen that it favored segregation or at least ministerial neutrality.

The net effect of three reference systems seems to favor the cause of integration. Were they equal in strength, and were there no contrary forces internal to any of them, this conclusion is obvious. The minister would then feel committed to support the official national policy of his denomination; his knowledge that fellow ministers were similarly committed would support him, and the local hierarchy would encourage him to make this decision and reassure him should his congregation threaten disaffection. These external influences would reinforce his own values, resulting in forthright action in stating and urging the Christian imperatives. However, internal inconsistencies in the PRS and the SRS restrain what on first examination appears to be an influence toward the defense of integration.

The Professional Reference System

Two overriding characteristics of the PRS minimize its liberalizing influence. First, most of its components cannot or do not impose sanctions for non-conformity to their expectations. Second, those parts of the PRS that can impose sanctions also impose other demands on the minister, inconsistent with the defense of racial integration before members who, in large part, believe in racial separation and whose beliefs are profoundly emotional.

The Inability to Impose Sanctions

The national and regional associations that serve as the official "voice of the church" are not organized to confer effective rewards or punishments on individual ministers. Especially is this true in the case of failure to espouse national racial policy or to act decisively in the presence of racial tension. This is even more true of the local ministerial association; it does not presume to censure or praise its members. Conversely, the local church hierarchy is an immediate source of sanctions. It has the responsibility of recommending or assigning parishes, and of assisting the pastor in expanding the program of his church.

The probability and the nature of sanctions from fellow ministers among whom one has personal contacts and friends are somewhat more difficult to specify. However, it does not appear likely that he is subject to sanctions if he does not conform to their expectations by liberal behavior on racial matters. Should he indorse and actively support segregationist and violent elements, this would be another matter. If he is silent or guarded, however, it is not likely to subject him to sanction. The active integrationists in Little Rock expressed disappointment at the inaction of their associates while at the same time suggesting possible mitigating circumstances. There is no evidence that personal or professional ties had been damaged.

Among the various components of the PRS, then, only the local ecclesiastica, which does not exist for some, and, to a considerably lesser extent, fellow ministers, are conceivable sources influencing the minister's decision to be silent, restrained, or forthright.

Conflicting Expectations and Mitigated Pressures

The role of the minister as community reformer is not as institutionalized (i.e., it does not have as significant a built-in system of rewards and punishments) as are certain other roles associated with the ministry. The minister is responsible for the over-all conduct of the affairs of the church and is judged successful or unsuccessful according to how they prosper. He must encourage co-operative endeavor, reconciling differences, and bring people together. Vigor and high morale of the membership are reflected in increased financial support and a growing membership, and his fellow ministers and his church superiors are keenly sensitive to these evidences of his effectiveness. His goal, elusive though it may be, is maximum support from all members of an ever growing congregation.

The church hierarchy keeps records. It hears reports and rumors. It does not like to see divided congregations, alienated ministers, reduced membership, or decreased contributions. Responsible as it is for the destiny of the denomination in a given territory, it compares its changing fortunes with those of rival churches. In assigning ministers to parishes, it rewards some with prominent pulpits and punishes others with posts of low prestige or little promise. However exalted the moral virtue the minister expounds, the hierarchy does not wish him to damn his listeners to hell—unless somehow he gets them back in time to attend service next Sunday. Promotions for him are determined far less by the number of times he defends unpopular causes, however virtuous their merit, than by the state of the physical plant and the state of the coffer.

Now it is especially commendable if the minister can defend the cause and state the imperative with such tact or imprint that cleavages are not opened or loyalties alienated. If, however, the moral imperative and church cohesion are mutually incompatible, there is little doubt that the church superiors favor the latter. One administrator told two of his ministers, "It's o.k. to be liberal, boys; just don't stick your neck out." Indeed, ecclesiastical officials advised younger ministers, systematically, to "go slow," reminding them of the possibility of permanent damage to the church through rash action.

Under these circumstances pressure from the national church to take an advanced position on racial matters loses much of its force. The minister is rewarded *only* if his efforts do not endanger the membership of the church: "Don't lose your congregation." Similarly, the prospect of an unfavorable response from his congregation protects him from the (possibly liberal) church hierarchy; he need only point to what happened to Pastor X, who did not heed the rumblings in his congregation. The higher officials, themselves keenly aware of local values and customs, will understand. And his fellow ministers, too, are, after all, in the same boat. They give him sympathy, not censure, if he says, "My hands are tied." An informal rationale develops that reassures the pastor: "These things take time," "You can't change people overnight," "You can't talk to people when they won't listen." There is strong sympathy for the forthright pastor who is in real trouble, but he is looked on as an object lesson. Thus the ministers reinforce each other in inaction, despite their common antipathy to segregation.

The Self-reference System

We still must reckon with the demands the minister imposes upon himself. It is obvious that the actor has the power of self-sanction, through guilt. A threatening sense of unworthiness, of inadequacy in God's sight, cannot be taken lightly. Similarly, to grant one's self the biblical commendation "Well done" is a significant reward. We have said that the self is an influence favoring action in support of desegregation. Can the inactive integrationist, then, either avoid or control the sense of guilt?

Our data are not entirely appropriate to the question. Nevertheless, four circumstances—all of which permit of generalization to other cases—appear at least partially to prevent the sense of guilt. These include major characteristics of the ministerial role, several ministerial values and "working propositions," certain techniques for communicating without explicit commitment, and the gratifying reactions of extreme opposition forces.

The Role Structure

The church, as an institutional structure, sets criteria by which the minister may assess his management of the religious enterprise; it does *not* offer criteria by which to evaluate his stand on controversial issues.[10] This encourages, even compels, the minister to base his self-image, hence his sense of worth or unworth, on his success in managing his church. Thus, if church members do not share his goals, three types of institutionalized responsibilities restrain him in reform.

In the first place, the minister is required to be a cohesive force, to "maintain a fellowship in peace, harmony, and Christian love," rather than to promote dissension. Thus some ministers prayed during the Columbus Day services that members "carry no opinion to the point of disrupting the Christian fellowship."

Second, he is expected to show a progressive increase in the membership of his church. Pro-integration activity, lacking mass support, is likely to drive members to other churches.

Finally, his task is to encourage maximum annual giving and to plan for the improvement and expansion of the plant. It is hardly surprising that several inactive integrationists who were engaged in vital fund-raising campaigns shrank from action that might endanger their success.

Working Propositions

The minister makes certain assumptions about his work that reduce the likelihood of guilt when he does not defend moral convictions that his members reject. He is, first, a devotee of education, by which he means the gradual growth and development of spiritual assets—in contrast to his counterpart of an earlier period, who was more likely to believe in sudden change through conversion. He also believes that communication with the sinner must be preserved at all costs ("You can't teach those you can't reach") and for long enough to effect gradual change in attitude and behavior. A crisis, when feelings run high, is not the time to risk alienating those one wishes to change. For example, Pastor X acted decisively but, in so doing, damaged or lost his pastorate: "Look at him; he can't do any good now."

Communication Techniques

The minister may avoid committing himself unequivocally.[11] Some use the "every man a priest" technique, for example, the stating of his own opinion while expressing tolerance for contradictory ones and reminding his listeners that their access to God's truth is equal with his. Others use the "deeper issues" approach; generalities such as the brotherhood of man, brotherly love, humility, and universal justice are discussed without specific reference to the race issue, in the hope that the listener may make the association himself. Still another course is to remind listeners that "God is watching," that the question of race has religious significance and therefore they should "act like Christians." There is also the method of deriding the avowed segregationists without supporting their opposites. The "exaggerated southerner" technique, which may be supplementary to any of the others, involves a heavy southern drawl and, where possible, reference to an aristocratic line of planter descent.

These techniques do not demand belief in integration as a Christian imperative. Further, except for the "every man a priest" technique, they do not commit the speaker to integrationist goals as religious values; the listener may make applications as he chooses. The speaker, on the other hand, can assure himself that the connections are there to be made; he supplies, as it were, a do-it-yourself moral kit.

Reaction of the Opposition

The ministerial body in Little Rock, except for pastors to dissident fundamentalist sects, is defined by agitated segregationists as a bunch of "race-mixers" and "nigger-lovers." For example, the charge was made that the peace prayers were intended to "further integration under a hypocritical veneer of prayer" and that the sect pastors sponsored prayers for segregation "to show that not all of the city's ministers believe in mixing the races." Indeed, ministers of major denominations were charged with having "race on the mind" so that they were straying from, even rejecting, the biblical standard to further their un-Christian goals.

The effect of opposition by segregation extremists was to convince certain inactive integrationists that indeed they *had* been courageous and forthright. The minister, having actually appropriated the opposition's evaluation of his behavior, reversing its affective tone found the reassurance he needed that his personal convictions had been adequately and forcefully expressed.

Were the force of the membership reference system not what it is, the professional reference system and the self-reference system would supply support to integration that was not limited to "law and order" appeals and the denunciation of violence. However, since "Don't lose your congregation" is itself a strong professional and personal demand, the force of the PRS is neutralized, and the pressure from the SRS becomes confused and conflicting. Inaction is a typical response to conflicting pressures within both the internal and the external system.

It is not surprising, then, that most Little Rock ministers have been far less active and vocal in the racial crisis than the policies of their national church bodies and their sense of identification with them, as well as their own value systems, would lead one to expect. Rather, what is surprising is that a small number continued to express vigorously the moral imperative as they saw it, in the face of congregational disaffection, threatened reprisal, and the lukewarm support or quiet discouragement of their superiors and peers.

---

1. This study was supported by a grant from the Laboratory of Social Relations, Harvard University. The authors wish to express their gratitude to Professor Samuel A. Stouffer for his suggestions. Two brief popular accounts of aspects of this study have appeared previously: "Men of God in Racial Crisis," *Christian Century,* LXXV (June 4, 1958), 663-65, and "Vignettes from Little Rock," *Christianity and Crisis,* XVIII (September 29, 1958), 128-36.

2. For example, local ministerial groups issued such statements in New Orleans, Louisiana; Richmond, Virginia; Dallas and Houston, Texas; and Atlanta, Macon, and Columbus, Georgia. For a review of national church statements see "Protestantism Speaks on Justice and Integration," *Christian Century,* LXXV (February 5, 1958), 164-66.

3. A 1956 National Opinion Research Center poll indicated that only one in every seven white southerners approves school integration (H. H. Hyman and P. B. Sheatsley, "Attitudes toward Desegregation," *Scientific American,* CXCV [December, 1956], 35-39). A 1956 survey by the American Institute of Public Opinion showed that in the Middle South—including Arkansas—only one in five whites approved of school integration (M. M. Tumin, *Segregation and Desegregation* [New York: Anti-Defamation League of B'nai B'rith, 1957], p. 109).

4. By showing that the actor may have a predisposition toward either a particularistic or a universalistic "solution" to role conflicts in instances where the particularistic-universalistic dimension is relevant, Stouffer and Toby link the study of personality to that of role obligations in a way rarely done (Samuel A. Stouffer and Jackson Toby, "Role Conflict and Personality," *American Journal of Sociology,* LVI [March, 1951], 395-406). This study, however, treats the personal predisposition as a determinant of conflict resolution rather than a factor in conflict development. Much the same is true of Gross's analysis (Neal Gross, Ward S. Mason, and Alexander McEachern, *Explorations in Role Analysis: Studies of the School Superintendency Role* [New York: John Wiley & Sons, 1958], esp. chaps. xv, xvi, and xvii).

5. Thirteen additional interviews were held with the sect leaders of an openly pro-segregation prayer service. None of these were members of the ministerial association or were in personal contact with any ministers of the established denominations. A detailed report on them will be published.

6. Using the interview, three judges, the two authors and a graduate assistant, independently rated each respondent as either a segregationist or an integrationist. Agreement between the three raters was complete for twenty-seven of the twenty-nine cases.

7. Again, this is in contrast to the sect segregationists. One sect minister is president and another is the chaplain of the local Citizens' Council.

8. Our study of a modest sample of church members bore out the ministers' estimates of predominantly pro-segregation sentiment in their congregations.

9. Although groups make demands, impose sanctions, and significantly affect the actors' self-expectations and self-sanctions, nevertheless, we treat the self-reference system as an independent variable in role conflict. This system seems especially significant where personal action is contrary to the pressure of known and significant groups.

10. Blizzard does not find a "community reformer" or "social critic" role in the ministry (see Samuel W. Blizzard, "The Minister's Dilemma," *Christian Century,* LXXIII [April 25, 1956], 508-10).

11. For a full description and illustration of such techniques as used in Little Rock see our *Christians in Racial Crisis: A Study of Little Rock's Ministers* (Washington, D.C.: Public Affairs Press, 1959).

PHILLIP E. HAMMOND

The Campus Ministerial Mind

In one sense, the campus ministry has met the condition of recruitment. Fully 6 per cent of present-day Protestant seminarians plan eventually to be campus ministers.[1] Inasmuch as only 1 per cent of the current clergy are campus clergymen, church and college should have no trouble filling campus ministerial positions and doing so with considerable selectivity and/or expansion. Neither, it would appear, does the campus ministry have trouble filling counterpositions. Parish ministers, parishioners, and denominational officials—all of whom may have an interest in, and interaction with, campus ministers—are already "available" to play their parts. So it is with students, faculty, and administration on the campus. These role-partners, too, are already "recruited." By going to them, the campus minister, though he may have trouble *motivating* them to play their parts, has at least answered the question of who are the appropriate role-partners.[2]

From pp. 41-59 of Chapter 3, "The Campus Ministerial Mind" of *The Campus Clergyman* by Phillip E. Hammond, © 1966 by Phillip E. Hammond, Basic Books, Inc., Publishers, New York. Reprinted by permission.

But it is only in one sense that the recruitment condition is met. *How* it is met—with what kinds of people—is the subject of this chapter. We want, in these pages, to look at the nature of persons in the positions of chaplain and university pastor. We shall then see that, despite considerable variation within these ranks, a predominating *kind* of person is being recruited. A "campus ministerial mind" will emerge from the findings.

The Unorthodoxy of Campus Ministers

Clergy on campus are, of course, clergymen. As obvious as that appears, it bears repeating. For, though one of the aims of this chapter is to describe the different values and attitudes among campus ministers, we should remember that the great majority (87 per cent) are ordained, and most of the remainder have had some seminary exposure. They have chosen the ministry as a vocation, have trained for it, and thus share with all ministers a great many of the characteristics distinguishing the clergy from other occupations.

Campus ministers are not representative of all ministers, however. Whether through self-selection, recruitment policy, or experiences of the campus, those who minister to higher education differ systematically from their counterparts. They are politically more liberal, have more interest in news of national and world affairs (though less in denominational news), and reveal more support for the ecumenical movement. They are more critical of their denominations, have more formal education, and are more favorable to churches' taking stronger interest in social action. In these ways, the "mind" of the campus minister differs from that of his parish colleague. Evidence is found in Table 1.

The evidence is convincing. The parish minister data are recent, they include ten of the same denominations used in the present study, and they permit comparisons within several age groups. The last point is especially worth emphasizing because, though these dissimilarities might be widely acknowledged, they might also be attributed solely to the youthfulness of campus ministers, thus implying not a real but a spurious difference. Yet, in fact, denomination by denomination and age group by age group, campus and parish ministerial differences persist.[3] Campus clergy *are* systematically different from parish clergy.

How might the distinctions be summarized? Certainly one strong component underlying the items of Table 1 is the critical view of the organized church. Campus ministers more readily admonish their denominations for various faults. Another component is campus minis-

TABLE 1. *The Percentage of Campus Ministers and Parish Ministers Who Agree with Various Statements*

Statement	Campus Minister (N = 997)	Parish Minister (N = 3,928)*
POLITICAL ATTITUDES		
1. Strongly approve of the purposes of the United Nations	73%	57%
2. Strongly approve of the purposes of the AFL-CIO	21	11
BREADTH OF INTEREST		
3. Regularly read *Christian Century*	67	33
4. Regularly read *Christianity and Crisis*	44	6
5. Very interested in news of national and international affairs	75	62
6. Very interested in news of own denomination	35	68
7. Very or quite interested in news of other denominations	57	68
THE CHURCH AND SOCIAL ACTION		
8. Would very much like to see church-sponsored examination of major ethical issues†	66	57
9. Agree own denomination is too conservative in the field of social action	53	17
ECUMENICAL ATTITUDES		
10. Agree own denomination is not sufficiently ecumenical-minded	42	10
11. Strongly approve of the National Council of Churches	51	42
12. Strongly approve of the World Council of Churches	59	44
MISCELLANEOUS		
13. Agree own denomination does not have clearly defined policies	27	15
14. Have a Bachelor of Divinity degree	84	65
15. Have a Ph.D. degree	13	2
16. Choose, as closest to own belief regarding the Bible, "an infallible revelation of God's will" ‡	8	24

*These data were collected in 1960 by Robert E. Mitchell, then at the Bureau of Applied Social Research, Columbia University. His analysis appears in *The Professional Protestant* (forthcoming). The ten denominations he included are the same ten that include all but 29 of the 997 campus ministers of the present study. Mitchell's cooperation is gratefully acknowledged.

† The question to campus ministers read: ". . . see greater social education or action by Protestants."

‡ Other options: "inspired by God, but subject to historical criticism," and "a great history of religious experience, but not necessarily inspired by God." These two were chosen by 84 per cent and 7 per cent respectively of campus ministers, by 70 per cent and 3 per cent respectively of parish ministers.

ters' greater support of such agencies of change as the United Nations, the AFL-CIO, and the World Council of Churches. And a third component, overlapping the first and second, is a greater impatience with "denominationalism," with the present boundaries that separate the various churches. Were one to decide on a single term to describe how campus ministers differ from parish ministers, therefore, an appropriate choice might be "unorthodox." At least in the context of their work and organizations, campus clergymen are less orthodox than their parish equivalents. They are less traditional and favor more change.[4]

Civil Libertarianism

Additional available information suggests that campus ministers are not merely less orthodox than other ministers. Compared with some other groups, they score as unorthodox. For example, in a poll of the American public in 1954, Stouffer discovered that 89 per cent would fire from a college faculty a person who "admits to being a Communist." Only slightly fewer (86 per cent) of the community leaders (newspaper editors, club presidents, and so forth) would do the same.[5] A year later, in 1955, Lazarsfeld and Thielens asked the same question of social-science professors in American colleges and discovered that 44 per cent held this view.[6] In 1963, when asked if an admitted Communist should be fired from a faculty post, only 16 per cent of campus ministers said yes.

It is probably true that a question like this one, asked near the height of McCarthyism and in personal interview, will evoke a more restrictive answer. Had campus ministers been questioned in a similar climate and by an interviewer rather than mail questionnaire, their answers may have been less libertarian. However, if taboos regarding domestic Communism have relaxed in the last decade, it is by no means certain that taboos regarding atheists have. The following data, therefore, lend support to the proposition that campus clergymen are relatively libertarian. The question deals with an atheist, a person who wants "to make a speech . . . against churches and religion." Table 2 shows the proportions of the general public, community leaders, and campus clergy who would allow such a person "to teach in a college or university."[7]

Table 2

American public	12%
Community leaders	25%
Campus ministers (answering about a church-related college)	36%
Campus ministers (answering about a publicly supported college)	67%

Even in an area—atheism in a faculty—very important to them, campus ministers are more permissive than most Americans. But this point of view extends to other aspects of educational policy as well. Two questions dealing with proper classroom behavior, asked of social-science professors, were asked in identical or similar form of campus clergy. One inquired about the handling of "traditional values" in the lecture hall:

> *In teaching subjects which might require questioning of traditional values, which of these two approaches do you feel is a better educational policy for instructors to follow?*
>
> 1. After proper discussion, to argue in a measured way for their own points of view.
> 2. To give all sides of the question impartially without revealing their own views.

Social-science professors, in 1955, chose the first answer in 38 per cent of the cases;[8] twice that proportion (77 per cent) of campus ministers did so. Granted, a campus clergyman who wants students indoctrinated with a viewpoint and who trusts that the faculty share it with him might want that viewpoint argued in the classroom. But not many situations like that can exist when (as is the case) half of all campus ministers agree that higher education is "too secular, too cavalier with students' faith," and fully three-fourths agree that higher education "does not show realistic understanding of the religious enterprise." Furthermore, the item dealt with questioning *traditional* values. Presumably, the campus minister upholds the instructor's freedom to "argue in a measured way" for scientism, humanism, materialism, or what he will, as well as for traditional points of view.

Answers to the second question on classroom policy support this interpretation. It deals with the handling of value judgments and asked:

> *Everyone agrees that many areas in a college curriculum lend themselves to value judgments. In general, in handling such matters, which emphasis do you lean to?*
>
> 1. Value judgments should be discussed frequently in undergraduate teaching because of the educational value of such discussion.
> 2. Instructors should answer such questions honestly when they come up but not seek out a discussion of them.
> 3. Such discussions would probably better be saved for those places and persons that are best equipped to handle them.

Among social-science faculty, 68 per cent chose the first response; among campus ministers, 73 per cent. Again the data suggest that, compared with most people, campus clergymen are quite permissive or libertarian.[9] Here are additional contributing elements of the campus ministerial mind.

THE CAMPUS MINISTERIAL MIND

These last elements, it is true, are commensurate with the earlier ones regarding political, theological, and ecclesiastical unorthodoxy. But—to repeat an earlier sentence of this chapter—campus ministers are ministers. It is not surprising, therefore, to find this broader unorthodoxy expressed chiefly in the religious sphere. When one is seeking to describe the campus ministerial mind by what distinguishes it from other minds, here are the greatest differentiating characteristics—the radicalism, the unorthodoxy, the impatience with traditionalism, the willingness to hear all sides—but all of these redounding to the fact of the church. Unlike many radicals, those with the campus ministerial mind do not ignore the church; they criticize it. Unlike much unorthodoxy, the campus ministerial mind does not reject the church's heritage in favor of a new cult; it stays within the framework of the old even as it seeks change. And unlike libertarians in general, those with the campus ministerial mind are chiefly desirous that *religious* sides have hearings.

A consequence is that it is difficult for the campus ministerial mind —the unorthodoxy we are describing—to express itself without sounding critical of the church. But it is criticism from the "inside," so to speak, not the ignoring criticism from the outside. Perhaps not all, but many, campus ministers would agree with the Baptist chaplain who said in an interview:

> Some of us feel that the best thing the church can do for higher education is to lose its students for four years and quit assuming that somehow if we lay our hands on them and bring them inside that we are therefore going to save them. We feel this approach is not working, that the best thing we can do is simply expose students to the kinds of things a university is meant for—challenges and opportunities to expand their religious knowledge even outside the church, meaningful experience in worship, or in study. In other words, we should contribute to their religious life rather than to their church life. You would find within the majority of campus ministers on this campus the view that the church must lose itself in order to find itself.

This expression of the campus ministerial mind sounds, of course, a good deal like the unorthodox "Fellow Citizen" type of missionary who goes "not as a supervisor or director but as a fellow laborer. . . . It is no longer *our* attempt through *our* missionaries to carry on *our* work in distant lands."[10] But just as all missionaries do not see this as accurately descriptive of their task, neither do all campus ministers reflect equally the campus ministerial mind.

ROLE CONCEPTIONS OF THE CAMPUS MINISTRY: DIFFERENTIATED AND UNDIFFERENTIATED

The degree to which campus clergymen reflect the campus ministerial mind is a measure of their unorthodoxy (as this term is used here). Therefore, the "orthodox" persons—those least reflecting the campus ministerial mind—are orthodox in the sense that they conceive of their roles less as roles of *campus* clergymen. Instead, their task is seen to resemble more the task of the usual clergyman—the person serving the parish.[11]

The accuracy of this statement can be assessed. We can classify respondents' role conceptions—from those which most resemble the parish ministerial role to those which least resemble it. It should then turn out that respondents who conceive of their occupation in terms that differentiate it most from that of the parish minister are more unorthodox, more reflective of the campus ministerial mind. At the other extreme, respondents who conceive of their task in terms differing little from those they would use to describe the parish role should be least reflective of the campus ministerial mind.

Campus ministers were asked a number of questions applicable to a classification of role conceptions. Many of the questions dealt with the aims of the campus ministry—which of a number of listed goals are more important and which are less. Other questions inquired about respondents' motives for being clergymen on campus. These are alternative ways of asking "Why are you a campus minister?"—one asking persons what they consider desirable outcomes of a ministry in higher education, the other asking why they put themselves in the position of trying to bring about those outcomes. Together, these two types of questions tap respondents' conceptions of the role of the campus minister.

From these various questions, three were selected as indicating an *undifferentiated* conception of the campus ministry, and three were selected as indicating a *differentiated* conception. These six questions along with the proportions who agreed with each form Table 3.

One point was assigned for each *agreement* with a differentiating item and for each *failure* to agree with an undifferentiating item. The range

TABLE 3

Agreement Indicates Undifferentiated Role Conception		Per Cent
GOAL	prepare students for participation in the church	36
GOAL	help rebuild commitment to the church when it is shaken by the college experience	32
MOTIVE	the church expressed the desire to have its college ministry served	48
Agreement Indicates Differentiated Role Conception		
GOAL	facilitate students' religious growth even if they thereby become lost to the institutional church	56
MOTIVE	felt the opportunity for a creative witness is greater in campus–than in parish–ministry	69
MOTIVE	wished to avoid the routine tasks of the local parish	22

of scores, therefore, was 6 (very differentiated) to 0 (very undifferentiated). The number of persons in each category is shown in Table 4.

TABLE 4

Degree of Differentiation in Role Conception	Score	N=
Much	6	44
	5	168
	4	226
Moderate	3	229
	2	172
	1	83
Little	0	21
Failed to answer one or more of the six questions		54
Total		997

The Meaning of the Role-Conception Index

How are we to judge whether differentiation in conceptions of the ministerial role is adequately measured by the numbers of an index? In other words, how do we know that the index is valid? More broadly yet, how do we know what the index *means?* One answer is sometimes called face validity—the indicators of the index simply appear on face evidence to mean the same thing as the dimension underlying the distinction. Social science has relatively few indices made meaningful by face validity alone, however, so additional evidence is needed to be sure that an index is meaningful. To this evidence we now turn.

In addition to answering the three "motive" questions used in the index, campus ministers indicated the importance of six other motives they might have had for entering their special occupation. These included:

1. Felt the church was getting unfair hearing in the college community.
2. Had seen students lose interest in the church and wanted to remedy this.
3. Attracted to people who have doubts about religion.
4. Had some doubts myself and thought a campus ministry a better place to work toward their resolution.
5. Felt campus ministry offered more opportunity to think about and study theology.
6. Felt drawn by the intellectual element in this kind of work.

If we look at how persons with various role conceptions responded to these questions, several illuminating patterns are seen. First, the differentiated (23 per cent) and undifferentiated (19 per cent)[12] are alike in admitting to the first motive, though it is not very prominent for any category. The undifferentiated are somewhat more inclined to indicate the importance of the second motive (62 per cent of those with the least differentiated role conception, in contrast with 45 per cent of those with the most differentiated, say they wanted to remedy student loss to the church). But the other four motives are chosen much more often by the differentiated. "Attraction to doubters" is chosen by a majority (59 per cent) of the most differentiated but by very few (10 per cent) of the least differentiated. The most differentiated are most likely (21 per cent) to admit self-doubts; the least differentiated are least likely (0 per cent). The opportunity to think and study theology (66 per cent versus 24 per cent) and being drawn by the intellectual element (89 per cent versus 34 per cent) follow the same pattern; with each successive degree of differentiation in role conception, we observe higher rates of admitting to these motives. Together, these are the relationships we expect if a differentiated role conception means greater interest in the higher-education aspects of the ministry and less interest in "orthodox" pastoral aspects.

A second point about answers to these motive questions is this: Though the greatest difference is found with respect to the last-listed motive ("intellectual element"), even among the undifferentiated it ranks as the second most important motive.

And this leads to the third point: The differentiated in general admit to *more reasons* for being *campus* ministers.

We have some very reasonable evidence, then, for the validity of the role-conception index. Those scoring as differentiated on the index more nearly reflect the campus ministerial mind as seen by: (1) their greater admission to being drawn to that role by features unique to it, for example, intellectualism, agnosticism; (2) the fact that their motives are not so *different* from those of the undifferentiated as they are more salient or intense.

Similar points can be found in the differences in importance attached to the other "goals." "Being an available religious counselor" ranks first for all categories, but higher for the undifferentiated (100 per cent) than for the differentiated (77 per cent). All of the others, if differences exist, are more likely considered important by persons with more differentiated role conceptions, for example, "Instill in students a sustained intellectual curiosity" (68 per cent versus 19 per cent), "Develop close relationships with faculty" (48 per cent versus 24 per cent), or "Try to develop and articulate a theological basis for the campus ministry" (32 per cent versus 14 per cent).

There were many more questions which help to put flesh on the bones of a quantitative index. Several of these asked for agreement or disagreement with certain general criticisms of higher education. Another asked which of three labels a respondent would most likely use to describe his present ministry.[13] Still another is the question—already seen—asking whether an atheist should be allowed to remain on the faculty of a church-related school and on the faculty of a publicly supported school. And finally is the matter of whose opinions are considered more important in evaluating a campus ministry.[14] The relationships between these questions and the role-conception index can be summarized in this manner:

1. Persons with undifferentiated role conceptions of the campus ministry are more likely to judge higher education as too secular for students' faith, whereas those with differentiated role conceptions are more critical of the "applied" and "frilly" features they see in universities. Campus ministers of any role conception, however, are most critical of higher education for its apparent unrealistic understanding of religion.
2. The undifferentiated are far more likely to see themselves as "pastors"; the differentiated see themselves more as "religious voices" in the academy or as "teaching ministers."
3. The differentiated are more likely to allow atheism to be represented on college faculties, thus suggesting that, as campus ministers differ in "libertarianism" from the general public, so do differentiated campus clergy differ from undifferentiated.
4. In choosing important "evaluators" of their work, the undifferentiated select more from within the denomination (parish ministers and officials); the differentiated select more from higher education (administration, faculty, seminary teachers) and their colleagues.

Again the evidence supports the imputed meaning of the index: Differentiated role conceptions more nearly reflect the campus ministerial mind. Any remaining doubt should disappear, moreover, when it is pointed out that *every item used at the beginning of this chapter to distinguish the campus ministerial mind*—from that of parish ministers, of the general public, of community leaders, and of social scientists—*also distinguishes between the differentiated and undifferentiated in role conception.* The former, one might say, are more "campus ministerial" than the latter.[15]

Consider the following quotations from personal interviews with two university pastors, one a Methodist at a large state university, the other a Baptist at a small state school.

> *The Methodist:* Some conceive of the campus ministry in terms of a building, and the task is to get students to come and be active. Effectiveness, then, is judged in terms of where *we* are rather than in terms of where things are going on. They try to get students out of the environment of the university and increase their association with the church, rather than feel their way in to discover what the university is, what students are believing and what problems they are living with. This latter is an image of a mission that is hard for some to think of. Instead of gathering students away from this "devastating" university situation that corrupts their morals and robs their faith, it seems to me that the exciting part of the work is right at the other axis, where the normal flow of university life is.
> *The Baptist:* I think my major task is to break down students' ignorance of the church, to make them grow in this area as they are growing in other academic fields. This means tearing down a lot of superstitions that exist within our Protestant denominations. Some of the churches students come from have not been very inspiring; most of them have a second or third grade knowledge of their faith. We have to challenge them with what the church ought to be, and they've got a lot of growing to do. It would not bother me if the student rejects the church or tends to become an atheist. If he is beginning to question, this is fine; from there we can begin to build.

Campus ministers with differentiated conceptions of their role would agree with these two statements; those with undifferentiated conceptions would agree only in part.

The Sources of Different Role Conceptions

Chaplains and university pastors differ considerably in role conception. More than half (57 per cent) of the chaplains have differentiated role conceptions (that is, scores of 6, 5, 4) in contrast with 43 per cent of university pastors. But whether chaplains or university pastors, campus ministers from denominations with strong liturgical tradition (Lutheran,

Episcopal) or with more conservative theology (Southern Baptist, Presbyterian, U.S.) are less likely to be differentiated in their orientation to the campus ministry. (See Table 5.)

TABLE 5

Denomination	Per Cent Differentiated (scores of 6, 5, 4)	No. of Cases on Which Percentage Is Based
Disciples	69	32
United Church of Christ	61	69
Presbyterian, U.S.A.	57	103
Methodist	56	262
American Baptist	54	63
Lutheran (National Lutheran Council)	46	76
Episcopal	31	120
Southern Baptist	31	121
Presbyterian, U.S.	29	41
Miscellaneous*	29	28
Missouri Synod Lutheran	14	28

* Evangelical and United Brethren, Reformed Church, Unitarian, and others. See Appendix for description of how persons were selected.

But denomination and position as chaplain or university pastor by no means wholly determine role conception. Amount of formal education is another factor which cuts across denominational lines. The more education, the more differentiated is the orientation.[16] And, of specific interest to this discussion, another influence on role conception is the factor of specialized preparation for the campus ministry. By now, a number of seminaries offer courses designed to prepare campus ministers, several denominations and a private foundation offer "internships" enabling trainees to spend a year under the supervision of experienced campus clergy, and "workshops" or other short-term programs exist as devices to train campus ministers. The proportion in the study who have had each type of training is shown in Table 6.

In addition to these programs, however, an important source of training for the campus ministry is reading material, some bearing directly on religion in higher education, some more indirectly concerned, such as character education or the governing of higher education. The reading lists in seminary courses for campus ministers will typically contain materials of this sort, but we wanted to know how familiar campus ministers are in general with literature bearing on their work. They were asked, therefore, whether they had read certain books, the first three dealing with "religion" in education, the second three dealing with the values and attitudes of college students. These books, and the propor-

TABLE 6

TRAINING	
Internship *	5%
Seminary course(s)	22
Workshop	4
Training indicated but unspecified	1
No special training	68
	100%

*Persons who have been interns and had seminary courses are classed as having had an "internship." Those with courses *and* workshop are classed as having had "seminary course(s)."

tions who had read them, are listed in Table 7. The books on "religion" were more frequently read, as was anticipated, than "secular" books on college students' values. In constructing an index of special preparation, we therefore assigned a campus minister one point for each of these characteristics: (1) having read *two* or more of the first three books listed; (2) having read *one* or more of the second three books listed; (3) having had *any* type of specialized training. The highest score became 3 on this index, and the lowest 0. (See Table 8.)

One effect of specialized preparation for the campus ministerial role is greater differentiation in conceiving that role. Over half (55 per cent) of the persons with very high special preparation have differentiated role conceptions in contrast with fewer than a third (32 per cent) of those with very low special preparation. The first proportion increases to two-thirds among possessors of degrees beyond the B.D. who are from "liberal" or "non-liturgical" denominations, and the second proportion drops to one-fifth among those from other denominations possessing no more than a B.D. or Master's degree. The impact of special preparation is maintained in all of these categories. It is quite clear, in other words, that, irrespective of their denomination, campus ministers' education, and especially a certain kind of "education" conveyed through specialized training and literature, tends to produce differentiated conceptions of the campus clergyman's role. Insofar as churches

TABLE 7

	READ BY
Peter Berger, *The Noise of Solemn Assemblies*	68%
Alexander Miller, *Faith and Learning*	58
Walter Moberly, *The Crisis in the University*	55
Allan Barton, *Studying the Effects of College Education*	4
Rose Goldsen, *et al.*, *What College Students Think*	23
Philip Jacob, *Changing Values in College*	53

TABLE 8

SCORE		N=
3	Very high special preparation	181
2	High special preparation	351
1	Low special preparation	276
0	Very low special preparation	176
	Did not answer one or more questions	13
	Total	997

urge their campus clergy to take more formal education, and inasmuch as internships, seminary courses, and workshops are directly and indirectly supported by churches, then to this extent churches encourage differentiation of the sort discussed in this chapter.

Denominational officials, for the most part, would not blanch at this conclusion. They are aware of the specialized nature of the campus ministry and aware, therefore, of the necessity for unusual approaches to it.

---

1. As reported in a study of 17,565 seminary students by K. R. Bridston and D. W. Culver in *Seminary Quarterly,* V (Spring 1964), 2.

2. Cuninggim, *The College Seeks Religion,* argues that university personnel are not only available to play their parts but also willing and anxious to do so. In Chapter 5 we have more to say about this.

3. Using three age groups in ten denominations, each of the questions in Table 1 can be assessed 30 times. With 16 questions, 480 comparisons of parish and campus ministers are possible. Of these, 89 per cent reveal the difference contained in Table 1, though of the 11 per cent which do not, a quarter involve cells containing fewer than 10 cases.

4. The consequences of this difference for Protestant organizations are traced in P. E. Hammond and R. E. Mitchell, "Segmentation of Radicalism: The Case of the Protestant Campus Minister," *American Journal of Sociology,* LXXI (1965), 133-143. Of course, "orthodoxy" has many meanings in many different contexts. One of the justifications for the length of this section is to make clear what the term means here.

5. S. A. Stouffer, *Communism, Conformity and Civil Liberties* (New York: Doubleday, 1955), pp. 40-43.

6. Paul F. Lazarsfeld and W. Thielens, *The Academic Mind* (Glencoe, Ill.: The Free Press, 1958), pp. 391-392.

7. The full wording and answers are found in Stouffer, *op. cit.,* pp. 32-33. The question to campus ministers was slightly different: "Suppose now another man—one who advocates atheism and is opposed to all religious institutions as commonly understood—is teaching in a college. If it were a church-related college, do you think he ought to be released from his position?" Then: "If the college were publicly supported, should he be let go?"

8. Lazarsfeld and Thielens, *op. cit.,* p. 135, discuss this and the next question.

9. Indeed, in some schools the campus ministers may be in a position to be more protective of academic freedom than the faculty. For example, the [Little Rock] *Arkansas Gazette* reported on November 28, 1964, a faculty "resolution assailing the University [of Arkansas] administration for screening speakers." The resolution backed the university pastor of the Wesley Foundation, "who let a Communist official use the Wesley Foundation facilities to speak when the University denied the official the use of a building."

10. . . . Another sketch suitably descriptive of the campus ministerial mind, this one of a type of seminary student and therefore with an accented intellectual component, is found in H. R. Niebuhr, D. Williams, and J. Gustafson, *The Advancement of Theological Education* (New York: Harper, 1957), pp. 156-158.

11. Cantelon, *A Protestant Approach to the Campus Ministry,* pp. 14-15.

12. These percentages are for the extreme categories of "most" and "least" differentiation. Here, as with successive instances, the middle categories on the index of differentiation have correspondingly "middle" percentages.

13. The three: "a pastor to counsel people in the college community in matters of faith and vocation," "a teaching minister, to advance religious knowledge in the educational process," or "a religious voice in the academic community, to reveal added dimensions in secular education."

14. The question reads: "In his work, everyone knows persons whose evaluation he regards more than others. Here are several groups who may have opinion of your ministry. Please indicate the three whose opinion you consider the more important: parish clergy in your denomination; officials in your denomination; college administration; faculty; seminary teacher; other campus ministers."

15. It is instructive to note, however, that generally speaking even the least differentiated of campus ministers resemble "average," not "conservative," parish ministers; they resemble liberal, not conservative, community leaders, etc. For all of its diversity, then, the campus ministry has an occupational "culture."

16. Thus, 30 per cent of those with only a Bachelor's or Master's (chiefly M.Ed.) degree have differentiated role conceptions, 46 per cent of those with B.D., 50 per cent of those with B.D. plus Master's degree, and 59 per cent of those with a doctorate degree.

Chapter 4
Organization Characteristics: From Sect to Church

BENTON JOHNSON

On Church and Sect

Since Ernst Troeltsch formulated the church-sect typology more than half a century ago it has come to be regarded by most sociologists of religion as a singularly useful device for the analysis of the characteristics of organized Christian groups in relation to their environment.

Yet the typology as developed by Troeltsch has been subjected to a great deal of criticism. During the past generation many students have reworked it in various ways to make it more serviceable in sociological research. These attempts have been largely of two kinds. The first kind is best represented by Richard Niebuhr, who criticized Troeltsch's formulation for its classificatory or static character and sought to incorpo-

---

Reprinted from the *American Sociological Review* 28 (August 1963):539-49, by permission of the American Sociological Association.

rate it into a propositional scheme resting on the assumption that the sect type is inherently unstable and tends over time to develop into a church.[1] The second kind of attempt at reformulation has focused on the definition of the types themselves. Many students, among them Howard Becker,[2] Milton Yinger,[3] Peter Berger,[4] and D. A. Martin[5] have refined and expanded the typology to embody distinctions they deemed important.

If, as we believe, it can be shown that the definition of the typology remains ambiguous, then this ambiguity must be cleared up before the typology can be fruitfully used at the propositional level. In this essay we propose to show that a serious definitional problem does remain, to redefine the terms sect and church, to suggest guidelines for their proper use, and to illustrate the manner in which the distinction can be applied by using it to classify the major religious groups in American society.

Troeltsch's formulation of the typology is too well known to require extensive recapitulation. He conceived of church and sect as independent sociological expressions of two variant interpretations of Christian tradition. The sect, interpreting the teachings of Jesus in a literal and radical manner, is a small, voluntary fellowship of converts who seek to realize the divine law in their own behavior. It is a community apart from and in opposition to the world around it. It emphasizes the eschatological features of Christian doctrine, espouses ideals of frugality and poverty, prohibits participation in legal or political affairs, and shuns any exercise of dominion over others. Religious equality of believers is stressed and a sharp distinction between clergy and laity is not drawn. It appeals principally to the lower classes. The church, on the other hand, stresses the redemptive and forgiving aspects of Christian tradition. It compromises the more radical teachings of Jesus and accepts many features of the secular world as at least relatively good. It seeks to dominate all elements within society, to teach and guide them, and to dispense saving grace to them by means of sacraments administered by ecclesiastical office holders. Although it contains organized expressions of the radical spirit of Christianity in its monastic system, it does not require its members to realize the divine law in their own behavior. It is conservative and allied with the upper classes.[6]

Although this formulation has been criticized, almost no one has called attention to two of its most serious problems. First, Troeltsch arrived at his definitions of church and sect on the basis of an examination of the history of Christian Europe prior to about 1800. He therefore tended to assume that a Christian society would have a legally established, politically protected religious monopoly. He had before him primarily the cases of Catholicism, Lutheranism and Anglicanism, and he framed his definition of the church with these cases clearly in mind.

Within this historical context it was almost inevitable that alternative religious expressions would have the character of protest movements. Since they were often illegal, the very existence of such groups was a sign of public unrest and alienation. Troeltsch had groups like the Hussites and the Anabaptists in mind when he defined the sect type.

Even the most cursory review of the modern European or American religious scenes should suggest the artificiality of a church-sect distinction phrased in the above terms. In Europe, for example, there are few nations whose traditional churches can be said in any realistic sense to enjoy the regular support of most of the population. This is especially true in France, in England, and in the traditionally Lutheran areas of Germany and Scandinavia. On the other hand, although many of these nations have known profound unrest during the last 200 years, little of it, except perhaps in England, has found expression by means of sectarian religion.

Since the United States has no official religion, it cannot be said to have a church in Troeltsch's sense. There are a few withdrawn communities like the Amish and the Hutterites, and there are a few ambiguously radical active protest movements such as the Black Muslims or the Jehovah's Witnesses, but these sects make up only a tiny fraction of the religious bodies of the nation. The United States, unlike Europe, contains a large number of prosperous and popular religious organizations, but the vast majority of them cannot be validly classified as either churches or sects in terms of Troeltsch's typology.

Nevertheless, many have tried to apply the typology to the contemporary religious situation. But attempts to do this have revealed a second problem inherent in the typology. Troeltsch's definitions of sect and church each contain a large number of characteristics, or elements. Even when allowance is made for the fact that the United States has no official religion, or that modern European churches no longer command the allegiance of most of the population, it is clear that many of the remaining elements vary independently of each other.[7] Two examples are sufficient to document this. First, membership in the sect is supposed to be based on voluntary adherence. Yet several groups that researchers have not hesitated to call sects, e.g., the Amish, have in effect instituted ascribed membership. Second, the sacramental system of the Roman, Orthodox, Lutheran and Anglican communions is supposed to be characteristic of churches. But many modern Protestant groups often called churches completely lack this kind of sacramental system.

If elements vary independently, the classification of mixed cases becomes an almost impossible task. So far the major response to this difficulty has been to coin new types or subtypes on an *ad hoc* basis as important new mixed cases present themselves. As we have pointed out elsewhere, this is what Troeltsch himself did when he coined the term free church to describe latter-day ascetic Protestantism.[8] The trouble with most of these newer typologies is that they have never really stipulated all the elements under consideration and they have never succeeded in transcending the particular considerations that led to their development. In other words, they are as limited in their own way as Troeltsch's typology.[9]

One can go on creating new types and subtypes as further research and reflection bring to light the independence of more elements in the original formulation. But it is unlikely that this strategy will contribute to the major theoretical aim of sociology, which is to elucidate a variety of particular problems by means of a limited number of concepts and principles of general applicability. With this aim in mind we shall attempt to reformulate the typology in a manner that is both systematic and sufficiently abstract to enable it to be applied to a large number of circumstances both past and present.

Where we begin in the reformulation of the church-sect typology is an arbitrary matter provided the characteristics selected for incorporation within it are relevant to Christian groups. Since there is some merit in striving for as much continuity with customary usage as possible, we will try to embody one basic distinction which has figured prominently in most previous formulations of the typology.

To do this with clarity, however, it is useful to rely not on Troeltsch himself but on his close associate Max Weber.[10] According to Weber,[11] the world religions have been molded in large part by what he calls prophets, or charismatically legitimated bearers of distinctive religious teachings. Prophets regularly present a relatively systematized or cognitively rationalized cosmic image which in principle permits all events in heaven and earth, but particularly those affecting joy and suffering, to be interpreted in terms of a single framework of causal principles. Prophets often succeed in changing the cosmic image of the masses from one in which various deities and demons affect human destiny without regard to any over-all plan to one in which the cosmos is seen as a meaningful whole.

Weber distinguishes between prophets who promulgate the idea of a personal supramundane god who makes specific demands on men, and prophets who promulgate the idea of an impersonal cosmic law which can be appropriated by men. The first kind of prophet is called the *emissary* prophet and the second kind is called the *exemplary* prophet. Mohammed and the ancient Hebrew prophets are of the emissary type, whereas Buddha is of the exemplary type. Emissary prophecy conveys the idea that man's ultimate fate depends on how well he is a servant of the Lord's will. It has a strong ethical orientation, by which Weber means a disposition to regulate everyday conduct in terms of divinely given norms. Exemplary prophecy, on the other hand, tends to foster a relative lack of concern with ordinary mundane matters because its guiding idea is that individuals, through ascetic exercises, orgies, contemplation, or absorption of esoteric lore, can obtain power or other benefits which may be used for a variety of purely private ends. Emissary prophecy requires man to forget his own worldly interests and to join with others in promoting the ethical interests of the Lord.

The cosmic image promoted by emissary prophecy is of special interest to us because it constrains man to concern himself very seriously with questions of social policy, i.e., with the arrangements by which men live in society. Since the world is the Lord's principal theater of operations, how things are done there is likely to be a matter of the most intense concern to Him and therefore to His followers as well. They may be pleased with the way things are going or they may be displeased, but they are not likely to be indifferent. We would like to base the church-sect distinction on this consideration. *A church is a religious group that accepts the social environment in which it exists. A sect is a religious group that rejects the social environment in which it exists.* Since Weber emphasized that the world religions of the West were for the most part molded by emissary prophecy, whereas the religions of the Orient were molded by exemplary prophecy, we are safe in assuming that the church-sect distinction may be applied to most groups in the Jewish, Christian and Islamic traditions.[12]

We have deliberately defined church and sect at a very high level of generality. Its application is in principle limited only by the criteria contained in the foregoing discussion. But unless the distinction can be validly and reliably operationalized and applied by investigators, it will have no merit at all. It will therefore be helpful to suggest some guidelines for its proper use.

First, it is necessary to specify the group to be classified and the environment to which it is to be related. It would seem perfectly acceptable to use a congregation, a monastic order, or an entire religious body as one's basic unit. It must be stressed that the classification of a group will not necessarily depend on qualities intrinsic to the group but on the nature of its relationship to its environment. For example, the Catholic Church in Portugal is far more acclimatized to its environment than it is in Hungary.

Second, the distinction between church and sect involves a single variable the values of which range along a continuum from complete rejection to complete acceptance of the environment. Therefore, where one draws the cutting point between sect and church or how many additional distinctions one wishes to make are to some extent arbitrary matters.

Third, the distinction is well adapted to comparative analyses. One may compare a number of religious groups within a given environment in terms of where they fall on the continuum.[13] One may compare two environments in terms of the proportion of religious bodies within each that fall at certain points along the continuum. Or one may compare a given religious group with itself in another environment or with itself at a different point in time.

Fourth, the redefinition of church and sect in terms of a single variable of broad applicability means that no assumption is made about the manner in which other characteristics are related to any state of the defining variable. This strategy should alert investigators to the importance of specifying other variables to be included in their analyses. In the past the typology has tended to be applied very loosely, in part because of the formal deficiencies which we have already discussed. Consequently, generalizations about churches and sects have probably been made which may in fact be true only under special circumstances. The existing empirical generalizations in this area need to be reexamined. A good start in this direction has recently been made by Bryan Wilson.[14] He has shown by a comparative analysis of the development of Protestant sects in English-speaking nations that Niebuhr's hypothesis concerning the instability of sects probably applies only to groups that Wilson calls conversionist sects. These bodies tend to take on churchly characteristics with great rapidity because of their strong commitment to gaining converts and their relative lack of structural safeguards against environmental influences. Sects less interested in recruitment or better insulated or isolated from secular forces tend to retain sectarian characteristics more or less indefinitely. Wilson's careful investigations should stimulate more work along the same lines.[15]

Finally, although hard and fast criteria cannot be given for determining toward which end of the continuum given groups stand in any environment, a few rules of thumb appear consistently in the literature that fit our conception of church and sect very well. We shall make use of these indicators in applying the typology to contemporary American society. First, since a sect tends to be in a state of tension with its surroundings, we are safe in supposing that religions that have totally withdrawn from participation in a society or that are engaged in open attack on it are likely to fall close to the sect end. By the same token, we may assume that religions enforcing norms on their adherents that are sharply distinct from norms common in secular quarters should be classed as relatively sectarian. Churches, on the other hand, are comparatively at ease with the established values and practices of a society. Therefore we will probably be justified in classifying as churches those religions that comprehend the entire society or at least its dominant classes. Similarly, bodies permitting their members to participate freely in all phases of secular life should probably also be classified as churches.

Since many of the drawbacks of Troeltsch's typology only became apparent when it was applied to the United States, one criterion of the usefulness of the revised typology will be the ease with which it can be applied to the American scene. We will therefore illustrate how the typology can be used to classify the major religious groupings of American society. In principle, of course, it could just as well be applied to Europe, Latin America, other English-speaking nations, or indeed to any nation having religious bodies that meet our criteria.

The first step is to specify the environment to be used as the basic point of reference in classifying our religious groups. Although all societies contain a variety of subcultures, and the United States is no exception, most sociologists believe that this country does have a dominant value system. Since its content is well known, we need not describe it here. It has been adequately presented by Robin Williams,[16] Cora DuBois,[17] Gunnar Myrdal[18] and others. Will Herberg has referred to much the same constellation of values as the American Way of Life.[19] We propose to use the dominant value system of the United States as our basic environmental point of reference.

The most striking fact about the American religious situation is that the vast majority of religious bodies seem to accept the dominant value system. Herberg and others have argued this point quite convincingly.[20] Most groups, therefore, should be placed toward the church end of the church-sect continuum. To be sure, some religious groups are strongly at odds with the dominant value system. We identified some of them earlier in this essay. But these groups are few and small and most of them are not actively struggling against the very foundations of the social system. Many of them are groups that have historically elected to retreat from the world into communities of their own making.

There are several telling bits of evidence for the assertion that religion in the United States supports the dominant values. First, most religious bodies, though with varying degrees of enthusiasm, accept the basic norm of mutual toleration, which is essential if they are to coexist peacefully. Second, almost all of them allow their members to move about freely and to engage in most kinds of legal activity. Third, the United States lacks any serious, sustained social cleavages associated with religion. Although we will argue later that significant cleavages of a limited kind are associated with religion, differences in outlook among the religious bodies of this country are not nearly so great as those which have occurred from time to time in Europe. One need only recall the prolonged and bitter struggles between Huguenot and Catholic or between Anglican and Puritan to appreciate this fact.

Religion not only supports the dominant values, it is enormously popular in comparison to religion in most other industrial nations. In Europe, for example, the old state churches tended to identify themselves strongly with reactionary values and interests during the stressful period of the transition to industrialism and democracy. Partly for this reason and partly because of the historic weakness of popular sectarianism on the continent, reform movements tended to attack not only the old order but the Christian religion as well. Although many Christian leaders have made significant adjustments in their social outlook, religion has continued to remain controversial in the largest sense of the term in Europe and is still regarded with profound suspicion by a significant segment of the population, in particular the urban working class.[21] The United States is one of the few industrial nations of the world that has not undergone a marked decline in popular religious interest since the beginning of industrial development.[22]

These considerations make it plausible to suggest that we should regard the United States as the second major historical example since the beginning of the Christian era of a culture that has an essentially comprehensive and integrative religious system.[23] The first of these historical examples—represented by medieval Catholicism and perhaps by early Reformation Lutheranism—has long since been superseded in much of Europe by religiously based conflict and by popular alienation from religion.

The foregoing analysis, which classifies most American religious bodies as basically churchly, is a fruitful one for many purposes of crosscultural comparison. But it conceals a number of more subtle distinctions that may prove important for purposes of internal comparison. These distinctions concern the extent to which there appear to be reservations in the support given to the dominant values. Since the church-sect typology as conventionally applied to the American scene tends to obscure this phenomenon, it will be useful to suggest where several of the prominent religious traditions should be placed in relation to each other on the church-sect continuum. All of them are, of course, basically churchly.

Few would dispute that old-line Protestant denominations, such as the Methodists, the Presbyterians, the Congregationalists, and the Episcopalians stand very near the church end. Closely allied with these bodies are groups like the Baptists, the Disciples of Christ, the Evangelical-United Brethren and the Lutherans. These bodies, together with certain other smaller denominations, are to be regarded as the most churchly of all American religious groups. As Protestants they tend wholeheartedly to accept mutual toleration and the separation of church and state, two basic features of the American system. They are, in addition, bodies which are strongly identified with the relatively privileged segments of the population. Finally, with minor exceptions, they impose few if any distinctive expectations on their members. It is, for example, very easy to become and remain a Methodist or a Presbyterian. By the criteria we have suggested for determining where a religion should fall on the continuum, these groups seem clearly to belong very near the church end.

The same cannot be said, however, for the Roman Catholic Church in the United States. Although some observers have noted that American Catholicism has been obliged to take on characteristics which sharply distinguish it from European Catholicism, it has rarely been suggested that it should not be regarded as the sociological equivalent of, say, Congregationalism. There is a natural hesitancy to think of the lineal descendant of medieval Catholicism as anything but a sociological church. But a strict application of our criteria reveals that Catholicism cannot be regarded as among the most churchly bodies on the American scene. Although there are indications of a movement within Catholicism toward approval in principle of political democracy, religious pluralism and the separation of church and state, the Church in the United States has not apotheosized these landmarks of the American system to the extent that most Protestant groups have. There is, moveover, a sect-like quality in the official Catholic development of distinctively religious structures paralleling those of the secular society. We have in mind chiefly the educational system of the Church, as well as the numerous separate professional societies which it has fostered, especially among those vocations that are closely related to ideological concerns. For these reasons it is wise to classify Catholicism as somewhat more sectarian than most of the major Protestant bodies.

Judaism has usually not been classified as either sect or church because of the custom of applying the typology only within the Christian tradition. But Judaism was historically molded by a series of almost ideal-typical emissary prophets. We have, therefore, excellent reason to include it in our classification of American religions. Until recent times Judaism existed as an officially restricted sect that had been forced to withdraw from full participation in the larger society. Although the Jewish tradition always nurtured hopes for emancipation, it was not well prepared for the kind of emancipation that might require the close mingling of Jews with members of other religions on a basis of equality. In part this was due to the elaborate system of ritual segregation that served for centuries to draw the Jewish community closer together. Where traditional Orthodoxy persists it must be classified as a relatively sectarian form of religion. It is significant, however, that Orthodoxy has tended to decline rapidly wherever full emancipation has been readily available to the Jews.[24] This decline has been paralleled by the rise of Reform and Conservative Judaism, both of which have relaxed most of the religious restrictions against the full participation of Jews in secular society. These branches of Judaism tend also to be enthusiastic supporters of American values. They should probably be classified as more churchly than the Catholics.

Sociologists have devoted a great deal of attention to the study of religious groups which they have identified as sects. They have shown special interest in those modern revivalist groups which nowadays consist chiefly but not exclusively of the holiness and pentecostal movements. These are bodies that Wilson would call conversionist sects.

Even by our criteria these groups have certain sectarian characteristics. They disdain "worldly" things, they insist on the total commitment of their membership and they enforce a moral code more stringent than any code usually observed by nonmembers. But it is also clear that the opposition of these groups to the secular environment is partial and highly selective. They neither attack the society nor withdraw from it. Moreover, in many respects their members are less insulated from secular influences than good Catholics tend to be. They may forbid their members to patronize bathing beaches where the sexes swim together, but they usually allow them to attend the public schools. These groups, then, are sectarian only in the limited sense of being less churchly than bodies such as the Methodists. The same appears to be true of the Mormons, the Seventh Day Adventists, or more militant non-revivalist fundamentalist groups such as the Orthodox Presbyterians or the Christian Reformed.

We have elsewhere presented evidence for the view that many of these groups actively convey value orientations which Weber and Troeltsch would identify as ascetic Protestant.[25] Since most observers would agree that the ascetic Protestant tradition has been influential in setting the religious and even the institutional tone of the entire nation, we may be justified in considering almost all bodies within this tradition as belonging closer to the church end of the continuum than either Roman Catholicism or Orthodox Judaism. It may well be that one of the most important functions of the conversionist bodies in the United States, both now and historically, has been to socialize potentially dissident elements—particularly the lower classes—in the dominant values which are our basic point of reference. The differences sociologists have seen between the Protestant "churches" and the Protestant "sects" may be matters of taste, rhetoric and expressive symbolism in general far more than they are matters of basic value orientation.[26] The fact that the ascetic Protestant tradition has been so well able to adapt itself to the peculiarities of the various subcultures, including races and classes, with which its numerous branches have always been closely associated, may be one of the reasons underlying the popularity of religion in the United States.

The foregoing analysis has illustrated that with varying degrees of enthusiasm the great majority of American religious bodies support the dominant values. But one can easily make the mistake of supposing that this is the only relevant conclusion a sociologist can reach regarding the manner in which American religion is related to the environment as defined in terms of value orientations. Controversy over matters of social value and public policy is a regularized part of a democratic nation. To be sure, in this country these controversies seldom concern the dominant values themselves, which is perhaps one reason why American society has been politically more stable than many other industrial societies. But within the limits set by these values, important and deep-seated conflicts do exist in America. Moreover, for many purposes it is more important to know of the existence and bases of these conflicts than it is to know that most parties to them share a higher order of value commitments which serve to confine and restrain their disagreements. Like most groups in American society, religious bodies tend to share similar commitments at one level of generality. But if we shift our environmental point of reference down to the level of the major value-relevant cleavages in American society, a very different picture emerges.

It is a striking fact of American history since about the turn of the century that the ideological controversies between left and right, which have been waged on a variety of fronts and which are roughly reflected in the division between Republicans and Democrats, have also broken out in religious circles, particularly within Protestantism.[27] To be sure, in the seminaries and pulpits these controversies were sparked by theological issues, but it has turned out that the resulting theological factions have tended to line up on opposite sides of the fence in terms of political ideology as well.

Theologically, the dispute has centered around the validity of traditional supernaturalist doctrines. Liberalism, and to some extent neo-orthodoxy, has made important doctrinal modifications in response to recent developments in natural science, philosophy and historical research. These modifications have evoked strong negative reactions from groups that initially called themselves fundamentalists but presently seem to prefer the term conservative. They have dogmatically reasserted and even embellished the supernaturalist aspects of Protestant theology.[28]

There has been a marked elective affinity between theological and political liberalism on the one hand and theological and political conservatism on the other. These alignments have been brought to public attention most vividly in the social gospel movement that arose shortly after the turn of the century and in the strong fundamentalist backing presently being given to the various movements making up the "radical right."[29] But underlying these more visible and dramatic examples of recent political polarization is the fact that during the past half century most of the major Protestant groups have come to be associated with inter-denominational alliances that have grown up on the right and on the left. The National Council of Churches represents the relatively liberal viewpoint, and the National Association of Evangelicals and the American Council of Christian Churches represent the relatively conservative viewpoint. There is evidence, moreover, that political philosophy and to some extent party preference as well are closely related to theological position even among the ordinary parish clergy.[30] There is also evidence that the same relationships exist, though in attenuated form, among the more active laity.[31]

These facts strongly suggest that the liberal-conservative split within Protestantism cannot be overlooked by any researcher who wishes to investigate the actual manner in which religious bodies are related to the value climate of the contemporary United States. For many research purposes it will yield far more positive and meaningful results than will breakdowns based on denomination or on distinctions in the extent to which groups enthusiastically endorse the dominant values.

The church-sect distinction can be usefully applied in this context if we shift the environmental reference point to the generalized controversy between left and right over matters of value and social policy.[32] The leadership of most religious bodies can be roughly classified as predominantly conservative or liberal in a theological and ideological sense. Such a classification should not be attempted, however, in the case of withdrawn or hostile sects that have no use for *any* viable contemporary ideational system.

We can safely assume that the more extreme forms of liberalism or conservatism reflect a higher degree of dissatisfaction with the values and institutional status quo than do the milder forms. We can therefore distinguish between a churchly center group of relatively satisfied and therefore ambiguously liberal or conservative bodies and a more sectarian fringe group of relatively dissatisfied and therefore markedly liberal or conservative bodies. The former tend to be the groups we have previously labeled the most churchly bodies in America. Although there are important variations from region to region and even from parish to parish, in general the Congregationalists and the Methodists stand somewhat to the left of center, followed perhaps a notch or two to the right by the Episcopalians and the Presbyterians. The Baptists, the Lutherans, and the Disciples of Christ stand somewhat to the right of center.

At the extremes we may distinguish between the relatively sectarian bodies of the left and right. On the left are the Unitarians, many Quakers and certain Jewish bodies, especially those of Reform or Conservative persuasion. On the right are groups such as the Bible Presbyterian Church and several other small, aggressive fundamentalist bodies. While in recent years dissatisfaction has subsided on the left, it has risen markedly on the right. We may therefore speak of an increasingly sectarian trend within many Protestant groups. The denominations involved are in most cases those that were never prominently identified with theological liberalism, the social gospel or the National Council of Churches. The leadership of this large and growing sector of Protestantism did not therefore make the transition to a liberal or reform capitalist position.[33] In the years following World War II, when it began to appear that recent shifts in the value and institutional climate of the nation might become permanent, criticism of the status quo became progressively bitter in these circles. The strong mixture of religion and rightist politics coming from protest movements, such as Billy James Hargis' Christian Crusade, the spread of premillennial eschatology, and the new interest shown in the Christian school movement among groups previously supporting the public schools, are evidence of a sectarian intransigence in the face of social change. A stiffening posture toward everything that has become identified with the left may be found among many Baptists, Disciples of Christ, Mormons, and others.

Almost all the facts mentioned in the preceding discussion of American religion are well known to sociologists. But they have seldom been comprehended in a systematic manner within a single conceptual framework. It is hoped that our redefinition of the church-sect distinction with the suggested rules for its use and their illustrative application to the American situation will lead to the kind of ordering of our perspectives on religion that will stimulate the asking of questions of theoretical relevance.

---

1. H. Richard Niebuhr, *The Social Sources of Denominationalism,* New York: Henry Holt and Company, 1929, pp. 16-21.

2. Howard Becker, *Systematic Sociology,* New York: John Wiley and Sons, 1932, pp. 114-118.

3. Yinger has undertaken two different expansions of the typology. For his first effort see *Religion in the Struggle for Power,* Durham: Duke University Press, 1946, pp. 18-23. For

his second effort see *Religion, Society and the Individual,* New York: The Macmillan Company, 1957, pp. 144-145.

4. Peter L. Berger, "The Sociological Study of Sectarianism," *Social Research,* 21 (Winter, 1954), p. 474.

5. D. A. Martin, "The Denomination," *British Journal of Sociology,* 13 (March, 1962), pp. 1-14.

6. Ernst Troeltsch, *The Social Teaching of the Christian Churches* (translated by Olive Wyon), New York: The Macmillan Company, 1932, v. 1, pp. 328-349.

7. Peter L. Berger (*op. cit.,* pp. 469-470) is one of the few who have called attention to this very serious difficulty.

8. Benton Johnson, "A Critical Appraisal of the Church-Sect Typology," *American Sociological Review,* 22 (February, 1957), pp. 88-92.

9. Although Berger's typology is defined in terms of a single variable, it is not only inconsonant with prevailing usage, it is also very difficult to operationalize. Becker's typology is frequently referred to, but it is unsystematic, discursively developed and obviously limited to a few historical circumstances. Martin has proposed that Becker's term *denomination,* which Becker tended to regard as a transition type between sect and church, be regarded as a distinct sociological type. If one takes Troeltsch's typology as one's point of reference there is no doubt that the English and American bodies to which Martin refers cannot be called either churches or sects. But Martin's concept suffers from the same inadequacy as Troeltsch's: it is too closely bound to particular historical conditions to be of general use in the sociology of religion. This should not prevent investigators from profiting from the many insightful comments Martin makes about Anglo-American religion.

Yinger's second reformulation of the typology has been the most ambitious reworking yet to appear (*op. cit.,* 1957). He proposes to build a new typology applicable to all Christian bodies on the basis of two criteria. A close inspection of the typology reveals that he has not been successful. First, it is not clear why cross-classification of his criteria should yield six types instead of four. Second, in discussing each of his types the defining variables are in many cases completely overshadowed by extraneous characteristics which appear in fact to be the principal identifying elements. In short, it is almost impossible to discern just what combination of his two criteria each of his six types represents.

10. Although Weber used the terms church and sect and directly influenced Troeltsch to employ them in his major work on Christian social doctrine, his definitions are not free from the difficulties which we have just discussed. Instead of relying on these definitions, we will derive new definitions by drawing out some implications of another facet of Weber's sociology of religion.

11. Until recently only fragments of Weber's systematic treatment of religion have been available in English translation. Moreover, few sociologists have paid serious attention to this phase of Weber's work. Fortunately, an English translation now exists. See Max Weber, *The Sociology of Religion* (translated by Ephraim Fischoff), Boston: Beacon Press, 1963. The book contains an extended and useful introduction by Talcott Parsons.

12. But not all of them can be so classified by any means. Groups primarily concerned with offering specific benefits to individuals, e.g., Christian Science or other health-oriented bodies, should not be classified as either sect or church even if they regard themselves as Christian, Jewish or Islamic. Groups such as these are often referred to as cults, and some formulations of the church-sect typology have included a cult type. We are, however, in complete agreement with D. A. Martin (*op. cit.,* pp. 3-4) that the cult's outlook can hardly be called historically Christian. It reflects the cosmic image of exemplary rather than emissary prophecy. For this reason it should not be regarded as a part of the church-sect distinction.

13. Dynes' well-known church-sect scale is built on the assumption that bodies can be ranked along a continuum from church to sect. Dynes' scale, which is based on the

observations of Liston Pope, is a useful device provided one understands that it can be validly applied in its present form only to a certain set of religious bodies in a single cultural environment. See Russell R. Dynes, "Church-Sect Typology and Socio-Economic Status," *American Sociological Review,* 20 (October, 1955), pp. 555-560.

14. Bryan R. Wilson, "An Analysis of Sect Development," *American Sociological Review,* 24 (February, 1959), p. 4.

15. For example, our analysis of the American religious situation presented below suggests that Niebuhr's statement that churches cannot become sects needs to be questioned. It is at least conceivable that a church may adopt a stiffening posture toward its environment, i.e., take on certain sectarian characteristics, if the environment changes drastically. This is what the Catholic Church has done in communist nations and this is what a number of American religious groups seem to be doing, though to a lesser extent, at the present time.

16. Robin M. Williams, Jr., *American Society,* New York: Alfred A. Knopf, 1960, chapter 11.

17. Cora Du Bois, "The Dominant Value Profile of American Culture," *American Anthropologist,* 57 (December, 1955), pp. 1232-1239.

18. Gunnar Myrdal, *An American Dilemma,* New York: Harper and Brothers, 1944.

19. Will Herberg, *Protestant-Catholic-Jew,* Garden City, N.Y.: Doubleday and Company, 1960, pp. 75-90.

20. *Ibid.* The most detailed sociological presentation of this position has been made by Berger. See Peter L. Berger, *The Noise of Solemn Assemblies,* Garden City, N.Y.: Doubleday and Company, 1961, pp. 17-104.

21. For a good short summary of recent research on this phenonemon see Irenaeus Rosier, "El catolicismo en Europe en la aurora de una época nueva," in Rosier (ed.), *Essays on the Pastoral Problems of the Catholic Church in the World Today,* Rome: Institutum Carmelitanum, 1960, pp. 10-72.

22. The decline in popular religious interest has been particularly marked in the Lutheran countries and in France. For a good summary of the recent extensive sociological investigation of religion in France see F. Boulard, *An Introduction to Religious Sociology, Pioneer Work in France* (translated by M. J. Jackson), London: Darton, Longman and Todd, 1960.

23. This position has been stated in a slightly different way and from a somewhat different perspective by Talcott Parsons. See his "Some Comments on the Pattern of Religious Organization in the United States," in *Structure and Process in Modern Societies,* Glencoe: The Free Press, 1960, pp. 298, 310-311, 320.

24. Herberg, *op. cit.,* pp. 193-194.

25. Benton Johnson, "Do Holiness Sects Socialize in Dominant Values?" *Social Forces,* 39 (May, 1961), pp. 309-316.

26. Martin (*op. cit.*) makes a point that is closely related to this one when he argues that most of the English and American "sects" have in reality been what he calls denominations, which is to say that the features they have shared with such bodies as the Presbyterians or the Congregationalists have been far more numerous than the features they have shared with Troeltschean sects.

27. There is evidence of a similar, but of course far more controlled bifurcation within Catholicism. See Robert D. Cross, *The Emergence of Liberal Catholicism in America,* Cambridge: Harvard University Press, 1958. For an intriguing glimpse of issues currently being debated within this framework see the mimeographed transcripts of the public debates of William Buckley and William Clancy, East Paterson, N.J.: St. Leo's Holy Name Society, 1960. In general, the Catholic Church's posture on public issues cannot be clearly identified as either liberal or conservative. Since it has not been prominently associated with

the ideological drift toward liberalism, however, its general impact is probably more conservative than anything else.

28. One of the best recent treatments of liberalism, the social gospel, and the rise of neo-orthodoxy is Donald B. Meyer's *The Protestant Search for Social Realism. 1919–1941,* Berkeley and Los Angeles: University of California Press, 1960. Neo-orthodoxy has brought about a more conservative trend in theology but it has continued the strongly liberal trend in social outlook. See also N. F. Furniss, *The Fundamentalist Controversy, 1918–1931,* New Haven: Yale University Press, 1954.

29. The tendency of a minority of the clergy to lead or to affiliate with radical movements on the right and the left has been well documented. See Ralph Roy, *Apostles of Discord. A Study of Organized Bigotry and Disruption on the Fringes of Protestantism,* Boston: Beacon Press, 1953. See also Ralph Roy, *Communism and the Churches,* New York: Harcourt, Brace, 1960.

30. For example, a recent survey of all the Baptist and Methodist pastors of Oregon undertaken by the author reveals that 87 per cent of the theologically liberal pastors (N=68) also regard themselves as *politically* liberal, and that 93 per cent of the theologically conservative or fundamentalist pastors (N=179) also regard themselves as *politically* conservative. The same relationships are reflected, though in attenuated form, in party preference. Ninety-two per cent of theological conservatives and fundamentalists (N=165) have tended to vote Republican over the past five years, whereas only 52 per cent of theological liberals (N=58) have tended to vote Republican.

31. Benton Johnson, "Ascetic Protestantism and Political Preference," *Public Opinion Quarterly,* 26 (Spring, 1962) pp. 35-46; also "Ascetic Protestantism and Political Preference, Deep South" (forthcoming). In both studies the relationship between religion and political preference appears to be independent of occupational class.

32. Although the choice of this reference point will not illuminate all significant differences among denominations, there is good reason for supposing that it will shed far more light than any other perspective of comparable generality. Although most public issues never assume ideological significance, the liberal-conservative distinction has become relevant to a wide variety of issues ranging from foreign aid and the United Nations to labor policy, educational objectives, and mental health.

33. It is significant that the seminaries in which this transition did take place were the seminaries that produced clergymen for the churches of the middle and upper classes. Consequently, the social gospel movement never succeeded in rallying a large working-class following. On the other hand, the fundamentalist constituency has always been relatively working class and lower middle class in composition. For specific historical reasons not duplicated in most other nations, it has turned out that in recent years a very large segment of the Protestant laity in America has probably been subjected to ideational influences, even if ever so slight, that are at odds with the political perspectives likely to be current in their immediate class environment. The effect of this paradoxical phenomenon has yet to be investigated.

STEPHEN STEINBERG

Reform Judaism: The Origin and Evolution of a "Church Movement"

An early obstacle to systematic study of Reform Judaism is the difficulty of accommodating the Reform case to accepted sociological propositions concerning church and sect. At first glance one would surmise that the Reform group, having severed its relation with Orthodoxy, is a sectarian movement, analytically indistinct from Christian sects that arise out of schisms within established religious bodies. Yet certain elements usually associated with sects, such as literal adherence to Biblical teachings and apocalyptic ideological tendencies, are conspicuously absent. Of greater significance, while most religious movements seek to modify or transform societal norms and values, the Reform Movement is striking for its attempt to bring its norms and values into greater conformity with those of the larger society. This apparent ambiguity provides a useful point of departure for analysis of the Reform Movement, and a possible basis for the reformulation of theory. To state the question simply—is Reform Judaism a church or a sect?

From the *Journal for the Scientific Study of Religion* 5(Fall 1965):117-29. Reprinted by permission of the publisher and author.

This issue has been raised many times in terms of criticism of the church-sect typology as it was first formulated by Troeltsch and unsuccessfully redefined by subsequent sociologists. In a recent paper Benton Johnson offers a clear statement of the problem:

> Troeltsch's definitions of sect and church each contain a large number of characteristics, or elements . . . (many of which) vary independently of each other. . . . If elements vary independently, the classification of mixed cases becomes an almost impossible task. So far the major response to this difficulty has been to coin new types on an *ad hoc* basis as important new mixed cases present themselves. . . . The trouble with most of these newer typologies is that they have never really stipulated all of the elements under consideration and they have never succeeded in transcending the particular considerations that led to their development.[1]

Johnson proposes a refinement of the church-sect typology which he demonstrates to be both accurate and useful. This paper attempts to build upon Johnson's formulation by elaborating several distinctions that are undeveloped in the original scheme. These will provide a theoretical perspective that will allow comparisons between Reform Judaism and other kinds of religious movements.

The core of Johnson's thesis rests upon his one-variable definition of church and sect: "A church is a religious group that accepts the social environment in which it exists. A sect is a religious group that rejects the social environment in which it exists."[2] These definitions can be worded still more precisely. In Johnson's application of them, it becomes clear that the defining variable is not acceptance or rejection of the social environment, but a similar characteristic: whether or not there is a discrepancy or tension between the norms and values of the religious group and those of the surrounding society. This language is preferable because either society or the religious group may reject the values of the other, or both may occur at once. The sectarian nature of Judaism through most of its history in the Diaspora is as much a product of society's rejection of Jewish norms and values, as a calculated rejection of society on the part of Jews. Hence the concept of value tension is more accurate and more widely applicable than acceptance or rejection of the social environment. To apply this slight modification, a church is defined as a religious group that is in low tension with the social environment. A sect is a religious group in high tension with the surrounding environment.[3]

Consistent with Johnson's treatment, the concept of tension should be accorded both absolute and relative value. Hence, a religious group that comes into less tension is moving in the direction of becoming a church; however, if the state of tension is still high, the group must be classified as a sect. In other words, there is a continuum extending from low tension to high tension, with church and sect as the polar types. When the continuum is dichotomized, each half represents a church-like and a sect-like category. A further division along each half establishes the cutting-point for classifying a group as a church or a sect. This conceptualization is presented schematically below:

	less tension	more tension	
church	church-like	sect-like	sect

It should be added that the relative, rather than the absolute value of tension deserves emphasis. It is not of theoretical importance that "group X" is a church, but only that "group X" is in less tension with the surrounding environment than "group Y," or that "group X" is more church-like than "group Y."

The first step in elaborating Johnson's definition is to distinguish between two types of religious organizations: institutions and rump groups (schismatic groups). No sociological qualities should be attributed to either; rather, they should be defined in terms of some physical attribute, such as ownership of property. For the purposes of the present analysis, it will suffice to define an institution as a religious organization that possesses property. A rump group, in contradistinction, is a group that severs its connection with the institution and thereby forsakes its right to the property of the institution.[4] Of course, in time it may itself acquire property, whereupon it will *ipso facto* become an institution.

The relation of *both* institutions and rump groups to the larger society can be conceptualized in terms of the amount of tension between their values and the values of the dominant social system. Hence, cross-classifying these two generic types of religious groups with Johnson's criterion of church and sect, we arrive at the following calculation: both institutions and rump groups may come into either more or less tension with the surrounding environment. An institution that reduces the level of tension with society may be said to be in the process of becoming more churchly. This process is often called "institutionalization." Institutions that come into more tension with society manifest a tendency to become more sect-like. I will refer to this simply as institutional conflict. On the other side, a rump group that comes into more tension with society is a sect movement. Finally, rump groups that come into less tension with society from the time of their separation from the parent institution will be termed "church movements." The schematic presentation is as follows:

	Institution	Rump group
More tension	Institutional Conflict	Sect Movement
Less tension	Institution-alization	Church Movement

Social scientists have understandably focused attention on the two types that occur with greatest frequency. Typically, institutions are in a state of low tension with society. Through the process of institutionalization discordant elements of the religious institution become obscured before the emerging identity between fundamental aspects of the religious and secular cultures. In a stable social system, one normally finds an alliance, if not a fusion, between religious and social institutions. The religious institutions partake of and help to maintain the normative order of the larger society. Hence, most religious institutions are churches. In contrast, rump groups originate under conditions of instability and strain when the institution is not functioning to meet the needs of a significant proportion of its adherents. Hence, rump groups *typically* fall into greater tension with society as they break off from the religious institution, and are therefore sects.

However, not all institutions are churches and not all rump groups are sects. Two further possibilities exist:

First, a religious *institution* may come into greater tension with society and thereby move in the direction of becoming a sect.

Second, a *rump group* (from the time of its inception and not through the process of institutionalization) may come into less tension with society and thereby move in the direction of becoming a church. I have called this a "church movement."[5]

These will be shown to be not mere analytical possibilities, but empirical realities. My main objective is to demonstrate that the Reform Movement is an anomaly among religious movements in that it sought to modify institutional norms and values that were discrepant with those of the larger society. Afterwards, I will examine other anomalous features of this "church movement," and explore their implications for social theory. First, however, it will be helpful to briefly analyze Orthodox Judaism in order to uncover some of the social conditions that gave rise to the peculiar phenomenon of a religious movement that, in a sense, sought to eliminate those very qualities that made it a distinctive religious entity.

Orthodoxy: An Anachronism

How may a religious institution come into increased tension with the social environment? Established religions, as I have mentioned, are usually closely allied with the secular institutions. Under normal conditions they are able to adjust to changes in society. However, under conditions of rapid and extreme change in society, such adjustment may be impossible and a situation of greater tension will result. In this way, a religious institution whose values were once compatible with those of society may be thrust abruptly into a state of high tension with the surrounding environment.

Such was the case of Orthodox Judaism in Western Europe during the last half of the eighteenth century. During the Middle Ages the discrepancy between the traditional social system of the Jews and the norms and values of the accommodating European societies was, to be sure, of considerable magnitude. Tension was great, and according to Johnson's definition, Orthodoxy must be classified as a sect. But conflict between antagonistic elements of the two cultures was kept in bounds, ironically, by the physical and social isolation of the Jewish community. However, with the transformation of European society and the emancipation of the ghettoized Jew, the contradictions became more apparent. Tension with the (literally) surrounding society reached its crest and threw Orthodoxy into crisis. In his study of the Jewish community during this period, Jacob Katz writes:

> Traditional Jewish society . . . experienced a unique development. Instead of banishment and migration, changes now took place that left the society in the same place geographically, but that shattered, or at least distorted, its framework.[6]

In short, the elevation of the Jew to national citizenship and the breakdown of the ghetto walls made Jewish religious institutions vulnerable to the pressures of the developing nation-states, and resulted in even greater tension with the dominant social system.

While it is true that Orthodoxy had successfully adapted to disadvantageous social conditions during its long history in the Diaspora, it must also be said that the Emancipation represented a threat that was unprecedented in kind. A social revolution was taking place on all sides of the ghetto and within its midst, for the pressures that at first were imposed from outside soon began to foment from within. Although Jews had experienced centuries of religious persecution and enforced migration, their independent status as a nation in exile had never before been seriously challenged.

It is not necessary, in view of my limited objectives, to comment further upon the disintegration of the traditional Jewish community. Let it suffice to say that the value system of Orthodoxy was so discrepant with that of the enlightened society that adjustment *in its current form* was an impossibility. Two theoretical possibilities for a collective response existed. Either Orthodoxy could further isolate itself from the larger society—to reject society as well as be rejected by it, or it could transform (even to the point of abandoning) its norms and values to conform in greater degree to those of the dominant social system. In short, Judaism could move in the direction of becoming either more sect-like or more churchly. However, movement in one direction or the other was inescapable.[7]

The prospect of national citizenship, ending centuries of banishment and persecution, barred a collective withdrawal from society. In actuality, the crisis following the Emancipation precipitated a collective attempt toward accommodation. This began with the Haskala Movement in Western Europe and culminated in the American Reform Movement. These were "church movements" that aimed at greater conformity to the norms and values of secular society.[8]

The Reform Movement: An Anomaly among Social Movements

Rump groups typically originate, as Niebuhr has shown, when the discrepancy between individual and group values is a function of the institutionalization of the group to middle-class standards. As the institution adjusts its theological and social postures to conform to societal norms, it dispossesses a portion of its adherents whose values conflict sharply with those of both church and society. With the Emancipation, however, the Jewish religious institution was coming into greater tension with society at the same time that individuals were coming into less tension. This rare situation was the most important condition for an even more anomalous phenomenon: a rump group that aims at greater conformity to the values of the dominant social system. I have referred to this as a "church movement."

If the goal of the emancipated Jew was to conform to societal norms and values, why did this produce a religious rather than a secular response? Of paramount importance here was the Jew's desire to maintain some attachment with traditional culture. His hope was to venture out of the ghetto without going too far, to accept some of society's values without becoming altogether immersed in the dominant culture. Thus, the desire to remain apart was a necessary condition for the evolution of a church movement. Yet half integration is an ambigous, if not precarious goal, one that would inevitably create difficulties for the emerging movement.

The European Approach to Reform

The disintegration of the Jewish community following the Emancipation was never allowed to reach the point of absorption into the surrounding society. An intellectual elite who had penetrated into the enlightened society also moved to the forefront of Jewish community life. According to Katz, the emergence of this special class was the decisive event for checking the decay of the Jewish social system:

> The social turning point . . . is revealed in the emergence of a new type, the *maskil,* who added to his knowledge of the Torah a command of foreign languages, general erudition, and an interest in what was happening in the non-Jewish world. This type became increasingly numerous beginning with the 1760's, and it soon constituted a subgroup in Jewish society. It demanded for itself not only the right of existence, but also the privilege of leadership.[9]

This general erudition included a knowledge of, and dedication to, the rationalist principles of the Enlightenment which were acquired through the acceptance of the *maskilim* into the intellectual circles of "the neutral society." These principles eventually became translated into a liberal ideology that was to prove an effective rallying point for the Reform Movement.

Two general points should be made concerning the status and the role of the *maskilim.* First, many emancipated Jews began to identify with this intellectual elite. In effect, they "transferred their social goals to the context of the non-Jewish milieu"[10] through the intellectuals. This was an important development because once the *maskilim* achieved a degree of status within the Jewish community, their potential as a progressive leadership was enhanced.

Social status was a necessary, but not a sufficient condition for leadership. Obviously, the *maskilim* themselves had to resist the attractions of assimilation and devote their energies first to an intellectual reappraisal of Jewish tradition, and ultimately to a reconstruction of the Jewish community. While some *maskilim* defected permanently from Judaism, most followed the example of Mendelsohn, the foremost Jewish leader during this period, and "out of a sense of responsibility for the fate of Jewish society . . . agreed to undertake tasks which more or less delineated its course."[11] The *maskilim* became a distinctive element "whose identification with the values of the neutral society set them apart from the members of the traditional society, but whose attachment to the values and the culture of their original milieu did not allow them to divorce themselves completely from it."[12] This marked the appearance, virtually for the first time in Jewish history, of a marginal class of Jewish intellectual who sought to reconcile the antagonistic elements of his two worlds.

The *maskilim,* under some pressure from the secular authorities, set about the task of applying their rationalist principles to the traditional

Jewish institutions. In Western Europe the progressive elements eventually organized into the Haskala Movement which, "like the parallel non-Jewish Enlightenment movement . . . aimed not at reforming the evils of reality but at setting up a new reality in its place."[13] Progress along these lines, however, was circumscribed by the tradition-bound structure of European society. The locus for change was transferred to the American community.

The Reform Movement in America: The First Years

Although Reform Judaism is rooted in the intellectual and social transformation that occurred in Europe between 1750 and 1850, and had been transplanted, in an unmaturated form, from Germany, it first became a distinctive social movement and reached its fruition in the United States.

It should be noted that the situation in America before 1850 was not very different from that in Europe, at least with regard to the relation of Judaism to the wider society. The clash between the two value systems, even if this did not take the form of open conflict, was apparent to American Jews, most of whom had emigrated from Western Europe and had adapted in other respects to the new social environment. In addition, the American Jewish community had suffered a breakdown of the traditional system of controls similar to that experienced by its European counterpart. Writing about Jewish society around the middle of the nineteenth century, Moshe Davis concludes:

> At the end of this period, in 1840, American Jewry entered a new stage in its development. The dynamism of American life had released powerful forces. . . . The older methods of fines and bans lost their punitive powers. . . . Intermarriage, Jewish ignorance, and above all, the paralyzing indifference to the destiny of Judaism thoroughly upset Jewish religious institutional life. In the Colonial period, a Jew was zealously controlled from birth to death by the synagogue. Now a Jew could live or die as a Jew without regard for that control.[14]

It is not surprising that the crisis within the American Jewish community was so similar to the European pattern since the same disintegrating forces were operating in both environments.

However, one important condition was unique to America, and this helps to explain the unprecedented success of the Reform Movement. American society was structurally conducive to the advancement of rationalist principles and the reorganization of Jewish institutions. This claim is not overexaggerated. In European society the Reformers encountered unyielding opposition by the traditionalists. Not only did they face the internal sanctions of the Jewish community—"denunciation, punishment, and excommunication"[15]—but the traditionalist could also invoke the support of the secular authorities in suppressing deviation. In contrast, the freedom and religious diversity of American society precluded any such barrier to the mobilization of progressive elements within the Jewish community. Furthermore, the religious orientation of American society probably functioned indirectly to encourage the development of a liberal movement.

In general, the American setting was disastrous for the traditional system. Changes in American society had the effect of weakening the authority of the Jewish institutions. For example, the development of a system of state-controlled secular education deprived the synagogue of one of its chief functions. Moreover, the sheer increase in the number of synagogues paradoxically helped to undermine central authority, since synagogues were dispersed over a wide area and their memberships were socially different.[16] Finally, migration to America itself represented a breach from the past, and in his quest for social advancement, the immigrant was forced to abandon, at least temporarily, constricting social customs and religious rituals. However, his emotional attachment to Judaism endured, and this led him to seek an alternative that would allow him to retain his identification with the formal Jewish community. Thus, American Jews were psychologically prepared to accept the innovations that Jewish leaders proposed. In addition, conditions within the larger society were conducive for the development and success of a reform movement.

While there were sporadic attempts toward Reform before the influx of German Jews, it is clear that a desire simply to adapt to the American system of values was too ambiguous a goal to inspire organized action. In short, a collective movement was conditioned by the introduction of a system of generalized beliefs.[17] The unique contribution of the German intellectuals who migrated to America was that they invested this desire for social adjustment with religious significance. Once the rationalist principles of the Enlightenment were applied to traditional Judaism, "the traditional position could be attacked as wrong as well as inconvenient."[18] This ideology functioned to draw many uncommitted elements of the Jewish community into a cohesive social movement.

A critical evaluation of the entire traditional system was a principal feature of the new ideology. The conclusion was that most of Jewish tradition was grounded in superstition and antiquated custom. This new attitude provided ample justification for the abandonment of much traditional ritual and belief, and the formulation of a new system that was consistent with the social arrangements of modern society. This was the accomplishment of the intellectual leadership. The immoderacy of the early reformers, however, is astonishing even from the vantage point of contemporary Reform.

The Pittsburgh Platform reflects the general tenet of the Reform Movement during its first years. This historic document was a statement of Reform principles that emerged from a conference of Reform rabbis. It culminated a half century of controversy between traditionalists and progressives, and, by proclaiming a formal ideology, underscored the finality of the Reform defection from historical Judaism. The following passages are revealing of the rationalist philosophical strain in Reform ideology and illustrate the Movement's objective of greater conformity to the norms and values of Western society:

> We recognize in the Mosaic legislation a system of training the Jewish people for its mission during its national life in Palestine, and today we accept as binding only its moral laws and maintain only such ceremonials as elevate and sanctify our lives, *but reject all such as are not adapted to the views and habits of modern civilization.*
>
> We hold that all such Mosaic and Rabbinical laws as regulate diet, priestly purity and dress orginated in ages and under the influence of ideas altogether foreign to our present mental and spiritual state.
>
> We recognize in Judaism a progressive religion, ever striving to be in accord with the postulates of reason.[19]

These bold statements heralded major changes in doctrine and liturgy, the effect of which "was to make the social atmosphere of the synagogue that of a Protestant church of the upper and upper-middle classes."[20] The specific nature of these changes does not have to be considered here. Let it suffice to say that by 1885 Reform had completed the schism from the Orthodox institution, and by embracing principles and practices that were harmonious with the dominant value system, had substantially reduced tension with the surrounding society. It was, by my definition, a church movement.

The Later Stages of the Reform Movement

As I suggested earlier, conformity to American values and maintenance of a Jewish consciousness were, in some ways incompatible goals, especially for a social movement whose avowed method was to destroy the ancient symbols which represented and vitalized that consciousness. Could the Reform Movement follow their principles to their logical extreme without defeating their fundamental purpose of "preserving the historical identity of our great past?"[21] The issue concerning Jewish nationalism illustrates how this problem was resolved and the new direction of the Reform Movement in the twentieth century.

Jewish nationalism, stated in prayers and ritual as a longing for the end of the Dispersion and return to Palestine, and expressed socially by the conception of Judaism as a people as well as a religion, was the most formidable barrier to acceptance into the secular world. In Europe, Napoleon and other secular authorities had assembled Jewish leaders in order to establish whether Jews were loyal to the emerging nation-states. In addition, Jewish nationalism was contradictory to the Reform conception of Judaism as a universal and rational religion that was to join forces with modern humanism in realizing the utopia of the Enlightenment—"a Kingdom of truth, justice and peace among all men."[22] The authors of the Pittsburgh Platform were straightforward in their rejection of Jewish nationalism:

> We consider ourselves no longer a nation but a religious community, and therefore expect neither a return to Palestine, nor a sacrificial worship under the administration of the sons of Aaron, nor the restoration of any of the laws concerning the Jewish state.[23]

Even after the Zionist Movement came into existence, the official attitude of the Reform Movement was hostile to the creation of a Jewish state. Following the Balfour Declaration in 1917, the Central Conference of Reform rabbis passed a resolution which, although welcoming the Declaration as an act of good-will toward Jews, was clear in the renunciation of the concept of a national homeland:

> We hold that Jews in Palestine as well as anywhere else in the world are entitled to equality in political, civil, and religious rights but we do not subscribe to the phrase in the declaration which says, "Palestine is to be a national homeland for the Jewish people." . . . We hold that the Jews are and of right ought to be at home in all lands. . . . The mission of the Jew is to witness God all over the world.[24]

However, the anti-nationalistic position, notwithstanding the intellectual zeal with which it was enunciated, was accepted half-heartedly. The perseverance of nationalistic sentiment can be seen in the popular and official response to the persecution of European Jews. To quote Glazer again: "The solid majority, while they claimed to be members of a religion, not a 'people,' reacted to pogroms and persecutions abroad with somewhat more feeling than would have been justified by concern for co-religionists alone."[25] Finally, in 1935 the Central Conference replaced the anti-Zionist clause of the Pittsburgh Platform with a resolution that stipulated a neutral position with respect to Zionism and a determination to "continue to cooperate in the upbuilding of Palestine, and in the economic, cultural, and particularly spiritual tasks confronting the growing and evolving Jewish community there."[26] This was indicative of a more general trend away from the initial radicalism of the Movement.

In 1937 the Conference produced a new platform "whereby the debates and discussions of two decades were crystallized into a compromise program."[27] The Reform Movement had moved into the moderate camp. Crucial differences remained, to be sure, but the earlier radicalism was absent. The persecution of Jews abroad was only one factor. The feeling of spiritual emptiness that pervaded the Movement was another. A third factor was the emergence of the Conservative Movement and the liberalizing tendencies of the Orthodox synagogue. These changes meant that three religious bodies were competing for the loyalties of the more tradition-oriented East Europeans who, since 1881, were immigrating at an unprecedented rate. Finally, moderate leaders such as Mordecai Kaplan, were replacing the radical intellectuals of the first generation. Collectively, these factors led to a revival of many forgotten traditions, the reinterpretation of many Orthodox beliefs and their inclusion into Reform ideology, and a general modification of the extremism of the early Reform Movement.

This development is important from an analytical standpoint. The decline in the radicalism of Reform principles and practices signified, in effect, a corresponding increase in the discrepancy between religious values and the values of the larger society. Sects, as Niebuhr demonstrates, are in greatest tension with the surrounding society at the time of schism from the religious institution, and eventually become institutionalized to middle-class standards. The reverse pattern is found in a church movement (if it is possible to generalize from this single case). Church movements appear to be at their lowest point of tension at the time of their schism from the parent institution, and to come into more tension with societal values as their original aims are modified.

There is a logical basis for this generalization. While it is possible to conceive of a church movement which steadily reduces the level of tension with society, this is unlikely to be an empirical reality. Unlimited pursuit of its original aims would result in total integration into the secular society and were this the purpose, the movement would not have taken a religious form in the first place. Hence, a church movement is likely to confront internal conservative forces that either halt or revert its conforming tendency and thereby stabilize or increase its tension with the surrounding environment. Indeed, it would appear that a church movement, by its very nature, contains the seeds of moderation. As in the case of the Reform Movement, however, the rump group is likely to remain more churchly than the parent institution.

The Reform Movement suggests a second characteristic which distinguishes church movements from sect movements. Reform in Germany "began as a movement of Jews of high social status who wished to dignify Jewish religious services and make them decorous."[28] The leaders, as I have indicated, composed an intellectual elite, and their followers in America were also drawn from the upper classes. One Reform leader complained in 1932:

> Judaism has been alienated from the Jewish people. Its upkeep is today the concern of a class above a certain income level rather than of the masses and by and large this class is concerned only to the point of supplying the cost of the plant and the "spiritual leader" through whose professional expertness they may discharge their religious obligations.[29]

The Movement's trend, however, was to broaden its social base. Both out of a sense of moral obligation and out of organizational necessity, Reform leaders acted to make Reformism more palatable to the Jewish masses. This was particularly true during and subsequent to the East European migration. Hence, while sect movements are made up of "disinherited" individuals whose social and economic advancement has lagged behind that of the group, church movements originate as middle-class movements and appear to broaden their bases of support during their evolution.

Indeed, a church movement may be contrasted to a sect movement with respect to virtually all of the elements which analysts have used to characterize sects. In the beginning the Reform Movement emphasized a universal theology; with its development it became more parochial as it reinterpreted traditional doctrine and moved closer to historical Judaism. (Sects tend to move from parochialism to a position that emphasizes the universalism of the gospel.) While in the beginning the guiding principle for admitting proselytes was the Talmudic statement "Whoever renounces idolatry is a Jew," in time the requirements for converts became more rigorous. (Sects tend to restrict their memberships at first and later adopt a less discriminatory policy.) Practically the only characteristic which sect and church movements share in common is that both are rump groups. However, the circumstances of their origin and the direction of their development are antithetical.

Conclusion

That the origin and development of the Reform Movement was markedly different from the pattern observed for sects suggests that church movements constitute a meaningful theoretical type, one that should be included in theories concerning church and sect. It should be added, however, that the conditions that generated the Reform Movement rarely exist. While it is not uncommon for a religious institution to come into greater tension with a changing society, it rarely happens that the institution cannot adapt to the new situation, or in that event, that other institutional alternatives do not already exist.[30] In the case of Judaism, however, Orthodoxy could not quickly adjust to the sudden change, and individual Jews, unwilling to forsake their Jewish identity, had no institutional outlet for their social and religious needs. As a minority religion, Judaism had to create a new form for the Jew who wished to maintain his marginality between his religious culture and the secular order. The Reform Movement, then, is an anomalous case, and in this capacity helps to define the limits of current theory and suggests guidelines for its improvement.

---

1. Benton Johnson, "On Church and Sect," *American Sociological Review,* 28 (August, 1963), p. 541.

Charles Y. Glock argues in similar terms that the defining characteristics of sects are not universally applicable to new religious movements. He shows that for any characteristics, one can point to a religious group in which that characteristic is absent, but which would be classified as a sect by the other criteria. "On the Role of Deprivation in the Origin and Evolution of Religious Groups," in Robert Lee, ed., *Religion and Social Conflict,* New York: Oxford, 1964, pp. 24-36.

2. Johnson, *ibid.,* p. 542.

3. As indicated above, these definitions do not differ substantially from Johnson's formulation. For example, Johnson states: "Since a sect tends to be in a state of tension with its surroundings, we are safe in supposing that religions that have totally withdrawn from participation in a society or that are engaged in open attack on it are likely to fall close to the sect end. . . . Churches, on the other hand, are comparatively at ease with the established values and practices of a society." *Ibid.,* p. 544.

4. Rump groups do not always originate as dissenting elements that voluntarily break off from the parent institution. As in the case of the Anabaptists, a group of dissenters may be declared *persona non grata* by the authorities of the institution and their relation terminated by exclusion or formal excommunication.

5. This paper has profited from Glock's discussion of the origin and evolution of religious groups. Glock writes: ". . . not all religious groups emerge as sects. Some are churches in their original form. This was true of Reform Judaism in Europe and Conservative Judaism in America. Most Protestant groups were from their beginnings more like churches than like sects." *Op cit.,* p. 26.

6. Jacob Katz, *Tradition and Crisis: Jewish Society at the End of the Middle Ages,* New York: The Free Press, 1961, p. 227.

7. It should be made explicit that adjustment did not have to take a collective form. As often happens, individuals might realign themselves with groups whose values are consonant with their own. This, however, was not a realistic alternative for Jews, since denominationalism, practically speaking, was unknown to Judaism. The only other possibility for individual adjustment was conversion to Christianity or abandonment of religion altogether, but few Jews were willing to go this far.

8. In contrast, the Hasidic Movement in Eastern Europe, arising out of conditions of economic hardship and political repression, was a sectarian movement that included a theologically based rejection of societal norms and values.

9. *Op. cit.,* p. 246.

10. *Ibid.,* p. 251.

11. *Ibid.,* p. 257.

12. *Ibid.*

13. *Ibid.,* p. 260.

14. Moshe Davis, "Jewish Religious Life and Institutions in America," in Louis Finklestein, ed., *The Jews,* New York: Harper, 1949, p. 365.

15. Katz, *op. cit.,* p. 274.

16. Nathan Glazer, *American Judaism,* Chicago: University of Chicago Press, 1957, p. 34.

17. My analysis of the factors that conditioned the development of the Reform Movement has been guided by Neil J. Smelser's *Theory of Collective Behavior,* New York: The Free Press, 1962. According to Smelser, generalized beliefs help to mobilize people for collective action and thus are a necessary condition for the occurrence of a collective episode.

18. Glazer, *op. cit.,* p. 49. Glazer also suggests that the political and religious philosophy of the Enlightenment had special historical significance for Jews, since these ideas had freed them from medieval restrictions.

19. This document is reprinted in Glazer, *ibid.,* pp. 151-152.

20. *Ibid.,* p. 16.

21. This also was part of the Pittsburgh Platform, *ibid.,* p. 152.

22. From the Pittsburgh Platform. The entire sentence reads: "We recognize in the modern era of universal culture of heart and intellect the approach of the realization of Israel's great Messianic hope for the establishment of the Kingdom of truth, justice and peace among all men." *Ibid.*

23. *Ibid.*

24. Quoted in Beryl H. Levy, *Reform Judaism in America,* New York: Block Publishing Company, 1933, p. 134.

25. Glazer, *ibid.,* p. 54.

26. Quoted in Davis, *op. cit.,* p. 420.

27. *Ibid.*

28. Glazer, *ibid.,* p. 27.

29. Quoted in Levy, *op. cit.,* p. 77

30. In Christianity, for example, individuals who want to move into closer conformity with societal values can, and often do, cross denominational lines without altering their basic identification with Christian religion. Such a convenient option did not exist for Jews around the time of the Emancipation. Lacking an institutional alternative that would satisfy their desire for social adjustment, Jews were forced to create one.

BRYAN R. WILSON

The Pentecostalist Minister: Role Conflicts and Status Contradictions

Sects, as usually defined in the growing body of sociological literature on the subject, do not usually employ the services of a ministry.[1] In the pristine condition of the sect the ministerial role is divided into its separate functions—leadership in worship, prayer, social action; pastoral care; preaching; presidential duties; administration; welfare activities —and these are undertaken by elected or appointed members of the sect itself. The ministerial role is divided, and the functionaries are unspecialized, untrained, and usually unpaid, although here there is variation.[2] But there are groups which cannot be conveniently styled as other than sects which have, in fact, developed trained specialists as ministerial leaders. Such are the two principal Pentecostal groups in Great Britain, from one of which—the Elim Foursquare Gospel Alliance—are drawn the observations on which this paper is based.[3] These movements are apparently undergoing the familiar transformation from sect

---

Reprinted from the *American Journal of Sociology* 64 (March 1959):494-504, by permission of the author and The University of Chicago Press.

to denomination, although somewhat more slowly and irregularly than has been the pattern in American fundamentalist movements in the course of the last century.[4] The equivocacy of the Pentecostal minister's position is partly attributable to the transitional process.

Pentecostalism, in its modern form, had its English beginnings within the body of the Church of England and other denominations and in a number of earlier independent Holiness missions. The teachings of the Pentecostalists—that the Holy Ghost still quickens the faith of born-again believers and that the gifts of the Spirit, as described by Paul (I Corinthians, chaps. 13–15), and particularly the gift of tongues, are still granted—were harbored by some in the fundamentalist wings of the various churches, although these teachings remained alien even to the majority of these fundamentalists. Initially, the Pentecostalists were tolerated within other movements, but, as the teaching assumed increasing importance for its advocates, a separatist development occurred, even though most leading Pentecostalists recognized that this teaching was only an "added truth," a "fuller blessing," and not a truth essential to salvation. Some of the most influential remained in their own churches, where they felt they were most needed, and opposed any separate Pentecostalist movement. Nonetheless, such a movement developed almost unintentionally as a consequence of the intense revivalist activities of some who had espoused Pentecostal doctrines. The new movement lacked, in its early uncrystallized form, a clear articulation of its distinctive purpose and mission, but by revivalist techniques a growing following was built up, first in Northern Ireland from 1911 to 1920 and subsequently in England and Wales. Congregations brought into existence by revival could not be readily accommodated in existing churches, to whose congregations the fervor of the newly revived was often offensive.

The revival-recruited and the various independent missions which accepted Pentecostal teaching and practice became the core of the new sect. The revivalist leaders appear to have had no conscious aim, in the first place, to establish a sect. They did not imitate any model; it was the consequence of their attempt to "revive Christendom." The needs of the converted quickly imposed administrative obligations upon the leadership. The converted needed after-care, and functionaries other than revivalists had to be found to undertake what were essentially ministerial duties. In this important detail both the Elim church and, though to a somewhat lesser extent, the Assemblies of God differed from sects like the Brethren, the Christadelphians, and the Church of God in the British Isles and Overseas, in that they were congregations brought into being principally by revivalism and not in the same sense self-recruited seekers after truth. Their caliber was not that of the sturdy independent self-governing meeting houses; they had responded to a leader and still needed a pastor to shepherd the flock.

The appointment of honorary pastors and church leaders as functionaries distinct from revivalists followed. They were chosen as far as possible from local communities by the movement's leaders. This was the first shift in the accepted values and action patterns of the movement. The initial mission, the initial value-orientation, had been altered by the clientele itself.[5] In a sense the very methods of revivalism imply such an outcome and a weakening of the central value, the freedom of the Spirit, of the pioneer Pentecostalists. Yet the movement continues to be ideologically committed to this pristine value and finds need, from time to time, to assert that Pentecostalism's real contribution to the church of Christ is that, whereas all other aspects of its teaching are expressed by other branches of fundamentalism, in its emphasis on Spirit baptism and Spirit gifts, it has a real mission in fully restoring all true gospel to the community of the saved. Yet this is a subsequent rationalization; the movement appears to have emerged initially almost as an unforeseen consequence of the revivalist activities of a few prominent Pentecostalists. Revivalism was a technique inherited from the evangelicals of the nineteenth century and one appropriate to a mass society, but one, which, if successful, helps to produce mass movements, and this in itself implied serious modification of the activities of the small exclusive groups seeking personal experience of the Holy Ghost, in which Pentecostalism had had its beginnings.[6]

Elim quickly moved from the honorary pastor and lay leader to the regular minister appointed by headquarters and trained there in the movement's own Bible school. The honorary pastor had been a "Spirit-led" brother, but the minister was an appointee. In part the development of a trained ministry was a consequence of the particular interest of the leader of the Elim movement in helping poor boys to receive Bible-school training. Not all such young men could find outlet, subsequently, in overseas missions and revivalist work, although this appears to have been the original idea, and the movement came to find them work in "home missions" (as the ministerial positions were initially called, since "missioning" was respectable, whereas the movement was not yet committed to a ministry), although no guaranty was given of such placement. The process occurring was the familiar routinization, from voluntary service to service for a fixed stipend, as laid down by headquarters. Likewise, the continuing revival activities of the movement became routinized; typical was the discontinuation of the practice of asking for "love-offerings" to the revivalist, although asking for contributions to the campaign itself continued, since the revivalist was increasingly only an ordinary pastor within the movement, receiving his regular stipend while temporarily relieved of his normal duties. The movement had ceased to be simply a revival campaign but had become an established sect, with revivalism as the technique of recruitment. Ideally, the movement still had a "called ministry," but increasingly the real criterion determining who would actually minister was not that of Spirit-leading but that of Bible-school training.

The minister in Elim is now the legitimized functionary of the group, and it can be asked how far he embodies the values of the organization as expressed in the official ideology, in the actual practice of headquarters, and in the understanding of local congregations. These are not entirely consonant one with another, and it is principally the local minister who takes the strain. Revivalism, as we have noted, even though it feeds on the emotional release of the lower strata, weakened the early Pentecostal emphasis on the spontaneous freedom of the Spirit. A movement with a tradition of alertness to the call of the Spirit and a desire to get "on fire for God" had drawn unto itself a large body of followers with different backgrounds who needed to be awakened to such desires and experiences. The original values of the movement are no longer sustained from below but remain a significant ideological commitment and the *raison d'être* of the movement's separate existence. It is the ministry which must keep them alive, even though the Pentecostal tradition is essentially lay. The minister seeks to perpetuate a Pentecostal tradition in a revival-recruited congregation, but, if he succeeds, he jeopardizes his own position as a trained and appointed minister rather than one whose ministry derives from a congregationally observed Spirit-anointing.

The minister is himself restricted by the tradition of the free Spirit, insofar as this exists in his congregation, since inspirationalism, as in many earlier sects, contains values fundamentally opposed to any sort of institutionalized ministry,[7] or, if accepting a ministry at all, does so only at the Spirit's behest and in accordance with the gifts bestowed by the Spirit.[8] Modern Pentecostalism has retained the idea of Spirit utterance in its meetings but has regularized and institutionalized the circumstances and content of such utterance and brought the excesses and improprieties of the early period under control. However, there are, from time to time, warnings, in the literature produced for internal consumption, that the freedom of the Spirit must not be restrained. The criticism, although not pointed, can be directed only at ministers, who alone are in a position to bridle the Spirit. Thus the minister is responsible for infusing into his following a distinctive tenet of Pentecostalism and of encouraging Pentecostal phenomena—glossalalia being the most common—and is warned against checking spontaneous expression; yet he also has to keep order, guide Pentecostal demonstration, and prevent expression which might challenge his own leadership or bring his Spirit election into doubt. Clearly, the movement has not persisted for more than forty years without developing institutional mechanisms for the resolution of these role conflicts and rationalizations to justify ministerial decisions and leadership; in spite of this, the minister's task is, in the highly charged atmosphere of some Pentecostal meetings, a delicate one.

The intense conviction of the traditional Pentecostal doctrine of justification by faith alone and the priesthood of all believers, typical of sects, further induces equivocation of the role of the Pentecostal minister. Leadership in the sect is, paradoxically, less easily undertaken once it has become institutionalized, that is, as long as there is still commitment to the sect's peculiar value system. Institutionalization of roles implies a different basis of legitimation from that of charisma, but acceptance of the charismatic token as the basis of leadership is deeply imbedded in the Pentecostal teaching itself. In practice the ideal of the priesthood of all believers is only weakly held among contemporary Pentecostalists, who are generally people of limited ability, intelligence, and articulateness and who require very much to be ministered unto. Even so, the affirmation of this ideal is gratifying to some lay members, and hence the importance of providing opportunities for the ordinary individual to speak in tongues or prophesy. Pentecostalism provides these, even though it also seeks, institutionally, to circumscribe them; thus in recent years it has been cleverly explained that prophesying implies "forth-telling" rather than "fore-telling" and that such forth-telling must always be in accordance with biblical truth and be universally applicable rather than personal or particularistic.

The existence of a Bible school to which admission is easy for genuinely born-again youths and which stipulates no real educational prerequisites in some way reconciles the ideal of priesthood of all believers and the realities of the situation.[9] The circumscription of the minister's role is another means of achieving the same result: anyone may in fact distribute the emblems for the breaking of bread, since this is only a remembrance and not of any intrinsic merit. Lay members may preach, and some member is always called upon to begin prayers or "to lead in worship at the Throne of Grace"; and others are called to give testimony or tell of their healing. Some of these functions of leadership are themselves institutionalized lay functions and are supported by institutionalized roles appropriate to them, since usually deacons or elders are called to commence prayer and worship. The minister's choice is often spontaneous, in accordance with Spirit-leading, but for some more onerous tasks, such as organizing the singing of choruses, prearrangement is necessary. In either case, the minister learns to divide his functions and to share them in order to encourage members of the congregation to minister one unto another. He enjoys no *mystique* but is in many ways merely an agent of the movement's headquarters. In dividing his functions, he helps to retain the informality which is an especially prized feature of Pentecostal meetings; he reduces the "churchly" element and increases the involvement of the lay members. Likewise in evangelistic activities he seeks to get all his members at work in open-air testimony, house-to-house canvassing, leaflet distribution, and the old and infirm in the maintenance of a half-hour of prayer, morning and evening, for revival. All this helps to retain a sectlike atmosphere, but clearly the minister must strike a balance, lest he undermine his own position as leader.

Inevitably, the Pentecostal minister has discovered and perhaps even been taught ways of reconciling his own need to assert leadership with Pentecostalism's insistence on the spontaneous operation of the Spirit. There are institutionalized periods in each meeting for freedom of expression. The minister indicates such periods as occasions for prayer, supplication, or worship and elicits appropriate response; and he terminates such periods with some well-understood formula—often a formal, though spontaneous, prayer of his own. The mechanisms do not always work smoothly, and theoretically the meeting is open for Spirit operation at all times. Of all people, the minister must appear to be sensitive to the Holy Ghost and yet the meeting must not move beyond his control. Usually he does not publicly exercise Spirit gifts, or only perhaps in interpretation of some message in tongues (an intervention which helps to give him special control). Theoretically, it is now often claimed that ministers, almost qua ministers, are blessed with the gift of the discernment of spirits, which allows them to distinguish between true and false expressions of the Holy Ghost. This is a claim of considerable importance, a powerful rationalization of the minister's periodic need to guide and evaluate performance, and an attempt to limit this gift to the ministry, since no one is more dangerous to the group than the lay person who claims divine power to evaluate the charismatic utterances of his fellows. The minister uses his authority to bring all charismatic performances into accord with scriptural warrant, both in form and in content, and, to do this, he needs every scriptural support he can find for his own role.

Particular difficulties are posed by the methods of recruitment of Elim members for the minister's role in the upbuilding of stable congregations. Revival recruits often enjoy revival meetings more than stable church life and often respond to a revivalist in that role, or as a personality, more than to a regular minister. A crucial phase in the organization of churches following revivals is the transition from the campaign to the established church. There is, for the organization in general, the problem of the optimal length of the campaign and the best moment for the process of organizational conversion to commence—the conversion of the newly born-again believer into the stable and committed church member. Policy in Elim is to bring in a new minister at this time rather than to allow any of the revivalists (all regular pastors with churches of their own elsewhere) to continue in the new role.

Thus, whether it is consciously appreciated at Elim headquarters or not, the revivalist is spared the difficult operation of transforming his role to meet new requirements or, alternatively, of continuing his revivalist techniques when no longer called for and when, in addition to imposing a strain on him, they appear to have diminishing marginal returns, perhaps even to the point of bringing into operation the law of adverse effect. As a policy it also prevents the recruited from building up loyalty to an individual minister rather than to the movement as a whole. Yet the transition must not be too drastic, or recruits might feel that they have been brought into a movement whose character was misrepresented in the revival campaign. The minister who is to settle with the congregation must be "sold" to his congregation toward the end of the revival; he must share in its spirit and enthusiasm, and yet he must also begin the process of weaning the recruits from the intense excitement of the campaign. It is usually announced that "the campaign continues" at the new church buildings, and, indeed, Pentecostal meetings in established churches do retain a diminished flavor of revivalism, with more pronounced revival seasons fostered at special times of the year. The change of leader makes apparent the institutionalized nature of the relationship between pastor and following and aims at the commitment of the recruited to the movement rather than to a particular individual revivalist.

The minister must, of course, be acceptable to the members of the congregation, even though they do not choose him initially (and for subsequent appointments have only a veto, which is, in fact, hardly ever invoked, and serves merely as a paper safeguard of congregational rights). His task is particularly susceptible to disruption, especially in this transition from the campaign to the eventually established church; it is difficult to win genuine commitment to the movement. The commitment which tends to develop among the members is to the particular congregation of friends, with a campaign remnant of a sense of belonging to a wider and more amorphous body of "the born-again." The minister, clearly, seeks to promote these allegiances and to build up strong primary relationships in his congregation as an aid to its cohesiveness. He must not, however, build himself too fully into the structure of these relationships, lest on his eventual departure the group fall apart. Since Pentecostal meetings are brought into being by revivalists, and then receive a minister, they may lack the resilience of churches with a genuinely congregational polity which can survive the departure of a well-liked minister or the tenure of an unpopular one.

Elim members have less stake in the government of their own church, and, as "born-again" believers, their denominational commitment tends to be weak (although in recent years revival leaders have attempted to strengthen this allegiance during the campaign). Bad judgment on the part of a pastor can drive members to join other similar Pentecostal or fundamentalist churches and so be lost to the denomination. The minister's role is thus rendered more difficult by differential commitment to the movement between himself and the laity of a kind which does not occur among congregationally governed churches and is absent in non-ministerial sects.

A stable church is not easily established among social groups which are themselves unstable and consequently particularly susceptible to revivalist blandishments and the emotionalism of Pentecostal services. Petty jealousies and spites appear to be common in Elim churches, aggravated by the smallness of the groups and the frequency and intensity of their interaction. The primary-group character of Pentecostal assemblies provides an almost familial situation without any of the real bonds of the family and, consequently, often gives rise to "family" quarrels. And so the minister, while he must be sufficiently close to members to strengthen their commitment, must keep out of the quarrels and struggles for status of individuals within his church. He must check charismatic demonstrations manipulated by individuals or cliques for their own purposes and yet do so without giving offense, taking sides, or interfering with the "proper manifestations" of the Holy Ghost. Generalized warnings about back-biting and human pride are necessarily frequent, and ministers are sometimes obliged to discuss their performance privately with those who appear too prominent as the chosen voice of the Spirit, particularly those who too frequently manifest the gift of interpretation in the meeting and cause jealousy among other would-be interpreters (for, theoretically, many might receive the interpretation but only one is anointed by the Holy Ghost to deliver it). Sometimes some feel anointed but are forestalled by another before they can respond. These very problems of the Pentecostal teaching in operation themselves suggest a functional explanation of the emergence of the ministry, since without such an institutionalized role each assembly would probably succumb to internal dissensions and fractiousness.

Member commitment is volatile, and the establishment of a ministry helps to regulate relationships and minimize the threats which Pentecostalism's inspirationalism and subjectivism engender.

The role conflicts of ministers of other denominations are likewise experienced by Pentecostal ministers: the problems of social distance in the light of both private guidance and public and social performance of duty; the maintenance of enthusiasm and spontaneity in the face of long and routinized service (a particularly acute difficulty in the Pentecostal ministry); and the balancing of ministerial and administrative tasks.[10] But to some extent the role problems differ.

As against the liberal Protestant minister, the Pentecostal leader enjoys the support of the authority of Scripture, and he has, in most matters, the policy pronounced by the movement's headquarters as a guide. He is not faced with the difficulty of the minister of a congregationally organized church, whose conscientiousness may sometimes give offense to the very people who are his patrons. Yet the fact that the Elim minister is indisputably the agent at the local level of the movement's headquarters implies other conflicts. The Elim movement is loosely structured at the bottom and tight at the top; the mechanisms of control are institutionalized and unambiguous in the administration at headquarters, some being embodied in constitutional provisions and regulatory codes, but ill defined at the more informal local level. Thus in the matter of doctrinal conformity, the minister is specifically committed to headquarters, and his pulpit preaching is firmly circumscribed by formal rules; but no such attempt is made to insure correct doctrine in the laity, who need know little more than that they are born-again believers, eligible for Spirit baptism. The minister stands to bridge the gap between these two social systems of which he forms a part; he mediates the demands of headquarters to his own congregation, informs them of decisions, and builds up their confidence in "our movement" and "our God-blessed leaders."[11] There is no pretense of democratic participation of local people in the leaders' decisions, which are interpreted by ministers and literature as God-sent directives and opportunities. The minister's role in his church is diffuse and all-embracing, but in relation to headquarters it is specific and calculated; he is called upon to operate with the freedom of Spirit direction in his own church and yet to appear meticulous to headquarters. That these role obligations are separated tends to alleviate direct conflict, even if it does less to mitigate tensions felt by the man himself.[12] The disparities of behavior are understood and tolerated at headquarters, but the local congregation is far less aware of their minister's obligations to the movement's leaders. This lack of symmetry in knowledge of differing role obligations by those involved in the minister's role performance, does not reduce the value of role segregation as a mechanism in reducing role conflicts, but in the case of relatively tenderminded persons (and it can be reasonably supposed that the ministry contains many such) this might be a purely formal consideration. It may well increase tensions felt by the minister concerning role performance, for he is ideally committed to honesty and uprightness. Differential role obligations impair this self-image, as does inequality in the knowledge others have of his differing obligations.

When role-set members are aware of conflicting demands in a particular role, they free its incumbent from some obligation to them.[13] Where, however, the individual performs a bridge function, as does the Pentecostal minister, his diverse obligations are structurally implied, and the members cannot free him from them. In other occupational spheres the strain of such a situation can be partially dissipated by use of the very lack of knowledge among role-set members: the colleague group evolves a type of "shop talk" in which the overt values to which it subscribes are treated cynically or frivolously, a performance which has tension-reducing functions.[14] For ministers such an outlet is much less possible—the values of their professional role are too explicit. For Pentecostal ministers, whose allegiance is more intense and enthusiastic, it is even more unlikely, given the sectarian character of Pentecostal movements in England and the strength of the lay tradition.

There is conflict between the minister's commitment to the movement and his responsibilities to his own church members, which is parallel to the divergent if not conflicting obligations of many professionals to the professional ethic, on the one hand, and their clientele, on the other. The ministerial conference and headquarters' directives seek to impose rigorous moral standards, but the laity, in general, has little more than a conventional standard of Christian ethics. The leaders espouse a sectarian ethic of denial of the world and the minister acts as a socializing agent, persuading and disciplining the revival-recruited flock.[15] In public sermon and private counselling he exhorts his congregation to resist worldly associations and activities; at the same time, he must also be informal and friendly with everyone and, while maintaining his own status, must emphasize sectarian equality and brotherhood. He involves himself in the activities of the local people, even though his basic allegiance must always be to headquarters, which may move him at any time, permanently or temporarily, to another church.

He mixes very informally and visits homes frequently, yet he must take care not to favor one family above another or to jeopardize his commitment to the values and loyalties for which he is the agent of headquarters. A particularly delicate matter is the regulation of informal groups for religious praise and devotion. These are to be encouraged on scriptural warrant, yet there are difficulties. If the minister is invited to participate in their meetings, he must not become the property of any clique from which others are excluded and which might easily use him to confirm their own special blessedness. On the other hand, he will not want to have them meet too often without adequate supervision, for Pentecostal gifts and the concomitant emotionalism lend themselves to excesses and to manipulation. Yet religious impulses must not be dampened. He is thus likely to try to bring such informal and private activity into the compass of the church and to use the informal enthusiasm in the formal activity of the congregation, if this can be done without the alienation of others.[16]

The young unmarried minister must in keeping with the sect's expectations seek his mate within the sect. Only there is he, in any case, likely to meet young women, since all members, and certainly the minister, are supposed to keep their social activities within the sect. Within the assembly, however, courtship would conflict with the minister's wider affective role. Undoubtedly, this problem affects ministers of other movements, but the exclusiveness, emotionalism, and ministerial commitment to rigorous moral standards sharpen the conflict in the case of Pentecostalism. It is not surprising that the leaders of the Elim movement subject ministers' courtship and engagement to their approval and allow their termination only under extenuating circumstances. Nothing, short of disaffection, is likely to cause more disruption than a conflict between a minister's obligations to his congregation and to his bride-to-be. The congregation is in a sense jealous of the affection and attention which are necessarily expressed by him as their pastor. Thus his private activities have consequences for his public office and cannot be readily prevented from becoming almost the property of the entire group, to whom any extraneous commitment is likely to seem tantamount to a betrayal of sect allegiance.

In few if any other professions are the wives of *ordinary* practitioners committed to their husbands' work as are the wives of ministers—a consequence, perhaps, of the diffuse and affective character of the ministerial role. Because in the sect this is so important, there is good reason for the headquarters of Elim to seek to control in some degree the minister's selection of a wife.

It is headquarters' policy to move a minister who selects a fiancée from his local church, so that tensions in the home church are likely to be reduced, and the minister's role eased and likewise that of his bride. Diffuse and affective occupational roles always imply total allegiance to the work organization; this implicit loyalty is nowhere more demanded than in religious institutions, all of which, consequently, seek to regulate all the other affective roles of their functionaries. The Greek Orthodox church prohibits marriage for the priest; Roman Catholicism denies to the married access to the priesthood; in Protestantism the two roles are segregated as far as possible, and the ministerial role is more restricted. Even so, many clergymen choose to remain celibate. In the sect, without a ministry in the usual case, religious allegiance transcends both occupational and marital obligations for all members, but where a ministry has emerged as in Elim, occupational obligations are deemed to take precedence over those of marriage.

The tradition of the leadership of the Spirit is ill matched with a paid ministerial order, even though British Pentecostalism has accepted the ministry in steadily increasing numbers since early days. Ideally, the leaders within the church should be endowed with the gifts of the Spirit, and their functions should be divided along the lines suggested by Paul in his First Epistle to the Corinthians, on which Pentecostalism stakes much of its case.[17] From time to time it is suggested that Pentecostal ministers differ somewhat in their personal ministry precisely because of differential endowment by the Spirit, and it is always claimed that they possess one or more gifts. In meetings there is still what amounts to competition in demonstrating inspiration by the Holy Ghost, and in testimonies and even sermons frequent contrast is made between divine election and "futile" book-learning and schooling. Inevitably, the minister must identify himself with Pentecostal sectarianism, rather than with any conception of a ministerial profession. There is, too, a strong distrust of Catholic and Anglican priests, and the role of the ministry in the movement must always be distinguished from that of a priesthood, and its status consequently diminished.

Pentecostalists, however, in common with all sects which are not vicinally isolated, do, necessarily if involuntarily, accept the status system of the society at large and consequently their status assumptions oscillate between this and that of the sect itself. The professional minister is very differently placed in these two systems—there are pronounced status contradictions. Undoubtedly, the minister is accorded status in the sect because of symbols such as ministerial dress, which, up to a point, evoke responses more typical of society at large than of the sect and set him above the status ordering within the group. Yet he must not presume too much, and it is interesting that he will not infrequently conduct meetings, particularly midweek meetings, in ordinary dress. Pentecostalists never weary of debunking worldly social status and of emphasizing the unqualified significance of election by the Holy Ghost as the only status which really matters. But the minister is leader and identified with headquarters, and, as a saver of souls, he can lay successful claim to status based on achievement which sect members consider worthy.

Pentecostalists, like most sectarians, though despising the world, often accept worldly estimates of themselves or their activities when these are favorable, if, for example, an Elim minister is shown respect in public or in the press. The enjoyment of privileges in common with other ministers has not, however, been without its problems; this is particularly true of the exemption from military service granted to Pentecostal ministers in the second World War. This lifted the ministry from its lay following by according it privileges for which other members had to fight as rights of conscience in the law courts. In a sense, the ministry were taken into the "Establishment." Unambiguous ministerial example in asserting conscientious objection was eliminated, and few lay Pentecostalists did register objection to military service; ministerial control of the laity had been significantly impaired. More significant, however, is the clear distinction of status which this external administrative decision created between the ministry and the laity. To share the prerogatives and privileges of the ministers of other movements was at once a victory and a defeat; many, though gratified, were made uncomfortable by the implied association with what is often called a "worldly priesthood."

That the Pentecostal ministry has assumed conventional clerical garb indicates a search for status outside the movement and perhaps also inside. Yet the minister is aware that even though, as a minister, he enjoys relatively high status, as a Pentecostalist, his social status is low. And even high status is, for the sect, tainted: it were better to be despised among men. That ministerial aspirations are contradictory might well be inevitable in the transition of the movement from despised sect to accepted denomination.

There are clear limits to the extent to which the minister can identify himself with other ministers, and these are more or less defined by educational and salary differentials. The Pentecostalist has had a brief training in a college with an unlettered faculty, where the curriculum emphasizes practical training and scriptural knowledge rather than ancient languages and theological scholarship. Of all professions, the ministry has perhaps least professional solidarity and least uniformity of training. Denominational allegiances cut across professional identity and are of a far more radical kind than those which exist between different specialties in those professions which have more, and more rational, division of function. Pentecostalism, from the point of view of other ministers, has a spurious and contemptible form of ministry, to which most of them would prefer to deny ministerial status altogether. Likewise, to the general public there is incongruity in a minister with only an elementary education and ungrammatical speech with a marked regional accent.[18] The ministerial profession, in general, has been placed in an increasingly equivocal position as it has lost earlier functions and has found no highly specialized role of its own; moreover, it can barely maintain a reputation for learning, as knowledge itself has become more specialized and more widely distributed.[19] As a consequence ministers have probably become more sensitive about their professional status. All this retards the identification of the Pentecostal minister with the clerical profession and strengthens his identity with the sect. In practice, the Pentecostal minister comes into contact with few other ministers, and these usually on a self-selected basis of common acceptance one of another by fundamentalists. These are usually, in Britain, other Pentecostalists and Baptists, who join together to promote local campaigns and who accord each other parity of status. The Pentecostal minister is not usually invited into the local interdenominational councils and might be as much embarrassed by an invitation as would liberal ministers by his presence among them.

The status of the Pentecostal minister is contradictory because of a lack of consensus among those for whom his role has significance. It is insecurely fixed in the hierarchy of the organization, when the disparity of formal structure and ideological commitment is taken into account; it lacks distinctive ideological support; and it is unrecognized within the profession to which it might be said to belong. The contradictions in his status arise from the marginality of his role both within the profession[20] and within the movement, which has itself a certain marginality to the social order and which has not as yet passed from the status of sect to that of denomination.

---

1. See, e.g., E. Troeltsch, *Social Teachings of the Christian Churches,* trans. O. Wyon (New York: Macmillan Co., 1931), pp. 329 ff.; Howard Becker, in L. von Wiese and H. Becker (eds.), *Systematic Sociology* (New York: John Wiley & Sons, 1932), pp. 624 ff. On sect development and the circumstances in which ministerial tendencies occur in sects see B. R. Wilson, "An Analysis of Sect Development," *American Sociological Review,* February, 1959; cf. also n. 4 below.

2. Those who function as readers in Christian Science, for example, although performing no other significant leadership functions (with one or two exceptions concerning appointments), and not usually simultaneously serving as members of church boards, sometimes, if not always, receive an honorarium, which is, in practice, often given back to church funds.

3. The methods of study were participant-observation, both concealed and revealed, in a number of congregations, and in two revival campaigns, where Pentecostalist ministers were closely observed. Rigorous interviewing techniques are usually impossible in

research on sects, but in this case some ministers were willing to discuss at length their functions. Ministers were to some extent conscious of their own problems of role; most typically, they were aware of them only at the operational level, in knowing what was "appropriate behavior." Conversational remarks, pulpit pronouncements, and published articles all showed an awareness of, and even a sensitivity concerning, the difficulties of the ministerial role, although, of course, without any sophisticated sociological or analytical apprehension of the specific pressures and adjustive mechanisms involved. The observational and participant study was augmented by detailed content analysis of sect literature. The results of this and associated studies are shortly to be published under the title *Minority Religious Movements in Modern Britain.*

4. On this process see H. Richard Niebuhr, *Social Sources of Denominationalism* (New York: Henry Holt & Co., 1929); Liston Pope, *Millhands and Preachers* (New Haven, Conn.: Yale University Press, 1942); W. G. Muelder, "From Sect to Church," *Christendom,* 1945, pp. 350-62; E. D. C. Brewer, "Sect and Church in Methodism," *Social Forces,* XXX (May, 1952), 400-408; O. R. Whitley, "The Sect to Denomination Process in an American Religious Movement," *Southwestern Social Science Quarterly,* Vol. XXXVI (December, 1955). For a critical discussion see J. M. Yinger, *Religion, Society, and the Individual* (New York: Macmillan Co., 1957), esp. chap. vi. For modification and reassessment of this thesis see B. Johnson, "A Critical Appraisal of Church-Sect Typology," *American Sociological Review,* XXII (February, 1957), 88-92; B. R. Wilson, "Apparition et persistance des sectes dans un milieu social en évolution," *Archives de sociologie des religions,* V (January–June, 1958), 140-50; Wilson, "An Analysis of Sect Development," *op. cit.*

5. Analogous phenomena occur in other organizations (cf. B. R. Clark, "Organizational Adaption and Precarious Values," *American Sociological Review,* XXI [June, 1956], 327-36).

6. The bulk of those who embraced Pentecostalism while in previous fellowships differed from those who were won by subsequent revival campaigns in that the latter tended to be much more uniformly drawn from the lowest social classes, were less firmly grounded in a strong biblical tradition, and had a less vigorous and less articulated commitment to the moral and doctrinal standards of fundamentalism. Had Pentecostalism remained wholly in the possession of the independent missions and the "come-outers" from other denominations, it would have had far less need for a ministry. Revivalism, however, recruited a mass following for a particular leader. Few among the recruits showed capacities for effective leadership without training and institutional support for their position, and so arose problems establishing leadership with mediated responsibility from a following largely unsuited to undertake it. The bureaucratization of the movement, which has replaced the early simple charismatic revivalism, has created a hierarchy, but the organization remains highly centralized and somewhat autocratic.

In general, Pentecostalism still recruits almost entirely from the lower social classes and, typical of movements with mass appeal, tends to have a considerable turnover. The denominationalizing process is, as yet, more evident in internal organization than in external acceptance. In Britain the change of class position by whole groups and by institutions is less speedily effected than in the United States, and there is no evidence to suggest that Pentecostalism in Britain is gaining any ground among classes other than those to whom it made its initial appeal.

7. For a description of the free Spirit in earlier sects see, e.g., Norman Cohn, *Pursuit of the Millennium* (London: Secker & Warburg, 1957); G. Huehns, *Antinomianism in British History* (London: Cresset Press, 1951), esp. pp. 37-54.

8. The Catholic Apostolic church, founded by Edward Irving in London in the mid-nineteenth century, is an example of a church polity organized along lines suggested by Spirit gifts, according to the prescriptions of I Corinthians. Elements of this inspirationalism are widespread among Christian movements, for instance, as in the drawing of lots to determine performance of particular functions among the Moravians (see W. H. G. Armytage, "The Moravian Communities in Great Britain," *Church Quarterly Review,* CLVII [April–June, 1957], 141-52).

9. Such educational establishments are widespread among fundamentalist groups (see, e.g., W. E. Mann, *Sect, Cult and Church in Alberta* [Toronto: University of Toronto Press, 1955]).

10. For a discussion of the general role problems of ministers see James M. Gustafson, "An Analysis of the Problem of the Role of the Minister," *Journal of Religion,* XXXIV (July, 1954), 187-91.

11. These "bridge functions" of mediating roles are similar to the "bridge systems" in the process of socialization referred to in a highly suggestive article by K. D. Naegele, "Clergymen, Teachers and Psychiatrists," *Canadian Journal of Economics and Political Science,* XXII (February, 1956), 46-62.

12. Cf. Jackson Toby, "Some Variables in Role Conflict Analysis," *Social Forces,* XXX (March, 1952), 323-27; Robert K. Merton, "The Role Set: Problems in Sociological Theory," *British Journal of Sociology,* VIII (June, 1957), 106-20.

13. Merton, *op. cit.*

14. On colleague group cynicism see Everett C. Hughes, "Dilemmas and Contradictions of Status," *American Journal of Sociology,* L (March, 1945), 353-59.

15. An example of the strict ethical standard which ministers have sought to impose on the Elim laity is the strong recommendation by the ministerial conference in the 1930's of conscientious objection. Yet, in practice, few laymen became conscientious objectors.

16. Cf. the business executive's efforts to bring the energies of informal groups in industrial concerns to the service of the whole organization in Philip Selznick, *Leadership in Administration* (Evanston, Ill., and White Plains, N.Y.: Row, Peterson & Co., 1957), p. 8.

17. In modern Pentecostalism in England, the Apostolic church (not to be confused with the Irvingite Catholic Apostolic church referred to above) orders church leadership along these lines and claims, in consequence, to be more thoroughly Pentecostal than its two principal contemporaries.

18. Hughes (*op. cit.*) points out that, when people with new auxiliary characteristics seek entrance to a profession, they jeopardize the profession's own self-image, in that they may deviate from professional conduct and standards. Part of the hostility of other ministers doubtless originates here and also, as suggested below, in the fear of damaging the public stereotype of the profession.

19. Cf. S. H. Chapman, "The Minister, Professional Man of the Church," *Social Forces,* XXIII (December, 1944), 202-6; Joseph van Vleck, Jr., *Our Changing Churches* (New York: Association Press, 1937); Robert S. Michaelson, "The Protestant Ministry in America, 1850 to the Present," in H. R. Niebuhr and D. D. Williams (eds.), *The Ministry in Historical Perspective* (New York: Harper & Bros., 1956); S. I. Goldstein, "The Roles of an American Rabbi," *Sociology and Social Research,* XXXVIII (September, 1953), 32-37.

20. Cf. Walter I. Wardwell, "A Marginal Professional Role: The Chiropractor," *Social Forces,* XXX (March, 1952), 339-48.

SECTION III

The Church in Society

It may seem unnecessary to speak of the church as being "in society." As one undergraduate student put it, "Where else would it be?" The theological answer to that question is immediately forthcoming: the church is the Body of Christ and its essence is not dependent upon the social and historical limitations within which it must operate. Its location is not, therefore, understood in spatio-temporal terms. It is "eternal." Not all theologians, however, view the church in such a limited perspective. Richard Niebuhr discusses the "enduring problem" with which the Christian church has had to contend throughout its history in his insightful work, *Christ and Culture.*[1] The church does exist in a sociocultural setting and has, accordingly, proposed various responses to the problems which arise in adjustment to its environment. The church may be seen as *opposed* to the achievements of the human community, or it may be viewed as in fundamental *agreement* with human values. In between these two positions are varying arrangements which seek to provide a working relationship between the church and its cultural milieu. The church may be understood as something *above* culture; the church and culture may be viewed as existing in a *paradoxical* relationship where opposition is recognized but the claims of the church have priority; and, finally, the church may be viewed as the *transformer* of culture. In its historical development the church has adopted one or the other of these various relationships with its immediate environment (and in so doing provides, of course, the basis of the classification as church type or sect type discussed by Johnson in article 1, chapter 4).

In the more than twenty years since Niebuhr's work, theologians have increasingly shown a need to understand the church as a human community. In *Treasure in Earthen Vessels,* Gustafson succinctly summarizes this point of view:

> The Church can be defined as a human community with an historical continuity identifiable by certain beliefs, ways of work, rites, loyalties, outlooks, and feelings. Whatever else the Church is to the systematic theologian and Biblical exegete, it is a people with a history. It is a social entity with temporal and spatial dimensions. It is human, and shares many characteristics of other human communities such as nations, trade unions, and professions. As a human community it is subject to various modes of study and interpretation.[2]

A sociological investigation of the relationship of the church to other institutionalized areas of society does not, as Gustafson notes, "displace investigation from other points of view, or interpretation through other concepts. It seeks merely to make a contribution to our understanding of the community of Christians. . . ."[3] It is, in short, a simple recognition of the fact that the church, like other institutions, reflects, for example, the stratification system of the society. (Most sociological studies of the class structure of the church reveal that it does, about as well as any voluntary organization in society, accomplish what it purports to do: include segments of all levels of society into its membership.) The church is, also, a political organization (the clergy are well aware of this point). Church members, clergy and laity alike, are involved in the political decisions of a society *in their role* as church members and not just as citizens of the community. And in periods of economic recession or affluence the church becomes sharply aware of its dependence on the society's well-being. The church *in* society, then is the subject of Section III, with particular attention given to the relationship of the church to the stratification system, and the political and economic orders.

The Hammond article in the overview to section III raises a central question necessary to understanding the function of religion in society: does religion influence the direction of the society or is it better understood as a mirror of the larger cultural ethos? Hammond feels that it is imperative to clarify what we mean when we say that religion "influences" or "informs" the society. The demise of religious *authority* in many areas of the secular life of society is clearly recognized by those both within and outside the church. The *power* to make political decisions is not within the authority of any established religious group in the society. So, too, in the realm of ethical decisions. The recent change in abortion laws is sufficient evidence to support Hammond's point in this regard. But loss of authority (which is not a recent occurrence for the church) is not synonymous with loss of influence. The churches "may still exercise ethical influence, and they remain the developers and transmitters of nonempirical beliefs. In these ways, God is not dead, and religion does inform the culture."

The study of the relationship of religion to the stratification system of a society may, at first sight, seem to abrogate any remaining idea that religion has any priority in influencing the behavior of its adherents. The churches, like other voluntary organizations, reflect the stratification of the larger society of which they are a part. An understanding of a society's class structure is a far more complex task than is generally recognized. While the sophisticated magazines constantly make reference to "upper-class" behavior—as contrasted with "lower- or middle-class" behavior, sociologists are questioning whether or not a class structure can be clearly defined in some societies. Dennis Wrong states that "modern societies are unmistakably moving in the direction of maintaining considerable institutionalized inequality in the absence of a class system."[4] Texts in stratification often refer to the "relative absence" of classes in America. Stratification, nevertheless, remains "the sociologist's favorite independent variable"[5] since there are discernible associations between one's position in a defined class structure and other forms of social behavior. This is the case with the type church one attends and the nature of one's interest in religion. The first selection in chapter 6 by Erich Goode explores the known association between class affiliation and church participation. He points to the well-established relationship between class and degree of church participation: the higher the class the greater the participation in the church and the lower the class the less participation. But, equally important, studies have shown that not only are social class and church participation positively related, so, too, is church participation and participation in other voluntary associations. The question arises, then, of whether or not church and nonchurch participation are related to social class in the same fashion? The problem is to determine the nature of the relationship between the three variables rather than, as has been more often the case, simply to examine the relationship between class and church activity. Goode's conclusion is closely related to the studies in section I of this book concerning what variables should be used to measure religiosity. While all would not agree he, nevertheless, suggests that "some of the traditional measures of religiousness, such as church attendance, ought not even to be used at all."

The next two selections in chapter 5 examine the religious involvement of a particular segment of American society: the blacks. Not all blacks in this country are members of the lower class, but a disproportionate number (relative to their percentage of the total population) occupy the lowest levels of class designations in America. Blacks are largely perceived and treated as lower-class members. The history of discrimination and prejudice against blacks is highlighted in their educational, occupational, and religious segregation. The church, by virtue of its proclamation of the brotherhood of man, has been particularly vulnerable to its segregational stance—summed up in the overworked, but nevertheless accurate, phrase: "The most segregated hour in America is 11:00 A.M. on Sunday morning."

While tremendous strides have been made in the past decade toward an integrated society, the churches continue to remain basically all-white and all-black in their composition. Blacks have been elected to positions of leadership in predominantly white denominations, church commissions have been appointed to work toward the elimination of any segregation in given denominational bodies, and church funds (often under direct pressure) have been allocated to support the black man's effort to end segregation as a way of life in the United States. But the problem persists in the church (as in other areas of society, too) and is compounded by the development of the "Black Consciousness" discussed by James Cone in the second selection in chapter 5. Cone stresses the notion of liberation as the dominant element in Christian theology, and characterizes the post-Civil War black churches as institutions which have identified religion with piety rather than liberation. He argues that the emergence of a "Black Theology" is forcing the established black churches today to reconsider their role in the struggle for the black man's freedom. This reconsideration is necessary since "Black Power," "Black Consciousness," or "Black Theology" is clearly not the vocal emphasis of the established black churches. But "black is beautiful" and desirable *is* the theme of the Black Muslims, the subject of the selection by John Howard. The Black Muslims are one of the few religious movements to have their origin in America (the Mormons are another example).[6] They fully embrace the meaning of "Black Power," and not only understand the segregation of the black man but intend to see that he is freed from his suppression in the society of the "white devil." The movement is, of course, as Howard states, "a deviant organization even within the Negro community." Those who join the movement often do so over protests from family and friends. How many have joined the Black Muslims is unknown—estimates range from 5,000 to

100,000, or more. But their influence is not simply a function of size. The appeal of the movement (particularly strong for lower-class black males) stems, according to Howard's analysis, from an emphasis upon (1) black nationalism and (2) self-help. The first point is readily recognized by those familiar with the teaching of the Black Muslims. The second point is of particular interest since it does not receive as much publicity as the Muslims' avowed aim to establish a "new nation" within the confines of the United States. The Muslims encourage the "so-called Negro to give up those habits which have been spread among them by whites as part of the effort to keep them weak, diseased, and demoralized. The so-called Negro must give up such white fostered dissolute habits as drinking, smoking, and eating improper foods. The so-called Negro must prepare himself in mind and body for the task of wresting control from the whites." Those attracted by this ethic Howard has labeled "Protestant Ethic Muslims." The eventual fate of this religious movement is presently uncertain, but it has experienced much success in attracting those "Negroes who have already, through their own experiences in white America, developed a perspective congruent with that of the Muslim movement."

The studies in chapter 6 focus on two areas of concern in society where the church and the political system interact: civil rights and patriotism. These, of course, are only a small portion of the numerous points of contact between the religious and political structures of a society in which the "separation of church and state" does not mean, for example, that there is no support of religious bodies in this country by tax monies. Support for welfare agencies of the church,[7] federal assistance to church-owned hospitals, and busing of children for parochial education—all a part of church-state relations in American society—cannot, however, compete in terms of national interest with the role of the churches in the civil rights struggle in the society. It would be virtually impossible to find statements describing the official position of the major religious bodies which do not, at least in principle, support the idea of a fully integrated society with "equal justice for all." But as the study by Pettigrew and Campbell illustrated, when the issue is joined on the local congregational level, highly pragmatic matters and local mores do not necessarily coincide with official statements. A limited treatment of "Parishioners' Attitudes Toward Issues in the Civil Rights Movement" is provided by Fukuyama's study of 150 congregations of the United Church of Christ. He finds that official pronouncements, once again, do not filter down to the man in the pew. There are strong differences between black and white parishioners regarding the church's role in the civil rights struggle. The whites view the pastor in his traditional "shepherd" role while the blacks tend to see him as a "prophet," and less than one-third of the white parishioners felt that "working for social justice" was an "absolutely necessary" characteristic of the Christian life—as opposed to two-thirds of the black respondents. Fukuyama's conclusion that the black views the "Negro church as an instrument of social protest and change" is explored in greater detail by Gary Marx in his analysis of "Religion: Opiate or Inspiration of Civil Rights Militancy Among Negroes?"

Marx finds that the Negro church is not by any means homogeneous with respect to its conception of its role in the civil rights struggle. Whether or not members of Negro churches can be described as "militants" varies with church and sect-type groups, the degree of religiosity of adherents, and whether or not those who are religious have a temporal or other-worldly orientation. The study provides an excellent example of the necessity for clearly defining the variables used to describe "religious types" before attempting to depict attitudes or behavior as a function of religiosity.

The final selection by Robert Bellah argues for the existence of a "civil religion" which is institutionalized in its own right apart from the religion of the churches. The themes of this civil religion reach back to the founding fathers and come forward to the present time: America is Israel, God's favorite; we have made a "covenant" with God to carry out his work here on earth. The religious dimensions of our political sphere are seen in the words of Washington's first inaugural address and have been repeated in *every* presidential inauguration (with the exception of Washington's second). John Kennedy swore "before you and Almighty God the same solemn oath our forebears prescribed nearly a century and three quarters ago." He, too, stressed that "here on earth God's work must truly be our own." Thus there is provided a "transcendent goal for the political process" as exemplified in the American system. American civil religion has not been without its critics, of course, but Bellah maintains that it "is not the worship of the American nation but an understanding of the American experience in the light of ultimate and universal reality. . . ." He is hopeful that a "world civil religion" might emerge—"a genuine trans-national sovereignty" of which the American civil religion would be one part.

Three selections in chapter 7 provide an introduction to the Weberian thesis of the relationship of Protestantism to the rise of capitalism. There is little doubt that Weber himself would have been greatly surprised by the vast literature, from scholars in many fields, which has been devoted to the critical evaluation of his thesis. Sociologists of religion have been joined by historians, economists, and theologians in pointing out the weaknesses of the thesis, offering rebuttal, and, on occasion, completely disowning it. Sombart, Troeltsch, Tawney, See, and Samuelsson represent just a few of the critics who have responded to Weber's proposition.[8] What did Weber say to elicit such a profusion of scholarly concern? In his study of Max Weber, Bendix has succinctly summarized the thesis:

> Weber concluded that no one can say how the capitalist economic system would have originated without the Protestant ethic, while there is circumstantial evidence that the absence of such an ethic retarded economic developments elsewhere. . . . Weber's view was that this ethic had been a causal factor of uncertain magnitude whose importance could be denied only if the origin of the "capitalist spirit" in the West were explained more convincingly on some other ground.[9]

Weber found that religious ideas were not confined to religion. Changes in the religious sphere of a society may initiate changes in seemingly unrelated spheres such as economics. In examining the rise of capitalism he sought to show that the new religious outlook of the Protestant reformers, especially the Calvinists and the Puritans, were particularly conducive to the spirit of rationalistic capitalism. Weber considered first Luther's doctrine of man's "calling," i.e., his everyday task. Man's "calling"—whatever it might be, cobbler, prince, or priest —was from God, and the fulfillment of this "calling was a *religious* obligation." Catholic thought had not defined such everyday tasks as religious activity, which was more accurately portrayed in the work of monks and nuns. Luther thus introduced a new appraisal of the worthfulness of common labor. However, it was not Luther but Calvin who developed this viewpoint to its fullest implications. In Calvin's theology man stood alone before God and had, in the words of the Westminster Catechism, but one aim in life: "to glorify God and enjoy him forever." Furthermore, for the Calvinist, the great question of his life was: how can I know I am saved? The answer: be an instrument for God—be ceaselessly active to bring the total secular order into its proper purpose: the glorification of God. Such works by men were not, of course, the means of salvation, but did give the *assurance* of salvation. The harder the laborer worked, the more God was glorified, and the greater assurance one had of his salvation. The Protestant ethic had blessed the making of money. The tradesman as well as the priest could please God, and could please Him most by being frugal, avoiding worldly pleasures, and prospering. According to Weber, such an attitude toward work and the accumulation of wealth led to a rational view of the economic life which he characterized as the spirit of modern capitalism.[10]

Weber's interpretation was, in part, a reaction against the Marxian economic interpretation of history. Weber, unfortunately, was to suffer the same fate as Marx. Both came to be viewed, simplistically, as monocausalists in their methodology. Those who interpret Weber in this manner do so, however, only by disregarding his own concluding words in *The Protestant Ethic and the Spirit of Capitalism:*

> . . . it is, of course, not my aim to substitute for a one-sided materialistic an equally one-sided spiritualistic causal interpretation of culture and history.[11]

The first selection in chapter 7 by Greeley reviews eight empirical studies devoted to contemporary investigation of the Weberian thesis. Greeley concludes strongly that "nothing remotely approaching a confirmation of the Protestant Ethic hypothesis" is revealed in these studies. He feels (and many would agree) that studies often oversimplify Weber and the conclusions are not, therefore, based on an adequate test of the thesis. Greeley insists that a part of the difficulty with the studies he reviews is that sociologists do not know what Catholicism is. (Others have argued that Weber did not understand Protestantism, either.)[12]

Another valid criticism voiced by Greeley is that sociologists accept, almost as an "article of faith," the lower-class status of Catholics. Weber's study had been prompted, in part, by his observation that there were more Protestants than Catholics among "business leaders and owners of capital, as well as the higher grades of skilled labor, and even the higher technically and commercially trained personnel of modern enterprises."[13] Many studies since Weber (some not designed to test the Weberian thesis) have generally found Protestants to rank higher on measures of socioeconomic status than Catholics. These findings have been complicated by the fact, however, that Jews are often found to have higher status and experience higher rates of mobility than either Protestants or Catholics. The problem to which Glenn and Hyland address themselves in "Religious Preference and Worldly Success" is to examine data of national surveys from 1943 to 1965 to see what changes, if any, have occurred in the relative rates of upward mobility and consequent status for Protestants and Catholics. Their analysis strongly suggests that other factors must be given considerable attention in studying the effect of religion upon societal changes. They conclude that Catholics have, in recent years, experienced even more rapid advancements than Protestants and suggest that the explanation may be due to such influences as community size and regional location rather than to religion.[14]

The third selection in chapter 7 by Robert Bellah offers "Reflections on the Protestant Ethic Analogy in Asia." Noting the continuing influence of Weber's work Bellah provides a much needed cross-cultural investigation of the relationship between religion and economics. He stresses the fact that institutional arrangements in a society are as important for economic development as the presence or absence of the ideological motivation stressed by Weber in his early work. But even the combination of satisfactory institutional settings and the presence of a "work ethic" are not sufficient interpretations of recent examples of economic growth in Asian countries. What is needed is an understanding of the larger social and cultural factors behind "reformation itself . . . the 'transformation of the basic structure of society' and its 'underlying value system.' . . ."

Weber himself looked to England and America, and not Germany, as examples of the consequences of the Protestant Reformation. Germany, the birthplace of the Reformation, had lagged behind other countries in economic development due to the failure of needed institutional and value changes required for large scale societal reform. Such structural reforms are occurring in selected Asian countries today and provide a renewed interest in Weber's larger theoretical orientation of the relationship between religion and economic development.

---

1. H. Richard Niebuhr, *Christ and Culture* (New York: Harper Torch Books, 1956).

2. James Gustafson, *Treasure in Earthen Vessels* (New York: Harper and Row, 1961).

3. Ibid., p. 5.

4. Dennis H. Wrong, "Social Inequality without Social Stratification," *The Canadian Review of Sociology and Anthropology* 1 (February 1964):9.

5. Leonard Broom and Philip Selznick, *Sociology* (New York: Harper and Row, 1968), p. 153.

6. Black Muslims, citing their Islamic heritage, would argue that this point is not true, of course.

7. For an interesting documentation of this point see: Bernard J. Coughlin, *Church and State in Social Welfare* (New York: Columbia University Press, 1965), especially pp. 58-74.

8. For an excellent collection of the views of Weber's critics see: Robert W. Green, ed., *Protestantism and Capitalism: The Weber Thesis and Its Critics* (Boston: D.C. Heath, 1959).

9. Richard Bendix, *Max Weber: An Intellectual Portrait* (Garden City, New York: Doubleday, 1960), p. 103.

10. This analysis of Weber's thesis draws freely upon the excellent discussion of Kemper Fullerton, "Calvinism and Capitalism: An Explanation of the Weber Thesis," in Green, *op. cit.*

11. Max Weber, *The Protestant Ethic and the Spirit of Capitalism,* trans. Talcott Parsons (New York: Charles Scribner's Sons, 1930), p. 183.

12. See Winthrop S. Hudson, "Puritanism and the Spirit of Capitalism," in Green, *op. cit.*

13. Weber, *op. cit.,* p. 35.

14. Twentieth-century survey studies of the differences between Protestants and Catholics are valuable in their own right, but are largely an effort to see what social and economic differences may be attributable today to the Protestant religious viewpoint as opposed to the Catholic. Whatever the validity of Weber's original thesis it is not necessary to assume that the Protestant influence has carried on indefinitely.

An Overview

PHILLIP E. HAMMOND

Religion and the "Informing" of Culture

The passing phrase is no respecter of the abiding truth; religion too has its share of slogans. "Culture religion," "post-Christian era," "syncretistic religiosity," "religion no longer informs culture"—these are a few currently heard. Like many slogans, taken literally they can obscure as well as illumine. The clergyman seeing his community, even his parish, headed for ruin despite his warning may rescue some comfort from believing that in the nation at large "Christianity has lost its hegemony," that "the relationship of religion and culture has been subverted," that "God is dead."

But what do the phrases mean? To religionists as to social scientists, religion has always been a cultural phenomenon (though of course some

From the *Journal for the Scientific Study of Religion* 3(Fall 1963):97-106. Reprinted by permission of the publisher and author.

of the latter and most of the former have disagreed on what *else* religion is). Does the term "culture religion" connote therefore that religion is *only* a cultural thing? Much history, including contemporary, can be and is written with religion as a force in events. Does the phrase "religion no longer informs culture," mean, then, that history might better be written by ignoring religion since its impact is illusory?

In the United States, it is said,

> The traditional relation between religion and culture is for culture to stand under the judgment of the God to whom religion points. But in this newer American religiosity, the relation is inverted, subverted. Conventional religion is now validated in terms of the American Way.[1]

For most people presumably "the judgment of God" and "the American Way" are distinguishable. But what is the difference between them?

Some questions should be raised about these phrases. Admittedly they are not of one piece, yet they contain a common element, a current and pervasive view of American religion that can be misleading. These pages attempt to explicate that view. The significant referent of the phrases, it will be suggested, revolves around a change in the social structural location of ethical decision-making. Curiously then the change being pointed to is not recent, though its recognition may be; the "post-Protestant era" has been at hand since the Reformation.

The phrase "religion no longer informs culture" becomes the focus of the discussion.

The Meaning of the Phrase

Some possible meanings of "religion does (not) inform culture" can be dispensed with immediately:

(1) It is quite clear that in America in these times of almost universal self-designation as member of some religious tradition, affiliation with church, synagogue, mosque, temple, etc., is *not* understood as indicative of "informing." By the same reasoning neither is attendance in these religious organizations taken as a sign of potency. If it were, claims that religion had lost its edge would decrease, not increase. Indeed some of the phrase-users, like their analogues in the fine arts, take popularity as proof of impurity.

(2) It is equally clear that theological sophistication or awareness is not acceptable as a measure of religion's informing culture. Again, despite some nostalgia for the era of Bible-toting and -quoting, the fact must be that, absolutely and proportionately, more people today know

more theology. Simply the relative number of persons attending college and the number of theological-type paper-back books purchased support the contention.

(3) A third meaning of the phrase might be the philosophical or artistic excellence—the high quality—of theology. Religion fails to inform when the quality of its theology declines. One of those who claims that "God is dead," however, claims that such excellence is here.[2]

(4) Certainly a reasonable meaning of the phrase "culture is (not) informed by religion" suggests the possible *general* influence religion has had, and is having, on the affairs of man. But what person is prepared to argue that the Judaic-Christian tradition generally, and the Protestant tradition specifically, are *not* observable today in American economic goals, political procedures, judicial systems, and humanitarian welfare measures? Surely the values of contemporary American society are religiously rooted.[3] And if the response is that this "informing" is only indirect and "in the long run," then evidence is also available that even now, today, Americans behave differently according to which segment of that tradition they belong to, and how involved they are in it.[4]

(5) If, then, by "religion no longer informs the culture" is not meant any of the above, what does it mean? An answer is suggested in Vahanian's observation that "The Christian vocabulary has very little meaning for modern man . . . [Religion] fulfills civic ends."[5] That is, persons no longer behave *because* of religious motives; rather their motives are secular, civic, "American." "You will note the complete subversion of the relation of religion and culture implied here. The American Way becomes the ultimate value; religion is recommended by its terms."[6]

The Problem of the Meaning of the Phrase

But to assess religious motivation in this sense is an exceedingly difficult task. The Protestant clergyman who journeys South to "sit-in" and the indigenous clergyman who heads the White Citizens Council to defend against meddling Northerners are, to the observer, both "informed" by religion, or else neither is informed.[7] What other assessment is possible in the religiously *plural society,* unless of course one chooses to use "informing" to mean "conforming to principles as interpreted by a given religious community?" But that is another question, and admittedly not the one the phrase-users are discussing.

The phrase, however, it is agreed, still signifies some change. The problem of its meaning can be observed in the following statement.

> It is strange as well as ironic that a society where authority, both political and religious, is defined in terms of God's immediate and direct dominion should result in one where God's rulership is purely nominal or at best constitutional.[8]

But transcendental rulership *of society* has never been simply immediate and direct. *Individuals* may have non-empirical direction, may even preach to the multitudes of this direction—the basis of prophecy is *not* at issue here. But before transcendental (or any) direction becomes normative for society, it is translated by persons into socially structured power. Persons may coerce, or they may convince, thus exercising legitimate authority. Perhaps only they acknowledge that what they do is God's will; perhaps all of society so acknowledges. The fact remains, however, that the direction, whatever its source, gets manifested as empirical, socially structured power. No manipulation of language alters this fact.

When two or more of these "powers" (be they persons or groups) are in conflict, a decision must be reached regarding which is "right." If the contending factions are to remain in the same society after the decision is rendered, they must grant "legitimating power" to whatever procedure (king, priest, legislature, court, etc.) it is that decides the "right."

In this context, then, it is suggested that the phrase "religion no longer informs society" has reference to this legitimating power—the power to make decisions at times of conflict. This power is no longer "religious." The social structures that do determine ultimate legitimacy *for the society* do so in "non-religious" language, and have replaced organizations commonly thought to be religious. Churches, in other words, no longer make some decisions they once did. What kinds of decision are these?

Not for a long time has the church claimed to decide conflicts of a cognitive and empirical nature. The "right" way of building bridges and plotting planets has long since been institutionalized elsewhere. There is and has been, so to speak, a "culture-science." Religion no longer "informs" science.

Conversely, the church's claim has not been questioned in matters of a cognitive and non-empirical nature. Few if any other segments of society have challenged (and none denies) the religious organizations' leadership in developing, modifying and transmitting non-empirical beliefs. Though doubtlessly theology changes shape as other features of society change, the religious organization is free to espouse any belief, and free even to require assent to any belief on the part of members. Not the term "culture-religion" but "religious-culture" can apply here. Religion can and does inform culture in matters of a cognitive and non-empirical nature.

The one area where contention has existed, where the church once exercised authority but does no longer, is the area of ethics. Deciding the "higher good," a continuing problem for society, can be institutionalized in the church only as long as society is religiously homogeneous, only as long as society and church are coterminous. Under these conditions the church can be authoritative in ethical affairs, and the result is a "religious-culture." Under conditions of religious pluralism, however, the churches must relinquish that authority, and the result is a "culture-religion." Religion no longer informs society in the sense that religious organizations no longer resolve ethical conflicts.[9]

If spokesmen for one church claim divine sanction for demanding that the races be segregated, and spokesmen for another church by the same reasoning claim the opposite, then most assuredly it cannot be the church that decides the policy. And if it is the state (with its legislative and judicial procedures) that decides, then note that both sets of spokesmen, if they are to remain in the same society, *must* give higher allegiance to those decision procedures than to their own substantive positions.[10]

Stated that way—in terms of democratic process—the situation is well known. There is, however, another important way to state the situation: The essentially cognitive aspects and the essentially ethical aspects of religion, though perhaps intimately conjoined in the thinking of *persons,* in the religiously pluralistic *society* become separately institutionalized. That is, although within the *personality* ultimate beliefs about goodness and truth may be closely connected, *societal* decisions in these realms are made in different locations, by different people, at different times. One or all factions in an ethical dispute may be motivated by religious beliefs; resolution of that dispute, however, may occur quite removed from the place where those beliefs were nurtured.

Even the formal acknowledgement of this separation occurred early. As Salo Baron notes:

> Jefferson conceded . . . that in their "Metaphysical" aspects religious bodies might differ widely, but demanded that as social organizations they should all conform to the new political patterns of American democracy.[11]

In their "political patterns" religious organizations have had to relinquish their legitimating rights. But it is only their *legitimating* of ethics or behavior and not their *influence* that religious organizations have had to give up. When, therefore, it is said that

> the most fundamental change in the intellectual life of the United States is the apparent shift from biblical authority and religious sanctions to scientific and factual authority and sanctions[12]

there is a failure to see that (1) the change does not mean that organized religion no longer *influences* culture, (2) the change is in the sphere of ethics and not necessarily beliefs, and especially (3) the change is in the *social structural location for resolving conflicts* between contending ethical positions and not necessarily in the *source* or *motivation* for those ethical positions.

The third point, generally obscured in discussions of "culture-religion," deserves further comment. The remaining pages will outline a brief argument, the direction of which is indicated by Parsons when he says:

> In the United States there has appeared, though probably not yet fully matured, a new mode of institutionalization of the relations between religion and society, which, however, is not secularization in the sense that its tendency is to eliminate organized religion from the social scene, but is rather to give it a redefined place in the social scene.[13]

The Argument

The contention here—that the change revolves about the social structural location for deciding the higher good—has five parts: (1) The change connoted by the phrase "religion no longer informs culture" is not a recent change but began more nearly at the time of the Reformation and developed concurrently with religious pluralism, (2) the significance of the change is to be found in the changing social structural relations between churches and government. (3) One accompanying change has been the tendency of a "civic religion" to develop around the government. (4) Another accompanying change is found in the language used by persons to describe the motives for their behavior. (5) The churches' belated recognition of the change can be seen not only in proliferating alarms about the death of God, but also in the theological and political stances being taken by contemporary churches.

1. The Change Is Not Recent

"Almost every ancient religion was a state religion, its gods expanding and disappearing together with the state."[14] However, once theology removed the church as a necessary means of grace, once a religious leader articulated for followers their mutual belief that "the Lord hath more truth and light yet to break forth," then the way was open for religious heterogeneity. Whereas dissenters once were banished, now they are permitted. Immediately the problem then becomes: Suppose persons all claim transcendental direction but interpret it differently.

Who decides? Luther's answer, his ambivalence toward the state, has led to the suggestion that he "divided life into compartments, or taught that the Christian right hand should not know what a man's worldly left hand was doing."[15]

Another common answer was to substitute one Established Church for another. Certainly the three centuries following the Reformation saw no decrease in the number of migrating sects, i.e., people escaping from situations where their interpretations of God's will were not given equal status. But the fact remains that Protestantism facilitated in the Western World a large measure of theological liberty and thus heterogeneity.

And where there develops theological heterogeneity, it clearly is the case that authority relinquished by the church is assumed by the government. The struggle toward religious pluralism is too well known to elaborate in this essay. Of significance here, however, is the fact that in that struggle the government takes on the ethical decision-making that once was the church's.

> Often against the will of its founders Protestantism was driven into a direct alliance with the state. . . . it had to recognize the state's right to regulate ecclesiastical affairs. While adhering to the principles of universal Christianity and demanding the return to the other worldliness of the apostolic age, it thus accentuated, in practice, national unity as against the superior unity of Western Christendom.[16]

Not because it was Established, in other words, but because the seeds of religious liberty and heterogeneity had been sown whether or not it was Established, the church relinquished its ethical authority to the state. Culture-religion had begun, and not simply out of support for the status quo, but because the church was no longer to be the arbiter in cases of conflict over ethics.

2. The Change Is in the Relationship between Churches and State

The move away from religious homogeneity occurred over several centuries. It was the American experience, however, where a "liberty-infused culture" became most fully translated into a "liberty-providing social structure." It was the sustained interaction of persons with disparate beliefs, which beliefs potentially could lead to opposing behaviors, that required the government to assume decision-making power that once was the church's, or was shared with the church.

The government assumed decision-making power over behavior, however, and not beliefs. Only the essentially ethical aspects of religion, and not the essentially cognitive aspects, needed to be relinquished to the state. And only the power to resolve conflicts in behavior, not the creation and transmission of ethical guides for behavior, was to be the state's alone. The case of conscientious objection provides an illustration. A church may hold beliefs about the sanctity of life, the effect on others of passive resistance, etc. It may preach these beliefs to others. It may derive an ethical position which denounces violence. And its members may share this ethical position. But the members may not refuse to bear arms. Rather, the government exercises the right to decide the higher good and may grant them special status *if they register for it.* Failure to register, i.e., failure to acknowledge the government's right, is considered deviant and leads to imprisonment.

Some persons elect civil disobedience and go to prison. They may be the prophets of their age, or they may be "crackpots." For this reason the distinguishing mark of democratic procedure is not simply in the cultural beliefs about democracy nor even in the practice of majority rule, but is in the protection of minority rights. Still, however, the case of the civil disobedient must be decided, and it is the locus of that decision that is crucial here. It is the government.

3. A "Civic Religion" Has Emerged around the Government

When ultimate power to make ethical decisions is concentrated in the social structure, and when the exercise of this power is both visible and long-term, conditions exist for the emergence of a set of accompanying beliefs about that process of decision-making. When, therefore, the locus shifts from church (or person, in the charismatic leader case) to secular government, the beliefs shift accordingly. Something like this seems to have happened in the United States. Members of society, having granted that maintenance of democratic procedure has higher legitimacy than their own substantive positions, raise to hagiologic stature the persons thought to have conceived and instituted the procedure: the Washingtons, Jeffersons, and Lincolns. And the emerging beliefs make sacred the strategic locus of the decision process, chiefly the judicial system.[17] Like the doctrine of the divine right of kings, the new doctrine maintains the divine right of the majority and, ideally, the divine protection of the minority.

An analogue to this "civic religion," this "religion of democracy," is necessarily found in any integrated society. *It is only when churches and government are structurally differentiated, however, that the "civic religion" is seen as competing with "church religion."* When the essentially ethical aspects of religion are institutionalized apart from the essentially cognitive aspects, any set of "religious beliefs" developing around the ethical institution may appear to be a threat to the cognitive institution. To the latter it will seem that "religion no longer speaks to modern man," that "religion no longer informs the culture."

Though competition may inhere in the situation, however, conflict need not, if for no other reason than the fact that the reasons for, and objects of, devotion are different in the two belief systems. Does this mean that churches must engage in some heteronomous worship of the state? Certainly not, if by worship is meant the belief in the rightness of any governmental decision. If, however, by worship is meant the belief in the rightness of the *procedure* for deciding, then churches are in a position to exert influence precisely by articulating the two sets of beliefs, by revealing the relevance of profoundly held non-empirical beliefs for ethical action in the democratic social order. For presumably out of man's beliefs about what is true still come his convictions of what is good as well as the reverse. In a society where decision-making over conflicting "goods" is structurally separated from the institution of religious beliefs, however, this burden of relevance falls heavily onto churches. How well they carry the burden obviously varies.

4. The Language Used to Describe Motives Has Changed

One factor that makes the churches' burden more difficult is a linguistic change. People no longer justify their actions in the same words. Not simply have expressions with transcendent referents tended to disappear; the growth of scientific knowledge has undoubtedly led to changes in what persons seek for and accept as explanations of behavior. The replacement of notions of devil and sin by notions of mental illness may be more dramatic but is only one example of this change. The general "rationalization" of society, the increasingly utilitarian outlook of its members, has had the effect of diminishing the use of "religious" language.

No assertion is being made of course about the death of religion. Non-empirical meaning is still sought for the empirically unanswerable issues, and, as was shown above, decisions about the higher good are always "religious" in character. But this is the point; these latter decisions are no longer made by churches. Consequently, discussion of them are carried out not in "church language" but in secular language. The choice of words, however, ought not to obscure the fundamental change in the locus of decision-making or, if you please, the locus of interpreting God's will.

To quote again, then, the "shift from biblical authority and religious sanctions to scientific and factual authority and sanctions" is a misleading characterization. The relatively insignificant, recent linguistic change should not dim the older, significant redefinition of the churches' place in the legitimating process.

5. The Recent Change Is the Recognition of the Older Change

This lag in the language may have delayed recognition of the social structural change. Actually, the religious organizations' loss of authority in the realm of ethical decision-making is centuries old. Churches, it would appear, were slow to acknowledge their redefined place in society, and their belated recognition is manifested in part by slogans: "religion no longer informs culture," "God is dead," etc.

The slogans may be accurate as judgments on how well the churches carry their burden of relevance; they are not accurate as statements that the social structural role of churches in America is *recently* changed. For how early in the nation's life there came about the separate institutionalization of religious beliefs and ethics, even with the ensuing "sacredness" of the government, can be seen in Tocqueville's commentary. In 1831 that astute observer, had he been of the bent, could have written "Culture-Religion in America" or even "God is Dead in America." He is quoted variously here to illustrate that

(a) democracy and religious pluralism are joined:

> It may be asserted that in the United States no religious doctrine displays the slightest hostility to democratic and republican institutions. (I, 330)[18]
>
> In France I had almost always seen the spirit of religion and the spirit of freedom pursuing courses diametrically opposed to each other; but in America I found that they were intimately united, and that they reigned in common over the same country. (1. 337)

(b) beliefs become separated from ethics:

> In America religion is a distinct sphere in which the priest is sovereign, but out of which he takes care never to go. . . . Although the Christians of America are divided into a multitude of sects, they all look upon their religion in the same light. . . . [The clergy] endeavor to amend their contemporaries, but they do not quit fellowship with them. (II, 27-28)

(c) Americans may be heterogeneous in beliefs, but not in ethics:

> [Americans] differ in respect to the worship which is due from man to his Creator, but they all agree in respect to the duties which are due from man to man. Each sect adores the Deity in its own peculiar manner, but all the sects preach the same moral law in the name of God. (I, 331)

(d) The government, with its procedures for resolving conflicts, takes on a sacred quality:

> The men who live at a period of social equality . . . commonly seek for the sources of truth in themselves. . . . at such periods no new religion

> could be established . . . for such a purpose would be not only impious but absurd and irrational. . . . It may be foreseen that faith in public opinion will become a species of religion there, and the majority its ministering prophet. (II, 8-10)

(e) Finally, although churches cannot arbitrate disputes over ethics, they do exert influence, even in the ethical sphere:

> There is no country in the whole world in which the Christian religion retains a greater influence over the souls of men than in America. . . . religion exercises but little influence upon the laws, and upon the details of public opinion; but it directs the manners of the community, and by regulating domestic life, it regulates the state. (I, 331-332)

Taken together, Tocqueville's observations indicate that at least by early in the 19th Century this society had a recognizable "culture-religion," that Americans worshipped a "religion-in-general," that in the legitimating of ethics there was an "erosion of particularity."[19] And if the United States was to be one nation, one integrated society, this situation had to be.

The required change, however, let it be said again, was only in the structural location where decisions on competing ethical claims are made. The churches could still exert influence on its parishioners and the public at large, as could any other individual or organized collection of them. Furthermore, the churches still could claim authority in the realm of beliefs, even if some chose not to. The telling event is that Roman Catholics in America, though the church's ideology does not acknowledge it, have shifted their allegiance in the ethical sphere away from the church, as Fichter's data clearly indicate.[20]

As with the Roman Catholic Church only less so, Protestant Churches have retained a language that makes recognition of this change difficult and an orientation that makes it distasteful. The devout, motivated by religious ideals, cannot but feel frustrated when confronted with others who may be similarly devout but whose religious ideals indicate different behavior. The inclination has been to doubt the devoutness, the *religiousness* of the motivation. But precisely because such techniques do not remove the conflict, there develops the alternative of the persuasion. And playing by the rules of the persuasion game *of necessity* demands a greater commitment to the rules, the game, and the judge than to the message of which the player is persuaded.

To some observers of this situation the religious ideals appear to have not only no control but also no possible influence. But what Tocqueville noted in 1831 the churches have not yet grasped as well. Francis Wayland, in 1842, stated that in churches "men are told how they must feel, but they are not told how they must act, and the result, in many cases ensues, that a man's belief has but a transient and uncertain effect upon his practice."[21] He failed to see that a church *could not* tell a man how he must act. More poetically today it is said that God is dead, that religion no longer informs culture.

These pages have tried to show, however, that only in a special sense are these slogans accurate. Religion necessarily fails to inform only in the sense that churches have had to give up the authority to resolve conflicts in the ethical sphere.[22] They still may exercise ethical influence, and they remain the developers and transmitters of non-empirical beliefs. In these ways, God is not dead, and religion does inform culture.

This situation being the case, it is tempting to interpret the churches' renewed interest in biblical theology and their "search for political realism"[23] as indicating a growing awareness of their structural location in a society. Doubtlessly this is exaggerated. Many forces have contributed to these events. Yet recognition that (as Sumner put it) "the pulpit no longer speaks with authority" has probably had a role in the establishing of lobbies, the coordination of information campaigns, and the interdenominational efforts to concentrate influence. So, too, the awareness that religious beliefs in the religiously pluralistic society are not automatically reflected in predictable behavior has probably had a role in the re-examination of those beliefs. American churches' renewed concern for "truth," that is, may well reflect recognition of their changed location with respect to the "good."

---

1. Will Herberg, "Protestantism in a Post-Protestant America," *Christianity and Crisis,* 22 (February 5, 1962), pp. 5-6. The general theme we are to discuss is found in many places. Martin Marty, *The New Shape of American Religion,* Harper and Bros., 1959, and G. Vahanian, *The Death of God,* George Braziller, 1961, are two good examples.

2. Vahanian, *ibid.*

3. Talcott Parsons, *Structure and Process in Modern Society,* The Free Press, 1960, p. 311.

4. e.g., Gerhard Lenski, *The Religious Factor,* Doubleday, 1961.

5. Vahanian, *op. cit.,* p. 59.

6. Herberg, *op. cit.,* p. 5.

7. The poignant illustration comes from Peter Berger, *The Noise of Solemn Assemblies,* Doubleday, 1961.

8. Vahanian, *op. cit.,* p. 23.

9. A single, Established Church was involved in each of Troeltsch's instances of a "Christian Society." He noted that "all the ecclesiastical institutions soon found that they were unable to maintain and carry on their existence by moral force alone, and they were obliged to appeal to the civil power for aid. . . . In countries where the religious situation contains many different elements, the various ecclesiastical systems constitute a large body of opinion, in which each particular communion claims to possess the sole Truth, thus neutralizing the religious influence of all." Then, in the non sequitur fashion of some present-day observers, he adds, "The churches are losing their hold on the spiritual life of the nations. . . ." *The Social Teaching of the Christian Churches* (trans. Olive Wyon), The Macmillan Co., 1931, p. 1008.

10. An alternative, of course, is for the "defeated" faction to isolate themselves, migrate, or in some way become a new and separate society. Religion has played a huge role in these formations. Our remarks presuppose that in this day such an option will not be chosen. See Phillip E. Hammond, "The Migrating Sect," *Social Forces,* March, 1963.

11. Salo W. Baron, *Modern Nationalism and Religion,* Harper and Bros., 1947, p. 41.

12. Vahanian, *op. cit.,* p. 37, quotes uncritically this statement from the Hoover Commission report.

13. Parsons, *op. cit.,* p. 298.

14. Baron, *op. cit.,* p. 6.

15. As discussed by H. Richard Niebuhr. *Christ and Culture,* Harper and Bros., 1951, p. 171. Niebuhr's superb study of the church-society relationship documents the Christian theological responses to that relationship. Those responses are not, as some have assumed, necessarily *descriptive* of the relationship. To continue the metaphor then, disagreement may persist over whether one hand knows what the other is doing; there can be no question however that in the religiously pluralistic society the left has been separated from the right.

16. Baron, *op. cit.,* p. 15.

17. It is of some interest in this regard that the American public ranks Supreme Court Justices highest of some 90 occupations. See National Opinion Research Center, "Jobs and Occupations: A Popular Evaluation" in R. Bendix and S. M. Lipset, eds., *Class, Status and Power,* The Free Press, 1953, pp. 411-426. Of more significance is the continuing debate over the "proper" role of the judiciary—whether it is to "decide values." Though many analyses of this debate are available, its uniquely religious significance has yet to be documented.

18. All quotations from Alexis de Tocqueville, *Democracy in America,* 2 vols. (Trans. Henry Reeve).

19. Tocqueville was not alone in his 19th century observations of America. See Jerald C. Brauer, "Images of Religion in America," *Church History,* 30, March, 1961, pp. 3-18.

20. Joseph Fichter, *Southern Parish,* University of Chicago, 1951, pp. 259-271.

21. Quoted in Sidney Mead, "American Protestantism since the Civil War, from Denominationalism to Americanism," *Journal of Religion,* 36, January, 1956, p. 4.

22. Peter Berger, *The Precarious Vision,* Doubleday, 1961, elaborates a similar thesis at places, e.g., "Christian faith cannot be the basis of morality. . . . cannot be the basis for law and·order." pp. 173-174.

23. Donald B. Meyer, *The Protestant Search for Political Realism,* 1919-1941, U. of California Press, 1960, traces the churches' enormous though short-range change from their optimistic position in the first part of the century to a more "realistic" position at mid-century. In the terms of this essay, that change reflects (in addition to other things) the churches' belated recognition of their social structural relationship with political institutions in the democratic and religiously pluralistic society.

Chapter 5
The Church and the Stratification System: Class and Racial Differences

ERICH GOODE

Social Class and Church Participation

Social class and church participation have been found to be strongly and significantly related.[1] Numerous studies have revealed a positive association between these two variables.[2] Despite variation in the use of indicators, used, whether for class[3] or for church participation;[4] despite random fluctuations which occur in any set statistics as a result of sampling, and despite differences in the sociological traditions of the various researchers involved in these studies, this regularity obtains: the higher the class level, the greater the degree of church participation; the lower the class level, the less the degree of church participation.

Reprinted from the *American Journal of Sociology* 72 (July 1966):102-11, by permission of the author and The University of Chicago Press.

Much recent research on the topic of the relationship between religion and social status is concerned with the fact that several of the dimensions of religiosity vary positively by class, while others vary inversely.[5] This essay is concerned with only one of these dimensions —the ritualistic or "cultic"—yet conceives of it as being part of a more general dimension which includes all aspects of formal church activity. As will be demonstrated, religious ritual, such as church attendance, relates to other variables in a manner almost identical to non-ritualistic forms of church participation, such as church leadership or church organizational activity. They will be conceived of, therefore, as being parts of the same dimension. It must be kept in mind, however, that this will be demonstrated empirically and will not be "proved" by being assumed in the first place.

The main area of disagreement centers, not around whether the association exists or whether it is positive or negative—the data are too clear-cut for such a controversy to be long sustained—but around *why* this regularity should obtain. As to what the causal factors behind the relationship are is a question that has elicited some serious disagreement. One position is that the greater middle-class participation reflects a greater degree of religiousness and religious concern.[6] Others hold that the relationship is due to factors *extrinsic* to religion itself and that the greater level of church activity exhibited by the middle classes[7] is an artifact of some third variable.[8] An example of this position is that taken by Gerhard Lenski,[9] who maintains that the observed regularity is a function of the fact that members of the middle classes demonstrate a higher level of *overall* associational activity. They participate more in organizations of *all* kinds, the church being merely one specific example of a voluntary association.

This is a crucial question, and it deserves detailed exploration. It is, however, a complicated one; it contains several subtopics and relates behavior in a number of social spheres. There are at least two important conclusions of a study that demonstrates the dependence of the relationship between social status and church activity on general formal organizational participation. One is that church activity ought not to be treated as a separate, distinct, and unique aspect of social behavior, unconnected with other behavioral spheres of life which, because they are ostensibly non-religious in content, are assumed to be unrelated to "purely" religious manifestations. A demonstration of the more general position—that much religious behavior is secular in origin—would reduce the supposed insulation of societal institutions.

The second implication of this demonstration is a theoretical as well as a methodological one. Church activity cannot be seen as an indicator of religiosity if its relationship to other variables is dependent on nonreligious factors. This means, in practical terms, that when measuring degree of religiousness, church attendance should not be used; but it also points to the source of the causality of an important sociological relationship. In knowing this, we know a little more about the nature of social reality.

Unfortunately, Lenski, who introduced this hypothesis, presents no empirical evidence to support his assertion; until such time as data are brought to bear on this question, it will remain an unsupported assumption. It is, however, a reasonable one. A number of findings point to this conclusion, although they do not support it directly. For example, there is a clear and marked relationship between social class, again, regardless of the indicator used, and participation in non-church associations.[10] There is also a significant correlation between church and non-church activity.[11] It would seem reasonable, therefore, to assume that the latter two variables associate with social class in the same manner and to the same degree. This must remain an unsupported assumption, however, until the relationship of each is tested independently with other variables in such a way that "contamination" is eliminated. Two variables may be associated positively with one another, yet related in the opposite direction with a third variable. This kind of complex configuration of relationships is by no means rare in the sociological literature.

Several studies have attempted to test this three-variable relationship empirically, but in our opinion they fail to establish the precise nature of the association. One study holds that the link between social class and church activity is a function of the fact that individuals of middle-class status *attend* church more because they are far more likely to be church *members* than is true for those of laboring-class status.[12] That is, when the factor of *church membership* is controlled, the original relationship between social class and church participation will disappear. This thesis may be true by itself, but this particular question must be seen as a special case of a broader one; these figures are an artifact of another set of figures. Church membership should be seen as one measure of church activity, rather than regarded as the test variable itself. In order to determine the true nature of the relationship between these three variables, social class and church and non-church participation, we must find a study employing the last variable as the test variable which is seen as influencing the relationship between the first two variables.

Bernard Lazerwitz[13] has set out to explore the interrelationships existing between these three variables. He states: "With frequency of church attendance clearly associated with social status, questions still remain about the place of church attendance within the totality of an individual's activity in voluntary associations. Since church attendance and activity in voluntary associations both show increased frequencies with greater amounts of education, and more occupational status, several researchers have suggested studying church attendance within the context of all sorts of voluntary associations and trying to explain variations in church attendance by the same factors found to influence activity in voluntary associations."[14] This statement of purpose is followed by a number of empirical tests that purport to show that church and non-church activity both increase as the same set of sociological factors determining them increases.

The trouble is that the question of "contamination" still remains. The same sets of factors may increase together, but their relationship with one another has not been tested *independent* of third variables. More specifically, the relationship between social class and church activity has not been tested independent of over-all associational activity. Only parallel two-variable-relationship tables were run. Since Lazerwitz has not tested any relationship for spuriousness, the real causal connections between these variables is left unexplored. *Descriptively,* of course, his position is upheld by the data presented; analytically, however, no thesis is either supported or refuted by his tests.

One study, by Rodney Stark,[15] does make such a three-variable test of the relationship in question. Stark concludes from his data that, when the factor of general organizational participation is taken into account, the relationship between occupational level and church participation remains. At each level of associational activity, individuals of the white-collar occupational level attend church more than do those of the blue-collar occupational level.[16] The relationship, he claims, is therefore not a spurious one. Middle-class individuals actually do display a higher level of religiousness, a greater degree of religious concern, and their higher level of church activity measures this religiosity.

Unfortunately, Stark's methological errors mar his analysis. They are so serious that his conclusions cannot be accepted as definitive; they must be regarded as untested. Some of these errors are: (1) The main locus of interest in the three-variable test lies in the degree of *reduction* of the strength of the original relationship. Stark does not present a table showing the original relationship between social class and church participation. (2) The differences between the levels of church attendance of the two occupational levels in Stark's tables are actually quite small —from 4 to 8 percentage points of difference in weekly church attendance. (3) Only one indicator of each of the three variables used in the test is employed. For a relationship as complex as this, several indicators should have been used. Stark, in short, has not presented us with a true test of the actual relationship between social class and general associational participation and church activity.

I have recomputed Stark's figures so that his uncontrolled two-variable table can be presented and compared with the controlled three-variable table we presented originally.[17] The recombined figures and percentages for the uncontrolled relationship are presented in Table 1.

TABLE 1. *Church Attendance by Occupation*

Church Attendance	White Collar		Blue Collar	
	Per Cent	*N*	Per Cent	*N*
Attended in past week	55	145	46	255
Attended in past year	38	101	38	211
Not attended for year or more	7	19	16	91
Total	100	265	100	557

Table 2 is the original one presented by Stark. Not one of the independent "controlled" tests in Table 2 is significant at any level (with 2 degrees of freedom x^2 is 0.6, 3.8, and 5.7), whereas the uncontrolled relationship is significant at the .001 level (x^2=14.3). Using *h* as another measure of association,[18] the same picture emerges. For the respondents with no non-church organizations, the association between occupational level and church activity is .12; for those with one such organization it is .18, and for those with two or more it is .16. For the original uncontrolled relationship *h*=.21.

Unfortunately, a serious difficulty with both of these tests of significance is that the outcome of the test is determined in large part by the number of cases in each of the cells.[19]

TABLE 2. *Church Attendance by Occupation, Holding Voluntary Organizational Activity Constant*

Church Attendance	Number of Organizations Participated in (Per Cent)					
	None		One		Two or More	
	White Collar	Blue Collar	White Collar	Blue Collar	White Collar	Blue Collar
Attended in past week	53	45	54	46	56	52
Attended in past year	34	38	39	40	38	31
Not attended for year or more	13	17	7	14	6	17
Total	100	100	100	100	100	100
N	22	367	139	132	103	58

We can see that the original percentage differences in the church activity of the two class levels is slightly greater (9 per cent for weekly church attendance) than is true for the three variable relationships (an average of 6.7 per cent), but the differences are small in either case.

The Data

Because of the inadequacies and gaps in the available literature on this question, we set out to explore the relationship and provide a test of its precise nature in such a way that its findings may be accepted as more or less definitive. A secondary analysis of the data collected in two studies was made. We shall call these two the "Appalachian" and the "Congregational" studies. The Appalachian study is one phase of a general attitude survey conducted in the southern Appalachian area. The specifically religious phase of it was done in 1959. The headquarters of the broader project was Berea College, and it was conceived and designed by Thomas R. Ford, W. D. Weatherford, Earl D. C. Brewer, and Rupert B. Vance. The religious phase of the study was Emory University. It was designed and directed by Brewer. Six metropolitan areas, three of central cities, three of county areas outside central cities, and eighteen rural or non-metropolitan areas were chosen by a "modified area sample stratified by state economic areas, counties and subdivisions of counties or cities."[20] Within each of these areas, ten churches were chosen randomly. Five "church leaders" and five non-leader church members were selected for interviewing. In addition those selected designated five known non-members. Thus, the final sample was made up of one-third church leaders, one-third non-leader church members, and one-third non-members.

The final sample consisted of 1,078 individuals. It was almost entirely white and Protestant in composition, was largely rural, and was made up largely of blue-collar workers—manual laborers and farmers.[21] The Congregational study was made up entirely of church members.[22] In 1956 the Department of Urban Churches, a unit within the division of the National Council of Churches of Christ, authorized a study to determine the factors relating to the "effectiveness" of churches.[23] A schedule of topics to be covered was worked out by church-associated social researchers and sociologists. The actual questionnaire, originally designed for members of the United Lutheran denomination, was constructed by a group of researchers under the guidance of Charles Y. Glock, then director of the Bureau of Applied Social Research. It was adapted for Congregational use, making some changes in doctrinal questions.

In the fall of that year the thirty-seven superintendents of the Congregational state conference were asked to "nominate" churches in their conferences considered by them to be "effective" urban churches. Twenty-seven eventually were chosen. The ministers of these churches were then invited to participate in the study. Some declined, others were eliminated, and the final total of the first sample was reduced to twelve churches. Every church member in all except two churches was sent a mailed questionnaire; in the other two, every third member was asked to participate. The first sample was composed of 4,095 respondents. One suburban church was added a few years later and was made up of about 800 members.

The return rate varied from quite low to moderately high—from 27 per cent to 71 per cent—depending on the church in question. Because of the totally metropolitan makeup of the respondents, as well as the traditionally high status of Congregationalists, an abnormally high proportion of the respondents were white collar, college-educated, and high in income. The sample is therefore not representative of any general population, any urban population, or even any urban church population. This sample neatly complements the predominantly rural, southern, less well-educated sample included in the Appalachian study.

The results of these two studies agree and demonstrate the following empirical regularities:

1. *Church participation is significantly related to social class.*—The Appalachian study employed seven indicators of church activity: church attendance, participation in the Lord's Supper, money contributed to the church, number of memberships in church organizations, the holding of leadership positions in church organizations, attendance at church meetings of all kinds; and total number of religious activities within a period of time. Two measures of class were used: education and occupational level. These fourteen tables were all significant at the .001 level, with differences between high and low status levels in their church activity ranging from 8 to 43 percentage points. The second study, the Congregational study, employed three measures of church participation: church attendance, number of church financial contributions, and holding officerships in church organizations. The two indicators of class were: education and occupation. Of the six tables produced, five were significant at the .001 level; one was not significant. The percentage-point differences were from slightly negative to 17 points. These tables are collapsed and presented in Tables 3–6 to show the strength of the original uncontrolled relationship between social class and church activity.

2. *Non-church activity is significantly related to social class.*—The Appalachian study used number of non-church organizational memberships as its measure of non-church associational activity. The tables

produced by a cross-tabulation with the status measures were significant at the .001 level and represented from about 40 percentage points of difference. The Congregational study used as its indicator of non-church activity a number of non-church organizational memberships. When cross-tabulated with the two status measures, the differences were significant at the .001 level from 15 to 30 points of difference.

3. *Church participation is significantly related to non-church participation.* —The seven tables produced by the Appalachian study's indicators represented from about 15 to 30 points of difference, all significant at the .001 level. The Congregational study produced two tables, significant at the .001 level, the differences being from about 15 points.

These relationships corroborate previous findings that have related these variables. Our contribution, however, was to test the three-variable relationship between status and church and non-church activity.

4. *When general non-church formal organizational participation is controlled, the original uncontrolled relationship between class and church activity is greatly attenuated.*—In the Appalachian study's data, when education measured status, the mean point difference between the most and least educated levels with regard to their church activity—an average of all seven indicators—was 17.4 per cent. When the non-church-associational-participation control was applied to the relationship, this dropped to 9.9 per cent. When occupation was an indicator of status the original mean difference between white- and blue-collar workers (farmers excluded) in their church activity was 24.0 per cent after the control, the drop was small, to 19.4 per cent. The Congregational study's data agreed in substance with these findings. The original difference between the highest and lowest educational levels in their church activity was 7.0 per cent; this was reduced to 4.0 per cent after controlling for non-church organizational activity. The comparable figures when occupation measured status were 12.7 per cent and 10.5 per cent. The figures for these relationships are presented in Tables 3–6.

The reduction that resulted from this control was greater the greater the specificity of the control. Where the exact number of non-church organizations or the number of organization meetings was specified, the reduction in the relationships increased. Naturally, tables incorporating this degree of specificity are too clumsy to present in a paper of this scope.

One qualification must be registered here. This is the role of additional variables.[24] Clearly age, sex, denominational affiliation, and degree of urbanness all play some role in determining both religious and non-religious activity as well as in affecting the stratification variables. Does this regularity hold for women as well as for men? For urban and

TABLE 3. *Percentage "High" in Church Participation, by Education: Appalachian Sample*

	Disregarding Non-Church Activity		"Low" Non-Church Activity		"High" Non-Church Activity	
	Grade School	High School	Grade School	High School	Grade School	High School
Church attendance	43	63	38	49	58	71
Church associations	27	50	21	39	46	56
Church contributions	37	53	32	38	53	62
All church meetings	34	47	29	35	47	54
Lord's Supper	45	66	39	55	63	73
All religious activities	21	29	18	18	30	35
Church leadership	33	54	27	45	50	60
*N**	511	567	380	208	125	355

Note. – Indicator for a "high" level of church participation: church attendance: once a week or more; church associations: three memberships or more; church contributions: one hundred dollars or more given in the past year; all church meetings: one hundred or more attended in the past year; Lord's Supper: partaken at least once in the past year; all religious activities: six or more in the past week. Indicator for non-church activity: "low": attended no meetings of non-church organizations in the past year; "high": attended at least one meeting of non-church organization in the past year.

**N's* for all of the following tables vary somewhat due to non-response.

for rural dwellers? For Catholics and Protestants, for sects and "old-line" denominations? For all age groups? Clearly an entire monograph, and not merely a paper of this scope, would be necessary to answer these questions. The author cannot go into these complex questions because of space limitations, except to point out that the Congregational study's sample was limited to urban and suburban dwellers and to a single denomination, the Congregational Christian Church; naturally,

TABLE 4. *Percentage "High" in Church Participation, by Occupation:* Appalachian Sample*

	Disregarding Non-Church Activity		"Low" Non-Church Activity		"High" Non-Church Activity	
	Blue Collar	White Collar	Blue Collar	White Collar	Blue Collar	White Collar
Church attendance	49	77	40	65	62	82
Church associations	39	56	27	46	55	60
Church contributions	44	67	38	53	53	73
All church meetings	38	61	29	54	50	64
Lord's Supper	51	80	41	71	66	84
All religious activities	20	45	15	36	27	49
Church leadership	41	64	31	54	54	69
N	522	254	295	78	223	176

*Farmers were eliminated because of their ambiguous occupational status. They were not eliminated from the education table because they could be arranged educationally. *N's* and percentages in the two tables do not match perfectly, therefore.

TABLE 5. *Percentage "High" in Church Participation, by Education: Congregational Sample*

	Disregarding Non-Church Activity			"Low" Non-Church Activity			"High" Non-Church Activity		
	No College	Some College	College Graduate	No College	Some College	College Graduate	No College	Some College	College Graduate
Church attendance	56	55	55	55	53	55	57	56	55
Church contributions	43	45	51	39	35	43	50	53	54
Church leadership	29	36	43	26	26	37	34	43	45
N	1,658	1,288	1,811	789	454	347	688	752	1,372

Note. – Indicator for a "high" level of church participation: church attendance: attendance three times a month or more; church contributions: contributes regularly to at least three church funds; church leadership: holds an officership in at least one church organization. Indicator for non-church activity: "low": mentions membership in fewer than two non-church organizations; "high: mentions membership in two or more non-church organizations.

this does not eliminate the influence of all of the variables mentioned, but it does suggest that they might not make our conclusions invalid.

A second qualification that must be entered here is the fact that the class differences in church activity did not entirely disappear; they were only reduced significantly. Clearly, then, the relationship is not completely spurious. Class still affects church activity to some degree even when this crucial third variable is controlled. We therefore cannot eliminate its role in the relationship, though it can be seen as less determining than was true previously.

The last qualification relates to the *direction* of the relationship. Although we have designated over-all organizational participation as the general dimension under which we may subsume church participation, it is conceivable that church activity causes non-church activity, that is, that because one attends church one feels compelled to participate in other organizations as well. Although our thesis is a more plausible one, within the confines of this paper we cannot eliminate the alternative argument.

TABLE 6. *Percentage "High" in Church Participation, by Occupation: Congregational Sample*

	Disregarding Non-Church Activity				"Low" Non-Church Activity				"High" Non-Church Activity			
	Lab	Sales	Mgr	Prof	Lab	Sales	Mgr	Prof	Lab	Sales	Mgr	Prof
Church attendance	49	55	52	58	49	56	50	57	53	53	52	59
Church contributions	38	45	52	50	33	38	39	42	43	52	58	54
Church leadership	25	33	42	42	22	29	32	36	30	36	48	46
N	570	931	714	1,921	319	474	249	678	244	457	458	1,231

Note. – Prof = professional; mgr = managerial; sales = sales and clerical; lab = manual labor.

IMPLICATIONS

Our findings strongly suggest that church activity, such as attendance at church ritual, cannot be seen as an unambiguous reflection of religiosity, that is, as a measure of religious feeling. Church participation clearly means something quite different for members of the white-collar occupational level than it does for manual laborers. To judge by the evidence, for the former it is in part an extension of their over-all associational participation. It appears that church activity has become secularized to such an extent that it can be subsumed, at least partially, under general associational activity; it is quite possible that to this extent religious activity has lost much of its uniqueness historically, much of its separateness from the other institutions in society. It does not seem to be experienced as a special and exclusive form of sociation.

Working-class church members, however, display a quite different pattern of religiosity. They participate less in formal church activities, but their religious activity does not appear to be nearly so secularized. It is more specifically religious in character. This is indicated by the fact that on a number of other religious dimensions, dimensions not dependent on extraneous non-religious variables, individuals of manual-status levels appear to display a considerably higher level of religious response. This is true particularly of psychological variables, such as religious "salience," the greater feeling that the church and religion are great forces in the lives of respondents.[25] It is also true for "religiosity" as measured by a higher level of religious concern,[26] and for religious "involvement," the extent to which the individual is psychologically dependent on some sort of specifically religious sociation in his life.

This is not to say that these two measures of religion, formal church participation and religious "involvement," are different and equally valid indicators of religiosity, each one measuring a different type of religiousness, each one bearing a different relationship to stratification variables. It is to say, rather, that some of the traditional measures of religiousness, such as church attendance, ought not even to be used at all. Church activity is not really a "pure" measure of one particular kind of religiosity; it is not a measure that can be considered specifically religious in character. Its strength and degree depend in such a large measure on non-religious factors that it cannot be said to measure a purely religious variable; secular variables are intertwined with it.

This also means that we must now shift a large part of the burden of the explanation of the different levels of church activity of the various class levels from religiousness specifically to organizational activity per se. Instead of asking: "Why are the middle classes more religious than the laboring classes?" or "Why do those of middle-class status attend church more?" we must ask, rather: "Why are the middle classes more active in voluntary organizations?" or "Why do they participate more in social activities of all kinds?" This makes the question a more general one, one less tied to one specific institution. We should seek the explanation at a higher level of generality than has been true in the past. This is not an explanation, of course, but it does point to where one might be found. What we have done is not to solve a question but to reroute questions about a specific relationship to a more fruitful area of inquiry.

---

1. This research was supported by Public Health Service grant 1-F1-MH-23, 474–01. I would like to thank Professors William J. Goode and Terence K. Hopkins for critical comments. I am grateful, in addition, to the research directors of the studies whose data this essay employs. They will be referred to when the data are cited.

2. To cite only those studies, a few of which use church attendance as their indicator of the dependent variable: Anton T. Boisen, "Factors Which Have To Do with the Decline of the Rural Church," *American Journal of Sociology,* XXII (September, 1916), 187; William G. Mather, Jr., "Income and Social Participation," *American Sociological Review,* VI (June, 1941), 381; Harold F. Kaufman, *Religious Organization in Kentucky* (Agricultural Experiment Station Bulletin 524 [Lexington: University of Kentucky, 1948]), p. 43; John A. Hostetler and William G. Mather, *Participation in the Rural Church* (Agricultural Experiment Station Paper 1762 [State College, Pa.: Pennsylvania State College, October, 1952]), p. 55; Wendell Bell and Maryanne T. Force, "Religious Preference, Familism and the Class Structure," *Midwest Sociologist,* IX (May, 1957), 84; Bernard Lazerwitz, "Some Factors Associated with Variation in Church Attendance," *Social Forces,* XXXIX (May, 1961), 306. At least one study demonstrated little or no association between these variables: Louis Bultena, "Church Membership and Church Attendance in Madison, Wisconsin," *American Sociological Review,* XIV (June, 1949), 348-89. An attempt has been made to "integrate" the contradictory findings of a positive and negative association between them: Harry C. Dillingham, "Protestant Religion and Social Status," *American Journal of Sociology,* LXX (January, 1965), 416-22. Since the relationship is, according to my own survey of the literature, overwhelmingly found to be positive, no such procedure appears to me to be necessary. With regard to his point that there is a difference between examining church activity and social status on the individual level and comparing these variables using denominations as the unit of analysis, our own data point to the lack of importance that denominational differences have in this relationship.

3. The most common indicators of this variable are education, occupational level, and income. The number of categories employed, the points at which the classes are divided from one another, and the labels used to characterize the groups depend on the theoretical and methodological characteristics of any given study in question. It is not our intention to enter into the controversy over definitions and indicators of social class.

4. The various indicators of church participation that have been used by these and other studies are: church attendance, church membership, number of church-association memberships, attendance at meetings of church associations, financial contributions to the local church, total number of religious activities within a specified period of time, etc. What is important to note about these various indicators is that the same empirical relationships should obtain, regardless of the specific indicator used.

5. For a discussion of these dimensions, see Charles Y. Glock, "On the Study of Religious Commitment," *Review of Recent Research Bearing on Religious and Character Formation,* research supplement to the July–August, 1962, issue of *Religious Education,* pp. S-98-S-110. For empirical tests of the relationship of these dimensions with social class, see: Yoshio Fukuyama, "The Major Dimensions of Church Membership," *Review of Religious Research,* II (Spring, 1961), 154-61, and Nicholas J. Demerath, "Social Stratification and Church Involvement," *Review of Religious Research,* II (Spring, 1961), 146-54.

6. Michael Argyle, *Religious Behavior* (Glencoe, Ill.: Free Press, 1959), p. 147, and Rodney Stark, "Class, Radicalism and Religious Involvement in Great Britain," *American Sociological Review,* XXIX (October, 1964), 698-706.

7. Some researchers claim that there is a decline in church participation when the upper class is compared with the middle classes. It must be stressed here that methodological questions of stratification are not at issue. Our own data will stress the differences between the white-collar and the manual classes and avoid altogether the questions of what comprises the "upper class" and what their possibly unique religious-participation patterns are.

8. Paul F. Lazarsfeld has pioneered in the theoretical development of three-variable analysis. See his "Interpretation of Statistical Relations in a Research Operation," in Lazarsfeld and Morris Rosenberg (eds.), *The Language of Social Research* (Glencoe, Ill.: Free Press, 1955), pp. 115-25, and Lazarsfeld, "Evidence and Inference in Social Research," *Daedalus,* LXXXVII (Fall, 1958), 117-24.

9. *The Religious Factor* (Garden City, N. Y.: Doubleday & Co., 1961), p. 44 n., and "The Sociology of Religion in the United States," *Social Compass,* IX (1962), 313-14.

10. Mirra Komarovsky, "The Voluntary Associations of Urban Dwellers," *American Sociological Review,* XI (December, 1946), 688; Leonard Reissman, "Class, Leisure and Social Participation," *American Sociological Review,* XIX (February, 1954), 76-84; Basil G. Zimmer, "Participation in Urban Structures," *American Sociological Review,* XX (April, 1955), 219; John M. Foskett, "Social Structure and Social Participation," *American Sociological Review,* XX (August, 1955), 433-36; Morris Axelrod, "Urban Structure and Social Participation," *American Sociological Review,* XXI (February, 1956), 15; John C. Scott, Jr., "Membership and Participation in Voluntary Associations," *American Sociological Review,* XXII (June, 1957), 321-23; Charles R. Wright and Herbert H. Hyman, "Voluntary Association Memberships of American Adults," *American Sociological Review,* XXIII (June, 1958), 289.

11. Harold F. Kaufman, *Participation in Organized Activities in Selected Kentucky Localities* (Agricultural Experiment Station Bulletin 528 [Lexington: University of Kentucky, 1949]), pp. 20-21, 48; Louis Albert Ploch, "Factors Related to the Persistences and Changes in the Social Participation of Household Heads" (M.S. thesis Pennsylvania State College, 1951), p. 78; Basil G. Zimmer and Amos H. Hawley, "Suburbanization and Church Participation," *Social Forces,* XXXVII (May, 1959), 353; Bernard Lazerwitz, "Membership in Voluntary Associations and Frequency of Church Attendance," *Journal for the Scientific Study of Religion,* II (Fall, 1962), 74-84; Earl D. C. Brewer, "Religion and the Churches," in Thomas R. Ford (ed.), *The Southern Appalachian Region: A Survey* (Lexington: University of Kentucky Press, 1962), p. 214.

12. Lee G. Burchinal, "Some Social Status Criteria and Church Membership and Church Attendance," *Journal of Social Psychology,* XLIX (February, 1959), 53-64.

13. Lazerwitz, "Membership in Voluntary Associations and Frequency of Church Attendance."

14. *Ibid.,* p. 74.

15. Stark, *op. cit.*

16. *Ibid.,* p. 700.

17. There was a slight error in Stark's computations, since no figures can be 53 per cent, 34 per cent, and 13 percent of 22.

18. W. Allen Wallis and Harry V. Roberts, *Statistics: A New Approach* (Glencoe, Ill.: Free Press, 1956), pp. 282-84.

19. Hanan C. Selvin, "A Critique of Tests of Significance in Survey Research," *American Sociological Review,* XXII (October, 1957), 524.

20. The following account was given to me in a personal letter from Professor Brewer.

21. Other details about the study may be found in Brewer, *op. cit.,* pp. 201-18. The author wishes to thank Professor Brewer for his generosity in sharing the data cards from this study.

22. One methodological consequence of this is that the difference in the church activity among the class levels is smaller than is true of general population samples.

23. This account was taken from Yoshio Fukuyama, "The Major Dimensions of Church Membership" (Ph.D. dissertation, University of Chicago Divinity School, 1960), pp. 216 ff. We would like to express our appreciation to Dr. Fukuyama for letting us use the data cards from this survey.

24. It is interesting that in a recent article on religious activity and social status which stressed the importance of controlling additional third variables, over-all associational activity was not even mentioned as one important enough to control (see Dillingham, *op. cit.,* pp. 416, 421-22).

25. Demerath, *op. cit.,* p. 153.

26. Clifford Kirkpatrick, "Religion and Humanitarianism," *Psychological Monographs,* LXIII, Whole No. 304 (1949), 13.

JAMES H. CONE

Black Consciousness and the Black Church: A Historical-Theological Interpretation

Since the rise of Black Power and its multifarious expressions in black life, it is no longer possible to ignore the once invisible black minority in American society. The black insurgency of the 1960's means that the invisible has become visible, demonstrating the untruth of the assumption that America embodies one community with a common destiny for all. New voices are making themselves heard, and they are calling into question the American Dream—that rhetoric about brotherhood, equality, and "the land of the free and the home of the brave." Black people are forcing this society to deal with the *new black men,* the persons of color who have no intention of integrating into the whiteness of this culture, but are moving with power in the direction of a new humanity as defined by the forces of liberation in the oppressed black community. My purpose is to examine this new black expression, seeking to analyze the effect of blackness on the black church and placing special emphasis on the theological implications of black presence in America.

From the *Annals of the American Academy of Political and Social Science* 387 (1970):49-55. Reprinted by permission of the publisher and authors.

Black Consciousness: A Definition

Perhaps the most appropriate description of this new black mood is the concept of black consciousness, which is to say that black people are aware of the meaning of their blackness in the context of whiteness. They know that their color must be the defining characteristic of their movement in the world because it is the controlling symbol of white limitations placed on black existence. Black consciousness is recognizing that the social, economic, and political status of black people in America is determined by white people's inability to deal with the presence of color.

Black consciousness is the black man's self-awareness. To know blackness is to know self, and to know self is to be cognizant of other selves in relation to self. It is knowing the criterion of acceptance and rejection in human encounters. To be conscious of his color means that the black person knows that his blackness is the reason for his oppression, for there is no way to account for the white racist brutality against the black community except by focusing on the color of the victim.

To know *why* one is the victim of inhumanity is only the first step toward self-awareness. The next step is the *limit* that a man sets on the encroachments against his humanity. To know self is to define self, and this means nothing less than telling the enemy that he can go so far, but no farther. It is impossible to be human without fighting against the forces that seek to destroy humanity. In the black context, this means that the black man knows that the knowledge of his being places him in conflict with those who refuse to recognize his humanity. Black consciousness, therefore, is not only the knowledge of the source of black oppression; it is the black man's willingness to fight against that source. Black consciousness is Black Power, the power of the oppressed black man to liberate himself from white enslavement by making blackness the primary datum of his humanity. It is the power to be black in spite of whiteness, the courage to affirm being in the midst of nonbeing.

Black Consciousness and Black History

To understand the present impact of black consciousness on black life, it is necessary to proceed in the direction of a definition that does not sidestep history. To know self is to know the historical self, and for black people, this involves the investigation of other black selves who lived in a similar historical setting. Our present being is defined by the being of our fathers, what they said and did in a white racist society. It is only through ascertaining what the responses of our fathers were to white strictures placed on their existence that we can come to know what our responses ought to be to white people who insist on defining the boundary of black being. Oppressors are inclined to blot out all past events that are detrimental to their existence as rulers, giving the impression that their definition of humanity is the only legitimate one in the world. Black consciousness means rejecting the white oppressor's definition of being by re-creating the historical black being that is an antithesis of everything white. It is recognizing that our feelings about America are not new, but stem from past black rebels who prepared the world for our presence. In the words of Earl Ofari: "Black radicals such as W. E. B. DuBois, William Trotter, Marcus Garvey, Malcolm X, and Stokely Carmichael simply made modifications on the foundations which the earlier black radicals laid."[1] The earlier black radicals were black people who could not reconcile themselves to slavery, and thus chose to risk death rather than to accept the European definition of man. Nat Turner, Denmark Vesey, and Gabriel Prosser are prominent examples. They put into practice Martin Delany's comment: "Every people should be the originators of their own designs, the projectors of their own schemes, and creators of the events that lead to their destiny—the consummation of their desires."[2]

Black consciousness did not come into being with Stokely Carmichael and his articulation of Black Power in the spring of 1966. It began with the slave ships, the auction blocks, and the insurrections. It began when white people decided that black people and their children should be slaves for the duration of their lives. It is not possible to enslave a people because of their blackness and expect them not to be conscious of color.

Black consciousness, however, is more than color consciousness; it is using one's color as a means of liberation. This is the meaning of every black attempt to say yes to what whites regard as evil, and no to their definition of good. It is not enough to thank God for making us men, but, as Delany would say, we must thank him for making us *black* men. This is what black consciousness means, as defined by the black historical context.

Black Theology and Black Consciousness

What does black consciousness have to do with theology? This question forces us to consider the relationship between black self-identity and the biblical faith. It is not surprising that white American theology has not inquired into this relationship, because it has pursued the theological task from the perspective of white enslavers. White religious thinkers seem to have been blind to the theological significance of black presence in America. But if we intend to speak about God and his involvement in world history, and particularly in America, the black experience is an indispensable symbol for discerning divine activity.

God and Liberation

The theological perspective that defines God as unquestionably identified with the liberation of the oppressed from earthly bondage arises out of the biblical view of divine revelation. According to the Bible, the knowledge of God is neither mystical communion nor abstract rational thought; rather, it is recognizing divine activity in human history through faith. The biblical God is the God who is involved in the historical process for the purpose of human liberation, and to know him is to know what he is doing in historical events as they are related to the liberation of the oppressed. To know God is to *encounter* him in the historical liberation process as experienced in the community of the oppressed.

In the Bible, revelation, history, and faith are bound together. Revelation refers to God's self-disclosure; history is the arena of divine revelation; and faith is the perspective that enables the community to discern divine activity. To know God, then, is to have faith in him. Faith is the divine-human encounter in the historical situation of oppression, wherein the enslaved community recognizes that its deliverance from bondage is the Divine himself at work in history. To know God is to know the actuality of oppression and the certainty of liberation.

In the Old Testament, the liberation-theme stands at the center of the Hebrew view of God. Throughout Israelite history, God is known as he who acts in history for the purpose of Israel's liberation from oppression. This is the meaning of the Exodus from Egypt, the Covenant at Sinai, the conquest and settlement of Palestine, the United Kingdom and its division, and the rise of the great prophets and the second exodus from Babylon. This is also why salvation in the Old Testament basically refers to "victory in battle" (I Sam. 14:45). "He who needs salvation is one who has been threatened or oppressed, and his salvation consists in deliverance from danger and tyranny or rescue from imminent peril (I Sam. 4:3, 7:8, 9:16). To save another is to communicate to him one's prevailing strength (Job 26:2), to give him the power to maintain the necessary strength."[3] Israel's Savior is God himself, whose sovereign rule is guiding the course of human history, liberating the oppressed from the oppressors.

The theme of liberation in the New Testament is present in the appearance of Jesus Christ, the Incarnate One who takes upon himself the oppressed condition, so that all men may be what God created them to be. He is the Liberator par excellence, who reveals not only who God is and what he is doing, but also who we are and what we must do about human oppression. It is not possible to encounter this man and still remain content with human captivity. That is why Paul says, "For freedom Christ has set us free" (Gal. 5:1). The free man is the man who rebels against false authorities by reducing them to their proper status. The Christian Gospel is the good news of the liberation of the oppressed from earthly bondage.

Black Consciousness and the Christian Gospel

If the Gospel of Christ is pre-eminently the gospel of the liberation of the oppressed, then the theological assessment of divine presence in America must begin with the black condition as its point of departure. It is only through an analysis of God as he is revealed in the struggle for black liberation that we can come to know the God who made himself known through Jesus Christ. Any other knowledge of God is, at best, irrelevant and, at worst, blasphemy.

The presence of black people in America, then, is the symbolic presence of God and his righteousness for *all* the oppressed of the land. To study theology is to take the radical black perspective wherein all religious and nonreligious forms of thought are redefined in the light of the liberation of the oppressed. Elsewhere, I have called this "Black Theology."[4]

What is Black Theology? Black Theology is that theology which arises out of the need to articulate the significance of black presence in a hostile white world. It is black people reflecting religiously on the black experience, attempting to redefine the relevance of the Christian Gospel for their lives. It is a mood, a feeling that grips the soul of a people when they realize that the world is not as they wish it to be. White people are cruel, disorderly, and violent against black people. To study theology from the perspective of Black Theology means casting one's mental and emotional faculties with the lot of the oppressed so that they may learn the cause and the cure of their humiliation.

More specifically, Black Theology is the theological explication of the blackness of black people. Its task is:

> to analyze the black . . . condition in the light of God's revelation in Jesus Christ with the sole purpose of creating a new understanding of black dignity among black people, and providing the necessary soul in that people to destroy white racism.[5]

This means that Black Theology is revolutionary in its perspective. It believes that black people will be liberated from oppression, not when white people decide to "love" them, but only when black people decide that the oppressors have gone too far. Something must be done about that! The purpose of Black Theology is to place the actions of black people toward liberation in the Christian perspective, showing that Christ himself is participating in the black struggle for freedom. This is what Black Theology means.

Black Consciousness and the Black Church

If black consciousness is the working out of the biblical faith along the lines of Jesus' identification with the oppressed, what is the role of the church, and particularly the black church? Abstractly, the church of Christ is the people of God, that community which lives on the basis of the resurrected Christ. Concretely, it is the community of sufferers in any society which believes in, and lives on the basis of, a reality of liberation that is not recognized by the ruling class. The church is that community which refuses to accept things as they are and rebels endlessly against the humiliation and oppression of man. It is the community through which the Oppressed One has chosen to make his will known to the world. It is a liberating community whose chief task is to be to the world that visible possibility of God's intention for man. It is not possible to be for Christ and not to be for his people, the oppressed and unwanted in society.

Relating this concept to our contemporary situation in America, Black Theology affirms that the church of the Oppressed One must be a black church, a community that is totally identified with the goal of all oppressed people as symbolized in the condition of black people. There can be no *white* churches because the white reality is the work of him who seeks to destroy humanity by enslaving men to false ideologies regarding race. The church of Christ must be black, that is, it must be related to the realities of human misery and to what that means to people of color in a white society.

Historically, the black denominational churches bore witness to the possibility inherent in color when they regarded blackness as a symbol for the liberation of man. While the white institutional churches were pussyfooting, compromising, and reconciling themselves with the question of black oppression, the appearance of the black churches in America in the eighteenth and nineteenth centuries represented an oppressed people coming to terms with the brutal realities of the world. These early black religionists knew that the world was not as it ought to be, and that its imperfection was to be found in white oppression of the blacks. With this perception of things, they defied the "unity" of the church by refusing to allow themselves to be used as religious sanctions of an ungodly social order. At a time when an affirmation of blackness made death a "live" possibility, they said "no" to whiteness and "yes" to blackness. The affirmation of blackness was present, not just in the color of the people assembled, but in the name they chose to define their institution—the *African* Methodist Episcopal Church, the *African* Methodist Episcopal Zion Church, the *Colored* Methodist Church, and the like.

As the Bible teaches us, the name of a person or institution must not be taken lightly. It connotes definition, style, and the reason for being. To name something is to limit it, to locate it, and to decide the scope of its presence in the world. Therefore, when black people, almost without exception, used "African" in the definition of their religious communities, they said something about their view of the world and God's involvement in it. If they thought it important to define the meaning of their spiritual community by focusing on their racial identity, this meant that they believed that either the God of Jesus Christ must meet them at the point of the blackness of their existence, or he is unrelated to reality as they know it to be. Either God is involved in the black condition, participating in its liberation, or he is a murderer and a liar. This is probably what the Reverend Nathaniel Paul had in mind when he said:

> The progress of emancipation . . . is . . . certain: It is certain because that God who has made of one blood all nations of men, and who is said to be no respector of persons, has so decreed. . . . Did I believe that it would always continue, and that man to the end of time would be permitted with impunity to usurp the same undue authority over his fellows, I would . . . ridicule the religion of the Savior of the world. . . . I would consider my Bible as a book of false and delusive fables, and commit it to flame; Nay, I would go still further: I would at once confess myself an atheist and deny the existence of a holy God.[6]

Unfortunately, the post-Civil War black church did not sustain the zeal of its fathers. It compromised—consoled and pacified black people as they endured new forms of white oppression. For the most part, its leaders denied blackness, pretending that religion was basically concerned with the next life—some heavenly reality that nobody is concerned about anymore, except perhaps a few preachers who use it to mulct oppressed people of the little money that they have.

This critique of the black church is not for the purpose of writing off its significance in this new age of the emerging black revolution. Some "ultrablacks" discard the black church, but I remind them that there can be no revolution without the masses, and the black masses are in the churches. I do not believe that slavery is meant for man, and, given the proper ideological frame of reference—I am not sure what this would be, but we blacks are working on it—and political circumstances, short of suicide, all enslaved people will take what belongs to them. The purpose of the church is to provide the religious dimension inherent in all struggles for freedom. Therefore, Black Theology's critique of the post-Civil War black church is not a putdown but a call to face reality, in order that the church may move in the direction laid down by its fathers.

Garvey in the 1920's, the Black Muslims in the 1930's, Powell in the 1940's, King in the 1950's, and Malcolm X in the 1960's served to remind the black church of what its role in the society ought to be. Any church that fails to focus on black liberation as the sole reason for its existence has denied the Lord and Savior Jesus Christ and aligned itself with the antichrist. It is significant that black people in white denominations are realizing this, and that the black laity in so-called black churches are beginning to urge their leaders to act accordingly or to quit. Both groups are making decisions about the world, about people and their desires and needs, and they are determined either to reshape existing institutions along the lines of black liberation or to destroy them.

The leaders of the traditional black churches are especially nervous at this point. They have been accustomed to thinking of their churches as having always been black. How could we ever forget that in America? But what the black church is being made to realize is that blackness has new content, and it involves more than skin color. It means sharing in the condition of those who are oppressed and participating in their liberation. Unless the black church redefines its present existence in the light of the fathers who fought, risking death, to end slavery, the judgment of God will descend upon it in the persons of those who affirm with Brother Eldridge Cleaver:

> We shall have our manhood. We shall have it or the earth will be leveled by our attempts to gain it.[7]

---

1. Earl Ofari, "The Roots of Black Radicalism," *Negro Digest* (August 1969), p. 18.
2. Quoted in *ibid.,* p. 21.
3. F. J. Taylor, "Save," in Alan Richardson, ed., *A Theological Word Book of the Bible* (New York: The Macmillan Company, 1960), p. 219.
4. See James H. Cone, *Black Theology and Black Power* (New York: Seabury Press, 1969).
5. *Ibid.,* p. 117.
6. Quoted in B. E. Mays, *The Negro's God* (New York: Atheneum, 1968), p. 42.
7. Eldridge Cleaver, *Soul on Ice* (New York: McGraw-Hill, 1968), p. 61.

JOHN R. HOWARD

The Making of a Black Muslim

You were black enough to get in here. You had the courage to stay. Now be man enough to follow the honorable Elijah Muhammad. You have tried the devil's way. Now try the way of the Messenger.

Minister William X, in a West Coast Black Muslim mosque

The Lost-Found Nation of Islam in the Wilderness of North America, commonly known as the Black Muslim movement, claims a small but fanatically devoted membership among the Negroes of our major cities. The way of the "Messenger" is rigorous for those who follow it. The man or woman who becomes a Muslim accepts not only an ideology but an all-encompassing code that amounts to a way of life.

A good Muslim does a full day's work on an empty stomach. When he finally has his one meal of the day in the evening, it can include no

From *Trans-action,* December 1966, pp. 15-21. Reprinted by permission of the publisher.

pork, nor can he have drink before or a cigarette after; strict dietary rules are standard procedure, and liquor and smoking are forbidden under any circumstances. His recreation is likely to consist of reading the Koran or participating in a demanding round of temple-centered activities, running public meetings or aggressively proselytizing on the streets by selling the Muslim newspaper, *Muhammad Speaks.*

Despite allegations of Muslim violence (adverse publicity from the slaying of Malcolm X supports the erroneous notion that Muslims preach violence), the member's life is basically ascetic. Why then in a non-ascetic, hedonistically-oriented society do people become Muslims? What is the life of a Muslim like? These are questions I asked in research among West Coast members. Specifically, I wanted to know:

What perspective on life makes membership in such an organization attractive?

Under what conditions does the potential recruit develop those perspectives?

How does he happen to come to the door of the temple for his first meeting?

The Black Muslims are a deviant organization even within the Negro community; the parents or friends of many members strongly objected to their joining. So how does the recruit handle pressures that might erode his allegiance to the organization and its beliefs?

Presenting my questions as an effort to "learn the truth" about the organization, I was able to conduct depth interviews with 19 West Coast recruits, following them through the process of their commitment to the Nation of Islam.

Two main points of appeal emerged—black nationalism and an emphasis on self-help. Some recruits were attracted primarily by the first, and some by the second. The 14 interviewees who joined the organization for its aggressive black nationalism will be called "Muslim militants." The remaining five, who were attracted more by its emphasis on hard work and rigid personal morality, may be aptly termed "Protestant Ethic Muslims."

Muslim Militants: Beating the Devil

Of the 14 Muslim militants, some came from the South, some from border states, and some from the North. All lived in California at the time of the interviews; some migrated to the state as adults, others were brought out by their families as children. They varied in age from 24 to 46, and in education from a few years of grade school to four years of college. Regardless of these substantial differences in background, there were certain broad similarities among them.

At some point, each one had experiences that led away from the institutionally-bound ties and commitments that lend stability to most people's lives. Nine had been engaged in semi-legal or criminal activities. Two had been in the military, not as a career but as a way of postponing the decision of what to do for a living. None had a stable marital history. All of them were acutely aware of being outsiders by the standards of the larger society—and all had come to focus on race bias as the factor which denied them more conventional alternatives.

Leroy X came to California in his late teens, just before World War II:

> I grew up in Kansas City, Missouri, and Missouri was a segregated state. Negroes in Kansas City were always restricted to the menial jobs. I came out here in 1940 and tried to get a job as a waiter. I was a trained waiter, but they weren't hiring any Negroes as waiters in any of the downtown hotels or restaurants. The best I could do was busboy, and they fired me from that when they found out I wasn't Filipino.

Leroy X was drafted, and after a short but stormy career was given a discharge as being psychologically unfit.

> I tried to get a job, but I couldn't so I started stealing. There was nothing else to do—I couldn't live on air. The peckerwoods didn't seem to give a damn whether I lived or died. They wouldn't hire me and didn't seem to worry how I was going to stay alive. I started stealing.
>
> I could get you anything you wanted—a car, drugs, women, jewelry. Crime is a business like any other. I started off stealing myself. I wound up filling orders and getting rid of stuff. I did that for fifteen years. In between I did a little time. I did time for things I never thought of doing and went free for things I really did.
>
> In my business you had no friends, only associates, and not very close ones at that. . . . I had plenty of money. I could get anything I wanted without working for it. It wasn't enough, though.

Bernard X grew up in New York City:

> As a kid . . . you always have dreams—fantasies—of yourself doing something later—being a big name singer or something that makes you outstanding. But you never draw the connection between where you are and how you're going to get there. I had to—I can't say exactly when, 13, 14, 15, 16. I saw I was nowhere and had no way of getting anywhere.
>
> Race feeling is always with you. You always know about The Man but I don't think it is real, really real, until you have to deal with it in terms of what you are going to do with your own life. That's when you feel it. If you just disliked him before—you begin to hate him when you see him blocking you in your life. I think then a sense of inevitability hits you and you see you're not going to make it out—up—away—anywhere—and

> you see The Man's part in the whole thing, that's when you begin to think thoughts about him.

Frederick 2X became involved fairly early in a criminal subculture. His father obtained a "poor man's divorce" by deserting the family. His mother had children by other men. Only a tenuous sense of belonging to a family existed. He was picked up by the police for various offenses several times before reaching his teens. The police patrolling his neighborhood eventually restricted him to a two-block area. There was, of course, no legal basis for this, but he was manhandled if seen outside that area by any policeman who knew him. He graduated in his late teens from "pot" to "shooting shit" and eventually spent time in Lexington.

William 2X, formerly a shoeshine boy, related the development of his perspective this way:

> You know how they always talk about us running after white women. There have always been a lot of [white] servicemen in this town—half of them would get around to asking me to get a woman for them. Some of them right out, some of them backing into it, laughing and joking and letting me know how much they were my friend, building up to asking me where they could find some women. After a while I began to get them for them. I ran women—both black and white. . . . What I hated was they wanted me to do something for them [find women] and hated me for doing it. They figure "any nigger must know where to find it. . . ."

Things Begin to Add Up

Amos X grew up in an all-Negro town in Oklahoma and attended a Negro college. Because of this, he had almost no contact with whites during his formative years.

> One of my aunts lived in Tulsa. I went to see her once when I was in college. I walked up to the front door of the house where she worked. She really got excited and told me if I came to see her anymore to come around to the back. But that didn't mean much to me at the time. It is only in looking back on it that all these things begin to add up.

After graduating from college, Amos joined the Marines. There he began to "see how they [the whites] really felt" about him; by the end of his tour, he had concluded that "the white man is the greatest liar, the greatest cheat, the greatest hypocrite on earth." Alienated and disillusioned, he turned to professional gambling. Then, in an attempt at a more conventional way of life, he married and took a job teaching school.

> I taught English. Now I'm no expert in the slave masters' language, but I knew the way those kids talked after being in school eight and nine years was ridiculous. They said things like "mens" for "men." I drilled them and pretty soon some of them at least in class began to sound like they had been inside a school. Now the principal taught a senior class in English and his kids talked as bad as mine. When I began to straighten out his kids also he felt I was criticizing him. . . . That little black man was afraid of the [white] superintendent and all those teachers were afraid. They had a little more than other so-called Negroes and didn't give a damn about those black children they were teaching. Those were the wages of honesty. It's one thing to want to do an honest job and another thing to be able to. . . .

With the collapse of his career as a public school teacher and the break-up of his marriage, Amos went to California, where he was introduced to the Muslim movement.

> I first heard about them [the Muslims] in 1961. There was a debate here between a Muslim and a Christian minister. The Muslims said all the things about Christianity which I had been thinking but which I had never heard anyone say before. He tore the minister up.

Finding an organization that aggressively rejected the white man and the white man's religion, Amos found his own point of view crystallized. He joined without hesitation.

Norman Maghid first heard of the Muslims while he was in prison.

> I ran into one of the Brothers selling the paper about two weeks after I got out and asked him about the meetings. Whether a guy could just go and walk in. He told me about the meetings so I made it around on a Wednesday evening. I wasn't even bugged when they searched me. When they asked me about taking out my letter [joining the organization] I took one out. They seemed to know what they were talking about. I never believed in nonviolence and love my enemies, especially when my enemies don't love me.

Muhammad Soule Kabah, born into a family of debt-ridden Texas sharecroppers, was recruited into the Nation of Islam after moving to California.

> I read a series of articles in the Los Angeles *Herald Dispatch,* an exchange between Minister Henry and a Christian minister. It confirmed what my grandfather had told me about my African heritage, that I had nothing

> to be ashamed of, that there were six thousand books on mathematics in the Library of the University of Timbucktoo while Europeans were still wearing skins. Also my father had taught me never to kow-tow to whites. My own father had fallen away. My parents didn't want me to join the Nation. They said they taught hate. That's funny isn't it? The white man can blow up a church and kill four children and the black man worries that an organization which tells you not to just take it is teaching hate.

Protestant Ethic Muslims: Up by Black Bootstraps

The Protestant Ethic Muslims all came from backgrounds with a strong tradition of Negro self-help. In two cases, the recruit's parents had been followers of Marcus Garvey; another recruit explicitly endorsed the beliefs of Booker T. Washington; and the remaining two, coming from upwardly mobile families, were firm in the belief that Negroes could achieve higher status if they were willing to work for it.

When asked what had appealed to him about the Muslims, Norman X replied:

> They thought that black people should do something for themselves. I was running this small place [a photography shop] and trying to get by. I've stuck with this place even when it was paying me barely enough to eat. Things always improve and I don't have to go to the white man for anything.

Ernestine X stressed similar reasons for joining the Muslims.

> You learned to stand up straight and do something for yourself. You learn to be a lady at all times—to keep your house clean—to teach your children good manners. There is not a girl in the M-G-T who does not know how to cook and sew. The children are very respectful; they speak only when they are spoken to. There is no such thing as letting your children talk back to you the way some people believe. The one thing they feel is the Negroes' downfall is men and sex for the women, and women and sex for the men, and they frown on sex completely unless you are married.

Despite their middle-class attitudes in many areas, Protestant Ethic Muslims denounced moderate, traditional civil rights organizations such as the NAACP, just as vigorously as the militant Muslims did. Norman X said that he had once belonged to the NAACP but had dropped out.

> They spent most of their time planning the annual brotherhood dinner. Besides it was mostly whites—whites and the colored doctors and lawyers who wanted to be white. As far as most Negroes were concerned they might as well not have existed.

Lindsey X, who had owned and run his own upholstery shop for more than 30 years, viewed the conventional black bourgeoisie with equal resentment.

> I never belonged to the NAACP. What they wanted never seemed real to me. I think Negroes should create jobs for themselves rather than going begging for them. That's why I never supported CORE.

In this respect Norman and Lindsey were in full accord with the more militant Amos X, who asserted:

> They [the NAACP and CORE] help just one class of people. . . . Let something happen to a doctor and they are right there; but if something happens to Old Mose on the corner, you can't find them.

The interviews made it clear that most of the Protestant Ethic Muslims had joined the Nation because, at some point, they began to feel the need of organizational support for their personal systems of value. For Norman and Lindsey, it was an attempt to stop what they considered their own backsliding after coming to California. Both mentioned drinking to excess and indulging in what they regarded as a profligate way of life. Guilt feelings apparently led them to seek Muslim support in returning to more enterprising habits.

Commitment to Deviance

The Nation of Islam is a deviant organization. As such it is subject to public scorn and ridicule. Thus it faces the problem of consolidating the recruit's allegiance in an environment where substantial pressures operate to erode this allegiance. How does it deal with this problem?

The structural characteristics of the Nation tend to insulate the member from the hostility of the larger society and thus contribute to the organization's survival. To begin with, the ritual of joining the organization itself stresses commitment without questions.

At the end of the general address at a temple meeting, the minister asks those nonmembers present who are "interested in learning more about Islam" to step to the back of the temple. There they are given three blank sheets of ordinary stationery and a form letter addressed to Elijah Muhammad in Chicago:

> Dear Savior Allah, Our Deliverer:
> I have attended the Teachings of Islam, two or three times, as taught by one of your ministers. I believe in it. I bear witness that there is no God but Thee. And, that Muhammad is Thy Servant and Apostle. I desire to reclaim my Own. Please give me my Original name. My slave name is as follows:

The applicant is instructed to copy this letter verbatim on each of the three sheets of paper, giving his own name and address unabbreviated at the bottom. If he fails to copy the letter perfectly, he must repeat the whole task. No explanation is given for any of these requirements.

Formal acceptance of his letter makes the new member a Muslim, but in name only. Real commitment to the Nation of Islam comes gradually—for example, the personal commitment expressed when a chain smoker gives up cigarettes in accordance with the Muslim rules even though he knows that he could smoke unobserved. "It's not that easy to do these things," Stanley X said of the various forms of abstinence practiced by Muslims. "It takes will and discipline and time, . . . but you're a much better person after you do." Calvin X told of periodic backsliding in the beginning, but added, "Once I got into the thing deep, then I stuck with it."

This commitment and the new regimen that goes with it have been credited with effecting dramatic personality changes in many members, freeing alcoholics from the bottle and drug addicts from the needle. It can be argued, however, that the organization does not change the member's fundamental orientation. To put it somewhat differently, given needs and impulses can be expressed in a variety of ways; thus, a man may give vent to his sadism by beating up strangers in an alley or by joining the police force and beating them up in the back room of the station.

"Getting into the thing deep" for a Muslim usually comes in three stages:

Participation in organizational activities—selling the Muslim newspaper, dining at the Muslim restaurant, attending and helping run Muslim meetings.

Isolation from non-Muslim social contacts—drifting away from former friends and associates because of divergent attitudes or simply because of the time consumed in Muslim activities.

Assimilation of the ideology—marking full commitment, when a Muslim has so absorbed the organization's doctrines that he automatically uses them to guide his own behavior and to interpret what happens in the world around him.

The fact that the organization can provide a full social life furthers isolation from non-Muslims. Participation is not wholly a matter of drudgery, of tramping the streets to sell the paper and studying the ideology. The organization presents programs of entertainment for its members and the public. For example, in two West Coast cities a Negro theatrical troupe called the Touring Artists put on two plays, "Jubilee Day" and "Don't You Want to Be Free." Although there was a high element of humor in both plays, the basic themes—white brutality and hypocrisy and the necessity of developing Negro self-respect and courage—were consonant with the organization's perspective. Thus the organization makes it possible for a member to satisfy his need for diversion without going outside to do so. At the same time, it continually reaches him with its message through the didactic element in such entertainment.

Carl X's experiences were typical of the recruit's growing commitment to the Nation. When asked what his friends had thought when he first joined, he replied: "They thought I was crazy. They said, 'Man, how can you believe all that stuff?'" He then commented that he no longer saw much of them, and added:

> When you start going to the temple four or five times a week and selling the newspaper you do not have time for people who are not doing these things. We drifted—the friends I had—we drifted apart. . . . All the friends I have now are in the Nation. Another Brother and I get together regularly and read the Koran and other books, then ask each other questions on them like, "What is Allah's greatest weapon? The truth. What is the devil's greatest weapon? The truth. The devil keeps it hidden from men. Allah reveals it to man." We read and talk about the things we read and try to sharpen our thinking. I couldn't do that with my old friends.

Spelled out, the "stuff" that Carl X had come to believe, the official Muslim ideology, is this:

The so-called Negro, the American black man, is lost in ignorance. He is unaware of his own past history and the future role which history has destined him to play.

Elijah Muhammad has come as the Messenger of Allah to awaken the American black man.

The American black man finds himself now in a lowly state, but that was not always his condition.

The Original Man, the first men to populate the earth, were non-white. They enjoyed a high level of culture and reached high peaks of achievement.

A little over 6,000 years ago a black scientist named Yakub, after considerable work, produced a mutant, a new race, the white race.

This new race was inferior mentally, physically, and morally to the black race. Their very whiteness, the very mark of their difference from the black race, was an indication of their physical degeneracy and moral depravity.

Allah, in anger at Yakub's work, ordained that the white race should rule for a fixed amount of time and that the black man should suffer and by his suffering gain a greater appreciation of his own spiritual worth by comparing himself to the whites.

The time of white dominance is drawing near its end. It is foreordained that this race shall perish, and with its destruction the havoc, terror, and brutality which it has spread throughout the world shall disappear.

The major task facing the Nation of Islam is to awaken the American black man to his destiny, to acquaint him with the course of history.

The Nation of Islam in pursuing this task must battle against false prophets, in particular those who call for integration. Integration is a plot of the white race to forestall its own doom. The black bourgeoisie, bought off by a few paltry favors and attempting to ingratiate themselves with the whites, seek to spread this pernicious doctrine among so-called Negroes.

The Nation of Islam must encourage the American black man to begin now to assume his proper role by wresting economic control from the whites. The American black man must gain control over his own economic fortunes by going into business for himself and becoming economically strong.

The Nation of Islam must encourage the so-called Negro to give up those habits which have been spread among them by the whites as part of the effort to keep them weak, diseased, and demoralized. The so-called Negro must give up such white-fostered dissolute habits as drinking, smoking, and eating improper foods. The so-called Negro must prepare himself in mind and body for the task of wresting control from the whites.

The Nation of Islam must encourage the so-called Negro to seek now his own land within the continental United States. This is due him and frees him from the pernicious influence of the whites.

The Problem of Defection

Commitment to the Nation can diminish as well as grow. Four of the members I interviewed later defected. Why?

These four cases can be explained in terms of a weak point in the structure of the Nation. The organization has no effective mechanisms for handling grievances among the rank and file. Its logic accounts for this. Muslim doctrine assumes that there is a single, ultimate system of truth. Elijah Muhammad and, by delegation, his ministers are in possession of this truth. Thus only Elijah Muhammad himself can say whether a minister is doing an adequate job. The result is the implicit view that there is nothing to be adjudicated between the hierarchy and its rank and file.

Grievances arise, however. The four defectors were, for various reasons, all dissatisfied with Minister Gerard X. Since there were no formal mechanisms within the organization for expressing their dissatisfaction, the only solution was to withdraw.

For most members, however, the pattern is one of steadily growing involvement. And once the ideology is fully absorbed, there is virtually no such thing as dispute or counter-evidence. If a civil rights bill is not passed, this proves the viciousness of whites in refusing to recognize Negro rights. If the same bill *is* passed, it merely proves the duplicity of whites in trying to hide their viciousness.

The ideology also provides a coherent theory of causation, provided one is willing to accept its basic assumptions. Norman X interpreted his victory over his wife in a court case as a sign of Allah's favor. Morris X used it to account for the day-to-day fortunes of his associates.

> Minister X had some trouble. He was sick for a long time. He almost died. I think Allah was punishing him. He didn't run the temple right. Now the Brothers make mistakes. Everyone does—but Minister X used to abuse them at the meetings. It was more a personal thing. He had a little power and it went to his head. Allah struck him down and I think he learned a little humility.

When a man reasons in this fashion, he has become a fully committed member of the Nation of Islam. His life revolves around temple-centered activities, his friends are all fellow Muslims, and he sees his own world—usually the world of an urban slum dweller—through the framework of a very powerful myth. He is still doing penance for the sins of Yakub, but the millennium is at hand. He has only to prepare.

The Nation of Islam does not in any real sense convert members. Rather it attracts Negroes who have already, through their own experiences in white America, developed a perspective congruent with that of the Muslim movement. The recruit comes to the door of the temple with the essence of his ideas already formed. The Black Muslims only give this disaffection a voice.

Chapter 6
The Church and the Political System: Civil Rights and Civil Religion

YOSHIO FUKUYAMA

Parishoners' Attitudes Toward Issues in the Civil Rights Movement

In 1964–65 when the nation's consensus on civil rights reached its peak with the passage of the first major Civil Rights Act since Reconstruction, the United Church of Christ conducted a survey of a sample of its churches to assess the religious orientation and social outlook of its parishioners. We are reporting in this monograph on an analysis made of data relating to attitudes held by this survey population on race relations and issues then being raised by the civil rights movement. We are particularly concerned with how parishioners of this denomination perceive the racial crisis of the nation and the degree to which black and white parishioners differ in their perception of the issues.

From *Sociological Analysis* 29 (Summer 1968):94-103. Reprinted by permission of the publisher.

Two hypotheses guide the ordering of our data in this analysis. First, we hypothesized that the official pronouncements of the denomination do not find corresponding support in the pews and second, that in spite of a common social class orientation, the attitudes of white parishioners are significantly different from those of black parishioners in this denomination.

Validation of the first hypothesis suggests a theory of the social function of resolutions and pronouncements made by voluntary associations on behalf of their members while support of the second hypothesis would help to identify the more critical issues which presently separate black and white Americans in their common struggle for racial justice.

The United Church of Christ is a Protestant denomination with over two million members in 7,000 congregations in the United States. It was formed in 1957 by the union of the Congregational Christian Churches and the Evangelical and Reformed Church. The Congregationalists trace their origin to the Separatists and Puritans of England and organized their first parishes in colonial New England. The Evangelical and Reformed Church is historically rooted in the Reformation tradition of Germany and its churches were most numerous in Pennsylvania and Missouri. Today, congregations of the United Church of Christ are found in every state of the union except Alaska, with its greatest numerical strength in the Northeast and North Central regions of the United States.

In matters of social policy, particularly in the area of race relations, the United Church inherited a traditionally liberal stance. The 19th century Congregationalists of New England were active champions of the Abolition Movement and in the years following the Civil War provided funds and teachers for the establishment of hundreds of schools for freedmen in the South through its American Missionary Association. The social pronouncements of the denomination have reflected increasing support for changes in social policies affecting Negroes, becoming more and more specific in recent years. The Congregational side of this denomination has had a significant number of Negro clergy and Negro churches since the Civil War and an increasing number of racially integrated churches.

In 1963, the Fourth General Synod of the United Church of Christ meeting in Denver passed unanimously one of the "strongest" statements ever made on civil rights by a Protestant denomination. In addition to giving its unequivocal support to the major demands then being made by the civil rights movement in such areas as public accommodations, voting, housing, employment and education, the statement also included the highly sensitive issue of intermarriage by making reference to the Negro's right "to gain acceptance as a person of worth who may marry whomever he loves and whoever loves him" and called for the denomination to become "radically committed" to the goals of the movement.[1]

It was in the light of this strong stand taken by the official plenary body of the denomination that some questions relating to specific issues in the civil rights movement were included in the survey design.

SURVEY DESIGN

The survey population reported here consists of 7,442 member and non-member participants of 150 congregations of the United Church of Christ. These parishioners were selected at random from three distinct groups in the denomination.

3,820 of the respondents were from 75 congregations in the Great Plains, an area extending roughly from Minneapolis to Denver, and represent churches which are often referred to as "town and country" churches by denominational officials.

3,446 additional parishioners belong to 68 congregations located in seven metropolitan statistical areas: Chicago, Cincinnati, Detroit, Hartford, Louisville, St. Louis and San Francisco.

Both the Great Plains and Metropolitan Area samples consisted almost exclusively of white respondents.

Since the original sample drawn failed to elicit a significant number of non-white respondents, a random sampling of predominantly Negro congregations was made. This third group yielded 176 respondents belonging to seven congregations.

The data was gathered during a period extending from the fall of 1964 to the summer of 1965 through a questionnaire mailed directly to each prospective respondent. After two weeks, a second letter and questionnaire was sent to each non-respondent. The final response rate varied from church to church, ranging from a low of 22.2 per cent to a high of 63.8 per cent.

The survey sample was drawn first by taking a random sample of all churches of the denomination located in the geographic areas included in the study. The pastor of each church falling into the sample was contacted and his cooperation in the survey requested. He was asked to provide the researcher with a current mailing list of all his parishioners. Every fourth person on these lists was sent questionnaires by mail.

The questionnaire, to be answered anonymously, consisted of 54 questions with multiple-choice responses, pre-coded for automatic data processing. Many of the questions asked for scaled responses reflecting different degrees of approval or agreement of ideas and behaviors. In addition to standard background items about the respondent's personal characteristics, the research instrument also inquired into his religious beliefs and practices, his attitudes toward a variety of social problems and his involvement in activities outside the church.

General Characteristics of Respondents

According to our data, the social style of the parishioners of the United Church of Christ reflects the dominant values of American middle class society. They are more likely to be members of educational (31%), professional (17%) and fraternal (27%) organizations than of labor unions (7%) or political parties (11%).

The Negro parishioner shares similar organizational interests outside the church, except that 65 per cent of them belong to some civil rights group as compared to a scant 2 per cent of the white parishioners.

Another indicator of the social style of our population is to be found in the periodicals they read. Six out of ten parishioners of the United Church of Christ read the *Reader's Digest* and the same proportion read *Life, Look* or the *Post.* In addition, seven out of ten Negro respondents reported reading *Jet* or *Ebony,* the high circulation Negro periodicals. Four out of ten read *American Home* or *Better Homes and Gardens* on the one hand and *Time, Newsweek* or *U.S. News* on the other.

Periodicals providing more intellectually sophisticated fare such as *Harper's, The Atlantic Monthly* or the *Saturday Review* claim only 6 per cent of these churchmen. While one parishioner in seven reported reading the *Wall Street Journal, Fortune* or *Business Week* regularly, politically liberal newsmagazines such as the *Reporter, New Republic* or *Nation* were read by less than 2 per cent.

The modal parishioner of the United Church of Christ is white, in his early forties, college educated and a member of a nuclear family. In addition to his reading habits and educational background, his middle class orientation is reflected in the fact that he is most likely to be employed in a white collar occupation and earning $8,600 annually. He is regular in his church attendance, accepts most of the traditional beliefs of his religion and looks to the church primarily to satisfy his personal and familial needs. He sees his minister most frequently in his pastoral role serving his privatized needs rather than in his prophetic role as a champion of social justice serving as a leader in the public sector.

The Negro parishioners of this denomination exhibit these middle class social characteristics to a greater degree than the white parishioners. As a group, they are slightly better educated and a higher proportion of them are employed in professional occupations. However, the consequences of job discrimination are reflected in the fact that in spite of his higher educational achievement and occupational status, his family income is not only lower than that of the white respondent, but a higher proportion of these incomes are earned by two or more members of the family.

The Negro parishioner also shares most of the religious characteristics of the white parishioner except at one significant point: his perception of the role of the clergy is markedly different. While most white respondents see their ministers primarily in their pastoral role, black respondents place their primary emphasis on the prophetic role of the clergy. In a list of 12 traditional attributes of clergy roles, only 20 per cent of the white respondents thought that their pastor spent "a lot of time" "working for social justice" while 77 per cent of the black respondents checked this item. This attribute of "working for social justice" ranked tenth in frequency among the 12 roles for the white respondents and first for the Negro respondents.

Furthermore, when asked to identify the essential characteristics of the Christian life, less than one-third of the white parishioners believed that "working for social justice" was an "absolutely necessary" characteristic while two-thirds of the Negro parishioners gave this item their highest priority.

These differences suggest that the traditional function of the Negro church as an instrument of social protest and change continues to be salient for Negro parishioners, even when they are members of congregations related to a predominantly white, middle class denomination. Some of the consequences of these differences in religious style will become evident as we examine our data relating to the attitudes of our survey sample toward issues in the civil rights movement.

Social Distance

To assess the attitudes of our parishioners toward the issues in the civil rights movement, we asked each respondent to fill in a modified version of the Bogardus Social Distance Scale. Each parishioner was asked, "To which steps in the scale below would you admit people in the various racial and nationality groups listed at the right?" The groups listed in the questionnaire were Englishmen, American Indians, Italians, Mexicans, Negroes and Orientals. The scale itself consisted of the following seven steps:

1. To close kinship by marriage
2. To my home as guests
3. To my club as personal chums
4. To my church as members
5. To my street as neighbors
6. To employment in my occupation
7. To citizenship in my country.

The relative order of these various steps was empirically determined and is reported in Table 1.

TABLE 1. *Responses of White Parishioners to the Social Distance Scale (N = 7,263)*

	Per Cent of Respondents Who Would Admit					
Social Distance Scale	English	Indian	Italian	Mexican	Negro	Oriental
Close kinship by marriage	82	32	49	21	9	20
My club as personal chums	78	51	62	46	39	42
My street as neighbors	83	63	73	54	47	62
My home as guests	83	71	75	64	58	68
Employment in my occupation	79	69	71	65	65	67
My church as members	84	76	77	72	69	74
Citizenship in my country	84	80	80	78	78	78

The responses to the Social Distance Scale by parishioners in the Great Plains and Metropolitan Area samples are summarized in Table 1. We see clearly that parishioners make significant differentiations in their responses, depending on the racial or ethnic characteristic of their reference group. Since nearly all the respondents reported in Table 1 are white, it is understandable why Englishmen are admitted to all steps in the scale by the large majority. (We did not approach a 100 per cent response due to non-responses from 14 to 20 per cent of our sample to various portions of the scale.)

The greatest degree of social distance is expressed toward Negroes, with only 9 per cent willing to admit Negroes "to close kinship by marriage." In fact, kinship through marriage is not approved by the majority of our sample for all non-English groups. The majority, furthermore, would not accept Mexicans, Negroes and Orientals into "my social club as personal chums" and less than half (47%) would admit Negroes "to my street as neighbors."

The majority are willing, however, to admit all groups to other steps in the scale, as guests in one's home, into church membership, as fellow workers and fellow citizens.

When this same scale is examined for Negro respondents, an entirely different pattern emerges. In Table 2 we see that the majority of the Negro respondents would admit all persons, regardless of ethnic background, to all steps in the Social Distance Scale. While some degree of reticence is expressed when it comes "to close kinship by marriage" and "to my club as personal chums," and a generally more favorable disposition is shown toward their own race, the black parishioner, unlike the white parishioner, does not express the kind of marked social distance toward others as evidenced in Table 1. There was no evidence, in 1964–65, to support a generalization which was to become more popular later that even the middle class Negro harbors strong feelings of antipathy toward the white man.

For the majority of the white parishioners of the United Church of Christ, attitudes of social distance toward Negroes are clearly evident, particularly when it comes to marriage, social activities and housing. The independent variables affecting these attitudes are those generally found in society as a whole.

For example, we found that the degree of social distance *vis-à-vis* the Negro was consistently greater among the metropolitan sample than among the sample drawn from the Great Plains. Conversely, we also found a slightly higher degree of social distance expressed toward American Indians by parishioners in the Great Plains than by those in metropolitan area churches. While this may give support to the hypothesis that the density of minority groups functions to increase prejudice, our data were not entirely consistent. Respondents in the San Francisco area, for instance, were significantly less prejudiced against Orientals

TABLE 2. *Responses of Non-White Parishioners to the Social Distance Scale*

	Per Cent of Respondents Who Would Admit					
Social Distance Scale	English	Indian	Italian	Mexican	Negro	Oriental
Close kinship by marriage	53	57	53	51	75	54
My club as personal chums	58	59	57	56	74	58
My street as neighbors	74	73	73	73	80	76
My home as guests	73	72	72	69	80	72
Employment in my occupation	73	73	72	72	78	73
My church as members	74	76	73	74	81	77
Citizenship in my country	74	74	74	74	78	76

TABLE 3. *Social Distances: Attitudes Toward Negroes by Sample Groups*

	Per Cent Who Would Admit Negroes						
Social Distance Scale	Lvle	Cinc	St. L	Chic	Detr	Htfd	SanF
Close kinship by marriage	6	4	5	8	10	7	18
My club as personal chums	19	26	26	35	35	45	56
My street as neighbors	22	30	36	40	42	49	67
My home as guests	27	41	40	55	55	70	75
Employment in my occupation	52	53	57	66	67	76	78
My church as members	45	50	58	66	66	81	84
Citizenship in my country	67	67	76	81	81	85	87
Cumulative score	238	271	298	351	356	413	465

than those in any of the other sample cities where the Oriental population is far less visible.

Secondly, the regional variable clearly affected the degree of social distance expressed by our various samples of parishioners. In Table 3 we have reported the percentage of those who would admit Negroes to various steps in the Social Distance Scale for the seven S.M.S.A.'s. Using the cumulative percentage scores for each city as an index, we have ranked the cities according to the degree of social distance expressed by parishioners in these cities. Thus Louisville with a cumulative score of 238 ranks highest in social distance while San Francisco with 465 ranks lowest. In most instances, the percentage of those who would admit Negroes for each step in the scale increases as one moves in the table from Louisville (where the highest degree of prejudice exists) to San Francisco (where the rate of prejudice was lowest). Chicago and Detroit showed almost identical scores.

The age of the respondent was positively related to prejudice: the older a person was, the less likely he was to admit Negroes to the various steps in the Social Distance Scale. In Table 4 we note that the proportion of parishioners who would admit Negroes to each step in the scale

TABLE 4. *Social Distance: Attitudes Toward Negroes by Age Groups*

	Per Cent Who Would Admit Negroes			
Social Distance Scale	Under 30	30 to 44	45 to 59	60 & over
Close kinship by marriage	17	10	6	4
My club as personal chums	52	46	36	15
My street as neighbors	57	49	43	33
My home as guests	70	66	58	36
Employment in my occupation	76	75	66	45
My church as members	78	77	70	55
Citizenship in my country	86	85	82	62

consistently lessens as one moves across the various age groups. For example, 57 per cent of those under 30 would admit Negroes "to my street as neighbors" as contrasted with only 33 per cent of those who are 60 or over. Three fourths (76%) of those under 30 would admit Negroes to their occupations as compared with less than half (45%) of the over 60 group. Younger parishioners were twice as likely to accept Negroes into their homes as guests and four times more likely to accept "close kinship through marriage" than the older group.

Finally, we found that differences between men and women were not differentiating but that the individual's socioeconomic status did show an inverse relationship to prejudice. That is to say, the higher one's S.E.S., the less social distance in our survey sample.

These findings make clear that the parishioners of the United Church of Christ reflect quite consistently the traditional values of American society as far as their attitudes toward minority groups are concerned. The variables of the American social system as identified by research in the past function consistently to increase or decrease the social distance perceived by this sample of Protestant Christians.

Issues in the Civil Rights Movement

Given the degree of social distance felt by white parishioners of this denomination toward Negroes, how do they feel about some of the issues raised by the civil rights movement? We have already made reference to the official support given by the United Church of Christ to the movement and its goals. In the questionnaire we asked each respondent to indicate the degree to which he approved or disapproved of selected statements which were then current in the rhetoric of the movement. Their responses are summarized in Table 5. That white and black parishioners differ sharply on most of the issues is clearly evident.

The modal white parishioner believes that the "Negro is right in demanding his full civil rights now" but also believes that the Negro "is trying to move too fast" to obtain these rights. Sixty-four per cent of them believe that "property values tend to go down" when Negroes move into white residential areas and nearly half of them (48%) believe that "Negroes are happier in Negro churches and Negro schools." Less than half of the white parishioners also agree with the statement that "on the whole, Negro children receive inferior education in comparison with white children."

The statements in Table 5 are ranked in the order of the differences between white and black responses so that those appearing at the top of the table are the issues which are joined and most differentiating

TABLE 5. *Civil Rights Issues: Summary of White and Negro Responses (N = 7,263)*

Statement	Per Cent Who Agree (Disagree)* White	Negro	Per cent difference
Negroes are trying to move too fast to obtain justice and equality	52 (24)	1 (97)	51 (73)
When Negroes move into white residential areas, property values tend to go down	64 (15)	14 (73)	50 (58)
Negroes are happier in Negro churches and Negro schools	48 (16)	8 (72)	40 (56)
Negro leaders today are working for the eventual mixture of races through intermarriage	18 (43)	6 (88)	12 (45)
Restaurant owners have a right to refuse service to a person because of his race	23 (59)	2 (97)	21 (38)
On the whole, Negro children receive inferior education in comparison to white children	45 (29)	81 (9)	36 (20)
The Negro is right in demanding his full civil rights now	50 (19)	85 (12)	35 (7)
We owe the Negro some kind of compensation for past injustices	15 (54)	48 (29)	33 (25)
Negroes should now be hired even if they are not fully qualified to make up for discrimination against them in the past	4 (81)	14 (75)	10 (6)
Negroes should be given jobs in proportion to their numbers in the population	15 (57)	15 (64)	0 (7)

* Percentage disagreeing with the statement is in parentheses.

while those at the bottom are issues over which there appears to be some degree of consensus among the two racial groups. The numbers in parentheses are the percentage of respondents who disagreed with each statement.

The pace of the Negro's demand for civil rights, residential housing and the perpetuation of segregated institutions are the issues which are joined between white and black parishioners. From 56 to 73 percentage points separate white and black responses to these statements.

On the other hand, proposals to hire unqualified Negroes and to hire Negroes in proportion to their numbers in the population are rejected by the majority of both groups, with differences ranging from 7 to 10 percentage points.

Although only 18 per cent of the white respondents agree that intermarriage is a goal of the civil rights movement, 43 per cent disagree with this statement. The statement on intermarriage was rejected by 88 per cent of the Negro respondents, a difference of 45 per cent over the white responses. This suggests that while the traditional fear of the white respondent to intermarriage is not a major part of the white parishioner's ideology, a large proportion are not yet willing to reject it completely.

Table 5 also shows that there is a high degree of consensus among Negro respondents for all the items except one: the issue of compensatory justice. Unlike the other statements to which responses ranged from 64 to 97 per cent, opinion on this issue was significantly divided. It should be noted, however, that nearly half the Negro respondents are in favor of "some kind of compensation for past injustices," a viewpoint shared by only 15 per cent of the white respondents.

The white parishioners do not reflect this high degree of consensus on the issues included in this survey. White responses range from 43 to 81 per cent, or an average of 55.3 per cent for the ten items in contrast to an average of 78.0 per cent for the Negro respondents.

Given the limitations of the Negro sample which represents a homogeneous middle class group, there was little evidence of disharmony within the group as far as the issues of the civil rights movement are concerned. Furthermore, the lower degree of consensus found among the white respondents suggests that though there are issues which seriously divide black and white respondents within this denomination, the white parishioners' commitment to the more traditional position of gradualism or maintenance of the *status quo* is more likely to be changed, for few issues seem to generate overwhelming support or rejection on their part.

The attitude of white parishioners toward property values underlines the particular sensitivity inherent in the housing issue. It is to be recalled that less than half of the white parishioners would admit Negroes "to my street as neighbors" in the Social Distance Scale. In Table 5 we find that 64 per cent believe that "property values tend to go down when Negroes move into white residential areas," a popular and all too pervasive rationalization for opposing open housing policies. In Table 6 we find an additional indicator of potential conflict over this issue. Federal non-discriminatory housing legislation is favored by 92 per cent of the Negro respondents but by only 36 per cent of the white, a difference of 56 per cent.

Table 6 also emphasizes the strong commitment of the Negro to all forms of federally oriented domestic policies. Except for the "ban on nuclear testing," a substantial majority of the Negro parishioners supported *all* the policies listed (urban affairs, education, employment, housing, and medical care) while not a single one of these domestic policies elicited the majority support of the white churchmen. The cabinet post for urban affairs and medicare were not yet realities at the

TABLE 6. *National Policies: Summary of Responses by White and Negro Parishioners*

National Policy	Per Cent Who Agree (Disagree)		
	White	Negro	Per cent difference
Ban on nuclear testing	37 (19)	47 (15)	10 (4)
Cabinet post for urban affairs	20 (16)	60 (3)	40 (13)
Federal aid to education	34 (38)	78 (9)	44 (29)
Federal non-discriminatory employment legislation	47 (15)	92 (0)	45 (15)
Federal non-discriminatory housing legislation	36 (22)	92 (0)	56 (22)
Medical care for aged through social security	46 (29)	84 (2)	38 (27)
U.S. participation in the United Nations	80 (3)	91 (1)	9 (2)

time of the survey. Only one white parishioner in five supported the urban affairs cabinet post and less than half favored medicare. Strong consensus was found only on the "U.S. participation in the United Nations."

SUMMARY AND CONCLUDING OBSERVATIONS

These findings lead us to the following observations about parishioner attitudes on issues raised by the civil rights movement:

1. It is clear that a cleavage exists between the official pronouncements of the denomination and the attitudes which prevail in the pews. In spite of the liberal and supportive stand taken by the denomination, the majority of the white parishioners of the United Church of Christ express varying degrees of social distance toward the Negro and resistance to the goals of the civil rights movement.

2. We have found that the issues which divide white and black parishioners most critically were those having to do with timing, housing and the perpetuation of segregated institutions. The white parishioner feels that the Negro is "trying to move too fast," is most threatened by the prospect of open housing and persists in his belief that the Negro would be "happier in segregated schools and churches."

3. We found no evidence to support the claim that middle class Negroes harbor deep seated prejudices about the white man. Nor did we find any evidence of disharmony among the Negro parishioners about what was believed to be the goals of the civil rights movement.

4. While the traditional religious beliefs and practices are supported by the majority of the parishioners in this study, the white parishioner's

emphasis on the pastoral ministry and the Negro parishioner's emphasis on the prophetic role of the minister resulted in significant differences for social action. There was evidence to suggest that the traditional role of the Negro church as an instrument of social protest and change continues to be salient even when the congregation is a part of a predominantly white denomination.

5. Finally, the lack of strong consensus on the part of the white parishioners of the United Church of Christ toward issues raised by the civil rights movement suggest that the situation is fluid and that the possibilities for change are latent. The direction in which these attitudes will change will undoubtedly depend on the direction taken by the movement and on the leadership within the churches.

---

1. United Church of Christ, *Minutes of the Fourth General Synod* (Denver, 1963), pp. 22-24.

GARY T. MARX

Religion: Opiate or Inspiration of Civil Rights Militancy Among Negroes?

The relationship between religion and political radicalism is a confusing one. On the one hand, established religious institutions have generally had a stake in the status quo and hence have supported conservatism. Furthermore, with the masses having an otherworldly orientation, religious zeal, particularly as expressed in the more fundamentalist branches of Christianity, has been seen as an alternative to the development of political radicalism. On the other hand, as the source of universal humanistic values and the strength that can come from believing one is carrying out God's will in political matters, religion has occasionally played a strong positive role in movements for radical social change.

This dual role of religion is clearly indicated in the case of the American Negro and race protest. Slaves are said to have been first brought to this country on the "good ship Jesus Christ."[1] While there was occasional controversy over the effect that religion had on them it appears that most slave-owners eventually came to view supervised

---

Reprinted from the *American Sociological Review* 32 (February 1967):64-72, by permission of the American Sociological Association.

religion as an effective means of social control. Stampp, in commenting on the effect of religion notes:

> . . . through religious instruction the bondsmen learned that slavery had divine sanction, that insolence was as much an offense against God as against the temporal master. They received the Biblical command that servants should obey their masters, and they heard of the punishments awaiting the disobedient slave in the hereafter. They heard, too, that eternal salvation would be their reward for faithful service . . .[2]

In discussing the period after the Civil War, Myrdal states that ". . . under the pressure of political reaction, the Negro church in the South came to have much the same role as it did before the Civil War. Negro frustration was sublimated into emotionalism, and Negro hopes were fixed on the after world."[3] Many other analysts, in considering the consequences of Negro religion from the end of slavery until the early 1950's reached similar conclusions about the conservatizing effect of religion on race protest.[4]

However, the effect of religion on race protest throughout American history has by no means been exclusively in one direction. While many Negroes were no doubt seriously singing about chariots in the sky, Negro preachers such as Denmark Vesey and Nat Turner and the religiously inspired abolitionists were actively fighting slavery in their own way. All Negro churches first came into being as protest organizations and later some served as meeting places where protest strategy was planned, or as stations on the underground railroad. The richness of protest symbolism in Negro spirituals and sermons has often been noted. Beyond this symbolic role, as a totally Negro institution, the church brought together in privacy people with a shared problem. It was from the church experience that many leaders were exposed to a broad range of ideas legitimizing protest and obtained the savoir faire, self-confidence, and organizational experience needed to challenge an oppressive system. A recent commentator states that the slave churches were "the nucleus of the Negro protest" and another that "in religion Negro leaders had begun to find sanction and support for their movements of protest more than 150 years ago."[5]

Differing perceptions of the varied consequences religion may have on protest have continued to the present time. While there has been very little in the way of empirical research on the effect of the Negro church on protest,[6] the literature of race relations is rich with impressionistic statements which generally contradict each other about how the church either encourages and is the source of race protest or inhibits and retards its development. For example, two observers note, "as primitive evangelism gave way to a more sophisticated social consciousness, the church became the spearhead of Negro protest in the deep South,"[7] while another indicates "the Negro church is a sleeping giant. In civil rights participation its feet are hardly wet."[8] A civil rights activist, himself a clergyman, states: ". . . the church today is central to the movement . . . if there had been no Negro church, there would have been no civil rights movement today."[9] On the other hand, a sociologist, commenting on the more involved higher status ministers, notes: ". . . middle class Negro clergymen in the cities of the South generally advocated cautious gradualism in race activities until the mid-1950's when there was an upsurge of protest sentiment among urban Negroes . . . but most of them [ministers] did not embrace the more vigorous techniques of protest until other leaders took the initiative and gained widespread support."[10] Another sociologist states, "Whatever their previous conservative stance has been, the churches have now become 'spearheads of reform.' "[11] Still another indicates: ". . . the Negro church is particularly culpable for its general lack of concern for the moral and social problems of the community . . . it has been accommodating. Fostering indulgence in religious sentimentality, and riveting the attention of the masses on the bounties of a hereafter, the Negro church remains a refuge, and escape from the cruel realities of the here and now."[12]

Thus one faces opposing views, or at best ambiguity, in contemplating the current effect of religion. The opiating consequences of religion are all too well known as is the fact that the segregated church is durable and offers some advantages to clergy and members that might be denied them in a more integrated society. On the other hand, the prominent role of the Negro church in supplying much of the ideology of the movement, many of its foremost leaders, and an institution around which struggle might be organized—particularly in the South—can hardly be denied. It would appear from the bombings of churches and the writings of Martin Luther King and other religiously inspired activists that for many, religion and protest are closely linked.

Part of this dilemma may lie in the distinction between the church as an institution in its totality and particular individual churches within it, and the further distinctions among different types of individual religious concern. This paper is concerned with the latter subject; it is an inquiry into the relationship between religiosity and response to the civil rights struggle. It first considers how religious denomination affects militancy, and then how various measures of religiosity, taken separately and together, are related to civil rights concern. The question is then asked of those classified as "very religious" and "quite religious," how an "otherworldly orientation"—as opposed to a "temporal" one—affects militancy.

In a nationwide study of Negroes living in metropolitan areas of the United States, a number of questions were asked about religious behavior and beliefs as well as about the civil rights struggle.[13] Seven of the questions dealing with civil rights protest have been combined into an index of conventional militancy.[14] Built into this index are a number of dimensions of racial protest such as impatience over the speed of integration, opposition to discrimination in public facilities and the sale of property, perception of barriers to Negro advancement, support of civil rights demonstrations, and expressed willingness to take part in a demonstration. Those giving the militant response to five or more of the questions are considered militant, those giving such a response to three or four of the questions, moderate, and fewer than three, conservative.[15]

Denomination

It has long been known that the more fundamentalist sects such as the Holiness groups and the Jehovah's Witnesses are relatively uninterested in movements for secular political change.[16] Such transvaluational movements with their otherworldly orientation and their promise that the last shall be first in the great beyond, are said to solace the individual for his lowly status in this world and to divert concern away from efforts at collective social change which might be brought about by man. While only a minority of Negroes actually belong to such groups, the proportion is higher than among whites. Negro literature is rich in descriptions of these churches and their position on race protest.

In Table 1 it can be seen that those belonging to sects are the least likely to be militant; they are followed by those in predominantly Negro denominations. Ironically those individuals in largely white denominations (Episcopalian, Presbyterian, United Church of Christ, and Roman Catholic) are those most likely to be militant, in spite of the perhaps greater civil rights activism of the Negro denominations. This pattern emerged even when social class was held constant.

TABLE 1. *Proportion Militant (%) by Denomination* *

Denomination	% Militant
Episcopalian	46 (24)
United Church of Christ	42 (12)
Presbyterian	40 (25)
Catholic	40 (109)
Methodist	34 (142)
Baptist	32 (658)
Sects and Cults	20 (106)

*25 respondents are not shown in this table because they did not specify a denomination, or belonged to a non-Christian religious group, or other small Christian group.

In their comments members of the less conventional religious groups clearly expressed the classical attitude of their sects toward participation in the politics of the secular world. For example, an Evangelist in the Midwest said, "I don't believe in participating in politics. My church don't vote—they just depends on the plans of God." And an automobile serviceman in Philadelphia stated, "I, as a Jehovah's Witness, cannot express things involving the race issue." A housewife in the Far West ventured, "In my religion we do not approve of anything except living like it says in the Bible; demonstrations mean calling attention to you and it's sinful."

The finding that persons who belong to sects are less likely to be militant than the non-sect members is to be expected; clearly this type of religious involvement seems an alternative for most people to the development of radicalism. But what of the religious style of those in the more conventional churches which may put relatively less stress on the after-life and encourage various forms of secular participation? Are the more religiously inclined within these groups also less likely to be militant?

Religiosity

The present study measured several dimensions of religious involvement. Those interviewed were asked how important religion was to them, several questions about orthodoxy of belief, and how frequently they attended worship service.[17] Even with the sects excluded, irrespective of the dimension of religiosity considered, the greater the religiosity the lower the percentage militant. (See Tables 2, 3 and 4.) For example, militancy increases consistently from a low of only 29 percent among those who said religion was "extremely important" to a high of 62 percent for those who indicated that religion was "not at all important" to them. For those very high in orthodoxy (having no doubt about the existence of God or the devil) 27 percent were militant while for those

TABLE 2. *Militancy by Subjective Importance Assigned to Religion* *

Importance	% Militant
Extremely important	29 (668)
Somewhat important	39 (195)
Fairly important	48 (96)
Not too important	56 (18)
Not at all important	62 (13)

*Sects are excluded here and in all subsequent tables.

totally rejecting these ideas 54 percent indicated great concern over civil rights. Militancy also varies inversely with frequency of attendance at worship service.[18]

TABLE 3. *Militancy by Orthodoxy*

Orthodoxy	% Militant
Very high	27 (414)
High	34 (333)
Medium	39 (144)
Low	47 (68)
Very low	54 (35)

Each of these items was strongly related to every other; when taken together they help us to better characterize religiosity. Accordingly they have been combined into an overall measure of religiosity. Those scored as "very religious" in terms of this index attended church at least once a week, felt that religion was extremely important to them, and had no doubts about the existence of God and the devil. For progressively lower values of the index, frequency of church attendance, the importance of religion, and acceptance of the belief items decline consistently until, for those scored "not at all religious," church is rarely if ever attended, religion is not considered personally important and the belief items are rejected.

Using this measure for non-sect members, civil rights militancy increases from a low of 26 percent for those labeled "very religious" to 30 percent for the "somewhat religious" to 45 percent for those "not very religious" and up to a high of 70 percent for those "not at all religious."[19] (Table 5.)

Religiosity and militancy are also related to age, sex, education, religious denomination and region of the country. The older, the less educated, women, Southerners and those in Negro denominations are more likely to be religious and to have lower percentages scoring as militant. Thus it is possible that the relationship observed is simply a consequence of the fact that both religiosity and militancy are related to some

TABLE 4. *Militancy by Frequency of Attendance at Worship Services*

Frequency	% Militant
More than once a week	27 (81)
Once a week	32 (311)
Once a month or more but less than once a week	34 (354)
Less than once a month	38 (240)

TABLE 5. *Militancy by Religiosity*

Religiosity	Very Religious	Somewhat Religious	Not Very Religious	Not at All Religious
% Militant	26	30	45	70
N	(230)	(523)	(195)	(36)

third factor. In Table 6 it can be seen however, that, even when these variables are controlled the relationship is maintained. That is, even among those in the North, the younger, male, more educated and those affiliated with predominantly white denominations, the greater the religiositv the less the militancy.

The incompatibility between piety and protest shown in these data becomes even more evident when considered in light of comments offered by the respondents. Many religious people hold beliefs which clearly inhibit race protest. For a few there was the notion that segregation and a lowly status for Negroes was somehow God's will and not for man to question. Thus a housewife in South Bend, Indiana, in saying that civil rights demonstrations had hurt Negroes, added: "God is the Creator of everything. We don't know why we all dark-skinned. We

TABLE 6. *Proportion Militant (%) by Religiosity, for Education, Age, Region, Sex, and Denomination*

	Very Religious	Somewhat Religious	Not Very Religious	Not at All Religious
Education				
Grammar school	17 (108)	22 (201)	31 (42)	50 (2)
High school	34 (96)	32 (270)	45 (119)	58 (19)
College	38 (26)	48 (61)	59 (34)	87 (15)
Age				
18–29	33 (30)	37 (126)	44 (62)	62 (13)
30–44	30 (53)	34 (180)	48 (83)	74 (19)
45–59	25 (71)	27 (131)	45 (33)	50 (2)
60+	22 (76)	18 (95)	33 (15)	100 (2)
Region				
Non-South	30 (123)	34 (331)	47 (159)	70 (33)
South	22 (107)	23 (202)	33 (36)	66 (3)
Sex				
Men	28 (83)	33 (220)	44 (123)	72 (29)
Women	26 (147)	28 (313)	46 (72)	57 (7)
Denomination				
Episcopalian, Presbyterian, United Church of Christ	20 (15)	27 (26)	33 (15)	60 (5)
Catholic	13 (15)	39 (56)	36 (25)	77 (13)
Methodist	46 (24)	22 (83)	50 (32)	100 (2)
Baptist	25 (172)	29 (354)	45 (117)	53 (15)

should try to put forth the effort to do what God wants and not question."[20]

A Negro spiritual contains the lines "I'm gonna wait upon the Lord till my change comes." For our respondents a more frequently stated belief stressed that God as the absolute controller of the universe would bring about change in his own way and at his own time, rather than expressing segregation as God's will. In indicating her unwillingness to take part in a civil rights demonstration, a Detroit housewife said, "I don't go for demonstrations. I believe that God created all men equal and at His appointed time He will give every man his portion, no one can hinder it." And in response to a question about whether or not the government in Washington was pushing integration too slowly, a retired clerk in Atlanta said: "You can't hurry God. He has a certain time for this to take place. I don't know about Washington."

Others who desired integration more strongly and wanted immediate social change felt that (as Bob Dylan sings) God was on their side. Hence man need do nothing to help bring about change. Thus a worker in Cleveland, who was against having more civil rights demonstrations, said: "With God helping to fight our battle, I believe we can do with fewer demonstrations." And in response to a question about whether Negroes should spend more time praying and less time demonstrating, an Atlanta clergyman, who said "more time praying," added "praying is demonstrating."[21]

Religion among the Militants

Although the net effect of religion is clearly to inhibit attitudes of protest it is interesting to consider this relationship in the opposite direction, i.e., observe religiosity among those characterized as militant, moderate, and conservative with respect to the civil rights struggle. As civil rights concern increases, religiosity decreases. (Table 7). Militants

Table 7. *Religiosity by Civil Rights Militancy*

	Militants	Moderates	Conservatives
Very religious	18%	24%	28%
Somewhat religious	48	57	55
Not very religious	26	17	16
Not at all religious	8	2	1
Total	100	100	100
N	332	419	242

were twice as likely to be scored "not very religious" or "not at all religious" as were conservatives. This table is also of interest because it shows that, even for the militants, a majority were scored either "very religious" or "somewhat religious." Clearly, for many, a religious orientation and a concern with racial protest are not mutually exclusive.

Given the active involvement of some churches, the singing of protest spirituals, and the ideology of the movement as it relates to Christian principles of love, equality, passive suffering,[22] and the appeal to a higher moral law, it would be surprising if there were only a few religious people among the militants.

A relevant question accordingly is: Among the religious, what are the intervening links which determine whether religion is related to an active concern with racial matters or has an opiating effect?[23] From the comments reported above it seemed that, for some, belief in a highly deterministic God inhibited race protest. Unfortunately the study did not measure beliefs about the role of God as against the role of men in the structuring of human affairs. However, a related variable was measured which would seem to have much relevance—the extent to which these religious people were concerned with the here and now as opposed to the after-life.

The classical indictment of religion from the Marxist perspective is that by focusing concern on a glorious after-life the evils of this life are ignored. Of course there are important differences among religious institutions and among individuals with respect to the importance given to other worldly concerns. Christianity, as with most ideologies, contains within it, if not out-and-out contradictory themes, then certainly themes which are likely to be in tension with one another. In this fact, no doubt, lies part of the explanation of religion's varied consequences for protest. One important strand of Christianity stresses acceptance of one's lot and glorifies the after-life;[24] another is more concerned with the realization of Judeo-Christian values in the current life. King and his followers clearly represent this latter "social gospel" tradition.[25] Those with the type of temporal concern that King represents would be expected to be higher in militancy. A measure of temporal vs. otherworldly concern has been constructed. On the basis of two questions, those interviewed have been classified as having either an other worldly or a temporal orientation.[26] The evidence is that religiosity and otherworldly concern increase together. For example, almost 100 percent of the "not at all religious" group were considered to have a temporal orientation, but only 42 percent of the "very religious." (Table 8). Those in predominantly white denominations were more likely to have a temporal orientation than those in all-black denominations.

Among the religious groups, if concern with the here and now is a relevant factor in overcoming the opiating effect of religion then it is to

TABLE 8. *Proportion (%) with Temporal (as against Otherworldly) Concern, by Religiosity*

Religiosity	% with Temporal Concern
Very religious	42 (225)
Somewhat religious	61 (531)
Not very religious	82 (193)
Not at all religious	98 (34)

be anticipated that those considered to have a temporal religious orientation would be much higher in militancy than those scored as otherworldly. This is in fact the case. Among the otherworldly religious, only 16 percent were militant; this proportion increases to almost 40 percent among those considered "very religious" and "somewhat religious" who have a temporal religious outlook. (Table 9). Thus it would seem that an important factor in determining the effect of religion on protest attitudes is the nature of an individual's religious commitment. It is quite possible, for those with a temporal religious orientation, that—rather than the effect of religion being somehow neutralized (as in the case of militancy among the "not religious" groups)—their religious concern serves to inspire and sustain race protest. This religious inspiration can, of course, be clearly noted among some active civil rights participants.

CONCLUSION

The effect of religiosity on race protest depends on the type of religiosity involved. Past literature is rich in suggestions that the religiosity of the fundamentalist sects is an alternative to the development of political radicalism. This seems true in the case of race protest as well. However, in an overall sense even for those who belong to the more conventional churches, the greater the religious involvement, whether measured in terms of ritual activity, orthodoxy of religious belief, subjective importance of religion, or the three taken together, the lower the degree of militancy.

TABLE 9. *Proportion Militant (%) by Religiosity and Temporal or Otherworldly Concern*

Concern	Very Religious	Somewhat Religious
Temporal	39 (95)	38 (325)
Otherworldly	15 (130)	17 (206)

Among sect members and religious people with an otherworldly orientation, religion and race protest appear to be, if not mutually exclusive, then certainly what one observer has referred to as "mutually corrosive kinds of commitments."[27] Until such time as religion loosens its hold over these people or comes to embody to a greater extent the belief that man as well as God can bring about secular change, and focuses more on the here and now, religious involvement may be seen as an important factor working against the widespread radicalization of the Negro public.

However, it has also been noted that many militant people are nevertheless religious. When a distinction is made among the religious between the "otherworldly" and the "temporal," for many of the latter group, religion seems to facilitate or at least not to inhibit protest. For these people religion and race protest may be mutually supportive.

Thirty years ago Donald Young wrote: "One function which a minority religion may serve is that of reconciliation with inferior status and its discriminatory consequences . . . on the other hand, religious institutions may also develop in such a way as to be an incitement and support of revolt against inferior status."[28] The current civil rights struggle and the data observed here certainly suggest that this is the case. These contradictory consequences of religion are somewhat reconciled when one distinguishes among different segments of the Negro church and types of religious concern among individuals.

---

1. Louis Lomax, *When the Word is Given,* New York: New American Library, 1964, p. 34.

2. Kenneth Stampp, *The Peculiar Institution,* New York: Alfred A. Knopf, 1956, p. 158.

3. Gunnar Myrdal *et al., An American Dilemma,* New York: Harper, 1944, pp. 851-853. About the North he notes that the church remained far more independent "but on the whole even the Northern Negro church has remained a conservative institution with its interests directly upon other-worldly matters and has largely ignored the practical problems of the Negro's fate in this world."

4. For example Dollard reports that "religion can be seen as a mechanism for the social control of Negroes" and that planters have always welcomed the building of a Negro church on the plantation but looked with less favor upon the building of a school. John Dollard, *Caste and Class in a Southern Town,* Garden City: Doubleday Anchor, 1957, p. 248. A few of the many others reaching similar conclusions are, Benjamin E. Mays and J. W. Nicholson, *The Negro's Church,* New York: Institute of Social and Religious Research, 1933; Hortense Powdermaker, *After Freedom,* New York: Viking Press, 1939, p. 285; Charles Johnson, *Growing Up in the Black Belt,* Washington, D.C.: American Council of Education, 1941, pp. 135-136; Horace Drake and St. Clair Cayton, *Black Metropolis,* New York: Harper and Row, 1962, pp. 424-429; George Simpson and Milton Yinger, *Racial and Cultural Minorities,* New York: Harper, rev. ed., 1958, pp. 582-587. In a more general context this social control consequence of religion has of course been noted throughout history from Plato to Montesquieu to Marx to Nietzsche to Freud to contemporary social theorists.

5. Daniel Thompson, "The Rise of Negro Protest," *Annals of the American Academy of Political and Social Science,* 357 (January, 1965).

6. The empirical evidence is quite limited. The few studies that have been done have focused on the Negro minister. Thompson notes that in New Orleans Negro ministers constitute the largest segment of the Negro leadership class (a grouping which is not necessarily the same as "protest leaders") but that "The vast majority of ministers are primarily interested in their pastoral role . . . their sermons are essentially biblical, dealing only tangentially with social issues." Daniel Thompson, *The Negro Leadership Class,* Englewood Cliffs, New Jersey: Prentice-Hall, 1963, pp. 34-35. Studies of the Negro ministry in Detroit and Richmond, California also stress that only a small fraction of Negro clergymen show any active concern with the civil rights struggle. R. L. Johnstone, *Militant and Conservative Community Leadership Among Negro Clergymen,* Ph.D. dissertation, University of Michigan, Ann Arbor, 1963, and J. Bloom, *The Negro Church and the Movement for Equality,* M.A. thesis, University of California, Berkeley, Department of Sociology, 1966.

7. Jane Record and Wilson Record, "Ideological Forces and the Negro Protest," *Annals, op. cit.,* p. 92.

8. G. Booker, *Black Man's America,* Englewood Cliffs, N.J.: Prentice-Hall, 1964, p. 111.

9. Rev. W. T. Walker, as quoted in William Brink and Louis Harris, *The Negro Revolution in America,* New York: Simon and Schuster, 1964, p. 103.

10. N. Glenn, "Negro Religion in the U.S." in L. Schneider, *Religion, Culture and Society,* New York: John Wiley, 1964.

11. Joseph Fichter, "American Religion and the Negro," *Daedalus* (Fall, 1965), p. 1087.

12. E. U. Essien-Udom, *Black Nationalism,* New York: Dell Publishing Co., 1962, p. 358. Many other examples of contradictory statements could be offered, sometimes even in the same volume. For example, Carleton Lee stresses the importance of religion for protest while Rayford Logan sees the Negro pastor as an instrument of the white power structure (in a book published to commemorate 100 years of emancipation). Carleton Lee, "Religious Roots of Negro Protest," and Rayford Logan, "Educational Changes Affecting American Negroes," both in Arnold Rose, *Assuring Freedom to the Free,* Detroit: Wayne University Press, 1964.

13. This survey was carried out in 1964 by the Survey Research Center, University of California, Berkeley. A non-Southern metropolitan area probability sample was drawn as well as special area samples of Negroes living in New York City, Chicago, Atlanta and Birmingham. Since the results reported here are essentially the same for each of these areas, they are treated together. More than 90% of the interviews were done with Negro interviewers. Additional methodological details may be found in Gary Marx, *Protest and Prejudice: A Study of Belief in the Black Community,* New York: Harper & Row, forthcoming.

14. Attention is directed to conventional militancy rather than to that of the Black Nationalist variety because a very small percentage of the sample offered strong and consistent support for Black Nationalism. As in studying support for the KKK, the Birch Society or the Communist Party, a representative sample of normal size is inadequate.

15. Each of the items in the index was positively related to every other and the index showed a high degree of internal validity. The index also received external validation from a number of additional questions. For example, the percentage belonging to a civil rights organization went from zero among those lowest in militancy to 38 percent for those who were highest, and the percentage thinking that civil rights demonstrations had helped a great deal increased from 23 percent to 58 percent. Those thinking that the police treated Negroes very well decreased from 35 percent to only 2 percent among those highest in militancy.

16. Liston Pope, *Millhands and Preachers,* New Haven: Yale University Press, 1942, p. 137. J. Milton Yinger, *Religion, Society, and the Individual,* New York: The Macmillan Company, 1957, pp. 170-173.

17. These dimensions and several others are suggested by Charles Y. Glock in "On the Study of Religious Commitment," *Religious Education Research Supplement,* 57 (July–

August, 1962), pp. 98-100. For another measure of religious involvement, the number of church organizations belonged to, the same inverse relationship was noted.

18. There is a popular stereotype that Negroes are a "religious people." Social science research has shown that they are "over-churched" relative to whites, i.e., the ratio of Negro churches to the size of the Negro population is greater than the same ratio for whites. Using data from a nationwide survey of whites, by Gertrude Selznick and Stephen Steinberg, some comparison of the religiosity of Negroes and whites was possible. When these various dimensions of religiosity were examined, with the effect of education and region held constant, Negroes appeared as significantly more religious *only* with respect to the subjective importance assigned to religion. In the North, whites were more likely to attend church at least once a week than were Negroes; while in the South rates of attendance were the same. About the same percentage of both groups had no doubts about the existence of God. While Negroes were more likely to be sure about the existence of a devil, whites, surprisingly, were more likely to be sure about a life beyond death. Clearly, then, any assertions about the greater religiosity of Negroes relative to whites are unwarranted unless one specifies the dimension of religiosity.

19. When the sects are included in these tables the results are the same. The sects have been excluded because they offer almost no variation to be analyzed with respect to the independent variable. Since virtually all of the sect members scored as either "very religious" or "somewhat religious," it is hardly possible to measure the effect of their religious involvement on protest attitudes. In addition the import of the relationships shown in these tables is considerably strengthened when it is demonstrated that religious involvement inhibits militancy even when the most religious and least militant group, the sects, are excluded.

20. Albert Cardinal Meyer notes that the Catholic Bishops of the U.S. said in their statement of 1958: "The heart of the race question is moral and religious." "Interracial Justice and Love," in M. Ahmann, ed., *Race Challenge to Religion,* Chicago: H. Regnery, 1963, p. 126. These data, viewed from the perspective of the activist seeking to motivate Negroes on behalf of the civil rights struggle, suggest that this statement has a meaning which Their Excellencies no doubt did not intend.

21. A study of ministers in Richmond, California notes that, although almost all questioned were opposed to discrimination, very few had taken concrete action, in part because of their belief that God would take care of them. One minister noted, "I believe that if we all was as pure . . . as we ought to be, there would be no struggle. God will answer my prayer. If we just stay with God and have faith. *When Peter was up, did the people march to free him? No. He prayed, and God did something about it.*" (Bloom, *op. cit.,* italics added.)

22. Non-violent resistance as it relates to Christianity's emphasis on suffering, sacrifice, and privation, is discussed by James W. Vander Zanden, "The Non-Violent Resistance Movement Against Segregation." *American Journal of Sociology,* 68 (March, 1963), pp. 544-550.

23. Of course, a most relevant factor here is the position of the particular church that an individual is involved in. Unfortunately, it was difficult to obtain such information in a nationwide survey.

24. The Muslims have also made much of this theme within Christianity, and their militancy is certainly tied to a rejection of otherworldly religiosity. The Bible is referred to as a "poison book" and the leader of the Muslims states, "No one after death has ever gone any place but where they were carried. There is no heaven or hell other than on earth for you and me, and Jesus was no exception. His body is still . . . in Palestine and will remain there." (As quoted in C. Eric Lincoln, *The Black Muslims in America,* Boston: Beacon Press, 1961, p. 123).

However, while they reject the otherworldly theme, they nevertheless rely heavily on a deterministic Allah; according to E. U. Essien-Udom, this fact leads to political inactivity. He notes, "The attainment of black power is relegated to the intervention of "Almighty

Allah" sometime in the future . . . Not unlike other religionists, the Muslims too may wait for all eternity for the coming of the Messiah, the predicted apocalypse in 1970 nothwithstanding." E. U. Essien-Udom, *Black Nationalism, op. cit.*, pp. 313-314.

25. He states: "Any religion that professes to be concerned with the souls of men and is not concerned with the slums that damn them, the economic conditions that strangle them, and the social conditions that cripple them is a dry-as-dust religion." He further adds, perhaps in a concession, that "such a religion is the kind the Marxists like to see —an opiate of the people." Martin Luther King, *Stride Toward Freedom*, New York: Ballantine Books, 1958, pp. 28-29.

John Lewis, a former SNCC leader and once a Baptist Divinity student, is said to have peered through the bars of a Southern jail and said, "Think not that I am come to send peace on earth. I came not to send peace, but a sword." (Matthew 10:34.)

26. The two items used in this index were: "How sure are you that there is a life beyond death?"; and "Negroes should spend more time praying and less time demonstrating." The latter item may seem somewhat circular when observed in relation to civil rights concern. However, this is precisely what militancy is all about. Still it would have been better to measure otherworldly vs. temporal concern in a less direct fashion; unfortunately, no other items were available. Because of this the data shown here must be interpreted with caution. However it does seem almost self-evident that civil rights protest which is religiously inspired is related to a temporal religious outlook.

27. Rodney Stark, "Class, Radicalism, and Religious Involvement," *American Sociological Review*, 29 (October, 1964), p. 703.

28. Donald Young, *American Minority Peoples*, New York: Harper, 1937, p. 204.

These data are also consistent with Merton's statement that it is premature to conclude that "all religion everywhere has only the one consequence of making for mass apathy" and his insistence on recognizing the "multiple consequences" and "net balance of aggregate consequences" of a given institution such as religion. Robert Merton, *Social Theory and Social Structure*, Glencoe: Free Press, 1957, revised edition, p. 44.

ROBERT N. BELLAH

Civil Religion in America

While some have argued that Christianity is the national faith, and others that church and synagogue celebrate only the generalized religion of "the American Way of Life," few have realized that there actually exists alongside of and rather clearly differentiated from the churches an elaborate and well-institutionalized civil religion in America. This article argues not only that there is such a thing, but also that this religion—or perhaps better, this religious dimension—has its own seriousness and integrity and requires the same care in understanding that any other religion does.[1]

THE KENNEDY INAUGURAL

Kennedy's inaugural address of 20 January 1961 serves as an example and a clue with which to introduce this complex subject. That address began:

From *Daedalus,* Winter 1967, pp. 1-21. Reprinted by permission of the publisher.

> We observe today not a victory of party but a celebration of freedom—symbolizing an end as well as a beginning—signifying renewal as well as change. For I have sworn before you and Almighty God the same solemn oath our forebears prescribed nearly a century and three quarters ago.
>
> The world is very different now. For man holds in his mortal hands the power to abolish all forms of human poverty and to abolish all forms of human life. And yet the same revolutionary beliefs for which our forebears fought are still at issue around the globe—the belief that the rights of man come not from the generosity of the state but from the hand of God.

And it concluded:

> Finally, whether you are citizens of America or of the world, ask of us the same high standards of strength and sacrifice that we shall ask of you. With a good conscience our only sure reward, with history the final judge of our deeds, let us go forth to lead the land we love, asking His blessing and His help, but knowing that here on earth God's work must truly be our own.

These are the three places in this brief address in which Kennedy mentioned the name of God. If we could understand why he mentioned God, the way in which he did it, and what he meant to say in those three references, we would understand much about American civil religion. But this is not a simple or obvious task, and American students of religion would probably differ widely in their interpretation of these passages.

Let us consider first the placing of the three references. They occur in the two opening paragraphs and in the closing paragraph, thus providing a sort of frame for the more concrete remarks that form the middle part of the speech. Looking beyond this particular speech, we would find that similar references to God are almost invariably to be found in the pronouncements of American presidents on solemn occasions, though usually not in the working messages that the president sends to Congress on various concrete issues. How, then, are we to interpret this placing of references to God?

It might be argued that the passages quoted reveal the essentially irrelevant role of religion in the very secular society that is America. The placing of the references in this speech as well as in public life generally indicates that religion has "only a ceremonial significance"; it gets only a sentimental nod which serves largely to placate the more unenlightened members of the community, before a discussion of the really serious business with which religion has nothing whatever to do. A cynical observer might even say that an American president has to mention God or risk losing votes. A semblance of piety is merely one of the unwritten qualifications for the office, a bit more traditional than but not essentially different from the present-day requirement of a pleasing television personality.

But we know enough about the function of ceremonial and ritual in various societies to make us suspicious of dismissing something as unimportant because it is "only a ritual." What people say on solemn occasions need not be taken at face value, but it is often indicative of deep-seated values and commitments that are not made explicit in the course of everyday life. Following this line of argument, it is worth considering whether the very special placing of the references to God in Kennedy's address may not reveal something rather important and serious about religion in American life.

It might be countered that the very way in which Kennedy made his references reveals the essentially vestigial place of religion today. He did not refer to any religion in particular. He did not refer to Jesus Christ, or to Moses, or to the Christian church; certainly he did not refer to the Catholic Church. In fact, his only reference was to the concept of God, a word which almost all Americans can accept but which means so many different things to so many different people that it is almost an empty sign. Is this not just another indication that in America religion is considered vaguely to be a good thing, but that people care so little about it that it has lost any content whatever? Isn't Eisenhower reported to have said, "Our government makes no sense unless it is founded in a deeply felt religious faith—and I don't care what it is,"[2] and isn't that a complete negation of any real religion?

These questions are worth pursuing because they raise the issue of how civil religion relates to the political society, on the one hand, and to private religious organization, on the other. President Kennedy was a Christian, more specifically a Catholic Christian. Thus, his general references to God do not mean that he lacked a specific religious commitment. But why, then, did he not include some remark to the effect that Christ is the Lord of the world or some indication of respect for the Catholic Church? He did not because these are matters of his own private religious belief and of his relation to his own particular church; they are not matters relevant in any direct way to the conduct of his public office. Others with different religious views and commitments to different churches or denominations are equally qualified participants in the political process. The principle of separation of church and state guarantees the freedom of religious belief and association, but at the same time clearly segregates the religious sphere, which is considered to be essentially private, from the political one.

Considering the separation of church and state, how is a president justified in using the word *God* at all? The answer is that the separation of church and state has not denied the political realm a religious dimension. Although matters of personal religious belief, worship, and association are considered to be strictly private affairs, there are, at the same time, certain common elements of religious orientation that the great majority of Americans share. These have played a crucial role in the development of American institutions and still provide a religious dimension for the whole fabric of American life, including the political sphere. This public religious dimension is expressed in a set of beliefs, symbols, and rituals that I am calling the American civil religion. The inauguration of a president is an important ceremonial event in this religion. It reaffirms, among other things, the religious legitimation of the highest political authority.

Let us look more closely at what Kennedy actually said. First he said, "I have sworn before you and Almighty God the same solemn oath our forebears prescribed nearly a century and three quarters ago." The oath is the oath of office, including the acceptance of the obligation to uphold the Constitution. He swears it before the people (you) and God. Beyond the Constitution, then, the president's obligation extends not only to the people but to God. In American political theory, sovereignty rests, of course, with the people, but implicitly, and often explicitly, the ultimate sovereignty has been attributed to God. This is the meaning of the motto, "In God we trust," as well as the inclusion of the phrase "under God" in the pledge to the flag. What difference does it make that sovereignty belongs to God? Though the will of the people as expressed in majority vote is carefully institutionalized as the operative source of political authority, it is deprived of an ultimate significance. The will of the people is not itself the criterion of right and wrong. There is a higher criterion in terms of which this will can be judged; it is possible that the people may be wrong. The president's obligation extends to the higher criterion.

When Kennedy says that "the rights of man come not from the generosity of the state but from the hand of God," he is stressing this point again. It does not matter whether the state is the expression of the will of an autocratic monarch or of the "people"; the rights of man are more basic than any political structure and provide a point of revolutionary leverage from which any state structure may be radically altered. That is the basis for his reassertion of the revolutionary significance of America.

But the religious dimension in political life as recognized by Kennedy not only provides a grounding for the rights of man which makes any form of political absolutism illegitimate, it also provides a transcendent goal for the political process. This is implied in his final words that "here on earth God's work must truly be our own." What he means here is,

I think, more clearly spelled out in a previous paragraph, the wording of which, incidentally, has a distinctly Biblical ring:

> Now the trumpet summons us again—not as a call to bear arms, though arms we need—not as a call to battle, though embattled we are—but a call to bear the burden of a long twilight struggle, year in and year out, "rejoicing in hope, patient in tribulation"—a struggle against the common enemies of man: tyranny, poverty, disease and war itself.

The whole address can be understood as only the most recent statement of a theme that lies very deep in the American tradition, namely the obligation, both collective and individual, to carry out God's will on earth. This was the motivating spirit of those who founded America, and it has been present in every generation since. Just below the surface throughout Kennedy's inaugural address, it becomes explicit in the closing statement that God's work must be our own. That this very activist and non-contemplative conception of the fundamental religious obligation, which has been historically associated with the Protestant position, should be enunciated so clearly in the first major statement of the first Catholic president seems to underline how deeply established it is in the American outlook. Let us now consider the form and history of the civil religious tradition in which Kennedy was speaking.

The Idea of a Civil Religion

The phrase *civil religion* is, of course, Rousseau's. In Chapter 8, Book 4, of *The Social Contract,* he outlines the simple dogmas of the civil religion: the existence of God, the life to come, the reward of virtue and the punishment of vice, and the exclusion of religious intolerance. All other religious opinions are outside the cognizance of the state and may be freely held by citizens. While the phrase *civil religion* was not used, to the best of my knowledge, by the founding fathers, and I am certainly not arguing for the particular influence of Rousseau, it is clear that similar ideas, as part of the cultural climate of the late-eighteenth century, were to be found among the Americans. For example, Franklin writes in his autobiography,

> I never was without some religious principles. I never doubted, for instance, the existence of the Deity; that he made the world and govern'd it by his Providence; that the most acceptable service of God was the doing of good to men; that our souls are immortal; and that all crime will be punished, and virtue rewarded either here or hereafter. These I es-

> teemed the essentials of every religion; and, being to be found in all the religions we had in our country, I respected them all, tho' with different degrees of respect, as I found them more or less mix'd with other articles, which, without any tendency to inspire, promote or confirm morality, serv'd principally to divide us, and make us unfriendly to one another.

It is easy to dispose of this sort of position as essentially utilitarian in relation to religion. In Washington's Farewell Address (though the words may be Hamilton's) the utilitarian aspect is quite explicit:

> Of all the dispositions and habits which lead to political prosperity, Religion and Morality are indispensable supports. In vain would that man claim the tribute of Patriotism, who should labour to subvert these great Pillars of human happiness, these firmest props of the duties of men and citizens. The mere politician, equally with the pious man ought to respect and cherish them. A volume could not trace all their connections with private and public felicity. Let it simply be asked where is the security for property, for reputation, for life, if the sense of religious obligation *desert* the oaths, which are the instruments of investigation in Courts of Justice? And let us with caution indulge the supposition, that morality can be maintained without religion. Whatever may be conceded to the influence of refined education on minds of peculiar structure, reason and experience both forbid us to expect that National morality can prevail in exclusion of religious principle.

But there is every reason to believe that religion, particularly the idea of God, played a constitutive role in the thought of the early American statesmen.

Kennedy's inaugural pointed to the religious aspect of the Declaration of Independence, and it might be well to look at that document a bit more closely. There are four references to God. The first speaks of the "Laws of Nature and of Nature's God" which entitle any people to be independent. The second is the famous statement that all men "are endowed by their Creator with certain inalienable Rights." Here Jefferson is locating the fundamental legitimacy of the new nation in a conception of "higher law" that is itself based on both classical natural law and Biblical religion. The third is an appeal to "the Supreme Judge of the world for the rectitude of our intentions," and the last indicates "a firm reliance on the protection of divine Providence." In these last two references, a Biblical God of history who stands in judgment over the world is indicated.

The intimate relation of these religious notions with the self-conception of the new republic is indicated by the frequency of their appearance in early official documents. For example, we find in Washington's first inaugural address of 30 April 1789:

> It would be peculiarly improper to omit in this first official act my fervent supplications to that Almighty Being who rules over the universe, who presides in the councils of nations, and whose providential aids can supply every defect, that His benediction may consecrate to the liberties and happiness of the people of the United States a Government instituted by themselves for these essential purposes, and may enable every instrument employed in its administration to execute with success the functions allotted to his charge.
>
> No people can be bound to acknowledge and adore the Invisible Hand which conducts the affairs of man more than those of the United States. Every step by which we have advanced to the character of an independent nation seems to have been distinguished by some token of providential agency. . . .
>
> The propitious smiles of Heaven can never be expected on a nation that disregards the eternal rules of order and right which Heaven itself has ordained. . . . The preservation of the sacred fire of liberty and the destiny of the republican model of government are justly considered, perhaps, as *deeply,* as *finally,* staked on the experiment intrusted to the hands of the American people.

Nor did these religious sentiments remain merely the personal expression of the president. At the request of both Houses of Congress, Washington proclaimed on October 3 of that same first year as president that November 26 should be "a day of public thanksgiving and prayer," the first Thanksgiving Day under the Constitution.

The words and acts of the founding fathers, especially the first few presidents, shaped the form and tone of the civil religion as it has been maintained ever since. Though much is selectively derived from Christianity, this religion is clearly not itself Christianity. For one thing, neither Washington nor Adams nor Jefferson mentions Christ in his inaugural address; nor do any of the subsequent presidents, although not one of them fails to mention God.[3] The God of the civil religion is not only rather "unitarian," he is also on the austere side, much more related to order, law, and right than to salvation and love. Even though he is somewhat deist in cast, he is by no means simply a watchmaker God. He is actively interested and involved in history, with a special concern for America. Here the analogy has much less to do with natural law than with ancient Israel; the equation of America with Israel in the idea of the "American Israel" is not infrequent.[4] What was implicit in the words of Washington already quoted becomes explicit in Jefferson's second inaugural when he said: "I shall need, too, the favor of that Being in whose hands we are, who led our fathers, as Israel of old, from their native land and planted them in a country flowing with all the necessaries and comforts of life." Europe is Egypt; America, the promised land.

God has led his people to establish a new sort of social order that shall be a light unto all the nations.[5]

This theme, too, has been a continuous one in the civil religion. We have already alluded to it in the case of the Kennedy inaugural. We find it again in President Johnson's inaugural address:

> They came here—the exile and the stranger, brave but frightened—to find a place where a man could be his own man. They made a covenant with this land. Conceived in justice, written in liberty, bound in union, it was meant one day to inspire the hopes of all mankind; and it binds us still. If we keep its terms, we shall flourish.

What we have, then, from the earliest years of the republic is a collection of beliefs, symbols, and rituals with respect to sacred things and institutionalized in a collectivity. This religion—there seems no other word for it—while not antithetical to and indeed sharing much in common with Christianity, was neither sectarian nor in any specific sense Christian. At a time when the society was overwhelmingly Christian, it seems unlikely that this lack of Christian reference was meant to spare the feelings of the tiny non-Christian minority. Rather, the civil religion expressed what those who set the precedents felt was appropriate under the circumstances. It reflected their private as well as public views. Nor was the civil religion simply "religion in general." While generality was undoubtedly seen as a virtue by some, as in the quotation from Franklin above, the civil religion was specific enough when it came to the topic of America. Precisely because of this specificity, the civil religion was saved from empty formalism and served as a genuine vehicle of national religious self-understanding.

But the civil religion was not, in the minds of Franklin, Washington, Jefferson, or other leaders, with the exception of a few radicals like Tom Paine, ever felt to be a substitute for Christianity. There was an implicit but quite clear division of function between the civil religion and Christianity. Under the doctrine of religious liberty, an exceptionally wide sphere of personal piety and voluntary social action was left to the churches. But the churches were neither to control the state nor to be controlled by it. The national magistrate, whatever his private religious views, operates under the rubrics of the civil religion as long as he is in his official capacity, as we have already seen in the case of Kennedy. This accommodation was undoubtedly the product of a particular historical moment and of a cultural background dominated by Protestantism of several varieties and by the Enlightenment, but it has survived despite subsequent changes in the cultural and religious climate.

Civil War and Civil Religion

Until the Civil War, the American civil religion focused above all on the event of the Revolution, which was seen as the final act of the Exodus from the old lands across the waters. The Declaration of Independence and the Constitution were the sacred scriptures and Washington the divinely appointed Moses who led his people out of the hands of tyranny. The Civil War, which Sidney Mead calls "the center of American history,"[6] was the second great event that involved the national self-understanding so deeply as to require expression in the civil religion. In 1835, de Tocqueville wrote that the American republic had never really been tried, that victory in the Revolutionary War was more the result of British preoccupation elsewhere and the presence of a powerful ally than of any great military success of the Americans. But in 1861 the time of testing had indeed come. Not only did the Civil War have the tragic intensity of fratricidal strife, but it was one of the bloodiest wars of the nineteenth century; the loss of life was far greater than any previously suffered by Americans.

The Civil War raised the deepest questions of national meaning. The man who not only formulated but in his own person embodied its meaning for Americans was Abraham Lincoln. For him the issue was not in the first instance slavery but "whether that nation, or any nation so conceived, and so dedicated, can long endure." He had said in Independence Hall in Philadelphia on 22 February 1861:

> All the political sentiments I entertain have been drawn, so far as I have been able to draw them, from the sentiments which originated in and were given to the world from this Hall. I have never had a feeling, politically, that did not spring from the sentiments embodied in the Declaration of Independence.[7]

The phrases of Jefferson constantly echo in Lincoln's speeches. His task was, first of all, to save the Union—not for America alone but for the meaning of America to the whole world so unforgettably etched in the last phrase of the Gettysburg Address.

But inevitably the issue of slavery as the deeper cause of the conflict had to be faced. In the second inaugural, Lincoln related slavery and the war in an ultimate perspective:

> If we shall suppose that American slavery is one of those offenses which, in the providence of God, must needs come, but which, having continued through His appointed time, He now wills to remove, and that He gives to both North and South this terrible war as the woe due to those by whom the offense came, shall we discern therein any departure from

> those divine attributes which the believers in a living God always ascribe to Him? Fondly do we hope, fervently do we pray, that this mighty scourge of war may speedily pass away. Yet, if God wills that it continue until all the wealth piled by the bondsman's two hundred and fifty years of unrequited toil shall be sunk, and until every drop of blood drawn with the lash shall be paid by another drawn with the sword, as was said three thousand years ago, so still it must be said "the judgements of the Lord are true and righteous altogether."

But he closes on a note if not of redemption then of reconciliation—"With malice toward none, with charity for all."

With the Civil War, a new theme of death, sacrifice, and rebirth enters the civil religion. It is symbolized in the life and death of Lincoln. Nowhere is it stated more vividly than in the Gettysburg Address, itself part of the Lincolnian "New Testament" among the civil scriptures. Robert Lowell has recently pointed out the "insistent use of birth images" in this speech explicitly devoted to "these honored dead": "brought forth," "conceived," "created," "a new birth of freedom." He goes on to say:

> The Gettysburg Address is a symbolic and sacramental act. Its verbal quality is resonance combined with a logical, matter of fact, prosaic brevity. . . . In his words, Lincoln symbolically died, just as the Union soldiers really died—and as he himself was soon really to die. By his words, he gave the field of battle a symbolic significance that it had lacked. For us and our country, he left Jefferson's ideals of freedom and equality joined to the Christian sacrificial act of death and rebirth. I believe this is a meaning that goes beyond sect or religion and beyond peace and war, and is now part of our lives as a challenge, obstacle and hope.[8]

Lowell is certainly right in pointing out the Christian quality of the symbolism here, but he is also right in quickly disavowing any sectarian implication. The earlier symbolism of the civil religion had been Hebraic without being in any specific sense Jewish. The Gettysburg symbolism (". . . those who here gave their lives, that that nation might live") is Christian without having anything to do with the Christian church.

The symbolic equation of Lincoln with Jesus was made relatively early. Herndon, who had been Lincoln's law partner, wrote:

> For fifty years God rolled Abraham Lincoln through his fiery furnace. He did it to try Abraham and to purify him for his purposes. This made Mr. Lincoln humble, tender, forebearing, sympathetic to suffering, kind, sensitive, tolerant; broadening, deepening and widening his whole nature; making him the noblest and loveliest character since Jesus Christ. . . . I believe that Lincoln was God's chosen one.[9]

With the Christian archetype in the background, Lincoln, "our martyred president," was linked to the war dead, those who "gave the last full measure of devotion." The theme of sacrifice was indelibly written into the civil religion.

The new symbolism soon found both physical and ritualistic expression. The great number of the war dead required the establishment of a number of national cemeteries. Of these, the Gettysburg National Cemetery, which Lincoln's famous address served to dedicate, has been overshadowed only by the Arlington National Cemetery. Begun somewhat vindictively on the Lee estate across the river from Washington, partly with the end that the Lee family could never reclaim it,[10] it has subsequently become the most hallowed monument of the civil religion. Not only was a section set aside for the Confederate dead, but it has received the dead of each succeeding American war. It is the site of the one important new symbol to come out of World War I, the Tomb of the Unknown Soldier; more recently it has become the site of the tomb of another martyred president and its symbolic eternal flame.

Memorial Day, which grew out of the Civil War, gave ritual expression to the themes we have been discussing. As Lloyd Warner has so brilliantly analyzed it, the Memorial Day observance, especially in the towns and smaller cities of America, is a major event for the whole community involving a rededication to the martyred dead, to the spirit of sacrifice, and to the American vision.[11] Just as Thanksgiving Day, which incidentally was securely institutionalized as an annual national holiday only under the presidency of Lincoln, serves to integrate the family into the civil religion, so Memorial Day has acted to integrate the local community into the national cult. Together with the less overtly religious Fourth of July and the more minor celebrations of Veterans Day and the birthdays of Washington and Lincoln, these two holidays provide an annual ritual calendar for the civil religion. The public-school system serves as a particularly important context for the cultic celebration of the civil rituals.

The Civil Religion Today

In reifying and giving a name to something that, though pervasive enough when you look at it, has gone on only semiconsciously, there is a risk of severely distorting the data. But the reification and the naming have already begun. The religious critics of "religion in general," or of the "religion of the 'American Way of Life,'" or of "American Shinto" have really been talking about the civil religion. As usual in religious polemic, they take as criteria the best in their own religious tradition and as typical the worst in the tradition of the civil religion. Against these critics, I would argue that the civil religion at its best is a genuine apprehension of universal and transcendent religious reality as seen in or, one could almost say, as revealed through the experience of the American people. Like all religions, it has suffered various deformations and demonic distortions. At its best, it has neither been so general that it has lacked incisive relevance to the American scene nor so particular that it has placed American society above universal human values. I am not at all convinced that the leaders of the churches have consistently represented a higher level of religious insight than the spokesmen of the civil religion. Reinhold Niebuhr has this to say of Lincoln, who never joined a church and who certainly represents civil religion at its best:

> An analysis of the religion of Abraham Lincoln in the context of the traditional religion of his time and place and of its polemical use on the slavery issue, which corrupted religious life in the days before and during the Civil War, must lead to the conclusion that Lincoln's religious convictions were superior in depth and purity to those, not only of the political leaders of his day, but of the religious leaders of the era.[12]

Perhaps the real animus of the religious critics has been not so much against the civil religion in itself but against its pervasive and dominating influence within the sphere of church religion. As S. M. Lipset has recently shown, American religion at least since the early-nineteenth century has been predominantly activist, moralistic, and social rather than contemplative, theological, or innerly spiritual.[13] De Tocqueville spoke of American church religion as "a political institution which powerfully contributes to the maintenance of a democratic republic among the Americans"[14] by supplying a strong moral consensus amidst continuous political change. Henry Bargy in 1902 spoke of American church religion as "la poésie du civisme."[15]

It is certainly true that the relation between religion and politics in America has been singularly smooth. This is in large part due to the dominant tradition. As de Tocqueville wrote:

> The greatest part of British America was peopled by men who, after having shaken off the authority of the Pope, acknowledged no other religious supremacy: they brought with them into the New World a form of Christianity which I cannot better describe than by styling it a democratic and republican religion.[16]

The churches opposed neither the Revolution nor the establishment of democratic institutions. Even when some of them opposed the full institutionalization of religious liberty, they accepted the final outcome with good grace and without nostalgia for an *ancien régime.* The American civil religion was never anticlerical or militantly secular. On the contrary, it borrowed selectively from the religious tradition in such a way that the average American saw no conflict between the two. In this way, the civil religion was able to build up without any bitter struggle with the church powerful symbols of national solidarity and to mobilize deep levels of personal motivation for the attainment of national goals.

Such an achievement is by no means to be taken for granted. It would seem that the problem of a civil religion is quite general in modern societies and that the way it is solved or not solved will have repercussions in many spheres. One needs only to think of France to see how differently things can go. The French Revolution was anticlerical to the core and attempted to set up an anti-Christian civil religion. Throughout modern French history, the chasm between traditional Catholic symbols and the symbolism of 1789 has been immense.

American civil religion is still very much alive. Just three years ago we participated in a vivid re-enactment of the sacrifice theme in connection with the funeral of our assassinated president. The American Israel theme is clearly behind both Kennedy's New Frontier and Johnson's Great Society. Let me give just one recent illustration of how the civil religion serves to mobilize support for the attainment of national goals. On 15 March 1965 President Johnson went before Congress to ask for a strong voting-rights bill. Early in the speech he said:

> Rarely are we met with the challenge, not to our growth or abundance, or our welfare or our security—but rather to the values and the purposes and the meaning of our beloved nation.
>
> The issue of equal rights for American Negroes is such an issue. And should we defeat every enemy, and should we double our wealth and conquer the stars and still be unequal to this issue, then we will have failed as a people and as a nation.
>
> For with a country as with a person, "What is a man profited, if he shall gain the whole world, and lose his own soul?"

And in conclusion he said:

> Above the pyramid on the great seal of the United States it says in Latin, "God has favored our undertaking."
>
> God will not favor everything that we do. It is rather our duty to divine his will. I cannot help but believe that He truly understands and that He really favors the undertaking that we begin here tonight.[17]

The civil religion has not always been invoked in favor of worthy causes. On the domestic scene, an American-Legion type of ideology that fuses God, country, and flag has been used to attack nonconformist and liberal ideas and groups of all kinds. Still, it has been difficult to use the words of Jefferson and Lincoln to support special interests and undermine personal freedom. The defenders of slavery before the Civil War came to reject the thinking of the Declaration of Independence. Some of the most consistent of them turned against not only Jeffersonian democracy but Reformation religion; they dreamed of a South dominated by medieval chivalry and divine-right monarchy.[18] For all the overt religiosity of the radical right today, their relation to the civil religious consensus is tenuous, as when the John Birch Society attacks the central American symbol of Democracy itself.

With respect to America's role in the world, the dangers of distortion are greater and the built-in safeguards of the tradition weaker. The theme of the American Israel was used, almost from the beginning, as a justification for the shameful treatment of the Indians so characteristic of our history. It can be overtly or implicitly linked to the idea of manifest destiny which has been used to legitimate several adventures in imperialism since the early-nineteenth century. Never has the danger been greater than today. The issue is not so much one of imperial expansion, of which we are accused, as of the tendency to assimilate all governments or parties in the world which support our immediate policies or call upon our help by invoking the notion of free institutions and democratic values. Those nations that are for the moment "on our side" become "the free world." A repressive and unstable military dictatorship in South Viet-Nam becomes "the free people of South Viet-Nam and their government." It is then part of the role of America as the New Jerusalem and "the last hope of earth" to defend such governments with treasure and eventually with blood. When our soldiers are actually dying, it becomes possible to consecrate the struggle further by invoking the great theme of sacrifice. For the majority of the American people who are unable to judge whether the people in South Viet-Nam (or wherever) are "free like us," such arguments are convincing. Fortunately President Johnson has been less ready to assert that "God has favored our undertaking" in the case of Viet-Nam than with respect to civil rights. But others are not so hesitant. The civil religion has exercised long-term pressure for the humane solution of our greatest domestic problem, the treatment of the Negro American. It remains to be seen how relevant it can become for our role in the world at large, and whether we can effectually stand for "the revolutionary beliefs for which our forebears fought," in John F. Kennedy's words.

The civil religion is obviously involved in the most pressing moral and political issues of the day. But it is also caught in another kind of crisis, theoretical and theological, of which it is at the moment largely unaware. "God" has clearly been a central symbol in the civil religion from the beginning and remains so today. This symbol is just as central to the civil religion as it is to Judaism or Christianity. In the late-eighteenth century this posed no problem; even Tom Paine, contrary to his detractors, was not an atheist. From left to right and regardless of church or sect, all could accept the idea of God. But today, as even *Time* has recognized, the meaning of the word *God* is by no means so clear or so obvious. There is no formal creed in the civil religion. We have had a Catholic president; it is conceivable that we could have a Jewish one. But could we have an agnostic president? Could a man with conscientious scruples about using the word *God* the way Kennedy and Johnson have used it be elected chief magistrate of our country? If the whole God symbolism requires reformulation, there will be obvious consequences for the civil religion, consequences perhaps of liberal alienation and of fundamentalist ossification that have not so far been prominent in this realm. The civil religion has been a point of articulation between the profoundest commitments of the Western religious and philosophical tradition and the common beliefs of ordinary Americans. It is not too soon to consider how the deepening theological crisis may affect the future of this articulation.

THE THIRD TIME OF TRIAL

In conclusion it may be worthwhile to relate the civil religion to the most serious situation that we as Americans now face, what I call the third time of trial. The first time of trial had to do with the question of independence, whether we should or could run our own affairs in our own way. The second time of trial was over the issue of slavery, which in turn was only the most salient aspect of the more general problem of the full institutionalization of democracy within our country. This second problem we are still far from solving though we have some notable successes to our credit. But we have been overtaken by a third great problem which has led to a third great crisis, in the midst of which we stand. This is the problem of responsible action in a revolutionary world, a world seeking to attain many of the things, material and spiritual, that we have already attained. Americans have, from the beginning, been aware of the responsibility and the significance our republican experiment has for the whole world. The first internal political polarization in the new nation had to do with our attitude toward the

French Revolution. But we were small and weak then, and "foreign entanglements" seemed to threaten our very survival. During the last century, our relevance for the world was not forgotten, but our role was seen as purely exemplary. Our democratic republic rebuked tyranny by merely existing. Just after World War I we were on the brink of taking a different role in the world, but once again we turned our back.

Since World War II the old pattern has become impossible. Every president since Roosevelt has been groping toward a new pattern of action in the world, one that would be consonant with our power and our responsibilities. For Truman and for the period dominated by John Foster Dulles that pattern was seen to be the great Manichaean confrontation of East and West, the confrontation of democracy and "the false philosophy of Communism" that provided the structure of Truman's inaugural address. But with the last years of Eisenhower and with the successive two presidents, the pattern began to shift. The great problems came to be seen as caused not solely by the evil intent of any one group of men, but as stemming from much more complex and multiple sources. For Kennedy, it was not so much a struggle against particular men as against "the common enemies of man: tyranny, poverty, disease and war itself."

But in the midst of this trend toward a less primitive conception of ourselves and our world, we have somehow, without anyone really intending it, stumbled into a military confrontation where we have come to feel that our honor is at stake. We have in a moment of uncertainty been tempted to rely on our overwhelming physical power rather than on our intelligence, and we have, in part, succumbed to this temptation. Bewildered and unnerved when our terrible power fails to bring immediate success, we are at the edge of a chasm the depth of which no man knows.

I cannot help but think of Robinson Jeffers, whose poetry seems more apt now than when it was written, when he said:

> Unhappy country, what wings you have! . . .
> Weep (it is frequent in human affairs), weep for the terrible magnificence
> of the means,
> The ridiculous incompetence of the reasons, the bloody and shabby
> Pathos of the result.

But as so often before in similar times, we have a man of prophetic stature, without the bitterness or misanthropy of Jeffers, who, as Lincoln before him, calls this nation to its judgment:

> When a nation is very powerful but lacking in self-confidence, it is likely to behave in a manner that is dangerous both to itself and to others.

> Gradually but unmistakably, America is succumbing to that arrogance of power which has afflicted, weakened and in some cases destroyed great nations in the past.
>
> If the war goes on and expands, if that fatal process continues to accelerate until America becomes what it is not now and never has been, a seeker after unlimited power and empire, then Vietnam will have had a mighty and tragic fallout indeed.
>
> I do not believe that will happen. I am very apprehensive but I still remain hopeful, and even confident, that America, with its humane and democratic traditions, will find the wisdom to match its power.[19]

Without an awareness that our nation stands under higher judgment, the tradition of the civil religion would be dangerous indeed. Fortunately, the prophetic voices have never been lacking. Our present situation brings to mind the Mexican-American war that Lincoln, among so many others, opposed. The spirit of civil disobedience that is alive today in the civil rights movement and the opposition to the Viet-Nam war was already clearly outlined by Henry David Thoreau when he wrote, "If the law is of such a nature that it requires you to be an agent of injustice to another, then I say, break the law." Thoreau's words, "I would remind my countrymen that they are men first, and Americans at a late and convenient hour,"[20] provide an essential standard for any adequate thought and action in our third time of trial. As Americans, we have been well favored in the world, but it is as men that we will be judged.

Out of the first and second times of trial have come, as we have seen, the major symbols of the American civil religion. There seems little doubt that a successful negotiation of this third time of trial—the attainment of some kind of viable and coherent world order—would precipitate a major new set of symbolic forms. So far the flickering flame of the United Nations burns too low to be the focus of a cult, but the emergence of a genuine trans-national sovereignty would certainly change this. It would necessitate the incorporation of vital international symbolism into our civil religion, or, perhaps a better way of putting it, it would result in American civil religion becoming simply one part of a new civil religion of the world. It is useless to speculate on the form such a civil religion might take, though it obviously would draw on religious traditions beyond the sphere of Biblical religion alone. Fortunately, since the American civil religion is not the worship of the American nation but an understanding of the American experience in the light of ultimate and universal reality, the reorganization entailed by such a new situation need not disrupt the American civil religion's continuity. A world civil religion could be accepted as a fulfillment and not a denial of American civil religion. Indeed, such an outcome has been the eschatological hope of American civil religion from the beginning. To deny such an outcome would be to deny the meaning of America itself.

Behind the civil religion at every point lie Biblical archetypes: Exodus, Chosen People, Promised Land, New Jerusalem, Sacrificial Death and Rebirth. But it is also genuinely American and genuinely new. It has its own prophets and its own martyrs, its own sacred events and sacred places, its own solemn rituals and symbols. It is concerned that America be a society as perfectly in accord with the will of God as men can make it, and a light to all the nations.

It has often been used and is being used today as a cloak for petty interests and ugly passions. It is in need—as is any living faith—of continual reformation, of being measured by universal standards. But it is not evident that it is incapable of growth and new insight.

It does not make any decision for us. It does not remove us from moral ambiguity, from being, in Lincoln's fine phrase, an "almost chosen people." But it is a heritage of moral and religious experience from which we still have much to learn as we formulate the decisions that lie ahead.

---

1. Why something so obvious should have escaped serious analytical attention is in itself an interesting problem. Part of the reason is probably the controversial nature of the subject. From the earliest years of the nineteenth century, conservative religious and political groups have argued that Christianity is, in fact, the national religion. Some of them have from time to time and as recently as the 1950's proposed constitutional amendments that would explicitly recognize the sovereignty of Christ. In defending the doctrine of separation of church and state, opponents of such groups have denied that the national polity has, intrinsically, anything to do with religion at all. The moderates on this issue have insisted that the American state has taken a permissive and indeed supportive attitude toward religious groups (tax exemption, et cetera), thus favoring religion but still missing the positive institutionalization with which I am concerned. But part of the reason this issue has been left in obscurity is certainly due to the peculiarly Western concept of "religion" as denoting a single type of collectivity of which an individual can be a member of one and only one at a time. The Durkheimian notion that every group has a religious dimension, which would be seen as obvious in southern or eastern Asia, is foreign to us. This obscures the recognition of such dimensions in our society.

2. Quoted in Will Herberg, *Protestant-Catholic-Jew* (New York, 1955), p. 97.

3. God is mentioned or referred to in all inaugural addresses but Washington's second, which is a very brief (two paragraphs) and perfunctory acknowledgment. It is not without interest that the actual word *God* does not appear until Monroe's second inaugural, 5 March 1821. In his first inaugural, Washington refers to God as "that Almighty Being who rules the universe," "Great Author of every public and private good," "Invisible Hand," and "benign Parent of the Human Race." John Adams refers to God as "Providence," "Being who is supreme over all," "Patron of Order," "Fountain of Justice," and "Protector in all ages of the world of virtuous liberty." Jefferson speaks of "that Infinite Power which rules the destinies of the universe," and "that Being in whose hands we are." Madison speaks of "that Almighty Being whose power regulates the destiny of nations," and "Heaven." Monroe uses "Providence" and "the Almighty" in his first inaugural and finally "Almighty God" in his second. See, *Inaugural Addresses of the Presidents of the United*

States from George Washington 1789 to Harry S. Truman 1949, 82d Congress, 2d Session, House Document No. 540, 1952.

4. For example, Abiel Abbot, pastor of the First Church in Haverhill, Massachusetts, delivered a Thanksgiving sermon in 1799, *Traits of Resemblance in the People of the United States of America to Ancient Israel,* in which he said, "It has been often remarked that the people of the United States come nearer to a parallel with Ancient Israel, than any other nation upon the globe. Hence OUR AMERICAN ISRAEL is a term frequently used; and common consent allows it apt and proper." Cited in Hans Kohn, *The Idea of Nationalism* (New York, 1961), p. 665.

5. That the Mosaic analogy was present in the minds of leaders at the very moment of the birth of the republic is indicated in the designs proposed by Franklin and Jefferson for a seal of the United States of America. Together with Adams, they formed a committee of three delegated by the Continental Congress on July 4, 1776, to draw up the new device. "Franklin proposed as the device Moses lifting up his wand and dividing the Red Sea while Pharoah was overwhelmed by its waters, with the motto 'Rebellion to tyrants is obedience to God.' Jefferson proposed the children of Israel in the wilderness 'led by a cloud by day and a pillar of fire at night.'" Anson Phelps Stokes, *Church and State in the United States,* Vol. 1 (New York, 1950), pp. 467-68.

6. Sidney Mead, *The Lively Experiment* (New York, 1963), p. 12.

7. Quoted by Arthur Lehman Goodhart in Allan Nevins (ed.), *Lincoln and the Gettysburg Address* (Urbana, Ill., 1964), p. 39.

8. *Ibid.,* "On the Gettysburg Address," pp. 88-89.

9. Quoted in Sherwood Eddy, *The Kingdom of God and the American Dream* (New York, 1941), p. 162.

10. Karl Decker and Angus McSween, *Historic Arlington* (Washington, D.C., 1892), pp. 60-67.

11. How extensive the activity associated with Memorial Day can be is indicated by Warner: "The sacred symbolic behavior of Memorial Day, in which scores of the town's organizations are involved, is ordinarily divided into four periods. During the year separate rituals are held by many of the associations for their dead, and many of these activities are connected with later Memorial Day events. In the second phase, preparations are made during the last three or four weeks for the ceremony itself, and some of the associations perform public rituals. The third phase consists of scores of rituals held in all the cemeteries, churches, and halls of the associations. These rituals consist of speeches and highly ritualized behavior. They last for two days and are climaxed by the fourth and last phase, in which all the separate celebrants gather in the center of the business district on the afternoon of Memorial Day. The separate organizations, with their members in uniform or with fitting insignia, march through the town, visit the shrines and monuments of the hero dead, and, finally, enter the cemetery. Here dozens of ceremonies are held, most of them highly symbolic and formalized." During these various ceremonies Lincoln is continually referred to and the Gettysburg Address recited many times. W. Lloyd Warner, *American Life* (Chicago, 1962), pp. 8-9.

12. Reinhold Niebuhr, "The Religion of Abraham Lincoln," in Nevins (ed.), *op. cit.,* p. 72. William J. Wolfe of the Episcopal Theological School in Cambridge, Massachusetts, has written: "Lincoln is one of the greatest theologians of America—not in the technical meaning of producing a system of doctrine, certainly not as the defender of some one denomination, but in the sense of seeing the hand of God intimately in the affairs of nations. Just so the prophets of Israel criticized the events of their day from the perspective of the God who is concerned for history and who reveals His will within it. Lincoln now stands among God's latter-day prophets." *The Religion of Abraham Lincoln* (New York, 1963), p. 24.

13. Seymour Martin Lipset, "Religion and American Values," Chapter 4, *The First New Nation* (New York, 1964).

14. Alexis de Tocqueville, *Democracy in America,* Vol. 1 (New York, 1954), p. 310.

15. Henry Bargy, *La Religion dans la Société aux États-Unis* (Paris, 1902), p. 31.

16. De Tocqueville, *op. cit.,* p. 311. Later he says, "In the United States even the religion of most of the citizens is republican, since it submits the truths of the other world to private judgment, as in politics the care of their temporal interests is abandoned to the good sense of the people. Thus every man is allowed freely to take that road which he thinks will lead him to heaven, just as the law permits every citizen to have the right of choosing his own government" (p. 436).

17. U.S., *Congressional Record,* House, 15 March 1965, pp. 4924, 4926.

18. See Louis Hartz, "The Feudal Dream of the South," Part 4, *The Liberal Tradition in America* (New York, 1955).

19. Speech of Senator J. William Fulbright of 28 April 1966, as reported in *The New York Times,* 29 April 1966.

20. Quoted in Yehoshua Arieli, *Individualism and Nationalism in American Ideology* (Cambridge, Mass., 1964), p. 274.

Chapter 7
The Church and the Economic Order: Religious Motivation for Economic Development

ANDREW GREELEY

The Protestant Ethic: Time for a Moratorium

It will be the contention of this paper that the Protestant Ethic hypothesis has no relevance to the study of contemporary American society. It will be further contended that many of the efforts to make this hypothesis relevant have been poorly conceived and even more poorly executed and that these efforts represent a misunderstanding of Protestantism, of Catholicism, and indeed of Max Weber.

We shall begin by commenting on a group of studies which have attempted to test the Protestant Ethic hypothesis and then proceed to an analysis of the peculiar phenomenon of the persistence of the hypothesis in the face of consistently negative findings. We shall not at this point attempt to formulate the hypothesis since the various authors

---

From *Sociological Analysis* 25 (Spring 1964):20-33. Reprinted by permission of the publisher.

of whom we will speak have somewhat different formulations. However, we can at least describe it by saying that those who look for empirical confirmation of the hypothesis tend to assume that Protestants will be more economically ambitious than Catholics because of the different orientations of the theology and the polity of the two religious bodies.

The first work we will comment on is that of Mack, Murphy, and Yellin.[1] The three authors summarize the theory as follows: "The Catholic ethic propounded a culturally established emphasis on otherworldliness; the rationale for the performance of earthly tasks was otherworldly; reparation for sins and purification through humility. Luther and Calvin sanctified work; they made virtues of industry, thrift and self-denial. Wesley preached that the fruits of labor were the signs of salvation. The culmination of the Protestant Reformation, then, was to give divine sanction to the drive to excel."

The three authors then point out that "the theoretical question which remains unanswered is whether the Catholic and Protestant faiths in contemporary American society exert a potent enough influence on behavior" to substantiate the operation of the Protestant Ethic in modern society. They, therefore, proceed to test the null hypothesis, "no significant differences will be found either in social mobility patterns or in aspiration level between samples of Protestant and Catholic Americans in several occupations." Using a non-random sample of 2,205 white males in three white-collar professions, the authors could find no evidence which would destroy their null hypothesis. In income goal, job orientation, intergenerational and intragenerational occupational mobility, there were virtually no differences between the two religious groups (out of 36 chi square tests, only two provided significant differences). They concluded that "whatever influence these two religious subcultures have upon their adherents in our society, so far as the Weberian thesis is concerned, is overridden by the general ethos." In short if there was any difference between Protestants and Catholics in their economic ambitions, the three authors could not find it.

We next turn to the work of Bernard Rosen[2] who was concerned with independence training of children and achievement and aspiration levels. He found that Greek, Jewish and Protestant children reached independence earlier and had higher achievement motivation than did French Canadian and Italian children. Rosen strove to explain this phenomenon in terms of ethnographic material about the native countries of the groups in question. He does refer to Weber and to the "puritan ethic" as a partial explanation of the difference and also to the strong influence of the Catholic Church on Italians and French Canadians (an influence which will be most encouraging news to the Church at least in the case of the former group). He further combines the scores of the French and the Italian groups on some items to form a "Roman Catholic score" but does not contend that religion is the sole cause of the differences he observed. Before his findings could be adduced to confirm any version of the Protestant Ethic hypothesis they would have to be replicated among the German, Polish and Irish Catholic ethnic groups. Rosen is apparently very well aware of this because he has written recently of the need to control for ethnicity when comparing Protestants and Catholics and has affirmed that Catholic ethnic groups often tend to differ more among themselves than does the Catholic average differ from the Protestant average.[3] Thus even though Rosen found different child-rearing practices and different motivational levels between certain Catholic ethnic groups and Protestants, he does not attribute these differences exclusively to a "Protestant Ethic" but more to the national background of the specific groups.

Also concerned with the influence of ethnicity are Seymour Martin Lipset and Reinhard Bendix.[4] Reanalyzing data collected by Stouffer in his civil liberties study (1955) they discovered, "That there is little or no difference between the occupational status achieved by third generation Catholics and Protestants, except that more Protestants than Catholics are farmers. On the other hand, among those with a recent immigrant background, Protestants are in higher positions than Catholics. Thus the occupational differences between the two religious groups disappear once the ethnic factor declines. . . . To put it another way, the Protestant immigrants come from ethnic groups with high status while the Catholics are members of ethnic groups with low status. The Protestants come from countries where educational attainment is high, the Catholics from poor countries in which the lower classes receive little education. Hence the difference between Catholic and Protestant immigrants may be related to ethnic rather than to religious factors, an interpretation that is given support by the fact that there is relatively little difference in the occupations of the first and second generation German-American Catholics and Protestants."[5]

With the work of Lipset and Bendix being as well known as it is, one wonders why there was no attention paid to the ethnic factor in more recent works. It is also worth noting, though it does not pertain directly to our topic, that Lipset and Bendix report that no trace of an effect of the Protestant Ethic can be found in England, Germany, and the Netherlands and that therefore Weber was probably right when he said that the effects of the Protestant Ethic on the Spirit of Capitalism had ceased to be important.[6]

Religion and Need Achievement

Now to McClelland's fascinating and ingenious book, *The Achieving Society.*[7] Having reviewed the available materials on need-achievement in Germany and the United States, McClelland concludes: "(1) More traditional Catholics do appear to have some of the values and attitudes that would be associated with lower N Achievement and (2) Other groups of Catholics exist at least in the United States and Germany which have moved away from some of these traditional values toward the 'achievement ethic.' Catholicism, while it may have been associated with attitudes promoting low N Achievement, is today a complex congeries of subcultures, some of which are traditional and others modernist in outlook."[8] He asks, "Which are the truly 'representative' Catholics? Which for that matter are the truly representative Protestants? . . . Predominantly traditionalistic, devout Catholic groups like the French Canadian almost certainly have a lower average N Achievement level than the general average among the white Protestant population. Similarly, upwardly mobile, rapidly assimilating Catholics almost certainly have higher N Achievement than the general white Protestant population. But general over-all differences are very small and depend almost entirely on the exact composition of the two groups compared."[9] Whether the Irish will like the implication that they are not as devout as the French Canadians (or the Italians) is a question which we will, for the present, pass over.

McClelland apparently based his conclusions in part on the work of Veroff, Feld and Gurin which was published, however, after *The Achieving Society.* Like McClelland they were interested in need-achievement, but unlike all previous investigators they had national sample data based on the TAT tests gathered in the Survey Research Center's study of American mental health.[10] Much to their surprise they discovered that while 48 per cent of the Protestants scored high in N Achievement, 57 per cent of the Catholics did (and 68 per cent of the Jews). They adduce several explanations for this difference, the most important of which has to do with the fact that they have a representative national sample. Some of their other explanations have to do with the size of Catholic families and the pressure on lower-class Catholics to support their families and the situation which Catholics find themselves in when they are isolated from the larger Catholic body in regions of the country which do not have many Catholics. Most of these speculations, while interesting, are based on rather small N's and in any case do not salvage the Protestant Ethic hypothesis. The three authors comment, "The hypothesis does seem to work simply only at the upper status positions of a well integrated, fairly prosperous economic structure in the established northeastern parts of the United States. Perhaps this region is more typical of the European structure Weber originally observed."[11] In any case, they conclude, "change in the tempo of capitalism in America, change in the Calvinist ideology in Protestant groups, change in direction of Catholic living in a highly mobile society, may all contribute to making the Protestant Ethic less generally discernible and outstanding as a way of life geared to achievement in modern America."[12] Indeed, so indiscernible as to be just about invisible.

Mack, Murphy, and Yellin; Lipset and Bendix; McClelland; and Veroff, Feld and Gurin—none of these works either as individual research projects, nor as a body of knowledge offers the slightest confirmation for the theory that Protestants are more achievement-oriented than Catholics in American society. It ought to be sufficient to report these findings and then forget about the whole business if we did not have two more recent works which claim to have saved the Protestant Ethic for contemporary society.

"Worldly Success"

The first such work is reported in an article by Mayer and Sharp[13] in the same issue of the *American Sociological Review* as the Veroff article. They begin with the usual description of Catholics: "The powerfully reinforced and traditional Roman Catholic Church tends to orient its members toward the hereafter; successful performance in the market place and the acquisition of symbols of economic achievement are of relatively little importance as an indication of the Catholic's status after death." To test the hypothesis they have available a large number of respondents from the Detroit Area Survey—9,000 respondents from five years of surveys. It would appear that on the measures of achieved status—income, self employment, high status occupations, median education, and median school years completed, Catholics are behind some Protestant denominations and ahead of others. But, the authors argue, this is not a fair picture since one must control for the status with which a given group begins. We would then expect a control for parental occupation, parental education, and parental income. But apparently the data available do not permit such a control and therefore the authors are forced to make up an index which will measure the "ascribed status" of each group. Such an index is based on the following indicators: per cent with no farm background, per cent born in cities of 50,000 or more, per cent not born in the rural south, per cent with native born fathers, per cent with fathers of northwest European stock, per cent born in the United States or Canada, per cent born in the Detroit area, per cent in

Detroit before age 15. The reader will note that six of these nine indicators are functions of whether one was born in Detroit. Since each indicator counts equally in the weighted index (except the last two which count for one and a half), it follows inevitably that the mere fact of having the largest per cent born in Detroit will put a group near the very top of the ascribed status index *regardless of anything else in its background*—including the occupation, education, and income of its forebearers. Since Catholics were most likely to be born in Detroit, their ascribed status is very high—only slightly behind the Episcopalians in fact. However, their achieved status is only medium so therefore their "net status" is very low indeed—just behind the white Baptists and just ahead of the Negro Baptists.

It is difficult to see how the authors can be satisfied with a status indicator which ranked Catholics equal to Episcopalians in ascribed status (and both behind Lutherans), which indicated that Catholics were strongly downwardly mobile—in the face of overwhelming evidence to the contrary—and which finally is based on indicators which are not only not independent, but which in great part are the function of one factor, a factor on which Catholics would be certain to score high no matter what their real SES background was. Instead of putting all denominations on an "equal footing" as they claim to do, the authors weighted the dice against the Catholics—one hopes unintentionally. As a result their analysis, which is at variance with most similar research, is hardly very useful.

The Religious Factor

The final work we will discuss is Gerhard Lenski's *The Religious Factor.*[14] If one goes through these pages, inspecting the data but not looking at Lenski's interpretations, the following facts emerge: (1) Passage from the working class to the middle class is no more common among Protestants than among Catholics.[15] (2) There is virtually no difference in ambitions between Protestants and Catholics.[16] (3) Negative attitudes toward work are no more common among Catholics than among Protestants (though Catholics are seven per cent more likely to have "neutral" attitudes and seven per cent less likely to have "positive" attitude, N = 111 and 106).[17] (4) There is no difference between Protestants and Catholics in the percentage self-employed.[18] (5) There is only a small difference (four per cent) between Catholics and Protestants in disapproval of installment buying and Catholics have a slight lead (two per cent) in keeping budgets.[19] (6) Catholics and Protestants are equally likely to approve saving.[20] (7) Catholics are just as likely to see God as endorsing economic effort as Protestants.[21]

Despite these findings, Lenski nevertheless concludes, "With considerable regularity Jews and white Protestants have identified themselves with the individualistic, competitive patterns of thought and action linked with the middle class and historically associated with the Protestant Ethic. . . . By contrast Catholics and Negro Protestants have more often been associated with the collectivistic, security-oriented working class patterns of thought and action. . . ."[22]

We may well ask how he is able to draw such a conclusion. For example even though there is no difference in the attitude toward saving in the two religious groups, he notes that Protestants are more likely to check more than one reason for saving and hence he argues that they are more favorably disposed to saving—a contention which to say the least is somewhat thin. However, his basic technique is to submit the similarities to multivariate analysis which will make the similarities go away. Now there is nothing wrong with this except that we must remember that Lenski's N's are very small and the multivariate framework he uses differs from item to item. Anyone who has worked with IBM cards knows that if you have small differences to begin with and a small N, you can prove almost any theory if you make enough cross tabulations. There is enough sampling variation to make anything look significant after a while—even the first letter of a person's name. An example can be found in the treatment of the similarity in self-employment:[23] "Differences between white Protestants and Catholics were generally quite small, *until an effort was made to limit comparisons to persons raised in similar settings.* [His italics] . . . When immigrant generation and region of birth were held constant, larger differences emerged. Among first and second generation immigrants, Protestants were twice as likely to be self employed as Catholics (15 per cent versus five per cent). Among third generation Americans raised outside the southern states, Protestants were three times as likely to be self-employed (12 per cent versus four per cent)." The N's on which these comparisons are based were 39, 71, 42, and 24—hardly enough to exclude sampling variation especially since we do not know how many other cross tabulations were attempted.

Another example: "Among college trained persons in middle class families where the head of the family earned $8,000 or more a year, 85 per cent of the Protestants (N = 20) perceived God as endorsing striving, but only 62 per cent of the Catholics (N = 13) shared this belief."[24]

One hesitates to be too severe on Lenski's use of small numbers, yet the worth of his book is often vitiated by it. There can be little objection to cross tabulations with small N's if the purpose is to explain away differences which appear in marginal tabulations. However, when one begins with 111 male Catholics and 116 male Protestants, it seems that detailed analysis of similarities displayed in marginal tabulations is extemely risky and can at best be reported with extreme caution, a caution which one does not always find in *The Religious Factor.* By not limiting himself to description and by attempting analysis with inadequate data, Lenski weakens the value of an otherwise important book. However, if we inspect his marginals, we can only conclude that they do not support the Protestant Ethic hypothesis and that the more subtle ventures of the author into analysis must be judged as "not proven" until he collects more respondents—preferably from a national sample.[25]

Religion and Upward Mobility

A word ought to be said about the work of Lenski's pupil, Weller. In his dissertation Weller reanalyzed more than 1,000 males from various phases of the Detroit Area study and found that Protestants were more upwardly mobile in occupation (though not so much in income) than Catholics. The relevance of this study (though not its sophistication in the handling of data—which is unassailable) is vitiated, however, by a flaw in design. Weller argues that the relevant question is the extent to which urban industrialism has narrowed the differences between Protestant and Catholic and that therefore a valid comparison would necessitate comparing only those that were born and raised in a large urban center. Thus all respondents born out of the metropolitan area were excluded from analysis. In effect, this excluded foreign-born Catholics and southern-born white Protestants. There were far more Protestants excluded than Catholics since Catholics were 34 per cent of the original sample and 52 per cent of the final sample, while Protestants were 58 per cent of the original and 48 per cent of the final. There are two flaws in this procedure. First of all, the question is not whether urbanism makes Catholics equal in mobility to Protestants but whether they are unequal at all; those Protestants who are excluded are precisely those who would be most likely to pull down the Protestant mobility rate, so that the effect of urbanism on them would be to make them more mobile and thus less like Catholics who according to Weller's hypothesis are the ones who ought to be benefiting from urbanism. Thus urbanism is used to prevent Protestants who might have a lower rate than Catholics entering into the analysis. However, the Protestant Ethic, if it has any effect, ought to have brought to the city precisely those southern whites who are most upwardly mobile.

Secondly, this procedure says in effect that children of native-born white Protestants have the same psychological and physical opportunities as do the children of foreign-born Catholics and hence must be included in the same sample while foreign-born Catholics and southern whites are equally disabled by not being born in the big city and hence must be excluded. However, in reality the southern white probably could be more fairly compared with the second generation Catholic rather than the first, because both have the advantage of speaking the language as a native and the disadvantage of coming from a cultural system (the south and the ethnic ghetto) which is part American and yet not part of the main stream of American society. If southern whites are to be excluded from the analysis, then so ought second generation Catholics.

Clearly it is not certain what a fair comparison ought to be, but until we know more regarding cultural backgrounds and how they affect mobility, it is not reasonable to arbitrarily exclude some groups from analysis and not others, especially when the exclusion is certain to work in favor of the hypothesis.

A National Sample Study

To conclude with a final investigation of the Protestant Ethic hypothesis, we will report two series of findings based on a large national sample of college graduates, studied by the National Opinion Research Center. As will be noted in Table 1, Catholics and Protestants show little difference on "security" items (slow sure progress and avoidance of pressure)

TABLE 1. *Occupational Values and Religion* *

				Statistical Significance		
Occupational Value	Protestant	Catholic	Jewish	P-C	P-J	C-J
Making a lot of money	21	27	38	01	01	01
Chance to be creative	50	50	64	no	01	01
Helpful to others	68	61	60	01	01	no
Avoid high pressure	15	17	15	no	no	no
World of ideas	39	35	50	no	01	01
Freedom from supervision	18	17	21	no	no	no
Slow and sure progress	33	32	25	no	05	no
Leadership	34	40	40	01	no	no
Same area	4	8	9	05	05	no
New area	10	11	11	no	no	no
Work with people, not things	57	55	56	no	no	no
N =	2,007	833	272			

*Answer to question: "Which of these characteristics would be important to you in picking a career?"

while Catholics actually lead Protestants on the desire to make money.[26] (And Jews lead Catholics which make the Jews the most "Protestant" and the Protestants least "Protestant.") Further, Table 2 shows that while Catholics are more likely to choose large corporations as employers (which might fit the security quest), they also are more likely to choose small companies and equally likely to choose self-employment. The Protestant lead is in primary and secondary education. These findings do not disappear under a control for sex, SES (an index based on parental income, education and occupation) and size of hometown. For example, Protestant males from large cities with a high SES background still overchoose primary and secondary education as careers which is hardly in keeping with the Protestant Ethic hypothesis. Nor does the Catholic inclination to self-employment undergo any major change under a similar control apparatus.

The Hypothesis Continues

Thus in eight separate studies done in the last decade we have nothing even remotely approaching a confirmation of the Protestant Ethic hypothesis. Yet is seems safe to say that the hypothesis is still very much alive and undamaged and will continue to generate research—and frustration—for some time to come. One might well wonder why.

At least one of the explanations seems to be sociologists are often tempted to an oversimplified approach to history and especially to that form of socio-economic historical analysis which Max Weber used. Indeed if one reads Weber carefully, one cannot escape a feeling of helplessness in the face of the naïveté which thinks his analysis would

TABLE 2. *Religion and Expected Employer*

Expected Employer	Protestant	Catholic	Jewish
Large company	25	33	26
Small company	7	11	21
Family business	2	3	4
Self-employed	7	8	14
Research organization	7	7	10
College	12	12	11
Educational system	36	27	27
Other education	—	—	—
Federal government	14	14	15
State or local government	5	7	4
Hospital, church, or welfare	9	6	4
Other	3	3	3
Total	127	131	139
N =	2,007	833	272

predict that there would be a difference in upward mobility between contemporary Catholics and contemporary Protestants. Weber—and his theory—are much too sophisticated for that.

The clearest statement of his ideas on the precise nature of the relationship between the Protestant Ethic and the Spirit of Capitalism are to be found in the author's Introduction in the edition of *The Protestant Ethic* translated by Talcott Parsons.[27] This appeared as the first pages of a final edition of the work shortly before Weber died. The essay may well have been the last thing he ever wrote on *religions-sociologie.* In any event it represented a re-examination of *The Protestant Ethic* in light of the years of research (including the work on Eastern religions) and controversy which has passed since its original publication.

The most important fact about this essay is that now Weber puts capitalistic rationalism and its Puritan ethic in perspective against the rationalizing tendency which had gone on in occidental society long before the Reformation. Only in the West, according to Weber, is there to be found a rational natural science, the rational historical scholarship begun by Thucydides, the rational harmonious music based on the harmonic third, the rational use of the Gothic vault as a means of distributing pressure and of roofing spaces of all forms, and the rational organization of legal and political systems.

Thus, argues Weber, it is not surprising that in the West there should develop a rationalized economic system complete with the separation of business from the household, the systematic keeping of books, the separation of corporate from personal property and, above all, the rational organization of the labor force.

What Weber seems to be saying in this Introduction is that capitalism represents an economic manifestation of a factor which has been at work in occidental society for a long time. Protestantism did not cause this factor to work in the economic order; rather Capitalism and Protestantism both are manifestations of the factor and hence related through a common antecedent cause. The similarity between the two should not be surprising. It was inevitable that certain forms of Protestant rationalism should be so congruent with certain forms of capitalistic enterprise that the Protestant Ethic would inevitably give considerable encouragement to capitalistic development and allow it to reach its logical conclusions.

One says, "What Weber seems to be saying" because he does not say this in so many words—he never says anything quite that clearly. However, it would appear that in this introductory essay—perhaps because of the controversy the earlier edition had stirred up—he was leaning over backward to insist that he did not claim that Calvinism had "caused" capitalism. He makes quite clear his position that capitalism can trace some of its causes to elements in the occidental spirit which long antedated the Reformation.

If one might hazard a comment, it seems that too much is made of the difference between the Calvinist ethic and the Medieval ethic as represented by the Scholastics. These latter were not nearly as other-worldly as some modern sociologists would have us believe. Certainly the dogmatic and moral conclusions of, let us say, Thomas Aquinas and John Calvin were different. But one wonders if the fact that the two of them were part of a common western intellectual tradition reaching back to Aristotle (at least) has not too often been overlooked. The confidence that one can understand reality and organize it in a rational manner did not enter the Western intellectual tradition in the 16th Century. The rationalist spirit of Calvin is not really so different (save in its conclusions) from that of Peter Abelard. If one reads Calvin in the original Latin, one is struck by the fact that he is very much a product of the Schools. R. H. Tawney may be wrong when he announces in typically dramatic fashion that the last of the Schoolmen was Karl Marx. A good case might be made for the claim that the last of the Schoolmen was John Calvin.

Whatever is to be said for the assumption by some sociologists that there is (or ought to be) a one-to-one relationship between Protestantism and economic rationalism, it should be clear that such an assumption is a drastic oversimplification of the theorizing of Max Weber.

Nor does this assumption show much comprehension for what Weber intended with his ideal-typical methodology. In his view, it is impossible for a social scientist to develop concepts which fit a given kind of conduct or a given form of domination in all instances and all particulars. But since he must have such concepts, he must construct ideal types at the cost of simplifying the complexity of historical data and exaggerating their uniformities. Such ideal types are just as scientific in sociology as the model of economic man is in economics. They are not descriptions of reality but rather abstract models against which reality can be judged. They are not generalizations but conceptual tools. Thus Weber's theory of the relationship between Protestantism and Capitalism would not, in his terms, be taken as a generalization for describing exactly what happened in the early centuries of our era, but rather as a concept, a model against which the events of those years in all their complexity could be examined. Weber did not deny pluralistic causation; quite the contrary, it was because of the fact of pluralistic causation that he found it necessary to insist on "atomistic isolation" of the ideal type method. One could not proceed scientifically, in Weber's view, unless one isolated one conceptual tool and analyzed all its implications. To try to describe the totality of pluralistic causation would be to run the risk of becoming bogged down in an "unscientific" morass of conflicting trends and countertrends. One had to abstract, but abstraction did not at all mean that one was insisting on just a single cause. It was the very multiplicity of causes which made abstraction inevitable.

It is obvious then that much of the criticism of Weber's work is irrelevant, at least within the framework he set for himself. He insisted time and time again both in the *Archiv* (as Fischoff tells us[28]) and in his later works that there were a multiplicity of causes at work in the development of capitalism and a multiplicity of relationships possible between religion and society. Weber had no intention of saying that Protestantism "caused" capitalism. Indeed in the revision of the *Protestant Ethic* he does not even claim that it was one of the "causes." In Fischoff's happy expression Weber was merely interested in the "congruency" between the two.[29] From the ideal typical viewpoint this is the best that can be expected.

As Yinger observes: "We may say that the essay establishes the fact that on a rather 'low' level of causation, the Calvinist ethic is properly seen as *a* cause of the capitalist spirit. Whatever the cause of Calvinism's interpretation of worldly activity, it is clear that it sponsored even in the beginning but especially after the middle of the 17th Century the activities of the new middle class. Although it did not create the new opportunities for trade and enterprise, it did furnish businessmen with an ideological weapon and a spiritual justification which were not unimportant in helping them come to power and in conditioning the nature of their activities."[30]

But it is one thing to say that Calvinism furnished spiritual justification to the middle class of the 17th Century and quite another to say that Protestantism makes for differential upward mobility patterns in the 20th. Such a conclusion may be correct (though as we pointed out, there is little data to suggest that it is) but it hardly follows logically from anything in Weber.

A second set of assumptions behind the survival of the Protestant Ethic theory represents an incredibly oversimplified approach to Catholicism. If sociologists tend to be naive about history, they are unbelievably uninformed about Catholic theology. Indeed anyone who knows something about Catholicism cannot help but writhe uncomfortably when he reads statements like, "The Catholic ethic propounded a culturally established emphasis on otherworldliness" or "The Powerfully reinforced and traditional Roman Catholic Church tends to orient its members toward the hereafter." The blunt fact is that most sociologists are uninformed about Catholicism and hence when they try to summarize what they take to be Catholic theology or practice end up with distorted cliches and caricatures which become truth if they are repeated often enough. (For examples of this that are especially disturbing, see the work of Reiss[31] on Catholic marriage teaching and the textbook of Hoult.[32]) This would not be so bad if the sociologists in question were aware of their ignorance, because then they would try to have someone check their statements for accuracy—as they would if they were dealing, let us say, with Islam. However it is to be very much feared that they do not even know that they are uninformed and hence continue to talk about Catholicism the way the proverbial blind men described the elephant.

David McClelland states, as though he had just discovered it, that Catholicism is a congeries of subcultures; but of course, one feels like saying, this ought to have been obvious to everyone. Within the Church of Rome there is and has been room for all kinds of divergent and paradoxical emphases to such an extent that simple statements about its position are extremely risky. But the prevailing mythology in social science has not yet adjusted to this fact; the massive monolith myth dies hard. So sociologists still think that if they find one manual that says, for example, that Catholics ought not to be interested in worldly gain, they have uncovered the official Catholic position as well as the practical orientation of most "good" Catholics. When someone tells them this is not so, they feel that the rules of the game have been violated.

On the particular subject of the Protestant Ethic, there can be no question that there is an eschatological, an otherworldly, a "Christ above culture" element in Catholic doctrine which would deemphasize worldly striving. But there is also—and the sociologists in question seem quite unaware of it—an incarnational, humanistic, "Christ in culture" orientation which would support worldly striving and which indeed springs from the same humanistic rationalism as does the Calvinistic ethic. Such doctrine can be found in Aquinas, in the ethics of Antonino, in the ascetics of Frances DeSales, and in whole approach to life which has been characteristic of the followers of Ignatius of Loyola. Indeed the rationalization of human striving attributed to the Calvinists can with equal justice be attributed to the Jesuits. Ignatius of Loyola was the last of the Calvinists (or the first of the Methodists).

One hopes that the recent dramatic shifts of emphasis within the Catholic community will persuade sociologists that Catholicism is a very complex phenomenon and will lead them, when they are of a mind to summarize "the Catholic ethic" in two sentences, to have someone familiar with the Catholic tradition read over the sentences and perhaps suggest a qualifying clause or two.

A third inexplicable element of the mystery of the Protestant Ethic myth is the inattention to sociological information which goes against its assumptions. For example, one looks in vain in the writings on the subject for references to the survey materials on Catholic social class. It still seems to be an article of faith among sociologists that Catholics are concentrated in the lower economic classes—despite the survey materials made available by Bogue,[33] Lazerwitz,[34] and the Gaffin[35] studies. One sees frequent reference to Liston Pope's article,[36] but nothing at all about the Bogue-Feldman data which suggest a dramatic change in the social position of Catholics since the Pope article was published. Indeed the fact that the section on religion in Bogue's *Population of the United States*[37] is not mentioned in any of the literature I have discussed is indeed mystifying, especially since an inspection of the tables which Feldman prepared for this chapter would suggest that within educational and occupational levels, Catholics make more money than Protestants—a finding which casts doubt on the Protestant Ethic hypothesis before any more data is collected.

A very recent large sample (12,000 households) studied by NORC enables us to get a close look at the relative economic positions of Catholics and Protestants. The marginal percentages reveal practically no difference in income, occupation, or education between the two groups. However, it could be argued quite properly that the marginal comparisons are not altogether valid since they do not take into account the fact that Negroes and non-city dwellers pull down the Protestant averages. Thus a valid comparison would be between whites from cities. I would add that a valid comparison would also control for age so as to eliminate the effect of the more recent Catholic migration to this country. Table 3 presents the effect of these three controls. It is to be noted that the same percentage of Catholics and Protestants earn more than $8,000 (the limen of the upper middle class) in the age brackets under 40. Thus among younger white males from metropolitan areas there is no difference in earning power between Protestants and Catholics.

It might be argued that the dissimilarity in the older levels results from the fact that the Catholic ethic leads to a reduction in drive during the later years. A more plausible explanation would be that the high

TABLE 3. *Income of Protestant and Catholic Males in Metropolitan Areas by Age*

	Per Cent Over $8,000 a Year	
Age	Protestant	Catholic
20-29	24 (559)	25 (350)
30-39	33 (621)	34 (498)
40-49	48 (567)	38 (439)
50-59	40 (438)	36 (265)
Over 60	26 (599)	20 (260)

performance of younger Catholics is the result of a gradual fading of the immigration experience in the Catholic population. Table 4 suggests that such a social change has in fact occurred and that the improving economic performance of Catholics is connected with the higher educational achievement of the younger Catholic population. We might remark, by the way, that the equality in education and income achieved by young Catholics from big cities would indicate that they are more upwardly mobile than Protestants because their parents (as represented to some extent by the older levels of the tables) had less.

TABLE 4. *College Education of Protestant and Catholic Males in Metropolitan Areas by Age*

	Per Cent College Graduates	
Age	Protestant	Catholic
20-29	17 (601)	15 (375)
30-39	21 (669)	15 (531)
40-49	15 (609)	10 (491)
50-59	12 (484)	7 (312)
Over 60	10 (613)	5 (290)

It is further incredible that some authors ignore the obvious ethnic differences within Catholic groups such as that between Irish and Polish Catholics. Yet American sociology has ignored ethnic groups within religions for two decades and there is no reason to think that this is going to change in the near future, despite the criticisms leveled at Lenski's work by Rosen[38] and Donovan.[39]

Yet one might ask why? I fear the answer has something to do with the need for "theory." Unfortunately there is not much theory in the sociology of religion. Instead of plunging into research that will enable us to fashion new theory, we turn to the past and obtain antecedent theory from the few people who seem to have fashioned it for the sociology of religion—which is to say Max Weber, Emile Durkheim, and Ernst Troeltsch. Even when the categories which these men devised have ceased to be fruitful in research projects, we continue to use them because they are "theory" and "theory" we must have. Thus the Protestant Ethic hypothesis as fashioned by contemporary sociologists is preserved—so that sociologists of religion will have some theory. It is high time for a moratorium.

1. R. W. Mack, R. J. Murphy, and S. Yellin, "The Protestant Ethic, Level of Aspiration and Social Mobility," *American Sociological Review,* 21 (June, 1956), pp. 295-300.

2. Bernard C. Rosen, "Race, Ethnicity, and the Achievement Syndrome," *American Sociological Review,* 24 (February, 1959), pp. 47-60.

3. In his review of Lenski's book in *American Sociological Review,* 27 (February, 1962), p. 111.

4. Seymour Martin Lipset and Reinhard Bendix, *Social Mobility in Industrial Society,* Berkeley: University of California Press, 1960, pp. 48-57.

5. *Ibid.,* pp. 50-51.

6. *Ibid.,* p. 55. The reference is to Weber, *The Protestant Ethic,* pp. 181-182.

7. David C. McClelland, *The Achieving Society,* New York: Van Nostrand, 1961.

8. *Ibid.,* p. 361.

9. *Ibid.,* p. 363.

10. Joseph Veroff, Sheila Feld, and Gerald Gurin, "Achievement, Motivation and Religious Background," *American Sociological Review,* 27 (April, 1962), pp. 205-217.

11. *Ibid.,* p. 217.

12. *Ibid.*

13. Albert J. Mayer and Harry Sharp, "Religious Preference and Worldly Success," *American Sociological Review,* 27 (April, 1962), pp. 218-227.

14. Gerhard Lenski, *The Religious Factor,* Garden City: Doubleday, 1961. My comments will be reserved to the data contained on pages 76-102.

15. *Ibid.,* p. 79 (Table 8).

16. *Ibid.,* p. 81.

17. *Ibid.,* p. 85.

18. *Ibid.,* p. 92.

19. *Ibid.,* p. 97.

20. *Ibid.,* p. 99.

21. *Ibid.,* p. 95.

22. *Ibid.,* p. 101.

23. *Ibid.,* p. 92.

24. *Ibid.,* p. 95.

25. The only solid differences that Lenski can find between Protestants and Catholics which might fit the Protestant Ethic hypothesis is that Catholics are much more oriented toward trade unions. Whether this is the result of Catholic "otherworldly" orientation is doubtful however. Indeed it might be more plausibly argued that it flows from an entirely different element in Catholic belief—an element promoted by the various social encyclicals.

26. Whether the desire to make money is a manifestation of the Protestant Ethic or not has been debated. That it is at least required (though not sufficient) does not seem to be doubted by Weber, c.f., *The Protestant Ethic and the Spirit of Capitalism,* New York, Scribners, 1958, p. 53.

27. *Ibid.,* pp. 13-31.

28. Ephraim Fischoff, "The Protestant Ethic and the Spirit of Capitalism: The History of a Controversy," *Social Research,* 2 (1944), pp. 61-77.

29. *Ibid.*

30. In the introduction to the Talcott Parsons translation of *The Protestant Ethic,* p. 9.

31. Ira L. Reiss, *Premarital Sexual Standards in America,* Glencoe: The Free Press, 1960, pp. 49-53.

32. Thomas F. Hoult, *The Sociology of Religion,* New York: The Dryden Press, 1958; see especially pp. 230-234 and 282-285.

33. Donald Bogue, *The Population of the United States,* Glencoe: The Free Press, 1957.

34. Bernard Lazerwitz, "A Comparison of Major United States Religious Groups," *Journal of the American Statistical Association,* 56 (September, 1961), pp. 568-579.

35. Originally reported in the *Catholic Digest,* but now available in John L. Thomas, *Religion in America,* Westminster, Maryland: Newman Press, 1963.

36. Liston Pope, "Religion and The Class Structure," *Annals of the American Academy of Political and Social Science,* 256 (March, 1948), pp. 84-91.

37. *Op. cit.,* pp. 688-710.

38. *Op. cit.*

39. In a review of the Lenski volume in the *Catholic Reporter* of Kansas City.

NORVAL D. GLENN
RUTH HYLAND

Religious Preference and Worldly Success: Some Evidence from National Surveys

The relationship of religion to economic and occupational success is the most viable topic of debate in the sociology of religion in the United States.[1] The issues raised by Weber in his famous essay on the Protestant Ethic continue to evoke vociferous exchanges. During recent years the controversy has become centered on the influence of religion in contemporary American society.[2] Some scholars who accept Weber's basic thesis object to its application, in modified form, to contemporary societies.

The focus of the present controversy is on the relative rates of upward mobility of Protestants and Catholics, since there is clearcut evidence that Jews, for reasons that may or may not be essentially religious, experienced more rapid upward movement for several decades than either Protestants or Catholics.[3] Although there are some "hard data" that throw light on the relative advancement of Protestants and Catho-

Reprinted from the *American Sociological Review* 32 (February 1967):73-85, by permission of the *American Sociological Association.*

lics, these data are somewhat contradictory, or at least are subject to contradictory interpretations. One national study found no difference between the upward mobility of Protestant and of Catholic men;[4] this finding has been interpreted to mean both that religious differences do not lead to differences in mobility and that the Protestants equalled the Catholics in spite of palpable handicaps.[5] A study in the Detroit metropolitan area found greater upward mobility of Protestants than of Catholics;[6] this finding has been interpreted both as an indication of the importance of the religious factor and as a mere reflection of sampling variability or differences in ethnic background.[7] One author, in reporting selectively the findings of a national survey, noted that an equal percentage of Protestant and Catholic men under age 40 in metropolitan areas had incomes of $8,000 or more; he used these data to support a claim that Catholicism is not detrimental to worldly success.[8] However, he could have selected data from the same survey to support the opposite conclusion.[9]

It is not our ambition to end the controversy once and for all in this article; a secondary analysis of national survey data not gathered for the purpose of assessing mobility cannot provide conclusive evidence. However, we are convinced that the potential of such an analysis to help resolve the controversy has not been realized. All too frequently partisans in the debate have judiciously selected national survey data to support preconceived conclusions. Never, to our knowledge, has anyone done a comprehensive, thorough and objective analysis of the relevant national data.[10] Although the analysis reported here is not completely comprehensive, we strive for an objective treatment of the most relevant information.

Using data from 18 national surveys conducted from 1943 to 1965, we first assess trends in the relative economic, occupational, and educational status of Protestants and Catholics. Then, we take a close look at the contemporary distributions, first for the nation as a whole and then with regional, age, and community-size controls. Finally we scrutinize the evidence concerning the relative persistence of Protestant and Catholic students in school and college. We also include data for Jews and, on occasion, for those with no religious preference, but the sample sizes usually allow reasonably confident conclusions only for Protestants and Catholics. In order to control influences related to race, we analyze data only for white respondents.

Seventeen of the surveys were conducted by the Gallup Organization (also known as the American Institute of Public Opinion) and one was conducted by the National Opinion Research Center. The two earliest polls (1943 and 1945) used quota samples; all of the others used some kind of probability sample.[11] Four of the surveys were selected expressly for this study; they were the four most recent Gallup polls using national probability samples which were available from the Roper Public Opinion Research Center when we started our research. The data from the other surveys were on hand for other purposes. In no case did we have any knowledge of the relevant frequency distributions before we selected a survey, and in no case did we exclude a survey after we examined the data.

POSTWAR TRENDS

Since the mid-1940's, the relative standings of white Protestants and Catholics in the country as a whole have changed dramatically (see Tables 1, 2, and 3). For instance, in 1943 Protestants were well above Catholics in economic status, whereas by 1964 Catholics were clearly above Protestants (Table 1). The differences between the proportions of

TABLE 1. *Distribution (%) by Economic Level of White Respondents to a 1943 NORC Survey and to Four Recent Gallup Polls, by Religious Preference*

Economic Level	1943 NORC Survey			
	Protestants	Catholics	Jews	Total
Upper	26.3	21.6	50.0	25.9
Middle	51.4	48.1	41.2	50.2
Lower	22.3	30.2	8.8	23.9
	100.0	100.0	100.0	100.0
N	1,638	485	67	2,190

Economic Level	Four Recent Gallup Polls (December, 1963 to March, 1965)			
	Protestants	Catholics	Jews	Total
Upper	35.9	41.0	58.0	37.8
Middle	41.5	43.3	26.7	41.5
Lower	22.7	15.6	15.3	20.7
	100.0	100.0	100.0	100.0
N	8,660	2,884	435	12,209

*The respondents to the 1943 NORC survey were divided into four economic levels largely on the basis of rent or, if they were home owners, estimated rental value of home. Here the two upper levels are combined into one. The Gallup respondents were divided into economic levels on the basis of the income data in Table 6. The upper level starts at $7,000 and the lower level is below $3,000.

The original 1943 NORC data give religious identification for church members only. The nonmembers had lower average status than the members; they were allocated between the Protestants and Catholics on the basis of information on church membership from a 1945 Gallup poll. Jewish members and nonmembers do not differ appreciably in economic status; therefore the 1943 Jewish data presented here are for members only.

Protestants and Catholics at both the highest and lowest economic levels around 1964 are statistically significant. Since the 1943 data come from a quota sample, they do not meet the strict requirements for tests of significance, but the difference in the proportions of Protestants and Catholics at the lowest level is so large that we are rather confident that it did not result solely from sampling error.

The change in relative economic status may not have been quite as great as these data suggest. We delineated in the 1964 levels on the basis of the income data in Table 6, whereas the levels for the 1943 respondents were determined at least partly on the basis of the interviewers' impressions of the life styles of the respondents and their families. Consequently the standards of placement of the 1943 respondents may have varied somewhat by community and region according to the average level of affluence. If so, the effect undoubtedly was to raise the Protestants relative to the Catholics, because Protestants were (and still are) disproportionately in the South and in small communities, where average incomes are relatively low.[12]

Nevertheless a marked change in relative economic status undoubtedly resulted from the pronounced changes in relative occupational and educational standings. The occupational changes are shown in Table 2.

TABLE 2. *Ratio of Actual to Expected Proportion of White Protestant, Catholics, and Jewish Heads of Households at Broad Urban Occupational Levels, 1945, 1953, and 1964**

	Protestants			Catholics			Jews		
	1945	1953	1964	1945	1953	1964	1945	1953	1964
Upper Nonmanual[1]	.99	.99	.94	.81	.82	.98	1.86	2.11	2.11
Lower Nonmanual[2]	.95	.92	.92	1.06	1.08	1.17	1.60	1.64	1.60
Upper Manual[3]	.89	.99	1.03	1.37	1.10	1.04	.86	.56	.22
Lower Manual[4]	.95	.95	.97	1.23	1.03	1.14	.57	.51	.49
N	1,748	4,178	7,150	587	1,616	2,462	121	286	341

*The 1945 data are from one Gallup poll, the "1953" data are from five Gallup polls ranging in date from October, 1953 to March, 1954, and the "1964" data are from four Gallup polls ranging in date from December, 1963, to March, 1965.

The "expected" proportion at each occupational level is the proportion of white heads of households of all religious preferences at that level.

1. Professional and semi-professional workers, businessmen, and executives.
2. Clerical and sales workers.
3. Skilled workers.
4. Service workers, operatives, and laborers.

The "expected" proportion of each religious category at each occupational level is simply the proportion of respondents of all religions at that level; accordingly ratios below and above unity indicate disproportionately low and high representation. Whereas Protestant representation decreased at both levels of nonmanual occupations and increased at both manual levels, Catholic representation increased sharply in nonmanual occupations and declined in manual work.[13] In 1945 and in 1954 Protestants were more highly represented than Catholics at the upper nonmanual level, but in 1964 representation of Catholics at this level slightly exceeded that of Protestants. Although the small N's do not allow us to place much confidence in the Jewish data, it appears that Jews gained on Christians during the two decades. According to the data, Jewish representation increased at the highest level, remained the same at the lower nonmanual level, and declined at both manual levels.[14]

The changes in representation at three broad educational levels were similar to the occupational changes (Table 3). Protestant representation increased at the lowest level and declined at the two higher levels, while Catholic representation declined at the lowest level and increased at the high school and college levels. Protestants ranked clearly ahead of Catholics in educational status in 1945, but by 1964 the relative standings of the two religious categories had become ambiguous. Catholics had moved ahead in median years of school completed (see Table 8) but were still underrepresented at the college level. During the 20-year period Jewish representation apparently increased at the college level and declined at all lower levels.

TABLE 3. *Ratio of Actual to Expected Proportion of White Protestants, Catholics, and Jews at Each Broad Educational Level, Ages 30 and Over, 1945 and 1964**

	Protestants		Catholics		Jews	
Educational Level	1945	1964	1945	1964	1945	1964
No more than 8 Years of School	.96	1.04	1.09	.95	.70	.55
At Least Some High School but No College	1.00	.97	1.08	1.11	1.11	.94
At Least Some College	1.05	.98	.75	.82	1.26	2.09
N	1,473	7,294	426	2,274	93	376

*The 1945 data are from one Gallup poll and the "1964" data are from four Gallup polls ranging in date from December, 1963, to March, 1965.
The "expected" proportion at each educational level is the proportion of white respondents of all religious preferences at that level.

It is clear that Catholics as a whole have experienced more net upward mobility during the postwar period than Protestants. In part, this is simply a matter of Catholics overcoming an initial disadvantage growing out of their more recent immigration. The Catholic immigrants, as all others, usually became employed at first at the lower occupational levels, and as long as they were incompletely acculturated in nonreligious American culture, many of their cultural characteristics may have impeded their upward movement. Culture not detrimental to worldly success in the home country became detrimental in the context of American culture; probably some of the culture of the Southern and Eastern Europeans in its original context was adverse to economic advancement. Consequently the acculturation of European immigrant groups during the past few decades has, in the absence of many new immigrants, tended in itself to close the socioeconomic gap between Protestants and Catholics.

However, Catholics are now pulling ahead of Protestants; their greater advancement is therefore more than just a catching-up process. If, as is widely believed, the values, beliefs and practices of Protestantism are more conducive to worldly success than those of Catholicism, then clearly the Catholics have some advantage that more than offsets their religiously-based disadvantage.

Catholics in the United States do have one obvious and important advantage. They are highly concentrated in the larger metropolitan areas in the non-Southern regions (Tables 4 and 5)—precisely the com-

TABLE 4. *Distribution (%) by Size of Community of Residence of White Respondents to Four Recent Gallup Polls, by Religious Preference**

Community Size	Protestants	Catholics	Jews	No Religion	Total
Rural	39.5	15.1	2.9	18.8	32.1
2,500–9,999	9.4	5.8	--	9.0	8.3
10,000–49,000	9.3	7.6	1.4	12.6	8.7
50,000–249,999	15.0	19.8	11.9	16.3	16.1
250,000–999,999	16.2	22.1	15.6	15.8	17.6
1,000,000 and over	10.5	29.5	68.1	27.4	17.2
Total	100.0	100.0	100.0	100.0	100.0
N	9,097	2,940	436	277	12,750

*Dates of the polls range from December, 1963, to March, 1965. Therefore, the data are essentially for 1964.

munities with the highest average incomes, most favorable occupational distributions, and highest average educational attainments.[15] Thus, if Catholics in each community only equal or approach their Protestant neighbors in these status variables, Catholics in the country as a whole will exceed Protestants by a fairly wide margin. Furthermore, the probability of upward mobility of sons of manual workers apparently varies directly with size of community of orientation.[16] Consequently, with other relevant factors held constant, one would expect upward mobility to be substantially greater for Catholics than for Protestants. If this were

TABLE 5. *Distribution (%) by Region of Residence of White Respondents to Four Recent Gallup Polls, by Religious Preference**

Region	Protestants	Catholics	Jews	No Religion	Total
New England	2.5	12.3	7.8	5.8	5.0
Middle Atlantic	16.7	39.0	70.1	11.9	23.6
East Central	18.4	18.6	5.7	18.4	18.0
West Central	12.7	8.4	1.1	8.3	11.2
South	34.4	7.8	7.1	14.8	26.9
Rocky Mountain	4.3	3.2	0.9	12.3	4.1
Pacific	10.9	10.6	7.1	28.5	11.1
Total	100.0	100.0	100.0	100.0	100.0
N	9,099	2,940	435	277	12,751

*Dates of the polls range from December, 1963, to March, 1965. Therefore, the data are essentially for 1964.

not the case, then indeed it would seem that religiously-related values, ethnicity, high fertility, or some other factor or factors were holding Catholics back. However, Catholics apparently *are* advancing more rapidly than Protestants, and one cannot tell from the greater Catholic mobility alone whether or not it is occurring *in spite of* religiously-based handicaps. For clues we turn to a detailed comparison of the contemporary status of Protestants and Catholics.

CONTEMPORARY STATUS DIFFERENCES BY RELIGIOUS PREFERENCE

Income, occupational, and educational distributions of whites by religious preference around 1964 are shown in Tables 6, 7, and 8.

Median family income was nearly $900 higher for Catholics than for Protestants, and the proportion of families with incomes below $3,000 was 7.1 percentage points greater for Protestants—a statistically significant difference. However, a slightly larger percentage of Protestant families were at the very highest income level. Jewish families ranked well above all other religious categories, and the respondents with no religious preference came from families than ranked only above Protestants in median income but only below Jews in the percentage with very high incomes.

The low economic standing of Protestants resulted partly from the lower earnings in each occupation and at each educational level in the South and in small communities,[17] but also from the fact that Protestants ranked lowest in summary measures of occupational and educational status.

TABLE 6. *Distribution (%) by Reported or Estimated Annual Income of Families of White Respondents to Four Recent Gallup Polls, by Religious Preference**

Income	Protestants	Catholics	Jews	No Religion	Total
Under $1,000	4.7	2.3	1.6	4.2	4.0
1,000–1,999	9.0	6.4	6.2	5.4	8.2
2,000–2,999	9.0	6.9	7.5	7.2	8.5
3,000–3,999	10.1	6.7	6.2	7.3	9.1
4,000–4,999	11.7	9.6	5.3	13.1	11.0
5,000–6,999	19.7	27.0	15.2	22.7	21.4
7,000–9,999	19.3	25.3	24.4	18.5	20.7
10,000–14,999	11.6	12.3	24.4	12.7	12.3
15,000 and Over	5.0	3.4	9.2	8.8	4.8
Total	100.0	100.0	100.0	100.0	100.0
Under $3,000	22.7	15.6	15.3	16.8	20.7
$7,000 and Over	35.9	41.0	58.0	40.0	37.8
$10,000 and Over	16.6	15.7	33.6	21.5	17.1
Median ($)	5,460	6,338	7,990	6,118	5,856
N	8,660	2,884	435	260	12,209

*Income was estimated by interviewer if respondent refused to report income. Income is reported or estimated for 1963 or 1964 depending on the date of the poll.

The only marked occupational difference between Protestants and Catholics was in the proportion of heads of households who were farmers. The two religious categories were about equally represented in upper-manual occupations, and Catholics were more highly represented in both nonmanual and lower-manual occupations. As one would ex-

TABLE 7. *Distribution (%) by Occupation of Head of Household Reported by White Respondents to Four Recent Gallup Polls, by Religious Preference**

Occupation	Protestants	Catholics	Jews	No Religion	Total
Professional and Semi-Professional Workers	12.8	13.1	27.6	38.7	14.0
Farmers and Farm Managers	10.8	2.2	0.3	1.8	8.2
Businessmen and Executives	13.5	14.3	31.4	6.3	14.1
Clerical Workers	6.6	8.9	9.4	2.7	7.2
Sales Workers	6.4	7.6	13.2	5.0	6.9
Skilled Workers	22.1	22.3	4.7	15.8	21.5
Operatives and Unskilled Workers	17.3	18.1	11.7	18.9	17.3
Service Workers	4.9	7.3	0.6	4.5	5.3
Laborers	5.5	6.2	1.2	6.3	5.5
Total	100.0	100.0	100.0	100.0	100.0
Non-manual Workers	39.3	43.9	81.6	52.7	42.2
Lower Manual Workers	27.7	31.6	13.5	29.7	28.1
Duncan's Socioeconomic Index	36.1	37.8	53.1	46.0	37.4
N	7,150	2,462	341	222	10,175

*Only those respondents reporting an occupation are included here. The dates of the polls range from December, 1963, to March, 1965. Therefore, the data are essentially for 1964.

TABLE 8. *Distribution (%) by Educational Attainment of White Respondents to Four Recent Gallup Polls, Ages 30 and Over, by Religious Preference**

Years of School Completed	Protestants	Catholics	Jews	No Religion	Total
0–7	15.5	14.1	9.5	9.0	14.8
8	22.4	20.4	10.6	23.2	21.5
1–3 High School	16.9	19.6	8.2	13.6	17.2
4 High School	28.4	31.9	35.7	21.5	29.3
1–3 College	8.2	6.2	15.4	9.6	8.0
College Graduate	8.7	7.9	20.5	23.2	9.2
Total	100.0	100.0	100.0	100.0	100.0
No more than 8 Years of School	37.9	34.5	20.1	31.2	36.3
At Least Some College	16.9	14.1	35.9	32.8	17.2
Median Years of School Completed	11.1	11.4	12.6	12.2	11.4
N	7,294	2,274	376	177	10,121

*Dates of the polls range from December, 1963, to March, 1965. Therefore, the data are essentially for 1964.

pect, Jews were highly represented in all nonmanual occupations except clerical workers, were less than proportionally represented in all urban manual occupations, and were virtually absent from the farm category.[18]

The educational data in Table 8, which are limited to respondents age 30 and older to exclude most persons who had not completed their formal education, show that Catholics slightly exceeded Protestants in median years of school completed and that a larger percentage of Protestants were at the lowest educational levels. However, Protestants were ahead of Catholics in one important respect—the percentage who had at least some college. Although the difference only borders on statistical significance, we show below that it almost certainly did not result from sampling error.[19]

These national data are useful for some purposes, but if we are to make even intelligent tentative inferences about the influence of religious factors, we must control for region and community size. Also desirable is control for age, since Catholics are somewhat younger than Protestants on the average.[20] Therefore, we present the data in Tables 9, 10, and 11 for young adults in non-Southern metropolitan areas with 250,000 or more residents. In order to avoid including a large number of people who had not completed their formal education, we use a different age range for education than for income and occupation.[21]

With these controls, Protestants ranked slightly above Catholics in summary measures of each variable. Jews ranked highest, well above each category of Christians in each variable; respondents with no religion ranked second in occupation and education and last in income.

TABLE 9. *Distribution (%) by Reported or Estimated Annual Income of Families of White Respondents to Four Recent Gallup Polls, Ages 20–39, in Non-Southern Metropolitan Areas of 250,000 or More People, by Religious Preference**

Income	Protestants	Catholics	Jews	No Religion	Total
Under $1,000	0.7	0.2	1.9	8.5	0.9
1,000–1,999	2.0	2.8	4.7	––	2.5
2,000–2,999	2.3	1.3	––	1.7	1.6
3,000–3,999	8.0	3.9	3.8	3.4	5.7
4,000–4,999	8.4	9.5	––	6.8	8.2
5,000–6,999	25.6	30.0	18.9	42.4	27.8
7,000–9,999	29.2	34.8	38.7	13.6	31.7
10,000–14,999	19.1	13.6	23.6	11.9	16.7
15,000 and Over	4.6	3.9	8.5	11.9	4.9
Total	100.0	100.0	100.0	100.0	100.0
Under $3,000	5.0	4.3	6.6	10.2	5.0
$7,000 and Over	52.9	52.3	70.8	37.4	53.3
$10,000 and Over	23.7	17.5	32.1	23.8	21.6
Median ($)	7,292	7,198	8,610	6,440	7,319
N	586	610	106	59	1,361

*Income was estimated by interviewer if respondent refused to report income. Income is reported or estimated for 1963 or 1964 depending on the date of the poll.

TABLE 10. *Distribution (%) by Occupation of Head of Household Reported by White Respondents to Four Recent Gallup Polls, Ages 20–39, in Non-Southern Metropolitan Areas of 250,000 or More People, by Religious Preference**

Occupation	Protestants	Catholics	Jews	No Religion	Total
Professional and Semi-Professional Workers	21.9	16.0	46.5	52.8	22.4
Farmers and Farm Managers	0.9	––	––	––	0.4
Businessmen and Executives	16.2	14.8	32.7	––	16.2
Clerical Workers	6.3	10.2	8.9	9.4	8.4
Sales Workers	7.8	11.9	6.9	––	9.3
Skilled Workers	22.8	22.7	5.0	15.1	21.1
Operatives and Unskilled Workers	14.5	10.6	––	5.7	11.3
Service Workers	7.1	11.8	––	13.2	8.9
Laborers	2.6	1.9	––	3.8	2.1
Total	100.0	100.0	100.0	100.0	100.0
Non-manual Workers	52.2	52.9	95.0	62.2	56.3
Lower Manual Workers	24.2	24.3	––	22.7	22.3
Duncan's Socioeconomic Index	43.5	41.9	62.5	52.0	44.7
N	588	586	101	53	1,328

*Only those respondents reporting an occupation are included here. The dates of the polls range from December, 1963, to March, 1965. Therefore, the data are essentially for 1964.

TABLE 11. *Distribution (%) by Educational Attainment of White Respondents to Four Recent Gallup Polls, Ages 25–44, in Non-Southern Metropolitan Areas of 250,000 or More People, by Religious Preference**

Years of School Completed	Protestants	Catholics	Jews	No Religion	Total
0–7	2.3	1.9	3.5	--	2.1
8	4.3	5.2	--	--	4.3
1–3 High School	14.1	17.9	--	3.6	14.4
4 High School	44.8	50.7	30.7	28.6	45.7
1–3 College	16.5	10.7	26.3	14.3	14.6
College Graduate	18.0	13.6	39.4	53.6	18.9
Total	100.0	100.0	100.0	100.0	100.0
No more than 8 Years of School	6.6	7.1	3.5	--	6.4
At Least Some College	34.5	24.3	65.7	67.9	33.5
Median Years of School Completed	12.7	12.5	14.8	14.5	12.6
N	693	689	114	56	1,552

*Dates of the polls range from December, 1963, to March, 1965. Therefore, the data are essentially for 1964.

One could easily use the Protestant and Catholic income data selectively, as Greeley did with similar data, to argue that the two religious categories had the same earning power. The percentages with incomes of $7,000 or more were virtually the same. However, a more detailed examination of the data reveals that below the $7,000 level Catholics were somewhat better off than Protestants, while at the level of $7,000 or more Protestants were decidedly more prosperous than Catholics. For instance, the proportion of Protestants with incomes of $10,000 or more was six percentage points greater—a statistically significant difference. The higher representation of Protestants at the lowest income level can be explained by their higher representation at the very lowest occupational and educational levels (Tables 10 and 11), which in turn probably resulted from a larger percentage of the Protestants being migrants from the South and from small towns and rural areas. The lower representation of Catholics at the highest income levels can be explained by their lower representation at the highest educational levels and in turn in professional, semi-professional, business, and executive occupations. We attempt to account for these differences below.

One could also use the occupational data selectively to show practically no Protestant-Catholic difference. The percentages of Protestants and Catholics in non-manual, upper-manual, and lower-manual occupations were almost identical. However, Protestants had a marked advantage within the nonmanual level; 38.1 percent of them, compared with 30.8 percent of the Catholics, were in professional, semi-professional, business, and executive occupations—a statistically significant difference.

As we have indicated above, this occupational difference can be attributed to the educational difference (Table 11). Similar percentages of Protestants and Catholics had completed the eighth grade, but the high-school dropout rate was substantially higher for Catholics. Of those who had completed high school, a substantially higher percentage of Protestants had started and completed college. Most of these differences approach but fall below statistical significance, but the difference in the percentages who had started to college is significant well beyond the 0.05 level.

Clearly, the differences in status between young metropolitan Protestants and Catholics grew primarily out of differential persistence in the educational process. This difference is so crucial that we scrutinize it carefully below. Before we do, however, it is important to point out that we cannot, from the data at hand, attribute the educational difference to religious or religiously-related influences, although Lenski's data from his Detroit study point toward a religious interpretation.[22] We cannot say that by controlling region, community-size, and age we are comparing people who have had equal opportunities for upward mobility. We know that more of the Catholics were offspring of immigrants, but, on the other hand, more of the Protestants were undoubtedly migrants from the South and from small towns and rural areas. Unfortunately, there is no way to assess accurately the relative importance of these two handicaps. Parental economic, occupational, and educational status is a crucial unknown, and thus uncontrolled, aspect of the opportunity structure, but the earlier data on Protestant-Catholic status differences suggest that this factor favored the Protestants.

Persistence in School and College

Some of the most important and interesting data presented by Lenski in *The Religious Factor* concern the relative dropout rates of white Protestants, white Catholics, Jews, and Negro Protestants. In his Detroit sample he found that Jews were least likely to have dropped out of a unit of school before completing it and that white Protestants, white Catholics, and Negro Protestants followed in that order.[23] The Protestant-Catholic difference was large enough that it probably did not result from sampling error, and it could not be explained by differences in parental status, because a larger percentage of the Catholics had middle-class parents. Weller, also using a Detroit sample, obtained similar results.[24] These data suggest that some difference in socialization may have given the Protestants a greater degree of "educational tenacity," which in turn might be a manifestation of the ability and willingness to defer gratification. As an alternative explanation, Lenski suggests that the larger average size of Catholic families may produce a Protestant-Catholic difference in average IQ and thus place Catholic students at a competitive disadvantage.[25]

Neither our recent national data nor our non-Southern metropolitan data agree with Lenski's findings on relative dropout rates. Nationally, about the same percentage of Protestant and Catholic respondents had completed the last unit of school they entered (59.5 and 60.2 percent), although the percentages for Jews and respondents with no religion were somewhat higher (66.8 and 67.9 percent). In the large non-Southern metropolitan areas, where we expected the greatest similarity to Lenski's findings, the percentage of Catholics who had not dropped out of a unit of school (69.5) was higher than the Protestant percentage (67.1) and virtually the same as the Jewish percentage (70.1). Only the percentage for those with no religion (82.2) differed much from the others. The differences between our findings and Lenski's are so great that it is unlikely that they resulted from sampling variability; they indicate that Detroit is not representative of the nation nor even of large non-Southern metropolitan areas.

Still our data do show important educational differences among Protestants, Catholics, and Jews. Though the respondents of each religion were about equally likely to have finished the last unit of school entered, on the average they had terminated their education at different levels. In the large non-Southern metropolitan areas, the young Jews ranked far above the young Protestants in educational attainments, and the Protestants in turn ranked well above the Catholics. If one looks only at the percentages who had entered and completed college, the same ranking obtained in the nation as a whole.

So important are these differences that we have analyzed data from eleven Gallup polls conducted in 1960 or later to gain confidence in our findings. Four of these are the polls on which our "1964" data are based, and the remaining seven were on hand for other purposes. Using data from each of these polls we compare Protestants and Catholics in: (1) percentage who had completed high school; (2) percentage who had started to college; and (3) percentage of those who had started to college who had finished. Then, using the eleven comparisons for each variable, we use a Wilcoxon matched-pairs signed-rank test to test the null hypothesis that no difference existed in the universe.

Apparently, about the same percentage of Protestants and Catholics had completed high school; the average on the eleven polls was 47.1 percent for Protestants and 46.9 percent for Catholics—of course the

Wilcoxon test does not reveal a significant difference. However, nine of the eleven polls show that a larger percentage of Protestants had started to college, and the difference is statistically significant. The average percentage shown by the polls is 17.6 for Protestants and 14.6 for Catholics. Of those who had started, the polls show that on the average 52.9 percent of the Protestants and 50.9 percent of the Catholics had graduated, but the difference is not significant.[26]

This analysis gives us a high degree of confidence that, among persons who were 30 years of age and older during the early 1960's, a larger percentage of Protestants than of Catholics had some college training. When it is remembered that there was a wide gap between Protestants and Catholics in all major status variables when these people were growing up, it becomes evident that differences in parental status may account for the greater college attendance of Protestants. Certainly there is ample evidence that nonmanual parents are more likely to instill in their children aspirations to go to college,[27] and of course these parents are usually more able to help pay the costs. If status differences of families of orientation do largely account for the differing rates of college attendance, then one would expect convergence of Protestant and Catholic college attendance rates with the convergence in income and occupation.

In order to estimate whether or not such convergence has occurred, we tabulated educational data for the youngest respondents (ages 20 through 25) to the six most recent Gallup polls included in the analysis. The N's of the Protestant and Catholic subsamples are fairly small (1182 and 492), but the data from these respondents suggest that the traditional difference in college attendance has been reversed. Whereas 33 percent of the Catholics had started to college, only 29 percent of the Protestants had done so. Although this difference in not statistically significant, it is unlikely that there was a substantial difference in the opposite direction in the universe, as there almost certainly was among persons aged 30 and older. Of those who had started to college, 40 percent of the Protestants and 36 percent of the Catholics had graduated, but, since many of the respondents were still enrolled in college, these percentages do not indicate relative dropout rates. Twenty-seven percent of the Protestants and twenty percent of the Catholics had not completed high school—a statistically significant difference.

The Catholic educational advantage at the young adult level can be attributed partially to the concentration of Catholics in large non-Southern metropolitan areas, where a larger percentage of the young respondents of all religions had finished high school (83 percent compared with 72 percent of the other young respondents) and had started to college (36 percent compared with 28 percent). However young Catholics in the large non-Southern metropolitan areas had almost attained parity with Protestants. The percentages who had completed high school were 84 for Protestants and 82 for Catholics, and the percentages who had started to college were 37 and 35.[28] These small differences are in sharp contrast to the wide Protestant-Catholic disparities among the older respondents (see Table 11). Among the young respondents in the South and in smaller communities, the Catholics were well ahead of the Protestants. Seventy-nine percent of the former and seventy percent of the latter had finished high school—a statistically significant difference; 31 percent of the Catholics and 27 percent of the Protestants had started to college. The Catholic advantage in this broad category of communities may have resulted from the more favorable distribution by community size of Catholics within it.[29] Given the magnitude of the overall Catholic lead, it is improbable that Protestants had a marked advantage in communities of any size.

If, as the above findings suggest, the last remnants of a Protestant educational advantage are disappearing, then serious doubts are cast on the belief that religiously-based and religiously-related influences have an important differential effect on the worldly success of Protestants and Catholics in contemporary American society. Parental status differences, which undoubtedly existed, are the most reasonable explanation for the educational differences among the older (over age 25) adults, and the educational differences can in turn account for the remaining Protestant advantage in income and occupation in the large non-Southern metropolitan areas. Therefore, one simply does not need to invoke a differential effect of religious factors to explain any of the data presented in this paper.

Summary and Conclusions

At the end of World War II, Protestants in the United States ranked well above Catholics in income, occupation and education; since then Catholics have gained dramatically and have surpassed Protestants in most aspects of status. A lingering crucial difference is in the percentages who have been to college. However, this may be only a residue of lower parental status, and even this difference seems to have disappeared among the youngest adults.

An important reason for the more rapid advancement of Catholics is their heavy concentration in the larger non-Southern metropolitan areas, where earnings, occupational distributions, educational opportunities, and rates of upward mobility are more favorable than in the typical home communities of Protestants. Protestants still rank above

Catholics in the large non-Southern metropolitan areas, but among young adults the gap in most aspects of status is not great. If the recent trend continues, Catholics in the nation as a whole will surge well ahead of Protestants in all major status variables in the next few years. However, Catholics may continue to lag slightly behind Protestants in their home communities.

Our primary concern here is with a Protestant-Catholic comparison, and therefore we refer only incidentally to the Jewish data. It is important to note, however, that Jews are maintaining a wide lead over other religious categories and apparently have improved their relative standing since World War II.

Our findings are consonant with the belief, expressed by Greeley and others, that religious influences do not handicap Catholics in their competition with Protestants. However, we must stress that these findings by themselves do not rule out a possible differential average impact of religious factors on the worldly success of Protestants and Catholics. The more favorable distribution of Catholics by region and community size could mask a religiously-based Catholic handicap, and there are reasons to believe that it does. In spite of the evidence presented here that Detroit is not typical of the country or of large metropolitan areas, one must not ignore Lenski's data showing greater upward mobility of Protestants. Even if one dismisses Lenski's findings as the result of sampling error or of peculiar Protestant-Catholic ethnic differences in Detroit, there remains the national study by Lipset and Bendix showing equal rates of upward mobility among Protestants and Catholics in spite of the greater mobility predicted for Catholics by their higher concentration in large communities. The Catholic handicap indicated by these data might be ethnic rather than religious; if so, it may have disappeared in recent years. However, religion itself should be important in at least one respect. The probability of upward mobility apparently varies inversely with number of siblings;[30] therefore the higher fertility of Catholics should give Protestants at least a slight advantage.

Analysis of national survey data for young adults during the next few years can provide more nearly conclusive evidence either for or against a differential impact of Protestantism and Catholicism on achievement. If it is found, as our data suggest, that the traditional differences in educational attainment are disappearing in each region and size of community, then sociologists should turn to more fruitful hypotheses concerning the relationship of religion to worldly status. Even if there should be some small remaining difference in Protestant and Catholic achievements, much of the recent attention devoted to Protestant-Catholic differences in mobility and aspirations could more fruitfully be directed to other topics.[31] This study shows that the effects of any

Protestant-Catholic differences in influence on worldly status are small in relation to the effects of other influences that on balance favor Catholics.[32] Any differential impact of Protestantism and Catholicism on income, occupation, and education explains at best only a small fraction of the variance. Our analysis provides no conclusive answer to the question that has commanded so much sociological attention in recent years, but it suggests that arriving at a more nearly conclusive answer is not very important.

---

1. Much of the debate deals not directly with economic and occupational success but with achievement motivation, deferred gratification, and similar variables that are assumed to underlie success.

2. For instance, see Raymond W. Mack, Raymond J. Murphy, and Seymour Yellin, "The Protestant Ethic, Level of Aspiration, and Social Mobility: An Empirical Test," *American Sociological Review,* 21 (June, 1956), pp. 295-300; Bernard C. Rosen, "Race, Ethnicity, and the Achievement Syndrome," *American Sociological Review,* 26 (February, 1959), pp. 47-60; Gerhard Lenski, *The Religious Factor,* rev. ed., Garden City, New York: Doubleday, 1963; Joseph Veroff, Sheila Feld, and Gerald Gurin, "Achievement Motivation and Religious Background," *American Sociological Review,* 27 (April, 1962), pp. 205-217; Albert J. Mayer and Harry Sharp, "Religious Preference and Worldly Success," *American Sociological Review,* 27 (April, 1962), pp. 218-227; Andrew M. Greeley, "Influence of the 'Religious Factor' on the Career Plans and Occupational Values of College Students," *American Journal of Sociology,* 68 (May, 1963), pp. 658-671; Marvin Bressler and Charles F. Westoff, "Catholic Education, Economic Values, and Achievement," *American Journal of Sociology,* 69 (November, 1963), pp. 225-233; Andrew M. Greeley, "The Protestant Ethic: Time for a Moratorium," *Sociological Analysis,* 25 (Spring, 1964), pp. 20-33; Ralph Lane, Jr., "Research on Catholics as a Status Group," *Sociological Analysis,* 26 (Summer, 1965); and Seymour Warkov and Andrew M. Greeley, "Parochial School Origins and Educational Achievement," *American Sociological Review,* 31 (June, 1966), pp. 406-414.

3. See Nathan Glazer, "The American Jew and the Attainment of Middle-Class Rank: Some Trends and Explanations," in Marshall Sklare, ed., *The Jews,* New York: The Free Press of Glencoe, 1958, pp. 138-146.

4. Seymour Martin Lipset and Reinhard Bendix, *Social Mobility in Industrial Society,* Berkeley and Los Angeles: University of California Press, 1959, pp. 48-56.

5. Lenski, *op. cit.,* p. 84.

6. *Ibid.*

7. Greeley, "The Protestant Ethic . . .," *op. cit.*

8. *Ibid.*

9. Our similar national data show important differences in the distributions of Protestants and Catholics above this level (see Table 9). Also, one could point out that Protestants equalled Catholics in spite of the heavy concentration of the former in the South and in the smaller metropolitan areas, where incomes in general were relatively low.

10. The best treatments of national data on status differences by religious preference are primarily descriptive rather than attempts to assess the relative impact of Protestantism and Catholicism on worldy success. See Hadley Cantril, "Education and Economic Composition of Religious Groups: An Analysis of Poll Data," *American Journal of Sociology,* 47 (March, 1943), pp. 574-579; Donald J. Bogue, "Religious Affiliation," *The Population of the United States,* New York: The Free Press of Glencoe, 1959, pp. 688-709; and Bernard Lazerwitz, "A Comparison of Major United States Religious Groups," *Journal of*

the American Statistical Association, 56 (September, 1961), 568-579. Lazerwitz's data are the most recent and come from two 1957 samples and one 1958 sample.

11. None of the samples are simple random samples, however; they are therefore not amenable to analysis with the usual textbook statistical formulae. The standard errors for the more recent Gallup polls are estimated to be usually about 1.4 to 1.6 times the standard errors for simple random samples. In addition, the recent Gallup samples are inflated about 100 percent by a weighting procedure used instead of callbacks; therefore the N's reported for the combined 1963, 1964, and 1965 data in the tables of this article are usually about twice the number of respondents represented. For statistical procedures for analysis of these samples, see Leslie Kish, *Survey Sampling,* New York: John Wiley and Co., 1965. We are indebted to Mr. Andrew Kohut of the Gallup Organization for additional guidance in analyzing the Gallup data.

12. See Tables 4 and 5. One should not place much confidence in the apparent increase, in Table 1, in the proportion of Jewish families at the lowest economic level. The Jewish samples for both dates are small and subject to considerable sampling variability, and the occupational and educational data in Tables 2 and 3 show an increase in the relative standing of Jews.

13. The underrepresentation of Protestants in 1945 and 1954 at all levels in Table 2 results from their overrepresentation in the farm category, which is not shown in the table.

14. The fact that Jewish representation declined from 1954 to 1964 in three of the urban levels and stayed the same in the other reflects decreased total representation of Jews in urban occupations as Christians became more urbanized.

15. For 1960 census data showing variation in income, occupation, and education by community size, see Leo F. Schnore, "Some Correlates of Urban Size: A Replication," *American Journal of Sociology,* 69 (September, 1963), pp. 185-193. The relationship between community size and median family income was monotonic, the median varying from $5,222 in urban places with 2,500 to 10,000 residents to $6,863 in urbanized areas with 3,000,000 or more residents. The relationship between community size and percentage of workers in nonmanual occupations was not as simple, but the percentages were generally higher in the larger classes of communities. Percentage of high school graduates did not vary consistently with community size, but the smallest percentage was in the communities with only 2,500 to 10,000 residents.

The median income of white persons with income in 1959 was $3,332 in the Northeast, $3,099 in the North Central Region, $3,322 in the West, but only $2,529 in the South. The percentage of employed white males in nonmanual occupations in 1960 was 39.4 in the Northeast, 33.7 in the North Central Region, 39.4 in the West, and 36.9 in the South. Median years of school completed by white persons 25 years old and older in 1960 were 10.8 in the Northeast and North Central Regions, 12.1 in the West, and 10.4 in the South. The more pronounced disadvantage of Southerners in income than in occupation and education reflects lower earnings within occupations in the South.

Bogue presents data from a 1955 NORC survey showing lower incomes for Protestants than for Catholics within broad occupational categories and educational levels (*op. cit.,* pp. 705-707). The variation in income within occupations by community size and region can account for this difference; therefore it is not, as Greeley argues ("The Protestant Ethic . . ., *op. cit.,* p. 32), evidence against an adverse economic effect of Catholicism.

16. Lipset and Bendix, *op. cit.,* chapter 8.

17. See footnote 15.

18. The respondents with no religious preference, or the heads of their households, had a bimodal distribution along the scale of occupational prestige. They had more than 2½ times their proportional share of the professional and semi-professional jobs and were slightly overrepresented as laborers and operatives and unskilled workers. In contrast, their representation was very low as farmers, businessmen and executives, and clerical workers. Although the sample size allows only a tentative conclusion, it seems that religious apostasy is most common at the upper end of the occupational hierarchy but more common at the bottom than in the middle.

Bogue's data agree with ours in showing a bimodal distribution but show a much larger percentage of the respondents with no religion as farmers and businessmen and executives (*op. cit.*, p. 703). Lazerwitz also shows a bimodal distribution and high representation of the no-religion respondents in the farm category (*op. cit.*, p. 574). These data are consistent with Lenski's finding of a curvilinear relationship between income and religious interest, with the smallest religious interest at the upper income level and the greatest at the middle levels. See Gerhard Lenski, "Social Correlates of Religious Interest," *American Sociological Review*, 18 (October, 1953), pp. 533-544.

19. Both Jews and respondents with no religion ranked well above Christians in educational status, and both had more than double the proportional representation as college graduates. Furthermore, the percentage who had finished of those who had started college was much higher for Jews and no-religion respondents than for Christians. The persons who said they had no religion had a bimodal distribution similar to their distribution along the scale of occupational prestige; they were highly overrepresented at the college level, slightly overrepresented at the eight-year level, and underrepresented at all other levels. Bogue and Lazerwitz report similar distributions.

20. See Leonard Broom and Norval D. Glenn, "Religious Differences in Reported Attitudes and Behavior," (forthcoming). Six of seven national surveys showed a larger percentage of Catholics below age 40.

21. In the case of income and occupation, our controls for age are imprecise, since the age data are for the respondents themselves, the income data are for their families, and the occupational data are for heads of households. However, most of the respondents were either heads of households or spouses of heads; the inclusion of a few young adults living with their parents probably affects the different religious categories in a similar manner. If there is any differential effect, it is probably to lower slightly the apparent relative standing of Catholics, since there is a wider Protestant-Catholic gap at the older ages.

22. *The Religious Factor*, chapter 6.

23. *Ibid.*, pp. 263-266. The percentages who did not drop out were 79, 61, 48, and 33 respectively.

24. Neil J. Weller, *Religion and Social Mobility in Industrial Society*, unpublished doctoral dissertation, University of Michigan, 1960, chapter 4, as cited by Lenski, *The Religious Factor*, p. 263. Weller found that 51 percent of the white Protestants but only 38 percent of the Catholics in his sample of 1100 men had completed their last unit of education.

25. A negative association of number of siblings with measured intelligence is well established and apparently is not simply the result of higher fertility at the lower socioeconomic levels. See Lipset and Bendix, *op. cit.*, p. 243.

26. When Jews are compared with Protestants, all of the polls show that a considerably larger percentage of the former had completed high school, and there is virtually no chance that this consistent large difference resulted from sampling error. The average percentage is 75.7 for Jews compared with 47.1 for Protestants. All but one of the polls show that a larger percentage of Jews had started to college, and the difference is significant (p.=0.002). The average percentages are 34.7 and 17.6 for Jews and Protestants respectively. Seven of the polls show a smaller college dropout rate for Jews; although this difference is not significant (p=0.108), the Catholic-Jewish difference is (p=0.013). On the average, the polls show that 59.7 percent of the Jews who had started to college had finished.

27. For instance, see Herbert H. Hyman, "The Value Systems of Different Classes: A Social Psychological Contribution to the Analysis of Stratification," in Reinhard Bendix and Seymour Martin Lipset, eds., *Class, Status and Power*, New York: The Free Press of Glencoe, 1953, pp. 426-442.

28. The Protestant N is 241; the Catholic N is 223.

29. Of the respondents to the four most recent Gallup polls included in this study, 54 percent of the Protestants who lived in communities with fewer than 250,000 residents were rural. The comparable percentage of Catholics was only 31.3. Forty-one percent of

the Catholics but only 20.5 percent of the Protestants lived in communities with 50,000 to 249,000 residents.

30. Lipset and Bendix, *op. cit.,* pp. 238-243.

31. Among the lines of inquiry that seem more fruitful is the study of the possible differential impact of different kinds of Protestantism on worldly status. For instance, a worthwhile project would be a rigorous test of Johnson's intriguing hypotheses concerning the effects of the Holiness sects. See Benton Johnson, "Do Holiness Sects Socialize in Dominant Values?" *Social Forces,* 39 (May, 1961), pp. 309-316.

32. It is possible that even the religious influences favor the Catholics, but we doubt that this is the case.

ROBERT N. BELLAH

Reflections on the Protestant Ethic Analogy in Asia

The work of Max Weber, especially the so-called "Protestant Ethic Hypothesis," continues to exercise an impressive influence on current research in the social sciences, as a glance at recent journals and monographs will quickly show.[1] The great bulk of this research is concerned with refining the Weberian thesis about the differential effects of Protestant compared with Catholic religious orientations in the sphere of economic activity. In recent years, however, there have been increasing though still scattered attempts to apply Weber's argument to material drawn from various parts of Asia. The present paper will not undertake to review these attempts with any completeness. Rather it will be devoted to a selective consideration of several different approaches to the problem with a view to determining some of their possibilities and limitations.

Perhaps the commonest approach has been to interpret the Weber hypothesis in terms of the economists' emphasis on the importance of

From *The Journal of Social Issues* 19 (January 1963):52-60. Reprinted by permission of the publisher.

entrepreneurship in the process of economic development. Weber's "Protestant Ethic" is seen as an ideological orientation tending to lead those who hold it into an entrepreneurial role where they then contribute to economic growth. We will consider shortly how serious this oversimplification of Weber's view distorts his intention. At any rate those who have taken this interpretation have proceeded to analyze various Asian religious groups to see whether examples of this-worldly asceticism, the religious significance of work in a calling and so forth have been associated with successful economic activity. Cases in which the association has been claimed include in Japan Jōdo and Zen Buddhists, the Hōtoku and Shingaku movements; in Java the Santri Muslims; in India the Jains, Parsis and various business or merchant castes and so forth.[2] David C. McClelland has recently subsumed a number of such examples under the general rubric of "positive Mysticism" within which he finds Weber's Protestant example to be merely a special case.[3]

Whether or not the claim to have discovered a religious ethic analogous to Weber's type case can be substantiated in all of these Asian examples, this general approach has much to recommend it. For one thing it calls attention to the motivational factor which historians, economists and sociologists have often overlooked. For another it calls attention to subtle and non-obvious connections between cultural and religious beliefs and behavioral outcomes. This latter point is one which some readers of Weber have consistently failed to understand, Kurt Samuelson being merely one of the more recent examples. The latter claims in refutation of Weber that since the puritan fathers did not espouse a materialistic dog-eat-dog capitalism their theology could not possibly have led to its development.[4] Milton Singer on the other hand proves himself a more discerning pupil of Weber when he argues that economic development is not supported merely by "materialistic" values but may be advanced by an "ethic of austerity" based perhaps in the case of India on the tradition of religious asceticism.[5]

But the application of the "entrepreneurship model" or motivational approach to Weber's thesis has, I believe, certain grave limitations. Some of the difficulty lies in the original essay itself when it is not grasped in its proper relation to the whole of Weber's work. One of the most serious of these limitations is emphasis on the importance of the motivational factor at the expense of the historical and institutional setting.

However important motivational factors may be they have proven time and again to be highly sensitive to shifts in institutional arrangements. The consequences for economic development depend as much on the institutional channeling of motivation as on the presence or absence of certain kinds of motivation. For example the entrepreneurial potential of the Japanese samurai, who from at least the 16th century comprised what most observers would agree was the most achievement oriented group in Japan, could not be realized until the Meiji period when legal restraints on their entering trade were abolished and their political responsibilities eliminated. Chinese merchants who made an indifferent showing within the institutional limitations of imperial China turned into a vigorous capitalist class under more favorable conditions in Southeast Asia. Clifford Geertz has shown how the Muslim Santri group in Java, characterized by a long merchant tradition and a favorable religious ethic, began to burgeon into entrepreneurship under favorable economic conditions early in this century only to wither on the vine when economic conditions worsened markedly during the great depression.[6] Gustav Papanek in a recent paper has indicated how several relatively small "communities" (quasi-castes) of traditional traders were able to spearhead Pakistan's remarkable industrial growth in recent years by taking advantage of highly favorable economic conditions which had not previously existed.[7] On the basis of such examples one might argue that there exists in most Asian countries a small but significant minority which has the motivation necessary for entrepreneurial activity. If this is the case, then, it would be advisable to consider motivation in close connection with institutional structure and its historical development.

In *The Protestant Ethic and the Spirit of Capitalism,* Weber himself seems to lean rather heavily on the motivational variable and this may be what has led some of his readers astray. In the later comparative studies in the sociology of religion, however, we get a much more balanced view and an implicit correction of emphasis in the earlier work. Following Weber's comparative studies a number of students have undertaken what might be called an "institutional approach," attempting to discern institutional factors favorable or unfavorable to economic development. Examples of this kind of study are Albert Feuerwerker's monograph *China's Early Industrialization,*[8] my *Tokugawa Religion,* about the inadequacies of which I will speak in a moment, Joseph Elder's dissertation on India,[9] and perhaps the most comprehensive in scope and historical coverage, Clifford Geertz's work on Java contained in a number of published and unpublished writings.[10] In all of these studies Weber's emphasis on the religious ethic continues to receive a central focus. It is seen, however, not simply in relation to personal motivation but also as embodied in or related to a wide range of institutional structures. Feuerwerker writes, "... one institutional breakthrough is worth a dozen textile mills or shipping companies established within the framework of the traditional society and its system of values."[11] And Geertz says in a similar vein:

> The extent and excellence of a nation's resources, the size and skill of its labor force, the scope and complexity of its productive "plant," and the distribution and value of entrepreneurial abilities among its population are only one element in the assessment of its capacity for economic growth; the institutional arrangements by means of which these various factors can be brought to bear on any particular economic goal is another . . . It is for this reason that economic development in "underdeveloped" areas implies much more than capital transfers, technical aid, and ideological exhortation: it demands a deep going transformation of the basic structure of society and, beyond that, perhaps even in the underlying value-system in terms of which that structure operates.[12]

My study of Tokugawa Japan taking a somewhat more optimistic approach to traditional society, stressed the extent to which traditional Japanese institutions were or could under certain circumstances be made to be favorable to economic development. In so doing I drew a number of parallels between certain aspects of "rationalization" in Japan and the rationalization Weber was talking about in the West. It was precisely on this point that Maruyama Masao's review on the April 1958 issue of *Kokka Gakkai Zasshi* was sharply critical.[13] Without denying that a number of the mechanisms I discussed, for example the concentration of loyalty in the emperor, may have been effective in bringing about certain social changes contributing to economic growth, he points out that they were far from rational in Weber s sense and indeed had profoundly irrational consequences in subsequent Japanese development, not the least of which were important economic inefficiencies.

With Maruyama's strictures in mind one is perhaps better able to deal with some remarks of Milton Singer near the end of his sensitive and illuminating review article on Weber's *Religion of India:*

> To evaluate Weber's conclusions is not easy. In view of the complexity of Hinduism, and of Asian religions generally, any characterization of them or any comparison of them with Western religion is going to involve large simplifications. Certainly Weber has brilliantly constructed a characterization based on an impressive knowledge of both textual and contextual studies. But one may wonder whether the construction does justice to elements of Asian religions. Some of these are: a strand of this-worldly asceticism; the economic rationality of merchants, craftsmen, and peasants; the logically-consistent system of impersonal determinism in Vedānta and Buddhism, with direct consequences for a secular ethic; the development of "rational empirical" science; religious individu-

> alism; and personal monotheism. Weber is certainly aware of all these elements and discusses them in his study . . . But in the construction of the "Spirit" he does not give very much weight to these elements. With the evidence today before us of politically independent Asian states actively planning their social, economic, and scientific and technical development, we would attach a good deal more importance to these elements and see less conflict between them and the religious "spirit."[14]

For Maruyama the mere *presence* of rational elements for which I argued in the Japanese case along lines quite parallel to those of Singer is simply not enough if they exist passively side by side with irrational elements (as they do in both Japanese and Indian cases) and are not pushed through "methodically and systematically" to their conclusion as they were in Weber's paradigmatic case of Protestantism. If Maruyama is right, and I am coming increasingly to believe that he is, then it becomes necessary to press beyond both the motivational and the institutional approaches and to view matters in an even broader perspective as the above quote from Geertz already hinted.

Concretely, this means that we are forced to take seriously Weber's argument for the special significance of Protestantism. The search through Asia for religious movements which here and there have motivational or institutional components analogous to the Protestant Ethic ultimately proves inadequate. The Protestant Reformation is not after all some mere special case of a more general category. It stands in Weber's whole work, not in the *Protestant Ethic* essay alone, as the symbolic representation of a fundamental change in social and cultural structure with the most radical and far-reaching consequences. The proper analogy in Asia then turns out to be, not this or that motivational or institutional component, but reformation itself. What we need to discern is the "transformation of the basic structure of society" and its "underlying value-system," to use Geertz's language. Before trying to discover some examples of this structural approach to the Protestant Ethic analogy in Asia it is necessary to note briefly that we see here an example of what must occur in any really serious confrontation with Asian examples: we are forced back to a reconsideration of the European case which provides us so many of the conscious and unconscious categories of our investigation.

The first consideration is that the development in Europe is neither even nor uniform. Developments in different countries and at different times have very different significance. As Reinhard Bendix has so clearly indicated it was Weber's growing discernment of the failure of structural transformation in important sectors of German society which led him to the Protestant Ethic problem.[15] As every reader of the famous essay knows the material is derived from England primarily, and not from Germany where the Reformation remained abortive in important respects and its structural consequences stunted. This is indeed the background for Weber's profound cultural pessimism. Interestingly enough one of the first Japanese to penetrate deeply into the structure of Western culture, Uchimura Kanzō, made a similar diagnosis. Writing in 1898 he said:

> One of the many foolish and deplorable mistakes which the Satsuma-Chōshū Government have committed is their having selected Germany as the example to be followed in their administrative policy. Because its military organization is well-nigh perfect, and its imperialism a gift of its army, therefore they thought that it ought to be taken as the pattern of our own Empire. . . .
>
> Germany certainly is a great nation, but it is not the greatest, neither is it the most advanced. It is often said that Art, Science, and Philosophy have their homes in Germany, that Thought has its primal spring there. But it is not in Germany that Thought is realized to the fullest extent. Thought may originate in Germany, but it is actualized somewhere else. The Lutheran Reformation bore its best fruit in England and America.[16]

These suggestions about European developments, which must in the present brief paper remain without adequate elaboration, have a further important implication. Germany is certainly one of the most economically developed nations in the world, yet it lagged, according to Weber, in some of the structural transformations which he discovered to be crucial in the development of modern society. Once the crucial breakthroughs have been accomplished it becomes possible for other nations to take some of them over piecemeal without the total structure being transformed. Possible, but at great cost, as the German case indicates.

These considerations bring us back to Maruyama's criticism of my work and the criticism of a number of Japanese intellectuals of American analyses of Japan in general.[17] Japan too, comparatively speaking, is one of the world's most economically advanced nations. Looking at economic growth as our sole criterion, we are inclined to consider Japan as a rather unambiguous success story. But to Japanese intellectuals who feel as acutely as Weber did the failure of modern Japan to carry through certain critical structural transformations which are associated with modern society, the evaluation of Japan's modern history is much more problematic. It would be convenient for social scientists and policy makers if economic growth were an automatic index to successful structural transformation. This does not, however, seem to be the case. Indeed where economic growth is rapid and structural change is blocked, or as in the Communist cases distorted, social instabilities result which under present world conditions are serious enough to have potentially fatal consequences for us all. A broader perspective than has often been taken would seem then to be in order.

As examples of the structural approach, which I believe to be the most adequate application of the Weberian problem to Asia, I may cite again the work of Clifford Geertz on Indonesia and especially a very suggestive recent article on Bali,[18] together with a highly interesting study of recent religious and social developments in Ceylon by Michael Ames.[19] In the Balinese case only the beginnings of the questioning of traditional assumptions are evident and the degree to which rationalization at the value level will have social consequence is not yet clear. In Ceylon Ames documents the existence of movements of religious reform which have gone far in changing some of the most fundamental assumptions of traditional Buddhism and replacing them with orientations supporting social reform. The degree to which the structural reform itself has gotten under way is not as yet clear. In Japan a century of ideological ferment has given rise to a number of tendencies and potentialities which need much more clarification, a problem on which the writer is currently working.[20]

There are indications from a number of Asian countries that traditional elements are being reformulated as part of new nationalist ideologies. Joseph Elder has presented some evidence that the Indian caste ethic is being transformed into a universalistic ethic of occupational responsibility detached from its earlier anchorage in the hereditary caste structure.[21] Such examples would seem to support Singer's argument as quoted above, as indeed in a sense they do. But it should not be forgotten that these reformulations have occurred under Western impact (not infrequently under Protestant Christian impact as Ames shows in Ceylon) and involve fundamental alterations in pattern even when based on traditional material, making them often formally similar to Western paradigms. This is not to imply that Asian cultures are inherently imitative but rather that modern Western Societies are not fortuitous cultural sports. Since they represent the earliest versions of a specific structural type of society it is inevitable that Asian societies should in some patterned way come to resemble them as they shift toward that type. Another set of problems arising from the structural approach have to do with the extent to which nationalism or communism can supply the ideological underpinning, the cultural Reformation if you like, for the necessary structural transformations. It is not possible to review here all the work done on these topics, some of which is certainly relevant to the present problem concern.

In conclusion let me say that the whole range of problems having to do with social change in Asia would be greatly illuminated if we had a comprehensive social taxonomy based on evolutionary principles of the sort that Durkheim called for in 1895.[22] Among recent sociologists I can think only of S. N. Eisenstadt as having made significant contributions to this end.[23] With such a taxonomy in hand we would be in a much stronger position to interpret the meaning of the results obtained by those currently concentrating on motivational and institutional research. We might also be in a better position to clear up profound problems both of science and policy which hover around the definition of the concept of modernization.

---

1. For example the current (April, 1962) issue of the *American Sociological Review* contains two articles explicitly claiming to shed light on "the Weberian hypothesis." Among last year's more important books in which the influence of Weber's work is very evident are Gerhard Lenski's *The Religious Factor,* New York: Doubleday and David C. McClelland's *The Achieving Society,* Princeton, New Jersey: van Nostrand. One might also mention Kurt Samuelson's scurrilous attack *Religion and Economic Action,* New York: Basic Books. That Weber can at this date generate such irrational hostility is in itself a kind of indication of his importance.

2. The influence of Jōdo Buddhism and the Hōtoku and Shingaku movements in Japan was discussed by Robert N. Bellah in *Tokugawa Religion,* Glencoe, Ill.: Free Press, 1957, Chapter 5. The Zen case in Japan was discussed by David C. McClelland, *op. cit.,* pp. 369-370 under the mistaken impression that the samurai in the Meiji Period were devotees of Zen Buddhism. The Santri Muslims of Java were treated by Clifford Geertz in *The Religion of Java,* Glencoe, Ill.: Free Press, 1960 and more especially in terms of the present context in "Religious Belief and Economic Behavior in a Central Javanese Town: Some Preliminary Considerations," *Economic Development and Cultural Change,* Volume IV, number 2, 1956. McClelland has discussed the Jains and the Parsis in *op. cit.,* pp. 368-369 and Milton Singer has discussed several Indian examples in "Cultural Values in India's Economic Development," *The Annals,* Volume 305, May, 1956, pp. 81-91. The latter article received further comment from John Goheen, M. N. Srinivas, D. G. Karve and Mr. Singer in "India's Cultural Values and Economic Development: A Discussion," *Economic Development and Cultural Change,* Volume VII, Number 1, 1958, pp. 1-12. Nakamura Hajime in a brief article entitled "The Vitality of Religion in Asia" which appeared in *Cultural Freedom in Asia,* Herbert Passin, Ed., Rutland Vt.: Tuttle, 1956, pp. 53-66 argued for the positive influence of a number of Asian religious currents on economic development. In his more comprehensive *The Ways of Thinking of Eastern Peoples,* Tokyo: Unesco, 1959 (An inadequate and partial translation of *Tōyōjin no Shii Hōhō,* Tokyo: Misuzu Shobō, 1949, 2 vols.) Nakamura takes a position very close to that of Weber. The types of argument put forward in the above very partial listing of work on this problem are quite various. In particular Clifford Geertz was careful to point out that the Santri religious ethic seemed suited to a specifically pre-capitalist small trader mentality which Weber argued was very different from the spirit of capitalism. This distinction could perhaps be usefully applied to many of the above cases of traditional merchant groups which seem to have some special religious orientation supporting their occupational motivations.

3. *Op. cit.,* pp. 367-373, 391.

4. *Op. cit.,* pp. 27-48.

5. "India's Cultural Values and Economic Development: A Discussion," *Economic Development and Cultural Change,* Volume VII, No. 1, p. 12.

6. "The Social Context of Economic Change: An Indonesian Case Study," Center for International Studies, MIT, 1956 (mimeo), pp. 94-119.

7. "The Development of Entrepreneurship," *The American Economic Review,* Vol. LII, No. 2, May 1962.

8. Albert Feuerwerker, *China's Early Industrialization,* Cambridge, Mass.: Harvard University Press, 1958.

9. Ph.D. Dissertation, Department of Social Relations, Harvard University, Joseph Elder, *Industrialism in Hindu Society: A Case Study in Social Change,* June 1959.

10. In addition to writings already cited see especially "The Development of the Javanese Economy: A Socio-Cultural Approach," Center for International Studies, MIT, 1956 (mimeo).

11. *Op. cit.,* p. 242.

12. "The Developments of the Javanese Economy . . .," pp. 105-106.

13. *Kokka Gakkai Zasshi* (The Journal of the Association of Political and Social Sciences), Vol. LXXII, No. 4, April 1958, Tokyo.

14. *American Anthropologist,* Volume 63, No. 1, 1961, p. 150.

15. *Max Weber: An Intellectual Portrait,* New York: Doubleday, 1960, Chapter II.

16. *Uchimura Kanzō Zenshū,* Tokyo: Iwanami Shoten, 1933, Vol. 16, p. 361-362.

17. Some illuminating remarks on this topic are to be found in John Whitney Hall's "Japan and the Concept of Modernization: Hakone and Aftermath," Mimeo, 1962.

18. "Internal Conversion in Contemporary Bali," Mimeo, 1961.

19. "An Outline of Recent Social and Religious Changes in Ceylon," *Human Organization,* forthcoming.

20. "Ienaga Saburo and the Search for Meaning in Modern Japan," Mimeo, 1962, is the first study concerned with this problem which the writer has completed.

21. *Op. cit.*

22. *The Rules of Sociological Method,* Glencoe, Ill.: Free Press, 1950, Chapter 4.

23. See his *From Generation to Generation,* Glencoe, Ill.: Free Press, 1956 and especially *The Political Systems of Empires,* Free Press, 1963.

SECTION IV

Religion and Social Change: Urbanization, Secularization, and the Future

"Unprecedented," "far reaching," and even "revolutionary" are terms commonly employed by scholars seeking to describe the magnitude of the changes which have altered the social structure of both the Western world and the so-called "newly emerging" societies. Weber may have been surprised, as previously noted, by the amount of attention given to his effort to link Protestantism with the emergence of a new industrial order. But the social scientist examining the Weberian thesis is, at the same time, demonstrating his concern with one of the major tasks confronting sociology and its sister disciplines: how to explain the modernization process which, in little more than two hundred years, has changed the Western world from a composite of basically agrarian societies to a community of highly industrialized nations. Sociology, particularly, has frequently been accused of giving excessive attention to the description of the static aspects of society while devoting minimal efforts to explaining the dynamics of social change. The accusation is only partially just. Various theories of change have been proposed and examined. Different variables have been put forth as necessary, but seldom sufficient, to explain how societies pass from one phase to another. Demographic variables such as population expansion have been stressed by some; technology has commanded perhaps an inordinate attention from many who see it as *the* explanatory variable; the polity has come in for its share of attention; and others, following Weber's lead, have emphasized the importance of ideological factors. Today, however, few scholars would give primacy to any one variable to the exclusion of others. Although each constituted a massive force in the change of the Western world to an industrial society, certainly the transformations in the economic order of the seventeenth and eighteenth centuries cannot be attributed simply to the "Protestant ethic" nor to a Marxian "class struggle" between the bourgeoisie and the proletariat. There is, instead, a growing recognition of the need to consider the interdependence of economic, political, religious, and other factors if we are to offer adequate theories of social change.

Religion, of course, not only affects but is greatly affected by social change. Whether religion is more active or passive in the changes occurring in a society is a subject of debate among those studying religion in its modern setting. Peter Berger tends to view religion as a "passive or reactive factor . . . in the structuring process of modern society."[1] On the other hand, Seymour Lipset feels that as a "value-generating institution, religion must affect the nature of political discourse seriously. Religion explains much of the variation in such nonpolitical aspects of behavior as work habits, achievement aspirations, and parent-child relations."[2] Others are simply puzzled by the discussion since the struggle of religious institutions to maintain some degree of autonomy and to preserve whatever degree of influence they have seems to be clearly a losing proposition. The data available to reach any definitive conclusion about the exact nature of the change in religion in response to the changes in the society are surely inconclusive at best. What is absolutely certain is that religion is no different from the other major societal institutions in one major respect: it finds itself forced to adapt to a changing environment. It is doubtful that religion has experienced any greater difficulties in this regard than the educational institution, for example. It may very well be more *resistive* to change than education (though some militant blacks might take issue with this); but as the studies in section IV illustrate, the processes of urbanism and urbanization,[3] on the one hand, and the growth of what is characterized as a "secular" society[4] on the other, have had a particular import for religion. There is evidence of changes in belief, organizational structures, and other facets of religion. Those who adhere to the "old time religion" foresee only disaster for the church in the changing society, and many sect-type groups actually welcome what they view as a general breakdown in the moral fiber of the society—it means that the "day of the Lord is at hand." The "new breed" of younger theologians, on the other hand, view religion's previous concern with transcendental matters as one reason for its diminished influence and eagerly look forward to new doctrines and new forms in which the church can find a place of prominence and influence in a post-industrial society.

The discussion by Talcott Parsons of "Christianity and Modern Industrial Society" in chapter 8 focuses on the differentiation of the church from the secular world resulting from the Protestant Reformation. He takes issue with Pitirim Sorokin's view that the Reformation was a step away from that which was inherently important in religion: an other-worldly orientation. Parsons argues instead that the denominational pluralism which resulted from the Reformation also gave autonomy to the individual conscience. Each man was now "on his own" with God. More importantly, he was free to view the secular society as a "legitimate field of action for the Christian." And, "precisely because he is a Christian he will not simply accept everything he finds there, he will attempt to shape the situation in the direction of better conformity with Christian values." Thus, the Reformation is viewed not as a step toward secularization (and in Sorokin's view *away* from religion) but rather a move toward a general institutionalization of Christian values —both within and outside the church.

The argument by Parsons of the positive consequences for religion of the differentiation process, still occurring in Western society, is a needed antidote for those who see the urbanization process as being primarily dysfunctional for religion. Gibson Winter, who feels that "the churches have prospered in the course of urbanization," presents, nevertheless, a picture of "The Dilemma of Metropolitan Protestantism" in the second selection in chapter 8. Even though Winter's study is less than ten years old, the problems which he outlines here have intensified in that period of time. There has been a continuing exodus to the suburbs by the more affluent middle-class church-goers with predictable consequences for decreasing numbers of churches remaining in the central city. Denominations are giving almost "exclusive attention" to building new churches in suburban areas, which are described as " 'high potential areas,' and they do not mean potential for prayer." Whether or not the prosperity evident in the suburban churches can provide a base for a missionary effort to recover the city is a concern of great importance for the leadership of the church,[5] but Winter's apt description of the suburban church offers only partial hope: "Assembled from no real community and witnessing to none, it merely contemplates its own budget."

Chapter 9 presents two essays which attempt (1) to delineate the meaning of secularization and (2) its particular meaning with respect to theology. In "The Concept of Secularization in Empirical Research"

Larry Shiner highlights some of the basic disagreements over just what secularization means. In the six different types of definitions which he investigates there is, at least, one common theme: religion and secularization tend to be viewed as polar terms. Shiner, along with many contemporary younger theologians, views this polarity as undesirable and urges the recognition of a definition of religion which allows some incorporation of secularism in any understanding of the religious phenomenon. Due to the generally negative connotations of secularization, from the religious point of view, Shiner suggests that it might be appropriate to drop the term for a more neutral one such as "transposition" or "differentiation." He is not, however, enthusiastic about the possibilities of acceptance of his proposal among social scientists.

"A Sociological View of the Secularization of Theology" is the problem to which Peter Berger addresses himself in the second selection for chapter 9. He points to the relative ease with which sociology can demonstrate "that large segments of traditional lore have become irrelevant (that is, subjectively meaningless and/or practically inapplicable) to the man in the street." What has replaced the "traditional lore" of ideas about God, man, and the world? A new *weltanschaung:* the scientific understanding of the total universe of phenomena—religion and man included. It follows, then, that any institution based on "reality presuppositions" which do not accord with the new perspective must accommodate, or face, gradual extinction. (As Berger notes, there is really not much that is new here. What is new is "the resonance of these ideas in a mass public.") His prediction of the future of the church as a result of this ideological struggle is *not* what one might anticipate: the end of institutionalized religion. Berger argues instead that "the probable fate of the secular theology," once it is past the stage of being "the latest word" in religion, will be its probable "absorption into the legitimating apparatus of the institution. . . ." His final nonscientific comments tap, once again, the problem raised in section I of the present work: must we give attention to the essence of religion as well as its functions? He argues that we must.

Bryan Wilson's study, "Secularization and the Clerical Profession," focuses on the professional leadership of the church and its response to the growth of a secular society in which the church must operate. His analysis is based on a sample of English clergymen and, thus, not necessarily generalizable to their American counterparts. As the previous studies in this work have indicated, however, practically every facet of the religious scene in England which he describes does have its counterpart in American religious life. Wilson, like Shiner, notes that one possible meaning of secularization is "transformation." In the midst of social change religious ideas, forms of worship, and other traditional characteristics of religion are not necessarily being secularized so much as simply changed to accord with the new environment. Man's religious dispositions are still present; he is, though, seeking new expressions for them. The clergy, however, find themselves subject to particular pressures as the result of change or secularization—whichever. They must continue to work with the laymen who "very often want only assurance and certainty of a kind which clerics feel increasingly less able to provide." This problem is magnified by the characteristics of English clergy: they are older, there are increasingly fewer of them, and fewer recruits.[6] Furthermore, among the latest recruits to the Anglican ministry there has been an increase in the proportion who are noncollege graduates (a feature which has not yet affected the Catholic church with its strict controls over educational requirements for its clergy). Compounding all these difficulties is the fact that those already in the ministry exhibit an increasing unwillingness to continue their ministries. Wilson briefly points to several responses to this situation facing the English clergy—all of which he characterizes as "defense mechanisms, mounted for professional survival."

The questions pertaining to the nature of secularity raised by Berger and Shiner in chapter 9 serve as an introduction to the material in chapter 10. The future of "church-oriented religion" in modern society is dubious, at best, according to Luckmann's analysis of religion in contemporary Western society. Basing his conclusions (though not without difficulty as he notes) upon the many studies of church-oriented religion in Europe and America, Luckmann argues that the religion of the churches has become a marginal phenomenon in modern society. That participation in the church (especially in the United States) is still very high cannot be denied. The more important point would seem to be, however, that the symbolic reality of traditional religion is no longer supported by the structure of modern society. Indeed, Luckmann argues that the remaining support for traditional religion as manifest in the churches comes from "social groups and social strata which continue to be oriented toward the values of a past social order." If his conclusions are accurate then the question immediately arises: what, if any, new forms of religion are coming into being to replace the traditional religion of the church?

The second selection in chapter 10 examines a new form and new symbols of the meaning of religion in contemporary society: the Underground Church. While the discussion by Theodore Steeman of "The Underground Church" focuses upon the Roman Catholic faith, many of the features of this movement have their counterpart in Protestantism and, to a lesser extent, Judaism. Indeed, one characteristic of those in the Underground Church is that denominational tags have little importance. Writing from the perspective of the Christian tradition Steeman states that "in the name of Christian renewal and authenticity one must go one's own way often without support from the institutional church and, as the case may be, against it. Initiative does not rest in the institutional church and its authorities and does not respect traditional structures." The Underground Church is not only willing, but feels an imperative necessity to by-pass the structures of the church as they have come to exist.[7] The emphasis is upon *involvement* in the world, and the present authority and structure of the church is perceived, more often than not, as impeding such direct involvement. Steeman maintains, nevertheless (and not everyone working in and studying the Underground Church would agree), that this new religious movement is "an intra-Church phenomenon" which, like the institutional church, is concerned with presenting the Christian message in a new form and content. Both, he argues, are a "part of the larger reality which is the church at large."

The existence of an Underground Church as a part of the contemporary religious scene is, perhaps, not even known to many of those who continue to participate in the traditional religion of the church. The same cannot be said for the subject of the third selection in chapter 10. The use of drugs by both young and old members of this society was one of the most widely publicized phenomena of the 1960s. The debate over the legality and propriety of drug usage continues to occupy the attention of the major institutions of the country from the federal government down to the poorest of the poor families in the ghetto. The legal matters involved in the use of drugs may have overshadowed the concern expressed in Huston Smith's question: "Do Drugs Have Religious Import?" But, for students of religion, the possible religious potentialities of mind-expanding drugs have come to occupy the attention of serious scholars—especially those pursuing the meaning of the religious experience. It should be noted that for many drug users the expectation of a "religious experience" is totally remote from their thinking. On the other hand, the drug user may, whether or not intended, report sensations and experiences which in some religions would be readily identified as a "religious experience." Certainly, however, as Smith notes, many (and prominent) theologians of the Christian persuasion disclaim any religious significance for drug-induced experiences. But, empirical data on drug usage (especially under controlled experiments) suggest, if nothing else, that some users have had experiences which are basically indistinguishable from mystical experiences reported by Christians in other eras. Other users have, of course, experienced only "hellish" results and would argue against any experimentation of this sort to induce an "awareness of God."

Religion is, as the present volume has emphasized throughout, a multifaceted phenomenon and the use of drugs to induce religious experiences can lead to an *overemphasis* upon experience to the exclusion of other dimensions of religiosity. The outcome of such activity can lead to an awareness that "the religious experience is a snare and delusion . . . no religion that fixes its faith primarily in substances that induce religious experience can be expected to come to a good end. What promised to be a short cut will prove to be a short circuit; what began as a religion will end as a religion surrogate." Nevertheless, Smith concludes that "if (as we have insisted) religion cannot be equated with religious experiences, neither can it long survive their absence" and thus the door must not be prematurely closed to the possibility that drugs can *aid* in the proper development of religious awe.

The final selection in chapter 10 explores yet another developing feature of the religious life in the United States: the interest in Eastern religions. Like the use of drugs, the relatively widespread appearance and serious interest in Eastern religions is a recent occurrence in the United States. Previous concern with Eastern religions was largely of a missionary nature: convert the "heathens." Today, however, Eastern theologies have a new appeal and have taken on a new meaning. King attributes this interest, in part, to certain features of contemporary American society: the increased tolerance for new manifestations of religion, the decline of the "manifest destiny" of Protestant America to "bring in the Kingdom of God," and the continuing exploitation and destruction of the natural environment. In such a milieu particular aspects of Eastern religions have appeal, e.g., "the East's sense of a close, even organic, relation to the environment and all its life-processes"; or, the view of man as a "microcosm" in a vastly larger "macrocosm" with which he must integrate and not necessarily dominate. But, as King is careful to note, there is a long religious and political heritage which would have to be overcome before the philosophy or theology of the Eastern religions could hope to occupy even a minor niche in the religious life of the United States: "all American Christianity is still *far* more fundamentalist at heart than most liberals realize." He is not, of course, advocating the continuation of a fundamentalist version of religion but is recognizing simply the reality of forces resistant to the widespread acceptance of new theologies in a country with a religious heritage such as the United States.

---

1. Peter Berger, "Religious Institutions" in Neil Smelser, ed., *Sociology: An Introduction* (New York: John Wiley, 1967), p. 359.

2. Seymour M. Lipset, "Political Sociology" in Neil Smelser, ed., *op. cit.,* p. 473.

3. A clarification of these often loosely defined sociological terms is in order here. *Urbanism* is a short-hand term for a complex phenomenon which may be defined as "a

pattern of existence which deals with (1) the accommodation of heterogeneous groups to one another; (2) a relatively high degree of specialization in labor; (3) involvement in nonagricultural occupational pursuits; (4) a market economy; (5) an interplay between innovation and change as against the maintenance of societal traditions; (6) development of advanced learning and the arts; and (7) tendencies toward city-based, centralized governmental structure." *Urbanization* is another short-hand term referring to "the processes by which (1) urban values are diffused, (2) movement occurs from rural areas to cities, and (3) behavior patterns are transformed to conform to those which are characteristic of groups in the cities." (See: Paul Meadows and Ephraim H. Mizruchi, eds., *Urbanism, Urbanization, and Change: Comparative Perspectives* [Reading, Mass.: Addison-Wesley Publishing Company, 1969], p. 2.) Such a way of life is not peculiar to the Western world and existed in various degrees prior to the Industrial Revolution. (See: Gideon Sjoberg, *The Preindustrial City* [Glencoe, Illinois: Free Press, 1960].)

4. Just what constitutes a "secular" society and the exact meaning of secularization is the subject of article 1, chapter 9, by Shiner. The nature of a causal relationship between the growth of modern societies with urban characteristics and secularization is extremely complex, and simple generalizations should be avoided. Harvey Cox, for example, sees the "rise of urban civilization and the collapse of traditional religion" as "closely related movements," but other data suggest the wisdom of a high degree of caution in such interpretations. (See: Harvey Cox, *The Secular City* [New York: Macmillan, 1965]; but see also, Herbert Gans, *The Urban Villagers* [Glencoe, Illinois: Free Press, 1962]; and, for cross-cultural perspectives, see Edward M. Bruner, "Urbanization and Ethnic Identity in North Sumatra," *American Anthropologist* 63 [June 1961]:508-21.)

5. Of course, Hadden's study (article 1, chapter 3) argues that the developing crisis in the church is between those leaders who wish to do more than "contemplate" their budgets and those laity who are content to do little else. An area of potential fruitful research in the sociology of religion is to explore the factors associated with the ability of some clergy to involve their churches in social action while others find themselves "without a pulpit" if they undertake such activity.

6. Wilson's stress on the increasing number of older Anglican clergy is accurate but calls for additional clarification. In the time period which he refers to, 1901–61, the life-span in Western society increased dramatically. Thus, the fact that in 1901 only 5.87 percent of Anglican clergy were 75 years or older while in 1961 11.97 percent were 75 or over can be partly attributed to the fact that the clergyman (as well as others) now lives longer. This would also have a tendency to reduce the demand for younger recruits.

7. Although, of course, such movements, to the extent that they are successful, come to take on institutional features themselves (see, for example, Thomas O'Dea, "Five Dilemmas in the Institutionalization of Religion," *Journal for the Scientific Study of Religion* 1 [October 1961]:32-39). They are, furthermore, minority movements affecting a very small proportion of those involved in the church. Nevertheless, the Wesleyan revival of the 18th century was, at the outset, a minority protest against the Church of England which in time came to be one of the largest Protestant bodies in the world. On the other hand, the Jesuit protest of the 16th century was successful but was incorporated *within* the main institutional features of the Roman Catholic Church. The outcome of the Underground Church is, at the present time, uncertain.

Chapter 8
The Church in an Urban Environment

TALCOTT PARSONS

Christianity and Modern Industrial Society

The present volume is conceived as a tribute to Professor Sorokin as a distinguished elder statesman of sociology, not only in the United States but also throughout the world. One of the highest achievements, particularly in a rapidly developing discipline in its early phases of development, is to serve as a generator and focus of creatively important differences of opinion. Such differences pose problems which, though not solved or in any immediate sense soluble in the generation in question, still serve to orient the thinking of professional groups. For such differences to be fruitful there must be a delicate balance of commonly accepted premises, which make a fruitful meeting of minds possible, and difference of interpretation in more particularized questions which are open to some sort of empirical test.

In the sociological profession today Professor Sorokin and the present author are probably defined predominantly as antagonists who have taken widely different views on a variety of subjects.[1] The objective of this chapter is to take explicit cognizance of one, to me crucial, field of such difference of opinion, but to attempt to place it within a framework of common problems in the hope that consideration of the difference may help others toward a fruitful solution of these problems.

In the highly empirical atmosphere of American sociology in recent times there has been a tendency to neglect the importance of the great problems of the trends of development of Western society and culture in a large sense, of its place relative to the great civilizations of the Orient, and similar problems. Within this field the problem of the role of religion and its relation to social values stands in a particularly central position. In my opinion it is one of Sorokin's great services to have held these problems consistently in the forefront of concern, and to have refused to be satisfied with a sociology which did not have anything significant to say about them. In this fundamental respect Sorokin stands in the great tradition of Western sociological thought. This emphasis coincides with my own strong predilections, shaped as they were by European experience under the influences in particular of Max Weber and Durkheim.

It can, I think, safely be said that we share the convictions, first, of the enormous importance of the general evolutionary and comparative perspective in the interpretation of social phenomena and, second, of the crucial role of religion and its relation to values in this large perspective. When, however, we turn to more particular problems of spelling out this context, differences of opinion emerge. A particularly important test case is that of the interpretation of the relations of religious orientation, values, and social structure in the course of that development in the modern Western world which has eventuated in modern industrialism. I propose to set over against a very schematic but I hope accurate outline of Sorokin's view, my own, which I think may be the kind of alternative which, though differing sharply from his view, may pose fruitful empirical questions on which future research may be expected to throw light. Only in this broadest contrast will I attempt to take account of the Sorokin position. My objective is not to present either a full statement or a critique of his conceptions as such, but to state my own as clearly as possible.

The heart of the Sorokin position which is relevant here I take to be his classification and use of three fundamental types of cultural orientation—the "ideational," "idealistic," and "sensate."[2] What may be called orientations in terms of the grounds of meaning on the one hand and values for social and personal conduct on the other, are treated as by and large varying together.

The ideational pattern is one which gives unquestionable primacy to transcendental and other-worldly interests in the religious sense. Reality itself is defined as ultimately beyond the reach of the senses, as transcendental. The goal of life must be to reach the closest possible accord with the nature of transcendent reality, and the path to this must involve renunciation of all worldly interests. Broadly speaking, other-worldly asceticism and mysticism are the paths to it. The ethical component which is so prominent in Christianity generally is not missing from Sorokin's conception. It takes, however, the form on which his later work has placed increasing stress: that of altruistic love, of pure personal selfless acts of love by individuals. In this discussion I would like to differentiate this form of altruism from the *institutionalization* of Christian ethics to become part of the structure of the society itself. It is the latter with which my analysis will be concerned.

The opposite extreme to the ideational pattern is the sensate. Here the empirical, in the last analysis the "material," aspect of reality is taken as ultimately real or predominant. In practical conduct the implication of a sensate view of the world is to make the most of the opportunities of the here and now, to be concerned with world success, power, and —in the last analysis—to put hedonistic gratifications first of all.

The idealistic pattern is conceived as intermediate between the two, not in the sense of a simple "compromise," but rather of a synthesis which can achieve a harmonious balance between the two principal components.

This basic classification is then used as the framework for outlining a developmental pattern leading, in the history of a civilization, from ideational to idealistic predominance and in turn from idealistic to sensate. Though very generally applied, the two most important cases dealt with in Sorokin's works are the civilization of classical antiquity and that of the Christian West. In both cases there was an early ideational phase which gradually gave way to an idealistic synthesis: in the classical that of fifth-century Greece, in the Western that of the high Middle Ages. The idealistic synthesis has then proceeded to break down into an increasingly sensate phase—in the classical case the late Hellenistic and Roman periods, in the Western the modern "capitalistic" or industrial period. Sorokin tends to regard the contemporary period, exemplified particularly in the United States, but also in the Soviet Union, as close to the peak of the sensate phase of development and destined for a general breakdown comparable to that of Greco-Roman civilization before a new ideational pattern can become established.

From one point of view the general developmental trend Sorokin outlines may be described as a progressive decline in the "religiousness" of the society and culture until a radical reversal is forced by a general societal breakdown. In the Western case the phase of early Christianity was the most religious, characterized by a primarily ascetic disregard for virtually all worldly interests, and the practice of brotherly love within the Christian community itself. Correspondingly, however, Christianity in this phase had little power to organize social relationships beyond the church. With the development of the idealistic phase, however, for a time it was possible to permeate secular life with at least an approximation of Christian ethics, but the balance was precarious and broke down relatively soon.

There may well be a considerable measure of agreement up to this point. Sorokin, however, clearly regards Protestantism, compared with medieval Catholicism, as primarily a step in the general decline of religiousness, and the secularism which has been prominent since the Age of the Enlightenment as the natural further step in the same direction. It is hence on the interpretation of Protestantism in the general process of Western social development and its sequel after the Reformation period that I would like to focus my own view. It will be necessary, however, to say a few things about more general theoretical orientation, and about the earlier historical phases as background for this analysis.

An Alternative Interpretation

There are two interrelated theoretical issues which need to be discussed briefly before entering into a historical analysis. These concern factors in the structure of a religious orientation itself on the one hand and the senses in which religious orientations and their institutionalization in the social system can undergo processes of structural differentiation on the other.

In the former respect Professor Sorokin seems to think primarily in terms of a single variable which might be called "degree of religiousness." This in turn tends to be identified with transcendental orientation in the sense of *other-worldliness* as defining the acceptable field of interest and activity. This is to say that, so far as religious interests are in any sense paramount in a motivational system, the religious person will tend to renounce the world and engage so far as possible in ascetic or devotional practices or mystical contemplation and purely spontaneous acts of love, reducing his involvement in "practical" affairs which involve institutionalized obligations to a minimum. He will therefore tend to be oriented to the reduction of all desires to participate positively and actively in worldly activities like political or economic functions. By the same token, positive commitment to such worldly interests and responsibilities is taken as an index of relative lack of religious interest.

Relative to the degree of religiousness we suggest the relevance of a second variable which we think is independent. This is the one which Max Weber formulated as the variation between other-worldly and inner-worldly orientation. Combined with a high degree of religiousness, the choice of one alternative leads to religious rejection of the world, the choice of the other to an orientation to mastery over the world in the name of religious values. There are further complications in the problem of a general typology of religious orientations, but suffice it to say for the present that I propose to explore the possibilities implicit in the hypothesis that Western Christianity belongs in the category of orientation which is high in degree of religiousness, with a predominantly inner-worldly orientation so far as the field of expected action of the individual is concerned. In ways I shall try to explain, this applies even to early and medieval Christianity, but becomes most clearly evident in "ascetic Protestantism." I feel that this hypothesis is excluded by Sorokin's assumption that religiousness *ipso facto* implies otherworldliness, supplemented only by spontaneous altruism.

The second main theoretical point concerns the question of differentiation. I think of religion as an aspect of human action. Like all other aspects, in the course of social, cultural, and personality development it undergoes processes of differentiation in a double sense. The first of these concerns differentiation within religious systems themselves, the second the differentiation of the religious element from nonreligious elements in the more general system of action. In the latter context the general developmental trend may be said to be from fusions of religious and nonreligious components in the same action structures, to increasingly clear differentiation between multiple spheres of action.

A special problem arises when we deal with a system over a sufficiently long period of time to include two or more stages in a process of differentiation. Structural parts of the system have to be named. It is in the nature of the process of differentiation that what was one part at an earlier stage becomes two or more distinct parts at a later. The simple logical question then is whether the name applied at the earlier stage is still used to designate any one of the parts surviving at the later. If the process is one of differentiation, clearly the surviving entity which carries the same name will be narrower in scope and more "specialized" in the later than it was in the earlier stage. It will then, by mere logic, have lost function and become less important than in the earlier phase. The problem then becomes one of analyzing the continuities, not only of the component called by the same name in the different stages, e.g., *religion,* but also of the senses in which the patterns of orientation given in the earlier stages have or have not been fundamentally altered in their significance for the system as a whole, considering the exigencies of the situations in which action takes place and the complex relations of this part to the other parts of the more differentiated system, e.g., the non-religious or secular.

It is my impression that Professor Sorokin has not given sufficient weight to these considerations and has tended to measure the influence of religion, from earlier to later stages, as if it were reasonable to expect maintenance of the same "degree of inclusiveness" in the direct "definition of the situation" for action which it enjoyed in the early stage of reference. Judged by this standard the degree of religiousness of Christian society has clearly suffered a progressive decline by the mere fact that the society has become functionally a more highly differentiated system of action than was the early "primitive" church.

The Setting of the Problem: Christianity—Society

As a first step it is necessary to outline a few essentials of the nature of the early Christian church and its relations to the secular society of the time. Its structure comprised, as is well known, a very distinctive synthesis of elements derived from Judaism, Greek philosophy, the Greek conception of social organization, and of course distinctive contributions of its own.

The Hebrew and the Greek patterns had in common the conception of a solidary, religiously sanctioned social unit, the organization of which was based on values fully transcending the loyalties of kinship. In the Hebrew case it was the confederation of "tribes" bound to Jahweh and to each other by the Covenant. These units became fused into a "people" whose main orientation to life was defined in terms of the Law given to them by Jahweh, a firm collectivity structure defining its role as the fulfillment of God's commandments. In the historical course, by what precise stages need not concern us here, two crucial developments occurred. First Jahweh became a completely universal transcendental God who governed the activities not only of the people of Israel but of all mankind. Second, the people of Israel became, through the exile, depoliticized. Their religion was the essential bond of solidarity. Since this was no longer expressed in an independent political community, it was not exposed to the "secularizing" influences so importantly involved in political responsibility.

On the Greek side the *polis* was a comparable solidary confederation, in the first instance of kinship lineages. It was the "political" society almost par excellence, but one which eventually came to be based on the principle of the universalistic equality of citizens. Religiously it was oriented not to a transcendental God but to an immanent polytheism. The conception of the ultimate unity of divinity emerged in Greek civilization, but essentially as a philosophical principle the necessity of which was demonstrated by reason.

Seen against the background of Judaism and in certain respects also of the Greek component, the most important distinctive feature of Christianity of importance here was its religious individualism. In Judaism the primary religious concern was the fate of the Jewish community as God's chosen people. In Christianity it became the fate of the individual soul; God was concerned with the salvation of individuals, not simply with the extent to which a social community as such adhered to His commandments.

This new conception of the relation of the individual soul to God might seem, given the fundamental transcendental character of the God of Judaism, to imply the virtual abandonment of concern with life in the world, to make the life of the Christian center primarily in devotional interests in preparing for the life to come. Indeed this strain in Christianity has always been a crucially important one and marks it off sharply from the main trend of Judaism. In this respect Christianity, however different its theological orientation, was closely analogous to Indian religion. But there was another aspect to Christian individualism: the fact that its adherents came to constitute a very special type of social collectivity on earth, the Christian church. The theological significance of the Christ figure as the mediator between God and man is central as defining the nature of man's relation to God, in and through the Church of Christ. It was the conception of the church which underlay the nature of the ethical conception of Christianity and was the basis from which the moral influence of Christianity could operate on secular society.

In theoretical terms this may be expressed by saying that the conception of the church, which implied the fundamental break with the Jewish law which Paul made final, constituted the *differentiation* of Christianity as a religious system (a cultural system) from the conception of a "people" as a social system. Given the Roman ascendancy in the secular society of the time, this differentiation was expressed in the famous formula "Render unto Caesar the things that are Caesar's"—i.e., the church did not claim jurisdiction over secular society as such.

At the same time this church was a solidary collectivity. The keynote here was the conception of "brothers in Christ." Its members were by no means concerned only with their respective personal salvations, but with the mission of Christ on behalf of mankind. This had the dual meaning of an obligation to extend the Christian community by proselytizing and, within it, to organize its internal relations on the basis in the first instance of mutual brotherly love.

Though, religiously speaking, this was a radically individualistic doctrine, it was not an anarchistic, but what we have come to call an "institutionalized" individualism. The Christian doctrine of the Trinity, compared with Jewish unitarianism, is intimately connected with this development. Instead of a single "line" of relationship between an ultimately transcendental God and man, God became related to man *through* the Christ figure who was both God and Man, and Christ became the head of the Church, the "essence" of which was formulated as the third person of the Trinity, the Holy Spirit.

As I interpret it, this implied, correlative with the differentiation of the church from secular society, a differentiation *within* the religious system itself, in the broadest respect between the aspect of devotion and worship on the one hand, and the aspect of the Christian's relation to his fellow men on the other. The Christian community was constituted by the fact of common faith and common worship, but the contexts in which worship was paramount were differentiated from the context of love and charity which bound the community together in bonds of human mutuality.

From the present point of view this differentiation was just as important as the first, and intimately connected with it. The Jewish law had held the individual to highly detailed prescriptions of conduct which were "rationalized" for the most part only in the sense that they were declared to be Divine commandments. Now, as a member of the church he was held to a set of principles of conduct—the obligation to act in accord with the Holy Spirit. And though obviously directly connected with his commitment to God through faith, conduct in this world could be made to a degree independent of this, above all, in the sense that detailed prescriptions of behavior were not taken as religiously given but only the general principles of ethical action. Thus action decisions in particular cases had to be left to the conscience of believers and could not be prescribed by a comprehensive religious law. The context of worship was an independent context which generated motivation to act in accord with the spirit, but was not exactly the same thing as this action.

This differentiation occurred, however, within a genuine unity. The key theological problem here was the doctrine of the Creation and whether it implied an ontological dualism. In the great formative period this came to a head in the struggle with Manichaeism, and Augustine's fundamental decision against the latter broadly settled the issue. The sphere of the church as that part of man's life on earth directly dominated by the Holy Spirit was then a point of mediation between the direct expression of Divine will through Christ and the rest of the

Creation. But the implication was that this remainder of the Creation could not be governed by an ontologically independent principle of evil and was hence inherently subject to Christianization.

Thus religious individualism, in the sense in which it became institutionalized in the Christian church, represented, relative to Judaism, a new autonomy of the individual on two fronts. In his own relation to God as an object of worship, the individual was released from his ascriptive embeddedness in the Jewish community. Whatever the relation of dependence on God implied in this, it was as an individual in the religious relation that he could be saved. There was also a new autonomy in his relation to the field of human action, in the first instance as a member of the church and in his relations to his fellow members in brotherly love. The church was an association of believers, manifesting their attachment to God in their conduct in this world. The church was thus independent, not an ascribed aspect of a total society. There was hence, through these channels, a basic legitimation of the importance of life in this world, but in a situation where the church could reserve a basic independence from those aspects of secular society not felt to be permeated with the Holy Spirit.

Life in this world clearly includes human society. Indeed the church itself is clearly a social entity. But the early Christians judged the secular society of their time, that of the Roman Empire, to be ethically unacceptable, so the Christian life had to be led essentially within the church. This was connected with the Chiliastic expectation of an imminent Last Judgment. But gradually this expectation faded and the church faced the problem of continuing to live *in* the world and of attempting to come to some sort of long-run terms with the rest of the society outside itself.

I have stressed both the social character of the church and its radical break from the Jewish community because the pattern I have sketched formed a basic set of conditions under which Christian orientations could exert a kind of influence on secular society different from that which was possible to religion in the Jewish pattern. First, proselytizing on a grand scale was possible without carrying along the whole society immediately. While conversion to Judaism meant accepting full membership in the total Jewish community, a converted Christian could remain a Roman, a Corinthian, or whatever; his new social participation was confined to the church itself. There were important points at which the church potentially and actually conflicted with the societies of the time, but most of them could be solved by relative nonparticipation in "public affairs."

If in this respect the church limited its claims on its members, it also maintained a position of independence from which further influence could be exerted. It established a "place to stand" from which to exert leverage, and it developed a firm organization to safeguard that place. But the process was not to be one of absorption of the secular society into the religious community itself; it was rather one of acceptance of the fundamental *differentiation* between church and state, but the attempt to define the latter as subject to Christian principles.

There were certainly tendencies to a radical rejection of secular society in principle, but at least for the Western branch of Christianity by the time of St. Augustine the door was opened to the possibility that a Christian society as a whole could be attained. The most important vehicle for this trend was the building into Christian thought of the Greco-Roman conception of natural law. This implied a differentiation of life between spiritual and temporal spheres and a *relative* legitimation of the temporal, provided it was ordered in accordance with natural law. From this point of view, Roman society could be defined as evil, not because it was a secular society as such, but because as a society it failed to live up to norms present in its own culture.

The other principal focus of the process of Christianizing of society lay in the implications of the attempt to universalize Christian adherence within the society. Christianity was gradually transformed from a sect that remained aloof and in principle expected a Christian life only for the segregated special group of its own members into *the* church which was the trustee of the religious interests of the whole population. In proportion as this happened, persons in positions of responsibility in secular society automatically became Christians, and the question could not but arise of the relation between their church membership and their secular responsibilities. The focus of the emerging conception was that of the Christian monarch. The great symbolic event in this whole connection was the coronation of Charlemagne by the Pope. The symbolism of this event was dual. It was an act by the head of the church of legitimation of secular authority, which could be interpreted as the definitive ending of the conception of aloofness on the part of the church, of the position that it could take no moral responsibility in relation to the secular sphere. It also symbolized the acceptance by the monarch of the obligation to act, in his capacity as chief of government, as a Christian. Church and state then symbolically *shared* their commitment to Christian values.

It is not, in my opinion, correct to interpret this as the subordination of secular authority to the church. It was definitely a putting of the seal of religious legitimacy on the differentiation of the two spheres and their fundamental independence from each other as organized collectivities. But a true differentiation always involves at the same time an allegiance to common values and norms. In terms of the ultimate trusteeship of these values, the church is the higher authority. Perhaps a good analogy is the administration of the oath of office to an incoming American President by the Chief Justice of the Supreme Court. This clearly does not mean that the Chief Justice is the "real" chief of government and the President his organizational subordinate. What it means is rather that the Supreme Court is the ultimate interpreter of the Constitution, and the legitimation of presidential office by the Chief Justice is a symbolization of the subordination of the Presidency to constitutional law, which is equally binding on the Court.

In very broad outline this seems to be the way the stage was set for the development of a process of the "Christianizing" of secular society, not, be it repeated, through absorption of secular spheres into the "religious life" in the sense of the life of the church or its religious orders, but by exerting influence on a life which remained by the church's own definition secular, hence, in the Catholic phase, religiously inferior to the highest, but still potentially at least quite definitely Christian.[3]

The first main phase was the medieval synthesis, which produced a great society and culture. But from the present point of view it must also be considered a stage in a process of development. The dynamic forces which led beyond the medieval pattern were in the present view inherent on both the religious and the secular sides. Brief consideration of some of the essential constituents which both went into the medieval synthesis and led beyond it will help to lay a foundation for understanding a little of the mechanisms by which a religious influence could be exerted on secular society.

First let us take the church itself. Differentiation of the church from secular society represented in one sense a renunciation of influence on secular life. There was no longer a detailed, divinely sanctioned law to prescribe all secular conduct. This may, however, be looked on as a kind of renunciation similar to that involved in a process of investment, a step toward a higher order of "productive" results in the future by a more roundabout process. Here resources are not simply mobilized to maximize shortrun production. Some current resources are diverted into temporarily "unproductive" channels in uses which prepare a later production effort. To do this, however, this set of resources must be protected against pressures for their immediate consumption. In the religious case the church was such a base of operations which was kept secure from absorption in the secular life of the time. Such pressures to absorption were indeed very prominent in the period after Constantine, in the West perhaps above all through the tendency of bishops to become heavily involved in secular political and economic interests.

The most important single fortress for the maintenance of the purity of religious orientation through this period was certainly the religious orders where segregated communities were devoted to a special religious life. Even this, however, had its this-worldly aspect, notably through the place taken by useful work in the Benedictine rule, which in many cases expanded into a generally high level of economic rationality. Furthermore the orders served as a highly important direct ground for the development of social organization itself; there were highly organized communities, administered in much more universalistic and less traditionalized ways than was most of the secular society of the time.

Secondly, however, that part of the church which served the laity through the secular clergy in the early medieval period underwent a major reform, significantly under monastic impetus. This of course is particularly associated with the Cluniac order and the name of Pope Gregory VII, himself a Cluniac monk. In one major aspect at least, it consisted of an extension of the monastic conception of purity of religious orientation to the roles of the secular clergy. There were two particularly important and closely related points here. One was the final defeat of the Donatist heresy and the firm establishment of the principle that priesthood was an office with powers and authority clearly separable from the person of the individual incumbent, or any particularistic network of relationships in which he might be involved. The second was the doctrine of clerical celibacy, which not only had not previously been enforced but also had not even been firmly established as a policy, and never was in the Eastern church.

These crucial reforms had two orders of significance. First, they served to consolidate and extend the independence of the church from secular influences. The particularly important extension was of course to the region of most direct and continuing contact with the laity through the secular clergy. Second, however, the structure of the medieval church came to serve, well beyond the Orders, as a model of social organization which could be extended into secular society. As Lea made so clear, in a society very largely dominated by the hereditary principle, clerical celibacy had a special significance.[4] Put in sociological terms, we may say that it made possible a social island which institutionalized a universalistic basis of role-allocation manifested in careers open to talent. The clergy was of course very far from being immune to class influence and at various times bishoprics and cardinalates were virtually monopolized by narrow circles of noble lineages. But this is not to say that the institution of celibacy and with it the barrier to inheritance of clerical office was unimportant.

There also was an intimate connection between the conception of clerical office which became crystallized in the Middle Ages and the building of much of Roman law into the structure of the church itself through canon law. In place of the relatively unrationalized and historically particularized Jewish law, the Christian church developed for its own internal use a highly rationalized and codified body of norms which underlay the legal structure of the whole subsequent development of Western society. Certainly the reception of secular Roman law in the late Middle Ages could not have happened without this.

Closely related to the church's use of Roman law was the place it made for the secular intellectual culture of antiquity. There is a sense in which this was already implicit in the place taken by Greek philosophy in theology itself. It was greatly reinforced by adoption of the conception of natural law as governing the secular sphere. Its medieval phase culminated in the very central place accorded to the work of Aristotle by Thomas Aquinas.

There was, however, also a structural aspect of the place of intellectual culture. Though in the earlier period it was only in the monasteries that the culture of antiquity was preserved and cultivated at all, as the medieval universities began to develop, the role of scholar and teacher assumed an important degree of independence both from the orders and from the hierarchy of the church. Though most of the schoolmen were monks, as scholars and teachers their activity was not directly controlled by their orders or chapters, nor by the bishops of the territories where they worked and taught. In terms of the crucial role of intellectual culture in later social development, notably through the rise of science, the structural basis of its independence is of an importance hardly to be exaggerated. This is perhaps the most critical single point of difference between the development of Western Christianity and of Islam, since in the latter case the influence of orthodoxy was able to suppress the independence of the scholarly class who had made such brilliant beginnings in the reception and extension of classical culture. The church's censure of Galileo should not be allowed to obscure the fact that, compared to other religious systems, Catholic Christianity made a place for an independent intellectual culture which is unique among all the great religions in their medieval phase.

There is one further important focus of the synthesis between medieval Christianity and the classical heritage. The universalism of Christianity held up a conception of moral order for Christendom as a whole, with Christendom ideally expected eventually to comprise all mankind. This matched and was without doubt greatly influenced by the Roman conception of a universal sociopolitical order governed by a single universal system of law, a natural law coming to be institutionalized as the law of a politically organized society.

In basic Christian thinking, the Roman Empire as the secular order of the world had never ceased to exist, But since Charlemagne it could be defined as the *Holy* Roman Empire, as the normative framework of a universal Christian society. The empirical course of political development in Europe was to be such as to make this dream of unity under law in some respects progressively less realistic, at least for a very considerable period. Nevertheless the importance of the conception of a universal order should not be underestimated.

I have argued above that Christianity originally involved a cultural "marriage" between Judaic and Greco-Roman components. Though the early church repudiated the secular society of the contemporary Roman Empire, the above considerations make it quite clear that the normative aspect of classical culture was not repudiated; essentially a fundamental trusteeship of this heritage was built into the basic structure of the Christian church itself. It became the primary source from which this heritage was rediffused into the secular world and became the basis for further developments which somehow had failed to materialize in the ancient world. It is essential to my general argument here that this was a genuine integration.

Perhaps particularly from a Protestant point of view it is common to think of medieval Catholicism as mainly a pattern of compromise between a set of religious ideals and the exigencies of life in the world. It is quite true that, as Troeltsch so clearly brings out, the conception was that of a series of levels of closeness to and distance from full contact with the Divine, with the monastic life at the top. But this is not to say that positive religious sanction was withheld from everything except devotional self-sacrifice, that for example natural law was thought of merely as a concession to human weakness. Very much on the contrary, a secular world governed by natural law was thought of as ordained by God, as the part of His Creation which was to serve as the field for man's activity. Secular society was, to be sure, a field of temptation, but also of opportunity to lead a Christian life. And an essential part of the Christian life came to be the control, if not the shaping, of secular society in the interest of Christian ideals.

Professor Sorokin is quite right, I feel, in regarding this as a synthesis rather than merely a compromise. But, as noted, it is my view that this was not the end of the road, the point from which the process of religious decline started, but rather an essential station on a road which has led much farther. A few more general things about the nature of the process need to be said. The point of view I am taking here is meant to be very far indeed from any idealistic "emanationist" conception of the process of social development.

A crucial initial point is the one stressed throughout, that the church was from the beginning *itself* a special type of social organization. We do not have to think of the cultural aspect of Christianity as socially "disembodied" and suddenly, by a kind of sociological miracle, taking over the control of a society. On the contrary, it developed, survived, and exerted its influence through the same kinds of processes of interaction between cultural and social systems which operate in other connections. First, we have noted, it maintained and consolidated its independence, and developed its own internal structure. Second, it became diffused so that, within the society in which it operated, it could assume that the whole population was, in the religious sphere, subject to its jurisdiction; it successfully eliminated all organized internal religious competition—by "propaganda" and various types of more or less political process.

It had in its own social structure institutionalized a set of values. Through the universality of membership in it, it had the opportunity to play a critical part in the socialization process for all members of the society. Though not directly controlling secular social organization, at certain levels of personality its "definition of the situation" and the importance of its special sanctions could, however imperfectly, be universalized. There was much revolt and much "backsliding," but relatively little indifference to the Christian point of view was possible. The long-run influence of such a set of forces should not be underestimated.

The church was not only an agency of reward for approved behavior and punishment of what it disapproved. It was a crucial focus of psychological support over a very wide range of human concerns—its role in administration of the *rites de passage* is a good index of this position. Finally it was a source of direct models, not only for values at the most general level, but for modes of organizing social relationship patterns at a relatively general normative level, in such fields as law, and careers open to talent.

This phase of the "Christianization" of secular society can, like others, be summed up in terms of a formula which has proved useful in other connections for the analysis of the progressive type of change in a social system.[5] Given a base in an institutionalized value system (in this case in the church) there have been three main aspects of the process. First there has been *extension* of the range of institutionalization of the values, above all through the influence on the laity through the secular clergy. Secondly, there has been a process of further *differentiation.* The church itself has become further differentiated internally in that its sacramental system has been more clearly marked off from its administrative system, and its system of prescriptions for the ethical life of Christians through the canon law more clearly differentiated from both the others. At the same time the differentiation of the church *from* secular society has become more clearly marked. There has been a process of disengagement of the church from secular society through much more stringent control of the political and economic interests of bishops and clergy, and through sacerdotal celibacy. The beginnings of a revived Roman civil law have greatly aided in this process by more clearly defining the normative order of secular society.

Finally, third, there was a process of *upgrading* in terms of fulfillment of the requirements of the value system. Internally to the church itself this is the primary meaning of its internal reform, the strengthening of its administration, the elevation of standards in the orders and among the secular clergy. Externally, it was the gradual pressure toward a higher ethical standard among the lay population. The immense lay participation in enterprises like the building of the cathedrals is the most conspicuously manifest aspect of the general wave of "religious enthusiasm" in the Middle Ages.

The Reformation Phase

Perhaps the most important principle of the relation between religion and society which was institutionalized in the Middle Ages was that of the *autonomy* of secular society, of the "state" in the medieval sense, relative to the church, but within a Christian framework. The Christianity of secular society was guaranteed, not by the subjection of secular life to a religious law, but by the *common* commitment of ecclesiastical and temporal personnel to Christian faith. The Reformation may be seen, from one point of view, as a process of the extension of this principle of autonomy[6] to the internal structure of religious organization itself, with profound consequences both for the structure of the churches and for their relation to secular society. It may be regarded as a further major step in the same line as the original Christian break with Judaism.

The essential point may be stated as the religious "enfranchisement" of the individual, often put as his coming to stand in a direct relation to God. The Catholic Church had emancipated the individual as part of its own corporate entity, from the Jewish law and its special social community, and had given him a notable autonomy within the secular sphere. But within its own definition of the religious sphere it had kept him under a strict tutelage by a set of mechanisms of which the sacraments were the core. By Catholic doctrine the only access to Divine grace was through the sacraments administered by a duly ordained priest. Luther broke through this tutelage to make the individual a *religiously* autonomous entity, responsible for his own religious concerns, not only in the sense of accepting the ministrations and discipline of the church but also through making his own fundamental religious commitments.

This brought faith into an even more central position than before. It was no longer the commitment to accept the particularized obligations and sacraments administered by the Church, but to act on the more general level in accordance with God's will. Like all reciprocal relationships, this one could be "tipped" one way or the other. In the Lutheran case it was tipped far in what in certain senses may be called the "authoritarian" direction; grace was interpreted to come only from the completely "undetermined" Divine action and in no sense to be dependent on the performances of the faithful, but only on their "receptivity." In this sense Lutheranism might be felt to deprive the individual of autonomy rather than enhancing it. But this would be an incorrect interpretation. The essential point is that the individual's dependence on the *human* mediation of the church and its priesthood through the sacraments was eliminated and *as a human being* he had, under God, to rely on his own independent responsibility; he could not "buy" grace or absolution from a human agency empowered to dispense it. In this situation the very uncertainties of the individual's relation to God, an uncertainty driven to its extreme by the Calvinistic doctrine of predestination, could, through its definition of the situation for religious interests, produce a powerful impetus to the acceptance of individual responsibility. The more deeply felt his religious need, the sharper his sense of unworthiness, the more he had to realize that no human agency could relieve him of his responsibility; "mother" church was no longer available to protect and comfort him.

An immediate consequence was the elimination of the fundamental distinction in moral-religious quality between the religious life in the Catholic sense and life in secular "callings." It was the individual's direct relation to God which counted from the human side, his faith. This faith was not a function of any particular set of ritual or semi-magical practices, or indeed even of "discipline" except in the most general sense of living according to Christian principles. The core of the special meaning of the religious life had been the sacramental conception of the earning of "merit" and this was fundamentally dependent on the Catholic conception of the power of the sacraments.

From one point of view, that of the special powers of the *church* as a social organization, this could be regarded as a crucial loss of function, and the Lutheran conception of the fundamental religious equivalence of all callings as secularization. My interpretation, however, is in accord with Max Weber's; the more important change was not the removal of religious legitimation from the special monastic life, but rather, the endowment of secular life with a new order of religious legitimation as a field of "Christian opportunity." If the ordinary man, assumed of course to be a church member, stood in direct relation to God, and could be justified by his faith, the *whole person* could be justified, including the life he led in everyday affairs. The counterpart of eliminating the sacramental mediation of the secular priesthood was eliminating also the special virtues of the religious. It was a case of further *differentiation* within the Christian framework.

Protestantism in its Lutheran phase underwent a process, analogous to that of the early church, of relative withdrawal from direct involvement in the affairs of secular society. With the overwhelming Lutheran emphasis on faith and the importance of the individual's *subjective* sense of justification, there was, as Weber pointed out, a strong tendency to interpret the concept of the calling in a passive, traditionalist, almost Pauline sense. It was the individual's relation to his God that mattered; only in a sense of nondiscrimination was his secular calling sanctified, in that it was just as good, religiously speaking, as that of the monk.

We have, however, maintained that the conception of the generalization of a Christian pattern of life was an inherent possibility in the Christian orientation from the beginning and it came early to the fore in the Reformation period in the Calvinistic, or more broadly the ascetic, branch of the movement. Here we may say that the religious status of secular callings was extended from that of a principle of basic nondiscrimination to one of their endowment with positive instrumental significance. The key conception was that of the divine ordination of the establishment of the Kingdom of God on Earth. This went beyond the negative legitimation of secular callings to the assignment of a positive *function* to them in the divine plan.

In terms of its possibility of exerting leverage over secular society this was by far the most powerful version of the conception of the possibility of a "Christian society" which had yet appeared. First, the stepwise hierarchy of levels of religious merit, so central to the Thomistic view, was eliminated by Luther. Then the individual became the focus not only of secular but also of religious responsibility emancipated from tutelary control by a sacramental church. Finally, precisely in his secular calling the individual was given a positive assignment to work in the building of the Kingdom.

The consequence of this combination was that, with one important exception, every major factor in the situation converged upon the dynamic exploitation of opportunity to change social life in the direction of conformity with religiously grounded ideals.

The basic assumption is that for Protestants the Christian commitment was no less rigorous than it had been for Catholics; if anything it was more so. In both Lutheran and Calvinistic versions the conception was one of the most rigorous submission of the individual's life to divine will. But in defining the situation for implementing this role of "creature," the Protestant position differed from the Catholic broadly as the definition of the preschool child's role relative to his parents differs from that of the school-age child's relation to his teacher. Within the family, important as the element of discipline and expectations of learning to perform are, the primary focus is on responsibility of the parents for the welfare and security of their children; the permeation of Catholic thought with familial symbolism along these lines is striking indeed.

In the school, on the other hand, the emphasis shifts. The teacher is primarily an agent of instruction, responsible for welfare, yes, but this is not the primary function; it is rather to help to equip the child for a responsible role in society when his education has been completed. To a much higher degree the question of how far he takes advantage of his opportunities becomes his own responsibility. Thus the function of the Protestant ministry became mainly a teaching function, continually holding up the Christian doctrine as a model of life to their congregations. But they no longer held a parental type of tutelary power to confer or deny the fundamentals of personal religious security.

If the analogy may be continued, the Lutheran position encouraged a more passive orientation in this situation, a leaving of the more ultimate responsibility to God, an attitude primarily of receptivity to Grace. (This is the exception referred to above—one of relatively short-run significance.) Such an attitude would tend to be generalized to worldly superiors and authorities, including both ministers and secular teachers. Ascetic Protestantism, on the other hand, though at least equally insistent on the divine origins of norms and values for life, tended to cut off this reliance on authority and place a sharper emphasis on the individual's responsibility for positive action, not just by his faith to be receptive to God's grace, but to get out and *work* in the building of the Kingdom. This precisely excluded any special valuation of devotional exercises and put the primary moral emphasis on secular activities.

Next, this constituted a liberation in one fundamental respect from the social conservatism of the Catholic position, in that it was no longer necessary to attempt to maintain the superiority of the religious life over the secular. Hence one essential bulwark of a hierarchical ordering of society was removed. The Christian conscience rather than the doctrines and structural position of the visible Church became the focus for standards of social evaluation. This should not, however, be interpreted as the establishment of "democracy" by the Reformation. Perhaps the most important single root of modern democracy is Christian individualism. But the Reformation, in liberating the individual conscience from the tutelage of the church, took only one step toward political democracy. The Lutheran branch indeed was long particularly identified with "legitimism," and Calvinism was in its early days primarily a doctrine of a relatively rigid collective "dictatorship" of the elect in both church and state.

Third, far from weakening the elements in secular society which pointed in a direction of "modernism," the Reformation, especially in its ascetic branch, strengthened and extended them. A particularly important component was clearly law. We have emphasized the essential continuity in this respect between classical antiquity and modern Europe through the medieval church. Broadly, the revival of Roman secular law in Europe was shared between Catholic and Protestant jurisdictions; in no sense did the Reformation reverse the trend in Continental Europe to institutionalize a secular legal system. In England, however, as Pound has emphasized, Puritanism was one of the major influences on the crystallization of the common law in the most decisive period. This is very much in line with the general trends of Protestant orientation, the favoring of a system of order within which responsible individual action can function effectively. The protection of rights is only one aspect of this order; the sanctioning of responsibilities is just as important.

Perhaps most important of all is the fact that the change in the character of the church meant that, insofar as the patterns of social structure which had characterized it by contrast with the feudal elements in the medieval heritage were to be preserved, they had to become much more generalized in secular society. This is true, as noted, of a generalized and codified system of law. It is true of more bureaucratic types of organization, which developed first in the governmental field but later in economic enterprise. It is by no means least true in the field of intellectual culture. The Renaissance was initially an outgrowth of the predominantly Catholic culture of Italy, but the general revival and development of learning of the post-medieval period was certainly shared by Catholic and Protestant Europe. It is a significant fact that John Calvin was trained as a lawyer. And of course, particularly in science, ascetic Protestantism was a major force in cultural development.

It is particularly important to emphasize the breadth of the front over which the leverage of Protestantism extended because of the common misinterpretation of Max Weber's thesis on the special relation between ascetic Protestantism and capitalism. This has often been seen as though the point were that Protestantism provided a special moral justification of profit-making as such, and of that alone. In view of the deep Western ambivalence over the conception of profit, the role of ascetic Protestantism in this context could easily be interpreted as mainly a "rationalization" of the common human propensity to seek "self-interest," which is the very antithesis of religious motivation.

First, it will be recalled that Weber was quite explicit that he was not talking about profit-making in general, but only about its harnessing to systematic methodical work in worldly callings in the interest of economic production through free enterprise. Weber was also well aware of a number of other facets of the same basic orientation to work in a calling, such as its basic hostility to various forms of traditionalism, including all traditional ascription of status independent of the individual, and its relation to science, a relation much further worked out by Merton.

Even Weber did not, however, in my opinion, fully appreciate the importance of the relation to the professions as a developing structural component of modern society, a component which in certain respects stands in sharp contrast to the classical orientation of economic self-interest.

The essential point is that private enterprise in business was one special case of secular callings within a much wider context. But it was a particularly strategic case in Western development, because of the very great difficulty of emancipating economic production over a truly broad front—on the one hand from the ascriptive ties which go with such institutions as peasant agriculture and guild-type handicraft, on the other hand from the irrationalities which, from an economic point of view, are inherent in political organization, because of its inherent connection with the short-run pressures of social urgency such as defense, and because of its integration with aristocratic elements in the system of stratification which were dominated by a very different type of orientation.

There is very good reason to believe that development of the industrial revolution *for the first time* could have come about only through the primary agency of free enterprise, however dependent this was in turn on prior conditions, among the most important of which were the availability of a legal framework within which a system of contractual relations could have an orderly development. Once there has been a major breakthrough on the economic front, however, the diffusion of the patterns of social organization involved need not continue to be dependent on the same conditions.[7]

Weber's main point about the Protestant ethic and capitalism was the importance of the subordination of self-interest in the usual ideological sense to the conception of a religiously meaningful calling; only with the establishment of this component was sufficient drive mobilized to break through the many barriers which were inherent not only in the European society of the time but more generally to a more differentiated development of economic production. Basically this involves the reversal of the commonsense point of view. The latter has contended, implicitly or explicitly, that the main source of impetus to capitalistic development was the *removal* of ethical restrictions such as, for instance, the prohibition of usury. This is true within certain limits, but by far the more important point is that what is needed is a powerful motivation to innovate, to break through the barriers of traditionalism and of vested interest. It is this impetus which is the center of Weber's concern, and it is his thesis that it cannot be accounted for by any simple removal of restrictions.

However deep the ambivalence about the morality of profit-making may go, there can be little doubt that the main outcome has been a shift in social conditions more in accord with the general pattern of Christian ethics than was medieval society, provided we grant that life in this world has a positive value in itself. Not least of these is the breaking through of the population circle of high death rates and high birth rates with the attendant lengthening of the average span of life. Another crucial point is the vast extension of the sphere of order in human relationships, the lessening of the exposure of the individual to violence, to fraud and to arbitrary pressures of authority.

So-called material well-being has certainly never been treated as an absolute value in the Christian or any other major religious tradition, but any acceptance of life in this world as of value entails acceptance of the value of the means necessary to do approved things effectively. Particularly at the lower end of the social scale, grinding poverty with its accompaniments of illness, premature death, and unnecessary suffering is certainly not to be taken as an inherently desirable state of affairs from a Christian point of view.

Another major theme of developments in this era which is in basic accord with Christian values is a certain strain to egalitarianism, associated with the conception of the dignity of the individual human being and the need to justify discriminations either for or against individuals and classes of them in terms of some general concept of merit or demerit. Certainly by contrast with the role of ascriptive discriminations in the medieval situation, modern society is not in this respect ethically inferior.

Also important has been the general field of learning and science. Perhaps the educational revolution of the nineteenth century was even more important in its long-run implications than was the industrial revolution of the late eighteenth century. It represents the first attempt in history to give large populations as a whole a substantial level of formal education, starting with literacy but going well beyond. Associated with this is the general cultivation of things intellectual and particularly the sciences through research. It is the marriage of the educational and industrial revolutions which provides the primary basis for the quite new level of mass well-being which is one major characteristic of the modern Western world. In both developments cultures with primarily Protestant orientations have acted as the spearheads.

The Reformation phase of Western development may be said to have culminated in the great seventeenth century, which saw the foundations of modern law and political organization so greatly advanced, the culmination of the first major phase of modern science, the main orientations of modern philosophy, and much development on the economic front. However important the Renaissance was, the great civilizational achievements of the seventeenth century as a whole are unthinkable without Protestantism. It coincided with a new level of leadership centering in predominantly Protestant northern Europe, notably England and Holland, and also with much ferment in Germany.

In spite of the very great structural differences, the essential principles governing the process by which society has become more Christianized than before were essentially the same in the Reformation period as in the earlier one. Let us recall that the Christian church from the beginning renounced the strategy of incorporation of secular society within itself, or the direct control of secular society through a religious law. It relied on the common values which bound church and secular society together, each in its own sphere, but making the Christian aspect of secular society an autonomous responsibility of Christians in their secular roles. My basic argument has been that the same fundamental principle was carried even farther in the Reformation phase. The sphere of autonomy was greatly enlarged through release of the Christian individual from the tutelage of the church. This was essentially a process of further differentiation both within the religious sphere and between it and the secular.

In all such cases there is increased objective opportunity for disregarding the values of the religious tradition and succumbing to worldly temptations. But the other side of the coin is the enhancement of motivation to religiously valued achievement by the very fact of being given more unequivocal responsibility. This process was not mainly one of secularization but one of the institutionalization of the religious responsibility of the individual through the relinquishment of tutelary authority by a "parental" church.

For purposes of this discussion the Reformation period is the most decisive one, for here it is most frequently argued, by Professor Sorokin among many others, that there was a decisive turn in the direction of secularization in the sense of abandonment of the values inherent in the Christian tradition in favor of concern with the "things of this world." As already noted, we feel that underlying this argument is a basic ambiguity about the relation of "the world" to religious orientations and that the Christian orientation is not, in the Oriental sense, an orientation of "rejection of the world" but rather in this respect mainly a source for the setting of ethical standards *for* life in this world. In line with this interpretation, the Reformation transition was not primarily one of "giving in" to the temptations of worldly interest, but rather one of extending the range of applicability and indeed in certain respects the rigor of the ethical standards applied to life in the world. It was expecting more rather than less of larger numbers of Christians in their worldly lives. It goes without saying that the content of the expectations also changed. But these changes indicated much more a change in the definition of the situation of life through changes in the structure of society than they did in the main underlying values.

Let us try to apply the same formula used in summing up the medieval phase to that of the Reformation. The most conspicuous aspect of extension was the diffusion of religious responsibility and participation in certain respects beyond the sacramentally organized church to the laity on their own responsibility. The central symbol of this was the translation of the Bible into the vernacular languages of Europe and the pressure on broad lay groups to familiarize themselves with it. The shift in the functions of the church from the sacramental emphasis to that of teaching is directly connected with this. This extension included both the elements of worship and that of responsibility for ethical conduct.

With respect to the church itself as a social system, the Reformation clearly did not involve further internal differentiation but the contrary. But it involved a major step in the differentiation of the religious organization *from* secular society. The Reformation churches, as distinguished from the sects, retained their symbiosis of interpenetration with secular political authority through the principle of Establishment. But the counterpart of what I have called the religious enfranchisement of the individual was his being freed from detailed moral tutelage by the clergy. The dropping of the sacrament of penance, the very core of Luther's revolt against the Catholic church, was central in this respect. Repentance became a matter of the individual's direct relation to God, specifically exempted from any sacramental mediation. This was essentially to say that the individual was, in matters of conscience, in principle accountable to no human agency, but only to God; in this sense he was *humanly* autonomous. This development tended to restrict the church to the functions of an agency for the generation of faith, through teaching and through providing a communal setting for the ritual expression of common anxiety and common faith.

There were two principal settings in which this differentiation of lay responsibility from ecclesiastical tutelage worked out. One was the direct relation to God in terms of repentance and faith. This was paramount in the Lutheran branch of the Reformation movement. The other was the primacy of moral action in the world as an instrument of the divine will, the pattern which was primary in ascetic Protestantism. In a sense in which this was impossible within the fold of Catholic unity on the level of church organization, both these movements become differentiated not only from the "parent" Catholic church but also from each other. Hence the ascetic Protestant branch, which institutionalized elements present from the beginning in Western Christian tradition, notably through Augustine, was freed from the kind of ties with other components which hindered its ascendancy as the major trend of one main branch of general Christian tradition. Clearly this is the branch which had the most direct positive influence on the complex of orientations of value which later proved to be of importance to modern industrialism.

The third point of upgrading is most conspicuous in the placing of secular callings on a plane of moral equality with the religious life itself. In crucial respects this shift increased the tension between Christian ideal and worldly reality. This increase of tension underlay much of the Lutheran trend to withdrawal from positive secular interests and the corresponding sectarian and mystical phenomena of the time. But once the new tension was turned into the channel of exerting leverage for the change of conduct in the secular world, above all through the imperative to work in the building of the Kingdom, it was a powerful force to moral upgrading precisely in the direction of changing social behavior in the direction of Christian ideals, not of adjustment to the given necessities of a non-Christian world.

The Denominational Phase

A common view would agree with the above argument that the Reformation itself was not basically a movement of secularization but that, in that it played a part in unleashing the forces of political nationalism and economic development—to say nothing of recent hedonism—it was the last genuinely Christian phase of Western development and that from the eighteenth century on in particular the trend had truly been one of religious decline in relation to the values of secular society. Certain trends in Weber's thinking with respect to the disenchantment of the world would seem to argue in this direction, as would Troeltsch's view that there have been only three authentic versions of the conception of a Christian society in Western history—the medieval Catholic, the Lutheran, and the Calvinistic.

Against this view I should like to present an argument for a basic continuity leading to a further phase which has come to maturity in the nineteenth and twentieth centuries, most conspicuously in the United States and coincident with the industrial and educational revolutions already referred to. From this point of view, the present system of "denominational pluralism" may be regarded as a further extension of the same basic line of institutionalization of Christian ethics which was produced both by the medieval synthesis and by the Reformation.

It is perhaps best to start with the conception of religious organization itself. Weber and Troeltsch organized their thinking on these matters within the Christian framework around the distinction between church and sect as organizational types. The church was the religious organization of the whole society which could claim and enforce the same order of jurisdiction over a total population as did the state in the secular sphere. The sect, on the other hand, was a voluntary religious association of those committed to a specifically religious life. The church type was inherently committed to the conception of an Establishment, since only through this type of integration with political authority could universal jurisdiction be upheld. The sect, on the other hand, could not establish any stable relation to secular society since its members were committed to give unequivocal primacy to their religious interests and could not admit the legitimacy of the claims of secular society, politically or otherwise, which a stable relation would entail.

This dichotomy fails to take account of an important third possibility, the denomination. As I conceive it, this shares with the church type the *differentiation* between religious and secular spheres of interest. In the same basic sense which we outlined for the medieval church, both may be conceived to be subject to Christian values, but to constitute independent foci of responsibility for their implementation. On the other hand, the denomination shares with the sect type its character as a voluntary association where the individual member is bound only by a responsible personal commitment, not by *any* factor of ascription. In the American case it is, logically I think, associated with the constitutional separation of church and state.

The denomination can thus accept secular society as a legitimate field of action for the Christian individual in which he acts on his own responsibility without organizational control by religious authority. But precisely because he is a Christian he will not simply accept everything he finds there; he will attempt to shape the situation in the direction of better conformity with Christian values. This general pattern it shares with all three of the church types, but not with the sect in Troeltsch's sense.

Two further factors are involved, however, which go beyond anything to be found in the church tradition. One of these is implicit in the voluntary principle—the acceptance of denominational pluralism—and, with it, toleration. However much there may historically have been, and still is, deep ambivalence about this problem, the genuine institutionalization of the constitutional protection of religious freedom cannot be confined to the secular side; it must be accepted as *religiously* legitimate as well. With certain qualifications this can be said to be the case in the United States today and, in somewhat more limited forms, in various other countries. From a religious point of view, this means the discrimination of two layers of religious commitment. One of these is the layer which defines the bases of denominational membership and which differentiates one denomination from another. The other is a common matrix of value-commitment which is broadly shared between denominations, and which forms the basis of the sense in which the society as a whole forms a religiously based moral community. This has, in the American case, been extended to cover a very wide range. Its core certainly lies in the institutionalized Protestant denominations, but with certain strains and only partial institutionalization, it extends to three other groups of the first importance; the Catholic church, the various branches of Judaism, and, not least important, those who prefer to remain aloof from *any* formal denominational affiliation. To deny that this underlying consensus exists would be to claim that American society stood in a state of latent religious war. Of the fact that there are considerable tensions every responsible student of the situation is aware. Institutionalization is incomplete, but the consensus is very much of a reality.

The second difference from the church tradition is a major further step in the emancipation of the individual from tutelary control by *organized* religious collectivities beyond that reached by the Reformation churches. This is the other side of the coin of pluralism, and essentially says that the rite of baptism does not commit the individual to a particular set of dogmas or a particular religious collectivity. The individual is responsible not only for managing his own relation to God through faith *within* the ascribed framework of an established church, which is the Reformation position, but for choosing that framework itself, for deciding as a mature individual *what* to believe, and *with whom* to associate himself in the organizational expression and reinforcement of his commitments. This is essentially the removal of the last vestige of coercive control over the individual in the religious sphere; he is endowed with full responsible autonomy.

That there should be a development in this direction from the position of the Reformation church seems to me to have been inherent in the Protestant position in general, in very much the same sense in which a trend to Protestantism was inherent in the medieval Catholic situation. Just as Catholics tend to regard Protestantism in general as the abandonment of true religious commitment either because the extension of the voluntary principle to such lengths is held to be incompatible with a sufficiently serious commitment on the part of the church (if you are not willing to coerce people to your point of view are you yourself *really* committed to it?) or because of its legitimation of secular society so that church membership becomes only one role among many, not the primary axis of life as a whole. But against such views it is hard to see how the implicit individualism of all Christianity could be stopped, short of this doctrine of full responsible autonomy. The doctrine seems to me implicit in the very conception of faith. Asking the individual to have faith is essentially to ask him to *trust* in God. But, whatever the situation in the relation of the human to the divine, in *human* relations trust seems to have to rest on mutuality. Essentially the voluntary principle in denominationalism is extending mutuality of trust so that no *human* agency is permitted to take upon itself the authority to control the conditions under which faith is to be legitimately expected. Clearly this, like the Reformation step, involves a risk that the individual will succumb to worldly temptations. But the essential principle is not different from that involved in releasing him from sacramental control.

This is of course very far from contending that the system of denominational pluralism is equally congenial to all theological positions or that all religious groups within the tradition can fit equally well into it. There are important strains particularly in relation to the Catholic church, to Fundamentalist Protestant sects, to a lesser degree to very conservative Protestant church groups (especially Lutheran), and to the vestiges of really Orthodox Judaism. My essential contention is not that this pattern has been or can be fully universalized within Judaeo-Christianity, but that it is a genuinely Christian development, not by definition a falling away from religion. But it could not have developed without a very substantial modification of earlier positions with Protestantism. In particular it is incompatible with either strict traditional Lutheranism or strict Calvinism.

It was remarked above that the Reformation period did not usher in political democracy, but was in a sense a step toward it. There is a much closer affiliation between denominational pluralism and political democracy. But before discussing that, a comparison between the two may help illuminate the nature of the problem of how such a system of religious organization works. Legitimists for a long period have viewed with alarm the dangers of democracy since, if public policy can be determined by the majority of the irresponsible and the uninformed, how can any stability of political organization be guaranteed? There is a sense in which the classical theory of political liberalism may be said to play into the hands of this legitimist argument, since it has tended to assume that under democracy each individual made up his mind totally independently without reference to the institutionalized wisdom of any tradition.

This is not realistically the case. Careful study of voting behavior has shown that voting preferences are deeply anchored in the established involvement of the individual in the social structure. Generally speaking, most voters follow the patterns of the groups with which they are most strongly affiliated. Only when there are structural changes in the society which alter its structure of solidary groupings and expose many people to cross-pressures are major shifts likely to take place. There are, furthermore, mechanisms by which these shifts tend, in a well-institutionalized democratic system, to be orderly.[8]

I would like to suggest that similar considerations apply to a system of denominational pluralism. The importance of the family is such that it is to be taken for granted that the overwhelming majority will accept the religious affiliations of their parents—of course with varying degrees of commitment. Unless the whole society is drastically disorganized there will not be notable instability in its religious organization. But there will be an important element of flexibility and opportunity for new adjustments within an orderly system which the older church organizations, like the older political legitimacy, did not allow for.

If it is once granted that this system of religious organization is not by definition a "falling away" from true religion, then its institutionalization of the elements of trust of the individual has, it seems to me, an important implication. On the religious side it is implicit in the pattern of toleration. Members of particular churches on the whole trust each other to be loyal to the particular collectivity. But if some should shift to another denomination it is not to be taken too tragically since the new affiliation will in most cases be included in the deeper moral community.

But such a situation could not prevail were the secular part of the system regarded as radically evil. The individual is not only trusted with reference to his religious participation, but also to lead a "decent" life in his secular concerns. Indeed I should argue, therefore, that for such a religious constitution to function, on the institutional level the society must present not a less but a more favorable field for the Christian life than did the society of earlier periods of Western history; its moral standards must in fact be higher.

There is a tendency in much religiously oriented discussion to assume that the test of the aliveness of Christian values is the extent to which "heroic" defiance of temptation or renunciation of worldly interests is empirically prevalent. This ignores one side of the equation of Christian conduct, the extent to which the "world" does or does not stand opposed to the values in question. If one argues that there has been a relative institutionalization of these values, and hence in certain respects a diminution of tension between religious ideal and actuality, he risks accusation of a Pharisaic complacency. In face of this risk, however, I suggest that in a whole variety of respects modern society is more in accord with Christian values than its forebears have been—this is, let it be noted, a *relative* difference; the millennium definitely has not arrived.

I do not see how the extension of intra- and interdenominational trust into a somewhat greater trust in the moral quality of secular conduct would be possible were this not so. The internalization of religious values certainly strengthens character. But this is not to say that even the *average* early Christian was completely proof against worldly temptation, *independent of any support from the mutual commitments of many Christians in and through the church.* Without the assumption that this mutual support in a genuine social collectivity was of the first importance, I do not see how the general process of institutionalization of these values could have been possible at all except on the unacceptable assumption of a process of emanation of the spirit without involvement in the realistic religious interests of real persons.

However heroic a few individuals may be, no process of mass institutionalization occurs without the mediation of social solidarities and the mutual support of many individuals in commitment to a value system. The corollary of relinquishment of the organizational control of certain areas of behavior, leaving them to the responsibility of the autonomous individual, is the institutionalization of the basic conditions of carrying out this responsibility with not the elimination, but a relative minimization of, the hazard that this exposure will lead to total collapse of the relevant standards.

Let us try to sum up this fourth—denominational—phase of the line of development we have traced in terms of our threefold formula. First I would suggest that the principle of religious toleration, inherent in the system of denominational pluralism, implies a great further extension of the institutionalization of Christian values, both inside and outside the sphere of religious organization. At least it seems to me that this question poses a sharp alternative. Either there is a sharp falling away so that, in tolerating each other, the different denominations have become fellow condoners of an essentially evil situation or, as suggested above, they do in fact stand on a relatively high ethical plane so that whatever their dogmatic differences, there is no basis for drawing a drastic moral line of distinction which essentially says that the adherents of the other camp are in a moral sense not good people in a sense in which the members of our own camp are. Then the essential extension of the same principle of mutual trust into the realm of secular conduct is another part of the complex which I would like to treat as one of extension of the institutionalization of Christian values.

So far as differentiation is concerned, there are two conspicuous features of this recent situation. First, of course, the religious associations have become differentiated from each other so that, unlike in the Reformation phase (to say nothing of the Middle Ages), when there was for a politically organized society in principle only one acceptable church, adherence to which was the test of the moral quality treated as a minimum for good standing in the society, this is no longer true. The religious organization becomes a purely voluntary association, and there is an indefinite plurality of morally acceptable denominations.

This does not, however, mean that Christian ethics have become a matter of indifference in the society. It means rather that the differentiation between religious and secular spheres has gone farther than before and with it the extension of the individualistic principle inherent in Christianity to the point of the "privatizing" of formal, external religious commitment, as the Reformation made internal religious faith a matter for the individual alone. This general trend has of course coincided with an enormously proliferated process of differentiation in the structure of the society itself.

In this respect the religious group may be likened (up to a point) to the family. The family has lost many traditional functions and has become increasingly a sphere of private sentiments. There is, however, reason to believe that it is as important as ever to the maintenance of the main patterns of the society, though operating with a minimum of direct outside control. Similarly religion has become largely a private matter in which the individual associates with the group of his own choice, and in this respect has lost many functions of previous religious organizational types.

There seem to be two primary respects in which an upgrading process may be spoken of. Approaching the question from the sociological side, we may note that the development of the society has been such that it should not be operated without an upgrading of general levels of responsibility and competence, the acquisition and exercise of the latter of course implying a high sense of responsibility. This trend is a function of increase in the size of organization and the delicacy of relations of interdependence, of freedom from ascriptive bonds in many different ways, of the sheer power for destruction and evil of many of the instrumentalities of action.

Responsibility has a double aspect. The first is responsibility *of* the individual in that he cannot rely on a dependent relation to others, or to some authority, to absolve him of responsibility—this is the aspect we have been referring to as his *autonomy* in the specific sense in which the term has been used in this discussion. The other aspect is responsibility *for* and *to,* responsibility for results and to other persons and to collectivities. Here the element of mutuality inherent in Christian ethics, subject to a commonly binding set of norms and values, is the central concern.

That the general trend has been to higher orders of autonomous responsibility is, in my opinion, sociologically demonstrable.[9] The central problem then becomes that of whether the kinds of responsibility involved do or do not accord with the prescriptions of Christian ethics. This is essentially the question of whether the general trend stemming from ascetic Protestantism is basically un-Christian or not. Granting that this trend is not un-Christian, the critical *moral* problems of our day derive mainly from the fact that, since we are living in a more complicated world than ever before, which is more complicated because human initiative has been more daring and has ventured into more new realms than ever before, greater demands are put on the human individual. He has more difficult problems, both technical and moral; he takes greater risks. Hence the possibility of failure and of the failure being his fault is at least as great as, if not greater than, it ever was.

There is a widespread view, particularly prevalent in religious circles, that our time, particularly some say in the United States, is one of unprecedented moral collapse. In these circles it is alleged that modern social development has entailed a progressive decline of moral standards which is general throughout the population. This view is clearly incompatible with the general trend of the analysis we have been making. Its most plausible grain of truth is the one just indicated, that as new and more difficult problems emerge, such as those involved in the possibility of far more destructive war than ever before, we do not feel morally adequate to the challenge. But to say that because we face graver problems than our forefathers faced we are doubtful of our capacity to handle them responsibly is quite a different thing from saying that, on the same levels of responsibility as those of our forefathers, we are in fact handling our problems on a much lower moral level.

Our time by and large, however, is not one of religious complacency but, particularly in the most sensitive groups in these matters, one of substantial anxiety and concern. Does not the existence of this concern stand in direct contradiction to the general line of argument I have put forward?

I think not. One element in its explanation is probably that new moral problems of great gravity have emerged in our time and that we are, for very realistic reasons, deeply concerned about them. My inclination, however, is to think that this is not the principal basis of the widespread concern.

The present discussion has, by virtue of its chosen subject, been primarily interested in the problems of the institutionalization of the values originating in Christianity as a religious movement, which have been carried forward at various stages of its development. But values—i.e., moral orientations toward the problems of life in this world—are never the whole of religion, if indeed its most central aspect. My suggestion is that the principal roots of the present religious concern do not lie in *relative* moral decline or inadequacy (relative, that is to other periods in our society's history) but rather in problems in the other areas of religion, problems of the bases of faith and the definitions of the ultimate problems of meaning.

The very fact that the process of the integration of earlier religious values with the structure of society has gone so far as it has gone raises such problems. The element of universalism in Christian ethics inherently favors the development of a society where the different branches of Christianity cannot maintain their earlier insulation from each other. The problem of the status of Judaism has had to be raised on a new level within the structure of Western society, one which came to a very critical stage in the case of German Nazism. It is a society in which all the parochialisms of earlier religious commitments are necessarily brought into flux.

But beyond this, for the first time in history something approaching a world society is in process of emerging. For the first time in its history Christianity is now involved in a deep confrontation with the major religious traditions of the Orient, as well as with the modern political religion of Communism.

It seems probable that a certain basic tension in relation to the "things of this world" is inherent in Christianity generally. Hence any relative success in the institutionalization of Christian values cannot be taken as final, but rather as a point of departure for new religious stock-taking. But in addition to this broad internal consideration, the confrontation on such a new basis with the non-Christian world presents a new and special situation. We are deeply committed to our own great traditions. These have tended to emphasize the exclusive possession of the truth. Yet we have also institutionalized the values of tolerance and equality of rights for all. How can we define a meaningful orientation in such a world when, in addition, the more familiar and conventional problems of suffering and evil are, if not more prevalent than ever before, at least as brought to attention through mass communications, inescapable as facts of our world?

It is the inherent tension and dynamism of Christianity and the unprecedented character of the situation we face which, to my mind, account for the intensive searching and questioning, and indeed much of the spiritual negativism, of our time. The explanation in terms of an alleged moral collapse would be far too simple, even if there were more truth it in than the evidence seems to indicate. For this would imply that we did not need new conceptions of meaning; all we would need would be to live up more fully to the standards familiar to us all. In no period of major ferment in cultural history has such a solution been adequate.

---

1. Cf. Sorokin, *Fads and Foibles in Modern Sociology and Related Sciences* (Chicago: Henry Regnery, 1956).

2. The most important general statements of his position are in *Social and Cultural Dynamics* (New York: American Book Company, 1937), Vol. I, Part 1, and *Society, Culture, and Personality* (New York: Harper, 1947), Part 7.

3. In this general interpretation I follow in particular Troeltsch. *Social Teaching of the Christian Churches.*

4. H. C. Lea, *The History of Sacerdotal Celibacy* (New York: Russell and Russell, 1957).

5. Perhaps the fullest statement of this scheme is contained in T. Parsons and W. White, "The Link between Character and Society," in S. M. Lipset and L. Loewenthal (eds.), *Culture and Social Character* (New York: The Free Press of Glencoe, 1961).

6. By autonomy I mean here *independence* of direct authoritarian control combined with *responsibility* defined in moral-religious terms. It is close to "theonomy" as that concept is used by Tillich.

7. This thesis is further developed in my two essays published as Chapters III and IV of *Structure and Process in Modern Societies* (New York: The Free Press of Glencoe, 1959).

8. Basing myself on the studies of voting behavior by Berelson, Lazarsfeld, *et al.,* I have analyzed this situation in " 'Voting' and the Equilibrium of the American Political System," in Eugene Burdick and Arthur J. Brodbeck (eds.), *American Voting Behavior* (New York: The Free Press of Glencoe, 1959).

9. Cf. Parsons and White, *op cit.,* for a brief statement of the case for this view.

GIBSON WINTER

The Dilemma of Metropolitan Protestantism

The major denominations of Protestantism are gradually becoming metropolitan in character; nevertheless, Protestant memberships are still more rural than would be expected in view of the growing concentration of people in the metropolis. A report for 1953 indicated that only 46 per cent of Protestant strength was in metropolitan areas, although 56 per cent of the total population resided in these areas at the time.[1] In view of the traditionally rural character of Protestantism, this is a reasonable showing. Certain denominations are, of course, markedly urban, whereas several large denominations continue to be primarily rural. In general, the churches have prospered in the course of urbanization, and are still growing.

A brief indication of recent religious growth may suggest the mental climate that pervades the churches. In the 1958 yearbook, contributions to most of the major bodies showed a gain of 11 per cent over the

From *The Suburban Captivity of the Church* by Gibson Winter, pp. 33-42.

preceding year.[2] Despite inflation, this is a notable gain. Church membership was 62 per cent of total population in 1956 as compared to 49 per cent in 1940. Opinion polls of attendance at church by adults indicated that 41 per cent of the respondents attended in the week preceding the interview in 1939 as compared to 51 per cent in 1957. Construction of new church buildings reflects somewhat more closely the state of the economy; however, comparing the lush years of 1928 and 1956, expenditures on new building show roughly a 400 per cent increase by 1956. These figures give some hint of the increase in religious interest.

The metropolitan problem of the churches is not a failure in organizational growth; the present rate of metropolitan expansion among the churches should soon bring their religious constituencies into line with general population trends. Metropolitan churches are confronted with a dilemma between organizational expansion and responsibility for the central city—at least, this is the superficial way in which the problem emerges. Satellite areas, as indicated above, are growing rapidly; the churches are capitalizing on this growth with an unprecedented expansion; simultaneously, however, the churches are losing contact with the central city areas—at least, this is true of the major denominations of White Protestantism. The metropolitan schism is present within the life of Protestantism: Negro and sectarian churches are multiplying in the central cities, but they are not in a position to come to grips with the social disorganization of the central city areas; for the most part they are small, inadequately staffed churches; ethnic churches are losing their ethnic traditions and their constituencies are moving to middle-class areas; the major White denominations are concentrated on the periphery of the city; the central city churches of these denominations recruit more than 50 per cent of their memberships from a great distance; these central city churches, meanwhile, lose members while satellite churches grow. Protestantism divides along racial lines and between blue-collar and white-collar populations. The major denominations, whose membership includes from 80 to 90 per cent of all Protestants, are being alienated from the peoples and problems of the central cities; the White branches of the major denominations are aligned with the middle-class, suburban side of the social-class and racial schism.

The schism in Protestantism is also reflected in the mixed attitudes of religious leaders toward metropolitan needs. Denominational leaders have watched the new residential areas surrounding the central cities with greedy eyes. These are largely middle- and upper-class residential areas; they have adequate resources for constructing church buildings; their residents are responsive to religious programs; in fact, denominational leaders call these "high potential areas,"—and they do not mean potential for prayer. In recent decades almost exclusive attention has been given to establishing churches in suburban areas. Denominations have joined forces for the development of new churches through federations and councils of churches; they have set up planning staffs for cooperative church extension, usually called comity.[3] Although comity programs for church extension vary considerably, all of them attempt to allocate new residential areas to different denominations in order to avoid duplication in expenditure and prevent over-churching of particular areas. Comity, to use a phrase from H. Paul Douglass, is a combination of ecclesiastical eugenics and planned parenthood. The growing co-operation on comity is an index of the extent to which organizational growth has been central to denominational concerns: the satellite areas have increased the demand for churches; denominational co-operation has attended to this demand.

Concentration on satellite areas is perfectly understandable in terms of the organizational interests of the denominations; central city areas, particularly the inner zones of the central city, confront the churches with innumerable problems; in fact, congregations have been retreating from these areas for decades, and only a few churches have been able to remain active in these parts of the cities. The central city is littered with decaying church buildings in areas of rapid population change. It has been difficult to obtain pastors for these churches; in fact, change of pastorate is almost an annual phenomenon. In recent years, however, the denominations have become aware that they were losing touch with central city areas, and that greed for growth was driving them to the outer zones of the central city. Programs of church extension have strengthened the major denominations in the satellite areas, but at the risk of losing touch with the heart of the metropolis. Policies of church extension, therefore, are arousing the anxieties of some farsighted denominational leaders: on the one hand, they are committed to a policy of extension on the growing perimeter of the cities; on the other, they sense that this policy is disengaging the churches from the center of the metropolis; since the whole central city is deteriorating rapidly, the net effect is to alienate the churches from the central cities.

Denominational leaders are troubled with problems even more serious than the schism between the central city and satellite areas. The preceding discussion has focused on this schism in the ministry to the city, but the alienation from metropolitan life runs much deeper, for the identification of congregational life with neighborhoods also means insulation from metropolitan concerns. At a meeting of City Churchmen of the United Church of Christ in 1958, John Osman said, "Religion today is challenged to create an urban civilization. . . . Religion has abandoned the city and left its redemption to business and industry.

. . . Only religion can regenerate our cities by making them a place for spiritual growth."[4] At the same meeting, Truman B. Douglas said, "Not only has American Protestantism failed to penetrate the culture of modern cities, it has largely refused to take that culture seriously, and it has withdrawn from the task of relating the Christian faith to the problems and needs of human beings in contemporary urban society."[5] These statements reflect a profound concern with the alienation of the churches from urban culture—the religious betrayal of the metropolis—and express the views of a prophetic minority in the churches.

The tension between the churches' responsibility for metropolitan life and their desire for suburban growth revealed itself at a meeting of Methodist leaders in 1959. John Wicklein of the New York *Times* headlined his report of the meeting with this statement: "The Methodist Church, the largest Protestant denomination in the country, is dying out in the cities."[6] His report also contains an observation made at this meeting by a Methodist leader: "In Boston five churches died in ten years, leaving only five surviving in the inner city."[7]

At this Methodist meeting, concern focused on the schism between central city and satellite areas; disengagement of Protestant churches from the central city is the most obvious and manifest form of alienation from metropolitan life, since the heart of the metropolis continues to be a significant center of population, a pivot of political power. The central city is the area which suffers most radically from the disorganizing effects of urban life; it is the area of most pressing personal and social need and the scene of repeated defeats for the churches. Every venture in the inner city involves exorbitant cost in personnel and money, with little hope of return in new members or funds. Every advance toward the satellite areas, on the other hand, promises unlimited return with minimal outlay. The organizational extension of Protestantism has followed the line of least resistance; church extension, thus, runs counter to the metropolitan responsibility of Protestantism, since it threatens to alienate the major White denominations from the central city areas. Denominations cannot continue their organizational growth without sacrificing their moral and religious responsibility to the total metropolitan area or to about one half of the metropolitan population. This is the dilemma which has faced Protestantism; its roots, however, lie deeper than the mistaken strategy of denominational leaders.

The metropolis has become an interdependent whole without adequate internal processes of communication to provide stability and direction. The most obvious symptom of this internal breakdown is the lack of political coherence in the metropolitan area—a void which has the most serious consequences for every aspect of metropolitan life, from park planning to police protection. The problem of the churches is that their strength centers in the fabric of a local community, for both parochial and congregational forms of religious organization emerged as expressions of cohesive, local communities in the villages of feudal Europe and in the local enclaves of medieval cities. When metropolitan changes practically dissolved neighborhood communities, the churches were left without any communal fabric to sustain their congregational life. Meanwhile, the breakdown of communication in the metropolitan area had created a search for insulated neighborhoods; hence, the neighborhoods in which the churches vested their basic unit of organization —parish or congregation—became the scene of a struggle for insulation. Segregation became the path to stability. While the metropolis needed new channels of communication, the more homogeneous communities on the fringe of the city were struggling to break communication with other groups in the metropolis. These citadels became dungeons for congregational and parochial life. The churches entered a period of suburban captivity, deserted the central city and aligned themselves with the status panic, becoming mere refuges for the fleeing middle classes. The churches, which should have facilitated communication, became instruments to block it.

The exodus from the central city reveals the struggle of middle-class people to fabricate some semblance of common life through a religious congregation. This struggle is a tragic story in the history of the Christian ministry to the metropolis, since it led to the unchurching of blue-collar people and the provision of ministry almost exclusively on the basis of power to pay—a ministry which was becoming increasingly costly in training and paraphernalia. The struggle for stability led to an uprooting of the congregations, since the emerging middle classes, which carried the weight of the Protestant population, were moving nearer and nearer to the edge of the city. The very dependence of congregational and parochial life upon a fabric of cohesive community made them vulnerable to the suburban captivity, for here at least they could find some semblance of common life to sustain their rituals. Nevertheless, the relationship of the major denominations to the middle classes was a two-way street, for the middle classes used the congregation as a platform upon which to build a sense of belonging and tradition, even as the major denominations used the middle classes as a pool for recruitment. In this way the exodus from the central city and the concentration on suburban growth were both products of the peculiar needs of the middle classes and the particular vulnerability of the major denominations in the changing metropolis.

The activity of the congregations of the major denominations and their appalling superficiality have often been noted by foreign observers; these visitors from afar look wistfully at church activities and budgets but stand aghast before the spiritual emptiness of these associations. This strange combination of vitality and emptiness can be understood in the light of the peculiar coalition between the major denominations and the emerging middle class. A wholly new style of religious life emerged in this coalition; in fact, the constellation of forces at work in the metropolis gave birth to the organization church. The bond between the organization church and the particular interests and needs of the white-collar ranks can be discerned, but the real problem remains as to whether this fabricated community can serve as a platform for a mission to the metropolis or must be abandoned for a renewed church.

The breakdown of local community meant the dissolution of the fabric which had made sense of congregational life, for without this communal fabric the congregation met in a vacuum, no longer a fellowship representing the community from which it was called. Assembled from no real community and witnessing to none, it merely contemplated its own budget. The same thing happened to the parish, for the parochial form had represented a geographical area in which economic, political, and communal interests intersected. When the residential area became a place for social and economic insulation, the parish became a highly segregated community which could barely survive the rapid population changes to which most metropolitan neighborhoods were subject. In either case, the breakdown of local community gave rise to an organization church as a substitute form of community. The principal difficulty lay in the fact that the organization church was neither a community of faith nor a truly universal form of organization which could bring together the conflicting and estranged elements in the metropolis, for the organization was anchored in a segregated context rather than a ministry. The organization church can be a platform for a mission and an appropriate form for reconciling diverse elements in the metropolis only insofar as it can be freed from the shackles of local enclaves. This is the real problem confronting Protestantism in the metropolis. The solution of this problem can pave the way for the churches to renew their ministry to the metropolis and ultimately to reopen communication in the metropolitan area.

This verdict—the essentially optimistic view that major denominations have a working base from which to launch a mission to the whole metropolis and to halt their flight into middle-class enclaves—has some warrant in recent developments among the churches. On May 1. 1960, Protestants, Catholics, and Jews joined together for a Conference on Problems of Housing in the Chicago Metropolitan Area. It was an historic occasion both because these groups have had relatively little communication and because they joined forces in confronting one of the most difficult problems in a metropolitan area. This interfaith venture into metropolitan communication over crucial problems of metropolitan community may come to nothing, but it is at least a straw in the wind. The great religious faiths which have emerged on the American scene are powerful forces for communication and renewal when they begin to look toward human needs in contemporary life. They can be vehicles of reconciliation and communication, even as the organization churches can provide the base for a totally new form of ministry to the metropolitan area. This is the promise of the churches in the metropolis, though at the moment no more than promise, since these same churches are largely preoccupied with organizational interests.

The subsequent discussion devotes little attention to the problems of interfaith communication, and even scants the difficulties of interdenominational union. Such omissions are justified in part by the attention being given to these problems by other writers, but more particularly by the importance of the central concern of this evaluation —that is, the actual fabric of the religious community in the metropolis and its potential for a mission to the metropolitan area. Ultimately, the only important question about any congregation or religious group is this: in what ways is it an expression of ministry in faith and obedience? The tragedy of the organization church has been its substitution of survival for ministry. Its promise lies in its resources for ministry in a mass society. The path to interfaith co-operation and interdenominational union will be found, as the title of a book by Visser t'Hooft so well expresses it, under *The Pressure of Our Common Calling.* This calling and our potentiality for fulfilling it will occupy the center of the stage at every point in this evaluation of the emergence of the organization church. It is from the inner grace of those called to the ministry that the organization church will find the strength to fulfill its role as a mission rather than a refuge from the metropolitan struggle for a human environment.

---

1. "Two Worlds of Church Life in the United States" by Glen W. Trimble, in *Information Service,* published by Bureau of Research and Survey, National Council of Churches, Vol. XXXVIII, No. 7, p. 1.

2. *Yearbook of American Churches for 1958,* edited by Benson Y. Landis (New York: National Council of Churches of Christ in the U.S.A., September 1957), p. 281.

3. *Church Comity* by H. Paul Douglass (New York: Doubleday, Doran and Co., 1929). See Chapters I–III for a study of the development of co-operative church extension.

4. Quoted in *Information Service,* op. cit., Vol. XXXVII, No. 15, p. 3.

5. Ibid., p. 4.

6. The New York *Times,* Mar. 15, 1959.

7. Ibid.

Chapter 9
Secularization: Its Meaning and Effects

LARRY SHINER

The Concept of Secularization in Empirical Research

Secularization, once branded *the* enemy, has suddenly become the darling of Protestant theology, and there are strong indications that some Roman Catholic theologians are softening. But why should such theological conundrums as "the secular meaning of the Gospel" or "secular Christianity" be relevant to the scientific analysis of religion? At the least, this recent theological attack on the received interpretation of secularization should inspire the analyst to reconsider the customary definitions and measures used in research. What *is* an index of secularization? Is it church attendance? Belief in immortality? The amount of private prayer? The number of scientists who believe in God? Or could it be that the indicators are more subtle, so much so that secularization

From the *Journal for the Scientific Study of Religion* 6(Fall 1967):207-20. Reprinted by permission of the publisher and author.

could even permeate what on the surface appears to be religious fervor? Is secularization a low score on a conventional index of religiosity? Or is it another form of religiosity? Or is it an independent process quite uncorrelated with religiosity? In both the empirical and interpretive work on secularization today, the lack of agreement on what secularization is and how to measure it stands out above everything else.

The following analysis is an attempt to bring the concept of secularization at least partially into focus by considering 1) its history, 2) its current definitions, 3) its use in empirical research, and 4) its weakness as an analytical tool and some possible alternatives.

An Historical Overview[1]

The English term "secular" comes from the Latin *saeculum,* which meant a generation, or an age, or the spirit of an age, and could also signify the span of a century. By the time of the Vulgate the Latin *saeculum* had already achieved considerable ambiguity, bearing both the religiously neutral sense of an immeasurably great span of time (e. g., *in saecula saeculorum,* I Tim. 1:17) and the religiously negative sense of "this world" which is under the power of Satan (e. g., *Et nolite confirmari huic saeculo,* Rom. 12:2). In the Middle Ages the idea of "this world" had itself been neutralized to some extent so that such concepts as "secular clergy" or the "secular arm" did not connote hostility to religion.

The first appearance of the form "secularization" (*saecularizatio*) in a sense approximating its present connotations was not until the negotiations for the Peace of Westphalia. Here the French representative introduced the term to signify lands and possessions transferred from ecclesiastical to civil control. Although most subsequent Roman Catholic discussions of secularization in this sense have regarded it as an unmitigated evil, not all the transfers in the 17th century were opposed by the Church, and the word retained in general a neutral and descriptive connotation.[2] By the 18th century, however, there were those who claimed that all ecclesiastical property should be at the disposition of the state as a matter of principle.[3] During the French Revolution, of course, this principle began to be carried out and expanded to all areas of life.

The best known use of the secularization terminology in a militant sense during the 19th century was by G. J. Holyoake and his freethinker's organization known as the "Secular Society." Holyoake called his program "Secularism," by which he meant "a practical philosophy for the people" intended to interpret and organize life without recourse to the supernatural.[4] Side by side with this aggressively programmatic meaning of "secularism" there has also grown up a usage which defines secularism as an attitude of indifference to religious institutions and practices or even to religious questions as such.

The historical sediment of most of these past meanings still clings to "secularism" and "secularization" as they are employed today in ordinary discourse. However, the dominant connotations, reflecting the long struggle against the tutelary function of the Churches and the Christian world view, are indifference, anti-clericalism, and irreligion. Beginning with Max Weber and Ernst Troeltsch, "secularization" was used as a descriptive and analytical term, and it was soon picked up by historians. Despite the relative neutrality attached to it in history and sociology during the first decades of the century, in theology it still designated a militant force to be combatted.

Since the Second World War, however, there has been an about-face among an increasing number of theologians. Dietrich Bonhoeffer and Friedrich Gogarten are the most significant of those who have argued that secularization is not only in part a result of Christian faith, but is also actually demanded and fostered in all areas of life by the freedom and responsibility laid on the man of faith. According to Gogarten, the independence of science and culture from the supposedly "Christian" world view is the logical and appropriate outcome of God's having turned the world over to man's responsibility.[5]

Many other theologians who are not ready to go as far as Bonhoeffer and Gogarten in celebrating the autonomy of man accept secularization as a positive development. This includes Catholic progressives who speak appreciatively of a secular society and look upon the medieval sacral society as an historical development necessitated by the Constantinian triumph but not as a phenomenon integral to the Christian faith. Although many of these more moderate Catholic and Protestant thinkers are "transformationists" who believe that secular society ought to be graced with the leaven of the sacred, it is clear that for them "secularization" is no longer a term of opprobrium but rather, an instrument of description and analysis.[6]

Types of Secularization Concept

If we put aside the special usage of economics and the legal definition derived from Westphalia, there appear to be six types of secularization concept in use today. Since what we are about to delineate are *types,* most of the actual definitions or usages one encounters in the literature will deviate to some degree or else represent combinations. Each is presented in terms of a brief definition which describes the kind of process involved and its theoretical culmination. Then a few examples are given before a critical assessment is attempted.

1. Decline of Religion

The previously accepted symbols, doctrines and institutions lose their prestige and influence. The culmination of secularization would be a religionless society. J. Milton Yinger, for example, terms secularization the process "in which traditional religious symbols and forms have lost force and appeal."[7]

Examples in research. One of the most significant general studies of American religion in the last few years, Glock and Stark's *Religion and Society in Tension,* makes use of a doctrinal version of the decline theory. The authors accept a definition of secularization as the replacement of "mystical and supernatural elements of traditional Christianity" by a "demythologized, ethical rather than theological religion."[8] They claim that some denominations are becoming relatively secularized in terms of the substantial percentage of members who either deny or are doubtful about many elements of their Church's historic creed.[9] Other studies have measured the decrease in clerical prestige, the number of marriages before clergymen, the amount of prayer or Church attendance, or the number of paintings with "religious" as opposed to "secular" themes.[10] Some, like Pitirim A. Sorokin, have put together a collection of such variables relating to belief and practice and developed a general theory of decline.[11]

Assessment. There are two major difficulties with the decline thesis. One is the problem of determining when and where we are to find the supposedly "religious" age from which decline has commenced. David Martin has noted that even secularists tend to take a utopian view of medieval religious life.[12] And as Gabriel Le Bras says of the term "dechristianization" which is widely used in France, such language presupposes a "christianized" France which never was. Moreover, although there has been a decrease in conventional forms of religious practice in France, Le Bras points out that there were in former times built-in premiums and liabilities relating to practice which may have produced large scale conventional acceptance of Christianity but little depth. Le Bras argues that in "dechristianized" France today there are, among practicing Catholics, probably more who participate voluntarily, faithfully and with an understanding of what they are doing than there were before 1789.[13]

Le Bras' suggestion regarding the seriousness of contemporary religious practice points to the other problems with the decline thesis: the ambiguity of most measures which are used. The easily measurable variables—church attendance, replies to belief questionnaires, proportion of contributions—are notoriously difficult to assess. Although the Glock and Stark study was a considerable improvement over past measures of belief, and although the refinements developed by Fichter, Lenski and Fukuyama have contributed much, the problem of the norm for doctrinal or practical deviation remains, as well as the question of whether such deviation from tradition is necessarily a decline.

Glock and Stark seem to accept the religious conservative's tendency to make "liberal theologically" the equivalent of "secularized." But is "liberal" theology really an adulteration of the historical faith? Or may it not be, as the best liberal theologians have always insisted, an interpretation of the essence of the tradition in the thought forms and language of today? Bultmann and others have even suggested that to repeat the old language and thought forms actually points men away from the genuine core of faith to peripheral matters and may demand an entirely unnecessary *sacrificium intellectus.* Moreover, far from being a mere capitulation or conformity to the reigning opinion of "this world," such an approach is viewed by its creators as the *only* way to face men with the real stumbling block of Christianity.[14] What can be the social scientist's justification for calling this effort to make a religious tradition more vital a "secularization" in the sense of a decline or subversion?

It is evident that part of the difficulty in measuring the decline of religion is the definition of religion itself.[15] As we proceed to examine other types of the secularization concept, the issue of the nature of religion will come up again and will finally have to be dealt with explicitly.

2. Conformity with "This World"

The religious group or the religiously informed society turns its attention from the supernatural and becomes more and more interested in "this world." In ethics there is a corresponding tendency away from an ethic motivated by the desire to prepare for the future life or to conform to the group's ethical tradition toward an ethic adapted to the present exigencies of the surrounding society. *The culmination of secularization would be a society totally absorbed with the pragmatic tasks of the present and a religious group indistinguishable from the rest of society.* Harold W. Pfautz has defined secularization as "the tendency of sectarian religious movements to become both part of and like 'the world.' "[16]

Examples in research. The classic statement of this position is Adolf Harnack's characterization of the early Church's growth in numbers and wealth, its emerging hierarchial organization, and its involvement with Greek thought as a "secularization."[17] Pfautz's analysis of Christian Science measures conformity to the world in terms of an "increasing traditional and purposeful-rational motivation, and decreasing affectual motivation."[18] In an important study of the general sect-church spectrum, Pfautz develops a more complex set of variables for measuring secularization in terms of demography, ecology, associational character, structural differentiation, and social-psychological texture. The movement across the typology is termed a "secularization" because it involves a constant increase in size, complexity, and rationalization of structures and modes of participation.[19]

By far the most provocative investigation of this type of secularization in America has been Will Herberg's *Protestant-Catholic-Jew.*[20] In his more recent Harlan Paul Douglas lectures he distinguishes between *conventional* religions (e.g., Judaism, Islam, Protestant denominations) and the *operative* religion of a society which actually provides its own "ultimate context of meaning and value."[21] Then he defines a secularized culture as one in which "conventional religion is no longer the operative religion in the sociological sense."[22] In his earlier book Herberg measured secularization by the degree to which nominal believers who belong to conventional religions actually reflect the outlook of the operative religion of American society.[23] In the second of his Douglas lectures, he modified Pfautz's typology of religious groups and concluded: "The series can now be completed: *cult—sect—denomination—socio-religious community—tri-faith system.* Beyond this, secularization cannot go."[24]

ASSESSMENT. As in the case of the decline thesis, the main difficulty with the idea of secularization as conformity to the world is the ambiguity of the measures applied. Moreover, simply by employing the Church/world or "this world/other world" dichotomy, the social scientist has taken over a particular theological framework as his own. In any given case we must ask whether something *integral* to a religious tradition is being surrendered in favor of "this world" or whether the change which is taking place may not be quite compatible with the main stream of the tradition. Is it a subversion of Islam or Christianity that one becomes increasingly concerned with the good life in "this world," or is it perhaps as much a shift of emphasis from certain elements in these traditions to other elements no less integral? And may not an apparent compromise with the world on the part of a religious group be part of a necessary differentiation within the group which leaves behind the affectional relationships of the "good old days" without breaking down the core of the tradition?

These observations are not meant to depreciate the usefulness of Pfautz's typology, but rather to question the value of terming the process one of "increasing secularization" when this implies a deviation or subversion from a more genuinely religious position. A similar objection may be made to Herberg's thesis, since what looks like secularization to Herberg appears to some religious liberals as the triumph of the "common faith" of America. The latter may be in some respects false or shallow, but it is a misleading (if not simply pejorative) use of the word to term the one religion "secularized" and treat the other as "authentic."

Although the three types of concept we will consider next have not been used as widely in empirical research as the two above, they are worth delineating in equal detail since they are more descriptive and also more suggestive in terms of the relationship between religious change and other variables.

3. Disengagement of Society from Religion

Society separates itself from the religious understanding which has previously informed it in order to constitute itself an autonomous reality and consequently to limit religion to the sphere of private life. The culmination of this kind of secularization would be a religion of a purely inward character, influencing neither institutions nor corporate action, and a society in which religion made no appearance outside the sphere of the religious group. Hannah Arendt defines secularization in one place as "first of all simply the separation of religion and politics."[25] The French theologian and social analyst Roger Mehl has described secularization as the "historical process which tends to contest the public role of religion, to substitute other forms of authority for religious authority, and finally to relegate religion to the private sector of human existence."[26]

Examples in Research. This understanding of secularization has been extensively investigated by historians, who see it as taking two forms, one intellectual-existential, the other institutional-social. Institutional secularization is usually traced in terms of the rise of the "secular" state and its gradual assumption of the educational and welfare functions once performed by the churches. A recent non-Western example of this is given in Donald E. Smith's *India as a Secular State,* where it is argued that the Indian government has been secularized in the sense that it has adopted an attitude of neutrality toward both individual and group religious belief and practice.[27] The social transformation which usually accompanies the secularization of the state has been analyzed in a variety of ways and has produced studies of the secularization of work, welfare, family life, etc. The intellectual-existential aspect of disengagement has probably been as extensively explored as any phenomenon of secularization. Bernhard Grotheuysen aptly describes the process as "the attempt to establish an autonomous sphere of knowledge purged of supernatural, fideistic presuppositions."[28] Concretely, one speaks of the secularization of science or ethics or art insofar as they are separated from ecclesiastical control or from the context of a particular version of the Christian world view.

ASSESSMENT. Although more specific than the thesis of decline or conformity with the world, the concept of secularization as disengagement suffers from parallel handicaps. Smith's argument that the Indian state is secularized because it is neutral on religious beliefs and practices has been criticized as overlooking the fact that the Hindu and Islamic faiths have never been a matter of purely private beliefs and practices. Smith's critics suggest that Indian secularity involves a strong dose of secularism, by which they mean a commitment to an ideology which seeks to embrace the whole of life and to replace the role once held by the religious communities.[29] A number of Christian thinkers have made a similar distinction between "secularization" or "secularity," which they take as signifying the rejection of religious or ecclesiastical tutelage of society, and "secularism" as signifying an all-embracing ideology which seeks to deny religious institutions or viewpoints any formative role in society. In reply, Smith acknowledges that the same sort of distinction is actually accepted by many Hindus and Moslems who find the relative restriction of their religious life to the private sphere fully consonant with the integrity of the faith.[30]

By its careful attention to the conceptual problem, Smith's work illustrates the pitfalls of defining secularization as disengagement. His work has also clearly raised the important question of how one decides when secularization in this sense has taken place and when we should speak rather of an internal adjustment within the religious tradition, or even of the triumph of one religion or religiously colored ideology over another.

One way of remedying the defects in the disengagement thesis is to substitute the more descriptive and neutral concept of *"differentiation"* that has been developed by Parsons and Bellah.

Parsons proposes "differentiation" as an alternative to the interpretation of modern society as undergoing a process of secularization in the sense of a "decline" of religion.[31] In an argument strikingly similar to that proposed by Gogarten, he points out that Christianity contains within itself the principle of differentiation between the community of faith and the social community as well as the differentiation within the religious community between faith and ethics. Similarly, in speaking of the Reformation's extension of the autonomy of the social and economic community and the Reformers' religious enfranchisement of the individual, Parsons notes that the Lutheran concept of the calling could be termed a secularization, but he prefers to see it as the "endowment of secular life with a new order of religious legitimation."[32] It is indeed true that many of the functions performed by the Churches and religious communities and many of the values of the Christian ethical tradition have been taken over by society at large and generalized. But this is not a sign that the Western religious tradition has collapsed; it is, rather, that the religious community plays an altered role in keeping with the general differentiation of society. Parsons is quite aware, of course, that Christianity has been facing a serious challenge to its understanding of man and the world.[33]

Bellah's version of the concept is intended as an overall framework for understanding religious evolution in general. He makes use of Voegelin's notion of the movement from compact to differentiated symbols, as well as describing differentiation within religious groups and between religion and other facets of society.[34] He refuses to consider even the rejection of the natural-supernatural schema and the gradual loss of concern for doctrinal orthodoxy a sign of "indifference or secularization," seeing it as simply a reflection of a new way of conceiving and practicing religion.[35] In this he would be supported by a good number of contemporary theologians. At the least, the concept of differentiation suggests that the idea of secularization as a disengagement of society from religion which reduces religion to insignificance may be a somewhat crude and value-charged designation of a much more complex and subtle phenomenon.

4. Transposition of Religious Beliefs and Institutions

Knowledge, patterns of behavior, and institutional arrangements which were once understood as grounded in divine power are transformed into phenomena of purely human creation and responsibility. In the case of disengagement, the institutions or social arrangements which are secularized are seen as something which did not necessarily belong to the sphere of religion, whereas in the case of transposition it is aspects of religious belief or experience themselves which are shifted from their sacral context to a purely human context. *The culmination of this kind of secularization process would be a totally anthropologized religion and a society which had taken over all the functions previously accruing to the religious institutions.* Writing of the secularization of historical interpretation, Adalbert Klempt speaks of secularization as the "transformation of conceptions and modes of thought which were originally developed by the Christian salvation belief and its theology into ones of a world-based outlook."[36]

EXAMPLES IN RESEARCH. Although it is difficult to find examples of "pure" transpositions with no admixture of other ideas or experience, some well-known theses have proposed the "spirit of capitalism" as a secularization of the Calvinist ethic, the Marxist version of the consumation of the revolution as coming from Jewish-Christian eschatology, psychotherapy as a secular outgrowth of confession and the cure of souls, etc. The classical treatment of transposition comes from Ernst Troeltsch, who spoke, for example, of "the complete severance of sexual feelings from the thought of original sin" which has been effected "by modern art and poetry" as "nothing else than the secularization of the intense religious emotions."[37] In another work he writes of the belief in progress as a "secularization of Christian eschatology."[38]

ASSESSMENT. The difficulty with the transposition thesis, of course, is the problem of identifying survivals or transmigrations. Is a supposed transposition really a Jewish or Christian belief or practice now appearing under the guise of a more generalized rationale, or is it something of separate origin and conception which has taken over some of the functions of the former religious phenomenon? We need only call to mind the sharp debate over the Weber thesis to envisage the kind of disagreements which can beset any particular thesis regarding a transposition. The wide-spread view that Marxism contains a transposition of some Jewish-Christian elements has also come under heavy attack.[39]

The German philosopher Hans Blumenberg has offered what is perhaps the most complete and also the most perceptive critique of the concept of secularization as transposition. Using as his test case the theory that the idea of progress is a secularization of Christian eschatology, he points out that neither is there proof of causal dependence, nor are the two ideas really the same in content; the parallel, rather, is one of function.[40]

Another fallacy implicit in the transposition thesis derives from its origin in the use of the term "secularization" for the transfer of ecclesiastical possessions from the Church to the princes. Is the vision of an ultimate consumation of history, for example, really the "possession" of Judaism or Christianity so that its later use by other movements must be regarded as a usurpation?[41] Blumenberg goes so far as to suggest that this way of conceiving secularization functions simply as a weapon of the theologians in their attack on the legitimacy of the modern world, and that its use by historians and sociologists reflects a fundamental uncertainty on their part as to the rightful place of the modern outlook. Whether or not one is willing to go that far, it must be admitted that Blumenberg has given us grounds for demanding that any reputed transposition theory pass strict methodological criteria.

5. Desacralization of the World

The world is gradually deprived of its sacral character as man and nature become the object of rational-causal explanation and manipulation. The culmination of secularization would be a completely "rational" world society in which the phenomenon of the supernatural or even of "mystery" would play no part. Historian Eric Kahler writes that secularization means "that man became independent of religion and lived by reason, face to face with objectified, physical nature."[42]

Examples in research. The classical statement of this view is Max Weber's concept of "disenchantment" (*Entzauberung*) which signifies an irreversible trend of rationalization leading to a view of the world as a self-contained causal nexus.[43] Among contemporary writers, Mircea Eliade has given us the most sensitive evocation of the loss (or suppression) of the sense of the sacred. Eliade too finds the root of desacralization in science, which has so neutralized nature and human life that no point can have "a unique ontological status" which integrates the whole.[44]

The proponents of the desacralization thesis do not agree as to how far this process can go. Some apparently feel that it will one day complete itself and religion, insofar as it is bound to an acknowledgement of the "sacred" or "holy," will disappear. Others hold that man is "incurably religious" and believe either that the sense of the sacred has been pushed into the unconscious for the time being or that it is in the process of finding new forms of expression.

Assessment. Although less global and simplistic than the decline thesis, the desacralization concept bears certain similarities to it. The inherent problem with the desacralization view is its assumption that religion is inextricably bound up with an understanding of the world as permeated by sacred powers. There is in the Hebraic faith, however, a definite desacralization of the world through the radical transcendence of the Creator, who alone is eminently holy and who has, moreover, given the world over to the dominion of man (Gen. 1:24). In Christianity the process is carried further through the separation of religion and politics and the notion of sonship through Christ in which man is free from the elemental spirits of the universe (Mk. 12:17 and Gal. 4:1 ff). This phenomenon of a religious tradition which itself desacralizes the world suggest that the desacralization view of secularization is not applicable to at least the Western tradition without qualification.

6. Movement from a "Sacred" to a "Secular" Society

This is a general concept of *social change,* emphasizing multiple variables through several stages. According to Howard Becker, its chief developer, the main variable is resistance or openness to change. Accordingly, *the culmination of secularization would be a society in which all decisions are based on rational and utilitarian considerations and there is complete acceptance of change.*[45] A theological version of this type of secularization concept has been developed by Bernard Meland, who defines secularization as "the movement away from traditionally accepted norms and sensibilities in the life interests and habits of a people."[46] Since Meland means by sensibilities a capacity to "respond appreciatively and with restraint to accepted ways of feeling or behavior," secularization does not refer merely to religious phenomena but to any traditional norms and perceptions.[47] Since this type of secularization concept is a general theory of social change rather than a theory of specifically religious change, it would take us well beyond the limits of the present inquiry if we were to examine the vast empirical literature that has grown out of it.

The Secular-Religious Polarity

Criticism of "Religion" Concept

Because the concept of secularization usually refers back to a secular-religious or sacred-profane polarity, our critique of it has often implied a parallel critique in certain definitions of "religion." It is evident that the criticisms made above were aimed at a view of religious phenomena which narrowly restricts them to certain external elements in the Western tradition, e. g., church attendance and financial support, conventional forms of public and private devotional practice, belief scales based on traditional creeds. The suggestion was also made that belief in the supernatural or in sacral powers pervading man and nature is not essential to all the kinds of phenomena we characterize as religious. My reasons for refusing to restrict the understanding of religion in any of these ways is twofold.

In the first place, the range of phenomena which have been considered religious is so varied that no single definition of the "essence" of religion can embrace them all. Consequently, it would be extremely difficult to discover a list of measurable indices of decline, subversion, transposition or other radical shift away from the "religious" toward the "secular." After examining some of the various ways of defining the polarity, David Martin concludes that it is impossible to develop criteria for distinguishing between the religious and the secular since it would be "an obvious absurdity" to combine "the metaphysical and mythopoetic modes of thought, the acceptance of miracle, belief in historical purpose, rejection of material benefits, and lack of confidence towards the world under the common rubric of religion."[48]

Secondly, most definitions of the essence of religion, even when they have not been crude combinations of practice and belief, have assumed that there exists an *entity* called "religion." This reification, as Wilfred Cantwell Smith has pointed out, is of recent origin even in the West, and many of its current connotations represent a polemical situation growing out of the Enlightenment.[49] This is perhaps why we not only have numerous Christian theologians denying that Christian faith is a religion (although Christianity may be), but we also have Jewish, Buddhist, Hindu and Muslim thinkers who refuse to consider their faith one of the "religions."

Paul Tillich has even suggested that the existence of a religious as opposed to a secular realm in human experience is an expression of "the tragic estrangement of man's spiritual life from its own ground and depth."[50] Thus, the notion of a religion as a separate part of culture presupposes an advanced stage of differentiation and reflects an attitude contrary to the way at least some of the adherents understand their own tradition. Therefore, I can sympathize with Smith's suggestion that we drop the substantive form "religion" altogether and use the concepts "faith" and "tradition" to convey respectively the interior and external aspects of what have been called "the religions."[51] This does not mean, of course, that we should give up the attempt to describe the quality or qualities which may be designated "religious," e. g., "ultimate concern," "openness for mystery," "apprehension of harmony," "commitment to creativity." But unfortunately, even the term "religious" continues to retain many connotations which would lead sensitive persons to hesitate to apply it to themselves or to their tradition.

Criticism of Polarity

Before leaving the problem of the definition of "religion" and the "religious" one further critical question needs to be raised. Must we think in polar terms at all? There are three disadvantages to a polar concept of the secular-religious type.

First, it tends to deceive us into taking a particular form of differentiation in the West as normative. Niyazi Berkes has pointed out that the usual dichotomy is based on the Western model of "church" and "state," which presupposes an institutionalized religion distinct from the political order. When we apply this "spiritual-temporal" polarity to non-Western situations where such differentiations did not originally exist, we falsify the data.[52]

Second, the secular-religious polarity easily encourages the assumption that an increase of activity in the so-called secular sphere must mean a corresponding decline in the religious area. But, as J. H. Hexter has remarked of this particular intellectual trap, there is considerable evidence that in some periods of history—the sixteenth century is one —*both* aspects of society rose to higher levels of intensity.[53]

Finally, the secular-religious polarity simply compounds the deception in the idea that religion is an entity of some kind. For if one does not begin by defining religion or the religious in terms of institutional or behavioral traits there will be no need to find a polar opposite. When "religious" is used to designate a certain quality of life or dimension of individual and social experience which concerns the whole man and the whole of society, this dimension may be as much in play in certain activities conventionally labeled "secular" as it is not in play in some that are conventionally labeled "religious."

Conclusion

During its long development the term "secularization" has often served the partisans of controversy and has constantly taken on new meanings without completely losing old ones. As a result it is swollen with overtones and implications, especially those associated with indifference or hostility to whatever is considered "religious."

On one hand, Martin has gone so far as to suggest that it has been a "tool of counter-religious ideologies," which define the "real" basis of religion and claim that religion so defined is in a process of irreversible decline. Martin believes the motives behind this are partly "the aesthetic satisfactions found in such notions and partly as a psychological boost to the movements with which they are associated."[54]

At the other end of the spectrum are the all too familiar clerical lamentations over the increase of "secularism." Blumenberg, as we have seen, even suggests that the concept of secularization has been a tool of those theologians and clerics who want to impugn the legitimacy of the modern world.

As if the conceptual situation were not confusing enough, the current enthusiasm in theology for styling one's version of Christianity "secular" muddies the conceptual waters almost to the point of hopelessness. As noted above, behind the present secular theology fad lies the work of several more sober theologians (Bonhoeffer, Gogarten, Michalson) who have worked out a sophisticated defense of secularization conceived in terms of man's coming into responsibility for his own destiny. To them, what Herberg calls a secularization of society is actually the triumph of "religion," whereas the legitimate outcome of faith would be the secularization of society in the sense of neutralizing conventional religiosity. Although Bonhoeffer and Gogarten do not style themselves "secular" theologians, the recent rash of books proclaiming "the secular meaning of the Gospel" or a "secular Christianity," or praising the "secular city" as the solely authentic place of Christian existence have made "secularization" once again an ecclesiastical battle slogan by stinging traditionalists and conservatives into a counter attack on this "secularization of Christianity."[55]

This accumulation of contradictory connotations would be enough of a handicap, but there is an even more serious one in the fact that so many different processes and phenomena are designated by the term "secularization." Often the same writer will use it in two or more senses without acknowledging the shift of meaning. Thus Weber could employ it not only for "disenchantment" but also for transpositions (spirit of capitalism), and at times even in the sense of becoming "worldly," as when he speaks of the "secularizing influence of wealth" on monasticism.[56]

The appropriate conclusion to draw from the confusing connotations and the multitude of phenomena covered by the term secularization would seem to be that we drop the word entirely and employ instead terms such as "transposition" or "differentiation" which are both more descriptive and neutral.

Since a moratorium on any widely used term is unlikely to be effected, however, there are two ways of salvaging "secularization" as a useful concept in empirical research. One, of course, is for everyone who employs it to state carefully his intended meaning and to stick to it.

The other is for researchers to agree on the term as a general designation or large scale concept covering certain subsumed aspects of religious change.

Three of the processes discussed above could be embraced significantly by the term "secularization" since they are not contradictory but complementary: desacralization, differentiation and transposition. To a certain degree they can also be seen as representing successive and overlapping emphases in Western religious history. Although the desacralization of nature and history, for example, seems to have generally preceded political and social differentiation, the former was not accomplished all at once. And it is evident that transposition cannot take place without the prior or concomitant occurrence of differentiation. To work out the exact bearing of and the measurement criteria for these sub-concepts is a task that still requires considerable reflection. I am afraid, however, that the careless and partisan use of "secularization" is so general that its polemical connotations will continue to cling to it despite the social scientist's efforts to neutralize it.

---

1. There are two discussions of the history of the concept of secularization available. Martin Stallmann, *Was ist Säkularisierung?,* Tübingen: J. C. B. Mohr, 1960, Chapt. I. Hermann Lübbe, *Säkularisierung, Geschichte eines ideenpolitischen Begriffs,* Freiburg, Karl Alber, 1965.

2. Stallmann, *op. cit.,* pp. 5-7.

3. *Ibid.,* p. 8.

4. For a short discussion of the background and principles of the movement see Eric S. Waterhouse's article on Secularism in the *Encyclopedia of Religion and Ethics,* Vol. XI, New York: Charles Scribner's Sons, 1921, pp. 347-50.

5. Gogarten's fullest statement of this position is to be found in *Verhängnis und Hoffnung der Neuzeit,* Stuttgart: Friedrich Vorwerk, 1953. Bonhoeffer's comments are found in *Prisoner for God,* New York: Macmillan, 1953, and *Ethics,* New York: Macmillan, 1955.

6. For a discussion of the main theological attempts to come to grips with the problem of secularization, see Larry Shiner, Towards a Theology of Secularization, *Journal of Religion,* Oct. 1965, pp. 279-95.

7. J. Milton Yinger, *Religion, Society and the Individual,* New York: Macmillan, 1957, p. 119.

8. Charles Y. Glock and Rodney Stark, *Religion and Society in Tension,* Chicago: Rand McNally, 1965, p. 116.

9. *Ibid.,* pp. 116-20.

10. Some examples may be found in Robert S. Lynd and Helen Merrell Lynd, *Middletown,* New York: Harcourt, Brace and Company, 1929, pp. 112, 120-21, 462; Daniel Lerner, *The Passing of Traditional Society,* Glencoe: The Free Press, 1958, p. 230; John T. Flint, The Secularization of Norwegian Society, *Comparative Studies in Society and History,* VI, 1964, pp. 325-44.

11. Pitirim A. Sorokin, The Western Religion and Morality of Today, *International Yearbook for the Sociology of Religion,* Vol. II, Köln und Opladen: Westdeutscher Verlag, 1966, pp. 9-43.

12. David A. Martin, Utopian Aspects of the Concept of Secularization, *Internatioanl Yearbook for the Sociology of Religion,* Vol. II, Köln und Opladen: Westdeutscher Verlag, 1966, p. 92.

13. Gabriel Le Bras, Déchristianisation: mot fallacieux, *Social Compass,* X, 1963, pp. 448 and 451.

14. Rudolf Bultmann, The New Testament and Mythology, in *Kerygma and Myth,* ed. by H. W. Bartsch, London, S. P. C. K., 1953, pp. 1-6. See also pp. 120-23 on the "real skandalon" of Christian faith.

15. Paul Tillich, Existentialist Aspects of Modern Art, in *Christianity and the Existentialists,* ed. by Carl Michalson, New York: Charles Scribner's Sons, 1956, pp. 133-38.

16. Harold Pfautz, Christian Science: A Case Study of the Social Psychological Aspect of Secularization, *Social Forces,* 34, 1956, p. 246.

17. Adolf von Harnack, *Monasticism: Its Ideals and History,* London: Willams Norgate, 1901, p. 112.

18. Harold W. Pfautz, *op. cit.*, p. 247.

19. Harold W. Pfautz, The Sociology of Secularization: Religious Groups, *American Journal of Sociology*, 61, 1955, pp. 121-28.

20. Will Herberg, *Protestant-Catholic-Jew*, New York, Anchor Books, 1960.

21. Will Herberg, Religion in a Secularized Society: The New Shape of Religion in America, *Review of Religious Research*, 3, 1961-62, p. 146.

22. *Ibid.*, p. 148.

23. Herberg, *op. cit.*, pp. 74-9, 82-3.

24. Will Herberg, The New Shape of American Religion: Some Aspects of America's Three-Religion Pluralism, *Review of Religious Research*, 4, 1962-63, p. 39.

25. Hannah Arendt, *Between Past and Future*, Cleveland: Meridian Books, 1963, p. 69.

26. Roger Mehl, De la sécularisation à l'atheism, *Foi et Vie*, 65, 1966, p. 70.

27. Donald E. Smith, *India as a Secular State*, Princeton: Princeton University Press, 1963.

28. Bernhard Grotheuysen, Secularism, *Encyclopedia of the Social Sciences*, 1934, XIII, p. 631.

29. Marc Galanter, Secularism, East and West, *Comparative Studies in Society and History*, 7, 1965, pp. 148-53.

30. Donald E. Smith, Secularism in India, *Comparative Studies in Society and History*, 7, 1965, pp. 169-70.

31. Talcott Parsons, Christianity and Modern Industrial Society, in *Sociological Theory, Values and Sociocultural Change*, ed. by Edward A. Tiryakian, Glencoe: Free Press, 1963, pp. 33-70.

32. *Ibid.*, p. 50.

33. *Ibid.*, p. 69.

34. Robert N. Bellah, Religious Evolution, *American Sociological Review*, 29, 1964, pp. 358-59.

35. Bellah, *op. cit.*, p. 73.

36. Adalbert Klempt, *Die Säkularisierung der Universalhistorischen Auffassung*, Gottingen: Musterschmidt, 1960, p. 7.

37. Ernst Troeltsch, *Protestantism and Progress*, Boston: Beacon Press, 1958, p. 96.

38. Ernst Troeltsch, *Der Historismus und seine Probleme*, Tübingen: M. C. B. Mohr, 1922, p. 57.

39. Reinhard Wittram, Möglichkeiten und Grenzen der Geschichtswissenschaft in der Gegenwart, *Zeitschrift für Theologie und Kirche*, 62, 1965, pp. 430-57. Henri Desroche, *Marxisme et Religions*, Paris: Presses Universitaires de France, 1962.

40. Hans Blumenberg, Säkularisation: Kritik einer Kategorie Historischer Illegitimität, in *Die Philosophie und die Frage nach dem Fortschritt*, ed. by Helmut Kuhn and Franz Wiedmann, München: Anton Pustet, 1964, pp. 249-50.

41. *Ibid.*, pp. 247-48.

42. Eric Kahler, *Man the Measure*, New York: Pantheon Books, 1943, p. 333.

43. Max Weber, Science as a Vocation, in *From Max Weber, Essays in Sociology*, ed. and trans, by H. H. Gerth and C. Wright Mills, New York: Oxford University Press, 1946, p. 139.

44. Mircea Eliade, *The Sacred and the Profane*, New York: Harper Torchbooks, 1961, p. 17.

45. Howard Becker, Current Secular-Sacred Theory and its Development, in *Modern*

Sociological Theory in Continuity and Change, ed. by Howard Becker and Alvin Boskoff, New York: Dryden Press, 1957, pp. 133-86. The most recent statement is contained in Becker's articles Sacred Society and Secular Society in *A Dictionary of the Social Sciences,* ed. by Julius Gould and William L. Kolb, New York: Free Press of Glencoe, 1964, pp. 613 and 626.

46. Bernard E. Meland, *The Secularization of Modern Cultures,* New York: Oxford University Press, 1966, p. 3.

47. *Ibid.,* p. 9.

48. David Martin, Towards Eliminating the Concept of Secularization, in *Penguin Survey of the Social Sciences,* ed. by Julius Gould, Baltimore: Penguin Books, 1965, p. 173.

49. Wilfred Cantwell Smith, *The Meaning and End of Religion,* New York: The New American Library, 1964, pp. 43 ff.

50. Paul Tillich, *Theology of Culture,* New York: Oxford University Press, 1959, p. 8.

51. Smith, *op. cit.,* pp. 139-81.

52. Niyazi Berkes, Religious and Secular Institutions in Comparative Perspective, *Archives de Sociologie des Religions,* 8, 1963, pp. 65-72.

53. J. H. Hexter, *Reappraisals in History,* New York: Harper Torchbooks, 1961, pp. 40-43.

54. David Martin, *op. cit.,* p. 176.

55. E. L. Mascall, *The Secularization of Christianity,* London: Darton, Longman & Todd, 1965. The other books alluded to are Paul Van Buren, *The Secular Meaning of the Gospel,* New York: Macmillan, 1963; Ronald Gregor Smith, *Secular Christianity,* New York: Harper & Row, 1966; Harvey Cox, *The Secular City,* New York: Macmillan, 1965.

56. Max Weber, *The Protestant Ethic and the Spirit of Capitalism,* New York: Charles Scribner's Sons, 1958, p. 174.

PETER L. BERGER

A Sociological View of the Secularization of Theology

Considerable public attention in this country has recently been focused on a movement in Protestant theology variously described as "radical," "secular," or just plain "new." This attention has gone far beyond the confines of organized religion proper, even attracting comment from such venerable theological journals as *Time, Newsweek,* and *The New Yorker.* The newsworthiness of the movement has been enhanced by its connection with several other developments of wide public interest, such as the civil rights movement, in which there has also been a "radical" involvement by religious figures; the so-called "youth problem," which supposedly involves widespread disillusion with societal values, religious and other; and the long-lasting news field day provided by the Vatican Council. By now, such bywords of the "secular" theologians as "death of God" or "post-Christian era" have become standard topics of discussion at businessmen's Bible breakfasts and in book re-

From the *Journal for the Scientific Study of Religion* 6(Spring 1967): 3-16. Reprinted by permission of the publisher and author.

views in the provincial press. To the extent that public issues in our society are largely determined by the mass media, it is possible to say that the "new" theology has become a public issue.

The spectacle afforded by the movement is strange. Indeed, it has all the characteristics of a man-bites-dog story. The phrase "secular theology" itself strikes with intriguing dissonance, while phrases such as "atheist theology" or "religionless Christianity" seem to come from a script for the theater of the absurd. The strangeness of the spectacle does not disappear on closer scrutiny. Professional theologians declare that their discipline must begin with the presupposition that there is no God. Clergymen, even bishops, charged with the performance of public worship proclaim the senselessness of prayer. Salaried employees of religious organizations state that these organizations are destined to fade away—and the sooner, the better. To an outside observer, say a Muslim scholar of western religion, all this might well appear as a bizarre manifestation of intellectual derangement or institutional suicide. An observer familiar with the background of these ideas can, of course, show that they did not spring from nowhere, but this still does not explain why they have attained their peculiar virulence at this time, nor how they can so plausibly present themselves as the wave of the future. We may assume that any adequate explanation of the phenomenon will have to be multifaceted. However, a sociological view of the matter (more specifically, a view in terms of the sociology of knowledge) can add something to our understanding of what is happening. Before we attempt this, though, a closer look at the ideational content of the phenomenon will be necessary.

The Ideational Content

While the roots of these ideas are in earlier developments, particularly in post-World War II controversies within German Protestant theology, their explosion into public view may conveniently be placed in 1963, when John Robinson's *Honest to God* was first published in England. The book immediately produced a violent public controversy there, which was repeated in other countries as the book was translated. In this country, not surprisingly, the book rapidly achieved bestseller status, and the attention paid to this controversy by the mass media attained the crescendo appropriate to the style of our cultural life. Since then, a number of American figures have either associated themselves, or been associated by others, with Robinson's overall theological stance—notably William Hamilton, Paul Van Buren, Gabriel Vahanian, Thomas Altizer, and, lately, Harvey Cox. Paul Tillich, apparently to his dismay, is widely regarded as a sort of elder statesman of the movement. While the movement continues to be definitely Protestant, it has found an echo both among *aggiornamento*-minded Catholics and among liberal Jews. It is safe to assume that the movement represents something much more significant than a curiosity of the Protestant imagination.

The various figures associated with the movement differ considerably in their precise positions and in the level of theoretical sophistication. All the same, it is possible to identify a central characteristic common to all of them—namely a denial, in various degrees and on different grounds, of the objective validity of the supernatural affirmations of the Christian tradition. Put differently, the movement generally shows a shift from a transcendental to an immanent perspective, and from an objective to a subjective understanding of religion. Generally, traditional affirmations referring to other-worldly entities or events are "translated" to refer to concerns of this world, and traditional affirmations about the nature of something "out there" (to use a phrase of Robinson's) are "translated" to become statements about the nature of man or his temporal situation. For example, the resurrection is no longer understood as a cosmic event, but as a symbol of human existential or psychological processes. For another example, Christian eschatology ceases to refer to the interventions of a transcendent God, but becomes an ethical perspective on current political affairs.

It is important to understand that this general characteristic of the "new" theology is anything but new. Rather, it stands in a direct continuity with classical Protestant liberalism at least as far back as Schleiermacher's "translation" of the Lutheran *"Christus pro me"* into a concept of "religious experience." It is instructive in this connection to read Adolf Harnack's great manifesto of Protestant liberalism, *Das Wesen des Christentums,* first published in 1900, and imagine what *Time* might say about it if it had just been written by a "radical" seminary professor. The immediate European antecedents of the new theology are commonly given as Rudolph Bultmann and Dietrich Bonhoeffer. In the latter case, it takes great selectivity to find legitimations for the current positions in Bonhoeffer's writings (mostly, in the fragmentary and, by their very nature, ambiguous writings of the underground period, particularly the correspondence from prison). In the case of Bultmann, however, the connection with classical liberalism is not hard to see. The Anglo-American theologians cannot even claim newness with respect to the degree of their "radicalness." If Bultmann is not already radical enough, there are such figures of comtemporary German-speaking theology as Friedrich Gogarten and Fritz Burl, not to mention once more, Tillich's daring "correlations" between the Christian tradition and modern secular thought. In addition to some of the conceptual tools, of which more in a moment, what is new here is, above all, the resonance of these ideas in a mass public. This fact by itself leads to the suspicion that there is a sociological dimension to the phenomenon.

In addition to the central characteristic indicated before, the secular theologians share a common presupposition, that the traditional religious affirmations are no longer tenable, either because they do not meet certain modern philosophical or scientific criteria of validity, or because they are contrary to an alleged modern world view that is somehow binding on everybody. In some cases it is not quite clear which of these two reasons (logically quite different) is the decisive one. Must the traditional affirmations be given up because we now know that they are false, or because we simply cannot put them over any more? Because of this confusion, the presupposition that the tradition is now untenable often hovers uneasily between questions of epistemology and of evangelistic tactics. Be this as it may, the conclusion typically comes out as a statement that "We cannot any longer . . ." maintain this or that element of the tradition, or cannot perhaps even maintain the tradition itself. This conclusion could, of course, result in the rejection of the theological enterprise as such or of the ecclesiastical institutions that embody the tradition—and we know that there are individuals who do just that.

The interesting thing about the secular theologians, however, is that they do *not* draw this conclusion. Not only do they continue to operate as theologians, but most of them do so within the context of traditional ecclesiastical institutions. That this creates a certain amount of practical strain is obvious and needs no elaboration here. The strain, however, is also theoretical. The problem of translation, consequently, is one of great urgency. In other words, if the situation is interpreted in such a way that "We cannot any longer," then a way must be found to deal with the tradition so that "We can again"—that is, can again exist as ecclesiastically involved theologians. It should be stressed as emphatically as possible that putting the problem in these terms *in no way* questions the sincerity of such an intellectual operation. On the contrary, the desire for sincerity is probably one of the strongest driving forces in this whole movement. The issue is not whether such an operation is sincere, but what theoretical procedures are required for it. In other words, given the problem of translation, where are the grammars?

Classical Protestant liberalism used various forms of philosophical rationalism or positivism to solve the same problem, as well as the newly refined tools of historical scholarship. To some extent, these methods are still used, both in the demolition and in the reconstruction phases of the translation enterprise. New conceptual tools have been added, derived from existentialism, psychoanalysis, sociology, and linguistic analysis (probably in declining order of importance). With the exception of the last, which understandably plays a greater part in the English branch of the movement and which in this country has been particularly employed by Van Buren, these conceptual machineries permeate the entire ideational complex and often overlap in both of the above-mentioned phases.

It is important to see that these conceptual mechanisms have two applications. They may be used by some writers in the movement on a high level of theoretical sophistication, and yet have an ideological correlate on a lower level of popular consciousness. Take the application of existentialism to our problem, for example. Concepts derived from existential philosophy, particularly Heidegger's, are the standard operating procedures of Bultmann's particular translation exercise—to wit, his famous program of "demythologization." With system and consistency, the entire transcendental frame of reference of the Christian tradition is demolished, that is, consigned to the mythological world view that "we cannot any longer" maintain. (His one lapse in consistency, as was immediately pointed out by some of his critics, was the retention of an acting God.) The major items so treated are then translated into terms that make sense within the frame of reference of an existentialist anthropology—a procedure, of course, of the most radical detranscendentalization and subjectivization imaginable. Thus transcendental ontology becomes immanent anthropology, and *Heilsgeschichte* becomes a kind of biography, the biography of the individual in terms of whose *Existenz* the reinterpreted tradition is still supposed to make sense. A similar procedure, employed with immense erudition and ingenuity, is at the center of Tillich's translation enterprise, and it is reiterated in one way or another (though rarely with the same intellectual force) by most of the figures in this movement. The sometimes awe-inspiring eggheadedness of the existentialist vocabulary must not be allowed to obscure the "pop" correlates of the movement. For example, existentialist *Angst* and alienation are not limited to seminary professors who have read Heidegger. To a remarkable degree, these experiences seem to be shared by suburban housewives. As a result, the translations undertaken by the seminary professors can be popularly applied by ministers with suburban housewives in their clientele. To use a Weberian term, there appears to be an "elective affinity" between certain ideas of Heidegger and the mentality of certain suburban housewives. The explanation of this, as we shall try to show presently, is to be sought *not* in a philosophical analysis of Heidegger, but in a sociology-of-knowledge perspective on the quasi-Heideggerian housewives.

Ideas derived from psychoanalysis (psychologism would probably be a better term) play a very prominent part in the translation procedures. The traditional religious affirmations are understood as symbols of (largely unconscious) psychological states and, as such, declared to have continuing positive significance. The optimistic twist to Freud's original understanding of religion that this entails is, in any case, consonant with (to pervert a phrase of Harry Stack Sullivan) the benevolent transformation that Freudianism underwent in America. Since psychoanalytically derived ideas are by now widely diffused in American society, almost instant relevance is guaranteed by an interpretation and, equally important, to an application of religion in these terms. At least part of the appeal of Tillich's theology may be explained by its ingenious combination of the conceptual mechanisms of existentialism and psychologism, both of them being ideational complexes that are, so to speak, "in the air" culturally. But, without in the least trying to denigrate Tillich's intellectual achievement in itself—for which one may have the highest respect, even if one totally disagrees with it—it should be emphasized that essentially similar procedures are employed on greatly inferior levels of sophistication. There, too, quasi-existentialist malaise is interpreted in psychologistic terms, psychotherapeutic measures are advocated to cope with the matter among people already predisposed to accept the diagnosis, and religion comes in as a "symbolization" in both the diagnostic and the therapeutic phases of the operation. There is, therefore, a very important link between Tillich and, say, Norman Vincent Peale—*not,* needless to say, in their statures as religious thinkers, but in the common relevance of their thinking in a psychologically inclined population. Louis Schneider and Sanford Dornbusch have given us an excellent analysis of this in their study of popular religious literature (*Popular Religion,* University of Chicago, 1958), and Samuel Klausner gives us a good picture of how the same relevance is being expressed in the programs of ecclesiastical institutions (*Psychiatry and Religion,* Free Press, 1964). Here, of course, the subjectivization of the traditional religious contents appears in pure form. Robinson's "Daddy on a cloud" has become a psychological datum, the "up there" is relocated "deep down within" human consciousness, and, in a truly impressive theoretical *salto mortale,* this very dissolution of theology into psychology is hailed as a vindication of religion.

Conceptual machinery derived from sociology can also be applied both diagnostically and therapeutically in the translation enterprise, and perhaps this is the point where I should acknowledge my own past share in both applications, with the added comment that these days I much prefer the diagnostic to the therapeutic role. Sociology can demonstrate easily enough that large segments of traditional religious lore have become irrelevant (that is, subjectively meaningless and/or practically inapplicable) to the man in the street. The conclusion may then be drawn that the remedy lies in reinterpreting the tradition so that it *will* be relevant (that is, subjectively meaningful and practically applicable). Cox's recommendation to the churches to "speak politically" is a good recent example of this—highly "relevant," of course, in a situation where churches and church people have been widely involved in the racial struggle, as well as, more recently, in the debate over American foreign policies. Here, particularly, the point should be stressed again that our analysis has *no bearing whatever* on the sincerity and intrinsic worth of these political activities. The point is, quite simply, that theology and ecclesiastical practice accommodate themselves to the reality presuppositions of the man in the street. The events and moral issues of Mississippi and Vietnam are real to the man in the street. The traditional religious affirmations about God, world, and man, very largely, are unreal. The sociologically derived programs for theology and church give cognitive as well as practical priority to the reality presuppositions of the man in the street over those of the religious tradition. Those with an inclination towards linguistic analysis as now fashionable in Anglo-American philosophy can perform essentially the same operation with different conceptual tools, for here too the reality of the man in the street is accorded a privileged cognitive status. There are some problems of application in both translation procedures, since, after all, there are significant variations within the species "man in the street." What is real and relevant to the young civil-rights worker is not necessarily so to the corporation executive. The general character of translation, therefore, will vary in accordance with the target audience addressed by the translators.

Whatever the particular conceptual machinery employed, the reinterpretation of the Christian tradition by the secular theologians entails an accommodation between the tradition and what is, correctly or not, taken to be modern consciousness. Nor is there any question as to where something must give way in this process, as between the two entities to be accommodated. Almost invariably, the tradition is made to conform to the cognitive and normative standard of the alleged modern consciousness. Our movement thus replicates to an amazing degree, in form if not in content, Feuerbach's famous program of reducing theology to anthropology.

The Infrastructure of the Movement

We have already indicated some of the practical consequences drawn from these theological developments. It would be very naive sociologically to think that there are not also practical, specifically social, roots for the theological developments. In other words, there is a sociologically graspable *Sitz im Leben,* a nontheoretical infrastructure, from which the theological ideas in question have sprung. Their self-avowed starting point is the disintegration of Christendom as a general and assumed universe of discourse in western culture. This disintegration, however, is itself an effect of broad historical forces that have created the modern world. Put differently, secularization in both society and consciousness is itself a phenomenon that must be explained. The usual explanations in terms of the growth of a rational and scientific world view (which is where Bultmann begins and where he is pretty generally followed by our secular theologians) are unsatisfactory for this reason, whatever their merits in particular cases. We strongly suspect that no explanation that remains only within the framework of the history of ideas is likely to serve as an adequate means to understand the phenomenon of secularization. The weakness of any such "idealistic" explanations is actually illustrated very well by the secular theologians as a case in point. Their general procedure is to relativize the religious tradition by means of certain modern ideas. It does not occur to them, on the whole, that these modern ideas, which serve as their criteria of validity or relevance, can themselves be relativized.

Let us grant Bultmann, for example, that people using electricity and radios generally find the miracles of the New Testament less than credible. Let us also leave aside here the question as to why, despite electricity and radios, these people still manage to find a place in their world view for luxuriant irrationalities of a nonreligious nature. Let us here even grant Bultmann (what should not be granted to him at all) that all these electricity- and radio-users share with him a scientific world view. But just this fact, if it were a fact, would cry out for explanation! And what equally cries out for explanation is the fact that Bultmann, and with him the entire movement, takes for granted the epistemological superiority of the electricity- and radio-users over the New Testament writers—to the point where the theoretical possibility that, after all, there may be a nonscientific reality that has been lost to modern man is not even considered. In other words, secularized consciousness is taken for granted, not just as an empirical datum, but as an unquestioned standard of cognitive validity. Otherwise, the possibility that there may be a cognitive need for modern consciousness to be *re*mythologized would at least make an appearance in the theological argument, if only for the purpose of rejecting it, not on tactical, but on epistemological grounds.

It is at this point that a sociology-of-knowledge perspective begins to be useful. The question as to who is ultimately right in his knowledge of the world—Bultmann, the electricity-using man in the street, or St. Paul—is, of course, bracketed in this perspective. What is asserted, though, is that all three exist and think in their own unquestioned worlds, that are themselves grounded in specific social infrastructures. Just as the religious tradition was grounded in such a specific infrastructure, *so also* are the ideas employed to relativize the tradition. The general blindness of the relativizing theologians to the relativity of their own debunking apparatus points directly to the need for analyzing the infrastructure of their own ideas.

Obviously, it is impossible here to discuss various possible explanations of the origins of secularization either in terms of the history of ideas or in socio-historical terms. We readily admit a certain partiality to the notion, frequently expressed by the theological figures that interest us here, that decisive impulses towards secularization may be found in Biblical religion itself. This notion, to our knowledge, was first elaborated systematically in Max Weber's understanding of the "disenchantment of the world," though, especially if one thinks in Weberian terms, it is well to keep in mind that this process was unintended and thus profoundly ironical. Nor is it our intent to quarrel with the various theories that explain the transformation of modern consciousness in terms of economic, technological, and social-structural terms. It is readily evident that so complex a phenomenon will have to be analyzed in multicausal terms, and it is evident, at least to me, that "ideal" and "material" factors will be found to interact dialectically in the historical chain of causes. However, there is one causal factor that is rarely emphasized in this connection and which we would consider to be decisive in the formation of an infrastructure capable of giving rise to modern secularized consciousness—namely, the pluralization of social worlds.

Christendom developed in a situation in which the great majority of people lived within the same overall social structure, as given in the feudal system, and the same overall world view, as maintained by the church as sole reality-defining institution. This is not to say that medieval society was monolithic or in a state of perfect equilibrium. There were strains within the social structure, as shown by the peasant uprisings, and there were challenges to the monopoly of the church, as expressed in the various heretical movements. All the same, Christendom provided both a social-structural and a cognitive unity that was lost, probably irretrievably, upon its dissolution at the beginning of the modern age. By the same token, the social world of Christendom was contained in a way that ours cannot possibly be. This, again, does not mean that there was no awareness of other worlds. There was always the world of Islam before the gates and the world of Judaism within the actual confines of the *res christiana.* These discrepant worlds, however, were only rarely capable of becoming threats to the unquestioned reality of the Christian world. The one was kept away at the point of the sword, the other carefully segregated, often enough also with the sword.

Our own situation, by contrast, is one in which discrepant worlds coexist within the same society, contemporaneously challenging each other's cognitive and normative claims. We cannot discuss here the various factors that have gone into this—the ideological schisms unleashed by the renaissance, reformation, and enlightenment; the opening up of strange lands (and ideas!) in the great voyages of discovery; the growth of highly differentiated and mobile social structures through urbanization and industrialization; the transformations of "knowledge" brought on by the invention of printing and, later, by mass literacy; the very recent impact of the mass media of communication; and so on. We can only stress the net result of this pluralization of worlds—that it has become very difficult to maintain, or, for that matter, to establish *de novo,* any monopoly in the definition of reality. Instead, our situation is characterized by a market of world views, simultaneously in competition with each other. In this situation, the maintenance of any certitudes that go much beyond the empirical necessities of the society and the individual to function is very difficult indeed. Inasmuch as religion essentially rests upon superempirical certitudes, the pluralistic situation is a secularizing one and, *ipso facto,* plunges religion into a crisis of credibility. The particular theological movement that interests us here must be understood, then, as emerging from a situation in which the traditional religious certitudes have become progressively less credible, not necessarily because modern man has some intrinsically superior access to the truth, but because he exists in a socio-cultural situation which itself undermines religious certitude.

We have so far avoided formulating our perspective in systematic sociology-of-knowledge terms, so as not to offend prematurely with the proverbial barbarity of the specialist's jargon. At this point, however, there must be at least some explication of the systematic features of the perspective. In this context, this must unavoidably be done in somewhat of an axiomatic manner. Let us first reformulate the above description of the background of our phenomenon in more systematic terms: The movement under consideration presupposes a *de-objectivation* of the traditional religious contents, which in turn presupposes a disintegration of the traditional *plausibility structure* of these contents. What does this mean?

De-Objectivation

Human consciousness emerges out of practical activity. Its contents, pretheoretical as well as theoretical, remain related to this activity in diverse ways. This does not mean that theoretical consciousness, or "ideas," are to be understood as mere epiphenomena or as dependent variables determined in a one-sided causation by nontheoretical, non-"ideal" processes. Rather, theories and ideas continually interact with the human activity from which they spring. In other words, the relationship between consciousness and activity is a dialectical one—activity produces ideas, which in turn produce new forms of activity. The more or less permanent constellations of activity that we know as "societies" are, therefore, in an ongoing dialectical relationship with the "worlds" that form the cognitive and normative meaning coordinates of individual existence. Religious worlds, as much as any others, are thus produced by an infrastructure of social activity and, in turn, act back upon this infrastructure.

The socially produced world attains and retains the status of objective reality in the consciousness of its inhabitants in the course of common, continuing social activity. Conversely, the status of objective reality will be lost if the common social activity that served as its infrastructure disintegrates. It is very important to remember that these social processes of reality-confirmation and reality-disconfirmation apply to contents that, by whatever criteria of validity, the scientific observer regards as true, as well as to those he regards as false. Thus, the objective reality of astrological forces is confirmed by the same social processes that, in another society, confirm the objective reality of the scientific world view. The sociologist, of course, is not in a position to judge between the rival cognitive claims of astrology and modern science; he can only point out that each will be taken for granted in the specific situations where everyday social experience confirms it. Human theories and ideas, then, require specific infrastructures of confirmatory social interaction if they are to retain what William James aptly called their "accent of reality." If such infrastructures are strong and enduring, then the theoretical constructions grounded in them take on an objective reality close to that of natural phenomena—they are taken for granted with the same unquestioning certitude given to the "facts of life" encountered in the physical universe. Again, this holds for religious ideation as much as for any other. It is as "natural" to be Catholic in a Catholic milieu, as to be a Muslim in Arabia. What is more, we have good reason to doubt an individual's "Catholic consciousness" if he is transplanted to Arabia, and to doubt a Muslim's religious certitudes in the reverse case.

The social infrastructure of a particular ideational complex, along with various concomitant maintenance procedures, practical as well as theoretical, constitute its plausibility structure, that is, set the conditions within which the ideas in question have a chance of remaining plausible. Within the plausibility structure, the individual encounters others who confirm, by their attitudes and by their assumptions, that the particular ideational complex is to be taken for granted as reality. Among these others there may be authority figures, officially accredited reality-definers, who will from time to time engage in especially solemn confirmations, frequently by means of terrifying and awe-inspiring ceremonies. If the individual should, for one reason or another, develop doubts about the officially defined verities, the plausibility structure will usually provide various mechanisms of "mental hygiene" for the eradication of doubts. Put simply, the plausibility structure is to be understood as a collection of people, procedures, and mental processes geared to the task of keeping a specific definition of reality going. It does not require great sociological sophistication to see that such a social and social-psychological matrix is a condition *sine qua non* of all religious ideation. It is precisely for this reason that religion is a communal or collective enterprise. At the risk of offending theological sensitivities, we can state this fact quite simply by appropriating the sentence, *"Extra ecclesiam nulla salus,"* with the slight modification that *"salus"* in our context does not refer to a superempirical destiny of the individual, but to the plausibility of the religious contents represented by any particular *ecclesia* within this empirically available consciousness.

Strongly integrated plausibility structures will produce firm objectivations, and will be capable of supporting world views and ideas with a firm status of objective reality within the consciousness of their adherents. As soon as plausibility structures begin to disintegrate, this status of objective reality begins to totter. Uncertainty, doubts, questions, make their appearance. What was previously "known" becomes, at best, "believed." In a further step, it is an "opinion," or even a "feeling." In other words, the particular contents of consciousness that used to be taken for granted as "knowledge" are progressively de-objectivated. In the case of religious contents, the process can be readily understood by contrasting the state of, say, "living in a Christian world," with a desperate "leap of faith" into a Christian position, and, finally, with having some sort of a Christian label attached to one's "religious preference" or "religious interest." These last two phrases, which need no explanation in an American setting, express what has taken place in the de-objectivation of the religious tradition with admirable succinctness.

The excursion into general sociology-of-knowledge theory has, we hope, been useful. It should be clearer now in what way a sociology-of-knowledge perspective may be applied to the situation that interests us here. The recent history of western religion makes a great deal more sense in this perspective, into which it has been placed only rarely, if at all. To my knowledge, the closest to it may be found in the work of some contemporary German sociologists, notably Arnold Gehlen, who coined the term, "subjectivization," for a broad range of modern cultural phenomena, and Helmut Schelsky, who applied Gehlen's notions to the sociology of religion. In any case, we would contend that our present religious situation can be understood much more readily if we apply to it the aforementioned concept of de-objectivation. The general background of the movement under consideration here is the reality-loss of the religious tradition in the consciousness of increasing numbers of people, something that is not to be ascribed to some mysterious intellectual fall from grace, but to specific and empirically available social developments. The secularization of consciousness and the pluralization of society must be understood together, as two facets of the same general and dialectical process. The important fact that this process has now burst beyond the confines of the western world and, as a result of modernization, has become a worldwide phenomenon, cannot be considered here, but should at least be kept in mind.

Defense or Accommodation?

The problem that poses itself as a result of the process of de-objectivation is simple—how to perpetuate an institution whose reality presuppositions are no longer socially taken for granted. The problem has an obvious practical side, which produces the headaches of all those responsible for the economic and general wellbeing of organized religion. There is an equally obvious theoretical problem of how to legitimize the continuing social existence of the institution and its tradition, in the absence of the massive reality-confirmation that previously sustained them. This, of course, is where the headaches of the theologians come in, or more accurately, of those theologians who continue to operate as legitimating functionaries of the institution. The manner in which our particular group of secular theologians has responded to the problem will be further clarified, we think, if we ask ourselves what options are possible in our situation in the first place.

There are two fundamental options, with variations within each—defense and accommodation. The institution may take on a defensive posture vis-à-vis the secularizing-pluralizing process, continue to affirm the old objectivities, and, as far as possible, go on with its own life and thought despite the regrettable developments on the "outside." Or the institution may accommodate itself to this "outside" in a variety of practical and theoretical compromises. Both options have been tried. Both entail considerable practical and theoretical difficulties.

The main practical difficulty of the defense posture is one of "social engineering." If one is to go on proclaiming the old objectivities in a social milieu that refuses to accept them, one must maintain or construct some sort of subsociety within which there can be a viable plausibility structure for the traditional affirmations. What is more, this subsociety must be carefully and continuously protected against the pluralistic turbulence outside its gates. Put a little rudely, one must maintain a ghetto. This is not easy under any circumstances. It becomes very difficult in a modern society with mass literacy and mass communications, unless the subsociety can exercise totalitarian control over its territory and its population. The theoretical difficulties are directly related to this. One can repeat the old legitimations as if nothing had happened, in which case one risks, sooner or later, a complete collapse of plausibility. Or one may carry on a ceaseless theoretical warfare, a kind of permanent apologetic, in which case one risks, sooner or later, contamination by the very reality one is trying to keep out.

The extreme case of this choice is the closed world of certain sects, which exist as deviant reality-enclaves within the surrounding social world with which they maintain only the minimal relations required for economic and political survival. The old-line Amish settlements or the Hasidic communities in New York may serve as illustrations. Less extreme cases are, of course, more common. The most important example is the Catholic church, which until very recently has confronted the modern world almost everywhere in a posture of determined defensiveness and, as a result, has had to spend a good deal of its institutional energy on the maintenance of Catholic subsocieties. It is hardly fanciful to suggest that the social engineering difficulties just indicated account in large measure for the *aggiornamento* now in process, setting loose disintregrating forces that, we suspect, the official promoters of the *aggiornamento* will find hard to control.

Within Protestantism and Judaism, orthodoxy and neoorthodoxy everywhere have had to go hand in hand with an energetic reconstruction of social milieus that could serve as plausibility structures for the reaffirmed objectivities of old. Thus, it is not so much a theological as a sociological imperative that led from the Barthian return to the tradition to the so-called "rediscovery of the church." To put it a little rudely again, one needs a pretty strong church as a social-psychological support if one is to believe what the Barthians want one to believe. We strongly suspect, incidentally, that the long dominance of neoorthodoxy in European Protestantism had much to do with political situations on the "outside" that made subsocietal self-enclosure morally appealing, and that the postwar decline in this domination is directly related to the loss of this essentially nonreligious appeal. In sum, orthodox or neoorthodox positions in our situation inevitably tend towards sectarian social forms for their maintenance, which will be successful to the degree that people can be motivated to be sectarians—a stand that is contingent upon many, mostly nonreligious, factors quite beyond the control of ecclesiastical authorities.

The accommodation posture is obviously the more "modern" one. But it too has its great difficulties, which can be summed up in the simple question, "Just how far should one go?" Usually, the answer is first given in tactical terms, just as the entire accommodation process typically begins with an effort to solve the tactical problem—that is, the problem of getting one's message across to a recalcitrant clientele. One then goes as far as one has to for the pastoral or evangelistic purpose at hand. The difficulty with such a procedure is that there is a built-in "escalation" factor. The clientele is likely to become more, not less, recalcitrant in the secularizing-pluralizing situation, and one is consequently obligated to ever-deepening concessions to the reality presuppositions of the people one wants to keep or win. The difficulty attains a new dimension, however, as these presuppositions begin to infect the thinking of the tacticians themselves—again, an almost inevitable outcome under the circumstances. The question is then no longer, "Just how far should one go?" but, "How far must *I* go to continue believing myself?" When this point is reached, the floodgates are opened to a veritable onslaught of relativizing challenges to the tradition. In sum, the intrinsic problem of the accommodation option is that, once taken, it has the powerful tendency to escalate to the point where the plausibility of the tradition collapses, so to speak, from within.

The fierce opposition to concessions of even a minor sort among ultraorthodox elements in the religious institutions may thus be said to rest upon a rather sound sociological instinct, which is frequently absent in their more "open-minded" opponents. Therefore, quite apart from one's own intellectual and moral sympathies, one cannot deny a good measure of sociological sense to the authorities that squelched the modernist movement in the Catholic church a half century ago, or, for that matter, to the conservatives in the church today who fear that the *aggiornamento* will open up a Pandora's box of ecclesiastical and theological troubles. The history of a couple of centuries of Protestant accommodation can hardly be reassuring to them.

THE CHOICE OF THE SECULAR THEOLOGIANS

But it is high time that we return to our secular theologians. How is one to understand their place in the general situation that we have tried to describe? Historically, as already mentioned, the "new" movement stands in a continuity with classical Protestant liberalism. While its theological propositions are hardly more radical than at least some made long ago by the generations of Ritschl and Harnack, their overall posture seems more radical precisely because the disintegration of the plausibility structures has greatly accelerated since the period of the classical liberals. In any case, whatever one may think of the newness of the "new" theology, it stands at an extreme pole of the defense-accommodation continuum of theological postures—so extreme that it is very hard indeed to imagine any further steps in that direction short of the final self-liquidation of the ecclesiastical-theological enterprise as such.

Accommodation with the secular theologians has become total. The reality presuppositions of our age have become the only valid criteria for the handling of tradition. From the viewpoint of the conservative apologetician, the secular theologians have surrendered to the enemy. The more moderate liberal positions may be characterized as a bargaining procedure with secularized consciousness: "We'll give you the Virgin Birth, but we'll keep the Resurrection;" "You can have the Jesus of history, but we'll hold on to the Christ of the apostolic faith;" and so on. The secular theology disdains such negotiation. It surrenders all. Indeed, it goes farther in its abandonment of the tradition than most people who do not identify themselves with it. For example, the secular theologians show a greater willingness to abandon belief in a life after death than does the unchurched man in the street, who commonly retains some lingering hopes in this matter. And, at least in America, it seems that theologians today have a greater propensity to proclaim themselves as atheists than the average, theologically untrained skeptic. The whole thing reminds one strongly of the old story of the drunkard who carefully walked in the gutter so that he could not possibly fall into it. The transformation of transcendence into immanence, and the change from objectivity to subjectivity, is completed. The paradoxical result is that one can now feel safe from the secularizing and subjectivizing forces threatening the tradition. The worst, so to speak, has already happened—one has pre-empted it to oneself.

It is important, we think, to understand that this posture can be very liberating. Quite apart from the general rewards of feeling oneself to be "with it," there is the liberation of "going all the way," being done once and for all with the agonies of compromise. Indeed, this liberating quality, we suspect, is psychologically very much the same as that which comes from the opposite movement of the "leap of faith." All "radical" decisions have this much in common psychologically: to quote the punch-line of a classic American joke, one is rid, once and for all, of "all those choices." In this case the choices include, at least, a good many theological ones. Every theologian must ask himself the question, vis-à-vis his tradition, "What do I believe?" And the answer, "Nothing!", can be as alleviating as the answer, "Everything!"

To think, however, that the fundamental problem of the *institution* can be solved in this manner is, obviously, mistaken. The practical and theoretical difficulties raised by secular theology for the churches are almost too apparent to elaborate. Practically, secular theology leads to programs of nonreligious activity that, by definition almost, are very hard to distinguish from similar programs launched under lay auspices. For example, it is not easy to retain any sort of marginal differentiation between psychotherapeutic or political-action programs sponsored by the churches or by purely secular organizations. The thought that one might just as well dispense with the "Christian" label is hardly avoidable sooner or later. There is thus a built-in self-defeating factor in all such programs of "secular Christianity." Very much the same problem arises on the level of theorizing. After all, a theoretical mind can usually stand only a certain amount of paradox. The particular paradox of engaging in the discipline of divinity while denying the divine is hardly likely to recommend itself to many people for very long.

Conclusions

Sociological prediction is dangerous business, as everyone knows who has tried it. We would not like to engage in it here. Yet some projections into the future are hard to avoid in an analysis such as this. If one projects a continuation of the movement under consideration here to the point where it becomes the dominant ideology within the Protestant community, one would also have to project that this community is on the brink of dissolution as an institution. This is not very likely, certainly not in America. There are powerful social functions carried on by the institutional complex of American Protestantism. Most of these, to be sure, are of an essentially nonreligious character, but there are strong reasons for maintaining at least a semblance of continuity with the traditional institutional legitimations. While in many ways American Protestantism is already secularized both in its social functionality and in its consciousness, there is no need to proclaim this from the rooftops as a theological verity. At the same time, the aforementioned difficulties for any sort of orthodoxity within our situation would certainly not lead one to expect a vigorous resurgence of antimodernism, unless, indeed, we are fated to undergo convulsions similar in intensity to those that brought the Barthian movement into a position of dominance in Europe in the 1930's. What is now happening in the Catholic community seems to support this. If one is to make a prediction at all, then probably the safest would be that there will be no reversal in the secularization and de-objectivation processes, but that the extreme legitimations of these will be considerably blunted as they are diffused through the community and become respectable. The probable fate of the secular theology, once its appeal as the *dernier cri* in religion has passed, would then be its absorption into the legitimating apparatus of the institution (which, incidentally, is exactly what happened with classical liberalism). We strongly suspect that this process of neutralization is already taking place as these "challenging new insights" are integrated in various ecclesiastical programs. In this process, there is nothing to prevent the "death of God" from becoming but another program emphasis, which, if properly administered, need not result in undue disturbances in the ongoing life of the institution.

A few slightly less than scientific words in conclusion. The foregoing analysis has moved with some care within a sociological frame of reference. It goes without saying that this imposes certain limits on one's view of these matters. The most important limit is that, of course, any question about the ultimate truth or error of the theological positions under consideration must be rigidly excluded from the analysis. When it comes to such questions of truth or error, the most that sociology can do is to make one aware of the socio-historical relativity of one's own cognitive presuppositions—an awareness that I, for one, would strongly recommend to the secular theologians. But I will take the liberty here of at least one little step beyond the proper limits of sociological inquiry.

If anyone should think that the previous analysis camouflages some strong position of certitude, I can only assure him that nothing could be farther from the truth. I cannot, I am afraid, lay claim to any certitudes, positive *or* negative, in the fundamental questions of religion. I can only claim a persistent and, at times at least, passionate concern for these questions. In speaking of de-objectivation and its consequences, therefore, I speak of something that involves myself. But perhaps it is precisely for this reason that I am somewhat less than amicably disposed towards those who claim to have reached the end of a road on which I still regard myself as traveling, regardless of whether they do so by proclaiming the "death of God" or His "undeniable" presence.

It seems to me that the essence of religion has been the confrontation with an *other,* believed to exist as a reality in the universe external to and vastly different from man—something that is indeed "out there," as Robinson puts it. The fundamental religious proposition, therefore, is that man is not alone in reality. Whether this is or is not part of the socially objectivated world view of a particular society is as irrelevant to its possible validity as, for instance, the absence from the world view of Zulu society of any notion of quantum theory is irrelevant to the validity of the quantum theory. The theological enterprise reduces itself to absurdity if it engages itself with the fundamental proposition of religion on any terms other than those of its validity. Is man alone in reality: Yes or no? If one is certain that the answer is "Yes," then, it seems to me, one could do better things with one's time than theology. In this respect one could learn from Marx. When he was certain that, with Feuerbach, the critique of religion was finished, he did not bother with it any more, but went on to concern himself with other things. But if one is *not* so certain that the religious proposition of an *other* confronting man in reality is only a gigantic illusion, then one can hardly dismiss the question about the validity of the proposition as irrelevant. In one way or another, inside or outside the traditional religious institutions, one will want to continue pursuing the question.

BRYAN WILSON

Secularization and the Clerical Profession

The loss of association with other major social institutions has not been accomplished without some effects on the religious profession itself. We have already seen that the clergy tend to have lost social standing. Scientists have increasingly replaced them as the intellectual stratum of society, and literature and the arts have passed almost completely out of the religious sphere. The scepticism of modern society has affected the clerical profession profoundly. The attempt to find other levels at which religious propositions are true—that is to say, levels other than the common-sense and literal level—has led to widely diverse clerical interpretations of religion in its contemporary meaning. Clerics have now come to disbelieve in the ultimacy of any answers which they can supply about social questions, as they did earlier about physical questions. As the range of empirical information has increased, acquisition of the knowledge of it and the skills to analyse it and interpret it pass

From *Religion in Secular Society* by Bryan Wilson (London: Penguin Books, Ltd., 1966), pp. 96-108. Reprinted by permission of Sir Issac Pitman and Sons, Ltd., London, England.

beyond the range of clerical education. The awareness of the relativity of modern knowledge has made the cleric more guarded and less confident in the intellectual content of religion. The man-in-the street, even if less concerned by this relativity in a society in which he is bombarded unceasingly with information and exposed mercilessly to persuaders, has developed a protective cynicism about what is being "put over."

One consequence of the expansion of modern knowledge has been its increased influence on theological studies. Without usually becoming expert in such disciplines, theologians have recognized how vulnerable is their discipline to influences from outside—of which archaeology, comparative religion, anthropology, psychology and sociology are perhaps the most relevant. Many of the early exponents of these disciplines were, necessarily, in societies in which intellectual roles were predominantly in clerical possession, clergymen. These subjects have increasingly passed out of the hands of clergymen together with older disciplines the personnel of which was once also ordained. The influence of these intellectual developments has been, however, to make the laymen's grasp of religious ideas more tenuous. It has been more difficult for the Churches to reconcile their traditional claims to wisdom and the increasing acceptance by the clergy of modern branches of knowledge which cast considerable doubt on what the Churches have for centuries been teaching. The man-in-the-street has not the permanent commitment to inquiry of the intellectual. He is not interested in the subtle shifts of academic debate, although clergymen of this cast of mind, and educationalists generally, often assume him to be. Thus what for the clerical inquirer is an interesting academic problem, and part of a long-sustained and continuing debate, may be merely a source of new confusion for the layman. The professional can afford to play an intellectual game. It is not difficult to present such discourse as thoroughly appropriate to his job, and, since heresy trials no longer occur, that his job is very secure. But laymen very often want only assurance and certainty—of a kind which clerics feel increasingly less able to provide.

That some clergy themselves become sceptical, and cease to believe in many of the things which laymen believe in as essentials of the faith, or believe in them in an entirely different way, can only be a source of confusion and despair to those who want to believe in certain, and usually simple, truths. A Bishop Barnes of Birmingham in the 1930s and 40s, a Bishop Pike of California, and a Bishop Robinson of Woolwich, in the 1960s, are only sources of bewilderment to ordinary believers, some of whom are impious enough to wonder why, if men think as they do, they continue to take their stipends from Churches which commit them, in honesty, to rather different beliefs. The alienation of the clergy is one of the remarkable phenomena of the Church of modern times. But even in this alienation from less intellectual laymen, the clergy have little chance of rapprochement with the secular intelligentsia, since they are committed to at least a framework of debate which is normally quite unacceptable to most other intellectuals in the secular society.

The speculative intellectuals among the clergy resemble in their professional position (and I make no judgement of the warranty of their specific ideas) the charcoal-burners or alchemists in an age when the processes in which they were engaged had been rendered obsolete, technically or intellectually. The clergy become a curiously placed intelligentsia, many of them uncertain of their own faith, uncertain of the "position" of their church on many matters, and unsure whether they agree with that position. The more advanced among them sometimes suggest that simpler men believe the right things for the wrong reasons. They themselves are institutionally entrenched but intellectually footloose. They have no real continuity with the actual beliefs of the past, but only with the forms, the rituals, the involvement in a persisting organization. At the same time they have no part in the faster-moving intellectual debate within their own society. Neither the scientists nor the literary intellectuals seek theological opinions, and least of all the social scientists.

Obviously there are many issues of a less specifically intellectual kind on which Church opinion is called for, and, even if not called for, is none the less freely given. In the moral field, which was once the area in which the Church's judgements held complete sway, Churchmen have become, as we have seen in the matter of birth control, much more aware of their own difficulties in making pronouncements on moral issues, without the benefit of "scientific" information. There is, then, no longer much confidence in God's word or in God's guidance about the issues arising in contemporary society. Thus before an Archbishop feels equipped to comment on the moral implications of television, he calls for an inquiry into its effects. What is surrendered by the Church, then, is the claim of religion to guide the course of social policy, the decisions of statesmen, the operation of social institutions, *and,* latterly, even the everyday behavior of the man-in-the-street.

The loss of general standing of the clergy in relation to other professions, and the diminution of their social influence, has been accompanied in England by their increasing average age as the accompanying table[1] illustrates for Church of England clergymen in England.

Thus, whereas in 1901 over 45 per cent of Anglican clergymen were under forty-five years of age, and only 17 per cent were more than sixty-five years of age, in 1961 just over 30 per cent were under forty-five years of age, and almost 27 per cent were over sixty-five years of age. No other profession would show an age distribution of this kind, and no other profession would have so high a proportion of members over the normal retiring age. An ageing profession may, it can be expected, be less efficient than one with a more normal age distribution, and this may hold for some branches of the work of the clergy, notwithstanding the fact that the clerical role has many noninstrumental aspects. Age may not much affect a priest's competence in the performance of ritual (and the Church has been growing steadily more ritualistic), but it might very much affect pastoral visiting, contact with the population and the ability to counsel them about "modern" problems.

TABLE 1. *Percentages of Anglican Clergymen by Age at Various Dates in the Twentieth Century*

	Years of age at appropriate dates						
Date	22–34	35–44	45–54	55–65	65–74	75+	Total No.
1901	20.23	24.91	20.90	16.43	11.66	5.87	23,670
1911	16.39	22.03	24.63	18.61	11.97	6.37	23,193
1921	10.70	19.47	23.95	24.01	14.27	7.60	22,579
1951	9.71	23.37	17.27	19.26	18.66	11.73	18,196
1961	15.28	14.71	25.19	17.90	14.95	11.97	18,749

One other feature of the statistics concerning the Anglican clergy is worth noting. That during the sixty years in which the number of clergy fell from 23,670 to less than 19,000 the population of the two provinces (Canterbury and York) to which the figures relate was growing steadily, from 30.6 millions in 1901, to 43.6 millions in 1961. Thus in a period in which the Anglican clergy in England have declined by more than 20 per cent, the population has increased by more than 40 per cent. Although in the same period there has been a remarkable increase in the numbers of Catholic priests in England, which very much more than "makes good" the losses in clerical professionals in the Church of England, there has still been an overall decline in the number of religious professionals. For England and Wales the number of religious professionals (including clergy of all religious bodies, monks, nuns, itinerant preachers, scripture readers, etc.) fell from over 56,000 in 1901 to a little over 51,000 in 1951.

The fall in relative, and absolute, numbers of clerical professionals in England clearly reflects a number of facts about contemporary religion, and the due weight of the various matters involved has yet to be assessed. It would appear that the religious profession has grown less attractive. Certainly there are fewer people coming forward for the Anglican ministry. In 1959 there were 757 candidates, which fell to 646 in 1961. Even a campaign under the slogan *Pray for Your Clergy—Pray for more Clergy* in 1962–3 took the figure up only to 737 in 1963, and it fell again to 656 in 1964.[2] Among the intake into the Anglican ministry, the age of entry itself has also risen; about 14 per cent of candidates recommended for Holy Orders in 1959 were thirty years of age or over, whereas in 1964 it was more than 20 per cent; and whereas 3 per cent of those recommended in 1959 were forty years or more, this figure was 12 per cent in 1964.[3] The "late entrants" constitute a similar proportion among both English and Canadian Anglican ordinands.[4] Clearly a profession which draws an increasing proportion of older entrants will *continue* to have an abnormal age-structure.

The diminished appeal of the clerical profession has had a further effect, at least in England, of attracting to it a decreasing proportion of men who are university graduates. In the four years from 1960 to 1964 the proportion of non-graduates among Anglican candidates rose from just over 50 per cent to just over 60 per cent of the intake.[5] Thus a declining educational level tends to characterize the Anglican ministry, at a time when almost all, if not all, other professions are characterized by increasing educational standards and more exacting professional qualifications. The Catholic Church, which more completely controls its own methods of professional education has not, of course, been exposed to changes of this particular kind. It may, however, especially in more affluent societies where there are, and have been over the past two decades, abundant work opportunities, have failed to draw forward candidates of the same quality as in the past. This, however, rests on the assumption that fewer candidates have been drawn forward. This appears to be true of the various religious orders. Since there are still many relatively non-affluent areas in which the Catholic Church is the dominant Church, this problem may not yet have become acute.

If recruitment to the religious profession becomes more difficult in an affluent society, the difficulty of retaining the recruited exacerbates the professional situation. We have very little detailed information about those who abandon their spiritual vocation. There is certainly considerable defection from the ranks of those who enter training for the priesthood; in America it has been estimated that "less than one-sixth of those entering the freshman year of [diocesan minor] seminaries eventually enter the priesthood."[6] In England a prominent Baptist, estimating that in a ten-year period the Baptist Church had lost 305 trained and ordained men from pastoral ministry, contended that "the central problem of our ministry lies, plainly, not in recruitment, but in the retention of our ministers."[7]

An important feature of the Protestant ministry in England has been the relative decline in the clerical stipend. In an inflationary society other incomes have tended to increase more rapidly than those of the *rentier* class (and the person with his freehold had some association with that class), and more rapidly than the stipends of the clergy. By the standards of other professions the ministry of the Established Church in England is badly paid. It bears little comparison with the medical and legal professions, as once it did, and stands now in rather closer relation to the schoolteachers. In America, where there is no establishment and where clerical stipends depend rather more closely on congregational generosity, the minister's salary has been more responsive to changing monetary values. The relative poverty of English Nonconformity (among Baptists, for example, the minimum stipend has in recent years been lower than the national average wage) is not reflected in the salaries of the American clergy in the same denominations among whom success as a clergyman may even be measured in monetary terms.[8] For Catholics, of course, with expectations of poverty, and with an obligation to celibacy which eliminates the expense of dependents, the stipendiary situation is, in both societies, radically different. The principal work on *Religion as an Occupation,* which is strictly Catholic in interpretation, has no direct mention of the payment structure of the Church: money reward is dismissed as irrelevant.[9]

Salary may be an uncertain test of the social evaluation of the ministry, although in England it must be acknowledged that the salary of the clergy has fallen relative to that of the professions with which they like to be compared, and that society at large makes no effort and voices no concern about clerical stipends. With ministerial salaries often lower than those of some of the better paid among industrial occupations, there is a tendency, despite frequent complaint of the deterioration of the quality of the clergy, for the past association of the clerical class with the gentry to be gently re-emphasized. Yet if the clergy are increasingly drawn in as late entrants to the profession, and are increasingly educated as priests after no higher education other than that of the theological college, in terms of modern objective criteria of social status their position increasingly approximates that of schoolteachers, whose ranks also include a high percentage of non-graduates, and whose professional qualifications in training colleges are conferred without very much rigour of selection.

The elaborate ranking scales which have sometimes been employed to assess status by asking people to place different occupational groups in order, may (perhaps particularly in the case of the religious profession) rather over-state society's actual evaluations. There are the spiritual affinities of the occupation which induce respondents to give relatively high rating to clerics, since people with any religious dispositions at all cannot but pay some attention to the traditional claim of all religious professionals to have the highest calling of all. In all traditional cultures religious functionaries tend to claim high status, and usually gain it, if only because of their access to higher and potentially dangerous sources of power. Fichter says that Catholic priests share the generally high status of clergymen in America: "the social position of clergymen is colored by two thousand years of church history."[10] Of ninety occupations which the respondents of the American National Opinions Research Center were asked to place in order of rank, clergymen came twelfth: physicians and academics were accorded higher status, but lawyers and architects were given lower status.[11]

The comparable English evidence, based on a more limited sample of respondents, placed clergymen fourth among thirty occupations, following surgeons, general practitioners, and solicitors, and immediately above university lecturers, grammar-school masters and dentists.[12] On the basis of this evidence it appears that most of those entering the priesthood of the Church of England are individuals who are rising in the social scale. Nearly ninety per cent of the ordinands in Coxon's extensive survey were the sons of men in occupations with lower social status than clergymen. Becoming a priest, then, if not exactly the "way to the top" (and within the clerical profession in the Anglican Church, prospects for promotion are very limited)[13] is none the less a way of enhancing one's status. Most ordinands, according to Coxon, identify with the middle class.[14]

It appears then, that on objective evidence English society accords its clergy relatively few of the material advantages normally associated with high social status, although subjectively it awards priests a reasonably high place in the social scale. The discrepancy reflects, perhaps, a pious sentiment and the traditional ascription of high status to religious professionals. High status must not be confused with high reward or with social influence. Social systems can, like that of Tonga, carefully dissociate real power from the elevated status of sacredness. The priest's work is not accorded much importance; society in general does not account its welfare to the efficacy of those who spend their lives praying for it, nor does it confer very high rewards on those who seek to bring men under the influence of God.

The decline in religious observance occurring in Western Europe, may yet leave the clergy as an entrenched profession with diminishing functions. It is true that the demands for the "service functions" of the clergy —baptisms, marriages and burials—show little sign of diminishing, and that some clerics report themselves as being overworked, and yet that work is for a declining number of religiously-committed people.[15] The priest's role in the secular society of England has steadily lost its social definition (it retains, of course, its theological definition). The search for social justification may in part be responsible for various trends evident among some of the clergy. Responses to the situation differ: some obviously see social work and welfare as their appropriate role, from work with youth groups to organizations like the Samaritans. Others see themselves as responsible for social protest against the political structure of society, and enlist themselves into movements like C.N.D. and Anti-Apartheid, substituting for traditional hymnology the music of protest. This appears to be one of the easiest ways for religious vocation to rediscover social relevance, though often with slightly *passé* reverence to nineteenth-century revolutionaries: even Roman Catholics display this tendency.[16] Similar manifestations are perhaps even more evident in the United States, where Marxist terminology (there is an especial fondness for the concept of "false consciousness") is to be found strewn throughout much recent, theologically-inspired social commentary.[17] Among parish priests and congregational ministers it is the younger elements who are most conspicuous in the Civil Rights movement and other activities of social protest, but the parish ministry—with dependence for the livelihoods on their lay following—are less likely to espouse radical causes than ministers serving in such roles as campus ministers or university teachers.[18]

Other ministers emphasize pastoral work in their communities and attempt to salve the abrasions which man living in highly institutionalized society is likely to suffer. While the more politically conscious clergy tend to manifest contempt for these "comfort functions" of the church, the American laity demand precisely this of their clergy.[19] Still others turn to ritual, as the irreducible religious function, capable of extension and elaboration, and the real professional expertise of the priest. The burgeoning of theological and quasi-theological academic and quasi-academic disciplines is another way in which churchmen keep their institutions alive. If they cannot fill the churches they might, in the sociology of religion seek out the reasons why people fail to attend or discuss the relation of worship and architecture, comparative liturgies or group therapy. All of these are the new responses, the defence mechanisms, mounted for professional survival. Not least important, there is the ecumenical movement.

---

1. *Facts and Figures About the Church of England,* No. 3, London, Church Information Office, 1965, p. 21.

2. *Men for the Ministry,* London, Church Information Office, 1965.

3. *Facts and Figures,* op. cit., p. 43.

4. A discussion of problems involved is contained in A. P. M. Coxon, *A Sociological Study of the Social Recruitment, Selection and Professional Socialization of Anglican Ordinands,* unpublished Ph.D. Thesis, University of Leeds, 1965.

5. *Men for the Ministry,* op. cit.

6. J. H. Fichter, *Religion as an Occupation,* Notre Dame, Ind., University of Notre Dame, 1961, p. 187.

7. R. E. O. White in *Baptist Times,* cited in E. J. Carlton, *The Probationer Minister—A Study among English Baptists,* unpublished M.A. Thesis, University of London, 1964, p. 30.

8. Philip J. Allen, "Childhood Backgrounds to Success in a Profession," *American Sociological Review,* XX, 2, 1955.

9. J. H. Fichter, op. cit.

10. ibid., p. 124.

11. Albert J. Reiss, *Occupations and Social Status,* Glencoe, Ill., The Free Press. 1961, p. 54.

12. Noel D. Richards, *An Empirical Study of the Prestige of Selected Occupations,* unpublished M.A. Thesis, University of Nottingham, 1962, cited in A. P. M. Coxon, op. cit., p. 254.

13. According to the analysis of Leslie Paul, *The Deployment and Payment of the Clergy,* London, Church Information Office, 1964, pp. 99 ff., only 8 per cent of clergy have posts above that of ordinary incumbents (1 per cent as Archbishops, Bishops, Deans and Provosts; 2 per cent as Archdeacons and Residentiary Canons, and 5 per cent as Rural Deans).

14. A. P. M. Coxon, op. cit., p. 236.

15. See Leslie Paul, op. cit., pp. 71 ff.

16. Fully manifested in the semi-Marxist Catholic periodical *Slant:* ". . . we hope to see emerging the full implications of Christian radicalism: to show that the Church's commitment to the creation of a fraternal society, its function as the sacrament of human community, the relations between its liturgy and a common culture, imply a revolutionary socialism." Vol. 2, No. 1, February–March, 1966.

17. For examples of this style of contemporary theological writing, see Harvey Cox, *The Secular City,* New York, Macmillan, 1965; Gibson Winter, "Theological Schools: Partners in the Conversation" in Keith R. Bridston and Dwight W. Culver, *The Making of Ministers,* Minneapolis, Augsburg Publishing Co., 1964.

18. Evidence is provided in Ernest Q. Campbell and Thomas F. Pettigrew, *Christians in Crisis,* Washington D.C., Public Affairs Press, 1959; and in Phillip E. Hammond and Robert E. Mitchell, "Segmentation of Radicalism—The Case of the Protestant Campus Minister," *American Journal of Sociology,* LXXI (2), September, 1965, pp. 133-43.

19. See Charles Y. Glock, Benjamin B. Ringer and Earl Babbie, op. cit.

Chapter 10
The Church and Religion in the Future: New Forms? New Content?

THOMAS LUCKMANN

Church-Oriented Religion in the Future

While our appraisal of the recent sociology of religion could not but turn critical, it was not undertaken for the sake of criticism. It served to demonstrate, rather, that the inability of the recent sociology of religion to provide an account of the place of religion in modern industrial society was to be attributed partly to the theoretical impoverishment, and partly to the methodological shortcomings, of that discipline. It would be wrong, however, to take this criticism as an invitation to declare the recent sociology of religion as incompetent, irrelevant and immaterial. It is true that church-oriented religion is merely one and perhaps not even the most important element in the situation that characterizes religion in modern society. In the absence of adequate research on that situation, *in toto,* it would be foolish to disregard the abundant data which recent research in the sociology of religion did provide on church-oriented religion in contemporary industrial societies. No attempt to theorize about religion in modern society can afford the luxury of leaving aside the material so assiduously collected—even if, as we suggested, it may fail to tell the whole story. It is reasonable, therefore, that we begin with a summary review and interpretation of that material.

During the past decades, and especially in the last ten years, many studies of churches, sects and denominations accumulated. Most studies originated in the United States, Germany, France, Belgium, England and the Netherlands, with a few coming from other countries such as Italy and Austria. In the European countries research concentrated, with a few exceptions, on Catholicism and the established or quasi-established Protestant churches. In the United States the sects received the major share of attention, although Judaism, Catholicism and the major Protestant denominations were not completely neglected.[1]

Despite the large number of studies it is not without difficulty that one may proceed to generalizations about the location of church-oriented religion in modern industrial society. With some exaggeration one may venture the remark that the wealth of data—in the absence of a common theoretical framework—proves to be more of an embarrassment than an advantage. Since most studies have concentrated on sociographic details it is easier to discern the local, regional, national, and doctrinal peculiarities of the churches than the common social characteristics of church-oriented religion. To add to the difficulties, some authors have ecclesiastic if not theological commitments. It is, therefore, sometimes necessary to disentangle the data from a certain bias in interpretation. The fact that we cannot present all findings in detail here compounds the difficulties. If we are to gain an overall picture of church-oriented religion in modern society as a first step toward an understanding of religion in the contemporary world, we must face the risk of some oversimplification. In order to minimize this risk, we shall present only such generalizations as are based on convergent rather than on isolated findings. Even after taking this precaution it is to be admitted that the generalizations cannot be taken as proven beyond all doubt. They are, however, conclusions favored by the weight of available evidence.[2]

In Europe it is common knowledge that the country is more "religious" than the city. This is generally borne out by the findings of research in the sociology of religion. From church attendance figures to religious burial reports, various statistics which can be taken as indicative of church-oriented religion show consistently higher averages for rural than for urban areas. On the basis of such statistics only a small proportion of the urban population can be described as church-oriented. It is of some interest to note, however, that there is a long-range trend toward a decrease of church-oriented religion in rural regions, too Consequently, the difference in church-oriented religion, while not completely leveled, is smaller now than several decades ago. It hardly needs to be added that this is merely part of a more general process. The transformations in the distribution of church-oriented religion are linked to increasing economic interpenetration of city and country, the growing rationalization of farming, the diffusion of urban culture to the country through mass media, and so forth. It should be noted, however, that these transformations do not proceed at an even rate. In addition to local and regional circumstances of economic and political character the specifically "religious" historical tradition of a region or congregation may speed up or retard the process.

According to another item of common knowledge women are more "religious" than men and the young and old more "religious" than other age groups. Research findings indicate that such opinions need to be revised at least in part. Indeed, women generally do better than men on various indices of church-oriented religion, and the middle generation is, in fact, characterized by lower participation and attendance rates than the young and the old. It is significant, however, that working women as a category tend to resemble men more closely in church orientation than, for example, housewives do. This hardly supports the view that women, children, and old people have something like a natural inclination for church-oriented religion. The findings represent an important aspect of the social distribution of church-oriented religion rather than being indicative of the psychology of sex and age. In general terms, we may say, that the degree of involvement in the work processes of modern industrial society correlates negatively with the degree of involvement in church-oriented religion. It is obvious, of course, that the degree of involvement in such processes is in turn linked with age- and sex-roles.

The involvement of the working population in church-oriented religion—while lower than that of the rest of the population—is, however, itself significantly differentiated. Among the various occupational groups can be found important differences in participation. The indices are generally higher for agricultural, white-collar and some professional groups. These differences coincide roughly with the distribution of church-oriented religion among social classes. Farmers, peasants, and those elements of the middle classes which are basically survivals of the traditional bourgeoisie and petite bourgeoisie are marked by a degree of involvement in church-oriented religion which is disproportionately higher than that of the working class.

In addition to church attendance, opinions on doctrinal matters and so forth, some recent studies in the sociology of religion also investigated participation in various nonritual activities of the churches, ranging from youth clubs to charitable enterprises. These studies indicate that in Europe only a small fraction of the members of congregations join activities that lie outside of the ritual functions of the churches. While those participating in these functions—whom we may collectively call the ritual core of the congregation—represent only a relatively small part of the nominal membership of the parish, they are yet more numerous than those otherwise active in the church. The size of that latter group, the hard core of active members, varies from region to region and from one denomination to the other. It can be said that the major factors determining these differences are the ecology of the community and the distribution of social classes and occupational groups within the parish. The role which these factors play in the selection of the "hard core" from the congregational membership as a whole, however, is not as important as the role these same factors play in the initial recruitment of the congregation from the reservoir of merely nominal members.

While some aspects of the relation between society and church-oriented religion are common knowledge, there can be little doubt that for the industrial countries of Western Europe the findings of the recent sociology of religion describe this relation with more precision. They establish a clear connection between the distribution of church-oriented religion and a number of demographic and other sociologically relevant variables. In the foregoing we described the most important of these. We must, however, draw attention to the fact that the figures vary from country to country and from denomination to denomination. By most criteria Catholicism exhibits higher rates of participation than Protestantism. Some part of this variation can be attributed to differences in the degree of industrialization characterizing Catholic and Protestant countries, respectively, to the presence or absence of a tradition of militant socialism, to different forms of church-state relations and other factors. At the same time, there are considerable national and regional differences which cannot be attributed directly to demographic, economic, or political factors. The level of participation in church-oriented religion seems to be exceptionally low in the case of Anglicanism. Or, to refer to another example, there are differences in the level of participation among French Catholic dioceses which can be attributed in part to sociologically rather intangible historical traditions. Note should be taken also of another factor, neglected in our present summary, that seems to be involved in the distribution of church-oriented religion: the proportion of the members of a denomination in the total population.

With certain exceptions, so-called diaspora congregations are characterized by relatively high attendance and participation figures.

These remarks should not obscure the overriding influence of economic, political and class variables in determining the distribution of church-oriented religion in present-day Western Europe. Before we proceed to draw conclusions about religion in modern society, the European data must be compared with the findings of research on religion in the United States.

For several reasons such comparison is difficult. First, the great variety of institutional expressions of religion in America has not yet been thoroughly and systematically investigated, although at least the major and most typical expresssions and some of the sects, fascinating to the sociologist for one reason or another, did receive attention. Second, among the studies that were carried out some were guided by a pronounced positivistic bias. The third and most important reason is the unique social and religious history of America. For this, more than for any other reason, caution is indicated in summary characterizations of church religion in America, especially if they are to be used for comparison with the European findings. A sizable number of processes and circumstances find no close parallel in European social history; for example, the absence of a feudal past and of a peasantry, the peculiar complex of conditions known as the frontier experience, the successive ethnically and denominationally distinct waves and strata of immigration, the rapid and nearly convulsive processes of urbanization and industrialization, the Negro problem and the early establishment of a dominant middle-class outlook and way of life. The religious history of the country includes equally distinct circumstances: the Puritan period, the early separation of church and state, followed by a persistent and peculiarly intimate relation between politics and religion, the era of revival movements, the prodigious development of sects and the transformation of sects into denominations.

If one views the findings of research on church religion in America against this historical background, it is surprising that they exhibit so much similarity to the European data. It is true that, at first, this similarity is not obvious. Fewer people seem to be involved in church religion than in Europe—if one bases the comparison on the European conception of nominal membership. Conversely, and no matter what criteria one uses, the figures for participation and involvement are much higher for the United States. The difference is especially striking in the case of Protestantism, since Catholic participation rates are relatively high in Europe, too.

Yet, on closer inspection, it appears that the same general factors determine the over-all social location of church religion, although the levels of participation may differ. The participation rates are again higher for Catholicism than Protestantism, especially if, in the latter case, one considers the major denominations rather than some of the smaller sects. And, again, differences between rural and urban areas can be found. The contrast between city and country exhibits a more complex pattern than in Europe and is not as striking, mainly because of Catholic concentrations in many metropolitan areas. The differences between men and women also follow the same lines, with the exception of the Jews. These differences, too, are less sharply drawn than in Europe. The differences in the involvement of the generations in church religion follow the European example only in part. Here, a number of factors, especially the pull of Sunday-school children on the parents—most pronounced in suburbia—complicates the basic pattern.

From the findings on church involvement of different occupational groups no consistent picture emerges. In any case, the data are too scarce to permit any generalizations. One may, perhaps, suspect that in this instance some deviations from the European pattern may be present. The differences between classes with respect to religion are less pronounced than in Europe. This may be attributable in part to the fact that class differences are less pronounced—and certainly less conspicuous—in general, despite an underlying structural similarity in the social stratification of the Western European countries and the United States. Although the major churches and denominations are, at the very least, middle-class oriented, the relatively sharp cleavage between a church-oriented middle class and an unchurched working class does not exist. This is, of course, not surprising, since the working class today merges almost imperceptibly into the outlook, way of life and religious pattern of the middle classes to a much greater extent than in Europe, although there are some indications of a process of *embourgeoisement* in the European working class. Such differences as still exist in the recruitment of church members and in participation are overlaid by the peculiarly American differentiation of prestige among the denominations. These differences find expression in the composition of membership of the denominations. Significantly enough, however, the status differences in the membership of the denominations are popularly much exaggerated. In this connection the Negro–White cleavage in Protestant churches and congregations deserves to be mentioned. These observations are not valid for one social stratum: the rural and urban proletariat, the term not being understood in its Marxist sense. It consists in large part of Negroes, Puerto Ricans, Mexicans and others. This stratum is socially almost completely invisible and nearly unchurched. Even Catholicism, whose influence on the working class generally appears to be stronger than that of Protestantism, appears to have lost or is loosing its hold on this stratum. But this stratum is not part of the middle-class oriented working population and those parts that are not unchurched tend to be attracted to sects that are marginal to Protestantism both theologically and in its orientation to society.

Ethnic churches played a significant role in American religious history. Today, ethnic churches for persons of European background have either disappeared or are of subordinate importance. Only churches linked to racial minorities persist on the religious scene. Their function depends, of course, on the position of the minorities in American society.

One of the most important developments in American church religion is the process of doctrinal leveling. It can be safely said that within Protestantism doctrinal differences are virtually irrelevant for the members of the major denominations. Even for the ministry traditional theological differences seem to have an ever-decreasing importance. More significant is the steady leveling of the differences between Catholicism, Protestantism and Judaism. This process should not be taken as a result of a serious theological *rapprochement.* Furthermore, several areas of fairly sharp friction remain between Catholicism and the other religious bodies, especially in matters of public policy. There can be little doubt, however, that Catholicism, Protestantism and Judaism are jointly characterized by similar structural transformations—a bureaucratization along rational businesslike lines—and accommodation to the "secular" way of life. In consequence of the historical link between this way of life and the Protestant ethos, the accommodation of Protestantism, as represented by its major denominations, has perhaps gone farther than that of the other religious bodies. It seems, however, that the difference is superficial.[3] It is to be noted that, despite the trend toward a leveling of ideological differences and the increasing irrelevance of doctrine for the membership, the *social* differences in the traditions of Protestantism, Catholicism and Judaism continue to play a role. According to some findings they may be destined for perpetuation by endogamy. The way of life and the social basis for some central dimensions of subjective identification remain linked to subcultures designated by religious labels.[4]

These observations may be summarized as follows. There are some aspects of church religion in America which are either unique or at least conspicuously different from the European situation. With one exception—the relatively high involvement of Americans in church religion—the differences seem less significant than the similarities. The correlations of various indices of involvement in church religion with demographic and ecological variables as well as with social role and status configurations follow a similar pattern in the European and American findings. This pattern represents the social location of church religion in the industrial countries of the West. If we may take these countries as paradigmatic, the pattern invites the conclusion that church-oriented religion has become a marginal phenomenon in modern society.

This conclusion meets one serious difficulty in the previously mentioned deviation from the pattern. The most "modern" of the countries under discussion, the United States, shows the highest degree of involvement in church religion. To compound the difficulties, the high American figures of overt participation represent, in all likelihood, a fairly recent upward movement rather than a decrease from a yet higher previous level. In the face of these circumstances it is obvious that no simple unilinear and one-dimensional theory of "secularization" in modern society can be maintained.

The difficulty is only apparent. In order to resolve it, it is only necessary to take into account the differences in the character of church religion in Europe and America. In Europe church religion did not undergo radical inner transformations and became restricted to a minor part of the population. As it continued to represent and mediate the traditional universe of religious ideas, its social base shrunk characteristically to that part of the population which is peripheral to the structure of modern society: the peasantry, the remnants of the traditional bourgeoisie and petite bourgeoisie within the middle classes, which are not —or no longer or not yet—involved in the typical work processes of industrial and urban society.[5]

In the United States, on the other hand, church religion has a broad middle-class distribution. The middle classes are, *in toto,* anything but peripheral to the modern industrial world. The distribution of church religion in America, nevertheless, does not represent a reversal of the trend toward "secularization"—that is, a resurgence of traditional church religion. It is rather the result of a radical inner change in American church religion. This change consists in the adoption of the *secular* version of the Protestant ethos by the churches which, of course, did not result from concerted policy but is rather a product of a unique constellation of factors in American social and religious history.[6]

Whereas religious ideas originally played an important part in the shaping of the American Dream, today the secular ideas of the American Dream pervade church religion. The cultural, social and psychological functions which the churches perform for American society as a whole as well as for its social groups, classes, and individuals would be considered "secular" rather than "religious" in the view the churches traditionally held of themselves.[7] Comparing the European and American findings on the social location of church religion and allowing for the differences in the character of church religion in European and

American society we are led to the conclusion that traditional church religion was pushed to the periphery of "modern" life in Europe while it became more "modern" in America by undergoing a process of internal secularization. This conclusion requires further interpretation.

The configuration of meaning which constitutes the symbolic reality of traditional church religion appears to be unrelated to the culture of modern industrial society. It is certain, at least, that internalization of the symbolic reality of traditional religion is neither enforced nor, in the typical case, favored by the social structure of contemporary society. This fact alone suffices to explain why traditional church religion moved to the margin of contemporary life. The findings contradict the notion that the challenge of overt antichurch ideologies plays an important role. If the churches maintain their institutional claim to represent and mediate the traditional religious universe of meaning, they survive primarily by association with social groups and social strata which continue to be oriented toward the values of a past social order. If, on the other hand, the churches accommodate themselves to the dominant culture of modern industrial society they necessarily take on the function of legitimating the latter. In the performance of this function, however, the universe of meaning traditionally represented by the churches becomes increasingly irrelevant. In short, the so-called process of secularization has decisively altered either the social location of church religion or its inner universe of meaning. As we have formulated it, it may appear that these two alternatives are mutually exclusive. This is the case only for their hypothetical, extreme forms. In fact, less radical transformations of both the social location and the meaning-universe of church religion may occur jointly.

The marginality of traditional church religion in modern society poses two distinct, although related, theoretical questions which must be answered by sociology. Since both questions refer to the problem of secularization as the term is commonly understood it will be useful to state the questions separately. First, it is necessary to identify the causes which pushed traditional church religion to the periphery of modern society and to give an account of the latter process in terms consistent with general sociological theory. Second, it is necessary to ask whether anything that could be called religion in the framework of sociological analysis replaced traditional church religion in modern society.

It is obvious that, until the present, the sociology of religion was only concerned with the first question. We said before that the sociology of religion found itself in a serious theoretical predicament when trying to give an account of secularization. Starting from the premise that church and religion were essentially one, its own findings led the discipline to the conclusion that religion, the term understood in its most general sense, becomes a marginal phenomenon in modern society—unless it ceases to be religion. The logic of the argument demanded that global causes be found for such a transformation. Since we need not accept the premise we can avoid that predicament. We need not look for global causes to account for the fate that befell the universe of meaning based upon a particular, historical, social institution. Whereas the problem is theoretically more restricted than commonly thought, it is, of course, still more relevant than, for example, a process of change from the extended to the nuclear family—at least if that process is viewed in isolation. Furthermore, this question is—as we just indicated—linked to the second, more important problem to be discussed. A few observations are, therefore, in order here.

In identifying the causes of secularization it does not suffice to refer to industrialization and urbanization as though these processes would automatically and necessarily undermine the values of traditional church religion. On the other hand, one cannot adequately interpret the decrease in church religion as a retreat before a historical wave of hostile ideologies and value-systems such as various types of "faith" in science. To postulate that the latter possess some inherent superiority—if only of a pragmatic kind—is sociologically downright naïve. It is more consistent with general sociological theory to view industrialization and urbanization as specific socio-historical processes which, however, led to encompassing changes in the total social structure. Once the nature of these changes is better understood it will be possible to specify more adequately the concomitant transformation in the pattern of individual life in society—and the decreasing role of traditional church religion in lending meaning to that pattern. It is often overlooked that the relation between industrialization and secularization is indirect. The corresponding explanatory schemes are, therefore, either too narrowly structural, deriving the change in one institution from changes in another, presumably more "basic" institution, or remain restricted to the history of ideas, interpreting the process as the replacement of one system of values by another, presumably more "powerful" one.

In suggesting that the relation between industrialization and secularization is indirect, we gain a different perspective on the process. The values which were originally institutionalized by church religion were not the norms of a particular action system. To put it differently, the values originally underlying church religion were not institutional norms but norms lending significance to individual life in its totality. As such they were superordinated to the norms of all the institutions that determined the conduct of individuals in various spheres of everyday life and spanned their biographies. Industrialization and urbanization were processes that reinforced the tendency of institutional specialization. Institutional specialization, in turn, tended to "free" the norms of the various institutional areas from the influence of the originally superordinated "religious" values. As we shall try to show later, the significance of these values for the individual decreased as they became irrelevant in his economic, political, and other activities. In other words, the reality of the religious cosmos waned in proportion to its shrinking social base; to wit, specialized religious institutions. What were originally total life values became part-time norms. In short, the decrease in traditional church religion may be seen as a consequence of the shrinking relevance of the values, institutionalized in church religion, for the integration and legitimation of everyday life in modern society.

If the answer we suggested to the first question referring to the problem of secularization is correct, one task for the sociology of religion consists in explaining the limited and modified persistence of church religion in the contemporary world. This task may be considered as solved, at least in part. The findings of the recent sociology of religion indicate, as we pointed out before, that traditional church religion came to depend more and more upon social groups and strata that are, in a sense, survivals of a past social order within modern society.[8]

The shrinking of church religion, however, is only one—and the sociologically less interesting—dimension of the problem of secularization. For the analysis of contemporary society another question is more important. What are the dominant values overarching contemporary culture? What is the social–structural basis of these values and what is their function in the life of contemporary man? For the sociologist it is not enough to trivialize the view that secularization refers to the retreat of religion before the onslaught of materialism, modern paganism and the like. He must ask, rather, what it is that secularization has brought about in the way of a socially objectivated cosmos of meaning. The survival of traditional forms of church religion, the absence, in the West, of an institutionalized antichurch, and the overwhelming significance of Christianity in the shaping of the modern Western world have combined in obscuring the possibility that a new religion is in the making. It is this possibility that we shall try to raise from a purely speculative status to the status of a productive hypothesis in the sociological theory of religion.

---

1. Notable are Fichter's studies of Catholic parishes. Fichter was influential in initiating the trend from purely sociographic studies to parish sociology and his studies served as a model for most recent Catholic as well as Protestant parish investigations. *Cf.* Joseph H. Fichter, S. J., *Southern Parish,* Vol. I., The University of Chicago Press, Chicago, 1951, and *Social Relations in the Urban Parish,* The University of Chicago Press, Chicago, 1954.

2. Considering the limitations of this study an attempt to document the following by a complete bibliography would be impossible. A large bibliography can be found in

Dietrich Goldschmidt and Joachim Matthes, eds., "Probleme der Religionssoziologie," Special Issue No. 6 of the *Kölner Zeitschrift für Soziologie und Sozialpsychologie.* For reviews of the field see Charles Y. Glock, "The Sociology of Religion," in Robert K. Merton, Leonard Broom and Leonard S. Cottrell, Jr., eds., *Sociology Today,* Basic Books, New York, 1959, pp. 153-177; Paul Honigsheim, "Sociology of Religion—Complementary Analyses of Religious Institutions," in Howard Becker and Alvin Boskoff, eds., *Modern Sociological Theory in Continuity and Change,* The Dryden Press, New York, 1957, pp. 450-481; Chester L. Hunt, "The Sociology of Religion," in Joseph S. Roucek, ed., *Contemporary Sociology,* Philosophical Library, New York, 1958; Gabriel Le Bras, "Problèmes de la Sociologie des Religions," in Georges Gurvitch, ed., *Traité de la Sociologie,* Vol. II., Presses Universitaires de France, Paris, 1960, pp. 79-102; Dietrich Goldschmidt, Franz Greiner and Helmut Schelsky, eds., *Soziologie der Kirchengemeinde,* Enke, Stuttgart, 1959; Richard D. Lambert, ed., "Religion in American Society," Vol. 332 of *The Annals of the American Society of Political and Social Science.*

3. *Cf.* Will Herberg, *Protestant, Catholic and Jew,* Doubleday, Garden City, 1955.

4. *Cf.* Gerhard Lenski, *The Religious Factor,* Doubleday, Garden City, 1961.

5. For an interpretation see Friedrich Tenbruck, "Die Kirchengemeinde in der entkirchlichten Gesellschaft," in Goldschmidt, Greiner and Schelsky, eds., *op. cit.* pp. 122-132; *Cf.* also Reinhard Koester, *Die Kirchentreuen,* Enke, Stuttgart, 1959, esp. p. 108.

6. A study which traces the symptoms of these changes has been done by Louis Schneider and Sanford M. Dornbusch, *Popular Religion—Inspirational Books in America,* The University of Chicago Press, Chicago, 1958.

7. For a description and interpretation of these functions see Peter Berger, *The Noise of Solemn Assemblies,* Doubleday, Garden City, 1961.

8. *Cf.* Tenbruck, *op. cit.*

THEODORE M. STEEMAN

The Underground Church: The Forms and Dynamics of Change in Contemporary Catholicism

The setting may be very simple: a family has invited some friends, relatives, and neighbors. They sit around the dining room table. The priest, a friend of the family, dressed in shirt and tie, presides over this meeting. He reads a passage or two from the Bible and opens a discussion. The liturgy can be adapted to respond to a personal situation—for example, the first communion of a child—or to a national calamity such as the death of Dr. Martin Luther King, Jr. Prayers are said, each contributing his own particular concern. There may be some singing.

The text of the canon for the mass is one of the twenty-odd mimeographed versions that are circulating now among priests and lay people. Each participant receives both bread and wine, the cup being passed around to everyone; the bread and wine were bought at a grocery store in the neighborhood. The children have had a sip of wine before so they know its taste. The atmosphere is relaxed, yet solemn. These are people

---

From *The Religious Situation: 1969*, ed. Donald R. Cutler (Boston: Beacon Press, 1969), pp. 713-22 from the essay "The Underground Church" by Theodore M. Steeman.

who know each other; they are friends, but what they do now is special, not simply a meal or a cocktail party. They *celebrate* a deeper concern for each other. The search is for community in Christ. The event is a manifestation of the Underground Church.

In some parishes the local clergy may take the initiative and go into homes, taking the mass kit and all the paraphernalia, and say the official liturgy; sometimes, however, the priest is "imported" from outside the local parish. The departure from the official liturgy in some cases may not go beyond the rejection of liturgical vestments, but it may go all the way to an almost completely extempore celebration. The theological tone may vary considerably. It may be determined by the experience of togetherness in the presence of the mystical Christ, or by a heavy emphasis on the Christian's social commitment. The group may be exclusively Catholic, but quite often it is not. A con-celebration of the mass by Catholic and non-Catholic clergy is now a realistic possibility. The small group, the informal setting, the freedom of expression, and the recognition of each other as brother and sister in Christ mark this kind of celebration as a reaction against, or a sign of dissatisfaction with, the official Sunday morning services in the parish churches.

Nobody knows how widespread this phenomenon, the *liturgical* Underground Church, is in the United States or in World Catholicism, but available data indicate that such groups exist all over the world.[1] Fr. Rocco Caporale reports the existence of several hundred groups in the United States. "In the Los Angeles area alone there are between thirty and forty of these groups, more or less permanent in nature. In the San Francisco Bay area their number is legion . . .".[2] Research in France and Chile led to the conclusion that the phenomena is indeed international. The question is not, therefore, whether such a thing as the liturgical Underground exists. The question is what it means, how we can make sense of it, how we can see it in a larger context.

Reference to a larger context is indeed necessary. Whatever the term "Underground" means, we should be careful not to limit the Underground Church to its liturgical expression. Even though the term is most often used to refer to the "group church" or the "home mass" movement, there is also a *theological* and an *ethical witness* Underground. William Hamilton has distinguished these three portions of the religious Underground,[3] and it would seem that there are in fact social realities corresponding to these ideas. There are small, intimate discussion groups which, in the same kind of atmosphere as the liturgical Underground, achieve a greater degree of theological openness and frankness in discussing matters of faith and morals than in previous years. Standard dogma is squarely challenged, and the question of what certain traditional formulations might possibly mean is asked openly. There is an amazing amount of open conversation about matters hitherto considered sacred and secure, not only on the level of professional theology, but at the level of the concerned layman. Such notions as papal infallibility, the divinity of Christ, and the real presence of Christ in the Eucharistic species, are freely discussed, and the "God is dead" theology is not without its impact.

One can also identify an *ethical* Underground. This means not only that many have decided to follow their own insight and conscience rather than accepting the Church's official teaching in such matters as birth control and sexual ethics, but also, as in the peace and civil rights movements, that some Catholics are following their consciences above and beyond and, if necessary, *against* the compromising attitudes of the institutional church. Social activists openly defy the prudent reserves of their bishops or the interests of the institutional church, criticizing it for its lack of social concern. Picketing a chancery to get the bishop to support the rights of the black man or of the draft resister is now a common thing in American Catholicism.

It may seem questionable whether we can refer to this variety of activities with the single term Underground Church. Apparently coined by Malcolm Boyd and given currency by *Time* magazine,[4] the term has the fallacy of suggesting a secrecy and subversiveness which are not always present. One can hardly say that the Berrigan brothers are "underground" in the same sense in which the French *Résistance* was "underground" during World War II. At the same time, however, the term does point to a common characteristic in the above described movements in the Church, so that even though one dislikes the term it still serves its descriptive purpose. This common characteristic is that in the name of Christian renewal and authenticity one must go one's own way often without support from the institutional church and, as the case may be, against it. Initiative does not rest in the institutional church and its authorities and does not respect traditional structures. When the hierarchy is very repressive, members of the Underground may proceed in secrecy and seeming subversiveness. I can accept Malcom Boyd's definition: "a contemporary Christian revolutionary movement in the U.S. bypassing official Church structures and leadership, and concerned with Christian unity and radical involvement in the world,"[5] but to cover more clearly the liturgical Underground I would read "community" instead of "unity," and I would add that reformulation of Christian doctrine is very much part of the movement as a whole.

The Liturgical Underground

The liturgical Underground is a good starting point for discussion, not so much because the liturgical aspect is more important by itself but because in the realm of the liturgy the movement is most visible and takes a social form most distinctly. More than in the realm of theological awareness or of social action it is in the liturgical Underground that the movement becomes Church, i.e., a form of typically and explicitly religious association, religious community. More than that: by moving the core ritual out of its traditional location in the Church, the liturgical Underground becomes most clearly an attempt to change the structure itself. The liturgy has to do with the Church as a corporate institution, with its self-awareness and with the ways in which the faithful identify with it. Emphasis on smaller, intimate groups, over and against the anonymous and impersonal parish, as the locus for liturgical celebration, means that the community is given preference over the institution. By making the community experience a primary criterion for the meaningfulness of the celebrated liturgy, the faithful, so to speak, take over from the institution and try to achieve a different type of church experience.

On the other hand, of course, to the extent that primary emphasis is placed on the liturgy, we cannot speak of a very radical departure from the traditional patterns of Catholic piety. The liturgical Underground as such seems to do little more than transfer the liturgy from the parish church to the home, perhaps thereby making the rite more meaningful to the individual's experience. But since the liturgy is *per definitionem* expressive celebration, it is still an open question whether the liturgical Underground goes beyond this to shape another kind of Christian awareness and of Christian presence. It could very well be that this phase of the Underground will turn out to be little more than a privatization of Christianity, a replacement of the Sunday morning ordeal by a Saturday afternoon delight, of the anonymous parish by a group of friends and relatives. An answer to this question, however, is only possible after a more extensive analysis of the Underground Church as a whole.

Regardless, the liturgical Underground reflects a profound and widespread dissatisfaction with the institutional church, more especially with the anonymity and powerlessness of the traditional, or slightly revised, liturgy as acted out in the parish churches. It also indicates a certain intent on the part of the faithful and lower clergy to experiment regardless of institutional approval of what they are doing. Disenchantment with the traditional liturgy and forms of worship is not itself amazing. Need for change was felt long ago and was officially recognized by Vatican II; the Church is even pledged to develop a more understandable, more meaningful liturgy. But the fact that in the Underground the initiative rests with the lower echelons of the Church's hierarchical structure is especially significant. It indicates not only that the changes the Church is pledged to are timely, if not too late, and that on the part of the laity there is a tremendous impatience in this regard, but that, in fact, the authority structure itself is being questioned. When one commentator on the Underground Church reveals his concern for the unity of Bishop, Eucharist, and Catholic, he may well have touched upon the real problem: whether the Catholic layman and lower clergy are willing to go along with the kind of institution the Catholic Church is.[6]

At this point, the real issue at stake in the phenomenon of the Underground Church becomes apparent. Whatever we think of the products of the movement, whether we can accept the group churches or not, whether we agree with the Underground type of theology or not, whether we can join the social concerns or not, there is an element of structural crisis that cannot be denied. The Underground is not simply built on particular issues; the phenomenon contains an element of structural crisis insofar as the changes are not only asked or demanded, but claimed as a right. The integrative patterns of the old institution are in jeopardy. The nature of the Church itself is under scrutiny and enters into a stage of experimentation. The liturgy is only a case in point. The liturgical Underground and its group churches point to a ferment deeper and more comprehensive. Rosemary Ruether is more to the point when she proposes the term "free church" to replace the rather awkward "Underground Church."[7] The tendencies are toward a much larger amount of freedom and initiative from below in all aspects of the life of the Church and thereby toward questioning the exclusive claims of the institution.

The "Church" in the Underground

Structurally speaking, the most important feature of the Underground Church is its disregard for traditional authority, vested concretely in the Catholic hierarchy and in the central government of the Church in Rome. For many people in the Underground this element does not carry much weight. They have just accepted the fact that the institutional church does not respond relevantly to present needs for change, and just go ahead and do whatever their Christian consciences prescribe, taking all the freedom vis-à-vis the institution they need to act out their commitments. In fact, some feel that we do not have to bother about the institution at all and that it is a waste of energy to do so. Yet, for the purposes of the present analysis this rejection of traditional authority is of major importance, for it shows how deep the changes are that we see happening in the Church.

William Osborne's distinction between ecclesiastical and religious reform may be helpful here.[8] Religious reform has to do with changes in the Church on the level of the religious life of the community.

Ecclesiastical reform, on the other hand, is the reform of the institution, of the organization. Osborne maintains that the two levels of change are clearly out of pace. The need for change as experienced by the community, by laymen, and by lower clergy, is much deeper and more comprehensive than the official leadership in the Church is willing to acknowledge. There have been changes in values, norms, life goals, and in the understanding of the core ritual in the community of the faithful, which are not accepted by the hierarchy. Thus there is a huge gap between the two levels; in fact there is almost no communication. Expressions of disregard for the institution reflect that some have given up attempting to bridge this gap.

But does this mean that we have to describe religious reform or the Underground Church as separating itself from the Church? Or can we describe this movement as a movement *in* the Church, and the Underground as something that is indeed happening *to* the Church? I think we must. There is no sign that the Underground Church considers itself as separate from or as having said farewell to the Church. Perhaps it may go in that direction in a later stage of development, but at present it appears that the Underground lives in deep loyalty to the church at large, in a critical loyalty that questions present structures but does not break the bonds of basic solidarity with the Church. I have, at present, no evidence of strong sectarian or schismatic tendencies; there seems to be no desire for separate organization. The Underground, rather, claims to be a reaffirmation of basic churchly realities; it stands over and against the institutional church with the claim of being more truly "Church" than the institution. It protests identifying the Church as the Catholic institution; the idea of separation, therefore, is somehow not part of its thinking. Fr. Hafner, in his description of the movement, mentions as one of its characteristics a deep suspicion of all forms of institutionalization.[9]

In fact, the Underground operates on a different concept of the Church. In the free church the liturgy, for example, is seen as the celebration of the community rather than as the administration of grace by the institution. The emphasis shifts fully from the institution to the community as the basic focus of the Church. This introduces, of course, a certain amount of vagueness into the conception of the Church; there are no definite boundaries. The Church consists of this vast body of people who call themselves Christians and who somehow participate in the stream of religious life that finds its origin in the New Testament. This Church is neither Catholic nor Protestant; it is simply Christian. It becomes actual when believers gather in the celebration of their common faith and when they engage in common action. This church "happens," to quote David Kirk.[10] The primary emphasis is on the Christian life in the Christian community.

The Underground concept of the Church is not necessarily *anti*structural, rather it is *pre*structural. Whatever structures exist are conceived as "functional," i.e., as serving the purposes of the community or as derived from the community; however, they have to be checked, for once structures develop a dynamic of their own they are likely to harm the community rather than to help it. Structures have to be flexible, changeable, and adaptable to the needs of the situation. They should never be thought of as embodying the life of the community, which might mean stagnation. The proper locus of the Christian faith is not in the structures but in the living and creative community, which may have to protest the existing structures.

To this way of thinking, of course, the question of institutional separation becomes irrelevant. The Underground Church would have to be more institutionalized in order to arrive at that stage. But neither do we have to speak of separation *de facto.* Sociologically speaking we have to accept the conclusion that the Christian Church presents three faces: the official Church, the experimental or Underground Church, and the Church of the people, the rank and file, the routine Christians.[11] Theologically speaking one should note the breakthrough in ecclesiology, sanctioned by Vatican II, which describes the Church primarily in terms of the people of God. These conceptions make it impossible to identify the Christian Church simply and uncritically with the institutional church or with organized Christianity. The institutional church itself does not now make this identification. Thus we can speak meaningfully about a "church at large" which is not fully in the institutional church or churches, whose reality extends beyond organized Christianity and which contains all Christian initiative in the present world. It is in this church at large that we can place the Underground Church as a "free church movement," to quote Rosemary Ruether, which tries to organize Christian initiative in a more original way than the institutions are able to. Thus the Underground Church moves with greater freedom than the institutional church is willing to grant in the realm of the church at large, more or less in tension with the hierarchy, but in the same realm.

This means that even though the Underground is characterized by a rejection of the traditional authority structures, it still can be seen as an intra-Church phenomenon. The Underground Church is a locus of change in the Church, a new effort to find ways and means to express the Christian message in intellectual and liturgical forms and in social action, and in this effort it protests the established forms of the institutional church. Even when the tension with the institution is considered to be immaterial, as Miss Ruether's concept of the free church would suggest, the institution is still there as part of the objective situation, albeit mostly as a negative pole of reference.[12] It is difficult to imagine that the institutional church will be unaffected by the phenomenon of the free church, for the free church must relate itself to the institution. Since both try to represent the Christian message they are bound to exist in tension with one another, being part of the larger reality which is the church at large.

Seen in this larger context, then, the Underground Church represents initiative from below. This is a more spontaneous kind of creativity, arising out of the community of the faithful. Here it is not Church officials dealing with the problems of adapting the Church to modern life, but laymen and lower clergy trying to develop a Christian style of life in which the modern Christian can live out his faith. The Christian community comes alive, and instead of waiting for orders from above, takes responsibility for the presence of Christ in modern society and for the credibility of the Christian message. The layman is taking his place in the Church. Christianity is taken seriously not only by those who have made it into their "vocation," but by those who used to belong to the rank and file, the passive audience. And they do so with such force and conviction that their initiative may lead to a total disregard for the traditional institutions, which do not seem to express adequately the Christian concerns of the modern layman.

---

1. Heuvel, Albert van den: Toward a New Style of Life (IDO-C, Rome, Italy) 68-19; *Time,* July 12, 1968.

2. Caporale, Rocco, SJ: Underground and Group Churches, an address given at the Boston College Institute on the Underground Church, Boston, Massachusetts, Apr 19-21, 1968.

3. Hamilton, William: quoted by Malcolm Boyd: The Underground Church, *Commonweal,* Apr 12, 1968, p 97.

4. *Time,* Sept 29, 1968.

5. Boyd, Malcolm: The Underground Church, *Commonweal,* Apr 12, 1968, p 97.

6. Haughey, John C, SJ: The Underground Church, *America,* May 18, 1968.

7. Ruether, Rosemary: Schism of Consciousness, *Commonweal,* May 31, 1968, p 327.

8. Osborne, William A: Catholic Reform in the United States; Too Late? (IDO-C, Rome, Italy) 67-14.

9. Hafner, George J: A New Style of Christianity, *Commonweal,* May 31, 1968, pp 331 ff.

10. Kirk, David: in a paper read at the Boston College Institute on the Underground Church, Boston, Massachusetts, Apr 19-21, 1968.

11. Heuvel, Albert van den: Toward a New Style of Life (IDO-C, Rome, Italy) 68-19.

12. Ruether, Rosemary: Schism of Consciousness, *Commonweal,* May 31, 1968, p 328.

HUSTON SMITH

Do Drugs Have Religious Import?

Until six months ago, if I picked up my phone in the Cambridge area and dialed KISS-BIG, a voice would answer, "If-if." These were coincidences: KISS-BIG happened to be the letter equivalents of an arbitrarily assigned telephone number, and I.F.I.F. represented the initials of an organization with the improbable name of the International Federation for Internal Freedom. But the coincidences were apposite to the point of being poetic. "Kiss big" caught the euphoric, manic, life-embracing attitude that characterized this most publicized of the organizations formed to explore the newly synthesized consciousness-changing substances; the organization itself was surely one of the "iffy-est" phenomena to appear on our social and intellectual scene in some time. It produced the first firings in Harvard's history, an ultimatum to get out of Mexico in five days, and "the miracle of Marsh Chapel," in which, during a two-and-one-half hour Good Friday service, ten theological students and professors ingested psilocybin and were visited by what

From *The Journal of Philosophy* 61 (October 1964):517-30. Reprinted by permission of the publisher and author.

they generally reported to be the deepest religious experiences of their lives.

Despite the last of these phenomena and its numerous if less dramatic parallels, students of religion appear by and large to be dismissing the psychedelic drugs that have sprung to our attention in the '60s as having little religious relevance. The position taken in one of the most forward-looking volumes of theological essays to have appeared in recent years —*Soundings,* edited by A. R. Vidler[1]—accepts R. C. Zaehner's *Mysticism Sacred and Profane* as having "fully examined and refuted" the religious claims for mescalin which Aldous Huxley sketched in *The Doors of Perception.* This closing of the case strikes me as premature, for it looks as if the drugs have light to throw on the history of religion, the phenomenology of religion, the philosophy of religion, and the practice of the religious life itself.

Drugs and Religion Viewed Historically

In his trial-and-error life explorations man almost everywhere has stumbled upon connections between vegetables (eaten or brewed) and actions (yogi breathing exercises, whirling-dervish dances, flagellations) that alter states of consciousness. From the psychopharmacological standpoint we now understand these states to be the products of changes in brain chemistry. From the sociological perspective we see that they tend to be connected in some way with religion. If we discount the wine used in Christian communion services, the instances closest to us in time and space are the peyote of The Native American [Indian] Church and Mexico's 2000-year-old "sacred mushrooms," the latter rendered in Aztec as "God's Flesh"—striking parallel to "the body of our Lord" in the Christian eucharist. Beyond these neighboring instances lie the *soma* of the Hindus, the *haoma* and hemp of the Zoroastrians, the Dionysus of the Greeks who "everywhere . . . taught men the culture of the vine and the mysteries of his worship and everywhere [was] accepted as a god,"[2] the *benzoin* of Southeast Asia, Zen's tea whose fifth cup purifies and whose sixth "calls to the realm of the immortals,"[3] the *pituri* of the Australian aborigines, and probably the mystic *kykeon* that was eaten and drunk at the climactic close of the sixth day of the Eleusinian mysteries.[4] There is no need to extend the list, as a reasonably complete account is available in Philippe de Félice's comprehensive study of the subject, *Poisons sacrés, ivresses divines.*

More interesting than the fact that consciousness-changing devices have been linked with religion is the possibility that they actually initiated many of the religious perspectives which, taking root in history, continued after their psychedelic origins were forgotten. Bergson saw the first movement of Hindus and Greeks toward "dynamic religion" as associated with the "divine rapture" found in intoxicating beverages;[5] more recently Robert Graves, Gordon Wasson, and Alan Watts have suggested that most religions arose from such chemically induced theophanies. Mary Barnard is the most explicit proponent of this thesis. "Which . . . was more likely to happen first," she asks,[6] "the spontaneously generated idea of an afterlife in which the disembodied soul, liberated from the restrictions of time and space, experiences eternal bliss, or the accidental discovery of hallucinogenic plants that give a sense of euphoria, dislocate the center of consciousness, and distort time and space, making them balloon outward in greatly expanded vistas?" Her own answer is that "the [latter] experience might have had . . . an almost explosive effect on the largely dormant minds of men, causing them to think of things they had never thought of before. This, if you like, is direct revelation." Her use of the subjunctive "might" renders this formulation of her answer equivocal, but she concludes her essay on a note that is completely unequivocal: "Looking at the matter coldly, unintoxicated and unentranced, I am willing to prophesy that fifty theobotanists working for fifty years would make the current theories concerning the origins of much mythology and theology as out-of-date as pre-Copernican astronomy."

This is an important hypothesis—one which must surely engage the attention of historians of religion for some time to come. But as I am concerned here only to spot the points at which the drugs erupt onto the field of serious religious study, not to ride the geysers to whatever heights, I shall not pursue Miss Barnard's thesis. Having located what appears to be the crux of the historical question, namely the extent to which drugs not merely duplicate or simulate theologically sponsored experiences but generate or shape theologies themselves, I turn to phenomenology.

Drugs and Religion Viewed Phenomenologically

Phenomenology attempts a careful description of human experience. The question the drugs pose for the phenomenology of religion, therefore, is whether the experiences they induce differ from religious experiences reached naturally, and if so how.

Even the Bible notes that chemically induced psychic states bear *some* resemblance to religious ones. Peter had to appeal to a circumstantial criterion—the early hour of the day—to defend those who were caught up in the Pentecostal experience against the charge that they were merely drunk: "These men are not drunk, as you suppose, since it is only the third hour of the day" (Acts 2:15); and Paul initiates the comparison when he admonishes the Ephesians not to "get drunk with wine . . . but [to] be filled with the spirit" (Ephesians 5:18). Are such comparisons, paralleled in the accounts of virtually every religion, superficial? How far can they be pushed?

Not all the way, students of religion have thus far insisted. With respect to the new drugs, Prof. R. C. Zaehner has drawn the line emphatically. "The importance of Huxley's *Doors of Perception,*" he writes, "is that in it the author clearly makes the claim that what he experienced under the influence of mescalin is closely comparable to a genuine mystical experience. If he is right, . . . the conclusions . . . are alarming."[7] Zaehner thinks that Huxley is not right, but I fear that it is Zaehner who is mistaken.

There are, of course, innumerable drug experiences that have no religious feature; they can be sensual as readily as spiritual, trivial as readily as transforming, capricious as readily as sacramental. If there is one point about which every student of the drugs agrees, it is that there is no such thing as the drug experience *per se*—no experience that the drugs, as it were, merely secrete. Every experience is a mix of three ingredients: drug, set (the psychological make-up of the individual), and setting (the social and physical environment in which it is taken). But given the right set and setting, the drugs can induce religious experiences indistinguishable from experiences that occur spontaneously. Nor need set and setting be exceptional. The way the statistics are currently running, it looks as if from one-fourth to one-third of the general population will have religious experiences if they take the drugs under naturalistic conditions, meaning by this conditions in which the researcher supports the subject but does not try to influence the direction his experience will take. Among subjects who have strong religious inclinations to begin with, the proportion of those having religious experiences jumps to three-fourths. If they take the drugs in settings that are religious too, the ratio soars to nine in ten.

How do we know that the experiences these people have really are religious? We can begin with the fact that they say they are. The "one-fourth to one-third of the general population" figure is drawn from two sources. Ten months after they had had their experiences, 24 per cent of the 194 subjects in a study by the California psychiatrist Oscar Janiger characterized their experiences as having been religious.[8] Thirty-two per cent of the 74 subjects in Ditman and Hayman's study reported, looking back on their LSD experience, that it looked as if it had been "very much" or "quite a bit" a religious experience; 42 per cent checked as true the statement that they "were left with a greater awareness of God, or a higher power, or ultimate reality."[9] The statement that three-fourths of subjects have religious "sets" will have religious experiences comes from the reports of sixty-nine religious professionals who took the drugs while the Harvard project was in progress.[10]

In the absence of (a) a single definition of religious experience acceptable to psychologists of religion generally and (b) fool-proof ways of ascertaining whether actual experiences exemplify any definition, I am not sure there is any better way of telling whether the experiences of the 333 men and women involved in the above studies were religious than by noting whether they seemed so to them. But if more rigorous methods are preferred, they exist; they have been utilized, and they confirm the conviction of the man in the street that drug experiences can indeed be religious. In his doctoral study at Harvard University, Walter Pahnke worked out a typology of religious experience (in this instance of the mystical variety) based on the classic cases of mystical experiences as summarized in Walter Stace's *Mysticism and Philosophy.* He then administered psilocybin to ten theology students and professors in the setting of a Good Friday service. The drug was given "double-blind," meaning that neither Dr. Pahnke nor his subjects knew which ten were getting psilocybin and which ten placebos to constitute a control group. Subsequently the reports the subjects wrote of their experiences were laid successively before three college-graduate housewives who, without being informed about the nature of the study, were asked to rate each statement as to the degree (strong, moderate, slight, or none) to which it exemplified each of the nine traits of mystical experience enumerated in the typology of mysticism worked out in advance. When the test of significance was applied to their statistics, it showed that "those subjects who received psilocybin experienced phenomena which were indistinguishable from, if not identical with . . . the categories defined by our typology of mysticism."[11]

With the thought that the reader might like to test his own powers of discernment on the question being considered, I insert here a simple test I gave to a group of Princeton students following a recent discussion sponsored by the Woodrow Wilson Society:

> Below are accounts of two religious experiences. One occurred under the influence of drugs, one without their influence. Check the one you think *was* drug-induced.

I

Suddenly I burst into a vast, new, indescribably wonderful universe. Although I am writing this over a year later, the thrill of the surprise and amazement, the awesomeness of the revelation, the engulfment in an

> overwhelming feeling-wave of gratitude and blessed wonderment, are as fresh, and the memory of the experience is as vivid, as if it had happened five minutes ago. And yet to concoct anything by way of description that would even hint at the magnitude, the sense of ultimate reality . . . this seems such an impossible task. The knowledge which has infused and affected every aspect of my life came instantaneously and with such complete force of certainty that it was impossible, then or since, to doubt its validity.

II

> All at once, without warning of any kind, I found myself wrapped in a flame-colored cloud. For an instant I though of fire . . . the next, I knew that the fire was within myself. Directly afterward there came upon me a sense of exultation, of immense joyousness accompanied or immediately followed by an intellectual illumination impossible to describe. Among other things, I did not merely come to believe, but I saw that the universe is not composed of dead matter, but is, on the contrary, a living Presence; I became conscious in myself of eternal life. . . . I saw that all men are immortal: that the cosmic order is such that without any preadventure all things work together for the good of each and all; that the foundation principle of the world . . . is what we call love, and that the happiness of each and all is in the long run absolutely certain.

On the occasion referred to, twice as many students (46) answered incorrectly as answered correctly (23). I bury the correct answer in a footnote to preserve the reader's opportunity to test himself.[12]

Why, in the face of this considerable evidence, does Zaehner hold that drug experiences cannot be authentically religious? There appear to be three reasons:

1. His own experience was "utterly trivial." This of course proves that not all drug experiences are religious; it does not prove that no drug experiences are religious.

2. He thinks the experiences of others that appear religious to them are not truly so. Zaehner distinguishes three kinds of mysticism: nature mysticism, in which the soul is united with the natural world; monistic mysticism, in which the soul merges with an impersonal absolute; and theism, in which the soul confronts the living, personal God. He concedes that drugs can induce the first two species of mysticism, but not its supreme instance, the theistic. As proof, he analyzes Huxley's experience as recounted in *The Doors of Perception* to show that it produced at best a blend of nature and monistic mysticism. Even if we were to accept Zaehner's evaluation of the three forms of mysticism, Huxley's case, and indeed Zaehner's entire book, would prove only that not every mystical experience induced by the drugs is theistic. Insofar as Zaehner

goes beyond this to imply that drugs do not and cannot induce theistic mysticism, he not only goes beyond the evidence but proceeds in the face of it. James Slotkin reports that the peyote Indians "see visions, which may be of Christ Himself. Sometimes they hear the voice of the Great Spirit. Sometimes they become aware of the presence of God and of those personal shortcomings which must be corrected if they are to do His will."[13] And G. M. Carstairs, reporting on the use of psychedelic *bhang* in India, quotes a Brahmin as saying, "It gives good bhakti. . . . You get a very good bhakti with bhang," *bhakti* being precisely Hinduism's theistic variant.[14]

3. There is a third reason why Zaehner might doubt that drugs can induce genuinely mystical experiences. Zaehner is a Roman Catholic, and Roman Catholic doctrine teaches that mystical rapture is a gift of grace and as such can never be reduced to man's control. This may be true; certainly the empirical evidence cited does not preclude the possibility of a genuine ontological or theological difference between natural and drug-induced religious experiences. At this point, however, we are considering phenomenology rather than ontology, description rather than interpretation, and on this level there is no difference. Descriptively, drug experiences cannot be distinguished from their natural religious counterpart. When the current philosophical authority on mysticism, W. T. Stace, was asked whether the drug experience is similar to the mystical experience, he answered, "It's not a matter of its being *similar* to mystical experience; it *is* mystical experience."

What we seem to be witnessing in Zaehner's *Mysticism Sacred and Profane* is a reenactment of the age-old pattern in the conflict between science and religion. Whenever a new controversy arises, religion's first impulse is to deny the disturbing evidence science has produced. Seen in perspective, Zaehner's refusal to admit that drugs can induce experiences descriptively indistinguishable from those which are spontaneously religious is the current counterpart of the seventeenth-century theologians' refusal to look through Galileo's telescope or, when they did, their persistence on dismissing what they saw as machinations of the devil. When the fact that drugs can trigger religious experiences becomes incontrovertible, discussion will move to the more difficult question of how this new fact is to be interpreted. The latter question leads beyond phenomenology into philosophy.

Drugs and Religion Viewed Philosophically

Why do people reject evidence? Because they find it threatening, we may suppose. Theologians are not the only professionals to utilize this mode of defense. In his *Personal Knowledge,*[15] Michael Polanyi recounts the way the medical profession ignored such palpable facts as the painless amputation of human limbs, performed before their own eyes in hundreds of successive cases, concluding that the subjects were imposters who were either deluding their physicians or colluding with them. One physician, Esdaile, carried out about 300 major operations painlessly under mesmeric trance in India, but neither in India nor in Great Britain could he get medical journals to print accounts of his work. Polanyi attributes this closed-mindedness to "lack of a conceptual framework in which their discoveries could be separated from specious and untenable admixtures."

The "untenable admixture" in the fact that psychotomimetic drugs can induce religious experience is its apparent implicate: that religious disclosures are no more veridical than psychotic ones. For religious skeptics, this conclusion is obviously not untenable at all; it fits in beautifully with their thesis that *all* religion is at heart an escape from reality. Psychotics avoid reality by retiring into dream worlds of make-believe; what better evidence that religious visionaries do the same than the fact that identical changes in brain chemistry produce both states of mind? Had not Marx already warned us that religion is the "opiate" of the people?—apparently he was more literally accurate than he supposed. Freud was likewise too mild. He "never doubted that religious phenomena are to be understood only on the model of the neurotic symptoms of the individual."[16] He should have said "psychotic symptoms."

So the religious skeptic is likely to reason. What about the religious believer? Convinced that religious experiences are not fundamentally delusory, can he admit that psychotomimetic drugs can occasion them? To do so he needs (to return to Polanyi's words) "a conceptual framework in which [the discoveries can] be separated from specious and untenable admixtures," the "untenable admixture" being in this case the conclusion that religious experiences are in general delusory.

One way to effect the separation would be to argue that, despite phenomenological similarities between natural and drug-induced religious experiences, they are separated by a crucial *ontological* difference. Such an argument would follow the pattern of theologians who argue for the "real presence" of Christ's body and blood in the bread and wine of the Eucharist despite their admission that chemical analysis, confined as it is to the level of "accidents" rather than "essences," would not disclose this presence. But this distinction will not appeal to many today, for it turns on an essence-accident metaphysics which is not widely accepted. Instead of fighting a rear-guard action by insisting that if drug and non-drug religious experiences cannot be distinguished empirically there must be some transempirical factor that distinguishes them and renders the drug experience profane, I wish to explore the possibility of accepting drug-induced experiences as religious without relinquishing confidence in the truth-claims of religious experience generally.

To begin with the weakest of all arguments, the argument from authority: William James did not discount *his* insights that occurred while his brain chemistry was altered. The paragraph in which he retrospectively evaluates his nitrous oxide experiences has become classic, but it is so pertinent to the present discussion that it merits quoting once again.

> One conclusion was forced upon my mind at that time, and my impression of its truth has ever since remained unshaken. It is that our normal waking consciousness, rational consciousness as we call it, is but one special type of consciousness, whilst all about it, parted from it by the filmiest of screens, there lie potential forms of consciousness entirely different. We may go through life without suspecting their existence; but apply the requisite stimulus, and at a touch they are there in all their completeness, definite types of mentality which probably somewhere have their field of application and adaptation. No account of the universe in its totality can be final which leaves these other forms of consciousness quite disregarded. How to regard them is the question—for they are so discontinuous with ordinary consciousness. Yet they may determine attitudes though they cannot furnish formulas, and open a region though they fail to give a map. At any rate, they forbid a premature closing of our accounts with reality. Looking back on my own experiences, they all converge toward a kind of insight to which I cannot help ascribing some metaphysical significance (*op. cit.,* 378-379).

To this argument from authority, I add two arguments that try to provide something by ways of reasons. Drug experiences that assume a religious cast tend to have fearful and/or beatific features, and each of my hypotheses relates to one of these aspects of the experience.

Beginning with the ominous, "fear of the Lord," awe-ful features, Gordon Wasson, the New York banker-turned-mycologist, describes these as he encountered them in his psilocybin experience as follows: "Ecstasy! In common parlance . . . ecstasy is fun. . . . But ecstasy is not fun. Your very soul is seized and shaken until it tingles. After all, who will choose to feel undiluted awe? . . . The unknowing vulgar abuse the word; we must recapture its full and terrifying sense."[17] Emotionally the drug experience can be like having forty-foot waves crash over you for several hours while you cling desperately to a life-raft which may be swept from under you at any minute. It seems quite possible that such an ordeal, like any experience of a close call, could awaken rather fundamental sentiments respecting life and death and destiny and trigger the "no atheists in foxholes" effect. Similarly, as the subject emerges from the trauma and realizes that he is not going to be insane as he had feared, there may come over him an intensified appreciation like that frequently reported by patients recovering from critical illness. "It happened on the day when my bed was pushed out of doors to the open gallery of the hospital," reads one such report:

> I cannot now recall whether the revelation came suddenly or gradually; I only remember finding myself in the very midst of those wonderful moments, beholding life for the first time in all its young intoxication of loveliness, in its unspeakable joy, beauty, and importance. I cannot say exactly what the mysterious change was. I saw no new thing, but I saw all the usual things in a miraculous new light—in what I believe is their true light. I saw for the first time how wildly beautiful and joyous, beyond any words of mine to describe, is the whole of life. Every human being moving across that porch, every sparrow that flew, every branch tossing in the wind, was caught in and was a part of the whole mad ecstasy of loveliness, of joy, of importance, of intoxication of life.[18]

If we do not discount religious intuitions because they are prompted by battlefields and *physical* crises; if we regard the latter as "calling us to our senses" more often than they seduce us into delusions, need comparable intuitions be discounted simply because the crises that trigger them are of an inner, *psychic* variety?

Turning from the hellish to the heavenly aspects of the drug experience, *some* of the latter may be explainable by the hypothesis just stated; that is, they may be occasioned by the relief that attends the sense of escape from high danger. But this hypothesis cannot possibly account for *all* the beatific episodes, for the simple reason that the positive episodes often come first, or to persons who experience no negative episodes whatever. Dr. Sanford Unger of the National Institute of Mental Health reports that among his subjects "50 to 60% will not manifest any real disturbance worthy of discussion," yet "around 75% will have at least one episode in which exaltation, rapture, and joy are the key descriptions."[19] How are we to account for the drug's capacity to induce peak experiences, such as the following, which are *not* preceded by fear?

> A feeling of great peace and contentment seemed to flow through my entire body. All sound ceased and I seemed to be floating in a great, very very still void or hemisphere. It is impossible to describe the overpowering feeling of peace, contentment, and being a part of goodness itself that I felt. I could feel my body dissolving and actually becoming a part of the goodness and peace that was all around me. Words can't describe this. I feel an awe and wonder that such a feeling could have occurred to me.[20]

Consider the following line of argument. Like every other form of life, man's nature has become distinctive through specialization. Man has specialized in developing a cerebral cortex. The analytic powers of this instrument are a standing wonder, but the instrument seems less able to provide man with the sense that he is meaningfully related to his environment: to life, the world, and history in their wholeness. As Albert Camus describes the situation, "If I were . . . a cat among animals, this life would have a meaning, or rather this problem would not arise, for I should belong to this world. I would *be* this world to which I am now opposed by my whole consciousness."[21] Note that it is Camus' consciousness that opposes him to his world. The drugs do not knock this consciousness out, but while they leave it operative they also activate areas of the brain that normally lie below its threshold of awareness. One of the clearest objective signs that the drugs are taking effect is the dilation they produce in the pupils of the eyes, and one of the most predictable subjective signs is the intensification of visual perception. Both of these responses are controlled by portions of the brain that lie deep, further to the rear than the mechanisms that govern consciousness. Meanwhile we know that the human organism is interlaced with its world in innumerable ways it normally cannot sense—through gravitational fields, body respiration, and the like: the list could be multiplied until man's skin began to seem more like a thoroughfare than a boundary. Perhaps the deeper regions of the brain which evolved earlier and are more like those of the lower animals—"If I were . . . a cat . . . I should belong to this world"—can sense this relatedness better than can the cerebral cortex which now dominates our awareness. If so, when the drugs rearrange the neurohumors that chemically transmit impulses across synapses between neurons, man's consciousness and his submerged, intuitive, ecological awareness might for a spell become interlaced. This is, of course, no more than a hypothesis, but how else are we to account for the extraordinary incidence under the drugs of that kind of insight the keynote of which James described as "invariably a reconciliation"? "It is as if the opposites of the world, whose contradictoriness and conflict make all our difficulties and troubles, were melted into one and the same genus, but *one of the species,* the nobler and better one, *is itself the genus, and so soaks up and absorbs its opposites into itself*" (*op. cit.,* 379).

THE DRUGS AND RELIGION VIEWED "RELIGIOUSLY"

Suppose that drugs can induce experiences indistinguishable from religious experiences and that we can respect their reports. Do they shed any light, not (we now ask) on life, but on the nature of the religious life?

One thing they may do is throw religious experience itself into perspective by clarifying its relation to the religious life as a whole. Drugs appear able to induce religious experiences; it is less evident that they can produce religious lives. It follows that religion is more than religious experiences. This is hardly news, but it may be a useful reminder, especially to those who incline toward "the religion of religious experience"; which is to say toward lives bent on the acquisition of desired states of experience irrespective of their relation to life's other demands and components.

Despite the dangers of faculty psychology, it remains useful to regard man as having a mind, a will, and feelings. One of the lessons of religious history is that, to be adequate, a faith must rouse and involve all three components of man's nature. Religions of reason grow arid; religions of duty, leaden. Religions of experience have their comparable pitfalls, as evidenced by Taoism's struggle (not always successful) to keep from degenerating into quietism, and the vehemence with which Zen Buddhism has insisted that once students have attained *satori,* they must be driven out of it, back into the world. The case of Zen is especially pertinent here, for it pivots on an enlightenment experience —*satori,* or *kensho*—which some (but not all) Zennists say resembles LSD. Alike or different, the point is that Zen recognizes that unless the experience is joined to discipline, it will come to naught:

> Even the Buddha . . . had to sit. . . . Without *joriki,* the particular power developed through *zazen* [seated meditation], the vision of oneness attained in enlightenment . . . in time becomes clouded and eventually fades into a pleasant memory instead of remaining an omnipresent reality shaping our daily life. . . . To be able to live in accordance with what the Mind's eye has revealed through *satori* requires, like the purification of character and the development of personality, a ripening period of *zazen.*[22]

If the religion of religious experience is a snare and a delusion, it follows that no religion that fixes its faith primarily in substances that induce religious experiences can be expected to come to a good end. What promised to be a short cut will prove to be a short circuit; what began as a religion will end as a religion surrogate. Whether chemical substances can be helpful *adjuncts* to faith is another question. The peyote-using Native American Church seems to indicate that they can be; anthropologists give this church a good report, noting among other things that members resist alcohol and alcoholism better than do nonmembers.[23] The conclusion to which evidence currently points would seem to be that chemicals *can* aid the religious life, but only where set within a context of faith (meaning by this the conviction that what they disclose is true) and discipline (meaning diligent exercise of the will in the attempt to work out the implications of the disclosures for the living of life in the everyday, common-sense world).

Nowhere today in Western civilization are these two conditions jointly fulfilled. Churches lack faith in the sense just mentioned; hipsters lack discipline. This might lead us to forget about the drugs, were it not for one fact; the distinctive religious emotion and the emotion that drugs unquestionably can occasion—Otto's *mysterium tremendum, majestas, mysterium fascinans;* in a phrase, the phenomenon of religious awe—seems to be declining sharply. As Paul Tillich said in an address to the Hillel Society at Harvard several years ago:

> The question our century puts before us [is]: Is it possible to regain the lost dimension, the encounter with the Holy, the dimension which cuts through the world of subjectivity and objectivity and goes down to that which is not world but is the mystery of the Ground of Being?

Tillich may be right; this may be the religious question of our century. For if (as we have insisted) religion cannot be equated with religious experiences, neither can it long survive their absence.

---

1. *Soundings: Essays concerning Christian Understandings,* A. R. Vidler, ed. (Cambridge: University Press, 1962). The statement cited appears on page 72, in H. A. William's essay on "Theology and Self-awareness."

2. Edith Hamilton, *Mythology* (New York: Mentor, 1953), p. 55.

3. Quoted in Alan Watts, *The Spirit of Zen* (New York: Grove Press, 1958), p. 110.

4. George Mylonas, *Eleusis and the Eleusinian Mysteries* (Princeton, N.J.: Princeton Univ. Press, 1961), p. 284.

5. *Two Sources of Morality and Religion* (New York: Holt, 1935), pp. 206-212.

6. "The God in the Flowerpot," *The American Scholar* 32, 4 (Autumn, 1963):584, 586.

7. *Mysticism, Sacred and Profane* (New York: Oxford, 1961), p. 12.

8. Quoted in William H. McGlothlin, "Long-lasting Effects of LSD on Certain Attitudes in Normals," printed for private distribution by the RAND Corporation, May, 1962, p. 16.

9. *Ibid.,* pp. 45, 46.

10. Timothy Leary, "The Religious Experience: Its Production and Interpretation," *The Psychedelic Review,* 1, 3 (1964):325.

11. "Drugs and Mysticism: An Analysis of the Relationship between Psychedelic Drugs and the Mystical Consciousness," a thesis presented to the Committee on Higher Degrees in History and Philosophy of Religion, Harvard University, June 1963.

12. The first account is quoted anonymously in "The Issue of the Consciousness-expanding Drugs," *Main Currents in Modern Thought,* 20, 1 (September-October, 1963): 10-11. The second experience was that of Dr. R. M. Bucke, the author of *Cosmic Consciousness,* as quoted in William James, *The Varieties of Religious Experience* (New York: Modern

Library, 1902), pp. 390-391. The former experience occurred under the influence of drugs; the latter did not.

13. James S. Slotkin, *Peyote Religion* (New York: Free Press of Glencoe, 1956).

14. "Daru and Bhang," *Quarterly Journal of the Study of Alcohol,* 15 (1954):229.

15. Chicago: Univ. of Chicago Press, 1958.

16. *Totem and Taboo* (New York: Modern Library, 1938).

17. "The Hallucinogenic Fungi of Mexico: An Inquiry into the Origins of the Religious Idea among Primitive Peoples," *Harvard Botanical Museum Leaflets,* 19, 7 (1961).

18. Margaret Prescott Montague, *Twenty Minutes of Reality* (St. Paul, Minn.: Macalester Park, 1947), pp. 15, 17.

19. "The Current Scientific Status of Psychedelic Drug Research," read at the Conference on Methods in Philosophy and the Sciences, New School for Social Research, May 3, 1964, and scheduled for publication in David Solomon, ed., *The Conscious Expanders* (New York: Putnam, fall of 1964).

20. Quoted by Dr. Unger in the paper just mentioned.

21. *The Myth of Sisyphus* (New York: Vintage, 1955), p. 38.

22. Philip Kapleau, *Zen Practice and Attainment,* a manuscript in process of publication.

23. Slotkin, *op. cit.*

WINSTON L. KING

Eastern Religions: A New Interest and Influence

It has been only in the twentieth century, and toward its midpoint at that, that Eastern religions might be said to have had any influence in the United States; and serious interest in them, even of the scholarly sort, is scarcely more than a generation older.

This interest and its possible influence have come upon us gradually and unintentionally, for the most part. In fact, the first form of American interest in Eastern religions was a quite negative one: the desire to learn about the Eastern "heathen" in order to convert them to Christianity, or, put otherwise, in order to destroy their religion. For outstanding as were the linguistic labors of an Adoniram Judson, and sincere as was his affection for the Burmese people, the ultimate motivation for his study of Buddhism was its subversion.

For a quite considerable period of time—indeed, for the better part of a century after Judson—the only knowledge of Asian religions pos-

From the *Annals of the American Academy of Political and Social Science* 387 (1970): 66-76. Reprinted by permission of the publisher and author.

sessed by most Americans was that gleaned from missionary accounts; and our scholars were only slightly better informed, for they were largely untouched by the late nineteenth- and early twentieth-century European scholarship on Asia—a few romantically interested individuals like Emerson and a bit of popular interest like that aroused by the World Parliament of Religions at Chicago in 1893 aside. Indeed, one might say that it was William James who indirectly prepared the way for the study of Eastern religions by presenting religious experience as a legitimate object of study in his *Varieties of Religious Experience.* So, too, several early twentieth-century European scholars, for example, Frazer, Westermarck, and Tylor, spread some information and aroused some "disinterested" inquiry concerning other religions by their studies of classical Mediterranean and primitive religions.

But the credit for the actual pioneering studies of Eastern religions in the United States lies with others: for example, Paul Carus, motivated by the Germanic hope for a genuine *Religionswissenschaft,* introduced D. T. Suzuki to America and presented his own demythologized version of Buddhism; A. J. Edmunds, in a kind of parallel-versions treatment, presented the (to him) startling likeness between the teachings of Buddha and Jesus; and Dwight Goddard brought out his Buddhist Bible in 1932. Works like these comprised the beginning of what has now become a small flood of literature, and of the substantial interest in things Eastern that characterizes our present situation.

For now, of course, there is a growing number of American scholars with a professional interest and training in Eastern cultures and religions, and the introduction of new courses in Asian civilizations is the wave of the immediate future in colleges and universities. Most university libraries are, or could easily be, well stocked with the translated scriptures of all of the major Eastern religions, and of some of the minor ones as well. Anthologies and interpretations of Eastern religions appear in increasing numbers. Paperback trade in university book stores, and even at the corner drug store, is brisk in such items as the Eastern-influenced poetry of Ginsberg and Snyder, the Zen-permeated novels of Kerouac and Salinger, the popular Eastern-religious essays of Watts, do-it-yourself yogist manuals, and the transcendental-meditation-inspired records of the Beatles. Such recently esoteric terms as nirvana, dharma (bums), karma, *satori,* "the sound of one hand clapping," and the like, have become almost household words. And there is a steady trickle of Eastern-inspired events like the following: an American going to Asia to become a Buddhist monk, or at least to practice meditation; hippie music and communities adopting Eastern themes and styles of living; American Quakers and Zen Buddhists holding a seminar in Japan; and establishment of Hindu and Buddhist meditation centers in the

United States, to say nothing of the aggressive efforts of groups like the Soka Gakkai (Nichiren Buddhists) of Japan to propagandize and proselytize in the United States.

Such, then, is the new climate. Our problem is its proper interpretation.

Origin, Interpretation, and Implications of the Phenomenon

In my opinion, the most illuminating way to study this twentieth-century phenomenon in America is an indirect one: first, to observe certain features of the American religious and cultural situation which provide the background for the Eastern-responsive mood in America; then, to note what there is in Eastern religion that seems to meet certain contemporary American needs; and, finally, to estimate the nature and depth of Eastern religious influence in America. That is the method that will be followed in the body of this paper.

The American Religious and Cultural Situation

First to be noted is what may be termed a negative, but essential, condition for the present interest: the breakdown of the militant Christian-missionary attitude toward all, but particularly Eastern, "heathen." For possessed of The Only Truth, who can be interested in another's error? But, with increasingly serious questions being raised about the absolute, watertight uniqueness of the Christian gospel, and with the accompanying weakening and changing of the Christian missionary impulse, the sectarian barrier to interest in and study of Eastern religions began to dissolve a generation ago.

A second factor, which is much more complex in nature and which has overtones and effects peculiar to America, is the transmogrification among us of the dominantly teleological Western-Christian sense of history. I use the word "transmogrification" deliberately to signify a change into something quite different—though, in this case, the result contains tragicomic semblances of its original essence.

We have been told repeatedly by biblical scholars and theologians that the distinctively Western historical sense grows out of the Judaeo-Christian linear-progressive view of human destiny. The simplest model of its form is a bee-line of Divine Purpose from the Beginning (in creation) to the (Terrible-Glorious) End in Judgment and the New Jerusalem. This is radically contrasted with the Hindu-Buddhist-Eastern cyclical view in which there is an endlessly repeated return to former states and conditions, with neither absolute beginnings nor absolute endings. And this linear-purposive character of the Western-Christian world view, we are further told, has been a fundamental determinant of Western values of life and cultural stance. Indeed, it is sometimes rather simplistically maintained that the inherent teleology of the Western-Christian view is the primary cause of the vitality and progressiveness of the West—as contrasted, again, with the opposite qualities of the East.

Despite some exaggerated claims of this sort, there is, undoubtedly, a very important cultural factor here. True, there are elements of cyclism in the Jewish tradition itself, as in the Book of Ecclesiastes. Further, the discernment of the actual historical outworkings of the Divine Purpose, even in the life of the Chosen People(s), put both Jewish and Christian imagination and faith in that purpose to many a severe test. In times of near-destruction or in a calamitous present, Jew and Christian were forced to the construction of such monstrosities (historically considered) as an imminent-but-not-now-visible day of judgment on their enemies; or of a secret historical connection between events which, despite all appearances to the contrary, bind these events into a meaningful, divinely purposed wholeness and a glorious consummation (*Heilsgeschichte*). Yet, the measure of the central importance of this teleology is precisely that such valiant efforts to make purposive sense of history *were* made, over and over again, despite tremendous rational-empirical odds.

It does seem to be true that this sense of history as a meaningful progression toward some future goal, even though varying from time to time in its emphasis and prominence, has basically determined the Western cultural attitude toward human life and destiny. And, as a result of a special, even unique, set of historical circumstances, American life-attitudes in particular have been deeply influenced by this linear-historical model. Thus, for a considerable period of time, American religion was strongly influenced by a rather concrete expectation of the Kingdom, so much so that one might almost speak of the *American* Kingdom of Heaven idea at certain points in the nineteenth century. For although it is true that there were probably always some who thought of the Kingdom's coming as sheerly apocalyptic and utterly transcendent (witness the Millerites and later Adventists), the millennial hope of a Kingdom of God on earth infused itself increasingly into the national culture. At least two major strands of Kingdom-ideology may be distinguished here: (1) America is a land of promise, providentially discovered and destined for a very special and glorious manifestation of Divine Purpose; (2) this Purpose will be manifested in the very near future, effected almost equally by Divine and human initiative.

The value—even necessity?—of human aid to bring in the Kingdom was largely a made-in-America feature, expressing the American sense of self-confidence and the optimism of a newly born nation. This sense of a splendid, man-aided destiny was further nourished by the openness of society for all classes; the tolerance shown most Christian sects—accorded, in actual fact, out of sheer pragmatic necessity, but often subsequently hailed as a mark of Divine favor and American virtue; the presence of abundant natural resources; and a growing evolutional optimism after liberal theologians had learned to accommodate Holy Writ to the *Origin of Species.* There were, of course, other derivative forms of this American version of Judaeo-Christian teleology, ranging from the immediate millennial hopes of special groups (Shakers, Perfectionists, and the like), through the expectation that some projected social reform would bring utopia—for example, temperance and the slaves' emancipation—to such secular-political formulations as the doctrine of manifest destiny.

But this is a picture of yesteryear. Today—two world wars and two lesser conflicts later—the eminently *un*manifest destiny of America in the world at large, the deepening of social conflict despite a plethora of ideals and reforms, and the growing sense of the infinity and impersonality of the environing universe have all combined to destroy, almost completely, this naïve American-Christian optimism and easy faith in inevitable progress toward some good Kingdom or other. Indeed, quite ironically, we find ourselves in the worst of all possible situations: though bereft of any clear or convincing sense of ultimate goals, or paths thereto, we are yet, inescapably, the heirs of the Judaeo-Christian linear-dynamic historical tradition: that is, we do not know where we are going or even where we *wish* to go, but are certain that our destiny is *not* an Eastern-style cyclic repetition of the past; and, as a result of the dizzy pace of present technical achievement, our "progress" toward this unknown future is ever more rapid and inexorable. In other words, the contemporary form of the Judaeo-Christian linear-historical heritage is demonic; it is possessed of all its inherent dynamism of movement, but possesses none of its classic sense of a beneficent Divine Purpose with which man may knowingly accommodate his efforts. We are driven by fate, not led by destiny.

Secondly, there is another, but not unrelated, tendency that may be described epigrammatically, and therefore too simply, as our turning from the intellectual to the visceral values. I shall characterize the cultural mood that this represents only generally by a very few examples, but it is quite culture-pervasive. One of these forms is our present unwillingness, by and large, to build, or to give credence to, any all-inclusive scheme of the universe. In philosophy, this is evidenced by the absence of system-builders—A. N. Whitehead and Paul Weiss aside. And, in its sphere, contemporary theology finds it almost impossible to provide either reality or meaning to the word "God," because, for many contemporary Americans, "God" no longer serves to enlighten and organize the universe, but, rather, represents a problem that they would sooner avoid. In many theological circles, "theology" is "relevant" only in direct proportion to the degree of its nonuse of the term "God" and its sensitivity to human values and emotions. Whatever results from the considerable theological ferment of the present, theology will be characterized much more by psychological and social concerns than by metaphysical systems. Even science is no longer the great explainer on a grand scale—presenting overarching theories of the origin, nature, and destiny of reality. In its various working forms, it is now, more humbly, content to deal with ongoing processes and with ascertaining how their discoverable bits and pieces fit together operatively—the results to be maximally exploited for concrete human benefit. Thus, our present cultural mood is existential, and more political and social than intellectual-speculative.

One further aspect of our cultural mood is worthy of note: a pervasive dissatisfaction with the manner in which we can and do relate to our environment, and with the kind of environment to which we must relate in a technological-metropolitan age. Many contemporary Americans are deeply depressed by the mechanized environments in which they work, the routinized nature of their occupations, and the impersonal exteriority of the relationships to fellow human beings that are forced on them by technology—and they do many foolish and desperate things to escape this Kafkaesque prison.

Part of this same sense of separation and alienation is the American experience, recognized or not, of our growing lack of any organic connection with the natural environment. This is, superficially, only a quantitative aspect of the increasing mechanization of our life, the growth of cities and reduction of countryside, and the expansion of the population. But, in a deeper sense, it is endemic to the Judaeo-Christian tradition as such—a congenital malaise with side-effects which are only now coming to light. For when man conceives himself to be the lord of the creation, for whose pleasure and benefit all else was created, his surroundings become for him only the sum of exploitable items. Thus, while it may be debatable whether Western science grew directly from the Divine command to arise and rule the earth, there is no doubt but that science and its resultant technology are now carrying out that exploitative mandate with a vengeance. In any case, a culture geared primarily to the exploitation of nature for man's pleasure and profit tends to alienate man spiritually from his environment, and it is an alienation which, to date, has not been healed by either the sportsman's or the romantic's superficial "love of Nature."

Eastern Religions' Appeal for our Contemporary Culture

The next question—what is there in Eastern religions that appeals to our present mood?—has already been implicitly answered in the preceding section. Here I shall note some specific features of Eastern religions which might well seem to speak effectively to our present cultural-religious situation.

One relatively superficial, yet important, feature of Eastern appeal can be noted at once: the elasticity of Eastern religio-philosophical language. This appeal is particularly strong for Americans who have been oriented or conditioned to Protestantism. One might put it thus: After two millennia of intellectualistic doctrinal disputation, and four centuries of dead-in-earnest Protestant biblical literalism, most of the poetry, and all of the flexibility, has gone out of the Christian vocabulary—especially in America, with its superliteralistic, fundamentalist tendencies. And, of course, the tighter and harder the doctrinal distinctions and the biblical literalism, the more disruptive was the subsequent scientific-philosophic conflict with categories of faith. In refreshing contrast, how easy, how flexible, how infinitely varied, how vast is the universe of religious language in the East! Here specific doctrinal terms are, on the whole, of no great consequence. If one finds one set of terms useless to him religiously, he may choose another more inclusive and "higher" set. For God, or Supreme Reality, has many names in the East, not just one correct one by which all men must be saved. Here, also, one is not confined to a small three-decker universe of a few thousand years' duration; for in Eastern cosmology, there are universes within universes, and their rise, existence, and fall are an eternal process. To sum up: a free-wheeling mystic permissiveness in language and concept pervades the whole—or so it seems at least—and the tight little worries about creed and the knotted doctrinal tangles of the West really do not matter in the presence of these transcendental Eastern experiences.

Another Eastern quality with potential for the West is obvious: the East's sense of a close, even organic, relation to the environment and all its life-processes. The dominant concept—or is it more an instinctual feeling?—about man in the East is that of man as a microcosm. He regards himself as a part of the world-process, completely integral to it; he arises from that process, his own mental-physical life processes exemplify it, and he returns to it in the end. The major Eastern cultures are sophisticatedly primitive, that is, they have become many-leveled in their apprehension and experience of the world, yet without thereby losing a sense of direct participation in its basic patterns, its sense life, and its dynamic vitality—even at the most abstruse heights of spiritual discipline. I may cite here the pervasive Indian-Hindu sense of the power of the universe creating and manifesting itself in the symbolic sexual union of god and goddess, of worshiper and worshiped; and of the ancient Brahmanical ritual conceived as microcosmic re-creation, integral, and perhaps even essential, to Nature's own perpetual self-renewal.

In this connection, there is also the Chinese sense of man as embodying in himself the Yang-Yin creative polarity of the universe, dramatically evident in the Chinese landscape-painting in which man is but one tiny part of the whole; the Taoist modeling of human life upon the effortless power of the natural order by a mystical openness to it; and the peculiarly intimate existential relation of Japanese religiosity to its environment, specifically in Shinto and Zen. And even when, on the sophisticated level, this relationship is mystically rather than animistically conceived, the microcosmic and organic concepts still hold. For Hinduism, in several of its forms, the core of human individuality, the *atman,* is, at the same time, identical with the ultimate Brahman, and the essential function of all religious words and activities is but to realize that identity existentially. Thus, the Taoist sage also sought to achieve an operative unity with the natural order in his life-style. And the Zen Buddhist—an heir of many Taoist values—seeks to realize the Buddha nature within every man and every part of the universe—in a spontaneous-unitive awareness in which all of the inner-outer, mind-matter, sentient-insentient dualities are transcended but not demolished. He becomes "one" with everything and everyone, but without losing his own identity.

The reasons why such an organic-relational view of nature and cyclical view of history may no longer appear as strange and repulsive as they once did to many Americans have been stated in the previous section. Alienated more and more from our natural environment by urbanization and technical progress—and with less and less natural environment with which to relate—we are belatedly asking ourselves whether trees and meadows may not have other and more significant uses than merely being destroyed to make way for a new highway, parking lot, or factory. Might they not be worth just enjoying? Has not the East, in its identification with, rather than exploitation of, nature, discovered a source of strength and peace sorely needed in the progress-wearied West? And though we still have our intellectual and emotional problems with historical cyclism, what better thing have we to put in its place? Certainly no sure and certain faith in a coming American Kingdom of God!

It is ironic, we may note in passing, that just as the organic relatedness to nature and the disciplines of passive contemplation are becoming attractive to the West, many in the East are discovering the attractiveness (and the political necessity) of the Western gospel of exploitative progressivism.

One other aspect of Eastern religiosity must be mentioned here, and it is, perhaps, the most significant of all in terms of possible influence in the West. I refer to what may be called the existential and intuitive-visceral orientation of the religious East, which finds its most characteristic and intensive expression in the meditative disciplines. Here, if anywhere, I am convinced, the East will make meaningful spiritual contact with the West; here, if anywhere, there are possibilities for a mutual meeting and joining—or should we say rejoining—of religious essences. For the West, too, once had its strong intuitional-mystical religious expressions.

Be that outcome as it may, there can be no doubt of the emphasis in the East upon the primacy of the visceral-intuitive approach to truth. Even philosophically this is true: for intuition—that immediate, sudden, and synoptic grasping of truth in one piece—is highly rated when it comes to wisdom-level truths. Practical and culturally conditioned truths, says the East, may be arrived at by lower-level logic, but when one comes to the essential and existential truth—that having to do with man's ultimate concerns—then only a species of intuition, or intuition in its highest form, can serve us. It may never quite be said that all intuitional results are infallible. Indeed, since "infallibility" relates mostly to doctrinal statements, what would it mean here? But there is never any doubt but that the truth, saving truth, comes by intuition rather than intellection. Perhaps Eastern intuition functions, in this sense, as does "revelation" in the Moslem-Christian West.

Of course, intuition is no stranger to the West. We, too, have our "moral certainties" and our "hunches" which are of vital importance, especially for science. With us, however, intuition is a subsidiary, rather than a central agency of intelligence; and it is completely conditioned by what it logically-rationally feeds upon day by day. But in the East, intuition rises above such relativities, and it is far more visceral than cerebral. Indeed, the East fully intends to involve the total person, at his deepest centers of existential being, in its quest for reality; it distrusts abstract intellectualism. And the true orthodoxy of Eastern religions, one that cuts across most creedal lines as though they did not exist, is that of meditational methodology. Though varying greatly in concrete detail and verbal context, all of the major meditational disciplines directly and deliberately involve the total psychosomatic organism in the quest for saving enlightenment. It is not that certain bodily sensations are of the essence—or mental states either, for that matter—but the total body-mind organism is seen as instrumentally necessary for the progressive integration and realization of true selfhood. Therefore, these disciplines pay considerable attention to such matters as psychological climate, bodily posture and exercises, and emotional utilization and control. They believe that the salvation which they seek is to be achieved in all of these areas.

Again, the attractiveness of such religions for the Westerner is obvious, particularly for the Protestant-oriented Westerner. The largely intellectualized, de-emotionalized religious "worship" of the average Protestant church, in which any undue bodily activity or emotional expressiveness is rigidly inhibited in the interests of a very quiet and respectable "reverence," seems to be a dried-up vestigial remnant of living religiousness when compared with the Eastern religiosity, which, in all its ranges, from orgiastic rite up to, and including, meditational intensity, is an affair of total existential participation. Thus, for those to whom the vigor of fundamentalist revivalism is no longer a viable sort of religiosity, such a pattern of existential totality of expression offers an attractive alternative. And, besides, such a methodology, which majors in method and minors in discussion, largely bypasses those doctrinal difficulties that negatively obsess the would-be religious Westerner.

Consequences for American Religious Life

Our basic question may now, finally, be asked: What will the practical consequence and significance of all this be for actual American religious life? And the answer to this is the most uncertain of all. It is relatively easy to indicate the qualities of Eastern religions that attract Americans and the points at which Eastern religiosity might make a decisive impression upon American religion, but it is most difficult to say with assurance whether all this will, indeed, make any significant difference in the end. Therefore, this concluding portion is highly tentative.

Some American interest in the East is a passing fad, and no more; in this area, Zen is out, and drugs are in. Or it represents a disillusioned, frantic, and therefore gullible, grasping at any straw within reach, provided only that it be of non-Western-Christian manufacture; thus, the "convert" espouses new beliefs whose like in Christianity he rejects as sheer superstition. It must also be observed that the results, to date, are not impressive either in quantity or in quality—if we are speaking about genuine religious influence of the East upon America. Most Buddhist influence is confined to first- and second-generation Japanese immigrants. The relatively few "native" Americans who have attempted to become Vedantist (or Buddhist, for that matter) are those on the culturally adventurous fringes of our society—mostly congenital dabblers in esoteric matters, people of the theater or the arts, and temporarily adventurous college students. But the solid mainstream of American life has been largely untouched.

Thus, for example, fundamentalist Christianity—and all American Christianity is still *far* more fundamentalist at heart than most liberals realize—has neither interest in, nor capacity for interest in, Eastern religions. The most that one can expect in the churches here, for some time to come, is an occasional Eastern finger-wetting in the form of a Sunday School class which devotes one unit of study to "other religions," or some church club that needs a program-filler and invites a local scholar to speak on Asian religions. And even the liberal churches that are much concerned with spiritual renewal from whatever source, whether orthodox Christian or not, never seriously consider Eastern religions as offering a resource. Nor do the promiscuous Unitarian minglings of Oriental Scriptures and theosophical writings with their inspirational readings have any great significance for personal religious life. For Catholics, their formidable Christian ecclesiastical-sacramental apparatus effectively prevents Eastern interest, and their own mysticism is too institutionalized, or too deeply buried in historical legend, to make meaningful contact with Asian mysticism.

The same matter may be put another way: we are immersed in the problems of our own expansive culture and history, and we instinctively expect the culture that produced the problems somehow to provide their solution. It always has in the past. It is too much, therefore, to expect that the Asian life-style—separated from the West for millennia, become so different in flavor, presuppositions, and goals, and, until recently, looked down upon by Americans as the essence of what we did *not* wish to become—should suddenly provide most Americans with any significant life-clues. Indeed, it can be said that even most of those who have forsaken traditional Jewish and Christian religiosity—save for the socially convenient *rites de passage*—would sooner have a made-in-America nonreligion than any foreign religious product of whatever sort. Home-grown unbelief is at least familiar and rational! And, to compound the difficulties, Eastern missionaries to the West are repeating in reverse the Western missionary mistake—identifying Eastern gospels with Eastern cultural contexts, complete with nationalistic coloring.

To make matters still worse, even among those Americans who have seriously and deliberately interested themselves in Eastern religions, there has often been an anomalous situation—they have turned to Eastern religions for the wrong reasons. This has been especially true for many would-be devotees of Zen, for, unfortunately, Zen has often been (and still is) peddled in America in the manner of religious snake-oil, as an easy cure-all for modern American religious diseases. In this presentation, the largely implicit, but essential, Buddhist presuppositions have been hidden from view or glossed over. It has been implied, or easily assumed, that the vicious business of theology is to be dissolved by psychosomatic gimmickry. By a bit of easy meditation and a few psychological twists, one could relax into a natural spontaneity that avoids all thinking and moral struggle. Thus, the pursuit of Zen has been, in actuality, an avoidance of religion, rather than a spiritual quest.

But even in Japan, more visceral though the spiritual quest may be, such a scheme does not work. And how much less likely it is to work for the Westerner who, whether he likes it or not, must deal with his moral, social, and intellectual problems head-on in coming to a satisfactory religious solution. For it seems quite obvious that a religious quest can never be successful if it is an evasion of one's existential problems, a side-stepping of the ultimate concerns as his culture presents them to him—unless he intends to forsake it altogether and live in another culture.

This raises the basic question of the actual viability of Eastern religiosity for America. Of course, it would be presumptuous to say that it cannot become an important American cultural ingredient, despite its slow and meager beginnings. Who could have predicted the wide spread of Christianity in 30 A.D. or of Islam in 632 A.D.? Nevertheless, some predictions may be ventured about possibilities and likely modes of influence.

It may first be surmised that an Eastern philosophico-religious component seems to have become a relatively permanent part of the American cultural scene. Though "Eastern studies" may turn out to be something of an academic fad, library holdings are too large, and professional interest in the Eastern cultures too well established, for America to subside into the completely ignorant disinterest in the East of two generations ago—to say nothing of the effects of continuing political and economic relations with Asia. To this extent, Eastern ideas have become a component part of our cultural heritage, though how important a part is another matter.

Further, the Hindu and Buddhist meditation and teaching centers in America, though at present few in number and of negligible influence, do represent a religious potential of some significance. Of course, one should not expect any massive conversional movement, despite enthusiastic reports of success on the part of Soka Gakkai, for example. But the promiscuously permissive religious mood of America offers no real obstacle to the establishment and activity of such centers, and if they persist for a generation or more, there will be both internal modification in the direction of an at-home-in-America style, as well as a wearing away of their present reputation of being an esoteric fad. It may be, therefore, that in another generation Buddhism and Vedanta will be seen as viable personal religious alternatives by a few, and as genuine components of American religiosity by the many.

I would make a further semiprojection that Eastern religion is more likely to join onto Western spiritual substance in the psychiatric and existentialist, rather than in the religious, sphere. Of course, the Jungian and Heideggerian interest in the East is not necessarily the wave of the future. But existentialist philosophy and behavioral disciplines have less doctrinal structure to encumber their contact with the East than does American religion. And the basically psychosomatic and humanistic meditational discipline of the East, which, as we have noted, is somewhat independent of doctrinal positions, is a natural point of meaningful contact, investigation, and even practice for pragmatic psychotherapy. This presumes, of course, a degree of flexibility of practice, a willingness to shed some cultural-doctrinal elements among Easterners, and an interest among Westerners that may not be present in actuality.

If we speak further of the modifications that may take place in Eastern spirituality come-West, there can be little doubt but that there must, and probably will, be a movement toward greater overt concern with social consciousness. At present, much of the attraction of Eastern religiosity consists, as noted above, in something closely bordering on "escapism." The mood of those seeking Eastern religious solutions, to date, is, on the whole, either one of reaction from the exteriority of a culture given wholeheartedly to scientific exploitation and material-technical progress which has forgotten all of its Christian-mystical heritage, or a mood of historical despair that seeks the non-historical solace of an organic universalism of the Taoist sort. But such a mood may well pass or destroy itself by its extremeness. A mere retreat to the psychic inside will not permanently deal with the problems of Westerners enmeshed in an inexorably expanding technological civilization. Therefore, if Eastern religiosity is to minister meaningfully to the (American) West, it cannot retain the usual come-West form of a socially passive, nonconceptual, turned-inward discipline which seeks to replace all else, but must in some manner combine its inner-organic spirituality with Western technical civilization and historical-rational sensibilities.

But this will take time. And time may be what the religious East does not have. Briefly, it can be put thus: Can Eastern religion exist long enough in its integrity to make an important contribution to Western (and American) culture? Some forms of Eastern religion are being completely destroyed, in their archaic forms at least, by Asian communism, before they have time to adapt to a newly open world—witness Tibet and China. And other forms of Eastern religion may be completely "corrupted" by the powerful invasion of Western-style technology and nationalism before a genuine encounter and mutual modification of Eastern and Western spiritual essences can take place—witness Japan and India. Nor is this latter danger less than the first, for as noted briefly above, the East, both Communist and non-Communist, is culturally pushing "Westward" as rapidly as possible. And I, for one, question whether the present feeble beginnings of Eastern religions in America, without an Asian fountainhead to nourish them for some generations to come, can achieve such strength and make such modifications as will enable them to exert any genuinely significant religious influence. Thus, in the end, the fate of Eastern religiosity in America depends fully as much upon what happens in Asia as upon what happens here in the next fifty years.

Chapter 11
Scientific Research in the Sociology of Religion

REX H. WARLAND

Quantitative Methods in the Sociology of Religion

Many readers of this volume may have been surprised to find that a reader in the sociology of religion contains several methods of analysis which are unfamiliar to them. No doubt such methods as Guttman scaling, factor analysis and multi-variate analysis may have caused some consternation on the part of many readers. Others may question the propriety of the application of these techniques which are presumed to aid the researcher in measuring religiosity, motives for religious participation, or even the essence of religion. These skeptics may wonder why the analysis of such concepts is not left to speculation and subjectivity rather than attempting to apply methods of precise measurement

---

This article was written especially for this book. Permission to reprint should be obtained from Charles E. Merrill Publishing Company.

and analysis in an effort to be objective. Indeed such criticisms have been raised in this book as well as elsewhere.[1]

To provide a better understanding, we will briefly discuss in this chapter several of the methods which appear in this volume. It is not our purpose to critically evaluate these methods or to explain in detail the technical aspects of these quantitative techniques. Rather, we wish to interpret the meaning of these methods and comment on the insight they may provide into the sociology of religion.

The chapter is divided into two parts. First, we will discuss several quantitative methods used in studies reported in this book to provide the reader with more information concerning the purpose and application of these methods. Then we will briefly review the present status of methods in the sociology of religion and speculate on future uses of quantitative methods by researchers interested in this area of sociology.

MULTI-VARIATE ANALYSIS

Two studies included in this reader have used multi-variate analysis. We will first examine the study by Erich Goode (chapter 5, article 1).

To review briefly, Goode is interested in the relationship between social class and church participation. Although numerous studies have established that a positive relationship exists between these two variables, i.e., the higher the social class, the more active one's church activity, Goode questions the bases for this relationship since he finds a lack of consensus among the explanations for why these variables relate to one another. This suggests to him that the relationship between class and church activity requires closer study.

Goode uses a multi-variate method which allows him to examine not two, but three, variables at one time.[2] In addition to social class and church participation, Goode also considers non-church formal organizational participation. First he establishes that each pair of variables—social class and church participation, social class and non-church activity, and church participation and non-church activity—are all positively related. Next Goode controls on non-church activity to see what happens to the original relationship between social class and church participation.

Let us look more closely at the way in which Goode introduces the third variable. A portion of table 3 from Goode's article is reproduced here (table 1). The relationship between church attendance and social class (measured by "grade school" and "high school") can be found under the heading "Disregarding Non-Church Activity." We observe that church attendance is 20 percent higher (63 percent–43 percent) for high school graduates than for those who attended only grade school.

TABLE 1. *Percentage "High" in Church Participation, By Education: Appalachian Sample**

	Disregarding Non-Church Activity		"Low" Non-Church Activity		"High" Non-Church Activity	
	Grade School	High School	Grade School	High School	Grade School	High School
Church Attendance	43	63	38	49	58	71
Lord's Supper	45	66	39	55	63	73
Church Leadership	33	54	27	45	50	60

*From Erich Goode, "Social Class and Church Participation," (chapter 5, article 1, of this book)

Non-church activity is then introduced as a control variable, i.e., a variable which we hold constant so its influence on the original relationship is eliminated. In controlling for non-church activity, Goode breaks this variable into two categories—"low" non-church activity and "high" non-church activity—and then examines the relationship of class to church participation *within* each category of non-church activity. We can see that when Goode controls on non-church activity, the relationship between church attendance and social class is weakened, for the original difference (20 percent) is reduced.[3] For those who are low on non-church activity, the difference is 11 percent (49 percent–38 percent) while the difference for the high non-church activity is 13 percent. The same pattern occurs for "Lord's Supper" and "Church Leadership" as well as most of the other church activities listed in Tables 3-6 of Goode's article. The finding that the relationship between social class and church participation is weakened when non-church activity is controlled suggests that the degree of relationship between class and church participation is influenced to some degree by non-church activity.

We can see that the use of this multi-variate method calls into question the interpretation of the original relationship between social class and church participation and suggests new theoretical interpretations and directions. Goode concludes from his findings that church attendance cannot necessarily be considered a measure of one's religiousness. In part, he suggests that white-collar church activity has become secularized to the extent that it can be considered a part of over-all white-collar secular organizational participation.

Some may question Goode's measures of church and social class, or his interpretation of the data. Yet use of multi-variate analysis makes it possible to more fully understand a simple relationship and raise provocative questions concerning a finding which most had accepted as fact. As debate over Goode's study proceeds, new insight and knowledge concerning the sociology of religion will surely follow.

The study by Goldstein (chapter 2, article 1) also uses multi-variate analysis. Without controls, differences among religious groups with respect to socioeconomic status are found. When several variables, including residence, education and occupation, are controlled, the socioeconomic status differences among the three groups diminish. In contrast to the approach used by Goode, Goldstein controls on two variables and then examines the original relationships. For example, when he controls on residence and education, he finds that differences in occupation status diminish for the three religious groups (table 7 in his article). Thus, multi-variate analysis assists Goldstein in concluding that both occupation and education play a more important role than religious affiliation in influencing income levels of these three religious groups.

Guttman Scaling

Now we turn our attention to research methods which aid in better understanding sociological concepts by specifying procedures to measure these concepts. Our first example is the study by Faulkner and DeJong (chapter 1, article 4). The study attempts to verify empirically that religiosity is characterized by five different aspects or dimensions of religious involvement suggested by Glock.

The authors measure the proposed dimensions of religiosity using five sets of items (i.e., the set of questions) which appear in the appendix of the article. For example, to measure the ideological dimension, the authors use five items which may be considered representative of prevailing conceptions of ideology. Thus, the reader is made aware of the precise meaning of the ideological as well as the other dimensions in this study. This is one of the major contributions of careful attention to measurement. It forces clarification of one's definition of a concept and ultimately leads to further specification and reconceptualization of concepts and theory.

The method used by the authors to evaluate the dimensions of religiosity is the Guttman scale technique, which is designed to determine if a set of items measure the same thing or tap the same dimension. To illustrate this application of the Guttman technique, let us consider the ritualistic scale of Faulkner and DeJong. This scale has five items which are summarized in table 2. These items represent several forms of religious behavior which can be considered indicators of the extent to which a person adheres to the ritualistic dimension of religiosity.

The basic idea of Guttman scaling is that if the items form a single dimension, then it will be possible to rank individuals along this continuum from greatest to least. The Guttman technique provides criteria to judge how well a set of items approximate a single dimension. In our example, if Person A feels more strongly about ritualism than Person B, he should give a positive response to at least all the items endorsed by B *plus* at least one more if a single dimension does exist. We would expect someone who is strongly ritualistic to endorse Item 1, which represents the most extreme or strongest ritualistic statement of the five items. If he believes it is not possible to develop a well-rounded religious life apart from the church, it is also very likely that he reads the Bible, attends services, prays, and wishes to be married by a religious official. However, someone who believes that he should be married by a religious official *does not* necessarily pray, attend church, etc. Thus, Items 1-5 on the ritualistic scale represent different degrees of adherence to ritualism, Item 1 being the strongest and Item 5 the weakest.

TABLE 2. *Items and Percent of Positive Responses for the Ritualistic Scale**

Item	Percent of Positive Responses**
1. Degree to which person feels it is possible to develop a well-rounded religious life apart from the church	21.3
2. Time spent reading the Bible and other religious literature	29.8
3. Extent of attendance at Sabbath worship services	45.9
4. Extent of participation in the act of prayer	63.8
5. Belief that marriage ceremony should be performed by a religious official	73.8

*From Joseph E. Faulkner and Gordon F. DeJong, "Religiosity in 5-D: An Empirical Analysis" (chapter 1, article 4 of this book).

**A positive response is defined as one which indicates a traditional religious response.

It may be observed in table 2 that the five items are ordered on the basis of the percent giving a positive response to the item. The most extreme item (Item 1) is endorsed the least (21.3 percent) while Item 5, the most moderate, is endorsed the most (73.8 percent). This indicates that people respond quite differently to these five items. To meet the criteria of a Guttman scale, these differences are necessary for they indicate that the items may be ordered with respect to the degree to which they are endorsed. The question is, "Are respondents endorsing the items with respect to the rank order of the items?" An example may help clarify this point.

To form a perfect Guttman scale, the following pattern of response must occur:

	Ritualistic Scale Items				
Person	1	2	3	4	5
A	X	X	X	X	X
B	0	X	X	X	X
C	0	0	X	X	X
D	0	0	0	X	X
E	0	0	0	0	X
F	0	0	0	0	0
Number Endorsing Item	1	2	3	4	5
Percent Endorsing Item	16.7	33.3	50.0	66.7	83.3

In this example Person A gives a positive response to all five items (indicated by an "X") on the ritualistic scale suggesting he strongly adheres to ritualistic religious behavior. Person B endorses 4 items but refuses to endorse Item 1 which is the most extreme. Thus he adheres less to ritualism than Person A. And so it goes to Person F who gives a negative response to all of the items (indicated by an "0") and may be considered the least ritualistic. Regarding the percent endorsing each item, it may be observed that there is a difference between the percentages of respondents endorsing the items. For example, only Person A and Person B respond positively to Item 2 (2/6 or 33.3%), but four persons of the six (66.7%) endorse Item 4. The reason for this can easily be ascertained from the pattern of responses; more people endorse the items as they become less ritualistic.

This is the essence of the Guttman model. One selects items to create a rank order from low to high and then determines by the pattern of their responses if persons may be assigned positions on the basis of the rank order. If so, one can easily determine the degree of adherence to the dimension being measured by one person relative to another. In short we have a single dimensional scale on which we can rank order the respondents from very ritualistic to not very ritualistic.

The details for how one exactly determines if a scale meets the Guttman criteria need not concern us here. Suffice it to say that difference with respect to the responses to the various items and "tolerable" aberration from the perfect Guttman scale are the important conditions that need to be met. All five scales in the Faulkner and DeJong article meet the minimum conditions and therefore may be considered by Guttman criteria to be unidimensional scales. One may argue that the items selected to measure these dimensions are not valid indicators of these dimensions. Indeed such questioning may ultimately lead to further specification and reconceptualization of these dimensions, and enhance our understanding of the concept of religiosity. Thanks to the Guttman technique, however, the authors have created unidimensional measures which allow them to carefully rank individuals with respect to their adherence to these aspects of religiosity.

Factor Analysis

A second type of method which aids us in the measurement of social and psychological phenomena is factor analysis. While the Guttman technique is concerned with a single dimension, factor analysis allows us to consider several dimensions simultaneously. This method is considerably more complex than those discussed earlier so it is impossible within the scope of this chapter to discuss the method in detail. But we can consider its meaning and purpose to assess its utility in the sociology of religion.

The study included in this reader which employs factor analysis is that by Gorlow and Schroeder (chapter 2, article 3). The basic idea of factor analysis is that if a number of items (attitude statements, series of questions on a test, etc.) are intercorrelated, the reason for this interrelation may be due to the presence of one or more underlying variables called factors. Put another way, factor analysis is a method which enables the researcher to identify general concepts which are representative of a much larger set of measures.

Consider the diagram below. In this diagram, F represents the factors and I the items. Items 1 through 5 (I_1–I_5) are parts of the underlying construct or variable represented by Factor 1 (F_1) while Items 6 through 8 are measures of Factor 2. We would expect to find Items 1-5 to be highly intercorrelated, and Items 6-8 to be highly intercorrelated, but we would expect I_1–I_5 to be weakly correlated with I_6–I_8 since they represent two different factors. These factors represent two distinct dimensions on which people may order themselves. By constructing these two factors, we reduce eight items to two factors as well as gain insight concerning the phenomena being investigated.

DIAGRAM 1. *Schematic Representation of Factor Analysis*

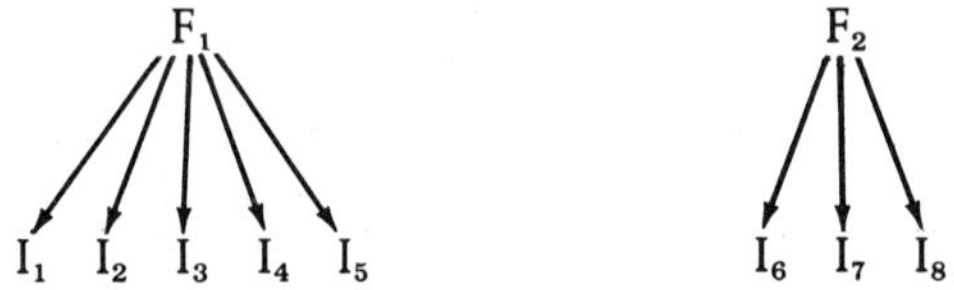

Let us return to the Gorlow and Schroeder study to see more specifically how factor analysis works and aids the researcher in his understanding of the sociology of religion. Gorlow and Schroeder report that during the first stage of their study, they developed 87 items concerning why people participate in religious activities. Rankings obtained from 129 subjects who were asked to indicate the degree of importance of each item or statement provide the data to be analyzed by this factor analysis. Next, Gorlow and Schroeder generate seven interpretable factors.[5] The technique used yields clusters of *people,* not clusters of items or motives.[6] Seven hypothetical religious types of people who have something in common are defined. Put otherwise, people who ranked the statements concerning reasons for religious participation in a similar way are clustered together on the factors. In terms of diagram 1, the people are the items (I) and the underlying similarity between them (defined by similar rankings of the reasons for religious participation) are the factors (F) or hypothetical types. These factors may be interpreted as that which holds the people together and measures the common tie between them with respect to motives for religious participation.

To characterize or interpret these seven "types," the authors relate the reasons for religious participation to each factor. After careful inspection of the reasons which appear in each factor, the authors offer an interpretation of the general meaning of the common patterns they perceive as present in the statements which define a general religious type of person. This method and its subsequent interpretation provide important insight concerning the nature of motivation for religious activities.

The first factor is labeled "Humble Servants of God." There are thirty-one different reasons for participating in religious activity listed under this factor. Several of these are reproduced in table 3.

To the left of each motive is a correlation coefficient (r) measuring the degree of association of the particular motive and the factor.[7] The higher the coefficient, the more closely the motive relates to the factor. Thus, "To be redeemed" is more closely related to Factor I than "To pray." However, on the basis of statistical criteria, all the motives which appear are considered by the authors as appropriate components of Factor I. Some correlations are positive while others are negative. The sign of the coefficient indicates if the particular motive of the persons clustering together on Factor I relates to redemption and experiencing the presence of God or not. Those reasons which are positively correlated with Factor I characterize persons who are religiously active for they wish to serve and experience God. Reasons which are negatively correlated with Factor I suggest these persons *do not* participate in religious activities because they consider themselves "humble servants of God," but because of tradition or self-improvement. Thus those who participate because they wish "To be an obedient servant" do not participate because they wish "To grow in the ability to value other people" or "To maintain traditions" and vice versa.

As one examines carefully all seven factors several things are apparent. For example, Factor I and Factor II appear to be negatively correlated, for many of the items which are positively correlated with Factor I are negatively correlated with Factor II and vice versa. It may also be noticed that some items correlate positively to more than one factor (e.g., "To experience God's love" correlates positively to Factor I and Factor VI). We may interpret this to indicate that this motive does not define a religious type as clearly as we would like, for it is a component of two general underlying types. When several items appear on two factors (like Factor I and Factor V) this suggests the Factors are correlated and represent somewhat the same thing. That is, "Humble servants of God" also tend to be "God seekers." Yet closer examination of the factors will show that each has uniqueness. For example, persons loading on Factor V place a higher value on an active relationship with God than those loading on Factor I.

These seven factors, therefore, represent different types of religious participants. Some are closely related, others are negatively related, but each provides insight into the different religious types. These religious types are further identified by personal, social and demographic variables (see table 2 of their article) which also suggest the usefulness of these types.

Again one can raise questions about the authors' interpretation of the factors. Indeed this is one of the difficulties with factor analysis. Yet the method has given us a different perspective of the original data which

TABLE 3. *Reported Motives Correlating With Loadings on Each Factor**

r	Motive Humble Servant of God (Factor I)
.64	To be redeemed
.52	To gain the promise of salvation
.48	To be an obedient servant
.45	To experience God's love
.29	To pray
–.50	To maintain traditions
–.42	To gain freedom
–.39	To grow in ability to value other people
–.30	To remain true to one's family teaching

*From Leon Gorlow and Harold E. Schroeder, "Motives for Participating in Religious Experience" (chapter 2, article 3 of this book).

offers some new interpretations and conceptualizations of this religious phenomena which enhances our understanding of religious participation.

Present and Future Status of Methods in the Sociology of Religion

As one may surmise by the publication dates of the studies just reviewed, quantitative methods have only recently been used in the sociology of religion. In fact, this volume brings together several of these applications for the first time. We have attempted to point out that careful and enlightened uses of quantitative methods can aid our understanding of sociological phenomena beyond intuition and speculation. These methods provide empirical tests of theoretical speculations, aid in the discovery of new and unanticipated relationships and patterns, and help define more precisely the meaning of concepts. Use of quantitative methods enables us to clarify our theoretical thinking, suggests new variables not considered before, increases confidence in our knowledge, and integrates our findings. In short, quantitative methods aid in the accumulation and acceleration of knowledge.

At present, the applications of more advanced methods and adherence to standards of scientific inquiry in the sociology of religion are still rather scarce. It is likely that we will see a proliferation of application of quantitative methods in the future, both those evidenced in this volume as well as others which have not been widely used by researchers working in the sociology of religion. Advances in measurement, including more precise estimates or reliability and validity should also become more common. Hopefully use of these methods will parallel the incidence of use in the general field of sociology. As the conceptualizations of religious behavior become more complex and refined, the methods should also become increasingly sophisticated.

Before closing, we must dutifully remind the reader that the ultimate utility of quantitative methods depends directly upon proper execution and careful precautions. Method can never be a substitute for thinking and imagination. As Blalock[8] has pointed out, proper application of quantitative methods should be accompanied by explicit statements of untested assumptions, admission of weakness, and careful statements of procedures. Method should be closely tied to theory if advances in knowledge are to occur. Whenever possible, statements and tests concerning reliability and validity should be presented. Such statements and tests are presently seldom included in studies dealing with the sociology of religion. We must always keep in mind that, although much of religious behavior is directly observable (e.g., church attendance, ritualistic activities), other aspects of religion are less amenable to measurement. Constructs such as religiosity and motives of religious participation must be measured indirectly by inferences from behavior, and thus be open to errors of measurement and interpretation. Only if these limitations are recognized and clearly understood, and the appropriate precautions taken, will quantitative methods be useful.

---

1. See the selection by J. P. Williams in chapter 1 of this volume. Objections to the use of sociological methods to understand the essence of religion have also been raised by E. Schillebeeckx, "Theological Reflections on Religio-Sociological Interpretations of Modern Irreligion," *Social Compass* 10 (September 1963):257-84.

2. The procedure used by Goode is known as the elaboration process of data analysis. For an excellent introduction to this method, see Morris Rosenberg, *The Logic of Survey Analysis* (New York: Basic Books, 1968).

3. The reader may wonder what interpretation might have been offered if the difference had *not changed* or *increased.* If there were no change in the original difference, this would suggest the control variable had no influence upon the original relationship. Had the difference increased, one might conclude that the control variable was weakening or suppressing the original relationship so that the removal of the influence of the control variable enabled the true strength of the relationship to emerge. For details, see Rosenberg, *op. cit.*

4. For a basic introduction to measurement in sociology as well as Guttman scaling and factor analysis, see Hubert M. Blalock, Jr., *An Introduction to Social Research* (Englewood Cliffs, New Jersey: Prentice-Hall, 1970).

5. Both logical and statistical criteria are used by the authors to select these seven factors. Initially, eight factors are extracted on statistical grounds, because any additional factors would have not, in the authors' judgment been statistically meaningful. The elimination of one of the eight factors extracted is for logical reasons, since this factor is not considered meaningful or interpretable.

6. Factor analysis may generate two major types of clusters. The R technique produces clusters of items, statements or measures which go together. The Q technique used by Gorlow and Schroeder generates clusters of people who have something in common.

7. More precisely the correlation coefficients in table 3 represent, on a scale from 0.0 to 1.0, how closely the rankings of a particular reason by each person studied relates to the degree to which each person is considered to be included in Factor I. Since the correlation coefficient between the ranking of the reason "To be redeemed" and the degree to which each person is considered a member of Factor I is closest to the maximum value of 1.0, we may consider this reason to most strongly characterize those persons who are members of Factor I. The item "To experience God's love" is correlated 0.45 with Factor I and therefore does not as strongly characterize those who cluster on this factor. Careful examination of the original table (table 1, chapter 2, article 3) will indicate that those reasons which do not correlate at least 0.26 with Factor I are considered unrelated to this factor. These reasons were judged not to be useful in understanding the similarities of those persons who cluster in Factor I.

8. Blalock, *op. cit.*, pp. 87-97.

Index